Jim Cowan's
Industrial Timeline

Jim Cowan's
Industrial Timeline

Jim Cowan

Thomas Owens, publisher

Jim Cowan's Industral Timeline

Published by Thomas Owens.

Printed in the United States of America.

First Printing, 2017.

Publisher's Note

A few years ago it came to my attention that one of my wife's uncles, a lifelong oil man, had meticulously compiled a timeline of man's industrial progress. The work was fascinating, for I had long been skeptical of the rather narrow, standard view of history focusing on the politicians and troublemakers.

Most of humanity is alive today because of industrial progress, as the carrying capacity of the planet was substantially lower before the technological mastery of nature achieved largely in the last 300 years. Based on the implications of physics alone, it is likely that we have exited the steep part of this growth, at least by the conventional measures of energy consumption per capita. Man's future technological progress will depend on doing more with the same or declining gross resources, and the information age we are currently experiencing is the perfect setting for these optimization efforts. The much-heralded "dematerialization" of the information age is enabled by the reality that few in advanced economies need worry much about their basic material needs.

Jim Cowan has lived through much of this progress, born in a small town in West Texas without running water or indoor bathrooms for much of his childhood. During his career, he worked his way up from rig mechanic to maintenance manager for one of the world's largest oil drilling companies. His timeline recognizes those who mastered nature for the benefit of their fellow human beings, often in obscurity. It is a valuable resource for anyone interested in science, industrial history, technology or engineering and tells the story of man's material struggle and triumph on God's good Earth.

"In the sweat of thy face shalt thou eat bread" was the judgment given to man in the Genesis narrative. That we all sweat much less than we used to for our daily bread is evidence of our debt to the Promethean individuals who brought forth the world of abundance we enjoy today. Jim's work is helpful in reminding us of the many blessings we enjoy in this tumultuous, but, in comparison our ancestors' struggles, truly golden age. May we not take our material abundance for granted, nor waste the luxury of leisure, but rather be worthy descendants of those giants on whose shoulders we stand.

Preface, Forward, Introduction, or Whatever....

For many years I have had a profound interest in industrial history. I have collected many books on the subject, and tidbits of information on scraps of paper (which all too often are soon lost). The remainder I kept in my head, where much of it remains today, as my retrieval system is not nearly as efficient as my filing system. Finally, in the early years of this century, I began compiling the information I had on hand, with whatever I could continue to acquire. I remember, one evening, telling my precious, very tolerant wife, that someday this Industrial TimeLine thing might grow to be 15 or even 20 pages long.

I appreciate any positive suggestions and input from readers regarding any items in this compilation. I usually tolerate any critical input, especially if I can use it in a positive manner.

The compiling of this work is simply a hobby of mine; therefore, if you don't like it, or don't like the way it is presented, I certainly hope you read and enjoy it anyhow.

May God Bless You!

James E. "Jim" Cowan
P. O. Box 601
Kilgore, Texas
75663-0601

Jim Cowan's Industrial Timeline
7500 BC–2016

7500 BC	**Boats made of reeds are now being made and used in the Middle East.**	
7500 BC	**The Sheguiandah quartzite quarry is operational on Manitoulin Island, in what will someday be southern Ontario, Canada.**	
6000 BC	**The first known beer is now being brewed in Mesopotamia.**	(see 5500 BC)
6000 BC	**It is generally thought that the wheel is first created and used about now, in Sumeria.** *"Yeah Bubba, it's simpul, tha wheel wuz made so them ole boys could get over to whur tha beer wuz."*	
5500 BC	**At this time, wine is being produced in Georgia and Persia, for those who don't like beer.**	(see 4500 BC)
5000 BC	**Egyptians begin using primitive man-powered and animal-powered mechanical dredges in their canals.**	
5000 BC	**The didgeridoo, a primitive musical instrument (huge flute?) is invented by the natives (Aboriginals) on the very large island that will someday be known as Australia.**	
4900 BC	**Egyptians create and are using the first metal handsaws, probably made of copper or bronze.**	
4500 BC	Wine is now being produced in Greece and other parts of Europe.	
4000 BC	Egypt; some of the first ropes made with tools are created… from reeds.	
3500 BC	**Cotton fabrics are now being used in the Indus Valley.**	
3200 BC	Egyptian drawings from this era, depict a man using a pick, digging a irrigation ditch. Wooden hoes as well as ox plows made of wood are now being used in the fields.	
3000 BC	**The first written languages are now being developed.**	
3000 BC	In Egypt; papyrus, a paper-like material is developed. It may be only paper-like, but it has to beat cave walls and clay tablets.	
3000 BC	At this time, the Egyptians are also using handmade metal nails to hold burial coffins together.	
3000 BC	**Mesopotamia; the process of kiln-drying clay bricks is developed.**	
3000 BC	**Ink is invented by the Chinese.**	
3000 BC	**Rice agriculture originates in India.**	
3000 BC	**About now, during the Bronze Age, it appears the first glass is created.**	
3000 BC	In the stone quarries in Egypt, some drilling is being done using a fire-hardened, hollow, wooden (later metal) tube. It is rotated by hand or bow-string, and is rotated on loose, hard mineral grains like crushed rubies or sapphires, which are sifted onto the surface being drilled. Most holes are drilled into stone about six inches by this method, although there is an instance recorded of a twenty foot hole being drilled this way.	(see 347) (see 1863)
2500 BC	**Glass beads for decoration and adornment are now being made and used in Egypt.**	

2000 BC	Sumeria; soap is invented about this time. However, only the very wealthy can afford this luxury.	(see 1825)
2000 BC	Egypt; wooden locks and keys are now being made and used to secure the royal Egyptian treasures.	
2000 BC	**About now, the Chinese begin using chopsticks to eat their food.**	(see 1500s)
1800 BC	Babylonia; the bathtub is invented and first used.	
1670 BC	The 3.35 mile (5.4 km) long and 45.5 foot (14 meter) high Rajsamand Dam in India is completed, for irrigation purposes.	
1500 BC	**In Asia Minor, the first known iron-smelting is now underway.**	
1500 BC	**The first known professional miller is already grinding grain in Egypt.**	
1300 BC	**The Phoenicians are now dredging canals at Sidon and Tyre.**	
1250 BC	About this time, desiring to shorten shipping routes by sending ships "overland" by way of canals, Egyptian Pharaoh Ramses II has a ship canal built between the Nile and the Red Sea, it is of sufficient width for two galleys to row past each other.	(see 550 BC)
1200 BC	Lebanon; ship builders from all over most of the known world come to local lumberyards, for the fine cedar lumber from the "Cedars of Lebanon."	(see 1000 BC)
1000 BC	**Nomadic tribes in the Middle East are now making cheese.**	
1000 BC	A type of guitar is now being played in the Middle East.	
1000 BC	Lebanon; Cyrus (Sirius), a local lumber merchant, sells a huge order of lumber to King Solomon for a temple he is building.	
880 BC	**King Ashurnasirpal II of Syria invents (or takes credit for) the inflatable life preserver.**	
870 BC	**In Assyria, the first-known pulley-wheel is now being used.**	
776 BC	**Olympus Greece; the first Olympian Games (Olympics) are held. The first known cheesecake is being served to the Olympic athletes.**	
753 BC	**This is the "traditional" date of the founding of Rome, the Eternal City. Damascus, Syria, has already been around for a couple of millennium or so.**	
750 BC	In ancient Greece and Rome, the diaphragm valve is being used to control the water level and temperature of their hot baths. It is a primitive but effective valve using a leather diaphragm manually closed over a weir.	

625 BC	**In Greece, metal coins are first introduced, replacing grain as the medium of exchange. The coins are stamped with the facsimile of an ear of wheat; coins are lighter and don't mold or rot.**
600 BC	Thales, a Greek, discovers that when amber is rubbed with silk, it becomes "electrically" charged and attracts objects.
550 BC	During this century, a 992 mile (1600 km) long canal is built in China, connecting Peking and Honshu; it is 97.5 ft. (30 m) wide, at its narrowest points. Twenty-five centuries forward, some portions of this canal will still be in use in the twenty-first century.
500 BC	**China; Confucius writes about 100 foot deep wells delivering water and natural gas through bamboo pipelines.**
450 BC	**In writing, Herodotus describes oil pits or natural seeps, in the area around Babylon.** (see 347)
400 BC	**In Greece; Hippocrates is now using willow tree bark to ease pain and fever.** (see 1850s)
400 BC	**About this time, the Chinese philosopher Mozi begins flying the first known kites. Soon the Chinese are sending people aloft in large kites, to survey activity on the ground.**
350 BC	**About mid-century, in the Peloponnesian War, Sparta, using a flame-thrower made from a hollow log, attacks the wooden stockade of Dilion.**
350 BC	**About this time, cast iron is invented in China.**
331 BC	**Alexandria; during the Ptolemaic Period, "modern" glass originates here. Artisans create "mosaic glass" using slices of colored glass to create decorative patterns.**
325 BC	**About this time, Alexander the Great is using burning torches soaked in petroleum to frighten his enemies.**
300 BC	**Heronis of Alexandria (the father of robotics) builds the world's first hydraulic system… but it is actually pneumatic.**
285 BC	**Egyptians light the first known lighthouse to warn ships.**
270 BC	**The "well-known" Greek Mathematician, Ktesibios, improves the water clock. The gadget is also called the "water thief," and has been in use in some form or another since the 16th century BC.** (see 250 BC)
250 BC	**Mesopotamia; to help prevent flooding, layered earthen terraces are now being built in Tell Helaf.**
250 BC	Byzantium; somewhat similar to the liquid-level control of Ktesibios, Philon uses a float regulator to control the level of oil in a lamp's reservoir.

247 BC	China; Qin Shi Huang, who would soon become the first emperor of the Qin Dynasty, imposes a standard measure for the axle-length of carts. Thus any cart might be able to travel over any of the deeply-rutted roads. When each locality has a customary axle-length of its own, through traffic has been hampered by the necessity, at frequent intervals, of either changing the axles of the cart or else trans-shipping the freight to another cart of the correct axle-length for the next portion of the journey.		

200 BC	The crank-handle is invented in China.	(see 810)
200 BC	The Romans build and use the first known weighing scale; the "Steelyard." Very much the same as our old cotton weighing scales.	
200 BC	In Greece, hydro (water) power is being used to grind grains.	
170 BC	In Rome, notes are recorded about the first known professional baker.	
100 BC	The sauna bath is invented, in Finland.	
101 BC	Egypt; Hero of Alexandria invents the baroulkos, or lifting crane.	
50 BC	Syria; during this century, glassblowing is invented by the Syrians.	

1 BC	**Three Wise Men head out on their camels following a certain bright star in the east.** *Note: these men aren't on racing camels, they'll only cover a few miles each day. They are probably looking at possibly a year-long trek across deserts, seeking their goal.*	
C	Israel; in Bethlehem, Jesus, the Christ, Savior of the world is born. Here the three wise men find him lying in a manger.	
D	Israel; just outside Jerusalem, on Golgotha (Latin: Calvary) hill, Jesus Christ is crucified by Roman soldiers, is interred in a borrowed grave. Then on the third day, rises to join his Father God in Heaven.	
25	**In China, the first known soy milk is now being produced.**	
43	On an island, off the west coast of Europe, just north of the Thames' boggy marshes, a Roman village is founded.	(see 121)
77	Speaking of artichokes - Pliny the Elder calls them "nature's monstrosities… which even the animals instinctively avoid."	
100	About this time; Plutarch describes oil bubbling from the earth in the area of Kirkuk.	
121	North of the Thames' boggy marshes, where the Roman village once stood, another village is started named Londinium.	

150	**Paper is first produced in China by Ts'ai Lun.** *"Ahhh Bubba, that'll be easier on the ball point when it comes along."*	
347	China; utilizing some sort of drill bit connected to the end of many connected bamboo poles, some Chinese folks drill down about 800 feet... searching for, and finding... crude oil.	(see 1848)
410	As the Gauls sack Rome, the Holy Roman Empire, for all practical purposes, draws to its end.	
500	Ireland; According to the "Book of Senchus Mor," an old journal written about this time, horizontal water wheels are now being used to power mills of various types.	
550	Middle East; during the 525 to 567 reign of Roman Emperor Justinian, the city of Dara is partially washed away by a flood in the river, a tributary of the Khabur, that flows through the city. The architect Chryses of Alexandria then builds the first "horizontal arch dam," complete with sluice gates in both the upper and lower portions, to allow slowly releasing the captured water during a flood, rather than letting the flood waters destroy the city. *NOTE: It seems the "horizontal arch dam" was then forgotten until modern times.*	
600	**About this time quill pens (probably goose quills) for writing first appear around Seville, Spain.**	
644	**Persia; the first known windmill is in use to grind grain, and soon other windmills are used to pump water.**	(see 1287)
686	**Buddhist priests in China produce the first printed book.**	
750	**8th century; due to the scarcity of wood, folks in Baku are now using dirt impregnated with oil (from local seeps) for heating.**	
808	**The Italians are being serviced by the first known bank.** *"Yeah Bubba, probably with toasters or cookware!"*	
810	The hand-crank is now a fairly commonly used device.	
850	Ahmad Al-Baladhuri, a ninth-century Arab traveler writing *The Conquest of the Countries*, describes that the politics and economy of Absheron has been well connected with oil, for a long time.	(see 950)
872	Legend has it that Oxford University is founded when, by happenstance, Alfred the Great meets some monks at Oxford, they all have a scholarly debate that lasts for several days.	(see 1200s)
950	Tenth century Arab traveler Abū Dolaf Al-Yanbū'ī visits Absheron, and describing the area's oil sources, writes that there are two major sources, one of black oil and one of white (clear) oil. White oil is exported to Iran, Iraq, and India as a valuable commodity.	(see 1150)
1023	In China, the first ever paper money is printed.	

1045	Movable type printing is invented by Bi Sheng in China.	
1100	Sugar from cane is now being granulated in the Middle East.	
ca1150	In Azerbaijan, a unique medicinal oil from Naftalan is being used for curing many various health problems. This oil is carried in wineskins through the area of modern Georgia to the Black Sea shore, then exported to other countries.	(see 1273)
ca1200	The first buttons are invented for clothing. *"Wal Slim, Ah wunder whin thay invinted buttonholes?"*	
1200	Having been made and used in China for the last eight centuries, paper only now reaches Europe, coming by way of Arab Spain.	
1215	Runnymede, England; the Magna Carta (Great Charter) is signed by King John, with strong "encouragement" (threats) from many English Barons. This "charter of liberties" guarantees fundamental rights, opening the way for more personal freedoms, therefore allowing for more commercial freedom.	
1249	Rodger Bacon invents his gunpowder formula. *If guns haven't been invented, how does he know it's gunpowder?*	
1250	The gun is invented in China... now there is a use for Rodger's gunpowder.	
1264	An English Bishop, Walter de Merton, establishes the first college at Oxford England.	(see 1400)
1268	The first European paper mill is built; in Italy.	
1268	The first known eyeglasses are invented.	
1273	Venetian Marco Polo, writes about visiting Baku, the Persian city on the shores of the Caspian Sea, and seeing oil being collected from seeps to be used for lighting and medicinal purposes. This is in modern day Azerbaijan.	(see 1290) (see 1594)
1280	Although the true inventor is unknown, mechanical clocks are invented, a move strongly opposed, I'm sure, by the BOSL, (The Brotherhood of Sundial Laborers).	(see 1335)
1290	Along about this time, the Venetian traveler Marco Polo writes of personally witnessing people flying aboard large kites, in China.	(see 1783)
ca1287	The windmill is invented. *"No Bubba, these folks don't know about the one in Persia."*	(see 644)

1300s	**The very first locks for ships are built and in use on the rivers of Germany.**	
1328	**The first known sawmill is now in use.**	
1335	**Powered by falling weights and springs, the first known mechanical clock appears in Milan, Italy.**	
1339	**All the streets in Florence, Italy are now paved, the only city in Europe to be so.**	
1391	NOW, THIS IS BIG!!! The first mass-produced sheets of toilet paper measure about two feet by three feet. These are first used by the Chinese Emperors. *"Yeah Bubba, thay must have had really big... uh... big... enniehow that's big paper."*	
1391	England; at Oxford, Merton Library is now built at Merton College.	
1400s	Europe; during this century, grenades are first used. They are hollow cannonballs, filled with gunpowder and small iron balls.	
1400s	**Italy; in Venice, the first clear glass, called cristallo, is invented; and soon is being heavily exported.**	
1400	**The piano is invented; it's called the spinet.**	(see 1709)
1400	**Golf balls are invented, but one wonders... why?**	
1400	**Near this time, the first glass mirrors are invented; made by using mercury to attach a very thin layer of tinfoil onto the glass.**	
1400	**There are now fifty-five universities across Europe, including Oxford, Bologna, and Paris.**	
1418	Italy; in Venice, Doctor and engineer Giovanni Fontana (+/-1395-1455) builds what may be the first "human-powered" land vehicle, other than a two-wheeled cart. Fontana's vehicle uses an endless rope connected to the four wheels by a gearing system.	(see 1420)
1420	Venetian Giovanna Fontana has diagrammatically represented his design for a hand-driven, floating dredger. It is a twin-scoop affair, with windlasses. It is not thought that it is actually built, but the design is very feasible.	
1421	**Hoisting gear is invented in Florence (Italy) and the Republic of Florence issues the first known patent to Brunelleschi for a canal boat equipped with cranes for handling heavy cargo.**	
1452	About this time, Leonardo DaVinci is born, the illegitimate son of a wealthy merchant and the daughter of a poor farmer.	
1452	**Johannes Gutenberg, a goldsmith by trade, prints what is now known as the GUTENBERG BIBLE. This is after he spends a decade perfecting the formulas for the metal for the type, the inks, and even the paper. Gutenberg never receives any proceeds from this venture, as his financier takes all his equipment as repayment for monies invested. With very few changes, Gutenberg's formulas will be in general use around the world until the mid-twentieth century, about five-hundred years.** *NOTE: Some sources say Gutenberg is a diamond polisher by trade, not that it matters.*	

1460s	The teenaged Leonardo Da Vinci moves to Florence, to live with his father. In 1468, the sixteen-year old Leonardo begins his apprenticeship to Verrocchio, as an artist. He strives, and excels far beyond his master's expectations. *NOTE: At this time, the professional trade unions (Guilds) are closed to illegitimates.*	
1469-70	Leonardo DaVinci continues to acquire great mechanical and engineering skills while studying under Verrocchio.	
1472	Probably due to Verrocchio's persuasion, Leonardo DaVinci is accepted and joins the Guild as a painter (artist), however he continues studying and working in Verrocchio's studio.	(see 1493)
1472	An Italian inventor comes up with a "carriage"… propelled by windmills. *"Yeah Bubba, I said windmills!!!"*	
1474	At this time, Venice is the heart of a commercial empire, and the Venetian Senate now passes the first-known written law to grant and protect patents.	(see 1624)
1475	In Germany and Italy, muzzle-loading rifles are invented.	
1492	Sailing for the Spanish flag, the Genoese Italian, Christopher Columbus, discovers the South American continent, forever he will think he was sailing by the coast of India. Given some sugar cane cuttings by his mother-in-law, Chris introduces sugar cane to the Caribbean, as he lands on an island, naming it Hispaniola, later known as the Dominican Republic and Haiti.	
1493	DaVinci designs a bicycle chain that is perfectible workable, similar to modern roller chain. He also sketches a pedal and chain driven bicycle; four hundred years before one will be actually built. *(Many "experts" consider these drawings a hoax)*	
1494	**Whiskey is invented; in Scotland.** *"Naw Bubba, Whusky weren't invinted in Caintuck."*	
1497	While sailing under the English flag, the Italian John Cabot sights in on North America, most likely Newfoundland; he then claims this territory for England.	
1498	**The toothbrush is invented.** *Sounds like a new industry to me.*	
1499	Spanish explorer Alonso de Ojeda discovers Lake Maracaibo, extending 110 miles into the northeast corner of South America.	
1500	It is calculated that some 35,000 separate editions of books have now been published. Probably between 15 and 20 million copies have been printed.	

1500	The "best guess" is that Europe's population is now about eighty million people.	
1500	**The coiled spring is developed as power for clocks and watches. Peter Henlein of Nuremberg Germany, invents the spring-driven "watch," so-called because originally it is primarily used by watchmen. It is about the size of our later alarm clocks, and has only one hand.**	(see 1502) (see 1600s)
1500s	Forks are now becoming a part of Italian tableware, in another century or so, they will be used in England, France, and the British colonies in North America.	
1500s	Jacque Cartier and his group sail about 500 miles up the St. Lawrence River, past the location of the present city of Montréal.	
1500s	By this time, estate auctions are commonplace in France and the Netherlands.	
1500s	**The Atlas, a collection of engraved and printed maps bound in a book, is invented. The French cartographer Gerhard Mercator publishes a book of his maps, featuring a picture on the cover of Atlas from Greek mythology, holding the world on his back. From this time onward, all similar books containing maps are referred to as an Atlas.**	
1500s	During this century, Paracelsus discovers zinc, calling it zinken.	
1501	Gerolamo Cardano, a mathematician, is born in Italy, he will later discover the principle of the universal joint. NOTE: The word "cardan" means driveline in some South American Spanish.	(see 1676)
1501	Amerigo Vespucci, sailing for the Portuguese flag, hits the coast of South America. Returning to Portugal, he tells his patron, Lorenzo de' Medici, that he has sailed to a "New World." Soon Amerigo's name is attached to that "New World" by some mapmaker.	(see 1507)

1502	**The coiled spring is developed as power for clocks and watches. The first known pocket watch is built by Peter Henlein of Hamburg, Germany. Called the "Nuremburg Egg," this large "pocket" watch is often carried by a small chain hanging from the neck.**	(see 1675)
1506	Christopher Columbus dies; believing to the end that his trans-Atlantic voyages had all been to Asia. Columbus never realizes he had sailed along South America's North and East coasts.	
1507	**April 25; St. Die France; cartographer Martin Waldseemüller publishes the first map depicting a separate Western Hemisphere, and a separate Pacific Ocean. He names the "new worlds," Americus or America, after their discoverer Amerigo Vespucci.**	
1510	Techichi dogs are introduced in the Northern Mexican state of Chihuahua, brought from Mexico City by traders.	(see 1801)
1517	October 31; Wittenberg, Germany; Martin Luther posts his 95 theses, setting out his positive views, on the door of the castle church. With this action, Christian Protestantism is born.	
1528	Pánfilo de Naváez, accompanied by Cabeza de Vaca, leads an attempt by Spain to conquer Florida.	

1530	England; the several various English craft Guilds (Unions) have gotten so wealthy and powerful, they have almost prohibitory apprenticeship fees. These are such that a craftsman would work for many years almost as an "indentured servant," just to pay the Guild fees. This year Parliament steps in and cuts the initial fees from forty shillings or about sixteen pounds sterling, down to two shillings, sixpence. This helps to keep skilled labor from becoming an "intolerable monopoly," as well as opening opportunities to many thousands of willing men.	
1531	Portugal; our beautiful Lisbon is really "roughed-up" by an earthquake this year.	(see 1755)
1536	The earliest known book on shipbuilding is dated from this year.	
1541	**North America; Francisco Vasquez de Coronado brings the first cattle into the region that will someday be known as Texas.**	
1543	July; the remnants of Hernando DeSoto's expedition find oil floating on the water between what is now Sabine Pass and High Island, Texas. They skim the oil and use it to help in caulking their boats.	
1543	Belgian physician Andreas Vesalius publishes *De Humanis Corporis Fabrica*, the first complete textbook of the human anatomy, marking the beginning of modern medicine.	
1543	Blasco de Garay, a Spanish naval Captain, installs a large copper boiler, side paddlewheels and all necessary connecting devices, on the Trinity, a 200 ton freighter. Reports are that this vessel moves without sails, oars, or such. *NOTE: Another source states that the captain put a steamship he invented on display at the port of Barcelona.*	
1550	**In Constantinople, the first known coffeehouse opens for business.**	(see 1592) (see 1600)
1550	**About now in France, nuts and bolts are invented, and of course, the wrenches to work them.**	
1564	**England; a storm fells a large tree, uncovering a strange black substance. Everyone thinks it is some type of lead, and chunks are soon used for marking and writing. Folks continue calling this substance "lead" for the next couple of centuries.**	(see 1779)
1564	**England; graphite comes into widespread use, especially for marking and writing, as it leaves a darker mark than lead. This upswing in usage is primarily due to the recent discovery of a large graphite deposit near Borrowdale.**	(see 1779)
ca1565	**The Frenchman, Jacques Besson, introduces a "multi-bucket lifting machine." It does not excavate, however, it provides a continuous transfer of material being removed; the laborers only have to dig the material and place the material in the buckets, to be raised to the surface and emptied.**	
1565	**St. Augustine, in what will be Florida, is founded this year, the first city in North America.**	

1568	**The first-known industrial exposition is held this year in Nuremberg, Germany.**	
1588	King Philip II of Spain sends the Spanish Armada of 130 ships out to conquer England.	
1592	Coffee is now declared to be a "Christian drink" by Pope Clement VIII. Up to now, many Catholics considered coffee to be the "wine of infidels."	(see 1652)
1594	Baku; in the village of Balakhani, a hand-dug oil well 35 m deep is re-entered in modern times and a stone with this date and signed by Allahyar Mahammad Nurogly is found in the well.	(see 1618)
1596	*Sir John Harington invents the flush toilet in his home in Kelston. His godmother, Queen Elizabeth I, pays a visit and places an order for herself. Its only small drawback is the straight discharge piping that allows offensive sewer odors up into the castle. The Good Queen is not impressed.*	(see 1775)
1600	**Farmers first begin using the "A-frame" triangular harrow for cultivation.**	
1600	**About this time, coffee is first introduced to Europe.**	(see 1652)
1600s	During the 1600s coffee brought from Ethiopia, is being cultivated in Yemen.	
1600s	**Early in this new century, Europeans first begin to harness the power of steam.**	
1600s	During the 17th century, a butcher in Coburg, Johann Georghehner, invents the "dachshund," or "little dog" sausage, and introduces it to the city of Frankfurt. Thus this sausage is known as the "frankfurter."	
1600s	William Gilbert coins the word "electricity;" he is also first to use the terms electric force, magnetic pole, and electric attraction.	
1600s	North America; early in this century, the Native Americans introduce the cranberry to English settlers.	(see 1817)
1600s	King Maximilian I of Bavaria (1573-1651) plainly states, "If you want troubles, buy a watch!"	
1605	**Germany; the first known newspaper is published by Johann Carolus.**	
1608	*The telescope is invented by Hans Lippershey in Holland.*	
1609	An English explorer, Henry Hudson, working for the DUTCH EAST INDIA COMPANY, explores the Hudson River. Hudson's favorable report leads to more exploration and settlement in North America.	
1610	**Galileo discovers the earth's true relationship to the sun… much to the consternation of his colleagues.**	
1611	**England; King James commissions a new Protestant translation of the Holy Bible into English, hence, the "King James Version."**	

1612	**Italian physician Santorio Santorio (Sanctorius of Padua) is the first to describe the thermometer's use in medical analysis.**	
1618	The great amount of black oil in the Baku area is mentioned by Italian traveler Pietro Della Valle as bringing much income to the Shah each year.	(see 1637)
1620	**Cornelus Drebbel invents the thermostat.**	(see 1624)
1620	Africa; natives of this continent are being captured and shipped to the coastal English colony of Virginia in North America.	(see 1710)
1621	The DUTCH WEST INDIA COMPANY receives its charter for a trade monopoly in parts of the Americas and Africa.	
1621	Massachusetts; this April, John Carver, governor of the new colony at Plymouth, makes an alliance with Massasoit Osamequin, chief of the Wampanoag tribe. The two leaders pledge not to hurt each other's people, and to unite in defense against each other's enemies. This treaty gives the Pilgrims a greater margin of safety and stays in effect until the outbreak of King Philip's War, in 1675.	
1623	Silver ore is discovered in Norway, and mining begins.	
1623	York, ME (part of the Massachusetts colony); America's first sawmill begins sawing logs into lumber.	
1624	**Cornelus Drebbel builds the first known submarine. It is made of wood, wrapped in leather and smeared with fat to help waterproof it. During tests, it remains submerged for several hours and keeps the dozen rowers inside almost dry.**	
1624	England passes a "Statue of Monopolies," to protect inventors' rights and their work.	
1625	**England; John Tilsley starts the first factory to manufacture metal pins; e.g., hat pins, straight pins, and others.**	

	1626	Pieter Schaghen writes a letter outlining the sixty guilder (about $24) worth of goods, purchase of Manhattan Island by the Dutch. This letter is often called the "Birth Certificate of New York."	
	1620s	France; about this time King Louis XIV establishes the corvée, a system of enforced peasant labor, and uses it to build a 15,000 mile (24,000 km) network of improved roads.	(see 1733)

1630	England; Beaumont designs and builds roads for local coal mines using heavy planks, over which horses will pull the loaded carts.	
1631	England; only one small mistake and the printers were heavily fined. It seems they left out the word "not;" and the seventh commandment now reads… "Thou shalt commit adultery." This printing will go down in history as the so-called "wicked bible."	

1634	Massachusetts; Boston Common is the first public park in the colonies of America.	(see 1636)
1636	Massachusetts; Harvard, the first college in North America, is established.	(see 1639)
1637	Russia; in a "List of Gun Stocks," Baku oil is noted as a "terrible weapon by ignition."	(see 1647)
1639	Tobacco prices are so very low this year that the General Assembly of Virginia Colony in North America orders that each tobacco farmer shall burn half his crop.	
1639	Dorchester, MA; the first public elementary school in America, The Mather School, is founded.	(see 1838)
1641	Boston; a British rope maker comes to town to serve the needs of colonial farmers and mariners.	
1642	**In France, Blaise Pascal invents an adding machine.**	
1643	**Evangilesta Torricelli invents the barometer.**	
1643	**Christmas Day; as the ship *Royal Mary* of the ENGLISH EAST INDIA CO. sails past an uncharted island in the Indian Ocean, the Captain, William Mynors names it "Christmas Island."**	
1644	Italy; this year, Antonio Stradivari is born. It is thought that he was born in Cremona.	(see 1666)
1646	Sweden; in the town of Karlskoga, a hammering trip "hammer mill" is established; it's known as "Boofors" (Bofors).	(see 1873)
1647	In the British colony of Massachusetts in North America, a law is passed requiring towns to form and fund public schools. This is to be known as "The Old Deluder Satan Law."	
1647	Baku; having traveled from Turkey, Evliya Çelebi examines and thoroughly describes local oil fields while here. Çelebi notes that Baku oil brings 7,000 tomans of annual income to the Shah's treasury, and is exported to Persia, central Asia, Turkey and India. *NOTE: Toman is an old Mongolian word meaning ten-thousand… ten-thousand of just what, I don't know.*	(see 1666)
1648	**Holland; the sewing thimble is invented.**	
1649	England; King Charles I loses his head, literally; and Parliament auctions off his art collection, the finest in the Western World, to bargain-hunters (mostly foreign), thus scattering these English treasures all around Europe.	(see 1676)
1650	**Otto von Guericke invents an air pump.**	

1650	There are estimated to be about 582,500,000 people on earth today.	(see 1677)
1650	**During this century, children first begin playing with string "telephones."**	
1650	**Ice cream first appears in Europe.**	
1650	Before this time, Porte de l'Enfer, a red ochre mine is already operating on the Mattawa River in what will someday be southern Ontario, Canada.	
1652	England; London's first coffeehouse opens.	(see 1701)
1658	Based on Galileo's designs, using weights and swinging pendulum, Dutch scientist Christiaan Huygens invents a pendulum clock. Huygens' clock is very accurate, losing only one second every three hours. The foliot clocks in current use, lose or gain a second every few minutes.	(see 1673)
1660	**Cuckoo clocks are now being made in the Black Forest region of Germany.**	
1662	Germany; the first mass-produced writing pencils are being made in Nuremberg.	
1663	**In London, the first known steam-powered sawmill opens for business.**	
1666	During the Great Fire of London, after four-fifths of the city has already burned, a machine utilizing a battering-ram is being used to demolish many, many buildings, to create a "fire-line," to hopefully stop the spread of the flames. This is the first known specific-built demolition machine.	
1666	The Dutch sailor and traveler Jan Struys is taken prisoner and enslaved in Persia. Struys often visited Baku with the merchant who owned him, and Struys writes in his book, Journey, about wells up on Besh Barmag mountain, lined inside with stones and white and black oil coming to the surface. *Note: this mountain is now in the Siazan region of Azerbaijan.*	(see 1723)
1666	The young Antonio Stradivari begins building his magnificent violins, known as Stradivarius violins.	(see 1760)
1668	**Isaac Newton builds his reflecting telescope.**	
1670	***Champagne is invented by Dom Pérignon, a blind monk.***	
1670	Germany; the candy cane is first created and used to help keep children quiet in church - the cane shape is to bestow a blessing.	
1671	**Gottfried Wilhelm Leibniz invents a calculating machine.**	
1673	**The Dutch scientist, Christian Huygens, produces the first known "heat engine," using ideas from a cannon, and a tethered piston, instead of a cannonball.**	(see 1675)
1674	**Robert Hooke designs a mechanism for rotating a telescope at a constant speed.**	

1674	In the first known such record, Louis Joliet makes a map showing coal in the British colonies of North America.	
1675	**In Holland, Christian Huygens is issued a patent for the pocket watch.**	
1675	China; Ferdinand Verbiest, a Flemish Catholic missionary, builds a two-foot model steam cart powered by an engine copied from Heron's aeolipile (steam engine).	
1675	England; glassmaker George Ravenscroft invents lead crystal (also called "flint" glass) by adding lead oxide to clear Venetian glass.	
1675	Englishman Stephen Gray distinguishes between conductors and non-conductors of electrical charges.	
1676	**Using Cardan's principles from the early 1500s, Robert Hooke invents the universal joint.**	(see 1695)
1676	England; the earliest known English auction catalog is dated this year. It is for a book auction.	(see 1734)
1677	Holland; in Delft, Antonie van Leeuwenhoek, uses his "microscope" …and decides there are no more than 13.3 billion persons on the planet earth. *NOTE: later, historians will estimate there are probably only about a half-billion or so at this time.*	(see 1830)
1679	**After he invents the safety-valve (pressure regulator), Denis Papin invents the pressure cooker.**	(see 1707)
1680	**Franciscan Friars open the first silver mines in the area near El Paso of the future State of Texas.**	
1681	**Europe's first great canal project opens for traffic. Louis XIV's Midi Canal uses 101 locks over its 150 mile (240 km) length to cross a 620 foot summit and connect the Atlantic and Mediterranean watersheds. A magnificent engineering and construction feat for this day and time.**	
1682	Fleeing from religious persecution in England; Josiah Franklin settles in Boston. Franklin then soon marries Abiah Folger, his second wife.	(see 1706)
1685	Germany; late February; George Frideric Handel (1685-1759) is born in Halle, and about a month later, in late March, Johann Sebastian Bach is born in Eisenach, and lives until 1750. Strangely, these two great Baroque composers never met each other.	
1690	**In Germantown, PA, William Rittenhouse makes the first paper in the British Colonies.**	
1695	Sir Isaac Newton contrives a universal joint to mount his telescope for maximum flexibility and ease of operation.	
1698	**The Englishman, Thomas Savery invents a steam powered pump.**	

1700	**The estimated population of Europe is now somewhat less that 150 million persons.**	
1700	By this time an international trading community has come into being, doing business all around the globe.	
1700	**During the past two centuries, the population of Paris has about doubled, to just less than a half million. London has grown from about 120,000 to almost 700,000 persons. During this period, a significant new English language word comes into use... suburbs.**	
1700s	During this century, Britain's Royal Navy ships are sheathed in copper from Wales, while carrying cannon manufactured from Welsh iron.	(see 1850)
1701	**Mr. Jethro Tull (not the musician) invents the seed drill for planting.**	
1701	In most of London's 2000 coffeehouses, a paper sheet is now printed each morning, recounting recent news events. *NOTE: this is the birth of the morning newspaper that we now know and appreciate.*	
1701	**In Richmond, VA, the first known coal deposit in the colonies is located.**	(see 1748)

	1705	**Thomas Newcomen invents a steam-powered pump to pump water from mines.**	(see 1712)
	1706	January 17; in Boston, MA, Benjamin Franklin is born, the tenth of seventeen children.	(see 1717)
	1706	England; Thomas Twining opens a shop on the Strand in London, selling various blends of tea.	(see 2010)
	1707	Denis Papin uses his safety valve as a regulating device on a steam engine.	(see 1718)
	1709	**Bartolomeo Cristofori invents the piano.** *"Hey Slim, whut 'bout thet 'spinet' back ther in 1400?"*	

1710	North America; twenty-five percent of the population of the Colony of Virginia is now comprised of slaves; most are from Africa.	
1711	**An Englishman invents the tuning fork, how else to tune the piano?**	
1712	**England; Thomas Newcomen invents and patents the atmospheric steam engine, this leads to increased research into engines.**	
1713	**France; M. D'Hermand invents a "crawler tread" trailer; to be pulled by goats. If he even built one, it was a "one-off."**	(see 1770)
1714	Tea is first introduced into the British colonies of North America.	
1717	**Eleven year old Ben Franklin invents "swim fins, or flippers" to help him swim.**	(see 1723)
1718	In North America, at the mouth of the Mississippi River, a settlement is founded, someday to become New Orleans.	

1718	By now, the safety valve is becoming a standard accessory of steam engines, and can be found on almost every steam engine.	
1720	Often hauling eight tons of cargo, the distinctive "Conestoga" covered wagons are now appearing across the British colonies of North America. The name is taken from the Pennsylvania region where German settlers originally introduced the wagon.	
1722	**Mr. French C. Hopffer patents the fire extinguisher. The extinguisher consists of a cask holding a liquid fire retardant, as well as a gunpowder canister made of pewter, with fuses connected. When a home fire is seen, the householder lights the fuses, (and runs rapidly away) igniting the gunpowder, which explodes, scattering the liquid retardant.** *"Yeah Bubba, I'd be runnin' too, cause the 'splosion'll also scatter chunks of the pewter canister, an' pieces of the wooden cask."*	(see 2010)
1723	Ben Franklin runs away to Philadelphia; leaving his apprenticeship contract with James, his older brother in Boston.	(see 1727)
1723	Peter the Great (1672-1725) of Russia issues special decrees regarding the order of oil extraction. In a letter to Major General Michael Matyushkin, Peter demands the sending of "one thousand poods of white oil, or as much as possible, and to look for an increase in production." Baku and Durbent, on the east coast of the Caspian Sea are annexed to Russia during Peter's Persian Campaign.	(see 1739)
1724	**Gabriel Fahrenheit invents the first mercury thermometer.**	
1724	**About this time, the Kentucky Rifle, the first true American Rifle, is introduced. These firearms are somewhat customized for use on the frontier.**	
1725	Having departed Philadelphia, at the pleasure of the "upper crust," William Bradford lands in New York City and soon publishes the first newspaper there.	
1725	In the British Colonies of North America, lobsters are so plentiful they are considered to be "poverty food," and are most commonly used to feed prisoners, slaves, and indentured servants.	
1727	**The first social club in the colonies, the Junto (also called the Leather Apron Club), is organized by Ben Franklin.**	(see 1728)
1728	Young Benjamin Franklin opens his own printing office in Philadelphia.	(see 1729)
1729	Ben Franklin encourages, recommends, and argues for a paper currency for the colony of Pennsylvania.	(see 1730)
1730	Philadelphia, PA; now age 24, and owning his own print shop, Ben Franklin publishes his own newspaper, the *PENNSYLVANIA GAZETTE*.	(see 1732)
1730	Philadelphia; St. John's Lodge, America's "Mother" Masonic Lodge is founded, Ben Franklin joins next year.	
1730	UK; Brothers Ralph and Robert Clarke, of Newcastle upon Tyne, buy an interest in a sailing vessel, a freighter.	(see 2012)

1731	Zwilling J. A. Henckels AG is founded as a cutlery making business.	
1731	March 14; Johann Wilhelm Buderus leases the Friedrichshütte Iron Works, near the Lahn River, north of Frankfurt, Germany. Buderus has already invested a lot in this firm and owns most of the operating capital.	(see 1753)
1732	Benjamin Franklin, aka Richard Saunders, first publishes *Poor Richard: An Almanak,* and will do so annually through 1758. Ben Franklin's printing shops are soon franchised from Boston to Barbados.	(see 1736)
1733	France; the National Department of Bridges and Roads is established by King Louis XV.	
1733	England; this is about the time that Parliament authorizes a system of privately-operated toll roads.	(see 1904)
1733	England; Mr. John Kay invents the flying shuttle.	
1734	London; young Samuel Baker is a "chancer," buying large lots of books and reselling them at a profit, usually. This year the twenty-one year old Baker puts out his first catalog to draw prospective customers to the tavern, where he sits with his books, until all are sold.	(see 1744)
1735	***The corkscrew is invented in England, by Samuel Henshall.***	
1735	**England; John Harrison invents the marine chronometer.**	
1736	During this year Ben Franklin becomes clerk of the Pennsylvania Assembly, then begins printing work for the Assembly; no conflict of interest here. Assemblyman Ben Franklin of Pennsylvania is appointed the first postmaster of the British colonies in North America. The first Postmaster General of the USA. Also, Philadelphia's Union Fire Company, basically an insurance company, is founded by Ben Franklin, et al, for "the better preserving our Goods and Effects from fire." The company's members are bound in "Friendship" to maintain buckets (used to douse fires) and cloth bags (used to rescue portable items from fires) to use to protect each other's property.	(see 1739 (see 1752)
1736	**Jonathan Pauls designs a practical tow/tug boat.**	
1738	Daniel Bernouli publishes *Hydrodynamica,* his book of hydraulic principles.	
1738	**J. F. Brondel invents the "valve-type" flush toilet.**	(see 1775)
1739	Ben Franklin begins his work with fireplace improvements.	(see 1743)
1739	Russia; the Russian academician I. V. Veytbreht publishes his treatise, "About the Oil," containing a good amount of information on Absheron oil.	(see 1741)
1740	The Harlowe family first enters the blacksmith business in Ashbourne, Derbyshire, England.	(see 1826)
1740	About this time, the world's first romance novel is printed.	
1741	Massachusetts; in Amherst, Jonathan Cowls establishes a lumber yard, using wood from the Cowls' family-owned forests.	

Poor Richard, 1733.

AN

Almanack

For the Year of Chrift

1733,

Being the Firft after LEAP YEAR:

And makes fince the Creation	Years
By the Account of the Eaftern *Greeks*	7241
By the Latin Church, when ☉ ent. ♈	6932
By the Computation of *W. W.*	5742
By the *Roman* Chronology	5682
By the *Jewish* Rabbies	5494

Wherein is contained

The Lunations, Eclipfes, Judgment of the Weather, Spring Tides, Planets Motions & mutual Afpects, Sun and Moon's Rifing and Setting, Length of Days, Time of High Water, Fairs, Courts, and obfervable Days.

Fitted to the Latitude of Forty Degrees, and a Meridian of Five Hours Weft from *London,* but may without fenfible Error, ferve all the adjacent Places, even from *Newfoundland* to *South-Carolina.*

By *RICHARD SAUNDERS,* Philom.

PHILADELPHIA:
Printed and fold by *B. FRANKLIN,* at the New Printing-Office near the Market.

1741	UK; Johnes Hanway, the director of the ENGLISH-RUSSIAN TRADING CO. investigates the condition of Baku's oilfields.	(see 1754)
1743	Benjamin Franklin goes to see an "Electrical Oddity" show… and he is hooked.	(see 1744)
1743	France; the champagne maker MOET & CHANDON is established.	
1744	**The first mail-order catalog in the US is issued by Benjamin Franklin, he is selling books.**	(see 1745)
1744	London; about this time, Sam Baker begins utilizing the auction method to resell the books he has purchased.	(see 1767)
1745	Ben Franklin performs his first known electrical experiments.	(see 1746)
1745	**Sheffield, England; it is about this time that the crucible process of steel making is invented.**	
1745	**Scotland; Edmund Lee, a millwright, invents and patents the fantail, a device for automatic control of windmills. The "fantail" automatically keeps a windmill's blades facing into the wind.**	
1745	Germany; E. G. von Kleist invents the leyden jar, the first known electrical capacitor.	

1746	**Forty year old Ben Franklin is now a household word throughout the colonies, he has already charted the Gulfstream, invented the fairly efficient Franklin Stove, and also invented the phonetic alphabet, which is a dismal failure.**	(see 1748)
1747	Hartford, CT; Col. Joseph Pitkin begins his successful forge business; making bar iron, and a mill for iron work.	(see 1750)
1748	**At forty-two and wealthy, Ben Franklin retires from his businesses, devoting more time to experimenting and inventing.**	(see 1749)
1748	John Newton, a seaman, has just left his post on deck, during a horrendous storm, when the crewman replacing him is violently swept overboard. Newton, a British slave trader now realizes his own helplessness and that only the Grace of God can save him.	(see 1753)
1748	The Swedish cartographer Pehr Kalm publishes a map of North America, showing the "oil springs of Oil Creek, PA."	(see 1767)
1748	The first coal production in the colonies begins in Richmond, VA.	(see 1769)
1749	In a cooking experiment he conducts on the banks of the Schuylkill River in Philadelphia, Ben Franklin roasts a turkey on an electric spit.	(see 1750)
1750	March; in a letter to a friend, Ben Franklin suggests the use of "lightning rods" to protect houses from lightning.	(see 1751)
1750	During this decade, Dr. J. P. Hale reports that the local Indians are using an "oil spring" in the Kanawha Valley of Western Virginia.	
1750	The British Parliament Act of 1750 shuts down Col. Pitkin's forge operation.	(see 1776)
1751	Axel Cronstedt, a Swedish chemist, isolates nickel, an extremely hard metal, and due to its hardness, names it "Nick," for the devil.	

1751	USA; Ben Franklin publishes his theory of electricity and his plans to test his theory.	(see 1752)
1751	France; the first recorded instance of the subject of "crossing the English Channel by means other than boat," is broached by the Amiens Academy.	
1752	June; Benjamin Franklin does his kite experiment and shortly afterwards invents the lightning rod. Then in December, Franklin designs a flexible catheter for his brother John, who suffers from bladder stones. *NOTE: Franklin always refuses to patent any of his inventions, preferring "just to contribute to the well-being of society."*	(see 1754)
1753	June 23, Germany; sixth-three year old Johann Wilhelm Buderus dies suddenly. Certainly he never realized what a successful, long-enduring business he had going. Buderus' wife, Elisabeth Magdalena, takes over management of the foundry and iron works, and will see it through many challenges, including the Seven Years War.	(see 1773)
1753	England; suffering a stroke that ends his days at sea, John Newton accepts a job at the Liverpool Customs Office. In his spare time, Newton begins to explore Christianity in depth.	(see 1764)
1753	North America; the first steam engine arrives in the colonies from England.	(see 1755)
1754	***The political cartoon is "invented" this year, when Ben Franklin publishes in his Philadelphia newspaper, his drawing of a snake separated in eight parts, with the caption, "We must join, or die;" encouraging the colonies to unite.***	(see 1760)
1754	**London; Johnes Hanway publishes his "Historical Essay About English Trade in the Caspian Sea."**	(see 1771)
1755	Portugal, November 1; an earthquake, immediately followed by a disastrous fire, then by a 50 foot (15.4 m) high tidal wave, hits Lisbon. About a quarter of Lisbon's population is killed, more than 60,000 persons. *NOTE: Modern scientific estimates of this earthquake place it at 8.5 on the Richter scale.*	
1755		
	North America; the first steam engine in the American colonies is installed for power to pump water from a mine.	
1756		
1756	Capt. Claude-Joseph Dubreuil de Villars is operating a sugar mill in New Orleans, but the granulation process remains a mystery to him.	(see 1759)
	Austria; Leopold Mozart is a court musician to Sigismund von Schrattenbach, the Archbishop-Prince of Salzburg. On January 27, Leo's wife gives birth to Wolfgang Amadeus Mozart. Leopold soon realizes his young son has an unbounded enthusiasm for music.	
1757	**John Campbell invents the sextant.** *"No, no, no Bubba, he didn't invent soup..."*	
1758	Switzerland; Jacques Gevril becomes the first exporter of Swiss timepieces, after the King of Spain has Gevril make a watch for him.	

1758	Osterfeld, Germany; the "St. Antony" ironworks is established nearby.	
1758	England; the MIDDLETON RAILWAY, in Leeds, is established by an act of Parliament; thus, the MIDDLETON can truly claim to be the world's oldest railway.	
1759	Austria; three-year-old Wolfgang A. Mozart can now play a harpsichord reasonably well.	(see 1760)
1759	In England, "Iron Mad" Wilkinson sets up his first factory.	(see 1779)
1760	LLOYD'S REGISTER OF SHIPPING is established in Great Britain.	
1760	Ben Franklin's favorite of his inventions is the Glass Armonica, consisting of 37 rotating crystal bowls. Mozart will someday write two compositions especially for this instrument.	(see 1780)
1760	**Small metal screws have been invented and are now being used for joining wooden pieces of furniture, etc.**	
1760	As George III becomes King of England, there are about a million and half inhabitants in the North American Colonies.	
1760	Cumbria, England; CURRAN IRON WORKS is established.	
1760	Austria; the violin is now being played by the four-year-old Mozart.	(see 1761)
1761	Germany; in Nuremberg, Herr Kaspar Faber builds the first factory (later FABER-CASTELL) to make erasers.	
1761	Austria; Mozart, now five years old, composes his first piece, "Minuet and Trio."	(see 1762)

	1761	England; the Duke of Buckingham sells a London "house" bearing his name to King George III, who only came to the throne last year. George bought the house for his wife, Queen Charlotte, and fourteen of their fifteen children will be born there. The "Queen's House" is extensively remodeled, and will someday soon be known as Buckingham Palace.	(see 1774)
	1762	The six year old Wolfgang Mozart goes on his first tour with his musical family. Often, he and his sister, Maria Anna, four years his senior, will play duets; sometimes with a cloth covering their hands to further impress the audience. For many years the Mozart family lives thusly, touring and playing their music all over Europe.	(see 1764)

1764	**James Hargreaves builds his "Spinning Jenny" to spin cotton fibers.**	
1764	England; on his fourth try, John Harrison invents a clock that allows precise longitude determination while at sea. Early this year, after a six and half week voyage to Jamaica, Harrison's clock is only five and one-tenth seconds slow.	
1764	England; the former seaman and slave trader John Newton now becomes an ordained minister.	(see 1772)
1764	This year Mozart plays for King Louis XV of France; and for England's King George III, in Buckingham Palace.	(see 1774)
1764	April 15; the British Parliament passes the "Sugar Act," to collect American revenue on molasses brought into the British colonies of North America from non-British colonies. In May, at a town meeting, James Otis, a Boston attorney, condemns the "Sugar Act" as "taxation without representation." In July, Otis publishes *The Rights of the British Colonies Asserted and Proved*.	(see 1770)

1764	In England, construction of the Bridgewater canal is now complete.	
1764	**Eli Whitney and John Hall each invent a milling machine to be used in making guns for the colonial government. Although both machines are very near the same time, the better-known Whitney is usually recognized as the inventor.**	
1765	Robert Fulton is born in Little Britain, Pennsylvania on November 14.	
1765	**About this time, John Wilkerson invents a boring machine for metal, powered by James Watt's steam engine.**	(see 1769) (see 1774)
1765	On a springtime Sunday afternoon walk on Glasgow Green, Watt's idea of a separate condenser just comes to him. Watt later said, "…in the course of one or two days the invention was thus far (as a pumping engine) complete in my mind."	
1765	Potatoes are first introduced into Europe.	(see 1769)
1765	Massachusetts; WALTER BAKER CHOCOLATE COMPANY is established in the town of Dorchester.	
1765	*Hydrogen gas is discovered by Henry Cavendish, an Englishman.*	
1766	**Joseph Priestly invents carbonated water.**	
1766	London; BAKER & LEIGH is founded, as Sam Baker takes George Leigh as his partner. Soon, Sam's nephew John Sotheby joins the auction firm.	(see 1778)
1767	New York; in his writings, Sir William Johnson mentions the Native American Indian practice of skimming oil.	(see 1778)
1768	**The *Encyclopedia Britannica* is first published, in a set composed of three volumes.**	
1768	England; the Royal Academy is established in London.	
1768	England; Richard Arkwright patents his spinning frame, he continues working on a water powered model.	
1768	October 23; in Paris, Nicolas-Joseph Cugnot demonstrates what is probably the first self-propelled land vehicle. His "steam artillery tractor," a three-wheeler, can haul as much as five tons at about 3 mph, but it loses all steam and needs watering after a mile and a half. The boiler overhangs the single front steering wheel, and it has only 15 degrees of steering. While trying to negotiate a turn, it rolls over, losing a battle with a brick wall (demolished the wall), got Cugnot jailed…the world's first ever traffic offense. He lost the fight, the public lost interest, and the idea lost steam… pun intended. Cugnot stops development at this time.	
1769	**Scotland; James Watt develops an improved, coal-powered, steam engine. When trying to sell his steam engine to industry, Watt has to be able to compare it to the power developed by a horse. By observing an average horse operating a winch for raising water, he then establishes horsepower (hp) as 33,000 ft. lb. of work per minute.**	
1769	England; Mr. Smeaton designs a (somewhat inaccurate) boring machine for the Carron Iron Works for machining cannon.	
1769	England; the WEDGWOOD POTTERY is founded.	
1769	Richard Arkwright's water frame, or water powered spinning frame, is patented this year.	
1769	Protesting the Stamp Act and "taxation without representation" some 200 colonists stage the Boston Tea Party.	

1770	England; writer and inventor Richard Lovell Edgeworth patents a steam-powered track system that clearly employs the principles of the modern crawler tractor, but as far as is known, he never uses the idea.	(see 1826)
1770	The population of the North American colonies is about 2,200,000 persons.	
1770	**Gen. George Washington acquires 250 acres of land in what is now West Virginia, "because it contains an oil and gas spring," making the future first president the first petroleum industry speculator in the colonies.**	
1771	The academician Samuel Gottlieb Gmelin (1745-1774) visits Baku and confirms that white oil was sublimated for production of kerosene in Surakhani, and describes the technique of the well's oil production.	(see 1781)
1771	UK; minister John Newton has written the words that become *Amazing Grace* as part of his sermon this New Year's Day.	(see 1829)
1773	**In one of the first recorded building implosion by explosives in the Western World, the Holy Trinity Cathedral in Waterford, Ireland, is brought down with 150 pounds of strategically placed gunpowder charges.**	
1773	Germany; the BUDERUS FRIEDRICHSHÜTTE business is carried through the economic downturn of the '70s by the outstanding management skills of J. W. Buderus II.	(see 1807)
1773	Austria; the waltz is taking Vienna by storm this year.	
1773	England; John Wilkinson comes up with the idea of making the boring bar heavier, running it through the cylinder being bored, and giving it support on the outboard end. Wilkinson will cast and bore all cylinders for Boulton and for Watt for many years, it's said, "almost without error."	
1774	Austria; Mozart is appointed concert master for the Archbishop-Prince of Salzburg; a position he holds for 3 years.	(see 1785)
1774	England; Joseph Priestley discovers oxygen, therefore discovering what makes things burn.	
1774	Switzerland; Georges Louis Lesage receives a patent on his invention of the electric telegraph.	
1774	**Alexander Cummings invents the "P" (or "U") drain trap, to prevent odors from the sewers from coming up into the house.**	
1775	April 18; the proverbial straw that breaks the camel's back… General Thomas Gage sends 800 British redcoats to Concord, MA, to seize armaments stored there by the colonists. April 19; Lexington, MA, at about 4 am, a small, ill-prepared group of local men and boys of all ages confront the Concord-bound British force. "Someone" fires the first shot, and in a couple of minutes eight colonists are dead and ten lie injured. *The American Revolutionary War is begun!!!*	
1775	Jacques Perrier invents a steamship.	
1775	November 10; in the British Colonies of North America, the Continental Congress today authorizes the formation of two battalions of Marines… these will be the first Leathernecks!!!	
1776	**July 4; the colonies in North America declare their independence from England.**	

IN CONGRESS, JULY 4, 1776.

The unanimous Declaration of the thirteen united States of America.

1776	**David Bushnell launches his hand-powered submarine, called the "Turtle."**	
1776	In England, a tram road is laid using cast iron angle bars laid on timber crossties.	
1776	Now, the Pitkin family squares things with the Brits by using their buildings to make gunpowder for the Continental Army during the American Revolution. The Pitkins will be industrial leaders for the next century or so.	(see 1834)

1777	England; British reformer Major John Cartwright (1740-1824) calls for the reform of Parliament, as well as calling for universal manhood suffrage in all parliamentary elections.	
1777	London; sixty-six year old Sam Baker dies this April. It has been previously decided that John Sotheby inherits Sam's partnership with Leigh. Soon the auction firm of Leigh & Sotheby is going strong.	
1778	London; the son of a humble "feather-bed beater," forty-eight-year-old James Christie is already well established as England's premier auctioneer.	
1778	Moravian missionaries have reported "oil wells, with the products of which the Seneca Indians carry on trade with Niagara" in the western portion of New York state.	(see 1785)

1779	**Englishman Samuel Crompton invents the "spinning mule."**	
1779	The word "graphite" comes into common usage as the name for mineral now being used for writing and marking.	(see 1890s)
1780	**Old Benjamin Franklin invents bi-focal eyeglasses.**	(see 1783)
1780	**Germany; Gervinus invents the circular saw.**	
1781	At Wylam, near Newcastle upon Tyne England, George Stephenson is born.	(see 1791)
1781	The planet Uranus is discovered by Herschel.	
1781	Admiral Marko Ivanović Vojnović (1750-1807), the chief of the Caspian expedition, finds signs of oil and gas on the bottom of the Caspian Sea near the island of Zhiloy (Chilov), near the Absheron peninsula. In 1781-1782 Vojnović charted a detailed map of the Eastern part of the Caspian Sea.	(see 1796)
1782	The "Gute Hoffnung" (Good Hope) ironworks is founded in Sterkrade, Germany.	
1782	Switzerland; the last known witch in Europe is burned at the stake.	
1783	**In England, Henry Cort invents the steel roller for steel production.**	
1783	**In Paris, France, the Montgolfier brothers are the first men to fly in a balloon, and old Benjamin Franklin is there to watch this spectacle.**	(see 1290) (see 1784)
1783	November 21; Jean-François Pilâtre de Rozier and the Marquis d'Arlandes rise into the heavens in "new" invention called a Montgolfier balloon. They drift over Paris, France, for twenty-five minutes, covering 5. 5 miles (9 km) before safely setting down. Although probably not the case, this event is hailed as the first time human beings have ever flown.	(see 1290)
1783	In Boston, Paul Revere begins making and selling copper bells and brass door hinges, his clients include the US Navy and US Mint.	
1783	September; the signing of the "Treaty of Paris," technically ends the Revolutionary War.	

1783	USA; in Connecticut, Mr. Benjamin Hanks patents the self-winding clock.	
1783	In the first recorded such event, Louis-Sébastien Lenormand uses a umbrella-type device to safely descend from a observation tower in Montpeilier, France. This is considered a "rigid" parachute, or a "aerodynamic braking device."	
1784	***The threshing machine is invented by Andrew Meikle.***	
1784	The BANK OF AMERICA is founded; the primary founding investors are women.	
1784	Half-joking, Ben Franklin publishes a paper advocating shifting the clocks in the summer, to create "daylight savings time." *"Yeah Slim, an' it's still a joke!!"*	(see 1790)
1784	John Jacob Astor, the twenty-one year old son of a German butcher, arrives penniless in the USA. His desire, above all else, is to get rich. He has a job beating beaver pelts with a stick to disperse moths and their eggs. Soon Astor will be buying pelts cheaply, one or two at a time from sailors at the docks, and promptly reselling them downtown at a profit.	(see 1799)
1784	England; Mr. Murdoch, an associate of James Watt, builds a steam engine model that runs 6 to 8 mph.	
1784	Having only recently settled in Kentucky, a family of poor, white, immigrants are attacked by Indians at their cabin in broad daylight. The father is shot and the savages are proceeding to tomahawk the six-year old son to death, when an elder brother shoots the savage from the doorway of the cabin, and the other Indians flee. The six-year old Lincoln boy grows up, marries, and one day he has a son... Abraham Lincoln.	
1785	Bath, England; George Stothert sets up shop as an ironmonger.	(see 1815)
1785	John Fitch has a wild idea about building a boat... now get this... powered by steam.	(see 1786)
1785	August 24; Wolfgang Amadeus Mozart receives notice that he has NOT been accepted into the Society of Composers.	(see 1787)
1785	During this decade, America, using English technology, begins a period of canal construction that will run for about eight decades. Most of these early projects were "lateral canals," paralleling a river, and built where the river was not navigable, often they were only eliminating portages around short, rough sections of the river.	(see 1817)
1785	England; steam power is used for the first time to spin cotton, as Edmund Cartwright invents the power loom.	
1785	In Pennsylvania, General William Irvine reports that "Oil Creek, PA, has taken its name from an oil or bituminous matter floating on its surface."	(see 1790)
1786	New York City, June 8th; the first commercial ice cream is made. *If this isn't a red letter day, I don't know what is!*	
1786	USA; John Fitch has a steam-powered boat operating on the Delaware River.	(see 1787)
1787	John Fitch now builds an even larger steamboat.	(see 1790)
1787	Czechoslovakia; Mozart's *Le Nozze di Figaro (The Marriage of Figaro)* debuts as a huge success in Prague.	(see 1788)
1788	Noah Webster first publishes *The Blue-Backed Speller*; about 300 editions will be published by 1824.	

Plan of Mr. Fitch's Steam Boat.

1788	Austria; this year, during a six-week period, Mozart composes three complete symphonies.	(see 1791)
1788	Britain sends the first shipload of convicts to their colony of Australia. *Look out Abos, here they come!!!*	
1789	**The German chemist, Martin Heinrich Klaproth discovers the element uranium, while assaying pitchblende ore.**	
1789	Samuel Slater sails back to America, after serving an apprenticeship in Britain. Having memorized the workings of Arkwright's spinning machines, Slater joins with Moses Brown, a Quaker merchant, trader and industrialist. In Rhode Island, they build the first American textile mills.	
1789	USA; Congress federalizes all existing lighthouses which have been built by the various colonies, also appropriating funds for more lighthouses, beacons, and buoys.	
1790	Britain; the Forth and Clyde Canal opens between Grangemouth and Falkirk Harbors, connecting Glasgow with the West Coast of Scotland.	(see 1822)
1790	The "Patents Act" of the United States becomes law this year. Then, The United States Patent Office issues its first patent to Wm. Pollard of Philadelphia for a machine that roves and spins cotton.	
1790	April 17; the world loses a printer, inventor and a great statesman when Benjamin Franklin dies at age 84. More than 20,000 people attend Franklin's funeral.	
1790	The Curran Iron Works employs over a thousand men.	
1790	While drilling a water well, crude oil is found near Elizabeth, WV.	(see 1806)
1790	Englishman Thomas Saint files the first known patent for a sewing machine. *NOTE: Many noted historians believe Saint only patented the idea, without ever building a functional machine. All future attempts to replicate his models have yielded faulty equipment.*	
1790	In Waterbury, CT, Mr. Henry Grilley begins making buttons of pewter.	(see 1802)
1790	Carrying paying passengers and freight, John Fitch's steamboat is running regular scheduled and advertised trips between Trenton and Philadelphia.	(see 1793) (see 1798)
1790	July 16; the Congress of the United States passes the "Residence Act," instructing the President to choose a location along the Potomac River for a permanent seat of government, ending its ten year stay in Philadelphia. President George Washington selects the confluence of the Potomac and the Anacostia Rivers for what will become the District of Colombia.	
1790	To protect the US coast against smugglers, President George Washington authorizes the construction of ten fifty-foot, two-masted Patrol boats.	
1790	Pennsylvania; Mr. Nathaniel Carey is skimming oil from springs near Titusville and delivering it on horseback to customers.	(see 1791)
1791	**England; John Barber invents the gas turbine.**	
1791	**France; the National Assembly of France passes a patent law this year.**	
1791	**After working 2 years part-time, 10 year old George Stephenson goes to work full-time in the coal mine pits, not yet having a chance to go to school.**	(see 1798)
1791	On Avery Island, LA, salt remaining from spring water evaporation is now being locally utilized.	
1791	In Essen, Germany, the "Neu Essen" ironworks is established.	
1791	Austria; December fifth, thirty-five year old Wolfgang Amadeus Mozart dies penniless in Vienna, ending a very busy year.	

1791	A map of Pennsylvania, made this year, shows a stream named "Oyl Creek."	(see 1795)
1792	**William Murdoch invents gas lighting.**	
1792	**English explorer George Vancouver begins surveying the Pacific coast from Oregon to Alaska.**	
1792	Jacques Nicholas Conté invents a hard, long-wearing pencil lead, made from clay mixed with graphite and covered with cedar wood.	
1792	**About this same time, someone in Australia also comes up with a good pencil lead.**	
1792	USA; in New York City, with twenty-four brokers, the NEW YORK STOCK EXCHANGE is founded.	
1792	USA; Bourbon County, VA, now becomes Bourbon County, KY.	
1792	The privately-built Lancaster Pike runs about 60 miles (96 km) between Lancaster and Philadelphia, PA.	(see 1795)
1793	**Robert Fulton first envisions powering boats with steam.** *Has Robert been hiding under a rock?*	
1793	This year the United States produces about 10,000 bales of cotton.	
1793	**Having invented a new way to spin thread, Hannah Slater, Samuel's wife, is the first woman to file for a patent in the new US patent offices.**	
1793	New Hampshire; Judge Samuel Blodgett begins building locks and canals on the Merrimack River, south of Concord, at Amoskeag Falls, planning to utilize the water power to operate textile mills.	(see 1804)
1794	**Last year Eli Whitney invented the cotton gin; this year, he is awarded a patent on it. Eli's ideas on interchangeable parts for muskets, actually start the idea of mass production in the US.**	
1794	**George Washington designates SPRINGFIELD ARMORY as the first US Arsenal.**	
1794	**A Welshman, Phillip Vaughn, invents the ball bearing.**	
1795	REXROTH is founded as a iron foundry and builder of steam hammers.	
1795	In Pennsylvania, the Lancaster pike is completed this year.	
1795	Reporting on Pennsylvania, the first US gazetteer, Joseph Scott, reports about Oil Creek and Seneca Oil.	(see 1806)
1795	Now, and for the next few years, crude oil is quoted at or about $16. 00 per gallon.	(see 1806)
1790s	Up to now; though many may try, very few are successful at milling sugarcane and producing raw sugar.	
1796	Christian Friedrich Martin is born in Germany into a family of many generations of guitar makers.	
1796	**One of the earliest steam dredges is now working in the port of Sunderland, England.**	(see 1835)
1796	RIZLA begins in business, making rolling papers, for rolling tobacco smoking items.	
1796	Marshal von Frederick Biberstein (1768-1826) noted: "...the Absheron peninsula contains an inexhaustible stock of oil."	(see 1803)
1797	Needing to make screws, Henry Maudslay invents the metal turning lathe, in England.	
1797	This year 550,000 pounds of sugar is exported from New Orleans.	

1797	The US Navy frigate *USS Constitution* is built, carrying a crew of 450 volunteers and forty-four cannons.	(see 1830)

1797	**The corrugated wash/scrub board, which can be stood in a wooden tub filled with hot water, is first introduced.**	
1797	**USA; Amos Whittemore patents a carding machine for wool.**	
1798	Eighteen year old George Stephenson takes it upon himself to attend evening classes to learn to read and write.	(see 1814)
1798	Kentucky; several states have granted John Fitch exclusive rights for steamboats on their waters. However, Fitch cannot secure financial backing, nor survive financially, and sadly, he dies broke, and broken hearted, here in Bardstown.	
1798	Europe; the Venetian author and adventurer, Giacomo Casanova, better known as a lover and seducer, dies this year. The freethinking libertine dies a very common death while working as a librarian for a Bohemian Count.	
1798	UK; Welsh farmer and businessman John Wilkinson installs a steam engine to power a threshing machine. John's idea catches on and gathers steam…	
1799	The first president of the United States, General George Washington dies, at age sixty-seven.	
1799	*The Fourdrinier machine for paper making is invented by Louis-Nicolas Robert, a Frenchman.*	
1799	PFERD is established as a manufacturer of abrasive products.	
1799	With a net worth of $100,000, John Jacob Astor is no longer beating beaver pelts; he now begins buying Manhattan real estate. Astor then begins ruthlessly expanding his fur dealing empire.	(see 1817)
1799	Egypt; the Rosetta stone is discovered.	
1799	Only in his late twenties, and going deaf, Ludwig von Beethoven is working on his first symphony.	
1799	As the French Revolution ends, Napoleon begins changing the face of Europe.	
1799	England; twenty-six-year-old George Cayley creates the first scientifically-based imagining of an airplane. It is around this time that he states, ". . . it is only necessary to have a first mover (engine) that will generate more power in a given time, in proportion to its weight, than the animal system of muscles."	
1800	England; Richard Trevithick builds his first steam powered vehicle for use on roads.	(see 1804)
1800	Charlotte, NC; gold mines in this area are the primary source of US gold, and will remain so for the next five decades.	
1800	The best guess is that there are a bit less than 200 million persons in Europe, more or less a quarter of the earth's inhabitants.	
1800	USA; Oliver Evans builds his first successful, non-condensing, high-pressure, stationary steam engine.	(see 1804)
1800	Canada; The first blast furnace for iron opens at Lyndhurst (or Furnace Falls), Leeds County, in southern Ontario. This facility uses ore from the nearby Bastard Township, and is soon abandoned.	(see 1813)
1800	Italy; Alessandro Volta invents the first electric battery.	

The eighteenth century is past history now, let us get into the nineteenth century…

1801	A French chemist, Philippe LeBon develops a usable coal gas, then patents a coal-gas fired internal combustion engine.	
1801	In the harbor of Brest, Robert Fulton demonstrates his "plunging boat" (submarine) for the French Admiralty, he stays underwater for four hours, at a depth of 25 feet (7.7 m). The demonstration is a unqualified success, but fails to garner financial support of the French government.	
1801	**Louisiana has 75 sugar mills and produces five million pounds of sugar. Sugar is now selling for eight cents a pound.**	
1801	Cane Ridge, KY; this August, 25,000 people come together for a Christian revival, the evangelists leading this meeting call it "The Second Great Awakening." This is an early "camp meeting," as they are beginning to be called. (*The population of Kentucky's largest city, Lexington is now 1,795.*)	
1801	Early this century, American traders along the Texas-Chihuahua border bring the little techichi dogs home to the US, and begin to breed them, now calling the species… Chihuahuas.	
1801	Philadelphia; the Fairmount Water works is now using steam-powered pumps to provide water for the citizens.	
1801	The first-ever census is taken throughout Great Britain.	
1801	Italy; to enable a blind friend to write, Pellegrino Turri invents a crude, but workable typewriter.	(see 1808)
1801	The first coal powered steam engine is now running.	(see 1803)
1802	E. I. Du Pont de Nemours opens its first gunpowder plant at Wilmington, DE.	
1802	Scotland; William Symington's 10 horsepower steam-powered paddle wheeler, the *Charlotte Dundas,* is the first practical tugboat ever built.	
1802	Waterbury, CT; Henry Grilley is joined by the Porter brothers, Abel and Levi. Now, as Abel Porter & Company, they're making buttons.	(see 1811)
1802	England; Sir Humphry Davy has created an electric arc light.	(see 1808) (see 1815) (see 1844)
1803	Lewis and Clark and their group make their westward search for the Northwest Passage, without the benefit of 4X4's, or motors for their boats.	
1803	**A metal point writing pen is patented, but never used commercially.**	
1803	In one of the greatest real estate deals of all time, the United States acquires more than 800 million acres from France, for less than three cents per acre. This transaction is often referred to as "The Louisiana Purchase."	
1803	Toledo, OH; local physician, Dr. Alan deVilbiss, has invented a spray device to replace swabs for applying medicine to oral and nasal passages.	
1803	Conn; Eli Terry incorporates interchangeable parts to rapidly produce clock parts in assembly-line style, while using waterpower to run his saws and lathes for building his wooden clocks.	
1803	Ohio; the last known wild buffalo (American Bison) in our state is killed this year.	(see 1830)
1803	Offshore oil production is reported in Bibi-Heybat Bay of the Caspian Sea of Azerbaijan, from two hand dug wells 18 meters and 30 meters from shore. This first offshore oilfield produces until 1825, when the now several wells are all ravaged by a bad storm.	(see 1807)

1804	England; Matthew Murray of Leeds invents a steam-powered locomotive that runs on rails of timber. Although it runs on wooden rails, Murray's is probably the **first railroad engine**, and it is viewed by Richard Trevithick before he builds his locomotive.	
1804	Cornwall, England; Richard Trevithick builds his first, very crude, locomotive, using a steam engine mounted on a wagon riding on steel rails. This little locomotive is locally known as "Capt. Dick's Puffer," due to the large excess of uncondensed steam exhausted. Mr. Samuel Homfray is funding Trevithick's steam locomotive research and development. This year Trevithick also builds a 40 psi steam locomotive for the Welsh Penydarren Railroad.	(see 1808)
1804	John Deere is born in Rutland, VT.	
1804	Paisley, Scotland; John Gibb develops "slow sand filtration" for water systems.	
1804	France; Joseph-Marie Jacquard invents the pattern-weaving loom. Jacquard, a French silk-weaver, invents a method of automatically controlling the warp and waft threads on a silk loom, by recording patterns of holes in a string of cards. *NOTE: this image of Jacquard was woven on one of his looms in 1839, and required 24,000 punched cards to create.*	
1804	New Hampshire; Mr. Benjamin Pritchett builds the first textile mill at Amoskeag Falls.	(see 1810)
1804	USA; Although it weighs 4,000 pounds, Oliver Evans has built his first steam-powered boat.	(see 1805)
1805	Oliver Evans fits powered wheels to the steam dredging barge he built to dredge the Schuylkill River in Philadelphia, he then drives it under its own power from his shop to the river. Evans predicts, "The time will come when people will travel in coaches powered by steam engines from one city to another almost as fast as birds can fly... 15 to 20 miles an hour."	(see 1812)
1805	Regularly scheduled stagecoach routes are fairly commonplace across western Europe by now, allowing overland travel and transport of mail. At this time, North America lacks any such road network.	
1806	March; Frederic Tudor arrives in Martinique with his shipload of ice from New England; the first ice ever exported from the USA.	
1806	March; the US Congress passes authorizing legislation for a "national road." This will be The Cumberland Road, which will connect the new state of Ohio with the Eastern seaboard.	(see 1815)
1806	Western Virginia; on the bank of the Great Kanawha River, David and Joseph, the Ruffner brothers, are making and assembling the crude equipment needed for drilling a well. The Ruffners' well is the first well known to be drilled, not hand-dug, in the western hemisphere. They are drilling for brine to be evaporated for the remaining salt in commercial amounts, for use by the rapidly growing population of our nation.	(see 1807)
1806	Benjamin Thompson (Count Rumford) invents a coffee pot using a metal sieve to strain out the grounds. Coffee lovers no longer need to chew their favorite brew. *"Yeah Slim, I'll drink a cuppa java to toast old Ben."*	
1806	Boston; here on Broad Street, Samuel Tuck opens his paint dealership: Paint and Color.	
1806	Salem, MA; shipwreck victims Mrs. Spencer and her son are penniless on the docks. The local folks hear that she can make candy, so they present her with a barrel of sugar. Soon she is making candy and selling it from the steps of a local church. Mrs. Spencer calls her candy "Gibraltar."	(see 1830)
1806	France; on November 21, Napoleon establishes "The Continental System;" prohibiting all trade with England.	(see 1807)

1807	The MALAYAN FIRE PISTON is brought to Europe from southeast Asia; it uses compressed air to ignite a small clump of tinder.	
1807	August; the first practical steamship, Robert Fulton's *Clermont*, a paddle wheeler, begins operating.	
1807	Germany; SOZISTAT J. W. BUDERUS SÖHNE is now founded.	(see 1835)
1807	Pennsylvania; oil from a spring on Hamilton McClintock's farm on Oil Creek is selling for one to two dollars per gallon.	(see 1808)
1807	England; March 25, the world's first passenger train (horse-drawn) begins making runs from Swansea to Mumbles.	
1807	July; becoming an ally of Napoleon, Russia now joins The Continental System.	(see 1810)
1807	Writing his "Sketches of a Tour of the Western Country," F. Cuming describes oil collection by blanket dipping.	(see 1808)
1807	Some of the streets of London England are now being lit by coal oil street lamps.	(see 1814)
1808	The Englishman Sir Humphry Davy proves aluminum's existence and gives it its name. Soon, Hans Christian Ørsted manages to produce a few drops of it.	(see 1809)
1808	USA; January 15; brothers David and Joseph Ruffner completed the 58 foot (17.85 m) deep well they began drilling by spring-pole in 1806. This well in western Virginia is tubed with wooden pipe to keep weaker salt water from mixing and diluting the brine they desired. Disappointingly, However, the Ruffners' well produces oil, instead of salt water. This soon leads to spring-pole drilling for oil.	(see 1810)
1808	Germany; the St. Antony Ironworks, the Good Hope Ironworks, and the Neu Essen Ironworks all merge to form the IRON MINING & TRADING CO, (English translation) in Sterkrade.	
1808	England; in London's Torrington Square, Richard Trevithick has built a circular railway. The 10 ton steam carriage called Catch Me Who Can runs up to 15 miles per hour.	
1808	Pellegrino Turri now invents carbon paper to use in the typewriter he invented a few years ago.	(see 1886)
1808	USA; concerning the planning of the nations transportation improvements, Secretary of Treasury Albert Gallatin issues a truly far-sighted proposal in his Report on the Subject of Public Roads and Canals.	(see 1825)
1809	In England, Sir Humphrey Davy is making the first known experiments with electric lighting.	(see 1815)
1809	USA; Cyrus McCormick, son of Robert, is born.	
1809	Europe; this year and next, Napoleon of France is now at the very peak of his power.	
1810	More or less contemporaneous with the spring-pole, this seems to be about when the "walking beam" is beginning to be used in salt drilling.	(see 1819)
1810	**The gyroscope is invented.**	
1810	Waltham, MA; having recently returned from a tour of British cotton mills, Francis Cabot Lowell partners with Paul Moody, a mechanic. Lowell and Moody proceed to build the first American cotton mill that cards, spins thread and weaves the cloth, all in the same building.	
1810	New Hampshire; Pritchett's textile mill is taken over by the AMOSKEAG COTTON & WOOL MANUFACTORY. Several other mills are currently under construction nearby.	(see 1822)
1810	December 31; Russia pulls out of The Continental System, resuming relations with Great Britain. Angered, Napoleon now plans to crush Russia militarily.	(see 1812)

1810	In America, there are now 173 "ropewalks," where the men walk backwards, pulling and wrapping the strands of rope together.	
1811	The KRUPP industrial empire begins in Germany on Nov. 20, as Friedrich Krupp and two partners found a factory for the manufacture of English cast steel and products made from this steel.	(see 1837)
1811	England; LLOYD'S OF LONDON is established to provide a worldwide system of "intelligence and superintendence" in all major seaports around the globe.	
1811	**The world's first steam-powered ferry boat, the *Juliana*, goes into service between New York City and Hoboken, NJ.**	
1811	November 8th; David Bradley is born in Groton, NY.	(see 1832)
1811	England; Peter Durand comes up with the idea of preserving food in tin canisters. Pete now sells his idea to John Hall and Bryan Donkin, who soon set up the first food canning factory.	
1811	All original partners of Abel Porter & Company retire; Hiram W. Hayden, M. Leavenworth, and William H. Scovill form LEAVENWORTH, HAYDEN, & SCOVILL.	(see 1820)
1811	On a farm near Union Bridge, MD, Mr. Jacob Thomas demonstrates a grain reaper he has designed and built.	
1811	England; in Nottingham, the Luddites are acting up. The Luddite movement is the reaction by textile mill workers in the Manchester-Leeds region, to the coming of steam-powered machinery replacing their skilled labor, and leaving them unemployed and hungry. The Luddites often break the frames of the looms and demand that mill owners shut down all steam-powered equipment, or all their frames will be broken.	(see 1812)
1812	New Egypt, NJ; British "redcoat" soldiers burn Christopher Foulks' snuff mill to the ground.	(see 1822)
1812	CITY BANK OF NEW YORK is established.	
1812	In Waterbury, CT, Aaron Benedict builds a factory and begins making bone and ivory buttons.	(see 1823)
1812	England; in April, hundreds of Luddites attack the BURTON POWER LOOM MILL in Lancashire. Two are killed by guards; the others then leave and set fire to the mill-owner's house. This violence is met with strong repression. In June, thirty-eight Luddites are charged and tried for various crimes, including "attending a seditious meeting"; all are acquitted. In August, eight men in Lancashire are sentenced to death and thirteen more exiled to Australia, for attacks on cotton mills. Fifteen others are executed for similar crimes. In an other few years, the Luddites will no longer be active in Britain.	
1812	England; the GAS LIGHT AND COKE COMPANY is chartered and now they introduce the first gas lights in London; their charter is opposed by BOULTON & WATT, manufacturers of steam machinery. This manufactured gas will soon be used in every major city in Europe and America, but the residual coal tar will remain an environmental problem well into the 21st century.	
1812	USA; the American, Colonel John Stevens publishes a pamphlet which contains "Documents tending to prove the superior advantages of Railways and Steam Carriages over Canal Navigation." He further states, "I can see nothing to hinder a steam carriage moving on its ways with a velocity of 100 miles per hour."	
1812	England; the world's first commercially successful steam locomotive, equipped with Blenkinsop rack and pinion drive, this year commences operations on the Middleton Railway. Distinctly opposed to experimental operations, this is the world's first regular, revenue-earning use of steam traction.	

1812	During the last half of this year, Napoleon invades Russia with a million-man force. However, with 160,000 men, Russia adopts a "scorched-earth" policy, burning most of Moscow to the ground before Napoleon's troops could do so. The brave French leader now deserts his huge army and hurriedly returns to Paris to take care of other business.	
1812	Massachusetts; a cabinet-maker in Concord, William Monroe makes the first wood pencils in America.	(see 1876)
1813	**The first newspaper in Texas is now being published in Nacogdoches.**	
1813	England; William Hedley builds and patents a 50 psi steam railroad locomotive that hauls 10 loaded coal wagons at 5 mph, or equal to a team of ten horses.	(see 1814)
1813	Canada; the second iron ore blast furnace in Ontario is built in Charlotteville Township in Norfolk County, but it was unsuccessful.	
1814	Kongsberg Våpenfabrikk (KV) is founded to help compensate for the depletion of the silver mines of Norway.	
1814	**James Fox builds the first metal planing machine (planer), patterning it after the actions of a wood planer.**	
1814	Samuel Colt is born.	
1814	**George Stephenson's "Blücher," a steam locomotive, pulls 30 tons up a grade at 4 mph; it also is the first to successfully use flanged wheels on rails. However, overall the "Blucher" is not an efficient machine.**	(see 1815)
1814	Just north of Marietta, OH, while drilling for salt water along Duck Creek, a disappointed Mr. McKee strikes oil instead. This 500 foot deep well often producing a barrel or more of oil each week, selling for 50 to 75 cents per gallon. (Hildreth 1833)	(see 1816) (see 1818)
1814	The US Library of Congress is created with a basis of 10,000 volumes sold to the government by Thomas Jefferson, after the British burned Washington.	
1814	John J. Woods of Poplar Ridge, NY, builds a plow with a replaceable cast-iron tip. This makes farming much easier, as up to now all plows have short-lived wooden tips.	(see 1833)
1814	The Battle of New Orleans is fought from December 23rd through January 8th, 1815. Although the Brits have twice the manpower, Andy and his boys win, but unknown to either side, the Treaty of Ghent is signed on December 24th, officially ended the War of 1812. Jackson, losing only seventy men to the Redcoats 2,000 plus losses, just puts the finishing touches on the war!!!	
1815	**Richard Trevithick builds the last of his several steam-powered vehicles, none of which have been commercially successful. However, he is on the right track and several others will follow him, improving on his ideas.**	
1815	Joseph Loane immigrates from England and begins sewing canvas sails for Baltimore's clipper ships in a small Baltimore shop.	
1815	England; while Humphry Davy is trying to produce a safety lamp for miners, George Stephenson develops a truly functional explosion-proof lamp.	(see 1825)
1815	Sidelined by the War of 1812, construction finally begins on The Cumberland Road, from Cumberland, MD, toward Wheeling, VA.	(see 1818)
1815	France; Louis Danzas joins Michel L'Evêque in the Etablissement de Commission et d'Expédition.	
1815	Bath, UK; George Stothert's eldest son, George Jr., is now running their highly successful ironmonger business.	(see 1860)

1815	Scotland; John Louden McAdam introduces the technique of using well-graded, compacted, broken limestone to build what is soon to be known as "water bound macadam." The limestone fines and dust fill the voids between the broken rocks and moisture binds the material into a dense, fairly impervious surface. However, due to having to break all rocks by manual labor, it is truly labor-intensive.	(see 1858)
1815	England; George Stevenson's second steam engine has six wheels and a multi-tubular boiler, a huge improvement!	(see 1825)
1816	In France, the stethoscope is invented by René Théophile Hyacinthe Laënnec.	
1816	Galveston Island, TX; at the local slave market, slaver Luis de Aury is selling negroes for one dollar per pound.	
1816	Mary Wollstonecraft Shelley pens her book… *Frankenstein.*	
1816	England; Robert Peel forms the first Parliamentary Commission; its charge is to investigate child labor practices.	
1816	Lighting the streets with gas made from coal, the Gas Light Company of Baltimore is founded, and the US manufactured gas industry is now underway.	(see 1818)
1817	Thomas Bond, a brick maker, establishes an earthenware kiln in Armitage, Staffordshire, UK, this is the forerunner to Armitage-Shanks Co. of the United Kingdom.	
1817	USA; a newspaper article makes the first known recorded reference connecting the cranberry to the Thanksgiving Holiday.	(see 2011)
1817	J. J. Astor's American Fur Company has now cornered the fur trade in the Great Lakes region, and in less than a decade, will dominate the fur trade in the Upper Missouri Valley region.	(see 1834)
1817	New York; construction begins on the Erie Canal.	
1817	USA; the US Secretary of Agriculture is authorized to reserve hardwood producing timberland solely for naval stores.	
1817	The first appearance of the two-wheeled principle, basic to our modern bicycling and motorcycling, comes as Karl Drais invents his "Dandy Horse," "velocipede," "Draisienne," or "running machine." Whatever it's called, it is "kicked off" with the feet and when you lose momentum, you lower your feet and walk it faster. It has a steerable front wheel, but it's only a fad and passes away after a short while.	(see 1863)
1818	Jordan Gatling's son Richard Jordan Gatling is born on their cotton plantation.	
1818	The gravel-covered highway, the Cumberland Road has reached Wheeling, VA.	(see 1833)
1818	Middlebury, CT; a "profile" woodworking lathe built by Thomas Blanchard does the work previously done by thirteen men.	
1818	The state of Massachusetts bans the hunting of popular food birds, robins and horned larks, as a conservation measure.	
1818	Kentucky; on Mr. Beatty's place over in the southeast another salt water well is producing oil. On the banks of the South Fork of the Cumberland River, the Beatty Well is soon producing nearly 100 barrels of oil per day.	(see 1820)
1818	The first locally made bricks are now being produced in Toronto, Ontario.	
1819	The first major oil well is drilled near Petroleum (is this a coincidence, or what), in Western Virginia near Parkersburg. Forty years hence, over in Pennsylvania, promoter Edwin Drake will drill "The First Oil Well," with a rig and crew from over here.	(see 1821) (see 1831)

1819	Hans Christian Øersted demonstrates that magnetic fields and electric current are closely associated.	
1819	The first gypsum mine in Canada opens on the banks of the Grand River near Paris, Ontario, this only the second discovery of gypsum in North America.	
1819	May 24th; Henry Disston is born in England.	(see 1833)
1819	**In Switzerland, the first-ever chocolate bar is made by François-Louis Cailler.**	
1819	A UK parliament committee expresses concern that steam engines and furnaces "…could work in a manner less prejudicial to public health."	
1819	A blast furnace is constructed in Marmora Township, Hastings County, Ontario. Iron ore is brought from the Blairton Mine in Belmont Township, over in Peterborough County. This furnace is operated unsuccessfully on several occasions until final closure in 1847.	
1820	Twenty-eight year old William Cecil is the first to build a continuously running engine, fueled by a 1:3 mixture of hydrogen and air.	
1820	This is about the time that artificial ice is first made, as an experiment.	
1820	Alexander Annin opens a small flag-making shop, on the New York City waterfront.	(see 1847)
1820	BALLANTINE'S BO'NESS IRON COMPANY begins business in Bo'Ness Scotland.	
1820	Cambridge Massachusetts; two local businessmen begin the first commercial production of varnishes in America. Their business will be the cornerstone of VALSPAR.	
1820	Topsfield, MA; the first known agricultural fair in America is held in this small rural town. Except for interruptions during the upcoming Civil War, this fair will run steadily into the 21st century.	
1820	Waterbury, Conn; a brass worker from Birmingham England comes to work with LEAVENWORTH, HADEN & SCOVILL. After a year or so, he quits and goes to work for Aaron Benedict.	(see 1823)
1820	Crude oil from the Beatty Well is now being shipped to several other southern states, and to Europe as well. Even though it wasn't drilled for oil, it certainly appears the Beatty Well would surely qualify as the first drilled well in North America to produce crude oil in commercial quantities.	(see 1825)
1821	England; even at this "modern" date, at the coronation banquet of King George IV, the King's Champion rides in full armor into Westminster Hall, to uphold that monarch's title "against all comers."	
1821	**James Watt improves the efficiency of "Newcomeris Reciprocal Pump," a steam engine.**	
1821	In Fredonia, NY, William A. Hart drills the first natural gas well in the USA.	(see 1831)
1821	England; an Englishman, Julius Griffiths receives the first patent on a passenger road locomotive.	
1821	Philadelphia; Charles Alexander and Samuel Atkinson (not the late Ben Franklin) establish the *Saturday Evening Post,* although it is in the same building as Franklin's paper was once housed.	
1821	Canada; the NORTH WEST CO. and the HUDSON BAY CO. merge, ending over a century of very fierce rivalry.	
1821	During the decade of the 1820s, the monorail is patented, in Great Britain.	
1821	A passenger railroad locomotive is patented by the Englishman, Julius Griffiths.	
1822	Having moved west a couple of years ago, Christopher Foulks begins producing snuff in Belleview, IL.	(see 1833)
1822	The Louisiana sugarcane industry is first introduced to steam powered milling equipment.	

1822	Leicester, MA; Joseph Bradford (J. B.) Sargent is born to Mr. and Mrs. J. D. Sargent.	
1822	UK; the Canal Union between Falkirk and Edinburgh is completed. Due to the 79 foot (24.3 m) elevation differential between it and the old Forth and Clyde Canal, the installation of eleven locks is necessary.	(see 1963)
1822	Having earlier partnered with David H. Mason, Matthias W. Baldwin now adds the engraving of printing rolls for textiles and bank notes to the bookbinder's tools they produce.	(see 1830)
1822	Massachusetts; Mr. Francis Cabot Lowell now harnesses the Merrimack River at Lowell, to power his textile mills. Lowell soon becomes the "cutting edge" textile manufacturing town of America.	(see 1825)
1823	Thaddeus Fairbanks, a wagon maker, mechanic, and builder, builds a foundry to produce two of his inventions, the cast iron plow and a stove.	
1823	About this time, Joel R. Poinsett, the first US Ambassador to Mexico, brings some flowering plants back to the US, they are named Poinsettias for him.	
1823	Aaron Benedict's factory in Waterbury, CT, begins making buttons of brass, as well as of bone and ivory.	(see 1827)
1824	Nicolas Léonard Sadi Carnot publishes his theory on the thermodynamic cycle of the heat engine; from this, Rudolph Diesel will someday design his engine.	
1825	**The greatest engineering feat of this era, the Erie Canal is completed, and will soon open for travel.**	
1824	Michael Faraday discovers the principles of absorption type refrigeration.	
1824	Erastus Fairbanks joins his brother Thaddeus in his iron business; they establish E & T FAIRBANKS CO. in St. Johnsbury, VT.	
1824	NOELL is founded in Würzburg, Germany, to specialize in hydromechanical equipment.	
1824	*The first known public opinion poll is taken, to assess voters' preferences in the presidential election between Andrew Jackson and John Quincy Adams.*	
1824	In the deep woods, west of the Sabine River, John Bevil builds a log cabin on the site of the future Jasper, TX.	
1824	England; in Newcastle, construction begins on the world's first locomotive workshop. Although it is not successful, David Gordon patents a steam-driven "machine" with legs, which more or less imitate the actions of a horse's legs and feet.	
1824	Rhode Island; discussing causes and remedies for soil erosion, Solomon and William Downs of Providence publish the Farmers' Guide.	
1824	UK; the London SPCA is formed, and begins enforcing the 1822 Humane Laws.	(see 1828)
1824	Massachusetts; on the Plymouth waterfront, PLYMOUTH CORDAGE COMPANY is established as a maker of rope and twine, and specializing in ship's rigging.	(see 1898)
1825	The *Curaçao*, the first practical steamship to sail, is built in Dover, England. It is a double paddle wheeler with two of the new one hundred and forty-seven horsepower steam engines.	
1825	George Stephenson builds the world's first public railway, the STOCKTON AND DARLINGTON. He builds his eight ton engine, "Locomotion No. 1;" it pulls 90 tons of coal at 15 mph (24 km) Stevenson plans ALL details of this railroad line, even designing all bridges, machinery, engines, turntables, switches and crossings; as well as being responsible for every step of their construction. *NOTE: At this time, ALL railroad passenger coaches continue to be pulled by horses.*	(see 1828)

1825	Twenty-four year old Benjamin Franklin Avery, with $400 capital and one ton of iron, establishes his business, with a plow factory in the Clarksville, VA, area.			
1825	UK; the government of Great Britain has awarded a patent for a cart to be used on soft soils. It has the wheels replaced by "tracks" on each side of the cart, affording better stability in soft soil. This system distributes the weight of the cart and contents over a much larger surface area than the wheels afford. This the earliest known documentation of a "crawler" machine. A few years hence, another Englishman uses the ideas in this patent, and installs "crawler" tracks on a 30 ton steam tractor, but it doesn't work out.			(see 1858)

1825	**After 4000 years, soap is finally inexpensive enough for most working people to afford it.**	
1825	Through his various electrical experiments, George S. Ohm, determines how to measure the amount of electrical power in a circuit, (Ohm's Law).	
1825	**London; William Sturgeon invents the electromagnet.**	
1825	**Circuses first begin using big tents for their performances, thus allowing the flexibility of shows in smaller venues, having no large arenas, or stadiums.**	
1825	New Hampshire; partially due to their inaccessibility to the markets, the entire project of several textile mills at Amoskeag Falls goes belly up.	

1825	New York; now open to traffic, Governor DeWitt Clinton officially opens the 363 mile (581 km) long, 83-lock Erie Canal, connecting Buffalo, on the Great Lakes to the Hudson River north of Albany, which flows on to the Atlantic Ocean. Freight rates drop, and trade booms, as crossing the state of New York now takes only days, instead of weeks.	
1825	New York; William Aaron Hart drills a well down to 27 feet, and begins producing natural gas, piping this through hollow logs to some nearby houses in Fredonia. This would be the first known commercial natural gas production and usage.	(see 1837)
1825	In Peterborough, Ontario, a brick factory is now in operation.	
1825	Texas; a seaport is established on Galveston Island.	(see 1839)
1826	Ashbourne, Derbyshire, England; the Harlowe's blacksmith shop is acquired by William Haycock, a clockmaker.	
1826	Maryland; on March 6th in Washington City, Peter Geiser is born to Mr. and Mrs. Daniel Geiser. Mrs. Geiser is distantly related to the Singer family of sewing machine fame.	(see 1850)
1826	The British inventor George Cayley, develops a continuous crawler track system he calls "the universal railway."	(see 1837)
1826	Samuel Morey has developed an engine that runs on a fuel mix of ethanol and turpentine.	
1826	Canada; the first recorded mention of a graveled street in Ontario is KING Street in Toronto.	
1826	Germany; Georg Ohm defines the relationship between power, voltage, current, and resistance in "Ohm's Law."	
1826 or 1827	**The photograph is invented by Joseph Claude Nicéphore Niépce, in France. Niépce uses a glass plate technology; taking almost eight hours to expose.**	(see 1839)
1827	Louisiana; there are now 226 animal-powered and 82 steam-powered sugarcane mills in the state.	(see 1843)
1827	Waterbury, CT; Hiram Hayden and M. Leavenworth sell out to William Scovill, and the firm now becomes J. M. L. & W. H. SCOVILL.	(see 1829)
1828	Until now, circus performers riding horses just wore their usual clothing. Then one day, bareback rider Nelson Hower's outfit goes missing. Hower performs wearing his long knit underwear (long johns) instead. Henceforth, wearing tights, often with leotards, becomes a permanent fashion statement for circus performers on horseback.	

1828	USA; New York passes the first state anti-cruelty to animals law.	(see 1835)
1828	Hawaii; the American missionary, Rev. Samuel Ruggles, buys some cuttings from Chief Boki's trees on the island of Oahu, and plants them in his yard on Kona. This is the beginning of coffee production on Kona.	
1828	UK; the London SPCA is almost bankrupt, but Lewis Gompertz bails 'em out.	(see 1832) (see 1840)
1829	Waterbury, Connecticut; Mr. Aaron Benedict, Israel Coe, and James Croft are now partners in Benedict & Coe. James Croft is very important to the brass industry in America, as he persuades Mr. Scovill's firm, as well as Benedict's firm to do their own brass rolling. The rolling processes, machinery, and many experienced workers are all imported from around Birmingham England. Historians consider that 1829-1830 is the passing of America's brass industry out of its experimental stage, with very rapid forward growth.	(see 1850)
1829	England; John Newton's *Amazing Grace* is first published with music.	(see 2009)
1829	USA; Mr. James Smithson, a wealthy British citizen, leaves "…the whole of my property, to the United States of America; to found at Washington an institution for the increase and diffusion of knowledge." The $515,169 gift is used to establish the Smithsonian Institution.	
1829	USA; William A. Burt invents the typographer, a predecessor to the typewriter.	(see 1866)
1829	England; George Stephenson and his son Robert build and launch their "Rocket," the very first practical steam locomotive. On October 28, at Rainhill Trials, Stephenson's "Rocket" locomotive reaches 29.1 mph (46.8 kph), winning the contest and earning a contract to mak ten trips a day over a 1.4 mile (2.24 km) track hauling thirteen tons for the Liverpool & Manchester Railway. For the next three decades the European locomotives will change very little.	(see 1837) (see 1893)
1829	Zanders Feinpapiere AG is founded in Germany, as a papermaker.	

1830s	Steel nibs for writing pens come into common usage.	
	That'll be a lot easier on the geese!!	
1830s	French engineer Aimé Thomé de Gamond has conducted geologic and hydrographical surveys and discovered that most soil under the English Channel is chalk, and would be fairly easy to bore through.	
	"Yeah Bubba, it seems the French are really interested in crossing over."	

1830	Charles Goodyear begins experimenting with raw rubber to turn it into a useable product.	(see 1839)
1830	Hydraulic powered elevators are in use in many US cities, but they limit the height of buildings.	
1830	Having worked on a accurate, stable platform scale for several years, one that a horse and loaded cart can drive on, and be accurately weighed; Thaddeus Fairbanks now applies for a patent on his scale, as orders are already pouring in.	
1830	Edwin B. Budding invents the reel-type lawn mower, based on the reel-type textile shearing machine he operates. He invents the "machinery for the purpose of cropping or shearing the vegetable surface of lawns… later to be called a lawn mower.	(see 1842)
1830	**Mr. Peter Cooper designs and builds the first American-built steam locomotive, the "Tom Thumb."**	(see 1845)
1830	**There are a total of twenty-three (23) miles (36.8 km) of railroad tracks in the USA.**	(see 1834)
1830	The first American train, "The Best Friend of Charleston" makes its initial run.	
1830	The scrapping of the *USS Constitution* is scheduled, prompting Oliver Wendell Holmes to write the poem christening the frigate as "Old Ironsides." This poem leads to public donations to preserve the unique craft for posterity.	

1830	New York; Prof. Joseph Henry of the Albany Academy builds a motor utilizing the electromagnet. At this time, there is no known practical use for this motor.	
1830	France; Barthélemy Thimonnier patents his own sewing machine; this is the first with a record of any practical success. Soon the French Army hires Thimonnier to make their uniforms. However, fearing for their livelihood, a mob of angry tailors ransack and burn down his factory, completely destroying his business.	(see 1834)
1830	The US government passes the Indian Removal Act, forcing Indians to surrender their lands East of the Mississippi River to the federal government, in exchange for land in the Indian Territory (the future state of Oklahoma).	
1830	Matthias W. Baldwin builds a model locomotive for the Peale Museum. This model leads to an order for a locomotive for the Philadelphia & Germantown Railroad.	(see 1831)
1830	In the USA, the production of steam-powered railroad locomotives is now beginning in earnest.	(see 1950)
1830	Now, Mrs. Spencer's son sells the "Gibraltar" candy business to John William Pepper, who develops a new candy made from blackstrap molasses. Pepper's new "Black Jack" is a stick candy to complement "Gibraltar."	(see 1890s)
1830	Very few of the great buffalo (American Bison) can now be found anywhere east of the Mississippi River.	(see 1835)
1830	The world's population is now about one billion, having doubled in the last fifty years.	(see 1930)

1831	Robert McCormick demonstrates a working version of a mechanical grain harvester. It is also commercially successful.	
1831	BALDWIN LOCOMOTIVE WORKS is established.	(see 1833)
1831	In West Virginia, natural gas is being moved via a wooden pipeline to be used as a manufacturing heat source by KANAWHA SALT COMPANY.	
1831	Michael Faraday builds the first electromagnetic generator.	
1831	Using the American-invented "swiveling truck," the Mohawk & Hudson, the second American train, makes its initial run. There is nothing similar to this swiveling truck being used in the English or European mainland railroads.	
1831	In the Kanawha Valley of Western Virginia, William "Billy" Morris, invents drilling jars, for freeing stuck pipe and down hole tools. Keep in mind that Drake's so-called "first oil well" in Pennsylvania is almost three decades away.	(see 1833) (see 1859)
1831	During the past decade, Stephen F. Austin has brought about 5,600 Anglo-American colonists into Texas.	
1831	Texas; on Oyster Creek, near Brazoria, William H. Wharton builds the first known frame house in Texas, on his Eagle Island Plantation. A few years hence, Wharton will be the first "foreign" minister of the Republic of Texas… to the United States.	
1831	Ontario; iron ore from the bogs near Colchester Township is used to feed the new blast furnace erected in Olinda (or Gosfield), South Township, in Essex County.	
1832	David Bradley goes to work for his older brother, C. C. Bradley in Syracuse, NY.	(see 1835)
1832	John Mathews invents an apparatus for charging water with CO_2 gas, making "carbonated" water. Carbonated beverages will soon become popular.	
1832	Sam Tuck's PAINT AND COLOR merges with the varnish manufacturer in Cambridge, making STIMSON & VALENTINE. They are more commonly known as "varnish manufacturers," however they import and retail paints, oils, glass, and beeswax.	

1832	Pushing up the Missouri River, the shallow-draft, side-wheeler *Yellowstone* reaches Fort Union, at the confluence of the Yellowstone and Missouri Rivers, in the future state of North Dakota.	
1832	UK; Lewis Gompertz is "drummed out" of the London SPCA…. for allegedly being a Jew and a vegetarian. Gompertz now proceeds to establish the Animals' Friends Society, heading this group until 1848.	
1832	USA; the Arkansas Hot Springs is established as a National Reservation; this sets a precedent for Yellowstone, then eventually for a National Park System.	
1832	Sweden; the 27-year-old son of a clergyman, Johan Theofron Munktell, is a "technical genius and innovator." Starts his own firm, soon building a machine for making coins and Sweden's first printing press. (see 1839)	
1833	THE CHARLES AND ELIAS COOPER FOUNDRY is established in Mt. Vernon, OH.	
1833	C. F. Martin and his family leave Germany for the USA, and C. F. MARTIN & CO. opens its first guitar shop in the "new world;" in New York City.	
1833	Fourteen-year-old Henry Disston comes to the US and gets employment as a saw-maker's apprentice. (see 1840)	
1833	Christopher Foulks moves his tobacco business to St. Louis, MO.	(see 1847)
1833	In London, Marcus Samuel founds a trading company, importing items for the Victorian households. Samuels decides to add oriental seashells to his inventory. His firm prospers and he's soon importing and exporting other merchandise.	(see 1880)
1833	USA; Mr. John Lane makes the very first steel plow.	
1833	Columbus, OH, is now the westernmost extreme of the Cumberland Road.	(see 1850)
1833	Dr. S. P. Hildreth, physician and scientist, has spent considerable time visiting and surveying the future petroleum producing areas of Ohio and Western Virginia. He writes this year in the *American Journal of Science* that, "It affords a clear bright light… and will be a valuable article for lighting the street lamps in the future cities of Ohio." Hildreth also states that the oil is being used for light as well as medicine, and as a lubricant for machinery.	
1833	**By law, slavery is now abolished throughout the entire British Empire.**	
1833	Baldwin completes the locomotive for the P & G RR last year, and it is placed in passenger service this January.	(see 1834)
1833	September 4; Benjamin Day of the *NEW YORK SUN* hires Barney Flaherty as the first ever newspaper carrier. This day will later be designated as Newspaper Carrier Day.	
1833	UK; the Royal "Commission on the Employment of Children in Factories" is established. This leads to the Factory Act, drastically changing child labor hours and allowing the appointment of an inspector and permanent Factory Inspectorate.	
1833	At Yale University, Professor Benjamin Silliman Sr. is currently experimenting with the distillation of crude petroleum.	(see 1840)
1834	An American engineer, Jacob Perkins invents an apparatus, an ether ice machine, which is the forerunner of our modern refrigeration systems.	
1834	The United States now has a total of 762 miles of railroad tracks.	(see 1840)
1834	As canal construction in America is reaching its zenith, the railroads are rapidly strutting their stuff, and this soon puts a "quietus" on the canal's supremacy.	(see 1836)
1834	Anticipating the imminent decline of the fur trade, J. J. Astor sells all his fur dealing holdings.	(see 1848)

1834	New York City; having spent the last few years working on it, inventor Walter Hunt makes a machine for "sewing, seaming, and stitching cloth." Hunt's machine introduces the "eye-pointed" needle, and the interlocked stitch, but he never patents it; for whatever reason.	(see 1846)
1834	Henry and James F. Pitkin begin making the "American Lever" watches; as it eventually works out, the Pitkins will train many of the early craftsmen who go to work for Waltham.	
1834	This year M. W. Baldwin builds five railroad locomotives. Now he's rolling!!!	(see 1835)
1834	In England, the "Poor Law" is intended to help the many persons now unemployed and impoverished by the side effects of the Industrial Revolution.	
1834	STEDMAN FOUNDRY & MACHINE COMPANY is established.	(see 1912)
1834	**Henry Blair patents a "corn planter." Blair is the second black person to ever receive a US patent.**	
1834	**France; the Fresnel lens for lighthouses is developed, dramatically improving lighthouse technology.**	
1835	William S. Otis invents the steam shovel, the first known mechanical excavator. *Isn't a steam dredge an excavator of sorts???*	(see 1796)
1835	David Bradley moves to Chicago.	(see 1854)
1835	Samuel Colt patents his revolving cylinder pistol in Europe.	
1835	One million bales of cotton are produced in the United States this year.	
1835	March 5; Charles Goodnight is born in Illinois. Some sources say it was 1836, but the Goodnight family bible states 1835.	
1835	Railroad Fever is sweeping America; it seems everybody wants railroads built, even though most folks have never seen one, including Abraham Lincoln, their most ardent American supporter.	
1835	Young Daniel M. Sechler begins his work as an apprentice to a carriage-maker in Milton, Pennsylvania.	(see 1839)
1835	The BUDERUS COMPANY now operates five iron works across Germany, producing cast-iron furnaces, ovens, cookware and irons.	
1835	Fourteen locomotives are produced by Baldwin this year.	(see 1836)
1835	England; Francis Pettit Smith and John Ericsson co-invent the propeller.	(see 1836)
1835	**Texas; Mr. Gail Borden Jr. draws the first topographical map of Texas.**	
1835	The AMERICAN FUR COMPANY currently has orders for 36,000 robes to be made from buffalo hides.	(see 1857)
1835	An Englishman, Charles Babbage, invents a mechanical calculator.	
1835	USA; Massachusetts is the second state to pass an animal anti-cruelty law.	(see 1838)
1835	On December 16th, a conflagration in a New York City warehouse rapidly spreads, and for fifteen hours volunteer firemen fight the blaze in high winds, sub-freezing temperatures that freeze water in hydrants and hoses. The "Great Fire of New York" destroys almost seven hundred (700) buildings, wiping out the New York financial center.	
1835	England; William Henry Talbot invents calotype or talbotype photography, utilizing paper treated with silver iodide.	(see 1839)
1836	April 21; after a long march from down in Gonzales, Texas, and now on the banks of the San Jacinto River, in an 18 minute battle Sam Houston "whups" the dickens out of General Antonio López de Santa Anna. *NOTE: Modern historians consider The Battle of San Jacinto as one of the five most important military battles in the history of the entire world.*	(see 1869)

1836	Illinois; hoping to find a better location to ply his trade, and having left his hometown of Rutland, VT, the thirty-two year old near-broke blacksmith, John Deere, settles in Grand Detour and opens his shop.	(see 1837)
1836	Crosby-Laughlin is founded.	
1836	**The screw propeller is first utilized on steamships.**	
1836	New York; General Thomas W. Harvey is granted two patents for operations and machines to greatly modernize and improve the manufacture of metal screws. Gen. Harvey acquires the Poughkeepsie Screw Company.	
1836	This year, Baldwin builds forty railroad locomotives.	(see 1861)
1836	December 16; the Republic of Texas grants the first government charter for a railroad, to the Texas Rail-Road, Navigation & Banking Company. This firm soon dissolves with no stock being sold, and no track having been laid.	(see 1838)
1836	Pennsylvania; ten years in the building, the 395 mile (632 km) Pennsylvania Mainline Canal opens. This waterway crosses over the Alleghenies at an elevation of 2,291 feet (705 m) above sea level, and includes a 900 foot (277 m) long railroad tunnel near Johnstown.	
1836	The Champlain & St. Lawrence, the first railroad in Canada begins operations.	
1836	Illinois; in Wilmington, the Eagle Hotel begins catering to stagecoach travellers on the future US Route 66.	
1836	For the first time, Absheron natural associated gas is researched from a scientific point of view, by scholar G. I. Gessi.	(see 1837)
1837	Mr. John Deere builds, tests and sells his first "self-polishing" plow share, using steel from a broken saw blade. EXTRA!! EXTRA!! Grand Detour, Illinois; in his one-man shop, local blacksmith Mr. John Deere, who has just recently settled here from Vermont, has successfully created a clean-scouring steel plow share by using a discarded piece of steel saw blade. Deere's new plow is creating quite a sensation amongst local farmers.	(see 1848)

	1837	Republic of Texas; a steamship first ventures up Buffalo Bayou (which will someday be the Houston Ship Channel) to what will eventually be the Port of Houston.	
	1837	James Nasmyth patents the first metal grinding machine.	(see 1839)
	1837	Samuel F. B. Morse demonstrates a very primitive telegraph, but Alfred Vale is impressed by Morse's demonstration.	
	1837	George Stephenson establishes a foundry, the Clay Cross Company Ltd. (Biwater Pipes & Castings).	(see 1848)

1837	This year, both Houston, TX, and Chicago, IL, become incorporated cities.	
1837	Tiffany & Young, "a stationery and fancy goods emporium," is established.	
1837	Brandon, VT; In one of the first practical applications of an electric motor, a local man, Mr. Thomas Davenport, uses an electric motor he has built, to power his shop machinery and to build the first known electric model railroad car.	
1837	Late this year, Poughkeepsie Screw Co. is making 800 gross of assorted screws, each week.	
1837	Friedrich Krupp's eldest son, Alfred, sends prototypes of Krupp's coin-minting machines to the US government.	(see 1848)

1837	Dmitry Zagryazhsky, a Russian inventor, has been working on a "carriage with mobile tracks." Up to this time, none of these crawler type, tracked vehicles have hardly moved past the paper drawing, or first prototype stage.	(see 1888)
1837	The CITY BANK OF NEW YORK almost goes under, but is bailed out by the nation's richest man, John Jacob Astor.	(see 1848)
1837	England; the electric telegraph is invented by Charles Wheatstone.	
1837	USA; the locomotive "Sandusky" is built for the MAD RIVER & LAKE ERIE RAILROAD. The total weight of the loaded engine and tender is 16,000 lbs (7,252 kg).	(see 1851)
1837	England; upon the death of King William IV, Victoria becomes Queen of England.	(see 1887)
1837	Russia's first public railroad begins operations between St. Petersburg, the Capital, and "The Tsar's Village" Tsarskoye Selo, fifteen miles (24km) away.	(see 1879)
1837	France; near Autun, the first attempts to mine oil shale begin, it must work, as these mines will operate until 1957.	(see 1848)
1838	Sixteen-year-old J. B. Sargent goes to work at the bottom, as a factory worker in his father's business making wool and cotton cards.	
1838	Houston; on June 11, the first theater in the Republic of Texas opens.	
1838	The Republic of Texas now grants a charter to the BRAZOS & GALVESTON RAILROAD COMPANY. This charter includes the provision that the republic "…shall have the sole power of regulating rates of tolls."	(see 1841)
1838	"Go to the West; there your capacities are sure to be appreciated." This is the actual advice given by newspaper editor Horace Greeley.	
1838	USA; this year Connecticut and Wisconsin pass anti-cruelty to animal laws.	(see 1913)
1838	From England, the first Atlantic crossing by a ship powered totally by steam and without any sails.	
1838	Massachusetts; the BOSTON & WEST WORCESTER RAILROAD is the first railway to charge "commuter fares."	(see 1895)

1839	**Charles Goodyear accidently discovers the "process of vulcanization of rubber."**	
1839	James Nasmyth invents the steam hammer, the first metal shaper.	(see 1891)
1839	**Alfred Vale creates the "Morse" code for telegraphers. Vale will receive neither compensation nor recognition for his creation.**	
1839	Twenty-one-year-old Richard J. Gatling invents a screw propeller for steamships, but someone else has patented one only months earlier. Gatling invents the seed sowing rice planter, which he later adapts to the wheat drill.	
1839	Daniel Sechler opens his own carriage-building shop, and business is good.	(see 1845)
1839	POUGHKEEPSIE SCREW COMPANY sells out to a firm recently established in Somerville, New Jersey.	
1839	England; the radical Chartist movement has been calling for more reforms… faster. This year Chartist riots break out in Birmingham.	
1839	Texas; on Galveston Island, a city has grown up around the port, the city of Galveston is incorporated this year, and is very soon the largest city in the state.	
1839	France; Louis Daguerre and Joseph N. Niépce co-invent daguerreotype photography.	

1839	Wales; Sir William Robert Grove conceives of the first hydrogen fuel cell.	
1839	Munktell's new facility is completed and they are building steam engines and other agricultural and industrial equipment.	(see 1844)
1840	Henry R. Worthington designs and builds the first direct-acting steam pump.	
1840	England; RANSOMES OF IPSWICH introduces a successful steam traction engine.	
1840	With $350 in capital, Henry Disston opens his own shop making saws.	(see 1850)
1840	**The first private home in America to have "indoor plumbing" installed is the home of the poet Henry Wadsworth Longfellow.**	
1840	**American now has 2,808 (4,493km) miles of railroad tracks; more than the entire continent of Europe.** *NOTE: Cattle guards, as we now know them, have been used rather sparingly up to this time. However, with the building of the Great American Railroads, the lowly cattle guard is now taking a quantum leap in popularity.*	(see 1844)
1840	Marietta, OH; one of the nation's first major petroleum brokers, BOSWORTH AND WELLS, is established.	
1840	France; Louis Danzas and his brother-in-law Edouard L'Evêque form the Maison de Commission et d'Expédition. In a few years they'll open a branch in nearby Mulhouse.	
1840	In the US there are now about thirty-one thousand (31,000) working sawmills.	(see 2000)
1840	*A collapsible-metal squeeze tube is invented by John Rand. This tube is a huge seller in Europe, for artists using it to store and dispense pigments*	
1840	This year, about one-fifth of all fuel wood sold in the US, or about 900,000 cords, is now being sold as steamboat fuel.	
1840	England; reform-minded groups are horrified by living conditions of many in London. In the next decade or so, this feeling reaches America. The European epidemics of typhoid and cholera kick up a lot of public interest in pure drinking water and sanitation standards in general.	
1840	Pennsylvania; at Centerville, natural gas is now being used for brine evaporation; the first recorded use of gas for manufacturing.	(see 1841)
1840	UK; Queen Victoria charters the Royal SPCA, formerly the London SPCA.	
1840	Germany; the "Sander'sche Maschinenfabrik" (SMF) or (Sander Engineering Works) is established in Augsburg.	(see 1841) (see 1844)
1840	England; The first postage stamps are used here on May Day. A two-pence stamp, as well as the so-called "Penny Black."	(see 1861)
1841	*The first pure uranium is isolated by the French chemist, Eugène-Melchior Péligot.*	
1841	*Adolphe Sax of Belgium invents the saxophone.*	
1841	Wirt County, WV; Oil is discovered in a well being dug on the Barney O'Neal farm. O'Neal bottles the oil, selling a three-ounce bottle for a quarter.	(see 1842)
1841	In Poland, the first known sugar beet processing factory is opened for business.	
1841	Nuremberg, Germany; Johann F. Klett opens EISENGIESSEREI UND MASCHINENFABRIK KLETT & COMPANY.	
1841	French scientist Eugene Melchior, isolates the first pure uranium, naming it for the planet Uranus.	

1841	January 4; the HARRISBURG RAILROAD & TRADING COMPANY is chartered, and is the first to begin actual railroad construction in The Republic of Texas. However, after some right-of-way grading and contracting for cross-ties, this project is abandoned, "due to a lack of funds, …. and the threat of invasion by Mexico."	(see 1850)
1841	The first westbound settlers move through the northern portion of the Great Plains on the Oregon Trail; this route will soon be a pipeline for emigration into America's northwest.	
1841	England; said to have the power of five horses, the portable steam engine shown by RANSOMES OF IPSWICH, has the special feature of waste steam piped into its chimney, so the steam "hopefully" puts out any sparks that might ignite the piles of hay or grain stalks or stubble in the fields.	
1841	Germany; Klett & Co. iron foundry and engineering works is established.	(see 1844)
1841	England; mechanical engineer and inventor Sir Joseph Whitworth devises a unified system of threading for bolts, nuts, screws, etc. Based on a 55 degree thread angle, with rounded roots and crests, the Whitworth system helps overcome dozens of various incompatible thread systems in use.	(see 1864)

1841	Canada; a limestone quarry opens at Thorold for the first natural hydraulic cement manufactured in Ontario.	
1842	Mr. Jerome Increase Case founds J. I. CASE CO. to build threshing machines. Eventually CASE becomes the world's largest builder of steam traction engines.	
1842	In Florence, Italy, NUOVO PIGNONE is established as a cast iron factory.	
1842	New York City begins servicing citizens through their first public city water system.	
1842	O'Neal takes two barrels of his oil to Cincinnati to use for lubricant in a flour mill. This is the first crude oil known to be used thusly.	(see 1846)
1842	A. Shanks develops the "Shanks' Pony," a lawn mower pulled by a horse.	(see 1850)

1842	Jefferson, GA; Crawford W. Long removes a tumor from Mr. James Venable's neck, using an ether-based anesthetic for the first time. Long will not reveal his method for several years.	(see 1849)
1842	May 17; August Thyssen is born into a wealthy family of German business-folk.	(see 1867)
1842	Mr. P. T. Barnum "discovers" Tom Thumb. Barnum is hired by, and then partners with, Dan Castello and W. C. Coup. Their first years operating profit is equivalent to 6 million 2007 dollars.	
1842	Germany; engineers from England lay out the city sewer system in Hamburg. The English system of house to house sewer lines is soon adopted in several other major European cities.	
1843	STANLEY TOOLWORKS begins operation.	
1843	Scotsman Alexander Bain, a clockmaker, conceives the idea of facsimile by wire, then patents a primitive, but workable, FAX machine. *"…'at's rat Slim, a fax machine!!"*	
1843	I. K. Brunel's GREAT *Britain* is launched, the first ship to use all three new technologies of steam engine, iron hull, and screw propeller. She weighs 600 tons less than a wood hulled ship of equal proportions.	(see 1846)
1843	Mr. Henry Wells and Mr. William Fargo begin operating railway service between Buffalo and Albany, NY.	
1843	Mr. Gail Borden invents his "terraqueous machine," a combination wagon/sailboat. It does well on land, but sinks when in water… the idea sinks also.	
1843	**Nancy Johnson invents and patents the hand-cranked ice cream freezer.**	

1843	Teas Nursery is established in Bellaire, Texas.		
1843	**Louisiana; Norbert Rillieux receives a patent on his "multiple-effect" evaporator, for processing syrup from sugarcane. We now have 408 steam-powered sugarcane mills, and 354 animal-powered sugar mills.**		(See 1846)
1843	Eagle Picher is founded.		

1843	England; flat broke, struggling author Charles Dickens, hoping to raise a bit of money to live on, spends a few weeks writing *A Christmas Carol*. Dickens manages to have it published and it sells for five shillings a copy.	
1843	UK; the House of Commons Select Committee on Smoke Nuisance recommends that "...all manufactories be removed to a distance of five to six miles from the city center."	
1844	Karl Benz is born in Germany.	
1844	As of the end of this year, there are 4,311 miles (6,898 km) of railroad tracks in the US	(see 1850)
1844	Ireland; Samuel Clegg and Jacob Samuda put their short-line, single-track Dalkey Atmospheric Railway, a branch of the Dublin and Kingstown Railway, in operation, probably the world's first "atmospheric" railway.	(see 1846)

1844	Mr. P. C. Van Brocklin starts a stove-making business on Dalhousie Street in Brantford, Ontario, Canada.	(see 1848)
1844	France; Jean Foucault makes an electric arc light powerful enough to light up the Place de la Concorde in Paris.	(see 1860)
1844	Germany; in Augsburg, the "Sander'sche Maschinenfabrik" is renamed the "C. Reichenbach'sche Maschinenfabrik."	(see 1857) (see 1898)
1844	Sweden; the Bolinder brothers, Jean and Carl Gerhard, found Kungsholmens Gjuteri & Maskin Verkstad in Stockholm. They focus on foundry and machine work, and have took over some machinery and assumed some customers of the recently closed engineering business of Samuel Owen.	(see 1874) (see 1853)
1844	Samuel F. B. Morse invents the electric telegraph.	
1845	Samuel Fitch builds the first turret lathe.	
1845	Mr. Peter Cooper of "Tom Thumb" locomotive fame, patents a gelatin treat that will eventually be known as Jell-O.	
1845	Sweden; the first successful safety matches are patented, but will not be manufactured for another decade.	
1845	B. F. Avery moves his company and factory to Louisville, Kentucky. Avery is now manufacturing a complete line of tilllage, planting, and cultivating implements.	
1845	This year, during a six week period, some 1,000 families cross the Red River into Texas, traveling Preston Road to make new homes in in the Republic of Texas. *"Yeah Bubba, 'at's tha' same Preston Road that runs through Dallas, even today."*	
1845	California joins the Union. The Republic of Texas joins as well, now becoming the "Great State of Texas."	
1845	Daniel Sechler heads West; for more than a decade he'll try several Ohio areas.	(see 1858)
1845	Daniel Halladay, aConnecticut machinist, invents the self-governing "wind-powered water pump." Halladay's invention will soon be known far and wide as a... windmill.	

1845	Across England, the many various local times plays havoc with railway schedules; railway companies now lobby for a Standard National Time.	
1845	USA; Robert William Thomson patents the first vulcanized rubber tire.	
1846	January; the Croydon Railway, another "atmospheric" railway begins operation; using a larger vacuum pipe than previous operators.	(see 1846) (see 1848)
1846	***The first slab of cast plow steel ever rolled in the US is shipped from Pittsburg, PA, to Moline, IL, for John Deere's new factory, set to open in 1848.***	(see 1848)
1846	May; British engineer, I. K. Brunel is so enamored with his own ideas of an "atmospheric" railway, paid no heed to the negative lessons of the earlier "atmospheric" short-line roads; and proceeds to begin service on his own 52 mile (83 km) South Devon Railway. However, Brunel's "atmospheric" line encounters the same serious problems as all the others.	(see 1848)
1846	HAZARD WIRE ROPE COMPANY is established.	
1846	Louisiana; an improved, three-bodied evaporator is patented by Rillieux this year; it is very successful, and produces a higher quality sugar cane syrup.	(see 1854)
1846	A revolution in printing is created when Richard M. Hoe rolls a cylinder over stationary plates of inked type, and uses the cylinder to make the impression on paper. Now, it will no longer be necessary to move and maneuver heavy type plates directly to the paper.	
1846	After a few years of experiments, General Thomas Harvey receives patents on completely automatic screw-making machines he has invented.	
1846	After much improvement on the sewing machine ideas already in existence, Elias Howe is granted an exclusive patent on his machine. He soon founds the HOWE SEWING MACHINE COMPANY of Bridgeport, Connecticut. Howe's patent is oft-infringed, but he prevails in courts and wins royalties from the usurpers. However, Howe was not the first with the idea, or the first to build a sewing machine.	
1846	Swedish engineer Alfred Nobel is working with "Nitroglycerine," recently invented by the Italian Chemist Ascanio Sobrero.	(see 1848)
1846	UK; the British government adopts as "standard gauge" the 4 ft. 8.5 in. of the STOCKTON & DARLINGTON tracks.	
1846	Using Nova Scotia coal, Abraham Gesner distills an illuminating oil he calls "Kerosene."	(see 1849)
1846	California; Mormon elder Samuel Brannan arrives in San Francisco aboard the ship Brooklyn, from the eastern US. Arriving with him are about 240 men, women and children, mostly Mormons, and a good stock of tools, a printing press, type and paper, as well as all machinery required for a grist mill.	(see 1847)
1847	Born in Bavaria in 1828, Levi Strauss now comes to America.	
1847	This year Cyrus McCormick moves way out west to Chicago, IL.	
1847	In Milwaukee, WI, James Decker and Charles S. Seville establish a firm manufacturing French buhrstones and flour milling supplies. Their business will someday evolve into Allis-Chalmers.	
1847	John E. Liggett, Christopher Foulks' grandson, joins the Foulks tobacco business.	(see 1858)
1847	The twenty-one-year-old New Yorker Edward P. Allis moves west to Milwaukee. He enters the leather business and is shortly a partner in a tannery, but soon becomes dissatisfied with the future prospects.	(see 1856)

1847	NYC; Alexander's sons have joined the flag-making business and now ANNIN & COMPANY is founded and moves uptown to Fifth Avenue.	(see 1849)
1847	In addition to opening the branch in Mulhouse, Louis Danzas acquires FRANGER & BERNARD.	
1847	Mishawaka, IN; William Gillen's Furnace Company fails financially, and James Oliver goes to work for St. Joseph Iron Company, a plow and casting maker.	(see 1855)
1847	Canada; Daniel Massey starts making farm implements in a village in the future province of Ontario.	(see 1857)
1847	San Francisco; this January, Sam Brannan starts a newspaper, the *California Star*.	

1848	The Rumely brothers, Meinrad and Jacob, set up a blacksmith shop and foundry in La Porte, IN.	
1848	**GOLD is discovered at Sutter's Mill in California.**	
1848	Illinois; having prospered in Grand Detour making his steel plows while in various partnerships, Mr. John Deere moves to the larger city of Moline. Once there, Deere forms a new, more substantial partnership, builds and fully equips a new factory.	(see 1850) (see 1929)
1848	Henry Knapheide, an immigrant from Westphalia, Germany, starts a wagon building business.	
1848	Johann Christian Wacker founds the WACKER blacksmith shop in Dresden, Germany.	
1848	New York; John Ellis and Platt Potter establish the SCHENECTADY LOCOMOTIVE ENGINE MANUFACTORY in Schenectady.	
1848	GOULDS begins designing and manufacturing pumps.	
1848	The BLODGETT COMPANY is founded.	
1848	In Chicago, a small Midwestern sales agency is established, later to become MORTON SALT.	
1848	UK; George Stephenson dies at Tapton House on August 12.	
1848	August; Brunel, the world's greatest proponent of the "atmospheric" railways, after losing half-million pounds sterling, finally admits "atmospheric" defeat.	
1848	Texas; G. A. Kelly builds his first plow in his blacksmith shop in Kellyville, in Marion County, near Longview.	(see 1884)
1848	In the Bowery district of New York City, two German immigrants establish the HAMMACHER SCHLEMMER store, with the vision of bringing the finest tools and hardware the world has to offer to the now booming construction trade.	
1848	BRUNSWICK is established.	
1848	The wealthiest man in America, John Jacob Astor, dies.	(see 1912)
1848	George Henry Corliss builds the first successful automatic release cutoff control, for the valve gearing of a steam engine. This brings about greatly improved engine efficiency.	
1848	The first sale of German made Krupp steel in the US; the BUFFALO & NEW YORK RAILWAY COMPANY buy two Krupp-made rail car axles.	(see 1849)
1848	Canada; Mr. C. H. Waterous buys into Van Brocklin's stove manufacturing business in Brantford, Ontario.	(see 1874)
1848	Texas; two hundred miles inland, the piney woods city of Jefferson have now developed into the state's leading port.	
1848	As US President James K. Polk leaves office, he announces the discovery of gold in Oregon Territory.	

1848	Russia; near Baku, in the Bibi-Eibat area of the Apsheron Peninsula, the first mechanically (using percussion tools) drilled oil well in history is completed at 21 meters (68.25 ft). As it is pre-dated by many hundreds of hand-dug oil wells in this region, its an exceptionally good crude oil producer. *NOTE: This 1848 Baku well is actually the beginning of our world's "modern" petroleum industry.*	(see 347) (see 1849) (see 1858) (see 1872)
1848	America's first "hit song" is Stephen Foster's "Oh Susanna."	
1848	Canada; the Wallace copper "mine" is discovered at White Fish River, on the north shore of Lake Huron. The first discovery of nickel in Ontario also occurs here, but there is never any production from these "mines."	
1849	H. W. AUSTIN & CO. is formed, later to become AUSTIN MANUFACTURING CO.	
1849	**The safety pin is finally invented by Charles Rowley of England and Walter Hunt of the USA.**	
1849	CHAS PFIZER & CO. opens as a fine chemical business.	
1849	*Eugene Bourdon invents the Bourdon Tube, which even today (2001) remains at the heart of mechanical measurement systems; thus BOURDON SEDEME.*	
1849	Concord, MA; after 22,000 cross-breeding experiments over the last decade, Ephraim W. Bull finally achieves his goal of developing the "perfect" sweet, tasty grape; the Concord grape. *"Bubba, Ole Eph musta been a real bull!"*	(see 1869)
1849	Crawford W. Long reveals his method for using a ether-based anesthetic for patients undergoing surgery.	
1849	Having worked in various businesses, J. B. Sargent now takes over his father's firm, J. D. SARGENT & COMPANY.	
1849	Flags made by ANNIN & CO. are flown at President Zachary Taylor's inauguration; starting a tradition that will continue well into the 21st century.	(see 2006)
1849	**Texas; the first newspaper in Dallas, the *Cedar Snag,* is now being published.**	
1849	**Detroit, MI; the Michigan State Fair, the first State Fair in the US, is held this year.**	
1849	The Somerville New Jersey Screw Company is reorganized, buying the screw-making equipment of General Thomas Harvey, and another business of Schenectady New York, and name the new company… UNION SCREW COMPANY.	
1849	**Germany; Frederick J. Miller begins his brewing business in his native country.**	
1849	KRUPP OF GERMANY delivers the "National Coin" to the Philadelphia mint for the price of $1,011.06.	(see WWI)
1849	Samuel Kier is now selling rock oil from his father's salt water well…. for medicinal purposes.	(see 1850)
1849	USA; a young Frederick E. Sickles invents the first steam steering "engine;" it will be used in the steamship *Augusta.*	(see 1866)

W. Hunt.
Pin.
Nº 6281.   Patented Apr. 10. 1849.
Fig. 1.   Fig. 2.   Fig. 4.   Fig. 3.   Fig. 5.   Fig. 6.   Fig. 8.   Fig. 7.

Railroads are rushing across North America…and across most land areas of the world.
Great steamships are rushing across the seas.
The "Forty-Niners" are rushing to Oregon and California.
The entire civilized world continues rushing forward with the INDUSTRIAL AGE!!!

1850s	As the double expansion steam engine is created, a fuel saving of almost 50% is realized.	
1850s	A British druggist, Joseph Swan experiments with incandescent light bulbs, but it will be many years before he is successful.	
1850s	USA; an average of 2,160 miles (3,456 km) of railroad track are laid each year of this decade, more than the rest of the entire world combined.	
1850s	France; chemist Charles Gerhardt experiments with salicin (from willow tree bark) as an anti-inflammatory and in the process, creates salicylic acid.	(see 1899)
1850	Fifteen year old James A. Folger first becomes involved in the coffee business.	
1850	February 10; Sidney Sherman is granted a charter to build and operate a railroad over the twenty miles between Harrisburg and Stafford Point, TX.	(see 1853)
1850	Better known as "hydraulicing," hydraulic mining is introduced in California.	
1850	**Lawn mowers are first mass-produced this year.**	(see 1900)
1850	William Fargo and Henry Wells establish the AMERICAN EXPRESS CO.	
1850	The city of London, England, is now using the "slow sand filtration process" for its potable water.	
1850	The world's population is +/- 1 billion, 165 million, having doubled in the last two centuries.	
1850	Henry Disston has survived fires and many other crises, and DISSTON is now recognized as the standard of quality for saws in the US A.	(see 1855)
1850	There are more rail manufacturers in the state of Pennsylvania than in all of Europe.	(see 1854)
1850	Pembroke, MA; Mr. E. S. Ritchie establishes his business making navigational instruments.	
1850	The LOUISVILLE & NASHVILLE RAILROAD is founded.	
1850	The American inventions of the cowcatcher, the railroad lantern, the "T"-rail, the brakes, and several others, come to fruition this year.	
1850	This forty-four year project nears its end as the Cumberland Road now reaches all the way out to Vandalia, IL.	
1850	PEABODY-HOLMES is founded in the UK.	
1850	A hot-water spa opens at the Geysers, a 40 square mile steaming valley near San Francisco, CA.	
1850	Mr. Richard Dudgeon builds his first hydraulic jacks.	(see 1855)
1850	The United States of America now has approximately 76 million acres of cultivated cropland.	(see 1900)
1850	Annual US lumber production is now 5.4 billion board feet.	(see 1910)
1850	General Thomas Harvey becomes associated with the screw company in Somerville, NJ.	
1850	Waterbury, CT; J. M. L. & W. H. SCOVILL now incorporates as SCOVILL MFG. CO., and will remain so until well into the next century.	
1850	February; the state of Texas issues a charter to the BUFFALO BAYOU, BRAZOS & COLORADO RAILWAY. This is the successor company to the HARRISBURG RAILROAD & TRADING COMPANY.	(see 1853)
1850	Having spent two years on it, Daniel Geiser has built the world's first grain thresher, and he patents it in '52.	(see 1854)
1850	Illinois; as his Moline shop now produces over 300 plows a month, it looks as though Mr. John Deere will be hard to stop.	(see 1853)
1850	There are now 9,021 miles of railroad tracks in the USA.	(see 1870)

1850	Mexico; the 6.8 mile or 11 kilometer line from Veracruz to Molino, that nation's first railroad, begins operations.	
1850	**In and around Natchez, MI, there are more millionaires than any other place on earth.**	
1850	There are now more Welsh folks employed in several various industries than are employed in agriculture. Going by this scale, Wales is the very first industrial nation on earth. A large amount of this industrial growth is due to the tremendous quantity of subsurface minerals. On another note, over the last five decades, the population of England and Wales has doubled from nine to eighteen million persons. Also, the proportion of people living in cities rose from 10% to 50% during this same half-century.	(see 1870s)
1850	Samuel Kier has now created a process for distilling crude oil, producing his "carbon oil."	(see 1851) (see 1857)
1850	USA; Joel Houghton invents a wooden, hand cranked machine that "splashes water on dishes," and receives the first patent for a dishwasher.	(see 1886)
1851	Indianapolis, IN; NORDYKE & MARMON MANUFACTURING COMPANY is founded, to build flour mill equipment.	(see 1900)
1851	In Homer, NY, William Brockway, a carriage builder, starts his company.	
1851	February; the SCHENECTADY LOCOMOTIVE ENGINE MANUFACTORY fails and is sold for taxes, in May the original owners re-open shop as the SCHENECTADY LOCOMOTIVE WORKS.	
1851	BROWN & SHARPE make the first vernier caliper.	
1851	In Hawaii, DOLE is founded.	
1851	Baltimore; C. Jacob Fussell opens the world's first wholesale ice cream factory. *"Bubba, Mr. Fussell was a fine, smart, man."*	
1851	**Mr. Isaac Singer invents the first efficient, domestic, sewing machine. Singer then establishes I. M. SINGER & COMPANY, to build and market the sewing machines.**	
1851	**California; a gold miner and a carpenter, build and open the world's first "Laundromat," consisting of a twelve shirt capacity washing machine, powered by ten donkeys.**	
1851	At the LONDON EXHIBITION, Mr. Joseph Whitworth's inventions stand alone in a class by themselves, above all the others.	
1851	Canada; the Tripp brothers recognize some potential in the "gum beds" in Ontario, but fail to develop them, finally selling the rights to James Miller Williams.	(see 1858)
1851	California, May 3; the "Great San Francisco Fire" is underway today.	
1851	California; the gigan-normus redwood tree, "Mother of the Forest," is felled by loggers working for George Gale, a carnival owner. The stormy reaction to this deed brings forth many requests for a national parks system. This 300 foot tall tree, with a 92 foot circumference, was perfectly symmetrical from base to top. The crew of five men take 25 days to saw through this 2,520 year old beauty.	
1851	USA; for the first time, trains are now being dispatched by telegraph. The locomotive "Gov. Merey" is built for the MICHIGAN SOUTHERN RAILROAD, the total weight of the loaded engine and tender is 67,000 pounds (30,390 kg).	(see 1860)
1851	UK; there are now estimated to be about 8,000 portable steam engines on British farms.	(see 1912)
1851	Carbon oil for use in household lamps is now being marketed by Samuel Kier.	(see 1854)
1851	Pennsylvania; Dr. Francis Brewer buys his first oil lease on some land owned by J. O. Angier of Titusville.	(see 1854)

1851	Canada; the first well is dug for petroleum near Oil Springs, Lambton County, in Ontario.	
1852	After acquiring American rights to the Bourdon gauge, Edward H. Ashcroft of Lynn, MA, founds the ASHCROFT CO. to manufacture pressure gauges for steam engines.	
1852	Henry and Clement Studebaker open a blacksmith shop in South Bend, IN.	(see 1855) (see 1858)
1852	Horace Smith and David Wesson become partners in… SMITH & WESSON.	
1852	Mr. Gail Borden is driven to bankruptcy by his failed "meat biscuit" business.	
1852	**Poorly designed, and it can hardly be called successful; however, a steam-powered airship is invented by Henri Giffard, in France.**	
1852	Illinois; EMERSON-BRANTINGHAM is founded in Rockford.	(see 1928)
1852	Connecticut, USA; having served an apprenticeship in a mercantile house in his native Germany, Isaac Sanger moves to New Haven to work in his uncle Jacob Heller's clothing store, while also working sometime at WALDHEIMER AND GROSSMIER, a men's clothing factory in New York City, gaining accounting experience.	(see 1857)

Mechanics' Magazine,
MUSEUM, REGISTER, JOURNAL, AND GAZETTE.
No. 1520.] SATURDAY, SEPTEMBER 25, 1852. [Price 3d., Stamped 4d.
Edited by J. C. Robertson, 166, Fleet-street.
SIR GEORGE CAYLEY'S GOVERNABLE PARACHUTES.
Fig. 2.
Fig. 1.

1853	In Germany, Johann Heinrich BORNEMANN begins his business building pumps.	
1853	February 7; the Texas legislature approves "an act to regulate railroad companies."	(see 1883)
1853	M. & J. RUMELY CO. is founded.	
1853	KVÆRNER BRUG is founded in Oslo, Norway.	
1853	Moline, IL; as his partnership dissolves, John Deere finally enters the plow business as a sole proprietor. Deere's sixteen-year-old son, Charles, will come on board next year.	(see 1857)
1853	New York; when a fussy patron in Saratoga Springs gripes that his sliced potato fries are too thick, Chef George Crum spitefully makes some very "super thin" fried potato slices, and creates the potato chip. Crum's patron, and the rest of the world, love them!!!	
1853	England; Sir George Cayley builds an improved version of his 1849 triplane glider.	
1853	August 1; Sid Sherman's railroad, the BUFFALO BAYOU, BRAZOS & COLORADO, begins operating between Harrisburg and Stafford, TX. This will be the original unit of the SOUTHERN PACIFIC system in Texas.	
1853	Having built steam and traction engines, Munktell now builds Sweden's first steam locomotive.	
1854	Francis and Philander Roots, brothers and woolen mill owners, stumble across the principles that drive the rotary positive displacement blower concept.	(see 1867)
1854	STANLEY TOOL WORKS begins manufacturing measuring tapes.	
1854	The GALION MACHINE WORKS is established in Galion, OH, primarily making small items for the B & O Railroad.	
1854	The W. A. RIDDELL CORP. (WARCO) is established in Bucyrus, OH.	
1854	Conrad Furst partners with David Bradley to form FURST & BRADLEY, agricultural implement manufacturers.	(see 1884)

1854	THE KUGLER COMPANY, a metal manufacturing business is founded in Geneva, Switzerland.	
1854	Daniel Halladay, a Connecticut mechanic, creates the first windmill with the now classic sunflower shape. He soon heads to Chicago and markets his windmills to the railroads.	
1854	David Dunbar Buick is born in Scotland on September 17th.	
1854	Louisiana; Moses Thompson develops an improved furnace capable of burning the wet bagasse (cane pulp) as fuel to power the sugar-mill's steam engines.	
1854	The first work obtaining the concession to build the Suez Canal begins.	(see 1859)
1854	Now there are 15,675 miles (25,080 km) of railroad track in the United States.	(see 1859)
1854	Vermont; Edwin Harrington (1825-1891) establishes his own machine tool business after decades of working in several machine shops around Southern Vermont.	(see 1867)
1854	Maryland; at the Hagerstown Fair, Daniel Geiser's thresher wins first prize in competition against a newly built Smith thresher, from New York.	(see 1855)
1854	The principles of fiber optics are demonstrated by John Tyndall.	
1854	Venango County, PA; George Bissell and Jonathan Eveleth lease 105 acres of Hibbard Farm land (owned by Brewer, Watson & Co.) for $5,000, to collect the surface oil. Bissell & Eveleth now establish the PENNSYLVANIA ROCK OIL CO., incorporated in New York; this is the first oil company in the USA.	(see 1855)

1855	In Germany, an engineer produces the first absorption-type refrigeration mechanism.	
1855	The world's first railway suspension bridge is built over Niagara Gorge by John Roebling. The $450,000 double-decked bridge is 825 feet long.	
1855	DISSTON is the first American saw manufacturer to bring experienced steel workers from England to build and open a crucible mill.	(see 1878)
1855	Frederick J. Miller migrates to the United States, buys the PLANK ROAD BREWERY in Milwaukee for $2,300. Miller begins brewing his Miller beer with yeast he brought with him from Germany.	
1855	John Moses Browning is born.	
1855	**Charles Goodyear invents the rubber dental plate.**	
1855	Now Danzas forms a partnership as DANZAS, OUZELET & CIE; giving them an office in Basel, Switzerland. This move is a real plus for the transport business.	
1855	From America, England imports the Enfield gun machinery and adopts what they style as the "American" interchangeable pieces system of gun-making.	
1855	Or maybe '56; anyhow it was about this time that Richard Dudgeon completes his first steam-powered wagon.	(see 1858)
1855	May; thirty-two-year-old James Oliver and co-worker Harvey Little each buy a quarter interest in a small foundry in South Bend, Indiana, a small town of 2,000 citizens. Six weeks later the St. Joseph River overflows and wrecks the foundry. By November, Oliver and Little are back in operation and now purchase the remaining half of the business from Emsley Lamb. Oliver and Little name their firm... South Bend Iron Company.	(see 1857)
1855	Texas; Mr. Simpson C. Dyer builds the first dam on the Brazos River, at the town of Towash in Hill County.	(see 1951)

| 1855 | Maryland; Peter Geiser establishes the GEISER COMPANY, and agrees to let JONES & MILLER of Hagerstown build the Geiser Threshers. Although still financially embarrassed, Peter manages to go to Ohio and Indiana, entering competition against the Pitts and other manufactured grain threshers. At each meet, Geiser wins every award for best performance. Geiser now grants manufacturing franchises to MUSSELMAN & VICTOR, then soon, Samuel Fitz in Hanover Pennsylvania is also given a franchise. | (see 1858) |

1855	A connection from the current cholera epidemic back to a contaminated water pump is made by London England physician John Snow.	
1855	Central America; the PANAMA RAILWAY is completed this year across the Isthmus of Panama.	
1855	As shown by RASE (Royal Agricultural Society of England) Fuel Efficiency Trial Results, steam engines have improved from burning 11.5 pounds of coal per horsepower hour in 1849, to now only burning 3.7 pounds of coal per horsepower hour.	
1855	Swiss chemist Georges Audemars invents acetate rayon, but it is very flammable, and not commercially viable.	(see 1884)
1855	Around the middle of this decade, California's wheat output exceeds its local consumption. Overall, the state's grain operations are beginning to evolve into a very different situation to the family farms of northern and Midwestern America.	
1855	Bissell & Eleveth reorganize PENNSYLVANIA ROCK OIL CO. as a corporation in Connecticut.	(see 1857)
1855	Canada's first phosphate (apatite) mine opens near North Burgess Township in Lanark County, Ontario.	(see 1870)
1856	The railroad reached the Mississippi River two years ago, and this year the first railroad bridge across the Mississippi is opened. Three years of construction completed, and the ROCK ISLAND Bridge opens to railroad traffic between the State of Illinois and the Territory of Wisconsin, on April 21. On May 6th, the steamer Effie Afton catches fire and sinks as she crashes into the new ROCK ISLAND Bridge. . . . the bridge also burns. This event leads to "Hurd vs. Rock Island Bridge company," with the young attorney Abraham Lincoln representing the bridge company. This drags on for more than a year, then the US Supreme Court rules for the bridge owners, thus effectively establishing the right of railroads to bridge navigable waters. Therefore the Mississippi River is no longer a barrier to the settling of the American West.	
1856	Young Stephen Wilcox, age 26, patents a water-tube boiler that is far superior to others, and is inherently safe.	
1856	**The first railroad on the west coast opens this year between Sacramento and Folsom, CA.**	
1856	William Rand opens a small printing shop inside Chicago's "Loop."	
1856	**The first consumer product sold on the installment plan is a Singer Sewing Machine. Margaret Hellmuth of New York City pays $50 down and then pays the balance of $100 over the next six months.**	
1856	Henry Bessemer begins making steel in England.	
1856	**George Easterly patents a "straddle-row" cultivator, drawn by two horses. It will be another fifty years before a double-row cultivator is built.**	
1856	The Illinois Central, with 700 miles of track, north and south across Illinois, plus a branch to Chicago, is now the longest rail line in the world.	
1856	PECK & WALTER COMPANY is taken over by J. B. and is renamed J. B. SARGENT & COMPANY.	
1856	Edwin Foden opens a modest engineering firm in Cheshire, England. This eventually becomes FODEN TRUCKS.	

1856	Four leading manufacturers of sewing machines pool their patents to license them for use by other manufacturers; for a fee of course, and the SEWING MACHINE COMBINATION is formed.	(see 1877)
1856	Homer Hamilton establishes a foundry and machine shop.	(see 1860)
1856	American citizen, Hiram Walker moves across the river to Canada.	(see 1858)
1856	USA; Mr. Gilbert Spaulding's SPAULDING & ROGERS CIRCUS is the first to have special-built railroad circus cars.	
1856	Milwaukee; Edward P. Allis sells his interest in the tannery and goes looking for new business opportunities.	(see 1861)
1856	Kerosene for use in lamps is now being sold in New York by Abraham Gesner's North American Kerosene Gas Light Co.	(see 1857)
1857	German immigrant, Mathias Klein sets up his blacksmith shop in Chicago and is soon making tools for the fledgling communications industry.	
1857	Ed Ashcroft works with George W. Richardson and develops the spring-loaded safety (pop-off) valve. Ed soon hires nineteen-year-old Charles A. Moore as the salesman of the valves and gauges.	
1857	George D. Roper, challenged from childhood by the loss of his left arm in a train accident, buys a 50% interest in the VAN WIE GAS STOVE CO.	
1857	Elisha Otis invents a safe, steam-powered elevator for tall buildings.	
1857	The TRAHERN PUMP CO. starts business making hand powered water well pumps.	
1857	Alexander Wilson founds the VAUXHALL IRON WORKS, a marine engineering firm, in Vauxhall, London, England.	
1857	In Cincinnati, OH, the R. K. LEBLOND CO. is established to manufacture machine tools.	
1857	A group of settlers build a family fort for protection, near the present site of Desdemona, one of the oldest extant Texas settlements west of the Brazos River.	
1857	George M. Pullman invents the Pullman Sleeping Car for the railroads passenger trains.	
1857	Richard J. Gatling invents a steam driven plow, a good and useful thing, but it never shows much of a profit.	
1857	Chambersburg, PA; T. B. Wood, a railroad mechanic, and Peter Housum, a millwright, join in a business that will become T. B. WOODS COMPANY.	(see 1897)
1857	In the USA, Joseph C. Gayetty invents toilet paper. *"No Bubba, Sairs an' Roebuck didn't invent turlit paper."*	
1857	Mr. John Butterfield lays out his Overland Stage Route from St. Louis Missouri to El Paso, TX, and on west to San Francisco, CA.	
1857	The BALTIMORE & OHIO Railroad first begins using lubricating oil from western Virginia wells.	
1857	Having been legal tender in the North American English colonies, and in the US until now, "pieces of eight" are demonetized by the US government.	
1857	Moline, IL; even though it is now one of the eight largest plow manufacturers, John Deere's business is almost brought to insolvency by the "Panic of 1857." However, by various maneuvers this year and next, his assets remain intact. During this mess, Deere's twenty-one year old son Charles takes the helm, and will lead this company for the next 49 years.	(see 1866)
1857	William Richardson first publishes the *TEXAS ALMANAC*.	
1857	Dayton, OH; PEASE, CLEGG & COMPANY, a manufacturer of tools and general machinery, begins operations.	

1857	Germany; having now become a PLC, C. Reichenbach'sche Maschinenfabrik is renamed… Maschinenfabrik Augsburg AG.	
1857	February; South Bend Iron Company is again damaged by flood waters, but they are soon back in production. They are buying scrap iron for 1.25 cents per pound, and making almost anything they can from the resulting cast iron. Products include window weights, kettles, pulleys, grates, and "bob shoes" (metal strips to fit under wooden sleigh runners) for the fledgling Studebaker Brothers Co. In June, James Oliver is issued his first US patent; "Improvements in Chilling Plow Shares," showing a new way to harden a plow point or plowshare.	(see 1860)
1857	This year 70,400 buffalo hides are delivered by riverboat to Kansas City, MO.	(see 1872-3)
1857	Canada; Alanson Harris buys a little factory in Beamsville, Ontario, and begins manufacturing agricultural implements.	
1857	Romania; at Bend, northeast of Bucharest, near the Carpathians, the first oil wells around here are drilled.	
1857	Samuel Downer and Joshua Merrill have now mastered multiple distillations, chemical treatments, and the cracking of crude coal oil. In three more years these processes will be applied to crude petroleum oil.	(see 1858)
1857	Pennsylvania Rock Oil Co. leases the Hibbard farm to Edwin Bowditch and Edwin L. Drake of New Haven, CT.	(see 1858)
1857	A good usable kerosene burning lamp is developed, providing clean burning light.	
1857	New York; on Canadaway Creek, near Fredonia, Preston Barmore drills two gas wells, using a eight pound gunpowder charge to frack one well at a depth of 122 feet. This is the first known instance of artificial fracturing of the underground formations.	
1857	Texas; with help from his former employer, Isaac Sanger opens the Baum & Sanger store in McKinney. McKinney has become a trading center for fur trappers and ranchers, and is somewhat larger than Dallas at this time.	(see 1858)
1858	John M. Studebaker returns from California, where he was building wheelbarrows for gold miners, and invests in his brother's black-smith business.	(see 1865)
1858	Rudolf Christian Karl Diesel is born.	
1858	**On the third attempt, a "successful" transatlantic telegraph cable is laid, but it is short lived, due the high voltage (2000) being used.**	
1858	Galion Machine Works adds a machine shop to their plant.	
1858	Near Petrolia, and Oil Springs, Ontario, Canada, the first commercial oil well in North America is drilled. On an area of Ontario's "gum beds," James M. Williams develops the first commercially successful oil well in North America.	(see 1860) (see 1872)
1858	The first eraser-tipped pencils are manufactured.	
1858	The H. W. Johns Manufacturing Co. is established to make fire-resistant roofing materials from asbestos.	
1858	The Foulks' tobacco business is now known as J. E. Liggett & Brother.	(see 1873)
1858	**Mr. Ezra Warner invents the first practical can-opener.**	
1858	**Hamilton E. Smith of Pittsburgh, PA, is issued a patent for a manual washing machine operated by rotating a crank that turns paddles on a vertical shaft inside a wooden tub. This is one of the earliest washing machine patents.**	

E. J. Warner,
Can Opener,
№ 19.063.   Patented Jan. 5, 1858.

1858	Dan Sechler settles down in Cincinnati, and tries other work in the iron industry for the next couple of decades.	(see 1877)

	1858	Canada; Mr. B. J. Coughlin (1836-1909) establishes the B. J. COUGHLIN COMPANY.	(see 1900s)
	1858	While on display at the American Institute Fair at the New York Crystal Palace, Richard Dudgeon's first steam wagon is destroyed by fire when the whole building burns down.	
	1858	Because of his "fear" of the American Temperance Movement, Hiram Walker opens a distillery in Canada.	(see 1919)

1858	Peter Geiser is now fully in business and this year grants franchises to George Frick, J. S. Moore, as well as McDOWELL & McKEE, to build the Geiser Threshers. Geiser's thresher and George Frick's steam engine are connected for the first time this year.	(see 1860)
1858	Australia; Cremorne Gardens in Melbourne; February first, George Coppin successfully ascends in a balloon, the first such ascent down under.	(see 1912) (see 1970)
1858	British anatomist Henry Gray releases his reference book *Gray's Anatomy*. This work will be considered the standard work of human anatomy for at least the next two centuries.	
1858	Crossing the Mystic River on a long wooden trestle, the SHORE LINE RAILROAD reaches the port of Mystic Connecticut.	
1858	The PENNSYLVANIA ROCK OIL CO. now evolves into SENECA OIL CO. and hires promoter Edwin Drake to drill an oil well on the bank of Oil Creek, near Titusville, PA.	(see 1859)
1858	California; an inventor builds and receives a patent for a steam-powered crawler tractor. He then displays it at the California State Fair, and it receives an award there. However, the inventor doesn't have the financial resources to make a success of his invention.	(see 1900)
1858	BAUM & SANGER begins to advertise, a relatively new concept in Texas.	(see 1859)
1859	April; the first actual construction work begins for the Suez Canal, connecting the Mediterranean Sea and the Red Sea.	(see 1869)
1859	Robert W. Gardner (as in Gardner-Denver) redesigns the "flyball" governor, for steam engines, some of his original customers are oil drillers with steam powered rigs.	(see 1927)
1859	New York lawyer, George Bissell and a New Haven (Conn) banker, lead a group of investors who decide to finance the drilling of a well for petroleum. They enter into an agreement with promoter Edwin L. Drake to have the drilling effected. Drake's drilling contractor uses his rig brought over from western Virginia, where he drilled brine wells, equipped with a six horsepower steam engine for power. Aug 28; Bissell and Drake's oil well (70 ft. or 21. 5 m. deep) comes in, near Oil City, PA … isn't that a coincidence? Now, was Drake a promoter or what, he hires experienced drillers and a rig from western Virginia, to come to Pennsylvania and drill "the first oil well." However; The crude produced from this one well soon exceeds the cumulative crude oil output of all Europe since the 1650s. This 70 foot deep well marks the beginning of the "modern" petroleum industry, and the Appalachian oil region will lead US crude oil production for the next three and one-half decades.	(see 1860) (see 1862)
1859	The first documented use of a bucket chain excavator on land, by Alphonse Couvreux, a French contractor. Later this same machine is used on the Ardennes railway.	
1859	June; The Comstock Lode is discovered near Virginia City Nevada, luring folks to search for both gold and silver ore.	
1859	The Great ATLANTIC & PACIFIC TEA COMPANY (A & P) is established.	(see 1914)
1859	San Antonio, TX; William Achatius Menger, a German immigrant, opens the MENGER HOTEL, soon to be known as "the finest hotel west of the Mississippi River."	
1859	Almost half of the railroads on this planet are in the US. About this time, the first actual cabooses are coming into use for train crews.	(see 1860)

1859	Council Bluffs, IA; the politician and railroad lawyer running for President meets General Grenville Dodge, and Honest Abe expresses his wholehearted support for a transcontinental railroad across America.		

	1859	Galveston; the first YMCA in Texas is established.	
	1859	France; Jean Joseph Étienne Lenoir creates the first ever true internal-combustion engine, running on coal dust ignited by a sparking ignition system. Although with its many drawbacks, it is not practical, it heralds a power source basically much lighter and compact than a steam engine.	(see 1860) (see 1876)
	1859	*Origin of the Species* is published by Charles Darwin.	
	1859	Ohio; fifteen-year-old John F. Byers moves from his birth state of Pennsylvania to Ravenna, where he begins working with his father in his machine shop.	(see 1873)
	1859	USA; the Reading Railroad is the first major rail company to abandon wood for coal, to burn in their locomotive engines.	
	1859	Canada; at this time, oil is being distilled from bituminous (coal) shales near Craigleith, in southern Ontario.	
1859	Texas; Lehman Sanger now joins his brother Isaac in the McKinney store. The Sanger brothers soon move to the new trading center of Weatherford. Next year, Lehman moves to Decatur to open a subsidiary store. Another brother, Philip Sanger leaves a position with a jobber who provides goods to peddlers in Savannah, GA.		(see 1866)
1860	Jean Joseph Étienne Lenoir builds an internal combustion engine. He builds +/- 500 of the 7:1 ratio air-gas engine, the first patented engine to actually be produced, but all have chronic electric ignition problems.		
1860	The Rumely Separator (thresher) wins first prize at the Illinois State Fair in Chicago.		
1860	Philip D. Armour opens a hog packing plant in Milwaukee, WI.		
1860	Almost doubling in the past five years, the railroads in the US now total 30,626 miles (49,001 km) of track.		(see 1864)
1860	America is now at its peak of 5,254 miles (8,406 km) of canals. Hence, canal mileage diminishes as the railroad competition grows, and their miles of track continue to increase.		
1860	To celebrate its one-hundredth anniversary, the Lorillard Co. randomly puts $100 bills in packs of its Century brand of tobacco.		
1860	Mr. Soloman Dresser, et al, form Vesta Oil Co. at Burning Springs in Western Virginia. Vesta is Mrs. Dresser's name.		
1860	Hartford, CT; three local ladies decide to take in "street urchins," the hard-luck, forgotten orphans of the industrial revolution. The actions of these ladies is the basic origin of Boy's Clubs.		
1860	Mr. Milton Bradley starts a lithography business in Springfield, MA. He soon introduces games to keep his business afloat.		
1860	The US Federal Ordnance Bureau officials turn down the Spencer Repeating Breech-Loading Rifle; arguing that soldiers would fire too fast and waste ammunition. However, near the Civil War's end it will be used extensively.		
1860	Cotton now accounts for two-thirds of the total exports of the United States of America.		
1860	Around this time, the Valentine brothers, Lawson and Homer, take over Stimson & Valentine. Shortly after, Mr. Charles Homer, brother of famed artist Winslow Homer, is hired as a chemist. His hiring leads to producing some of the "most perfect" varnishes ever. The company's name is soon changed to Valentine & Company.		

1860	About now Stothert begins building steam-powered jib-cranes for their own use, and for the expanding market.	(see 1896)
1860	July; Theodore Judah, a railroad engineer and enthusiast, sees Donner Pass and recognizes it as the ideal place to construct a railroad line through the Sierra Nevada mountains.	
1860	USA; as Abraham Lincoln is elected president, only 16% of the population now live in urban areas, however about 33% of America's income comes from manufacturing.	
1860	About this time, Mr. William Tod becomes associated with Homer Hamilton in Hamilton's foundry and machine shop. In addition to the various other machines and equipment they manufacture, they slowly begin building steam engines for the iron and steel industries.	(see 1893)
1860	South Bend Iron Company is renamed OLIVER, LITTLE & COMPANY, as Thelus Bussell, a machinist, is taken on as a partner. Soon Harvey Little retires, and it will be OLIVER, BUSSELL & COMPANY. Then on Christmas Eve, fire destroys the plant.	(see 1861)
1860	Canada; James M. Williams establishes the CANADA OIL COMPANY; this is the first "integrated" oil company; exploration, drilling, production, refining and marketing the products.	(see 1861)
1860	Texas; for tax purposes, the total assessed value of all the slaves in the state is $64,000,000.	
1860	USA; the nation's crude oil production is 500,000 barrels this year.	(see 1861)
1860	The GEISER MFG. CO. moves to Waynesboro, PA, on a parcel of land recently purchased by George Frick, who has sold his firm next to Geiser. Several more Geiser Thresher franchises are granted, including one to A. B. Farquhar, of York, PA. Due to the "dire straits" of America's civil economy, Peter Geiser is again "financially embarrassed;" however, Geiser's good friend, A. B. Farquhar prevails upon their friend Mr. J. I. Case to buy another block of Western Territory, for which Case pays Geiser $100. Geiser later states that this "windfall" saved him financially.	
1860	England; Sir Joseph William Swan makes a crude electric light bulb.	(see 1878)
1860	The DeBeukelaer family begins making and baking Belgium biscuits and wafers.	(see 2010)
1860	On December 20th South Carolina secedes from the Union; eleven other states will soon follow this path.	
1860	London; the idea of pairing battered, deep-fried fish with deep-fried potatoes (or chips) begins as thirteen year-old Joseph Malin suggests his family sell the combo on the streets. The idea spreads like wildfire. NOTE: Other sources say the fish and chips combo originates during the 1700s.	
1860	USA; a new locomotive built for the HUDSON RIVER RAILROAD, weighs in at 108,000 lbs (49,000 kg) with the engine and tender fully loaded.	(see 1880)
1860	April; the steamboat Venango carries the first ever cargo of crude oil from Pennsylvania's oil country to Pittsburgh.	(see 1861)
1860	May; A. B. Funk's 460 foot deep "Fountain Well" comes in, flowing 300 barrels a day.	(see 1861)
1860	The first phlogopite mica mine in Ontario, the Pike Lake Mine opens near North Burgess Township, in Lanark County.	
1860	Germany; inventor Nicholas Otto uses ethanol to power an engine he has built.	
1861	BUCYRUS MACHINE WORKS is founded in Bucyrus, OH.	(see 1880)
1861	In December, William Crapo "Billy" Durant is born.	

1861	Edward P. Allis buys out Decker & Seville, renaming the firm Edward P. Allis & Company. This year, Allis also buys the Reliance Iron Works, a small machine shop and foundry, specializing in flour-milling equipment.	(see 1868)
1861	NYC; Mr. Eberhard Faber, great-grandson of Kaspar Faber emigrates to the US and opens the first pencil factory here.	
1861	Louisiana now has 1,291 sugarcane mills, of which 1,027 are steam-powered.	
1861	*April 12; as the first shot is fired at Fort Sumter, SC, the US Civil War begins.*	
1861	USA; the first sea-mines are used to disable ships during the American Civil War.	
1861	France; Germain Sommeiller converts a steam-powered rock drill to work on compressed air… thus the first jack-hammer is built.	
1861	**The hand-cranked wringer is invented, to squeeze water from freshly washed clothes.**	
1861	A young George Armstrong Custer graduates last in his class at the West Point Military Academy.	
1861	March; having rebuild their plant, production resumes at Oliver, Bussell & Company.	(see 1864)
1861	In New York City, the first true department store is established by A. T. Stewart. However, following close behind are R. H. Macy, then Marshall Field in Chicago, and John Wanamaker in Philadelphia.	
1861	Canada; during his first two years of production, James Williams produces 1,500 cubic meters of crude oil.	(see 1910)
1861	Baldwin builds their one thousandth railroad locomotive this year.	(see 1880)
1861	USA; the total crude oil production of our great nation this year is 2,100,000 barrels.	
1861	France; as postage stamps are now used in nations around the world to pay for postal service, many folks are now collecting various postage stamps. Alfred Potiquet publishes the first known catalog for stamp collectors, or Philatelists as they are called.	
1861	On a business trip to the booming oil region in western Pennsylvania, Mr. John Eaton considers setting up a business there.	(see 1862)
1861	Pennsylvania; this October the Phillips #2 Well on the Tarr Farm comes in, and flows 4,000 barrels of crude each day.	(see 1862)
1861	November; on the sailing ship *Elizabeth Watts,* the first ever shipload of crude petroleum crosses the Atlantic, shipped to London England from Philadelphia.	(see 1820) (see 1863)
1862	Alphonse Beau de Rochas files is issued a French patent for laying out the four exact cycles (strokes) of the internal combustion engine.	
1862	The John Eaton Company (soon to be known as Oilwell Supply Company), is established in Oil City, PA, to furnish oilfield equipment in the area.	
1862	The "pacifist" Richard J. Gatling invents and perfects his Gatling Gun, mainly to help the south in the Civil War, the Navy will soon adopt this gun.	
1862	Wood, Taber & Morse is established in Eaton, PA, to build and sell steam engines.	
1862	In Virginia, fourteen shallow oil wells are now being pumped by "a series of interconnected rods." *Sounds like a "rodline and jerker" system to me.*	
1862	To help alleviate the many problems transporting crude oil, several individuals and firms are working at building pipelines.	(see 1880)

1862	Across southern Canada's oil fields and in the Appalachian region of the US, central powered pumping (rodline and jerker) systems are now beginning to be constructed.	(see 1865) (see 1880)
1862	Samuel Colt dies.	
1862	July 1; President Abe Lincoln signs the Pacific Railway Act into law. This subsidizes the construction of the Transcontinental Railroad, essentially authorizing the creation of the UNION PACIFIC RAILROAD.	(see 1869)
1862	**The Federal Calvary chasing Rebel troops toward Richmond, VA, encounter the first land-mines ever used in battle. These very successful mines were made by Mr. Gabriel Rains for the Confederacy.**	
1862	America's first National Park, Yellowstone, is opened. This park in Wyoming, Montana and Idaho, has more natural geysers and hot springs than are found in all the rest of the world combined.	
1862	Oil City, PA; the KRAMER WAGON WORKS is now building wagons especially designed for oilfield haulage. The OIL CREEK RAILROAD now reaches from Titusville to Corry, the first railroad in the Pennsylvania oil region. There are now more than twenty Allegheny River shipping companies in Oil City, most are shipping crude in barge tows to Pittsburgh.	(see 1863)
1862	To help pay for the Civil War, President Lincoln signs the first income tax law; three percent on income over $600 per year.	
1862	Avery Island, LA; the first true salt mining in North America begins on May 4th, after workers digging evaporated salt hit solid salt at sixteen feet deep. This salt is going to be used by the Confederacy in the war.	
1862	The first man-made plastic is made by Alexander Parkes.	
1862	England; American ports are blockaded during the American Civil War, severely disrupting the importation of cotton to Lancashire. Almost all textile mills are closed and many thousand mill workers left unemployed. This period is known as the "cotton famine."	
1862	Germany; Adam Opel's craftsman's shop is transformed as he turns it into a factory producing bicycles, sewing machines, and other "revolutionary" machines.	(see 1899)
1862	Pennsylvania; John Burns and the Ludovici brothers establish the HUMBOLDT REFINERY near the town of Plumer.	(see 1863)

1863	Two brothers-in-law, candle makers for the military during the civil war, accidently make P & G soap, and start PROCTOR & GAMBLE AND COMPANY.	
1863	Henry Ford is born.	(see 1947)
1863	WOOD, TABOR & MORSE is selling 3 horsepower steam engines for $350, and 20 horsepower engines for $1,500.	
1863	In Lockport, NY, Mr. Birdsill Holly, a hydraulic engineer and inventor, installs the first fire hydrant in the nation.	
1863	**In London, England, the world's first underground (subway) commences hauling passengers.**	
1863	Slaves in Virginia can be hired for thirty dollars a month, but a Confederate Army private draws only eleven dollars, and a Union private draws sixteen dollars.	
1863	West Virginia; in the Horseneck field, to "bring it in," Basil Childers first "torpedoes" a completed well, using nitroglycerine.	

1863	Germany; having become very fascinated with sewing machines during his travels across Europe, Adam Opel opens a factory to mass-produce them.	
1863	North America and Europe are covered by a roller skating craze, after James Plimpton builds the world's first practical four-wheeled roller skate.	
1863	On the outskirts of Birmingham England, Birmingham Small Arms Co. (BSA) is founded to manufacture firearms for the British military.	
1863	Union forces completely destroy the salt mining works on Avery Island, Louisiana.	
1863	Texas; having immigrated here from Germany in 1846, Jacob Brodbeck has now built a miniature flying machine (airplane) powered by coiled springs, complete with propeller, wings, and a steering rudder. Brodbeck is unable to get enough financial backing to build a full-scale prototype. While on a speaking tour in Michigan, trying to raise money, some of his drawings and plans are stolen. Tired and disgusted, Brodbeck abandons this project, and goes back home to Texas.	
1863	Russia; although "Fire Worshippers" from Persia, Burma, India and other locales have for centuries made pilgrimages to temples on the Absheron Peninsula, where natural gas escaping from the earth have maintained "eternal fires," just this year is the first time production of crude oil is recorded. This area is later known as the Surakhany oil field.	(see 1871)
1863	The first bicycle with pedals attached directly to the steerable front wheel comes along. This "Bone Shaker" or "Velocipede" only becomes moderately popular, before the fad passes away.	
1863	Rodolphe Leschot, a French engineer with early experience as a watchmaker, invents the diamond core drill bit, and puts it to use. This year Leschot is issued a patent in the USA for his bit.	(see 1869)
1863	Ohio; John D. Rockefeller establishes a refinery for crude oil, in Cleveland.	(see 1870)
1863	The first anti-pollution bill is passed; it prohibits the running of tar and distillery refuse into certain creeks in Pennsylvania.	(see 1864)
1863	Molybdenite is now being mined at Harvey hill, in Leeds County, Ontario, Canada.	
Civil War	Texas; due to a lack of newsprint, the *Victoria Advocate* is often being printed on butcher paper and wallpaper.	
Civil War	The United States (Union) Congress imposes a $2 per gallon excise tax on ethanol to help pay for the war.	
Civil War	About 6,000 union troops are being detained at Camp Ford, near Tyler, the largest Confederate POW camp in Texas.	
Civil War	During the four years of this war, 300 Geiser Threshers are built; George Frick builds 200 of them.	
Civil War	A giant mortar, "The Dictator," is mounted on a special small railroad flatcar. The gun weighs 17,120 pounds (7,766 kg) and it throws a 13 inch (33 cm), 200 pound (91 kg) shell (cannon ball) more than 2 1/2 miles (4 km). It operates on a branch line of the City Point & Petersburg Railroad, and is used by the Union Army in the siege of Petersburg, VA, from mid-1864 - March 1865.	
Civil War	The Studebaker brothers business is really booming, building wagons for the Union during the Civil War.	(see 1868)
1864	January 28th; Charles W. Nash is born to a farming family in DeKalb, IL.	
1864	Det Norske Veritas (DNV) is founded.	
1864	Leonard Bailey "revolutionizes" the wood plane, hence to be known as the BAILEY plane.	

1864	Nikolaus A. Otto and Eugen Langen form the N. A. OTTO & CIE.	
1864	P. D. Armour opens another plant, this one at Chicago's UNION STOCKYARDS.	
1864	Two more petroleum refineries are built in Marietta, OH; next year, another will be built.	
1864	February 17; the privately owned 25' (7.69 m) rebel submarine, the *H. L. Hunley*, attacks and sinks the 1,240 ton Union Navy steam sloop, *Housatonic*, in Charleston Harbor. The *Hunley*, Captain Dixon, and the crew of seven men never return. This is the world's first ever ship sinking by submarine attack.	
1864	William Rand and Andrew McNally form a partnership in a job-printing shop, mostly printing railroad tickets and timetables.	
1864	And now… 33,960 miles (54,336 km) of railroad track in the good old USA; with 16,000 (25,600) more currently under construction.	(see 1890)
1864	Confederate Army private salaries are raised from $11 to $18 per month.	
1864	THE STEVENS ARMS & TOOL COMPANY is established by Joshua S. Stevens	
1864	This year, OLIVER, LITTLE & COMPANY make and sell 1,000 plows; 100 of these are the patented steel share plows, selling for $17.50 each. Additionally they make and sell hundreds of "double shovels," and two dozen road scrapers, selling for $8 each. They also made 70 iron columns for the main building at Notre Dame University, rebuilding after a terrible fire. *NOTE: Many of these columns can still be seen at the University, 145 years later.*	
1864	USA; Mr. William Sellers sets the standard for bolts, nuts, and screws, which becomes the National Pipe Taper (NPT) thread. Sellers' 60 degree thread angle was in common use by early American clockmakers and enabling the American Industrial Revolution. These threads will someday become known as the American National Standard.	
1864	"Coal Oil Johnny" Steele begins his spending spree across the country, once spending $100,000 in one day.	
1865	**Approximately one-half of all crude oil shipped in the entire world, goes through Oil City, PA.**	
1865	AVELING-PORTER of England build their first steam-powered road rollers.	
1865	A commercial FAX system is operating in France.	
1865	Elisha Wells discovers the adaptability of the drop forge in forming interchangeable parts of fire locks for muskets.	
1865	James Noah Paxman joins with brothers, Charles and Henry Davey to establish DAVEY, PAXMAN AND DAVEY, ENGINEERS in Colchester, England.	
1865	April 9; the US Civil War comes to an end with the Lee's surrender at Appomattox Courthouse in Virginia.	
1865	April 14; President Abraham Lincoln is assassinated.	
1865	Initiated this year, the first railroad tank cars are wooden tanks mounted on railroad flatcars.	
1865	Sylvester Marsh receives sarcastic approval to build a cog railway to the top of 6,288 foot (1,935 m) Mount Washington, with some grades that are over 37%.	(see 1869)
1865	**Linus Yale, Jr., patents a drum-and-pin padlock that can be mass-produced.**	
1865	West Virginia; the PARKERSBURG GAS WORKS is producing gas and piping it to businesses and a few homes. This is NOT natural gas, but gas manufactured from coal, as most natural gas is flared at the wellhead as a nuisance.	
1865	SARGENT & COMPANY become the exclusive commission agent for MALLORY, WHEELER & Co., a maker of locks and hardware.	

1865	NOKIA starts business by building and operating a pulpwood mill. Later they get in the rubber business, making rubber boots.		
1865	New York; the first known patent for plywood is issued to a local man.		
1865	Illinois; in Moline, MOLINE PLOW WORKS is established as hay rakes and fanning mills are now being manufactured in a local blacksmith shop.	(see 1866)	

H.S. Maxim
Hair Curler
Nº 57354   Patented Aug. 21, 1866

Witnesses.   Inventor.

1865	Pennsylvania; the "Van Syckel" pipeline is built, connecting the Miller Farm on the Oil Creek Railroad to the US Well.	(see 1866)	
1865	Pennsylvania's total crude oil production this year is about 2,000,000 barrels.	(see 1880) (see 1892)	
1866	Torrington, CT; EXCELSIOR NEEDLE CO. is formed to manufacture sewing machine needles; later will make needle roller bearings.		
1866	Henry Sherwin and Edward Williams founds the SHERWIN-WILLIAMS CO., to make paints for carriages and buggies.		
1866	In use since 1840 up North, cable tool drilling rigs this year begin drilling in Texas.		
1866	**Lyne T. Barret drills the first producing oil well in Texas at Melrose in Nacogdoches county.**		
1866	The US ARMY officially adopts the Gatling Gun.		
1866	Twenty-six year old Hiram Maxim receives his first patent, for a hair-curling iron he invents.		
1866	After three years of work, Alfred Nobel invents dynamite, a controlled nitroglycerine explosive intended to make for safer construction worksites. Next year, Nobel licenses E. A. L. Roberts to use dynamite in "shooting" oil wells to increase their flow.		
1866	The Red Devil trademark is first used on cans of UNDERWOOD's Deviled Ham.		
1866	USA; mechanical engineer Christopher Sholes (1819-1890) invents a somewhat practical, modern typewriter. With the technical and financial support of his business partners, Samuel Soule and Carlos Glidden, a much improved version is made in a few years. Scholes' original machines have bad problems with the letter keys jamming. Another associate, James Densmore comes up with the "QWERTY" keyboard, commonly used into the 21st century.	(see 1874)	
1866	Mr. Henry Holt becomes partner in a publishing firm.		
1866	John Deere's catalog this year shows 31 implements, including walking and riding plows and cultivators, harrows, planters, grain drills, wagons, and buggies.	(see 1868)	
1866	In Pulaski, TN, the Ku Klux Klan is founded. Next year the violent and intimidating Knights of the White Camellia is organized. The common goal of both groups is to intimidate and weaken the Negro vote.		
1866	Mr. E. A. L. Roberts explodes a torpedo in a "dry hole" and establishes oil flow in a non-producing well. Roberts is issued a patent for his process. About 2,000 lawsuits are filed involving the patent, but it is said Roberts never lost a lawsuit.	(see 1868)	
1866	Charles Goodnight and Oliver Loving make their first cattle drive from Fort Chadbourne, TX, to the railhead at Dodge City, KS.		
1866	Henri Nestlé, a pharmacist, develops a food for babies who are unable to breastfeed. Nestlé's product, "Farine Lactée Henri Nestlé," saves the lives of many infants, and is soon being sold across Europe.		
1866	THOMAS GOGGAN AND BROTHERS of Galveston and San Antonio is established; the first music publisher in Texas.		

1866	England; COWANS SHELDON build their first railway recovery crane.	
1866	Illinois; MOLINE PLOW WORKS has now added breaking plows and cultivators to their farm implement line.	
1866	The first trans-Atlantic communications cable is completed, however it doesn't last long…	
1866	Robert Whitehead (1823-1905) invents the first known self-propelled torpedo.	(see 1869) (see 1884)
1866	UK; a steam steering engine, incorporating feedback, is now patented by J. McFarlane Gray and sees service on I. E. Brunel's *Great Eastern,* the largest and most advanced ship afloat.	(see 1873)

	1866	New York; Matthew Ewing and Hiram Bond Everest of Rochester found VACUUM OIL CO. Their lubricating oil is discovered by accident while distilling kerosene. Everest noticed that the residue from the distillation process was suitable for lubrication. Their oil is soon popular for use in steam engines and internal combustion engines. Ewing soon sells his interest to Everest to carry onward.	(see 1879)
	1866	This is a good year in Ontario, Canada; in Frontenac County, the Frontenac Lead Mine is opened at Loughborough Township. A well being drilled for oil at Goderich, gets no oil, but has the first production of salt in the province. Then the Richardson Mine at Eldorado is the first discovery of gold in Ontario.	

1867	N. A. OTTO & CIE. premiere the first model of their coffee grinder design (internal combustion) engine at the Paris Exposition 1867, it is very noisy, but wins first prize.	
1867	August 23; R. A. LISTER & COMPANY is founded by Robert Ashton Lister, in England.	
1867	Stephen Wilcox and his friend George Babcock establish BABCOCK, WILCOX AND COMPANY (B&W), to manufacture and market their water tube steam boilers. B&W is issued a patent for the "Babcock and Wilcox Stationary Steam Engine."	
1867	In France, NEYRPIC is founded and begins producing hydraulic turbines.	
1867	The Reverend Leonard H. Wheeler invents the Eclipse windmill, and L. H. WHEELER & SON of Beloit, Wisconsin is founded to manufacture the windmills.	
1867	**A. R. Starr and P. F. Edwards bring in an oil well at Oil Springs in Nacogdoches County, TX.**	
1867	In another good real estate deal, the US government buys Alaska from Russia for $7,200,000… less than two cents per acre… Seward's Folly.	
1867	Napoleon III of France has a chemist develop a food product "for the army, navy, and the needy classes of the population."	(see 1869)
1867	The Dominion of Canada is established.	
1867	Marietta, OH; a steam engine and oilfield equipment company is established that will eventually become PATTIN BROS. They will someday build gas engines.	
1867	California and Oregon produce 25,000,000 bushels of wheat, and no railroads to haul it away. That exceeds the value of the gold produced in these two "gold-producing" states.	
1867	April; Jack and Dan Casement have a force of about 10,000 building the Union Pacific's line westward. Now CHICAGO HOWE TRUSS BRIDGE COMPANY have more than 1,000 men supplying preformed bridge sections to the Casement's workers.	(see 1869)
1867	On December 7th, the first cable-pulled, elevated railway is demonstrated in New York City, by Charles T. Harvey.	(see 1871)
1867	At the Paris World's Fair, the Roots brothers' positive displacement blower receives the highest awards.	

1867	January 20; a meeting of petroleum exporters in NYC decides that the capacity of oil barrels shall not be less than 40, nor more than 46 gallons. Forty-two (42) gallons will be the final decision for a production and/or a market barrel of crude oil.	
1867	November 30; the first scheduled train from Sacramento arrives on the East side of the Sierra Nevada.	
1867	The "Western Tornado," a 21' 6" (6.61 m) tall Roots blower powers the New York City subway under Broadway Avenue.	(see 1873)
1867	In the entire US of A, there are eight ice manufacturing plants, of which three are in San Antonio, TX. Those plants are there primarily to service the many breweries in San Antonio. The many breweries are there primarily to serve the many German immigrants in the area.	
1867	**In Texas' earliest recorded baseball game, the Houston "Stonewalls" play the "Robert E. Lees" of Galveston.**	
1867	UK; Thomas Humber begins building bicycles, laying the foundation for a century of business.	
1867	Lawrence Johnston of Pease, Clegg, and Company builds a 10 foot (3.08 m) vertical boring mill, using a common friction disc for feeding the cutting tool. This same machine will be working well into the next century.	
1867	September 23; William Marsh Rice is murdered in New York City. Rice's will sets up Rice Institute in Houston, TX.	
1867	Having recently relocated his growing machine business to Philadelphia's industrial area, Harrington now ceases production of machine tools to focus solely on the manufacturing of hoists. The hoist business is very competitive, but Edwin prevails with the innovation of the spur-gear hoist, using anti-friction bearings, and pioneering the Westin-type brake.	(see 1968)
1867	Charles Pratt and Henry H. Rogers partner and form Charles Pratt & Company.	(see 1874)
1867	Germany; having a good technical and commercial education, August Thyssen founds Thyssen, Fossoul & Co. in Duisburg. Bicheroux, his brother-in-law, is his partner.	(see 1871)
1867	USA; the Master Car Builders Association is founded, primarily to simplify the interchange of rail cars among the various railroads.	
1867	USA; the Pullman Palace Car Company is chartered for the manufacturing of railroad passenger cars.	(see 1893)
1868	Moline, IL; Deere and Company incorporates this year and practically all stock remains in family hands. This years sales are $650,000.	(see 1900)

"Yeah Bubba, ...at's a lot uf plows 'n buggies."

1868	Studebaker Manufacturing Co. is formed from the family blacksmith and wagon business.	(see 1885)
1868	Millers Falls Mfg. Company is established.	
1868	**April; the Union Pacific constructs the largest windmill (wind-powered water pump) ever built, to pump water for its men and engines at Laramie, WY.**	
1868	Harvey S. Firestone is born.	
1868	Edmund McIlhenny, a banker, creates Tabasco Sauce on Avery Island, LA.	
1868	**The first micrometer caliper is made by Brown & Sharpe.**	
1868	Mitchell Mark is born, he will someday open the nation's first motion picture theatre, in Buffalo, NY.	
1868	**J. P. Knight, a railroad signal expert installs the world's first traffic light in front of Parliament in London, England. Intended mainly to allow pedestrians to cross the busy street, the red and green lensed gas lamps, must be manually positioned by a policeman. Within a few years one lamp explodes, injuring the policeman, and they are done away with.**	

1868	**Eli Janney Hamilton develops the automatic railcar coupler that is the forerunner to today's modern couplers.**	
1868	Adolph Coors migrates to America from his birthplace of Barmen, Russia.	
1868	KELLY, MORGAN & COMPANY is established to build the drilling equipment and drill water wells for local farmers.	
1868	**Near Chireno, the first oil pipeline in Texas is being laid.**	
1868	Dallas, TX; the steam-powered river freighter *Sallie Haynes* is built here and launched in the Trinity River, out just west of town.	
1868	The BAILEY CIRCUS, the first circus in Texas, is now formed.	
1868	Milwaukee; E. P. ALLIS & CO. is now one of the largest firms in the growing local metalworking industry.	(see 1870s)
1868	On January 16, the refrigerated railway car is patented by William Davis.	
1868	England; the TRADE UNION CONGRESS is established to defend workers' rights.	
1868	USA; the federal government establishes a eight-hour workday on all public works.	
1868	Robert Forester Mushet invents tungsten steel.	
1868	Pennsylvania; the John Benninghoff robbery near Petroleum Centre nets the robbers about a half-million dollars.	(see 1869)

	1869	STANLEY TOOL WORKS make their first STANLEY-BAILEY planes.
	1869	**May 10; the Atlantic and Pacific rail lines connect the East and West coasts of America, with the driving of a Golden Spike.**
	1869	Twenty-two year old George Westinghouse invents the air brake and founds the WESTINGHOUSE AIR BRAKE COMPANY.
	1869	The COOPER FOUNDRY is licensed to produce the CORLISS STEAM ENGINE.

1869	French clockmaker André Guilmet has the idea of putting gears on the pedals of a bicycle and joining them to the rear wheel with a metal chain.	
1869	JOHN EATON CO. and E. H. Cole join forces to form EATON & COLE to furnish oilfield equipment.	
1869	The first ALLIS steam engine is now in operation.	
1869	Thomas Adams gets a druggist to sell chewing gum he has made by adding sugar to chicle… chicle brought from Mexico by Antonio Lopéz de Santa Anna, the deposed Mexican President.	(see 1836)
1869	**The first reported steam distillation process plant used on land is built to supply fresh water to vessels stopping of the port of Aden, Yemen.**	
1869	New Hampshire; the specially designed steam locomotive "Tip Top," goes into service pulling tourists to the top of Mount Washington. This railway averages a 25% grade, one of the steepest in the world.	
1869	The nineteen-mile-long Suez Canal is completed, reducing many ocean voyages by as much as 5,000 miles (8,000 km). As almost 100 million cubic yards of earth were moved, this appears to be the largest single earthmoving project in history.	
1869	Chicago, IL; architect Frederick Law Olmsted lays out the suburb of Riverside, with open, monotonous lawns linking the houses of the community together. Riverside is the first ever known such suburb.	
1869	France; a few years ago, Emperor Napoleon III encouraged the development of a substitute for butter. Mr. Hippolyte Mège-Mouriès invents a paste made from animal fats, he calls it oleomargarine.	

1869	Michigan; David L. Garver patents the spring-tooth harrow, especially good for working rocky fields.		
1869	Collis Huntington acquires the CHESAPEAKE AND OHIO RAILROAD, then founds the town of Newport News, VA, as the deep-terminus for the C & O Railroad.		

D. L. GARVER.
Harrow.
No. 95,458.
Patented Oct. 5, 1869.

1869	Camden, NJ; Joseph Campbell, a fruit-seller enters into a handshake agreement with Abe Anderson, a maker of iceboxes. Thus forming the JOSEPH A. CAMPBELL PRESERVE COMPANY, producers of canned veggies, jellies, minced meats, etc. The products, which Joe sells from a horse-drawn wagon.	
1869	**An American Baptist preacher living in Yokohama, Japan, builds one of the earliest rickshaws, to transport his invalid wife around the city.**	
1869	Vineland, NJ; a communion steward, Dr. Thomas Bramwell Welch, successfully pasteurizes Concord grape juice, and produces an "un-fermented sacramental wine," for fellow parishioners. Welch's achievement is the beginning of the processed fruit juice industry. His product is marketed as "Dr. Welch's Grape Juice."	(see 1893)
1869	Lima, OH; LIMA MACHINE WORKS is established to produce agricultural and sawmill equipment.	(see 1878)
1869	The *Charles,* of Antwerp, Belgium, is the world's first known oil tanker, carrying 7,000 barrels of crude oil in iron tanks. Prior to this, crude is carried across the seas in 42 gallon wooden barrels. This has helped establish 42 gallons as the official and accepted worldwide unit of measurement for crude oil. Earlier this year, the British brig *Novelty* arrives in Boston, MA, carrying 84,000 gallons of molasses stored in bulk tanks similar to the *Charles'* tanks.	
1869	THE DAN CASTELLO CIRCUS is the first to travel to America's west coast over the newly-laid railroad tracks.	
1869	Western Pennsylvania; Mr. Henry John Heinz is making horseradish and selling it from the back of his wagon.	
1869	Ohio; in Cleveland, Edward Taylor Lufkin establishes the E. T. LUFKIN BOARD & LOG TOOL COMPANY.	(see 1883)
1869	Ohio; Mr. Amos Ives Root of Medina, establishes the A. I. Root Company. Root soon creates and begins manufacturing a new type of beehive; the first hive that makes it possible for beekeepers to harvest honey, without destroying the colony of bees.	(see 1903) (see 1917)
1869	A self-propelled torpedo driven by a pneumatic engine is demonstrated to the Austrian Navy by Robert Whitehead.	(see 1895)
1869	Connecticut; in New Haven, Thomas Thomas starts his oystering business with boats and a culling house. Oft-times, as many as fifteen men are working along the culling bench, grading the "delectable bivalves" by size, then bagging or barreling them for shipment locally or out across a oyster-hungry America.	
1869	Vermont; a Leschot diamond core drill bit is shipped from France and is put to use, successfully drilling shot blast holes in a marble quarry.	
1869	Greenspoint, NY; the owner of the local CONTINENTAL IRON WORKS, Thomas Fitch Rowland is issued a patent for his "submarine drilling apparatus," a fixed working platform for offshore drilling to about 50 foot depth.	
1869	Pennsylvania; the search for oil has now moved south to Armstrong, Clarion, and Butler counties of our state.	(see 1870)
1869	The Rockefeller, Andrews, and Flagler firm is now operating in Oil City, Pennsylvania, Cleveland, Ohio, and New York.	(see 1870)

1869	In Ontario, salt is now being commercially produced from a brine well near Seaforth.	
1870s	The RIDER ERICSSON water-cooled, hot-air engine starts in production, the 600-pound engine is rumored to produce more than one-half a horsepower.	
1870s	Milwaukee; Mr. E. P. Allis hires several outstanding inventors, who establish his company out front in sawmill machinery, flour mill equipment, and steam engines.	
1870s	The "basic process" of steel production (much the same as still used today) is developed in Blaenavon, South Wales.	(see 1913)
1870s	**Abijah McCall and F. Dusy invent their dirt scraper, the "fresno," in… Fresno, CA.**	
1870	As he now controls 10% of US oil refining, STANDARD OIL COMPANY (of Ohio) is founded by John D. Rockefeller.	(see 1871) (see 1872)
1870	In Akron, OH, Dr. B. F. Goodrich establishes the first rubber company west of the Alleghenies.	
1870	A. D. COOK PUMP COMPANY is established in Lawrenceburg, IN.	
1870	UK; DAVEY, PAXMAN & DAVEY produce their first steam engine; James Paxman has some steam engine experience.	
1870	**WOODWARD begins building steam engine governors.**	
1870	Elisha Wells and his sons Fredrick E. and Frank O. organize WELLS BROTHERS, to manufacture taps and dies, in Greenfield, MA.	
1870	ECLIPSE farm windmills are now available in 8' (2.46 m),10' (3.08 m), 12' (3.69 m), 13' (4 m) and 14' (4.30 m) diameter blade wheels. The larger ECLIPSE RAILROAD windmills are made in 16 foot (4.92 m) to 35 foot (10.77 m) diameter sizes.	
1870	In Japan, Yatarō Iwasaki (MITSUBISHI) establishes a shipping firm that soon diversifies into mining, shipbuilding, banking, insurance and others businesses.	
1870	**Mr. Aaron Montgomery Ward sends out his first one-page mailing list of 163 items to be purchased by mail.**	
1870	GOODALL RUBBER CO. is established in Trenton, NJ.	
1870	February 9; the United States Weather Bureau is established.	
1870	Australia; Tom Gale and John Allen are making balloon flights at Sydney. Gale soon moves to South Australia, and next year will make the first balloon ascent in that area.	
1870	The TENNANT COMPANY begins business as a cleaning company.	
1870	With less than two million Americans employed in manufacturing, the US still has nowhere near the industrial power of Great Britain.	
1870	Illinois; the "Great Chicago Fire" virtually burns the city to the ground… Was it really Mrs. O'Leary's cow that did it???	
1870	VALENTINE & CO. relocate to New York City, and soon acquire MINNESOTA LINSEED OIL PAINT CO. Before long they are operating a West Coast office with Whittier, Fuller & Company as representatives.	
1870	September 1; the UNION PACIFIC EASTERN DIVISION (UPED), now known as the KANSAS PACIFIC RAILWAY, has its tracks laid into Denver, CO.	(see 1872 (see 1873) (see 1876)
1870	Illinois; in Moline, the MOLINE PLOW WORKS incorporates with $300,000 capital, and George Stevens as president. MOLINE now introduces the first successful straddle-row cultivator, as well as the first successful grain drill.	

1870	USA; our nation now boasts 52,922 miles of railroads.	(see 1880)
1870	The Standard Oil Company is organized as a corporation in Ohio.	(see 1871)
1870	The Crawford Well in Emlenton, PA, is now producing 35 barrels of good crude oil each and every day.	(see 1871)
1870	Ontario; near Deloro, the province's first arsenic is being produced. Globe Graphite Co. is producing from North Elmsley Township, in Lanark County. It took them a while to get it going, but this year the first recorded shipment of apatite or phosphate in Canada from North Burgess Township in Lanark County.	
1871	**Abbot Q. Ross is issued the first US patent for a steam roller, although steamrollers have been manufactured in England for the past few years.**	
1871	**Phineas T. Barnum starts a traveling circus.**	
1871	Bovaird Supply Co. is founded.	
1871	Simon Ingersoll patents a steam powered rock drill.	
1871	German experts report large quantities of oil in Iraq.	
1871	November; Mr. M. F. Gale of New York City patents the first cigar lighter, truly a fantastic step, especially for cigar smokers.	
1871	Davey Paxman & Davey becomes Davey, Paxman & Company.	
1871	Fairbanks Morse is established in Beloit, WI.	
1871	During the Great Chicago Fire, William Rand buries two of their printing presses in the sand, thus saving Rand-McNally Co.	
1871	The B & O completes the longest railroad bridge in the world, between Parkersburg W. Virginia, and Belpre, OH.	
1871	There are now seven oil refineries operating in and near Parkersburg, WV.	
1871	**The West Virginia legislature passes the first law, anywhere, governing the care and inspection of oil wells.**	
1871	Kaufmann's Department Store is founded in Pittsburgh, PA.	
1871	As the Franco-Prussian War ends, Alsace becomes German; eventually Danzas becomes a Swiss company.	
1871	The petroleum industry is in panic; too much crude production from too many wells causes a 50% drop in the price of kerosene.	
1871	On April 20, the first steam-powered elevated railway begins operations in New York City.	
1871	Germany; in only four years, August Thyssen has quadrupled his investment in Thyssen, Fossoul & Co. He now leaves and founds his own business. With his father as partner, starts Thyssen & Company, an iron strip rolling mill in the city of Styrum.	(see 1878)
1871	In Pennsylvania, the Titusville Oil Exchange is established.	(see 1872)
1871	The first known spherical ball-type valve is patented in the USA by John Warren and assigned jointly to Mr. John Chapman, founder of Chapman Valve Company. This all-brass valve must not be commercially successful, as it is another seventy-five years before similar valves are readily available.	
1871	Russia; on the Absheron Peninsula, near Baku, the first Russian oil well is drilled. However in this area, for longer than anyone knows, oil has been produced from hand-dug pits, this method will be used in some places until 1923. In the area around Binagadi, more than 3,000 such pits have been productive over the years.	(see 1873)

MOSES F. GALE.
Improvement in Cigar Lighters.
No. 121,049.   Patented Nov. 21, 1871.

1871	The TEXAS & PACIFIC RAILROAD is chartered by the US Congress to build a line from Marshall Texas to El Paso, TX. However, yellow fever, high debts, the financial panic of 1873, acquisitions, and corporate reorganization all take their tolls.	(see 1873) (see 1876)
1871	California; the BEST MANUFACTURING CO. is established. Daniel Best soon develops a horse-drawn portable grain cleaner, soon to be replaced with his "link-belt combined harvester."	(see 1889)
1872	Albert Rand forms the RAND AND WARING DRILL AND COMPRESSOR CO.	
1872	THOMAS GREEN & SONS, LTD., Leeds, England begins building steam rollers.	
1872	Having produced mostly steel threshers up to now, RUMELY brings out their first portable steam engine this year.	
1872	MILLERS FALLS MFG. CO., is renamed MILLERS FALLS COMPANY.	
1872	England; R. A. LISTER & CO. is producing a small, very portable three horsepower steam engine.	
1872	Germany; OTTO & CIE. builds a new plant, called GASMOTOREN-FABRIK-DEUTZ for their successful engine, hiring Gottlieb Daimler and Wilhelm Maybach; putting three of the greatest mechanical engineers of all time, under one roof.	
1872	DAVEY, PAXMAN & DAVEY is exporting equipment to the KIMBERLEY DIAMOND MINES in South Africa.	
1872	Byron Jackson, a 31 year old inventor, forms the BYRON JACKSON MACHINE WORKS (BJ).	
1872	George Edward Holmgren, a Russian immigrant, comes to San Antonio from Florida, he soon becomes owner of SCHUHLE & NIXON ALAMO IRON WORKS.	
1872	**RAND-MCNALLY CO. produces their first maps.**	
1872	**Walter Scott of Providence, RI, converts a horse-drawn freight wagon and introduces the diner, strictly an American innovation.**	
1872	Russian Imperial authorities auction parcels of land around Baku to private investors and large scale oil exploration begins. Soon investors from across Europe and North America arrive, including the firms of NOBEL BROTHERS, the family Szuch, later known von Börtzell-Szuch, and the Rothschild family.	(see 1901)
1872	The Newton Gas Well near Titusville, PA, is now producing gas for 250 customers.	(see 1873)
1872	On the Laguna Seca (Dry Lagoon) Ranch, near Mission, the first orange seeds are planted for the first orange grove in Texas.	
1872	The first true railroad circus is now riding the rails, the entire train is comprised of seventy railroad circus cars.	(see 1885)
1872	WHITE SEWING MACHINE CORP. founder Thomas H. White and his wife have a new son, Rollin H. White.	(see 1894)
1872	Termed the "Cleveland Massacre," John D. Rockefeller takes over 22 competing companies, increasing Standard Oil's market share to 25%.	(see 1877)
1872-3	This year the KANSAS PACIFIC and the UNION PACIFIC carry 825,000 buffalo hides to the east for processing.	(see 1876) (see 1880)
1873	C. B. Solomon and S. T. Merrill buy the Eclipse windmill patent rights and form the ECLIPSE WINDMILL CO., but the Wheelers keep a chunk of the stock in this new company.	

1873	**Jacob David, a Reno, NV, tailor, has the idea to rivet the pocket corners of men's pants. He and Levi Strauss patent the idea. The first blue-jeans are made, they are called "waist overalls." These sell for six dollars in gold dust.**			
1873	Wisconsin; John Michael Kohler buys Sheboygan Union Iron & Steel Foundry, and establishes Kohler & Silberzahn.			
1873	Atlas Copco kicks off in Sweden.			
1873	The St. Charles Car Manufacturing Co. is founded to build railroad cars for the burgeoning railway industry.			

1873	At this time, there are 4,131 breweries in the USA. *"Ya know Bubba, 'at's a lotta beer!!"*	
1873	Texas; the first "mass transit" system in Dallas, mule-drawn streetcars, goes into service.	
1873	James T. Drummond's Drummond Tobacco Co. of St. Louis, a chewing tobacco maker, introduces Chesterfield cigarettes to the American public.	
1873	J. E. Liggett & Brother merge with George Smith Myers of Missouri, founding the Liggett & Myers Tobacco Company (L & M).	(see 1897)
1873	July 21; an unwelcome trend begins as Jesse James and his gang pull off the first known train robbery ever, at Adair, IA.	
1873	Henry's publishing firm is now Henry Holt & Company.	
1873	Spanner-Pollux is established.	

1873	Due to this year's financial panic, the New York Stock Exchange is closed for the first time in its history. This "panic" plays the Dickens with all business and industry, especially the very speculative railroad industry. James J. Hill sees opportunity and initiates a extremely complicated deal and acquires the bankrupt St. Paul Minnesota & Manitoba Railroad for only a small portion of its true value.	
1873	At the Vienna Exposition, the Roots blower wins the highest award for machinery.	(see 1914)
1873	In Texarkana, TX, the Texas & Pacific Railroad (T&P RR) is established.	(see 1876)
1873	Texas; the US federal government blasts holes in the "Great Raft," dropping water level in Big Cypress Bayou, and dealing a terrible blow to Jefferson's status as a leading port city. Then Jefferson is bypassed as the T&P RR lays track from Texarkana to Marshall… really knocking the props out from under Jefferson.	
1873	In Texas, the "Patrons of Husbandry," generally known as the "Grange," is organized by farmers (some 40,000 strong), to battle the "fearful rates of freight," and "efforts to control legislation and influence the courts," by the railroad companies.	(see 1883)
1873	California; the first cable-pulled cars begin operating in San Francisco.	
1873	Ohio; after the death of his father, John F. Byers took over the machine shops; this year he starts the J. F. Byers Machine Shop in Ravenna. About this time, Byers invents and patents an oatmeal cutter, which he sells to the local Quaker Oatmeal Company.	(see 1877) (see 1881)
1873	Russia; crude oil production begins in Turkmen province, near the east shore of the Caspian Sea. The production is small, but steady.	
1873	France; Jean Joseph Léon Farcot first uses the word "servo" in his book Le Servo-Moteur ou Moteur Asservi. Farcot describes the various designs of steam steering apparatus developed by the company of Farcot and Son. The Farcots have equal claims with Gray, as inventor of steam steering engines incorporating feedback. Joseph Farcot's work is an important advance in the development of control engineering and his book is the first in-depth account of the general principles of position control mechanisms.	

1873	The Commonwealth of Pennsylvania grants a $1,500 annual pension to Edwin L. Drake.	(see 1874)
1873	Sweden; now a leading steel producer, the corporate Boofors is now AB Bofors-Gullspång, and will soon be manufacturing weapons as steel produced by the Siemens-Martin process begins to be used for the manufacturing of guns.	(see 1884)
1874	September 1; William Dana Ewart, an Iowa farm implement dealer, patents the "link-belt chain," you know, like old horse-drawn planters used.	
1874	C. J. SMITH establishes his company in Milwaukee, WI, making baby buggy parts and other specialty hardware items.	
1874	RUSTON PROCTOR & CO. is established in England to build steam shovels.	
1874	J. F. Glidden of DeKalb, Illinois, invents the first barbed wire. (William Bush, October 5, 1921)	
1874	FISKE BROTHERS REFINING COMPANY is established in Toledo OH, about this time.	
1874	**Rocky Mountain Locusts invade the Western United States in a record-breaking swarm 1800 miles long.**	
1874	England; cousins Alfred Legrand and Robert Sutcliffe hand-drill a 174 foot (53.54 m) deep, 3 inch (76.19 mm) diameter water well. Thus begins LEGRAND INDUSTRIES, INC.	
1874	Philadelphia; the first zoo in the US opens.	
1874	The first Chris-Craft boats are built.	
1874	July 2; Alexander Graham Bell today conceives the idea of the telephone. However, he is supposed to be working to develop a harmonic telegraph method.	
1874	Bluffton, IN; Local merchant and noted inventor, William Blackstone designs and builds a special birthday present for his wife… a clothes washing machine. Blackstone then is building and selling his designed machines for the sum of $2.50.	
1874	The first telegraph system in Texas is established between Ft. Worth and Dallas.	
1874	About this time, J. D. Burton of England invents the "Full-Face" tunnel boring machine, to be used to bore under the English Channel.	
1874	England; RUSTON builds their first excavator.	
1874	Brantford, Ontario, Canada; Van Brocklin's stove business, of which he had sold all of his interest by 1857, is now part of the WATEROUS ENGINE WORKS.	(see 1881)
1874	Both ASTRAL OIL WORKS, and CHARLES PRATT & CO. become part of Rockefeller's STANDARD OIL CO.	
1874	Texas; about this time, one of the barbed-wire companies selling here says their product is "Light as air, stronger than whiskey, and as cheap as dirt."	
1874	Massachusetts enacts a very effective law limiting the work of women and children in factories to ten hours a day.	
1874	Pennsylvania; in the town of York, the YORK business is established.	(see 2005)
1874	Lacking the patience required for the marketing of his typewriter, Christopher Sholes sells all rights to James Densmore, who in turn contacts rifle manufacturer Philo Remington to market the machine. Although not an instant success, the "Sholes and Glidden Typewriter" is offered for sale this year. Over the next few years, Remington engineers "tweak" the machine, and typewriter sales take off.	
1874	There are now four railroad trunk lines into Chicago, all competing vigorously for traffic in and out of this large terminus.	

1874	USA; Charles Goodyear, Jr., invents the shoe welt stitcher to help speed up shoe manufacturing.	
1874	In Pennsylvania, the oil boom at Bradford is going in high gear.	(see 1878)
1874	In the southeastern corner of Kansas, near Scammon, the first underground shaft mine in the area is built. Previously all the below surface mining has been in little dinky gopher hole mines. Eventually there are almost 300 significant mines in this area.	
1874	Texas; having been bypassed by two railroads a couple of years ago, the citizens of Rusk, afraid that they might lose the Cherokee County seat to Jacksonville, get on the ball, organizing the Rusk Transportation Co. this May, to build their own railroad to Jacksonville, where it could connect with the International and Great Northern Railroad Co. (I&GN).	
1874	Sweden; the business of the Bolinder brothers is restructured with the more flattering moniker of J. & C. G. Bolinder Mekaniska Verkstads AB.	(see 1893)
1875	*The private Belle Plain Academy is established in Callahan County, TX.*	(see 1881)
1875	Walter P. Chrysler is born in Kansas.	
1875	S. Pennock & Sons of Pennsylvania gets into the road-building equipment business, and gets into the "good roads" movement, to lobby for road money.	
1875	In Columbus, KS, R. A. Long Company is founded as a lumberyard.	
1875	**Montgomery Ward & Co. is the first company in America, and maybe the world, to offer its customers a "satisfaction-or-your-money-back" guarantee.**	

1875	Swift & Company is incorporated.	
1875	In Marshall, TX; Marshall Pottery is established.	
1875	Guy F. Atkinson is born and he will live until 1968.	
1875	Twenty-five year-old Richard Joshua Reynolds (RJR) starts a chewing-tobacco manufacturing business in Winston, NC.	
1875	The Texas Panhandle is officially opened for settlement.	
1875	L. E. McKinnon begins making hardware for horse-drawn carriages, his business will eventually become Columbus McKinnon Co.	
1875	Germany; Eugen Langen re-invents sugar cubes for factory manufacturing. Previously, Jakub Kryštof Rad held a patent for a sugar cube press, invented in 1843 when his wife cut her finger chopping up a larger sugar loaf.	
1875	The first "disc-harrow" is introduced; it will be great for working on the plains.	
1875	By now, more than 2,000 washing machine patents have been issued, but the majority just plain don't work!!!	

1875	About this time, the population of Los Angeles, CA, is just a tad under 10,000 people.	(see 1900)
1875	Timothy C. Eastman buys the patent for the newly developed Bates Process refrigeration system for ships and rail cars. This October, Eastman exports his first shipment of 36,000 pounds of beef to England.	(see 1876)
1875	Champion Road Machinery Co. is founded.	
1875	The electric-powered dental drill is invented by George F. Green of Kalamazoo, MI.	
1875	Founded in 1836, Jefferson, TX, now boasts of a population of more than 30,000 persons.	
1875	A US patent is issued for a system to pump several oil wells, using only one centrally located steam engine. Connecting the walking beams of two or more wells to move in different directions at the same time, thereby counter-balancing each other; thus equalizing the strain on the engine. *"Yeah Bubba, Ah thank thet is the ole rodline 'n jerker systum!"*	(see 1913)

1875	Wisconsin passes a employers' liability law covering railroad workers.	
1875	Hamilton, MO; Rev. Penny, the local Primitive Baptist pastor, and his wife, are the proud parents of a new son, James Cash Penny.	
1875	UK; RUSTON, BURTON & PROCTOR produce their first steam-powered excavator.	
1875	The first "made in Canada" clay-working auger machine for brick manufacturing is made in London, Ontario.	
1875	Coal coke has now replaced charcoal as the primary fuel for iron-blast furnaces.	
1876	The Star of the USA centennial exposition in Philadelphia, is the 1400 hp CORLISS DOUBLE STEAM ENGINE that powers the entire exposition.	
1876	October; Alexander Graham Bell and Watson have the first two-way telephone conversation, over five miles of lines.	
1876	BRODERICK & BASCOM ROPE CORPORATION is founded in St. Louis.	
1876	In St. Louis, Adolphus Busch and his friend Carl Conrad introduce a new beer to the world… Budweiser.	
1876	**ORENSTEIN & KOPPEL (O&K) is founded in Germany and builds its first steam shovel.**	
1876	Albert G. Spalding, a pitcher winning 241 of the 301 games he pitched, leaves baseball using the ball he invented, and founds SPALDING, which for the next 100 years will manufacture the balls used exclusively by the major leagues.	
1876	In the first official National League Baseball game, Jim O'Rourke makes the first hit, as Boston goes on to win 6 to 5 over Philadelphia.	
1876	HOMESTAKE is founded by George Hearst, father of William Randolph, to develop the HOMESTAKE gold discovery in the Black Hills of South Dakota, and will begin mining operations next year.	(see 1951)
1876	A lecture by Sir Joseph Lister regarding airborne "germs" as a source of infection, has a profound effect on Robert Wood Johnson.	
1876	*The first typewritten manuscript ever submitted to a publisher; Mark Twain's* The Adventures of Tom Sawyer, *typed on a Remington.*	
1876	*Samuel Plimsoll invents the Plimsoll Line, a line painted on the hull and used to gauge how much cargo should be loaded on a ship.*	
1876	*This year Timothy Eastman is exporting three million pounds of refrigerated, dressed beef each month.*	
1876	Newark, NJ; Otto Bernz founds the OTTO BERNZ CO. to sell plumbers tools, furnaces, and torches. Bernz's gasoline torches branded "Always Reliable," are now appearing in use.	
1876	Captain W. S. Ikard brings the first Hereford cattle to Texas.	
1876	Dayton, OH; Lawrence Johnston changes PEASE, CLEGG & CO. into JAMES R. JOHNSTON & SON, with Lawrence Johnston as the president.	
1876	The nation of France conducts its first national census.	
1876	October 24; American clockmaker Seth Thomas patents the first small, mechanical, windup, alarm clock.	
1876	Jacob D. Cox, Sr., borrows $2,000 from his father and buys half of C. C. Newton's little twist drill business in western New York. Later this year, Cox convinces Newton to move their factory and business to the hustling and bustling port city of Cleveland, OH.	(see 1880)
1876	France; the young wheel-chair-bound Parisian, Alphonse Pénaud, completes his airplane. Collaborating with Paul Gauchot, their full-scale airplane features moth-like wings; as well as some very futuristic items such as a glazed cockpit, flight instruments, retractable wheels, and variable-pitch propellers; in this age of steam-power, an internal-combustion engine is specified.	

1876	November 20; today, the KANSAS PACIFIC RAILWAY is ruled bankrupt by the courts.	(see 1880)
1876	Germany; Nicholas Otto develops the first practical four-stroke, internal-combustion engine while assisted by Daimler and Maybach. Otto's engine has four cycles, intake, compression, ignition, and exhaust; thus giving higher power to weight ratios than earlier internal power to weight ratios than earlier internal-combustion engines, many not having comparable cycles. Thus these four cycle (or strokes) engines are to be known as "Otto cycle" engines.	
1876	Melville Bissell patents the carpet sweeper he has invented.	
1876	Until now, all wooden pencils are square. An American, Joseph Dixon, makes the first round pencils.	(see 1890s)
1876	Broke, Busted, and Bankrupt - but the T&P RR reaches Fort Worth… before all construction is stopped.	(see 1880)
1877	The WESTERN WHEELED SCRAPER CO. is formed, building the first horse-drawn wheeled scraper. In Iowa, a local contractor, Capt. C. H. Smith of Mt. Pleasant, has been interested for a while, in a "wheeled scraper." Smith gets with Dr. A. W. McClure and Capt. W. Beckwith and the three of them establish the WESTERN WHEELED SCRAPER CO. to manufacture… wheeled scrapers. The entire first year's production of 600 scrapers is delivered to Smith's firm, C. H. SMITH & CO. to complete their 40 mile (64 km) grading contract for the CB & Q RAILROAD.	(see 1891)
1877	Texas; a Post Office is established at Turkey Creek Village, or Schleicher, however, the settlement will soon be known as Cross Plains.	
1877	**Thomas Alva Edison sings "Mary had a little lamb" into his newly invented cylinder phonograph, thus, cutting the world's first recorded song. This early cylinder phonograph is also known as the tin foil phonograph.**	
1877	Henry Timken (1831-1909) converts his buggy factory in St. Louis to produce the Timken Buggy Spring, trying to keep up with the world-wide demand for the springs.	
1877	March 4; Garrett A. Morgan is born in Paris, KY. His parents are former slaves.	
1877	The AJAX ENGINE COMPANY is founded.	
1877	Russia; the "Zoroaster," the first steam-powered tanker in the world with a steel hull, is used to transport kerosene.	
1877	After three torturous years, the Rocky Mountain Locust plague ends in the Western United States.	
1877	November; with the purpose of furthering the sugar industry in our state, the LOUISIANA SUGAR PLANTERS ASSOCIATION is founded.	
1877	England; the first Wimbledon tennis tournament is played.	
1877	Dan Sechler returns full-time to carriage-making.	(see 1879)
1877	February 15; in Graham, TX, forty seasoned cattlemen meet under an old oak tree, and form an organization that will someday become the TEXAS AND SOUTHWESTERN CATTLE RAISERS ASSOCIATION.	(see 1878)
1877	Irishmen Michael O'Neil and Isaac Dyas open a dry goods store in Akron, OH, which becomes known as M. O'NEIL COMPANY.	(see 1912)
1877	The patents of the SEWING MACHINE COMBINATION expire, and they lose control of this lucrative industry.	
1877	Corry, PA; the AJAX IRON WORKS is established, manufacturing steam engines.	
1877	The average American coal miner now earns only $9.80 each week, about half his wages of eight years ago.	

1877	Milwaukee; without a doubt, the best catch ever made by Edward P. Allis, is hiring Edwin Reynolds as superintendent of Allis company shops. Reynolds had been the general superintendent for the CORLISS WORKS, one of the major builders of steam engines. As the CORLISS patents have expired sometime back, Reynolds is now free to build CORLISS-type engines, with some innovations of his own design; and that he does, and does it well.	
1877	JEFFREY MANUFACTURING COMPANY is founded in Columbus, OH.	(see 1928)
1877	The trademark "Quaker Oats" is registered by the QUAKER MILL COMPANY, for its breakfast cereal.	
1877	The LORILLARD REFRIGERATOR COMPANY is established in New York City.	(see 1901)
1877	Russia; Fyodor Abramovich Blinov creates a tracked vehicle he calls "wagon moved on endless rails." His wagon is horse-drawn, not self-propelled.	(see 1881)
1877	Whether "by hook or by crook," Rockefeller now controls NINETY (90) percent of American crude oil refining.	(see 1879)
1878	CHICAGO RAWHIDE CO. is founded (near the Chicago stockyards) to make flat leather belts to drive industrial machinery.	
1878	Louis Chevrolet is born in France on Christmas Day.	
1878	Henry Disston dies after a long illness and a stroke.	
1878	*Texas; in Brown County, J. M. Bloodworth opens the first store in the village of Cross Out.*	(see 1879)
1878	Albert Champion is born in France.	
1878	England; Joseph Swann (the druggist) has some fairly successful tests of his incandescent light bulbs.	
1878	Fort Griffin Town, Shackelford county; the TEXAS CATTLEMAN ASSN. (later the TEXAS & SOUTHWESTERN CATTLE RAISERS ASSOCIATION) is founded.	
1878	June 15; Palo Alto, CA; Eadweard Muybridge, collaborating with Leland Stanford, places 12 box cameras, 21 inches apart, alongside the racetrack, and makes the first photographs of the strides of the trotter horse, Abe Edgington. These pictures confirm that when trotting, all hooves of a horse are sometimes off the ground at the same time. Beginning further studies of animated motion photographs.	(see 1888)
1878	ROBBINS & MYERS is established.	
1878	Thomas Crapper, a British Sanitary Engineer invents the modern flush toilet. WRONG!!!! Mr. Crapper only sells the toilets.	
1878	New York; the BUTLER-LARKIN COMPANY is established to manufacture downhole drilling tools.	
1878	Three miles north of New Braunfels, TX; Henry Gruene builds his mercantile store at a crossing on the Guadalupe River, it is soon surrounded by a busy village.	
1878	Frank W. Woolworth begins selling five cent items.	
1878	Gold is discovered near Leadville, CO, in the Western US	
1878	J. B. SARGENT & CO. has grown, now having 16 acres of floor space, and 1,700 workers, receiving 15 cents an hour for an average sixty-hour work week.	
1878	George Selden, an attorney and part-time inventor in Rochester, NY, builds a crude three-cylinder engine, but he will never perfect it. But Selden is the first to apply for a patent on the idea of using a gasoline engine to power a carriage; to be called an "automobile."	
1878	Having attended the Royal Agriculture College in England, 25 year old Alfred Rowe moves to the Panhandle of Texas. There he begins buying acreage for his RO Ranch, partnering with two of his brothers. Rowe continues living in a dugout in Donley county, buying cattle with the guidance of Charles Goodnight.	

1878	A Mid-West office is opened in Chicago by Valentine & Company.		
1878	Lima Machine Works builds the first "Shay type" steam locomotive.	(see 1891)	
1878	Along about this time, Al Stewart, a traveling wholesale grocery salesman carries "Mrs. Stewarts Bluing," which he makes at home using a formula he has acquired. Meanwhile, in Minneapolis, MN, a young salesman of silk materials, Luther Ford opens the first "Five and Ten Cent Bazaar" west of Pittsburgh, PA. Ford's business is poor, so he begins a wholesale business selling notions, toys and fireworks. Al Stewart soon encounters Luther Ford, and sells him the rights to "Mrs. Stewart's Bluing."	(see 1883)	
1878	Reading, PA; George William Clewell invents the ice cream scoop, or dipper. Hopefully this will save many bent spoons.		
1878	The first telephones in Texas are installed by Galveston newspaper publisher, Col. A. H. Belo.		

1878	**Wanamaker's of Philadelphia is the first department store in the US to install electric lighting; delighting their customers, who are accustomed to browsing the aisles of wares by the glow of oil lamps.**	
1878	Texas; on October 7, buffalo hunter J. Wright Mooar bags a rare albino buffalo near Snyder.	
1878	England; Sir Joseph William Swan demonstrates a successful carbon-filament lamp bulb at Newcastle. It will be another ten months before Thomas A. Edison comes out with his "original" light bulb.	(see 1879)

1878	Germany; in a separate situation, August Thyssen begins processing products (materials) manufactured by Thyssen & Co.	(see 1883)	
1878	Ohio; Dayton café owner and mechanic James Ritty takes a voyage to Europe. Having become friends with the ship's engineer, and spending considerable time studying the mechanics of the engine room, Ritty's impression is that the same basic type mechanism that counts the revolutions of the propeller shaft could be used to operate a "cash register." Returning to Dayton, he soon conceives the method, and builds "James Ritty's New Cash Register and Indicator." Ritty patents two somewhat different styles, which are only mildly successful. Although Ritty's goal is to cut down on the pilferage of cash receipts from his own café, he does sell a few machines to other businesses, shipping one all the way to Duluth, MN.	(see 1881)	
1878	The Eaton, Cole & Burnham Co. becomes the Oil Well Supply Company.		
1878	Venezuela; the first drilling for crude oil takes place on Lake Maracaibo.	(see 1880)	
1879	The McCormick Harvesting Machine Company is founded in Chicago.		
1879	Rand Drill & Compressor changes the name to Rand Drill Co., then introduces the first Rand air compressor.		
1879	Cross Out, Brown County, TX, becomes Cross Cut when the Post Office opens there.		
1879	R. M. Downie and his brother build the first mobile, steam-powered drilling rig, selling it to drill water wells.		
1879	October; Thomas Edison tests his first bulb using carbonized cotton thread as a filament; on Dec 31st, he gives the first successful demonstration of these light bulbs.		
1879	**BJ moves to San Francisco, their engineers then develop the first deep-well turbine pump and the original submersible pump.**		
1879	About this time George and Rufus Brown operate Brown Brothers Tobacco Co., the largest tobacco company in Mocksville, NC.		
1879	In a one-room log cabin in Grafton, TX, Amon Giles Carter, Sr., is born. The family soon moves to Bowie, TX.		

1879	**The first coffee sold in sealed tin cans in the US is sold by CHASE & SANBORN.**	(see 1900)
1879	One of the first central sugarcane mills (sugar factory) in Louisiana is the VERMILION ROSE HILL COMPANY. This is the beginning of the trend to central mills; getting away from a small mill on each sugarcane plantation.	
1879	Desiring to work for one of the leading machine makers of Europe, Mr. Rudolf Diesel joins the staff of SULZER BROS. in Switzerland.	
1879	Manchester, England; CROSSLEY builds their first natural gas engines… to run on coal gas.	
1879	Dan's outfit, SECHLER & COMPANY incorporates, and before long they are the world's largest producer of all types of horse-drawn vehicles, from sporty phaetons to funeral coaches. Eventually they are the largest exporter of carriages in America, shipping their products world-wide.	
1879	The railroads of Russia now have a total of 12,500 miles (20,125 km) of track in use.	
1879	**Mr. Milton Bradley invents the "one-armed" paper cutter, similar to the ones still used in offices in the 21st century.**	
1879	England; Edward Leveaux invents the automatic player piano, he receives the patent in 1881.	
1879	Pennsylvania; the Tidewater Pipeline is completed from Bradford to Williamsport, a run of 100 miles.	(see 1880)
1879	STANDARD OIL COMPANY buys VACUUM OIL CO. from Everest, but he remains on as manager.	(see 1887)
1880s	France; Comte Albert de Dion finances mechanics Bouton and Trépardoux in their production of steam carriages.	
1880s	In this decade, Cyrus McCormick introduces his franchise agreement. This contract sets the pattern for retail distribution of farm equipment and later for construction equipment. McCormick thus builds a strong network of independent dealers, whose first loyalty is to the MCCORMICK brand of farm equipment. Basically, this same agreement used well into the 21st century by most equipment dealers.	
1880s	Over the past decade, and through this one, "tricycles" are coming into considerable usage (by those who can afford them) and some mechanical innovations invented for the tricycle are rack and pinion steering, band brakes, and the differential, just to name a few. The upcoming invention of the motorcar just might make use of some of these.	
1880	**In this year alone, over 10,000 patents are issued for "labor-saving" devices of all sorts.**	
1880	Bucyrus, OH; Daniel P. Eells gets several relatives and business associates together to form the BUCYRUS FOUNDRY AND MFG. CO, "to carry on the business of a foundry and of manufacturing machinery and railroad cars."	(see 1882)
1880	LINK-BELT MACHINERY CO. is formed to build rail shovel cranes.	
1880	*Cross Plains, TX, now has twenty-five residents, a cotton gin, a grist mill, a wagon maker, and a general store.*	
1880	Solomon R. Dresser starts business, after patenting a cylindrical packer to seal off crude oil from water underground; during America's first oil boom.	
1880	Edward Ashcroft sells his interest in ASHCROFT CO. to Charles Moore, who joined with partners to form MANNING, MAXWELL AND MOORE, in New York City. M. M. & M. will continue to produce Ashcroft branded gauges.	
1880	In Sweden, Karl Gustaf De Laval devises the first mechanical cream separator.	
1880	L. S. Starrett starts in business in Athol, MA.	
1880	The family owned HATZ ENGINE CO. is founded.	

1880	CLARK BROS. Is founded in Belmont, NY, as a manufacturer of agricultural and timber machinery.	
1880	MORSE EQUALIZING SPRING CO., later to be MORSE CHAIN, is founded.	
1880	In Germany, Werner Von Siemens company perfects a light bulb.	
1880	The automatic screw machine is invented by BROWN & SHARPE.	
1880	As the ECLIPSE WIND MILL CO. is again reorganized, the Wheelers keep over half the stock in ECLIPSE WIND ENGINE CO. At this time, C. H. Morse, a partner in FAIRBANKS MORSE & CO., buys a 20% interest in ECLIPSE. FAIRBANKS MORSE then becomes the general agent for ECLIPSE windmills.	

1880	Joe Juneau and Richard Harris discover gold in Alaska, starting the first gold rush in American Alaska. During the next two decades, about a billion dollars worth of gold will be mined here, not a bad return for the $7,200,000 that the US spent to buy "Seward's Folly" from Russia. In Alaska; the ALASKA JUNEAU and the TREADWAY mines both begin producing gold this year.	
1880	FISHER CONTROLS is established as a maker of governors for steam-powered equipment.	
1880	Denver, CO; George W. Robinson establishes the ROBINSON BRICK COMPANY.	
1880	Mr. Milton Bradley expands and begins making jigsaw puzzles.	
1880	April 3; DODGE MANUFACTURING CO. is incorporated by Warren H. Dodge.	
1880	Texas; construction begins on the Port Aransas jetties, and dredging the pass to twelve feet deep, at low tide.	
1880	Although primitive, it is an improvement over the ear-trumpet; R. G. Rhodes creates a hearing aid.	
1880	England; as the firearms market slumps, BSA begins manufacturing bicycles and tricycles.	
ca1880	Australia; David Waugh and Sydney Josephson go partners in an engineering works in New South Wales.	(see 1891)
1880	London; Marcus Samuels Jr., and his brother Sam, now have the business their father started. They export British textiles and machines and import rice and china pottery. Marcus Jr. is interested in the booming oilfield in Azerbaijan (a part of Russia). Soon Junior is making his own deals in lighting and lubricating oils… competing with Standard Oil and the Rothschilds.	(see 1897)
1880	Plymouth, OH; about this time, J. D. Fate, a brickyard worker from Pennsylvania, and his partner Gunsaullus, settle here to establish their business.	
1880	The five thousandth Baldwin railroad locomotive is built this year.	(see 1913)
1880	Western Pennsylvania; H. J. Heinz makes his first batch of fruit preserves.	
1880	After four struggling years, Jacob Cox buys out Newton's half of CLEVELAND TWIST DRILL CO. and is left with $9,000 debt. Frank F. Prentiss, Cox's nephew, joins the company as its first real salesman, leaving Cox to design machines and operate the business, as well as look after the bookkeeping.	(see 1886)
1880	Having begun operations as a branch line of the UNION PACIFIC, this year after bankruptcy, the KANSAS PACIFIC RAILWAY is now history, as it is now truly a part of Jay Gould's UNION PACIFIC RAIL ROAD. This year, Jay Gould acquires control of the TEXAS AND PACIFIC RR and resumes westward construction as Mr. Grenville Dodge is named construction engineer for the project.	
1880	USA; a new locomotive going into service this year for the NEW YORK, PENNSYLVANIA & OHIO RAILROAD, has a total weight of 160,000 pounds (72,574 kg) with the engine and tender fully loaded. This is 10 times the weight of 1837.	(see 1895)
1880	There are now 93,267 miles of railroad tracks in this country.	(see 1890)
1880	USA; crude oil production is now flourishing in the Allegheny National Forest region.	(see 1881) (see 1892)
1880	On November 8th, Edwin L. Drake dies in Bethlehem, PA, at age 61.	(see 1881)

1880	Today, very few buffalo, or American Bison, remain on the southern prairies of North America.	(see 1884)
1880	Mr. John Charter of the CHARTER GAS ENGINE COMPANY invents the first practical liquid-fueled tractor. Charter's machine is lightweight, more maneuverable, and more economical than the established practice of using livestock for motive power.	(see 1887)
1880	The "Little Giant" excavators are now being built by the VULCAN STEAM SHOVEL CO.	
1880	Ontario, Canada; one day the Lacey Mine near Southborough Township will be one of the planet's largest producers of phlogopite mica. Commercial production has now begun, and some of the mica crystals are 9 feet in diameter in this Frontenac County mine.	
1881	William Boeing is born in Detroit, MI.	
1881	**J. W. Miller, a tool dresser, develops a self-contained, mobile, shallow oil well spudder.**	
1881	*Belle Plain College is established in Callahan County, TX.*	
1881	Jacob Herbrand and three others found HERBRAND TOOLS, in Freemont, OH.	
1881	*The city of Abilene, TX, is founded in March; the* ABILENE REPORTER NEWS *is established in June.*	
1881	William Church, a stranger, suggests that PHELPS-DODGE invest in copper mining; then shortly after they begin the MORENCI mine in Arizona.	(see 2003)
1881	**The first electric street lights in the US are lit on Ganson Street in Buffalo, NY.**	
1881	Ruben Hills and his brother Austin begin roasting coffee beans.	(see 1900)
1881	By the end of this year, 110 million pounds of beef are exported from the US to Great Britain. This disturbs the British, as the imported US beef is selling for less than their domestic beef or mutton.	
1881	Tunneling begins as France and Britain have agreed to build a tunnel under the English Channel. Soon however, Britain "pulls the plug," concerned that invaders from the continent might use the tunnel for a military route.	
1881	As President James A. Garfield is dying from an assassin's bullet, Alexander Graham Bell hurriedly "throws together" an apparatus to try and locate the bullet in his body. Although unsuccessful in this first usage, this apparatus is the world's first metal detector.	

	1881	The twin sons of C. H. Waterous organize a branch of Waterous Engine Works in Winnipeg, Manitoba, Canada. Here Waterous manufactures sawmill machinery, steam-powered fire-engines, and other varied equipment. Within a few years this Winnipeg branch is moved to South St. Paul, MN, USA.	(see 1898)
	1881	STANDARD OIL CO. organizes the National Transit Company.	(see 1882)
	1881	England; the world's first coin operated machines (of any type) are introduced in South London.	

1881	Ohio; having just established the JOHN F. BYERS MACHINE COMPANY last year, Byers now moves into a larger shop facility, here in Ravenna, and will soon be introducing hoisting equipment.	(see 1891)
1881	Ohio; W. J. Tappan now sells his coal and wood-burning stoves all around the Bellaire area.	(see WWI)
1881	Texas; more miles of railroads are constructed in the great state of Texas this year than anytime before or after.	
1881	France; Alexandre Pinguély establishes a crane manufacturing company, PINGULEY.	
1881	Ohio; James Ritty moves his cash register factory from the room above his café to new larger quarters with ten employees. Continuing to concentrate more on operating his café, Ritty sells his cash register business, lock, stock and barrel, to Jacob H. Eckert for $1,000. Although unsuccessful, Ritty was on the right track, as his mechanical ideas were the foundation for successful cash registers for many decades to come.	
1881	The Russian Fyodor Blinov begins work on a steam-powered tracked vehicle.	(see 1888)

1881	The first electric streetcar is introduced.	
1882	Mr. L. S. Starrett goes to Europe, on a selling trip, and soon starts exporting a large portion of his products.	
1882	Henry J. Kaiser is born.	
1882	BUCYRUS assumes manufacture of the Thompson Railroad Shovel, the first railroad-style, non-rotating, steam shovel; and on June 3rd, Bucyrus ships their first railroad steam shovel to the Northern Pacific Railroad.	
1882	Cabot Corporation is founded.	
1882	Texas; a post office is opened at Cottonwood, in Callahan County.	
1882	Franklin Mfg. Company is established in St. Paul, MN, and shortly renames itself American Mfg. Co.	(see 1892)
1882	Flushing, Long Island, NY; James Harvey Williams opens a small forge shop and soon pioneers the concept of standardized industrial hand tools.	
1882	In Beaver Falls, PA, the Downie brothers establish the Keystone Portable Steam Driller Co. Ltd.	
1882	**The earliest hydraulically powered excavator is built by the British firm, Sir W. G. Armstrong & Company, to construct docks at Hull, England; the hydraulic medium used is water.**	
1882	**Henry Perky produces the first commercially manufactured breakfast cereal… Shredded Wheat.**	
1882	**W. H. Dodge's "split pulley" patent is issued.**	
1882	**John L. Sullivan becomes the last bareknuckle heavyweight boxing champion, as he knocks out Paddy Ryan.**	
1882	Sargent & Co. ends their venture with Mallory Locks, as Burton Mallory died in '78, and business has faded rapidly.	
1882	The Crocker & Curtis Electric Motor Co. is now producing a two-bladed electric desk fan, recently invented by Dr. Schuyler S. Wheeler.	
1882	Valentine & Company open a plant in their old hometown of Boston, where they first began.	
1882	In the village that will someday be Hurley, SD, Mahlon E. Layne begins his drilling career. His first rig is powered only by his muscles. Layne soon designs his own horse-powered and steam-powered drilling rigs.	(see 1901)
1882	To better serve the cattle business, the St. Louis & San Francisco Railroad extends its line to Tulsa, OK.	
1882	Plymouth, OH; the Fate & Gunsaullus Co. begins making clay extruding equipment for brickmaking.	(see 1892)
1882	The Standard Oil Trust is organized.	(see 1885) (see 1890)
1882	Philadelphia; German immigrant Charles F. Zimmerman invents and receives a patent for the "autoharp;" actually it is not a harp at all, but a "chorded zither" with 36 or more strings.	
1882	June 6; in New York City, Henry W. Seely receives the patent for the electric iron, at this time called the electric flatiron. Seely's iron uses a carbon arc to heat the iron surface; not real safe, but it works.	(see 1892)

W. H. DODGE & G. PHILION.
SEPARABLE PULLEY.
No. 260,462.   Patented July 4, 1882.
(No Model.)

1883	**G. Daimler receives a patent for his "gas engine with hot tube ignition."**	
1883	KOHLER & SILBERZAHN introduce their "Horse Trough/Hog Scalder/add four legs and it's a bathtub." *"No Bubba, 'at's no joke!!"*	
1883	Retired inventor, Mr. JOHN BEAN creates a new insecticide spray pump for orchards.	
1883	Ludvig Fredholm established ELEKTRISKA AKTIEBOLAGET in Stockholm, to manufacture electrical generators and lighting.	
1883	WOLVERINE begins making and marketing work shoes and boots.	
1883	The predecessor to FAG bearings is founded in Schweinfurt, Germany.	
1883	April 1; in the booming cow town of Tascosa, TX, two dozen cowpunchers of the LX, LIT, and LS ranches go out on strike for higher wages. This is a short-lived incident, as the cowboys soon get hungry and go back to work, some for less pay than before.	
1883	Joseph Francis Joy is born in Cumberland, MD.	
1883	Texas; in the southwest corner of Eastland County, Pioneer, TX, is established.	
1883	In St. Paul, MN, the AMERICAN MANUFACTURING CO. begins producing hoisting equipment.	
1883	October 11; meeting in Chicago, the General Time Convention (precursor to the American Railway Association) adopts four Standard Time Zones; Eastern, Central, Mountain and Pacific, for rail service in the US and Canada. Now they can synchronize their clocks.	
1883	**Regardless of what the Yanks say, the French *did* invent cigarette lighters,** they are actually modified oil lamps, and weigh about two pounds, so there!!	
1883	A printer working on a regular telephone book runs out of white paper and uses yellow paper instead to finish the job. This is the first "yellow pages."	
1883	**Twenty-four old Francis Peabody and a partner open a retail coal business in Chicago, with a $100 investment.**	
1883	Schweinfurt, Germany; the ball-bearing industry is originated as Friedrich Fischer invents the ball grinder, starting the city's industrialization and rise to eminence as "the ball bearing town." FRIEDRICH FISCHER CO. is soon founded.	
1883	Kinderdijk, the Netherlands; in this village, SMIT-SLIKKERVEER manufactures the first machine for electric power generation in the Netherlands.	
1883	BUCYRUS ships the first "dipper dredge" from their factory.	(see 1893)
1883	John Crawford, an Irish immigrant, arrives in America, and soon sets up shop in Parkersburg, Western Virginia.	
1883	The first LUCCHESE BOOTS are marketed.	
1883	Cincinnati, OH; Bernard Henry "Barney" Kroger opens a grocery store, his first.	
1883	**Near Medicine Hat, Alberta, Canada, railroaders drilling for water find natural gas instead. A harbinger for the petroleum industry in Alberta.**	
1883	Oil and gas drilling begins in Alberta, Canada, using technology imported from the US, and adapted to local conditions.	
1883	August 26; Krakatoa, the island volcano begins erupting, with forces increasing by the hour.	
1883	Dan Gardner, Eugene Williams, rancher Samuel Lazarus of the FA Ranch, and businessman A. P. Busch, Jr., of St. Louis, form the PITCHFORK LAND & CATTLE CO.	(see 1884)
1883	F. A. Gower, an American living in France, successfully flies his "fish-shaped" balloon across the English Channel; using a oil-powered, bronze, steam engine for steering. On a future flight, Mr. Gower crashes and drowns in the Channel.	

1883	From his savings of $50, sixteen year old George S. Parker takes $40 to publish and market "Banking," a game he has invented. He soon establishes the George S. Parker Company in Salem, MA.	(see 1888)

	1883	In far west Texas, Robert Ellison, a sixteen year old cowboy is the first to see the Marfa Lights, or at least the first to tell others about seeing them.
	1883	Pittsburgh Plate Glass Co. is founded. The PPG plant at Creighton, PA, is the first commercially successful plate glass factory in the US.
	1883	Brooklyn, NY; a recent Irish immigrant, the youthful Benjamin Moore begins his paint manufacturing business here.
	1883	On July the fourth, the world's first known rodeo is held in the small town of Pecos, TX.

1883	The Cherokee Strip Live Stock Association is formed. This corporation will last for forty years, operating on land leased from the Cherokee Nation.	
1883	July 30; Luther Ford begins manufacturing "Mrs. Stewart's Bluing," and his first recorded sale is today. Ford plans to expand the bluing distributorship all across the Midwest region.	(see 1925)
1883	Huber Manufacturing is now building the Barnhart Steam Shovels at its plant in Marion, OH.	(see 1884)
1883	The Pennsylvania Railroad (Pennsy) begins placarding their cars carrying explosives and poisonous chemicals.	
1883	Texas; the office of the State Engineer is created to investigate railroad abuses. Although this office is abolished after its initial two-year run, it is still considered the forerunner to the Texas Railroad Commission.	(see 1891)
1883	Omaha, NE; Mr. Kiewit, the local bricklayer, and his two sons start a small construction company here in town.	(see 1884)
1883	Michigan; Mr. E. T. Lufkin moves E. T. Lufkin Board & Log Tool Co. from Cleveland, OH, to Saginaw.	(see 1920)
1883	Germany; a local mechanical engineering firm is purchased, this is the foundation for Maschinenfabrik Thyssen & Company; now rolling sheet iron and galvanizing it.	(see 1891)
1883	California; the Stockton Wheel Company is founded by Benjamin Holt and his three brothers. Their main business is building and selling wagon wheels and carriage bodies. These best selling items soon take a back seat to their new invention; a ten foot diameter wheel mounted on a ten foot long axle, enabling loggers to tie logs to the axle and pull them from the forest with large teams of horses and mules.	(see 1886)
1883	New Jersey; a small generating plant sends electricity through overhead wires to Thomas A. Edison's electric light bulbs in a store, the railroad station, 40 homes and 150 street lights; thus making Roselle the first town lighted by Edison's light bulbs.	
1883	In Hastings County, Ontario, actinolite mining is now underway.	
1884	Marion, OH; Huber Manufacturing changes its name to Marion Steam Shovel Company.	
1884	Henry Royce establishes a electrical and mechanical business in England.	(see 1904)
1884	Alanzo Pawling & Henry Harnischfeger found Harnischfeger Corp. (P & H)	
1884	Harry Ferguson is born.	
1884	John H. Patterson founds the National Cash Register Company, then makes one of the first mechanical cash registers.	
1884	Brothers Peter and Andrew Kiewit forms Keiwit Bros., a masonry contracting company, in Omaha.	(see 1890)

1884	Some of the items EATON & COLE are making in their own shop and selling are cable tool rigs and tools, steam engines, under-reamers and fishing tools.	
1884	May; the first RINGLING BROS. CIRCUS is thrilling audiences, featuring five of the seven Ringling brothers. There are NO animal acts, only juggling, some tumbling, and a few jokes. Ringling Bros. will continue to travel by horse-drawn wagons for six more years.	
1884	The largest centrifugal pump in North America is built by ALLIS.	
1884	**Aluminum is still considered a semi-precious metal, total US production this year is 125 pounds.**	(see 1886)
1884	**SPALDING becomes the first American manufacturer of golf clubs.**	
1884	**An insurance broker, Lewis Edson Waterman invents the first proper fountain pen.**	
1884	DAVID BRADLEY MANUFACTURING CO. is formed as David Bradley and his son J. Harley Bradley, buy Conrad Furst's interest in FURST & BRADLEY.	(see 1895)
1884	During a 90 day period this summer, 825,000 head of North-bound Texas cattle plod past a set point in the Indian Territory, just north of the Red River. Also this summer, Ike Pryor (an orphaned cotton-picker) trails fifteen herds of 3,000 head each north. Ike is offered $700,000 for his cattle.	
1884	**Albert Blake Dick invents the mimeograph process for copying written papers; he and Thomas Edison partner with a handshake deal.**	
1884	RAND-MCNALLY CO. acquires DENOYER-GEPPERT CO., a leading school map and globe manufacturer.	
1884	KELLY PLOW COMPANY is established in Longview, TX, by G. A. Kelly.	
1884	**The WEIR BROTHERS build their first commercial water distiller, for use on ships at sea.**	
1884	**Due to extreme damage caused to the environment, hydraulic mining is outlawed in California.**	
1884	Texas; the PITCHFORK RANCH sells its first cattle; 288 head of 3 year old steers are sold to Tom Trammell for thirty-five dollars a head.	(see 1935)
1884	SARGENT & COMPANY begin manufacturing and selling their own bench planes and block planes for wood working.	
1884	DANZAS contracts with the Swiss Post Office for international postal deliveries. DANZAS is now guaranteeing twenty-four hour Switzerland to London mail service.	
1884	England; Nipper, a stray fox terrier and bull terrier mix, fond of chasing rats and nipping ankles, is born in Bristol, Gloucester.	(see 1887)
1884	Wisconsin; the story goes, that a CASE dealer near Racine was unable to repair a faulty CASE brand thresher. Mr. J. I. Case goes down to get the problem sorted out, but being unable to repair the problem himself, Case torches the machine, burning it to the ground. Case then orders the customer a new replacement thresher, and it arrived the very next day… *Now, folks, that is customer service!!!*	
1884	The XIT Ranch now covers 3,050,000 acres of the Texas Panhandle.	
1884	Baltimore, MD; with their considerable experience gained while working several years in various local shops, Charles White and Arthur Middleton start their own little machine shop. Because of their good reputation, they were able to open the shop on borrowed money; White once remarked, "You bet! We hustled to make our paper good."	
1884	Washington, DC; while delegates from twenty-five nations meet for the International Meridian Conference, Greenwich, England, is adopted as the zero meridian, to be used as the worldwide standard of time zones.	

1884	Having worked on the project for sixteen years, Naval Commander John Adams Howell develops the Howell Torpedo.	
1884	Japan; HONJO COPPER SMELTERY starts up in business.	
1884	Japan; YAMADA CABLE WORKS begins operations, making copper cables.	
1884	USA; George Eastman patents his paper-strip photographic film.	
1884	Texas; the state legislature enacts a law prohibiting "malicious fence cutting."	
1884	Cleveland, Ohio; CLEVELAND FROG & CROSSING COMPANY is established to manufacture a patented railroad switch frog, permitting a train travelling on one track to cross the rails of an intersecting track.	(see 1949)
1884	Charles Parson patents a steam turbine.	
1884	The buffalo, or American Bison, of our northern prairies are now almost gone; the last shipment of hides on the NORTHERN PACIFIC goes to the east this year.	
1884	Grover Cleveland is elected President of the United States of America.	
1884	Cyrus McCormick passes on, but his son Robert carries the business forward, until merging with Deering Harvester.	(see 1902)
1884	Illinois; the three-wheeled Flying Dutchman™ style plow is introduced by MOLINE PLOW WORKS, INC.; this popular style is soon well known around all the farming areas of the world.	
1884	USA; the federal government establishes the US Bureau of Labor Statistics.	
1884	Canada; out on the prairies of Alberta, the village (pop. 500) of Calgary is incorporated as a town. The Calgary and District Agricultural Society is formed as well.	(see 1891)
1884	France; originally trained as an engineer, and an assistant to Louis Pasteur at one time, chemist Hilaire de Chardonnet invents rayon from nitrocellulose, as an alternative to real silk during an epidemic affecting silkworms. The material is extremely flammable, but denitrating the fibers with ammonium sulfide improves this quality without weakening the fibers.	(see 1891)
1884	Sweden; (AB) Bofors-Gullspång opens its cannon building workshop.	(see 1894)
1884	Discovery of the Kingdon Lead Mine in Fitzroy Township, Carleton County, becomes Ontario's largest lead producer for more than the next eight decades.	(see 1970)
1885	This year STUDEBAKER MFG. CO. production tops 75,000 wagons, by far the largest wagon builder in the world. *"Hey Bubba, 'at's 205 waggins a day, thank about it!!"*	
1885	**J. D. Adams invents the horse-drawn road grader.**	
1885	GOLDBLATT TOOLS (masonry tools) starts in business.	
1885	Germany; G. Daimler files for patent on his "Reitwagen," the world's first gas-engine motorcycle.	(see 1886)
1885	John Secor of NYC begins experimenting with internal combustion engines, subjecting them to tests trying to achieve maximum power from minimum fuel.	
1885	Billy Durant partners with J. D. Dort and organize the COLDWATER ROAD CART COMPANY.	
1885	In Minneapolis, Albert Butz patents the furnace regulator and alarm.	
1885	Texas; Dr. Charles Alderton, working at the soda fountain of the Old Corner Drug Store in Waco, concocts a new drink… Dr. Pepper. *Note: Coca-Cola is still a few years in the future.*	(see 1893)

1885	Albert G. Fuller is born on a farm in Nova Scotia, Canada.	
1885	Robert Wood Johnson and his two brothers form a partnership making surgical dressings and soon will incorporate as JOHNSON & JOHNSON.	
1885	L & M is the largest manufacturer of plug chewing tobacco in the world.	
1885	Germany; Herr G. Georg Schäfer sets up a mechanic shop that soon expands into a factory, the BALL BEARINGS WORKS GEORG SCHÄFER & CO.	
1885	Rietberg, Germany; KONRAD STÜKERJÜRGEN KG is founded as a water well drilling company.	
1885	Sterling County, TX; the Weekly Observer, Robert Lee's local newspaper, is now being published by Mr. George Cowan.	
1885	The CANADIAN PACIFIC RAILWAY is completed.	
1885	ELLICOTT MANUFACTURING CO. is founded in Baltimore, to build dredges.	
1885	The DIEBOLD FIREBRICK COMPANY is formed.	
1885	USA; W. H. Bundy invents the printing time clock for workers. Later, in some countries, "to Bundy" is generic for to "clock in or to clock out."	
1885	Iron ore mining in the UK is now at its peak.	
1885	ROYAL DUTCH discovers crude oil in Sumatra.	(see 1892)
1885	Germany; Adam Opel expands his business into building pre-assembled bicycles.	(see 1886)
1885	Germany; Karl Benz (1844-1929), son of a locomotive engineer, builds his first automobile powered by an internal-combustion engine.	(see 1886)
1885	Thomas "Captain" Baldwin is credited with inventing the collapsible parachute, although he never patents it.	
1885	The American beef cattle business is truly booming. As British beef and mutton are still losing ground to American beef, British financiers invest heavily in US cattle herds and ranches, often coming over the pond to oversee and operate them.	
1885	There are now fourteen "true" railroad circuses crisscrossing America on the tracks.	(see 1900)
1885	James Trane begins his family business.	
1885	Kansas; the PITTSBURG & MIDWAY COAL CO. is founded in Pittsburg.	
1885	Canada; the mining of marl for the manufacture of portland cement begins at the first quarry at Strathcona, in Lennox and Addington counties in Ontario.	
1886	BROWNING POWER TRANSMISSION (gears, sprockets, etc.) starts business.	
1886	The first CHAMPION grader appears.	
1886	**January 29; Germany issues a patent to Karl Benz for the first automobile powered by an internal combustion engine. Karl's tricycle-type vehicle will travel nine mph. Benz's vehicle is generally considered to be the first automobile.**	
1886	**Germany; Gottlieb Daimler builds the world's first FOUR-WHEELED engine powered vehicle.**	
1886	The Statue of Liberty, a gift to the USA from France, is unveiled in New York Harbor.	
1886	**A coal mining operation begins at what will soon be Thurber, TX.**	
1886	At the STOCKTON WHEEL CO, Benjamin Holt builds his first LINK BELT COMBINED HARVESTER (combine).	(see 1891)
1886	Tiona, PA; Mr. W. C. Norris begins production of wooden sucker rods for pumping oil wells.	
1886	In Stuttgart, Robert Bosch founds the WORKSHOP FOR PRECISION MECHANICS AND ELECTRICAL ENGINEERING, later to become ROBERT BOSCH GmbH.	

1886	The M. Rumely Co. introduces its first steam traction engine, a straw burner.	
1886	Albert Butz founds the Butz Thermo-Electric Regulator Co.	
1886	Former Brush Electric Co. executive W. H. Lawrence forms the National Carbon Company.	
1886	Frank and Charles, the Duryea brothers, begin experimenting with gasoline engines in their spare time.	
1886	The young Charles Martin Hall develops a method to make aluminum oxide, he now goes in search of financial backing to proceed.	(see 1888)
1886	S. C. Johnson is established as a manufacturer of parquet flooring and soon S. C. develops a very good floor wax.	
1886	Morrison Patent Wire Rope Co. is founded. In a couple of years they will change the name to Williamsport Wire Rope Company.	
1886	The Manville Covering Co. is founded to use asbestos as a heat insulating material.	
1886	Smith Premier Typewriter Co. creates the first typewriter that writes both upper and lower case letters.	

	1886	Richard W. Sears makes $5,000 selling watches from unclaimed freight he has bought, then partners with watchmaker Alvah C. Roebuck in the watch business.	
	1886	**Texas; George Dullnig, a Bexar county rancher, strikes oil while drilling for water, but he never attempts commercial production.**	
	1886	Columbus, OH; on the eighth day of December, the American Federation of Labor (AFL) is founded.	
	1886	**Josephine Cochrane of the US, invents a more practical, usable dishwasher.**	
	1886	**Keyboard typesetting is invented by Ottmar Mergenthaler, in the USA.**	
	1886	Spain; the open-cast Rio Tinto silver mines first begin producing.	
	1886	Carl Reed begins manufacturing tacks, nails, and brads in Worcester, MA. This is the origin of Reed & Prince.	

1886	New Mexico Territory; in the southeast, the Cowden family establishes the JAL cattle ranch in Monument Draw.	(see 1928)
1886	Business has been bad for Cleveland Twist Drill and at one point, Cox tries to sell the entire outfit for only $75,000. He finds no takers, so they continue to struggle onward.	(see 1894)
1886	USA; on May 31st, the standard gauge of four feet, eight and one-half inches is adopted by the southern railroads.	
1886	Mr. John Deere dies this year, and the bold smitty's company is now making thousands of plows, cultivators, and many other farm implements every year. It will be another four decades before they enter the tractor business.	
1886	In Lansing, MI, nineteen year old Ransom E. Olds builds his first steam-powered car.	
1886	Tennessee; September 14; previously, all typewriters used carbon paper, now George K. Anderson of Memphis patents typewriter ribbon.	
1887	The Minneapolis Threshing Machine Company gets to thrashin', as they bring out Victory separators (threshers) as well as steam engines this year.	(see 1888)
1887	Conrad Hilton is born on Christmas Day, in San Antonio, NM.	(see 1924)
1887	John Fowler & Co. Ltd., in Leeds, England builds their first steam rollers.	

1887	OHIO OIL COMPANY is founded.	
1887	**A. G. EDWARDS begins business, as a financial and investment consultant with the unusual belief, "It's all about our clients."**	
1887	German physicist Heinrich Hertz, demonstrates the process of electromagnetic radiation through space, proving that radio waves travel as fast as light waves.	
1887	**Olin J. Garlock patents his first industrial sealing system.**	
1887	The TIDE WATER OIL COMPANY is founded.	
1887	**The first commercial mimeograph machine is marketed by A. B. DICK CO. with his partner Thomas Edison's support.**	
1887	CANNON TEXTILE MILLS is established.	
1887	**Garner, TX; eleven-year-old William Albert Thomas invents the domino game of forty-two (42).**	
1887	**September 20; Mr. John Charter receives patent 370,242 on his engine; the first successful internal-combustion, liquid fuel, engine.**	
1887	When Mark Barraud dies, his dog Nipper goes to Liverpool to live with Mark's brother, artist Francis Barraud.	(see 1895)
1887	England; Queen Victoria celebrates her Golden Jubilee this year.	
1887	VACUUM OIL founder Hiram B. Everest and his son Charles M. Everest are charged with conspiracy to destroy the BUFFALO LUBRICATION OIL CO, by bribing Buffalo employees to damage and destroy buildings and machinery. Both Hiram and Charles Everest are found guilty.	(see 1899)
1888	Benjamin Harrison becomes President of the United States of America.	
1888	Robert Gilmour LeTourneau is born in Richland Vermont.	
1888	The MINNEAPOLIS THRESHING MACHINE CO. built its first steam traction engine.	
1888	La Verne Noyes starts building AERMOTOR windmills in San Angelo, Texas, and sells 24 units.	
1888	John Bean's son-in-law, David Crummey is the first president of BEAN SPRAY PUMP CO.	
1888	LINK-BELT ENGINEERING CO. is founded.	
1888	John Dunlop, a veterinarian in Ireland makes air filled rubber tires for his son's bicycle, and applies for a patent for his pneumatic bicycle tire. These are considered to be the first commercially successful pneumatic tires.	
1888	Thomas Edison now has incandescent light bulbs that last 550 hours (120 years later they will only last 4 times that, on the average).	
1888	W. W. Gibbs, the vice president of UNITED GAS IMPROVEMENT CO., a gas lighting firm, realizes the potential of electricity, and forms the ELECTRIC STORAGE BATTERY COMPANY.	
1888	**Thought to be the first skeletal steel skyscraper ever built, the Tower Building is completed in New York City.**	
1888	Thomas Edison, using B&W boilers in his laboratory, writes that a B & W boiler is "the best boiler God has permitted man yet to make."	
1888	Backed by Alfred E. Hunt et. al., Charles M. Hall opens a small plant and on Thanksgiving day produces the first commercial aluminum, using Hall's own method.	(see 1907)
1888	North Wales; J. K. SMIT & SONS DIAMOND TOOLS LTD. is established.	
1888	**George Eastman receives a patent for his roll-film camera, and registers his trademark… KODAK. Eastman's KODAK markets its first box camera. The camera and a roll of 100 exposure film sells for $25.**	(see 1949)

1888	**The world's first electric streetcar system begins carrying passengers in Richmond, VA.**	
1888	**Marvin C. Stone of Washington, DC, patents his hand-rolled invention, the wax-paper drinking straw.**	
1888	George's brother Charles Parker joins him and in a couple of years their company will be renamed PARKER BROTHERS.	
1888	Washington DC; some scientists and explorers meet here to organize "a society for the increase and diffusion of geographic knowledge," and the National Geographic Society is founded. *"...My, my, my, Slim. . . at's a mouthful!"*	
1888	HAISS BROTHERS COAL COMPANY begins operations in New York City.	(see 1890)
1888	Louisiana; Huddie "Lead Belly" Ledbetter is born in Mooringsport on January 15th.	
1888	Late in this decade, Episcopal Bishop William D. Walker of North Dakota takes a trip to Russia. While there Bishop Walker sees the elaborate Russian Orthodox chapel cars on the Siberian Railway. These chapel cars provide occasional church services for the people of eastern Siberia living in or near towns with railroad stations and sidings. Towns very often lacking a church building.	(see 1890)
1888	Showing people walking in a garden, "Roundhay Garden Scene" is a two-seconds-long moving picture. Therefore, inventor Louis Le Prince of France is credited with the very first motion picture.	(see 1895)
1888	Texans love their sports, and this year the East Texas League (baseball) is founded, this league will operate until 1941, and WWII.	
1888	Nikola Tesla invents the AC electric motor and transformer.	
1888	In Russia, Fyodor Blinov completes his steam-powered, self-propelled crawler, tracked tractor, and begins testing his baby.	(see 1896)
1888	November 9; in shaft No. 2 of the SANTA FE MINING CO, near Frontenac, KS, a terrible explosion kills 150 miners.	

	1888	Across America now there are about 80,000 freight cars using 39 various types of couplers, most of which cannot intercouple. Last year The Master Car Builders Assn. adopted an automatic coupler, reducing the various designs to a dozen or so, all now able to intercouple.	
	1888	Louisiana; about this time the first rotary drilling for crude oil is taking place.	
	1888	Texas; he's been self-supporting for the last couple of years, and the 18 year old Walter B. Sharp is now using a crude early rotary drilling rig and contracting and drilling water wells in and around the Dallas area.	(see 1893)
	1889	January 1; New York; the grand opening ceremony of the recently completed Poughkeepsie Bridge. This 212-foot-high, 6,767-foot-long double-tracked "Great Bridge" across the Hudson is the longest railroad bridge in North America.	(see 1974)

1889	Andrew Lawrence Riker founds the RIKER ELECTRIC VEHICLE COMPANY, soon to become one of the country's largest builder of electric cars and trucks.	
1889	J. W. Miller incorporates STAR DRILLING MACHINE CO. of Akron Ohio, to build his cable-tool drilling rigs, or "spudders."	
1889	SOUTH PENN OIL CO. is formed in Pennsylvania.	
1889	J. W. Earl, a Michigan lumberjack, moves his family to California and begins building carriages, wagons, and racing sulkies.	

1889	**Jonas Wenström invents the three-phase electrical system for generators, transformers, and motors.**	
1889	C. J. SMITH & SONS gets into the bicycle business.	
1889	S. PENNOCK & SONS is reorganized as the AMERICAN ROAD MACHINERY CO. (ARM) and the marketing branch, GOOD ROADS MACHINERY COMPANY.	
1889	A forerunner company to ACF, builds the first railroad tank car, called a "tub car."	
1889	**Edwin Ruud invents the home water heater.**	
1889	Sterling, IL; the Charter Tractor is introduced by the CHARTER GAS ENGINE COMPANY. One hundred years hence, this will be considered the first successful gasoline-powered tractor ever built.	
1889	As a youngster, John C. Edelbrock goes to work for SECHLER & COMPANY as an office boy.	(see 1910)
1889	July 8th; the first issue of the *WALL STREET JOURNAL* is published.	
1889	**HOLT MFG. CO. of Stockton, CA, begins building wheeled steam traction engines.**	
1889	**Having purchased the Remington steam engine rights, Daniel best begins building steam traction engines, and combines.**	(see 1890)
1889	Japan; the NINTENDO CO. is founded to make handmade hanafuda playing cards.	
ca1889	**The first horse-drawn riding cultivators are introduced.**	
1889	Josephine Cochran of Shelbyville, IN, has spent a decade building prototypes and now produces a practical dishwashing machine.	
1889	The XIT Ranch introduces Angus cattle to Texas.	
1889	Paris, France; having found no one in Europe to build the elevators for his tower in time for the EXPOSITION UNIVERSELLE, Gustave Eiffel invites Elisha Otis to Paris to help design and build the three elevators. These same three elevators are still operating well into the twenty-first century.	
1889	USA; Mr. H. D. Lee founds the H. D. LEE MERCANTILE CO. in Kansas. Soon LEE is manufacturing overalls, jackets, and dungarees to meet the needs of a growing nation.	(see 1924)
1889	England; into the Perkins family of Peterborough, a son, Frank, is born on February 20. Frank's father is a second generation engineer, and the family business is BARFORD & PERKINS, manufacturers of agricultural machinery and road rollers.	(see 1932)
1889	The first commercial natural gas wells in Ontario are discovered near Port Colborne and Gosfield Townships in Essex County.	
1889	In Renfrew County, on the shore of Whitefish Lake, graphite is discovered. This will become the Black Donald Mine, Ontario's richest graphite mine.	
1889	Daniel Best patents his steam harvester.	
1890s	Alexander G. Bell concentrates on his kite flying experiments and trying to progress to manned flights.	
1890s	During this decade, young George Burkinshaw goes to work sweeping floors at the PEPPER CANDY COMPANIE. George soon works up to candy-maker, and will eventually buy the business, including the original recipes.	(see 1965)
1890s	In Europe; a Belgian racecar driver and a French nobleman duel in electric automobiles. The Belgian eventually sets a new record of 65.79 miles (105.26 km) per hour.	(see 1927)

1890s	USA; wooden pencil manufacturers in America begin painting their pencils yellow, as they are using the highest quality graphite in the world, imported from China; and yellow is considered the "Royal" color in China.	
1890s	USA; oil companies first begin drilling "offshore," from long wooden piers attached to the shore.	(see 1937)
1890s	Jacob Valk invents the wrecking ball in the late 1800s.	
1890s	Late in the 1800s, the first asbestos is now being mined in Quebec, Canada.	
1890s	**Both Nikola Tesla and G. Marconi are now seriously listening for extraterrestrial communication, voices or sounds.**	
1890s	By the late 1800s, B. F. Avery is the largest plow manufacturer in the world.	
1890	England; William Paxman joins his father in DAVEY, PAXMAN & CO.	
1890	In Warren, Ohio, PACKARD ELECTRIC CO., is founded to make incandescent light bulbs and electrical items.	
1890	EMERSON ELECTRIC MANUFACTURING CO. is founded.	
1890	The MOLINE PLOW COMPANY is established.	
1890	John Dunlop sells his tire idea to William Harvey Du Cros, who starts the DUNLOP RUBBER COMPANY.	
1890	February 26; Chauncey (Chance) M. Vought is born on Long Island, NY.	
1890	The ROUSE-DURYEA CYCLE CO. is founded in Peoria, Ill.	
1890	Peter J. Kiewit is born, he is the Peter Keiwit best known for developing PKS into a major contractor.	
1890	In the late 1800s Harry Cobey establishes PERFECTION COBEY, to manufacture farm machinery and bodies for trucks.	
1890	EA merges with WENSTROMS & GRANSTROMS ELEKTRISKA KRAFBOLAG; forms ALLMÄNNA SVENSKA ELEKTRISKA (ASEA).	
1890	INDIANAPOLIS CHAIN & STAMPING CO. (IC & SC) is formed to manufacture bicycle chain.	
1890	Four Armstrong brothers found the ARMSTRONG BROS. TOOL CO., to make parts, tools, and equipment for bikes.	
1890	The ELECTRIC STORAGE BATTERY CO. installs the first practical storage battery in the GERMANTOWN ELECTRIC LIGHTING COMPANY in Philadelphia.	
1890	**The DURANT-DORT CARRIAGE COMPANY is the US's largest carriage builder, producing 50,000 horse-drawn vehicles yearly.** *"Hey Slim, thet's jest 137 ever day, not like Stude's 175 waggins."*	
1890	An unusually warm winter causes a shortage of natural ice to harvest, thus helping to "kick-start" the mechanical ice-making industry.	
1890	FAIRBANKS, MORSE & CO. assume control of the ECLIPSE firm, although for several more years the windmills will also be distributed from the Beloit Company.	
1890	Fred B. Kilmer, (father of poet Joyce Kilmer) the JOHNSON & JOHNSON scientific director, introduces baby powder - Johnson's Baby Powder.	
1890	January 2; the FARMERS & MERCHANTS NATIONAL BANK opens in Abilene, TX.	
1890	Kentucky; Nathan B. Stubblefield demonstrates his "wireless telephone" (radio) to a few friends on his farm.	(see 1892)
1890	Young Herman Hollerith wins the contract for the US census, using his recently invented "statistical piano" (calculator) punch-card reading machine.	
1890	ROYAL DUTCH PETROLEUM is established to develop a oilfield in Sumatra.	

1890	Beaumont, TX; CONNS is established as a small plumbing and heating business.		
1890	One of the least desirable illegal immigrants arrives as the Mexican Boll Weevil swims across the Rio Grande, and begins its century of wrecking havoc in the cotton fields of the southern United States.		
1890	April; having recently returned from Russia, Bishop Walker contracts with the PULLMAN PALACE CAR CO. for construction of a chapel car. This November Bishop Walker takes possession of the Episcopalian chapel car named "Church of the Advent - the Cathedral Car of North Dakota."		
1890	The KUBOTA CORP. is organized as an iron casting foundry in Japan.		
1890	**A Missouri doctor creates peanut butter.**		
1890	**Davis mountains; John Z. Means and C. O. Finley kill the only Grizzly bear ever known to be taken in Texas.**		
1890	After losing considerable money on failed inventions such as a nail-feeder, a racing-sulky speedometer, and a 24 hour clock; Alfred and Charles G. Harris invent an automatic sheet-feeder to eliminate the labor-intensive work of hand-feeding paper into printing presses. These jewelers soon design a new printing press to better interface with their "automatic sheet feeder."		
1890	The National Woman Suffrage Association and the American Woman's Suffrage Association, consolidate forces as The National American Woman's Suffrage Association, for a united front pushing for women's voting rights.		
1890	Across the US there are 163,597 miles of railroad tracks transporting freight and passenger trains.	(see 1900)	
1890	USA; the federal congress passes the Sherman Anti-trust act.	(see 1892)	
1890	There are now over eight thousand and seven hundred miles of railroad track in Texas.	(see 1900)	
1890	John Burton invents the electric cattle prod.	(see 1891)	

1890	The state of Michigan now has 2,200 lumber mills, cutting 4.2 million board feet of lumber each year.		
1890	January 25; Nellie Bly completes her 'round the world trip in 72 days, eight days shorter than the fictional Phileas T. Fogg in Jules Verne's novel, *Around the World in Eighty Days*. Bly, a *New York World* reporter traveled by trains, ships, horses, man-powered carts, boats, and burros during her jaunt.		
1890	Early in this decade, at the docks around the Great Lakes, iron-ore carrying boat Captain Richard Thew usually has problems handling the iron ore once it is dumped on the docks. The railroad steam shovels now used are very heavy, cumbersome, and only have 180 degrees of swing, leaving a huge amount of hand-shovel work and repositioning of its tracks.	(see 1895)	
1890	In California, the fifty-four mile long Sanger Flume is completed. This is the longest log floating flume ever built.		
1890	The GEORGE HAISS MFG. COMPANY is founded in New York City, to build various types of coal-loading equipment.	(see 1913)	
1890	Duluth, MN; NATIONAL IRON WORKS FOUNDRY & MACHINE SHOP is organized.	(see 1896)	
1890	Ohio; in Cleveland, Theodore A. Willard starts a business that will eventually be the WILLARD STORAGE BATTERY COMPANY.		
1890	Chicago; four sons of an Scottish immigrant blacksmith begin a business making and selling bicycle parts, as well as the tools and equipment used in the manufacture and repair of bicycles.	(see 1895)	

1890	New York; mining tycoon Daniel Guggenheim and his wife Florence have a new son, Harry.	
1890	John D. Rockefeller has now gained control of about 90% of America's oil-refining business, pretty much monopolizing the industry.	
1890	California; the LEVI STRAUSS & CO. INC., San Francisco factory now has 500 employees.	(see 1902)
1890	New York; Moses L. Orberdorfer begins manufacturing bronze pumps in his small facility on East Water St. in Syracuse. His pumps are used as engine lube oil pumps for engine cylinder walls in the early motorcar, aircraft and motorboat industries.	(see 1922)
1890	Having spent the last year or so raising funds, in August the AMERICAN BAPTIST PUBLICATION SOCIETY now contracts with the BARNEY & SMITH CAR CO. shops of Dayton, Ohio, to build the Baptist's first rail chapel car.	(see 1891)
1890	Canada; the Ontario Bureau of Mines is organized this year.	
1891	December 1; at the YMCA in Springfield, MA, Canadian grad student James Naismith invents the game of basketball.	(see 1896)
1891	Sid Richardson is born in Athens, TX.	
1891	Young Albert Champion opens his first shop.	
1891	Charles L. Brown and Walter Boveri establish BROWN, BOVERI & CIE (BB&C), in Switzerland.	
1891	Switzerland; Carl Eisner builds the first SWISS ARMY multi-tool knife for the military.	
1891	The Duryea brothers begin full-time work on gasoline engines, building the first American car next year.	
1891	October 26; to supply gas for his carbon-black business, Godfrey Cabot completes his first natural gas well, on the Joseph Smith lease in Armstrong County, PA.	
1891	May 5; in New York City, Russian composer Pyotr Tchaikovsky is the featured artist on opening night at Carnegie Hall.	
1891	In Fort Wayne, IN, the WAYNE PUMP COMPANY is organized.	
1891	Leading implement makers, Daniel Massey's MASSEY MANUFACTURING CO. of Toronto and A. HARRIS SON & CO., also of Ontario, merge to form MASSEY-HARRIS COMPANY. At the time of the merger, these two companies have over fifty percent of Canada's farm implement business.	
1891	In Finland, AHLSTROM build their first pumps.	
1891	MARELLI COMPONENTI ELETTROMECCANICI is founded in Italy.	
1891	USA; Whitcomb Judson invents the zipper, but it will be two more decades of improvements before it is faster and easier than buttons.	
1891	In Cascade Canyon Colorado, railroad engineer Moore thinks he has it under control…	
1891	LEIDECKER TOOL COMPANY is established, by J. J. Leidecker, L. D. Shryrock, Clint Moore, and G. T. Braden.	
1891	LELAND STANFORD JUNIOR UNIVERSITY opens in California, named for L. S., Jr., who died in 1884, at almost sixteen years of age.	
1891	Mr. George Merck establishes a drug company.	
1891	In Ft. Wayne, IN, the WAYNE OIL TANK CO. is founded.	
1891	Pennsylvania; the school principal, Mr. McKaskey, patents his idea of building clocks with a device to ring classroom bells.	(see 1894)
1891	Dayton, OH; Lawrence Johnston builds his first gas engine for his shop's own use. However, due to demand, JAMES R. JOHNSTON & SON are soon manufacturing several sizes of natural gas engines.	

1891	LIMA LOCOMOTIVE & MACHINE CO. (LIMA) is the result of the reorganization of LIMA MACHINE WORKS.	(see 1894)
1891	Texas; beginning this year, the Texas Fever Cattle Quarantine is put in place to keep Texas and southern cattle apart from northern herds, unless owners could show proof the Texas cattle had been dipped to kill the ticks that carry and transmit the fever. During this time, one of the newly invented electric cattle prods is being used on the Englishman, R. D. Cordwent's ranch out in Callahan County.	
1891	Australia; Sydney Josephson opens a branch office in Brisbane for WAUGH & JOSEPHSON; soon building and move their operations into a new modern facility on Unwins Bridge Road, and will remain there for six decades.	(see 1920)
1891	Texas; after a decade and a half of arguing and battling, the Texas Railroad Commission is finally created to try and rein in the powerful railroad companies.	
1891	Near Benson, AK, Mr. John Olson discovers "fuller's earth," a type of clay very useful for giving cloth, fur, etc, more body when used by a "fuller" of cloth. Thus, fullers is written with a lower case "f."	
1891	This year, the WESTERN WHEELED SCRAPER CO. relocates to Aurora, IL, from Mt. Pleasant, Iowa.	(see 1901)
1891	Ohio; incorporating this year, Byers moves into a much larger facility in Ravenna.	(see 1905)
1891	Germany; August Thyssen begins creating a complementary business at the GEWERKSCHAFT DEUTSCHER KAISER coal mine in Hamburg, thus expanding into a integrated iron and steel working plant on the River Rhine.	(see WWI)
1891	Canada; May 2; with forty-six original members, the Calgary Board of Trade is established.	(see 1950)
1891	France; Hilaire de Chardonnet begins manufacturing his artificial silk, or rayon.	(see 1924)
1891	New York; Jesse W. Reno invents the "inclined elevator" or escalator and installs it at the Old Iron Pier on Coney Island.	
1891	California; the "self-leveling" combine, for use on hillsides, is introduced by the STOCKTON WHEEL CO. These are extremely large machines, requiring teams of 18 or more horses for motivation.	
1891	This spring, the Baptists' first rail chapel car, the Evangel, is completed and put into service.	
1891	The INTERNATIONAL BROTHERHOOD OF ELECTRICAL WORKERS, or IBEW is established this November.	
1892	The SUPERIOR ENGINE AND COMPRESSOR COMPANY is founded.	
1892	AXELSON starts in business.	
1892	**This year 20,000 AERMOTOR windmills are sold.**	
1892	John Froelich builds the first usable gasoline tractor, with a Van Duzen engine mounted on a wooden frame and a steam traction engine running gear. At one point it is coupled with a Case threshing machine, and works 52 ½ days, threshing 62,000 bushels of wheat without a major breakdown. *It looks like the first tractor is a good one!!!*	(see 1893)
1892	**EMERSON ELECTRIC sells their first electric fan…** *A Very Cool Move!*	
1892	Walter B. Templeton invents the railroad track jack, the SIMPLEX.	
1892	**Rudolf Diesel patents the internal combustion engine named for him; his first engines run on peanut oil for fuel.**	
1892	*W. C. Norris produces the first metal sucker rods, to use to operate bottom hole pumps.*	

(No Model.)   J. W. RENO.
                    ENDLESS CONVEYOR OR ELEVATOR.
No. 470,918.   Patented Mar. 15, 1892.

1892	**The J. I. Case Co. develops a gasoline tractor, but carburetion and ignition problems prevent it from becoming a commercial success.**	
1892	**BB&C is the first company to transmit high-voltage AC power.**	
1892	Copp Bros. Co. Ltd. Of Hamilton, Ontario, obtains rights to manufacture products of Arm Co. in their plant, making the "Steel Champion" Grader.	
1892	A. T. Brown invents a pneumatic bicycle tire, and later sells the patent to the Dunlop brothers in England.	
1892	Helios Electric Co. is formed in Philadelphia, PA, manufacturing batteries and power supplies.	
1892	Oilwell Engineering (Oilwell) acquires Continental Tube Works of Pittsburgh, PA.	

1892	***The Duryea brothers build the first car in America.***	
1892	The G & B Street Railway begins operating from Denver to the suburb of Cherrelyn. The rail car is pulled by a horse on the fifteen minute trip uphill to the suburb, then the horse rides with the passengers on the 3 minute ride back down to Denver, thus the Gravity & Bronco name. It will operate thusly until 1910.	
1892	**James Dewar, a scientist at Oxford University invents the "vacuum flask."**	
1892	The American Manufacturing Company changes its name to American Hoist and Derrick Co.	
1892	In Stockton, CA, Holt Manufacturing Company incorporates.	
1892	**About 1,000 people witness a public demonstration of Nathan Stubblefield's radio in Kentucky, later this year he will give a public demonstration in Washington, D. C. Having transmitted voices and music, (his son whistles and plays the harmonica) Stubblefield now patents his invention, forms a company to promote it, sells some stock, but having no business acumen, he does no more.**	(see 1908)
1892	Ithaca, NY; pharmacy owner Lester Platt pours cherry syrup over vanilla ice cream for a customer. The customer names the creation a "Cherry Sunday," for the day on which it was first served.	
1892	Texas; the Aransas Harbor Terminal Railroad is chartered to connect Aransas Pass to Harbor Island.	
1892	France; Trépardoux devises the "De Dion Axle" for power transmission of their heavy steam units.	(see 1894)
1892	The United States Rubber Company is established by Charles R. Flint.	(see 1940)
1892	Texas; in McCullough County, Jeff Benson takes a seventy-eight (78), yes, that is a seventy-eight point, white-tailed buck. Over a century down the road, the exact location of the kill will still be argued by nearby Mason and Menard counties.	
1892	Holland; J. B. August Kessler, backed by Henri Deterding, starts an oil field in Northern Sumatra, Indonesia. They build all their infrastructure, including oil tankers to transport the crude oil. This is the birth of Royal Dutch Petroleum.	(see 1897)
1892	Watertown, NY; inventor and lawyer Henry D. Perky's experiments with business partner William H. Ford finally come to fruition, as they succeed in making a machine that shreds whole wheat.	(see 1928)
1892	The J. D. Fate Co. is founded as J. D. buys out Gunsaullus. Fate continues building clay working equipment.	(see 1909)
1892	This year Pennsylvania State University begins offering "a short course in making ice cream."	
1892	After only a decade, the Standard Oil Trust passes a formal resolution to dissolve itself, with strong encouragement of the US federal government regulators.	(see 1895)

1892	June 4; the Sierra Club is founded; Scottish-born American John Muir says it is "…to make the mountains glad." Muir serves as the club's president until his death in 1914. Not all that many folks really seem to care if the mountains are glad, or not.	
1892	Texas; HOCHHEIM INSURANCE COMPANY is founded and begins insuring the citizens of this great state.	
1892	This year both CROMPTON & CO. and GENERAL ELECTRIC CO. introduce hand irons using electrical resistance for heat.	(see 1952)
1892	USA; this year Pennsylvania produces 32 million barrels of crude oil, the state's all-time high.	(see 1895)
1892	The first known steel derrick for drilling is built, at 72 feet tall, it can be ordered through the Oil Well Supply Co.'s catalog starting in 1900.	(see 1985)
1893	MORSE POWER TRANSMISSION (gears, sprockets, etc.) is founded.	
1893	**Germany; Karl Benz patents "Double-pivot" steering, & begins making 4-wheel VICTORIA cars.**	
1893	James B. Hill claims to have built the first ditching machine at Bowling Green, OH.	
1893	FAIRBANKS MORSE build their first fuel burning engine, which is claimed to be the first commercially successful gasoline engine ever produced.	
1893	California; in November Harley Earl is born to J. W. Earl and his wife, in Los Angeles.	
1893	JAMES B. PETTER & SONS is founded in England.	
1893	**COLOMBIAN builds their first bolted steel storage tanks.**	
1893	F. L. Maytag begins producing farm implements in Newton, IA.	
1893	In Atlanta, a druggist, John S. Pemberton patents a green health drink called COCA-COLA.	
1893	September; Frank Duryea takes to the streets of Chicopee, MA, in one of the earliest American gasoline cars; by this time, his brother Charles is in Peoria, IL, building bicycles.	
1893	**Milton Hershey makes his first 5 cent HERSHEY chocolate bars.**	
1893	David H. McConnell a traveling book salesman, gives out free cologne to the ladies to "get his foot in the door;" he soon finds the free cologne is more popular than the books he sells.	
1893	Iowa; in Waterloo, John Froelich et al, found the WATERLOO GASOLINE TRACTION ENGINE CO., building farm tractors.	(see 1918)
1893	Chicago; Standing 264 feet high, carrying 36 cars, each holding 60, for a total of 2,160 riders; G. W. G. Ferris introduces his Ferris Wheel, or the Chicago Wheel, at the Columbian Exposition. The WILLIAM TOD CO. build and install the two engines powering this original Ferris Wheel.	
1893	At the Colombian Exposition, the MINNEAPOLIS Threshers earn the first premiums and awards.	
1893	Ninety-one year old Birdsill Holly dies with more patents to his name than anyone else, except Thomas A. Edison.	
1893	Winston, NC; George Brown and his brother-in-law Robert Williamson form BROWN & WILLIAMSON TOBACCO CO.	
1893	Richard W. Sears and Alvah C. Roebuck establish SEARS, ROEBUCK & CO. and soon issue their first catalog, but customers should be very wary of some of their claims.	
1893	Lorenzo Coffin, a civil war chaplain leads the crusade resulting in passage of the Railroad Safety Appliance Act of 1893, mandating air brakes and automatic railcar couplers, almost immediately the accident rate is reduced by 60%.	
1893	Mr. T. L. L. Temple buys 7,000 acres of timberland in Angelina County, TX.	
1893	**The first American automobile sold for export is a $400 Olds Gasoline Steam Carriage, shipped to Bombay, India.**	(see 1897)

1893	Having outgrown the Ohio facility, Bucyrus moves to a new plant in South Milwaukee, WI, and incorporates as the Bucyrus Steam Shovel & Dredge Company of Wisconsin.	
1893	According to some folks, the first rotary drilling is being done about this time.	
1893	Germany; Sulzer Bros. acquire Rudolf Diesel's Swiss patent rights.	
1893	Mr. Ariens starts his ironworks business; it will be successful until the Great Depression.	
1893	Wayne Oil Tank Co. wins the "Best Self-Measuring Oil Pump" Gold Medal Award.	
1893	Thirty-six year old Arthur W. Savage patents his lever action rifle.	
1893	With thousands sampling grape juice at the Chicago World's Fair, the drink becomes a national favorite. Thomas Welch's son, Dr. Charles Welch quits his dental practice and gives his complete attention to marketing grape juice, now dropping the "Dr." from the Welch's labels.	(see 1918)
1893	June 20th; sixty-nine year old Leland Stanford dies in his sleep at his home in California.	
1893	Corsicana, TX; the American Well and Prospecting Co. is drilling water wells for the city. The city fathers are very upset when oil is discovered while one well is down to 1,035 feet (318.46 m) and crude oil begins rising to the surface.	(see 1894)
1893	John "Jack" Mack and his brother Augustus F. Mack purchase the Fallesen & Berry factory to build their carriages.	
1893	California; the first well for crude oil is drilled at Los Angeles.	(see 1895)
1893	A Yankee, Mr. Greenleaf Whittier Simpson, builds and begins operating a refrigerated packing plant in Ft. Worth, TX.	
1893	Augsburg Germany; the invention of the diesel engine develops over the next four years in cooperation with M. A. N.	
1893	National Supply Company is founded.	
1893	At work, Henry Ford is promoted to Chief Engineer at Edison Illuminating Co; at home, his son Edsel is born.	(see 1895)
1893	Thomas Edison introduces motion pictures this year.	
1893	Henschel & Son of Germany receives the First Prize for locomotive design at Chicago's World's Fair.	(see 1904)
1893	UK; Lister introduces a new universal steam generator, also the Lister-Babcock Milk Tester.	
1893	N. Tesla and Westinghouse Corporation win the contract to light the Chicago World's Fair. Spiteful at losing the contract, Thomas A. Edison refuses to allow Tesla to use "his light bulb." Tesla invents his own type of light bulb, and manufactures 200,000 bulbs in just six months and has them ready in time for the fair.	
1893	May 10; it is believed that the New York Central Railroad's "Empire State Express" reaches the speed of 112.5 mph (180 kph), near Batavia, NY.	(see 1897)
1893	Stockton, CA; the largest combined harvester (Combine) ever built, is built locally by the Holt Manufacturing Co. This machine cuts a fifty foot (15.38 m) swath, while pulled by thirty-six head of horses for propulsion and cutting power.	
1893	January 6; today in the Cascade Mountain village of Scenic Washington, the Great Northern Railway drives its final spike.	
1893-4	USA; during this time of financial depression, the Pullman Company cuts wages and working hours, thus precipitating a notorious labor strike.	(see 1897)
1893	A Swedish engineer, Weyland, designs his country's first internal combustion engine. This is a one cylinder, four-stroke, paraffin-burning engine. Bolinder builds Weyland's engine, first marketing it this year. As it is not very successful, it is only produced for a short time.	(see 1906)

1893	Texas; Walter B. Sharp takes his $3,000 savings and his drilling rig and heads for Beaumont. There, Sharp is prospecting for oil, and drilling for the GLADYS CITY OIL AND GAS MANUFACTURING COMPANY for their first test for oil. This first well is up Spindletop Hill, but is abandoned at 418 feet, due to quicksand. Now tired and broke, but characteristicaly independent, he walks the 300 miles back to Dallas, rather than wiring his dad for money or help.	(see 1895)
1894	The merger of BUCKEYE SUPPLY CO. of Ohio and NATIONAL SUPPLY of West Virginia, forms the NATIONAL SUPPLY COMPANY.	
1894	The CONSOLIDATED RUBBER TIRE CO. begins as Edwin S. Kelly, of Springfield, OH, begins producing rubber carriage tires, designed by his partner Arthur Grant; these are an instant success.	
1894	CASE introduces their gigantic steam engine, "Hercules," which soon becomes a star of RINGLING BROS. CIRCUS parades.	(see 1895)
1894	George Roper becomes sole owner of the Van Wie Stove Co. and 10 days later it is completely destroyed by fire and he rebuilds as the ECLIPSE GAS STOVE CO.	
1894	New York City; the ELECTROBAT COMPANY begins operations building electric cars in what is probably the first real automobile factory, in Philadelphia, Pennsylvania.	
1894	**The largest customer of the US Post Office is MONTGOMERY WARD & COMPANY of Chicago.**	
1894	JOSEPH REID GAS ENGINE CO. is founded in Oil City, PA.	
1894	Mr. T. L. L. Temple opens a sawmill deep in the pine forests of Angelina County, TX.	(see 2004)
1894	CHICAGO PNEUMATIC is founded.	(see 1901)
1894	**The first electric excavating machine, a placer dredge, is built by BUCYRUS.**	
1894	**Sir Charles Parsons fits his steam turbine to a ship, transforming sea travel.**	
1894	**In the first sports film ever, Thomas A. Edison films a boxing match between Jack Cushing and Mike Leonard.**	
1894	**UK; Marks and Spencer open their first actual store.**	
1894	**Marius Berliet begins his experiments with the "automobile."**	
1894	Established to build equipment for electric driven trains, The HUBLEY MFG. CO. of Lancaster, PA, is incorporated.	
1894	SAVAGE ARMS COMPANY is established in Utica, NY, by A. W. Savage.	
1894	Through the end of year, BUCYRUS has sold more than 170 power shovels, 24 of them are now being used to dig the Chicago Drainage Canal.	
1894	The first oil boom in Texas, and the first oil boom west of the Mississippi, begins June 9th as the "water" well drilled for the city of Corsicana comes in as a good oil well.	(see 1898)
1894	Commerce, TX; William L. Mayo establishes East Texas Normal College (later East Texas State University). Mayo will run this school mostly by himself for many years.	
1894	Daniel Best better adapts his "steam-logger," for use in the timber country. Best now markets 2hp to 200hp steam engines for use on dairy farms, irrigation, and for installation in boats.	
1894	August; Waynesboro, PA; Fred Frick, with his brothers, Amos and A. O., begin manufacturing clocks.	(see 1900)
1894	France; Trépardoux resigns from the de Dion business due to de Dion and Bouton "piddling" with petrol, or gasoline engines, which he considers to be heresy.	
1894	William C. Mack has been building wagons in his plant in Scranton, PA; he now joins his brothers in their business. Soon the Macks' focus is all on wagons, as carriages are phased out. Shortly they will begin experimenting with steam and electric vehicles.	

1894	Chicago, IL; JOHNSTON & JENNINGS is established, building foundry equipment and stokers.	(see 1950)
1894	Ohio; despite the major depression of last year CLEVELAND TWIST DRILL has now wiped out their entire debt, and are now growing. Through necessity, their manufacturing floor space is expanded ten-fold.	(see 1904)
1894	Rollin H. White graduates from Cornell University with degrees in both mechanical and electrical engineering. Rollin now joins the family business as it is expanding into bicycles, machine tools, and roller skates.	(see 1900)
1894	England; the Manchester Ship Canal is now opened to traffic.	
1894	Sweden; (AB) Bofors-Gullspång is acquired by Alfred Nobel.	(see 1896)
1895	Ignaz Schwinn & Adolph Arnold found "ARNOLD, SCHWINN & CO." in Chicago.	
1895	Holyoke, MA; William G. Morgan creates a new game called "Mintonette." Soon a demonstration is given at the YMCA in nearby Springfield, and the name "Mintonette" is replaced with the name "Volleyball." *Hmmmmm... "Mintonette"... Hmmmmm...*	
1895	Horace and John Dodge apply for their first patent, for bicycle ball bearings, and form their first company, EVANS AND DODGE.	(see 1901)
1895	Having overcome their engine problems, J. I. CASE begins producing several sizes of two-cylinder gasoline tractors.	(see 1912)
1895	With a two hundred dollar investment, John C. Lincoln founds the LINCOLN ELECTRIC COMPANY, to build electric motors of his own design.	
1895	The *first* person to even consider air-filled rubber tires for cars, **Andre Michelin has twenty flats in a 350 mile (560 km) race, and air-filled rubber tires are considered a flat-out failure...** *...pun intended!!*	
1895	JAMES B. PETTER & SONS produce their first oil-burning engines.	
1895	WIRTH is founded in Germany.	
1895	USA; *Field & Stream* magazine is first published.	
1895	C. J. SMITH & SONS is the largest US manufacturer of bicycle parts, soon to be the world's largest.	
1895	ARMSTRONG BROS. begin making tool holders for lathes, and soon were devoting full time to their manufacturing.	
1895	A. T. Brown and friend Charles Lipe conceive an idea for a two-speed gear for bicycles, but it is too expensive for commercial success.	
1895	Charles Clarence Hobart brings HOBART ELECTRIC MFG. CO. to Troy, OH.	
1895	Twelve year old Joe Joy goes to work in the coal mines.	
1895	The DURYEA MOTOR WAGON COMPANY is established by Charles Duryea.	
1895	On Thanksgiving Day, the *Chicago Times-Herald* race (probably the first sponsored auto race in America) is won by Frank Duryea in his Motor Wagon. The Duryea and a Benz are the only entrants finishing the 54 mile (86. 4 km) trek along Lake Michigan, out of 89 cars entering. Their average speed is about ten miles-per-hour... *WOW!!!! The Great Chicago Car Race is actually a test of innovation and durability, not speed. No kidding???*	
1895	The Italian, Guglielmo Marconi, utilizing a long-wire antenna, develops a practical radio system for long-distance communication.	
1895	DAVID BRADLEY MFG. COMPANY moves from Chicago to near Kankakee, IL.	(see 1899)

H. E. & J. F. DODGE.
BICYCLE BEARING.
No. 567,851. Patented Sept. 15, 1896.

1895	**In the USA, up to now, Benz has sold a total of 271 autos, the French bicycle maker Armand Peugeot has sold 270, the Duryeas are not yet in production, and Henry Ford is still building his first car.**	(see 1901)
1895	Michael L. Benedum, a lease man for SOUTH PENN OIL and J. C. Trees, a independent driller, form BENEDUM-TREES, an exploration and production partnership.	
1895	MARSHALL POTTERY CO. is established in Marshall, TX.	
1895	**The German scientist Wilhelm Conrad Röntgen is the first to use X-rays.**	
1895	A thousand or so different varieties of barbed wire are now in use.	
1895	The first issue of Horseless Age Magazine guesses that there are 300 self-propelled vehicles planned, built, or a-building at this time.	
1895	BUCYRUS reorganizes as the BUCYRUS COMPANY.	(see 1896)
1895	December 23; the Harris brothers, Al and Charles, incorporate the HARRIS AUTOMATIC PRESS CO., in Niles, OH.	
1895	Adam Opel dies; his company is now the largest European manufacturer of sewing machines, and also produces over two thousand bicycles annually.	
1895	GARANT is established as a family tool-making operation.	
1895	SAVAGE ARMS COMPANY begins production of the Savage Model 1895 rifle.	
1895	The little dog Nipper dies, but Francis has already introduced the dog to his phonograph, and notes his quizzical response. In 1898, Francis records the scene on canvas.	(see 1897)
1895	France; Bouton introduces a one cylinder petrol (gasoline) engine that has been tested up to 3,500 rpm, and will power their "sporting tricycles" for the next few years.	
1895	Having long studied the ore-handling problems encountered on the Great Lakes docks, ore-boat Captain Richard Thew conceives a unique machine to overcome most of the difficulties and drawbacks. Assisted by experienced shovel designer H. H. Harris, Thew builds his first machine at the VARIETY IRON WORKS in Cleveland, OH. This is a fully-revolving, steam-powered excavator with a 5/8 yard shovel attachment. It is capable of swinging in a full circle, as opposed to the 180 degree swing of existing rail shovels. The unit is mounted on four steel traction wheels, so it can propel and steer itself without railroad tracks, thus tremendously reducing the amount of elbow-grease and hand shovel work required.	(see 1899)
1895	Texas; as the first oil is shipped from CORSICANA OIL DEVELOPMENT COMPANY, it is the first crude producer to utilize a railroad tank car to ship its oil.	(see 1897)
1895	This year's issue of the *Encyclopedia Britannica* mentions Mr. Obed Hussey of Ohio as having built a grain reaper with the first known cutting tool of a sickle knife running through a guard mechanism.	
1895	The first four-wheeled motor car in England is built by Frederick Lanchester.	
1895	The popular drink Coca-Cola is now on tap in every US state and territory. A US soldier stationed in Cuba recently invented the "Cuba Libre".... rum and coke. Using equal parts lime juice and rum to coke, he made a drink that will live on.	
1895	In Chicago, the Armstrong Brothers Tool Company introduce the first tool holders for lathes.	(see 1900)
1895	John D. Rockefeller retires from business this year.	
1895	Mr. Lyman T. Davis creates his specialty dish... Wolf Brand Chili.	
1895	This year, George Selden is issued the first US patent for an automobile.	

1895	Pennsylvania; a local flour merchant, Franklin Baker receives a shipment of fresh coconuts as payment of a debt. Unable to find a buyer for the coconuts, Baker buys a small coconut processing business.	(see 1927)
1895	July 9; John Lee Love, a black inventor, is issued a patent on an improved plasterer's hawk. Love's new model has a detachable handle, folds up, and is made of aluminum.	(see 1897)
1895	Ludwig Obry of the Austrian Navy invents a gyroscopic device to use in guiding torpedoes.	(see 1908)
1895	This year, California produces 1,200,000 barrels of crude petroleum.	(see 1896)
1895	France; the Lumière brothers invent a portable motion picture camera, weighing only about 11 pounds (5kg). This year they present the first ever motion picture to an audience of more than one person.	(see 1910)
1895	There are now about 300 motorized vehicles, or horseless carriages, operating on the trails, roads, and byways of America.	(see 1905)

Le cinématographe Lumière: projection.

	1895	USA; the St. Louis, Vandalia & Terre Haute Railroad has a new locomotive weighing 219,000 lbs. (99,336 kg), with engine and tender fully loaded. This more than twice the weight of 1860.	(see 1902)
	1895	USA; across the Appalachian region, the engines powering oil well pumping operations are now being converted from steam to well-head gas power. The central powered pumping systems are now very common in the oil country.	(see 1897)
	1895	Using hot water, bitumen is extracted from bituminous sand in a project at Carpinteria, CA.	(see 1901)
	1895	Texas; up and running again, Walter Sharp drills some shallow oil wells in the Sour Lake area, bringing in limited quantities of crude oil. Within another year Sharp builds a small refinery in this area. Sharp's little refinery slightly precedes Cullinan's "first refinery in Texas," which begins operations in another couple of years or so.	(see 1897)

1896	J. B. Hill becomes associated with the Van Buren Foundry and Machine Company, who are building his ditchers on a royalty basis.	
1896	**Tired of his papers being scattered all around Boston, Thomas Briggs invents the stapler.**	
1896	Deutag Drilling is incorporated in Bad Bentheim, Germany.	
1896	**Leo Hirschfield introduces the Tootsie Roll.**	
1896	There are now 300 bicycle manufacturing companies in the USA, and 101 of these are in Chicago.	
1896	**G. Daimler builds the world's first truck. The Daimler Phoenix is a 1 1/2 ton truck powered by a four horsepower engine.**	
1896	There are four million bicycles on the streets and sidewalks of America.	
1896	On March 4, the US Patent Office issues their first patent for a "power sled" for use on snow. Moses, William, and Joseph Runnoe of Crested Butte, CO, have developed a power sled with an endless track of chain and eight steel crossbars supported by spring straps. The crossbars (cleats) have spurs on the outer edges for traction.	(see 1914) (see 1921)
1896	**In Corsicana, TX, Collin Street Bakery begins baking its famous DeLuxe® fruit cakes.**	
1896	May; Samuel P. Langley launches his 13 foot (4 m) long, steam-powered aerodrome "Model 5"; the unmanned "drone" is airborne for more than a half-mile. Later this year Langley flies his two steam-powered models of flying machines as far as 4,200 feet (1292 m).	
1896	The National Carbon Co. markets the very first battery for consumer use: "The Columbia," six inches tall, used to power home telephones.	

1896	Halsey W. Taylor's father dies of typhoid fever caused by contaminated drinking water.
1896	**After hand-building it himself, Henry Ford runs his first car, an experimental, ethanol-fueled quadricycle; on Detroit streets.**
1896	Detroit; after running his first car more than a thousand miles around town, Henry Ford sells it to Charles Ainsley for 1,000 bucks. Ford now takes the money and begins building another car. Some years later, Ford tracks down the fellow who had bought his first car from Ainsley, and buys it back for one hundred dollars.
1896	Evansburg, PA; George B. DeArment, a blacksmith, begins spending all his time improving farrier's tools, starting the CHAMPION BOLT & CLIPPER CO.
1896	ALLIS comes out with their first triple expansion steam engine.
1896	Germany; the "oil pioneer" Anton Raky establishes INTERNATIONALE BOHRGESELLSCHAFT AG.
1896	Charles Duryea sets up a small factory to build motorcars for profit; the brothers build and sell thirteen vehicles this year.
1896	George Washington Carmack discovers gold in the Yukon Territory of Northwest Canada.
1896	September 15; as a publicity stunt, a head-on locomotive collision is staged by the MKT Railroad. More than 30,000 spectators arrive to see the event. At 4:00 p. m., the trains are speeding together; on impact, the boilers burst (contrary to the railroad mechanic's beliefs), sending metal chunks into the crowd. Two persons are killed, and many others are injured. The crash site, a few miles from the village of West, TX, is named "Crush," for the MKT station agent who conceived the idea, Mr. William G. Crush.
1896	New York City; street vendor Italo Marchiony creates the ice cream cone and has a mold for making them patented in 1903.
1896	**The world's first convention bureau is established in Detroit, MI.**
1896	**The first Ft. Worth Fat Stock Show & Rodeo is held in Fort Worth, TX.** (see 1897)
1896	Carl Reed founds REED MANUFACTURING COMPANY.
1896	**G. Marconi sends sound by "radio," more than a mile distance.**
1896	Forty-eight year old Otto Lilienthal dies soon after a crash in his glider. Over the past several years, Lilienthal, a German inventor, has made over 2,000 flights in gliders he designed and built.
1896	Reorganizing, the BUCYRUS STEAM SHOVEL & DREDGE CO. OF WISCONSIN becomes simply.... the BUCYRUS COMPANY.
1896	Mr. Rudolf Diesel is credited with the designing of the mechanical supercharger, for the internal combustion engine.
1896	Bristol, England; Henry Stothert, a son of George Jr., is now building railroad locomotives in his local plant. (see 1900)
1896	Having moved to more spacious quarters on South Market Street in Brantford, the WATEROUS ENGINE WORKS is now manufacturing equipment for power plants, sawmills, and pulpwood mills. (see 1898)
1896	January 16; in the first ever "five on five" college basketball game, the University of Chicago beats the University of Iowa, 15 to 12. The coaches, Amos Alonzo Stagg and Henry F. Kallenberg, had been acquainted years ago at the YMCA in Springfield, MA.
1896	Japan; YOKAHAMA CABLE MANUFACTURING CO. is founded with 50,000 yen capital.
1896	UK; the Progress Chain Harrow, that folds to make its own sledge for transporting, is introduced by Lister.

No. 746,971. I. MARCHIONY. PATENTED DEC. 15, 1903.
MOLD.
APPLICATION FILED SEPT. 22, 1903.
NO MODEL.

1896	National Iron Works Foundry & Machine Shop becomes National Iron Company.		(see 1958)
1896	Clarholz, Germany; Franz Claas builds the first hay balers in this country. These balers are situated immediately behind the stationary threshing machine, to bundle the straw.		(see 1913)
1896	UK; Britain's first commercial vehicle (truck) is the one-ton Thorneycroft steam van.		
1896	USA; Utah passes a law regulating work in mines to eight hours per day per person.		
1896	Russia; after years of successful testing, Fyodor A. Blinov shows his self-propelled steam tractor at a Farmers Exhibition.		(see 1901)

1896	California; Gus Kratzmeyer opens a foundry in Bakersfield.	(see 1899)
1896	USA; in New York City, driver Henry Wells is jailed, as his car collides with a bicycle ridden by Evelyn Thomas, breaking her leg. This is the first-ever reported automobile accident in the country.	(see 1900)
1896	Sweden; having played the major role in transforming Bofors, the former iron and steel producer, into a modern cannon manufacturer and very active chemical industry participant, Alfred Nobel passes away this December after less than three years at the helm.	(see 1898)
1897	Two brothers, Louis and John Clark found the Pittsburg Motor Car Co., and build a gas-powered tricycle.	
1897	Kemmerer Mine opens in Wyoming.	

1897	***The first automobile company in Michigan; Ransom Eli Olds founds the Olds Motor Car Co., produces four cars this year, and sells them for $1,000 each, however, eight years later, he will leave Olds Motor Car Co.***		
1897	Corsicana is the first city in Texas to use natural gas as fuel for heating and lighting.		(see 1898)
1897	Corsicana; the first oil refinery in the Great State of Texas is being built this year.		
1897	**Lord Kelvin, Scottish mathematician and physicist, former president of the Royal Society states, "Radio has no future."**		
1897	**The Kilgore Machine Co. of Minneapolis patents a hydraulic shovel using direct-acting cylinders, five machines are built and one of those is shipped to Mexico.**		
1897	*Little Lytle Lake is built near the small West Texas town of Abilene.*		
1897	September; the citizens of Cheyenne, WY, produce the world's first organized rodeo, soon to be called Cheyenne Frontier Days, grand-daddy of all rodeos.		
1897	**Charles Nash drives a car for the first time, and is interested in the commercial potential of the machine.**		
1897	Theodore Gary & Co. purchases the Macon, MO, telephone exchange.		
1897	The "plug tobacco war" starts with Drummond Tobacco Co. and Liggett & Myers against Jim Duke and his American Tobacco Co. monopoly. Mr. John Liggett dies this year.		(see 1898)
1897	Now handling mostly kerosene, fuel oils, and some gasoline, Marcus Samuels and his brothers now own six crude oil tankers, and they rename their firm, Shell Transport & Trading (after their father's sea shells). Standard Oil is still shipping its crude oil in leaky wooden barrels.		(see 1903)
1897	Jell-O, Peter Cooper's gelatin treat, is finally being marketed.		
1897	The J. M. Smucker family begins making and selling jams and jellies on the family farm near Ohio.		
1897	Seattle; Mr. C. C. Filson begins his business selling rugged clothing to the miners headed North to Alaska.		
1897	Parkersburg, WV; Parkersburg Rig & Reel Co. is established to manufacture drilling rigs, tanks, and auxiliary items.		

1897	Art Dorrance, General Manager of CAMPBELL PRESERVE CO., reluctantly hires his 24 year old nephew, Dr. John T. Dorrance, a European schooled chemist. Soon, young Dr. J. T. Dorrance invents condensed soup…	
	And… as they say, "the rest is history."	
1897	Russia conducts its first national census this year.	
1897	March; near Nottingham, England, the MIDLAND RAILWAY's Engine No. 117 achieves 90 mph (144.8 kph).	(see 1938)
1897	USA; on September 1, in Boston, the nation's first electrified subway system begins carrying passengers.	
1897	Mr. T. B. Wood's business in Pennsylvania is incorporated as TB Wood's Sons.	(see 1900)
1897	November 23; a patent for a very-improved pencil sharpener is issued to John Lee Love.	
1897	California; in a small shop on 5th street in Los Angeles, Mr. S. D. Sturgis builds a motorcar for J. Philip Erie. Sturgis and Erie are the first persons to drive an automobile on the streets of LA.	(see 1904)
1897	Connecticut; in Willimantic, the BARROWS VEHICLE CO. builds a 2-passenger, 3-wheel, front-wheel-drive electric car, for a couple of years.	
1897	As George M. Pullman dies, his company has a virtual monopoly of all sleeping car services across the USA; and running many dining and parlor car services, as well.	
1897	In Detroit, the Ackerman automobile is built by the W. K. ACKERMAN COMPANY, however, only for a short time.	
1897	The first patent is issued for "bandwheel power" for use in central power pumping systems for oil wells.	(see 1950)
1897	In Germany, ZETTELMEYER is established by Hubert Zettelmeyer.	
1897	Ontario; production begins at the Long Lake zinc mine in Olden Township in Frontenac County.	
1897	Texas; Walter B. Sharp is one of the early drilling contractors at Corsicana, as the first commercial oil field is being developed here. Having taken his younger brother James R. Sharp into his business, they soon meet J. S. Cullinan, and all are eventually associated in the development of the TEXAS COMPANY.	
1898	**E. D. ETNYRE & Co. is established and produces the worlds first road oiler.**	
1898	**During the Spanish-American War, the US seizes Guantanamo Bay, Cuba, and establishes a naval base there.**	
1898	Frank Seiberling founds the GOODYEAR TIRE & RUBBER CO., honoring Charles Goodyear, who has been dead for thirty years.	(see 1921)
1898	AMERICAN SOCIETY FOR TESTING AND MATERIALS (ASTM) is established.	
1898	The Reverend Burrell Cannon organizes the EZEKIEL AIRSHIP CO. in Pittsburg, TX.	
1898	The DURYEA MFG. CO. is chartered in Peoria, IL.	
1898	Conrad Hubert, a Russian immigrant, founds the AMERICAN ELECTRICAL NOVELTY AND MANUFACTURING CO.	
1898	Having retired 5 years ago, 61-year-old Henry Timken un-retires to invent the tapered roller bearing, to be forever known as a Timken bearing.	
1898	Using a mule-drawn scraper, W. A. Bechtel begins grading railroad beds in Oklahoma Indian Territory.	

(No Model.)
J. L. LOVE.
PENCIL SHARPENER.
No. 594,114.
Patented Nov. 23, 1897.

WITNESSES:
INVENTOR
John Lee Love.
ATTORNEYS.

| 1898 | Germany; Sulzer Bros. builds their first diesel engine; a 4 stroke, 260mm (10. 23") cyl., developing 19.7 horsepower. | |

	1898	**Electric storage batteries powers the USN's first submarine.**	
	1898	**The first recognized land speed record of 39.24 mph (62.78 kph), is set by an electric car.**	
	1898	Hammermill Paper Company is established in Erie, PA.	
	1898	Leaving his medical practice, Dr. Edwin J. Fithian and John Carruthers found the Carruthers-Fithian Clutch Company, to manufacture friction clutches for oil-pumping engines.	(see 1899)
	1898	January 31; seventeen pulp and paper mills merge to form International Paper Co.; soon IP is supplying 60% of all newsprint used in the US, and also exporting.	
	1898	In North Carolina, Mr. Caleb Bradham formulates Pepsi-Cola.	

1898	Eighteen west coast canning companies merge to form the California Fruit Canners Assn.; one of their premium brands is Del Monte.	
1898	Travelers Insurance of Hartford, CT, issues the first auto insurance policy to Dr. Truman Martin of Buffalo, NY, to cover his auto against damage caused by frightened horses.	
1898	**Richard Gatling attaches electric motors to some of his Gatling Guns and achieves a rate of fire exceeding 3,000 rounds per minute.** *"Shucks Slim, 'ats only fifty rounds a second!"*	
1898	**Brakes for bicycles are finally introduced, and it's about time.**	
1898	The James Duke monopoly wins the "plug tobacco war" and he buys Drummond, and next year, Liggett & Myers will join the Duke trust.	
1898	September; the first diesel engine built in the US is a two cylinder, sixty horsepower model, built by the Bush-Sulzer Bros. Diesel Engine Company.	
1898	US President William McKinley initially imposes the federal excise tax to help finance the Spanish-American war.	
1898	December 25; the J. S. Cullinan Co. begins operating a refinery (the second in the state) in Corsicana, TX.	
1898	Corsicana is the first municipality in Texas to treat its dirt streets with crude oil. The Corsicana field now has 287 producing wells.	
1898	Paris, France; Swiss waiter and party planner Cesar Ritz opens the Ritz Hotel. Celebrities and royalty of all sorts flock to the Ritz. Soon the word Ritz is synonymous with a "new style" or a "glitzy style."	
1898	Classmates and Princeton graduates and engineers Robert M. Thomas and Hobart D. Betts first begin selling rigid conduit to electric wholesalers.	
1898	Germany issues a patent (backdated to 1895) to Count von Zeppelin for a "steerable air vehicle with several carrying bodies."	
1898	Cuba; in the Spanish-American War, twenty-five year old Pvt. Charles Walgreen, a former drugstore employee, dies of yellow fever, has an out-of-body experience, then lives and decides to make the most of his life. He is soon discharged and establishes Walgreen Drugs.	
1898	Biloxi, MS; Edward Adolf Barq, Sr., creates the first known "root beer" beverage, and calls it Barq's Root Beer.	
1898	Germany; Weimar is established as a builder of railway wagons and cranes.	

1898	Campbell Soup executive Herberton Williams attends the Cornell University and University of Pennsylvania football game, and is so impressed by Cornell's flashy red and white uniforms that he convinces the company to change their can labels to red and white labels.	
1898	Having bought the rights to the Lutzmann automobile, Opel now sells them as Opel-Lutzmann vehicles.	
1898	WASHINGTON CONDENSED MILK CO. opens a condensing plant in Kent, WA, and in 18 months it is bankrupt.	
1898	Commissioned by the US NAVY, the J. P. Holland Torpedo Boat Company launches the first practical submarine with a successful test. The Navy then orders six more submarines.	
1898	UK; a three and one-half horsepower Phaeton is the first car built by the Thomas Humber Company.	
1898	Waterous Engine Works introduces the first gasoline-powered pumper, revolutionizing fire-fighting, even though it is still horse-drawn or sometimes, hand-drawn.	(see 1909)
1898	During the last six years, Oliver Heaviside contributes to the mathematical analysis of control systems; thus he is generally considered to be the inventor of operational calculus.	
1898	France; Marie and Pierre Curie discover "radium," as a product of uranium decay.	
1898	Colorado; in Sinbad Valley, Tom Dolan reactivates the Colorado Rajah Mine, on Roc Creek. This year several tons of uranium ore from Colorado are shipped to France for testing and processing.	
1898	USA; the first coin-operated telephone in the world is installed in Chicago, IL.	(see 1902)
1898	Germany; the IRON MINING & TRADING COMPANY, the SANDER'SCHE MASCHINENFABRIK, and KLETT & COMPANY IRON WORKS all merge to form one very large iron, engineering and fabrication firm.	
1898	In San Antonio, TX, Mr. G. H. Lutz builds the "Lutz Steam Car."	
1898	Mr. Edwin Prescott invents the roller coaster.	
1898	The PLYMOUTH CORDAGE COMPANY of Massachusetts is now the world's largest manufacturer of rope and twine.	(see 1964)
1898	Indiana; manufacturers George C. Harwood and Charles G. Barley partner, forming the MARION IRON & BRASS BED COMPANY.	(see 1905)
1898	Sweden; (AB) Bofors Nobelkrut is founded as a wholly-owned subsidiary of (AB) Bofors-Gullspång, and is soon a successful general organic-chemical and explosives producer.	(see 1911)
1898	West Lynn, MA; the GENERAL ELECTRIC CO. is building experimental gas, electric, and gas-electric cars.	(see 1902)
1898	Philadelphia; the "General Electric," a light runabout with light weight batteries is built by GENERAL ELECTRIC AUTOMOBILE CO. for a couple of years.	
1898	Massachusetts; the American Waltham motorcar is produced this year and next by the AMERICAN WALTHAM MFG. CO.	
1899	The forward-looking Charles H. Duell, director of the United States government patent offices, attempts to have the patent offices closed permanently, as he says, "Everything useful that can be invented, has been invented."	
1899	In Germany, Adam Opel builds his first motorcar, the "Opel-Patent-Motorwagen system Lutzmann."	
1899	The OLDS MOTOR VEHICLE CO. and OLDS GASOLINE ENGINE WORKS merge to form OLDS MOTOR WORKS. Olds then builds the first specific factory for automobile production in the US, in Detroit.	(see 1901)

1899	February 12; the temperature in Tulia, TX, drops to -23 degrees F. Thirty-four years hence, Seminole, TX, will match this record Texas cold spell.	
1899	St. Charles Car Manufacturing Company merges with twelve (12) other railroad car builders, forming the American Car & Foundry Company. (AC&F)	
1899	Packard & Weiss is formed to build autos, after Alexander Winton rebuffs James W. Packard's ideas for improving the Winton automobile. The first Packard motor car is built in the Packard Electric Company subsidiary plant, the New York & Ohio Company. They then start the Ohio Automobile Company.	(see 1912)
1899	"Mile-a-minute" Murphy, paced by a locomotive, is the first man known to go 60 mph on a bicycle.	
1899	Carruthers-Fithian is incorporated as Bessemer Gas Engine Company.	
1899	Birmingham Rail & Locomotive Co. is established in Birmingham, AL.	
1899	H. R. Worthington Co. merges with Laidlaw-Dunn-Gordon Co., a manufacturer of gas compressors.	
1899	The Clarks move Pittsburg Motor Car Co. to Ardmore, PA, and rename the company Autocar.	
1899	Sebastian Spering Kresge founds S. S. Kresge Co.	
1899	A. L. Barber and J. B. Walker buy the design rights to the Stanley Brothers steam automobile, with this, Walker founds the Locomobile Co. of America. Locomobile (locomotive and automobile) first builds steam cars, but in a few years begin experimenting with gasoline internal combustion engines.	
1899	October 5; Mr. E. H. R. Green brings the first gasoline powered automobile to Dallas, TX; driven by Jesse Illingsworth, it is a 1899 model St. Louis gasoline car, surrey style, built by George P. Dorris. Dorris accompanied the car from St. Louis to the railhead at Terrell for its unloading. October 6; the first known intercity automobile trip in Texas is made as Green drives from Terrell to Dallas, averaging about six miles per hour.	(see 1906)
1899	Conrad Hubert files for two patents for his "Electric Hand Torch," the forerunner of the world's first flashlight.	
1899	Pennsylvania; May 30; the South Fork Dam breaks today, completely destroying Johnstown.	
1899	Templeton, Kenly & Co. is founded.	
1899	**Arthur O. Smith (son of C. J.) develops the world's first pressed steel automobile frame.**	
1899	Menck & Hambrock is founded in Germany to build power shovels.	
1899	Dallas; on Young street, the Olive and Myers Mfg. Co. begins business, building furniture.	
1899	John Harris is trying to develop a process to make artificial rubies, and he accidently cuts the steel plate he is working on. This event leads him to develop the acetylene torch for cutting and welding.	
1899	August; the Edison Company offers Henry Ford the position of General Superintendent of the company on the condition that Ford would give up playing with his gasoline engine, and "devote himself to something really useful"... electricity. Ford has faith in his engine, as well as his ideas of cars, and on the fifteenth he quits his current job at Edison and with no money, goes into the automobile business full time, starting Detroit Auto Company. This is Henry's first go at running his own business and it soon fails.	
1899	July 1; three Christian traveling men meet, pray, and form the Gideons; to place Holy Bibles in hotel rooms, hospitals, and prisons, around the world.	

1899	David D. Buick sells his plumbing fixture company to STANDARD SANITARY MFG. CO. (later to be AMERICAN STANDARD) and begins building gasoline engines for farm and marine uses.	
1899	**J. G. Leyner invents the pneumatic jackhammer, but miners refuse to use it because of the excess dust it causes.**	
1899	Mr. J. H. Muzzy and E. F. Lyon found the MUZZY-LYON COMPANY in Detroit, shortly they set up a subsidiary company, the MOGUL METAL CO., to manufacture new bearing alloys. Muzzy and Lyon have the radical idea that different bearing metals are needed for low or high speed, light or heavy loads, and blended to suit the application. They also begin to manufacture replaceable die-cast bearings for engines, instead of pouring the Babbitt directly into the engine block.	
1899	July 11; the "Societa Anonima Fabbrica Italiana Torino" or FIAT, is formed in Torino, Italy.	(see 1900)
1899	The early Pennsylvania fields are playing out, and Godfrey Cabot moves to West Virginia, completing his first well on Sept. 17. CABOT has had continuous natural gas operations in West Virginia ever since then. Godfrey is soon selling gas to third parties for domestic use and to pipeline companies.	
1899	Findlay and Battle found FINDLAY MOTOR METALS, soon renamed GLACIER ANTIFRICTION METAL CO.	
1899	September 6; Kent, WA; the first fifty-five cases of Carnation Sterilized Cream (later Carnation Evaporated Milk) is produced by the PACIFIC COAST CONDENSED MILK COMPANY, in the recently acquired plant of the bankrupt Washington Condensed Milk Company.	
1899	Mr. David Bradley dies.	(see 1910)
1899	Martha White's self-rising flour with "Hot Rize" is first marketed.	
1899	In England, Charles C. Wakefield (later Sir Charles) establishes CASTROL to produce high-quality engine oils.	
1899	CORSICANA PETROLEUM CO. is formed as a crude oil producer for the CULLINAN refinery at Corsicana, TX.	
1899	Durham, NC; the DURHAM FURNITURE CO. LTD. begins operations in a new 3-story, 20,000 square foot factory.	
1899	USA; William Gray builds the first public, pay telephone, and installs it in a Hartford, CT, bank.	
1899	READING GLOVE & MITTEN MANUFACTURING COMPANY is founded.	
1899	CORBITT MOTOR TRUCK COMPANY is established.	
1899	Grand Saline, TX; Wylie Post is born.	(see 1930)
1899	Edward G. Budd begins working to develop stainless steel bodies for railroad cars.	
1899	Making minor improvements to their Model 1895, Savage introduces their Model 1899, and will remain virtually unchanged for its lifespan.	
1899	Francis Barrand registers his painting of Nipper as "Dog looking at and listening to a phonograph."	(see 1902)
1899	France; Bouton introduces a petrol powered quadricycle.	
1899	In Glasgow, Scotland, Norman Fulton and T. B. Murray establish the ALBION MOTOR CAR COMPANY.	
1899	Mollie Wright Armstrong becomes the first female optometrist in Texas, and only the second in the nation.	
1899	Captain Richard Thew, et al, incorporate the THEW AUTOMATIC SHOVEL COMPANY, at Lorain, OH.	(see 1912)
1899	New York City; on May 20, possibly the world's first speeding ticket is given to automobile taxicab driver, Mr. Jacob German for speeding along at twelve (12) miles (19.2 km) per hour… by a NYC policeman… on a bicycle.	

1899	AJAX adds natural gas engines to its product line.		
1899	Serving 1897-1901, US President William McKinley is the first sitting president to ride in an engine powered car. This year he rides in a steam-powered Locomobile, driven by automotive pioneer Freelan O. Stanley, co-inventor of the Stanley Steamer automobile.		
1899	**According to US government statistics, forty-eight (48) barrels of crude oil are produced in Texas this year.**		
1899	Texas; prominent San Antonio businessman George Brackenridge donates 199 acres of wooded land to his city.		(see 1914)

	1899	Germany; Felix Hoffmann perfects Gerhardt's recipe for salicylic acid. BAYER begins distributing aspirin powder to doctors for their patients' use.	(see 1915)
	1899	UK; Britain has three motor vehicle related deaths, as a driver, a passenger, and a motorcyclist are killed in three separate, unrelated accidents.	
	1899	Chicago; the AMERICAN ELECTRIC VEHICLE CO. builds the American Electric car for the next three years or so.	
	1899	Germany; Friedrich Lutzmann, a farmer from Dessau, comes to town and makes a contract with Adam Opel. They start a automobile factory in Anhalt. Adam's sons (the Opel Brothers) will work a couple of years with Lutzmann, in Russelsheim, building up the production of their automobiles, producing their first model, the Opel patent car engine system, called the "Lutzmann."	(see 1901)
	1899	Lakewood, NJ; a new three-lane bowling alley is opened on the campus of Georgian Court University. This bowling alley continues to be enjoyed regularly more than 110 years hence.	
	1899	Missouri; a patent for the motor-driven vacuum cleaner is issued to John S. Thurman of St. Louis.	

1899	California; A. J. Webster and Wm. Busse buy Kratzmeyer's foundry, renaming it KERN COUNTY FOUNDRY & MACHINE WKS.		(see 1900)
1899	For the next 17 years, the BAKER MOTOR VEHICLE CO. produces the Baker electric car.		
1899	Partners Canfield and Chanslor are now shipping 70,000 barrels of crude oil each month from Coalinga, CA. These men are also operating BAKERSFIELD IRON WORKS at 24th and M St., not too far from the KERN COUNTY FOUNDRY & MACHINE WORKS location.		(see 1912)
1899	Ohio; the CLEVELAND MACHINE SCREW CO. is building and selling a small 2 person electric automobile.		
1899	The Standard Oil Company is reorganized as a holding company in New Jersey.		(see 1900)
1899	Maine; the BELKNAP MOTOR CO. of Portland, is producing the Chapman electric car, also known as the Electromobile, built by Mr. W. H. Chapman.		
1899	VACUUM OIL CO. creates the "Mobil" trademark, the red flying Pegasus. It is called "Mobilgas."		(see 1907)
1899	New York; for five or six years, the KENSINGTON AUTOMOBILE CO. is producing gas, steam and electric powered vehicles.		
1900s	The ALLEN-BRADLEY COMPANY is formed in Milwaukee, WI.		
1900s	Mr. Watson Jack (1870-1928) is now the primary owner of the B. J. COGHLIN COMPANY. The firm's name is changed to WATSON JACK COMPANY.		(see 1933)
1900s	Mr. P. K. Saunders, a South African mining engineer, uses the ancient concept of the leather diaphragm valve to develop the first modern diaphragm valve.		

1900	Just about now, EXCELSIOR NEEDLE CO. becomes TORRINGTON MANUFACTURING COMPANY.	
1900	January 8; W. C. Coleman launches the HYDRO-CARBON LIGHT COMPANY in Wichita, KS, where he rents the lamps to businesses and residences; Coleman also maintains the rented lamps.	
1900	The UTAH CONSTRUCTION CO. is established.	
1900	March; ground is broken for an electric-powered subway in Manhattan, NY.	
1900	In Germany, Benz produces the first "honeycomb" radiator.	
1900	EATON & COLE build their first draw-works, or hoisting mechanism, for a drilling rig.	
1900	John Mack has researched and experimented for some years with his own designs for motorized wagons, and finally opens a truck and bus factory with his brothers. The first motorized vehicle produced was a 40 horsepower, 20 passenger bus, built for sight-seeing firm HARRIS & MCGUIRE. Eight years later it will be converted to a truck, and will eventually rack up more than a million miles. As John Mack later states, "The first Mack was a bus, and the first bus was a Mack." The Macks are also doing automotive repair work in their plant.	(see 1903)
1900	COOPER enters production of natural gas internal combustion engines.	
1900	In East Texas, the LEBUS BLACKSMITH SHOP is established.	
1900	Christian Schramm and Emil Maerky form SCHRAMM & MAERKY, fixing elevators in Philadelphia.	
1900	Morris W. Kellogg starts his pipe fabrication business.	
1900	About this time, Marmon enters the automobile business as the MARMON CAR COMPANY.	(see 1908)
1900	Carl D. Browne builds an airplane factory and a prototype aircraft, in Freedom, KS, but never flies the plane. In 1902 this factory closes.	
1900	The ELECTRIC STORAGE BATTERY CO. introduces a new battery especially for the many electric taxicabs that are plying the larger cities, they call it "Exide," short for "Excellent Oxide."	
1900	Fredrick E. Wells leaves WELLS BROTHERS to start a new pipe threading business with his son.	
1900	In Germany, CARLSHÜTTE begin building their steam shovels.	
1900	SUMITOMO METALS is founded in Japan.	
1900	"Borrowing" the gasoline motor from his wife's washing machine, Col. Edwin George builds the first known gasoline powered lawn mower, but Ed's in the doghouse for sure.	(see 1915)
1900	In Akron, OH, 31-year-old Harvey Firestone and 12 employees begin producing tires, and the FIRESTONE TIRE & RUBBER CO. is established.	
1900	Now five trans-continental railroad routes connect the Eastern US with the West, with a total trackage of 201,000 miles (321,000 km) across and throughout the United States of America.	(see 1910) (see 1916)

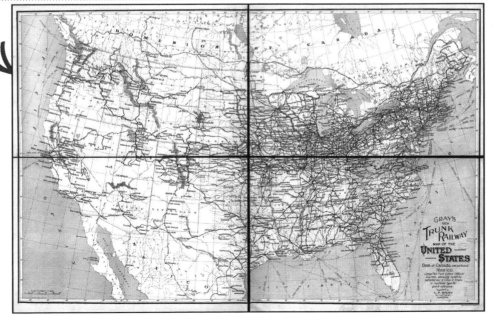

1900	Chicago; Thomas Lovejoy founds LOVEJOY TOOL WORKS, to manufacture tooling and machinery for the railroad and steel industries.	
1900	The American public rates the Bible as their favorite book, and the second favorite is the SEARS & ROEBUCK catalog.	
1900	FAIRBANKS-MORSE puts the first FMZC engine (hit & miss type) to work powering a pump jack out in the oil patch.	

1900	Johan Vaaler invents a paper clip in Norway, unaware of the British "Gem" style clip already in use throughout Europe.	
1900	New York; the world's first automobile show is held in Madison Square Garden.	
1900	With a population of 3,439,202, New York City is the world's second largest city, only behind London with its 5 million or so persons.	
1900	**PACKARD installs the first steering wheel on an automobile, as its tiller is replaced.**	
1900	Netherlands; the electro-cardiograph is invented by W. Einthoven.	
1900	LEIDECKER TOOL COMPANY now has nine branches around the petroleum producing area.	
1900	The NEW YORK KEROSENE OIL ENGINE CO. of NYC have been building surrey-type motor carriages, powered by small, hot-bulb type, four-stroke, one cylinder, kerosene oil engines. However, to date, there are no sightings of diesel engine powered highway vehicles.	
1900	It is estimated that there are now 5000 forging plants in England.	
1900	The SOUTHERN PACIFIC has trains operating from Portland, OR, and Ogden, UT, running into New Orleans.	
1900	PPG acquires a paint manufacturing company; this is the foundation of PPG's coatings business.	
1900	Adam Opel's son signs an agreement and begins building the "Opel-Darracq;" an Opel body on a Darracq chassis, powered by a two-cylinder engine.	
1900	**HILLS BROTHERS are the first to vacuum pack coffee in metal cans.**	(see 1906)
1900	Having built a few one cylinder automobiles, Berliet now builds his first two cylinder model.	
1900	New York; there are more than 130 brick-making plants along the Hudson River Valley's clay deposits. The ongoing growth of NYC keeps them all busy.	
1900	Saturday, September 8; before this year's devastating hurricane, Galveston is a larger city than Houston. Houston soon has a growth surge, mostly due at first to the many industries and families desiring to be further inland than the island. Several thousands die in this natural disaster.	
1900	**Oxygen-acetylene cutting at 6,000 degrees Fahrenheit is discovered.**	
1900	Although not registered as a trademark, the Nipper picture is being used in advertising, since Barrand sold the copyright for 100 pound sterling to the GRAMOPHONE COMPANY. Emile Berliner registers the Nipper picture as a US trademark for his Camden NJ based business.	(see 1902)
1900	From 76 million acres in 1850, the United States of America now has approximately 319 million acres of cultivated cropland.	
1900	With a four-horse team pulling a single moldboard "sulky" wheeled plow, a farmer can plow 40 acres in about 55 hours.	(see 1936)
1900	At the San Francisco World's Fair, Frick Clocks win First Prize for timepieces.	(see 1910)
1900	More than 100,000 acres of the Texas panhandle are now covered by Alfred Rowe's RO Ranch. Alfred has improved his 15,000 head herd by breeding his Longhorns with Hereford and with Durham stock.	

1900	Having won dozens of international awards for high quality varnishes, VALENTINE & CO. now have offices in Pennsylvania, as well as in Paris, France.	
1900	The population of the US has tripled during the past half-century.	
1900	There are now about 8,000 motorcars owned in the USA. Half of these were bought new this year.	(see 1901)
1900	VISSER & SMIT is established to construct water distribution pipelines.	
1900	Largely due to the SOUTHERN PACIFIC RR, Los Angeles, CA, now boasts more than 100,000 persons.	
1900	Bristol, UK; the building of iron-hulled ships is added to Stothert's locomotive manufacturing here. Robert Pitt joins the business, and STOTHERT & PITT is established.	
1900	Having been incorporated only two years ago, Tulsa, OK, now has a population of 1,400 citizens.	(see 1980)
1900	Mr. Edward H. Harriman takes control of the SOUTHERN PACIFIC RAILROAD, which will be operated in tandem with the soon to be acquired UNION PACIFIC RAILROAD.	(see 1901)
1900	USA; twenty genuine railroad circuses are now travelling around our great nation.	(see 1910)
1900	**The first flax crop in Texas is planted near Victoria, in south Texas.**	
1900	Rollin White patents a "flash-boiler" that allows steam to be raised rapidly, leading to development of White's Stanhope brand steam car.	
1900	Stockton, CA; HOLT MANUFACTURING CO., is the leading producer of grain combines in the US, and California's largest producer of steam engines.	
1900	UK; over the past several decades, British workers are organizing themselves into associations, or unions, these actions lead to the formation of the Labour party this year.	
1900	As the bicycle parts business has become unprofitable, the Armstrong Brothers cease distribution and close their retail store. Having decided to devote 100% to manufacturing, they move to a new facility at 617 Austin Avenue in Chicago.	(see 1902)
1900	UK; in the *London Times* newspaper, outlined in a little box, this simple advertisement runs: *"Men wanted for Hazardous Journey. Small wages, bitter cold, long months of complete darkness, constant danger, safe return doubtful. Honor and recognition in case of success. Sir Ernest Shackelford."* Shackelford's advertisement draws many responses from all over England.	(see 1914)
1900	TB WOOD'S SONS enters the power transmission industry.	(see 1936)
1900	California; the crude oil discovery on the Kern River, near Bakersfield, causes the foundry business to boom and A. J. Webster doubles his work force from 15 to 30 men.	(see 1901)
1900	Italy; FIAT opens their first factory; it is 12,000 sq m, with 150 employees; and this year produce 30 of their 3 1/2 hp cars.	(see 1902)
	The dawning of the Twentieth Century…	

1901	As the new century dawns, Singer is selling a million sewing machines annually, all around the world.	

	1901	Turn of the Century; as Mark Sullivan states in *Our Times*, "...in nearly every village and town in America, especially in the Midwest, the local mechanical genius devoted his whole being to this new device," referring to the automobile.	
	1901	The Dodge Bros., Horace and John, open a shop in Detroit, MI.	(see 1902)
	1901	As this new century dawns, almost half of the world's total crude oil production is from the Baku area of Russia.	
	1901	A-Car is still building trucks and cars. This year Autocar introduces the first drive-shaft driven car in the USA.	
	1901	***Ninety-one-year-old John Bean creates the "Magic Pump."***	
	1901	Michigan; Alfred Humphrey opens General Gas Light Co., in Kalamazoo, manufacturing and selling the newly invented gas lights.	

1901	May; the J. M. Guffey Petroleum Company is formed.	
1901	Warner Gear Company is founded.	
1901	Thompson Products is founded.	
1901	Frank and Perry Remy establish Remy Electric Co. building dynamos (generators) and magnetos.	
1901	**The first Western Hemisphere gusher - Spindletop blows in at Gladys City near Beaumont, TX. Brought in by a young Austrian, Anthony Lucas, the Spindletop well flows 84,000 barrels per day. As the well blows in, the pressure blows several tons of 4" (100 mm) pipe up and out over the top of the wooden derrick, knocking off the water table and the crown block as it goes. Soon this well is producing more crude oil than all other wells in America, combined. In one month, Beaumont's population jumps from 9,000 to 30,000.** *NOTE: This gusher is only 30 yards from the well that Walter Sharp had to abandon due to quicksand, at 418 feet, back in 1893.*	(see 1902)
1901	**BB & C builds the first steam turbine in Europe used to produce electricity.**	
1901	**IC & SC introduce the first double roller chain for industry.**	
1901	Mr. Frank Poor becomes a partner in a small company that renews burned-out light bulbs.	
1901	New York City; the Ajax, a light weight, 2 passenger electric car is being built by the Ajax Motor Vehicle Co., until 1903.	
1901	George Roper acquires the American Foundry Co.	
1901	Cousins, Everett and Clinton Cushman have ideas for improving the two stroke engine, begin manufacturing farm equipment and two-cycle boat engines in Lincoln, NE.	(see 1909)
1901	Out of work and out of money, Henry Ford, his wife and son move in with his parents. Then, driving his personal car, Ford beats Alexander Winton in a race, attracting investors who help him to form Henry Ford Company.	(see 1902)
1901	**The curved-dash Oldsmobile is the first American car to be manufactured in quantity.**	(see 1902)
1901	Oscar Hedstrom, a engine designer, and George Hendee, a bicycle racer, build a bicycle powered by a Hedstrom designed, 1 3/4 hp, single cylinder engine, this is the first Indian motocycle, built by their new Hendee Manufacturing Company. *NOTE: The Hendee Mfg. Co. always built Indian motocycles, not motorcycles. This was always distinctive in their advertising.*	(see 1907)
1901	**G. Marconi succeeds in producing wireless voice communication across the Atlantic Ocean.**	
1901	**International Paper issues firm instructions forbidding the cutting of trees below a certain size.**	

1901	Macmaster-Carr begins in the supply business in Chicago.	
1901	The Tokheim Oil Tank & Pump Co. is established in Ft. Wayne, IN.	
1901	J. W. Duntley, a foundry foreman with ideas for pneumatic tools, partners with Charles Schwab, the young steel tycoon, and founds Chicago Pneumatic.	
1901	June; Schenectady Locomotive's "big shop" and seven other locomotive builders are merged to form the American Locomotive Co. (ALCO)	
1901	**The double-edged safety razor is invented by King Camp Gillette. This September, Mr. Gillette co-founds the American Safety Razor Company.**	
1901	**Hubert Booth invents a compact and modern vacuum cleaner.**	
1901	Jasper, TX; the beautiful new, Victorian styled Swann Hotel is opened to guests.	
1901	H. W. Johns Manufacturing Co. and the Manville Covering Co. merge to form the H. W. Johns-Manville Co. in NYC.	
1901	To exploit the extensive tracts of longleaf pines in the area, Amos Hodge establishes a sawmill in Zavalla, TX. This is in addition to other sawmills nearby, as well as Mr. Benton McMillian's turpentine plant.	
1901	Connecticut passes the first statewide automobile (speed) legislation in the US; "On country highways, 15 mph (24 kph); on highways within city limits, 12 mph (19.2 kph)."	
1901	Although water-well driller Mahlon E. Layne has six rigs drilling in a five state region, he pulls up stakes in South Dakota and heads for the Spindletop oil boom in southeast Texas.	(see 1902)
1901	The George A. Burts Refining Company is organized to use much of the crude oil from the Spindletop Field.	
1901	**The electric washing machine is invented by Alva Fisher in the USA.**	
1901	Charles Goodnight sells the "Cross J Ranch" to Bigbee and North.	
1901	Olive & Myers Mfg. Co. is manufacturing mattresses in its new three-story brick building at 197 Polk Street in Dallas.	
1901	E. H. Harriman takes over the bankrupt Union Pacific Railroad; soon straightening out the oxbow south of Omaha, NE, using Dey's original line.	
1901	May 14; the first water from the Colorado River flows through Charles Rockwood's first canal to irrigate the desert.	
1901	**Warren Bros. Paving builds the world's first modern asphalt plant.**	
1901	In a merger, the Victor Talking Machine Co. (Victor) is formed; with Nipper the dog, and the Victor Phonograph is its logo.	(see 1902)
1901	Texas; as Swift and Armour are both building major packing plants in Ft. Worth, G. W. Simpson sells out and returns to Boston, MA.	
1901	Tulsa, OK; oil is discovered just North of here, at the small village of Red Fork.	
1901	**Texas; Corsicana is the first town in the state using natural gas for lighting and as fuel for heating buildings.**	
1901	Maine; after building them for a while, Alvin O. Lombard patents a steam-powered, track-type tractor to use for towing logging sleds in the wintertime. Lombard's tractor is truly a mechanical success, but lacking resources, sadly it is never promoted outside the logging industry. Sadly, only about 200 of the Lombard tractors are ever built.	(see 1904) (see 1908)
1901	Around the world, prior to now, more than 100 patents have been issued for the use of tracks on mobile equipment. However, it seems that all of these failed to work out, when working in the field. Alvin Lombard's tractors are probably some of the most successful.	

1901	Australia; Harry George Hawker, age 12, works in a garage building engines, but he will soon emigrate to England.	(see 1910)
1901	By now about 1,000 tractors of all sorts have been built by more than twenty different separate manufacturers.	
1901	The two fierce rivals in the wheeled scraper business, Western Wheeled Scraper Co, and F. C. Austin Mfg. Co. join to form a marketing corporation named the Austin-Western Road Machinery Co, to be headquartered in Chicago, IL.	
1901	Though small in stature, James J. Hill is a giant of American railroading, he now controls the Great Northern, the Northern Pacific, and the Burlington. Hill's three railroads primarily serve the Pacific Northwest.	
1901	About now, the first known, and recorded use of the word "tractor." It's from the Latin word "trahere" meaning "to pull."	(see 1906)
1901	A current advertisement for Lorillard Refrigerator Co.'s ice boxes calls them the "highest priced refrigerators made." Claimed as customers are Andrew Carnegie as well as George Vanderbilt, who installed five Lorillard refrigerators in his Biltmore Mansion in Asheville, NC, back in 1894.	
1901	Germany; separating from Lutzmann, Adam Opel signs a contract with Alexandre Darracq, a Frenchman.	(see 1902)
1901	Toledo Scales improve their pendulum weight scales by using gravity instead of a spring tension mechanism. The new scales are more resistant to changes in temperature and also lasts much longer.	
1901	Buffalo, NY; the Buffalo Electric Carriage Co. is building runabouts and big expensive cars with a range of 75 miles per charge. A local rival is the Buffalo Electric Vehicle Company, also building electric automobiles.	
1901	A transatlantic radio transmission is received by Marconi's radio receiver.	
1901	Miles, WI; the Heil Rail Joint Welding Company is founded by Julius P. Heil.	(see 1905)
1901	Webster's Kern County Foundry & Machine Works is now operating seven forges.	(see 1903)
1901	USA; this year there are 14,800 automobiles registered in this country.	
1901	The electric "Bachelle" automobile is built this year and next by Otto Bachelle of Chicago. The Crowdus Automobile Co. of the same city makes the electric "Cyclecar" with a range of 50 miles per charge, on through 1903.	
1901	Sweden; blacksmith and mould maker Per Alfred Stenberg establishes a foundry in the southern town of Emmaboda.	(see 1922) (see 1929)
1902	Willis Carrier invents and introduces refrigerated air conditioning to the world.	
1902	Wisconsin; Manitowoc Co., Inc. is formed.	
1902	Blodgett develops the first gas-burning ovens.	
1902	C. Jim Stewart, blacksmith and Joe R. Stevenson, carriage maker, combine their talents, and $300 each, and establish C. Jim Stewart & Stevenson Company.	
1902	The Packard's Ohio Automobile Co. now becomes the Packard Motor Car Company.	
1902	Studebaker Mfg. Co. builds an electric horseless carriage.	
1902	The Minneapolis Steel & Machinery Company is founded.	
1902	Lufkin, TX; the Lufkin Foundry & Machine Co. is established, making railroad & sawmill equipment.	
1902	Van Buren Foundry & Machine Co. merges with Heck & Marvin Co., becoming Van Buren, Heck & Marvin, established to build J. B. Hill's ditcher in Findlay, OH.	

1902	**DODGE BROS. build 3000 transmissions on an order from R. E. Olds, for the very first OLDS automobiles.**	(see 1903)
1902	Max Grabowsky establishes the RAPID MOTOR VEHICLE COMPANY, to build one cylinder motor trucks.	
1902	Rev. Burrell Cannon's WHEEL airship, built by the EZEKIEL AIRSHIP CO. of Pittsburg, TX, makes its short but realistic flight. Soon, his airship is blown off a flatcar and destroyed by winds in Texarkana, while on its way to the St. Louis World's Fair.	
1902	H. R. Worthington develops the first gas-engine-driven gas compressor.	
1902	David Dunbar Buick establishes the BUICK MFG. COMPANY.	
1902	LOCOMOBILE hires Andrew Lawrence Riker, and begins building 2- and 4-cylinder gasoline-engined cars.	
1902	SCHRAMM & MAERKY is dissolved, Maerky departs; however, Chris Schramm and his son Henry to run the business.	
1902	German scientist Arthur Korn builds the forerunner to the modern FAX machine.	
1902	*POPULAR MECHANICS* magazine begins publishing.	
1902	POTAIN starts in business building tower cranes.	
1902	**MAYTAG is the world's largest manufacturer of threshing machine feeders.**	
1902	Major Ernest "Billy" Barlow forms THOMAS BARLOW SONS in Durban, South Africa.	
1902	A. O. SMITH begins making vehicle frames for the PEERLESS AUTOMOBILE CO.	
1902	Less than 100 are sold of the first diesel engine built in the US; a 3 cylinder, 55kw model from Adolphus Busch's firm.	
1902	King Edward VII's royal farrier orders a set of farrier's tools from CHAMPION BOLT & CLIPPER CO. because of their superior reputation.	
1902	**July 1; Nipper listening to the phonograph first appears on a record label.**	(see 1929)
1902	Bryan D. Horton, electrical engineer, establishes the MCBRIDE MFG. CO., later renamed DETROIT FUSE & MFG. CO, manufacturing and marketing enclosed fuses and fuse switches.	
1902	Five businessmen in Two Harbors, Minnesota found MINNESOTA MINING & MANUFACTURING CO. (3M) to mine corborundum and make sandpaper and abrasive wheels.	
1902	Fall; the GULF REFINING CO. OF TEXAS is organized to process the oil produced by GUFFEY, then the GULF refinery at Port Arthur, TX, is built.	(see 1907)
1902	NATIONAL SUPPLY (NATIONAL) buys out CALIFORNIA SUPPLY CO.	
1902	Henry Ford withdraws from HENRY FORD COMPANY; Henry M. Leland (a manufacturer of precision auto parts) reorganizes the company and it soon becomes… CADILLAC AUTOMOBILE COMPANY.	(see 1903)
1902	**Barney Oldfield goes a mile a minute in Henry Ford's car No. 999.**	
1902	The first of a new species is born, the Teddy Bear.	
1902	Sir Hiram Maxim backs the LONDON GENERAL AUTOMOBILE CO. and the first Maxim car is built; it is a medium sized, sixteen-horsepower vehicle.	
1902	AIR LIQUIDE is founded in France as Georges Claude and Paul Delorme invent the process of "liquefaction of air." French physicist George Claude invents neon light.	(See 1904)
1902	UK; the long established JAMES CYCLE CO. decides to build a "motorised-cycle," and clips a Minerva one-hp, two-stroke engine on a standard James bicycle frame, and they have the first James motorcycle.	
1902	Alexander Y. Malcomson now owns six coal yards in Detroit, MI.	

1902	Shell Transport & Trading forms a joint venture with Royal Dutch Petroleum.	
1902	Whittier, CA; twenty-year-old Herman C. Smith starts a blacksmith shop.	
1902	Animal Crackers are introduced; the box is fitted with a string, to be hung from a Christmas tree.	
1902	Having drifted from Iowa down to southeast Texas in the wake of Spindletop, Howard Robard Hughes, Sr., now partners with Walter B. Sharp and starts a drilling company. Immediately, like all other drillers, they are having problems with the existing flat, fishtail bits that wear out very fast while scraping a hole through rock.	(see 1906)
1902	Mahlon Layne, along with O. P. Woodburn, a mechanical engineer, moves the entire Layne Company to Texas. In Texas, Layne meets salesman, Mr. P. D. Bowler, and the three begin developing better drilling rigs, better well screens, and better centrifugal pumps. Mahlon Layne sketches his design for a "pitless water pump" on the wall of a farmhouse in El Campo, TX.	(see 1907)

1902	Archer-Daniels Linseed Co. begins as George A. Archer and John W. Daniels start a linseed crushing business.	
1902	Arthur I. Jacobs "busts his knuckles" using an old style drill press and declares, "There must be a better way to build a chuck." A few days later, Jacobs has developed the first drill chuck with a toothed sleeve and key, and he soon founds the firm that will be the Jacobs Chuck Mfg. Co.	(see 1954)
1902	Ruben Wright buys the Reed Mfg. Company.	(see 2006)
1902	*McClure's* Magazine begins publishing the series on Standard Oil Co. by Ida Tarbell.	(see 1903) (see 1911)
1902	Pittsburgh Plate Glass is one of the earlier American manufacturers to operate in Europe.	
1902	France; the Audibert & Lavirotte manufacturing plant in Lyon is acquired by Berliet, who now start making a four-cylinder automobile, with a steel frame instead of wood, and with a honeycomb radiator.	

1902	Carl Frederick Malzahn moves to Perry, OK, and with his sons Charlie and Gus, opens a blacksmith shop; eventually becoming Charlie's Machine Shop.	
1902	Prominent scientist Simon Newcomb, states, "Flight by machines heavier than air is impractical and insignificant; if not utterly impossible."	(see 1903)
1902	France; the rear-engined Bouton quadricycle has a six horsepower engine, soon to be replaced with a eight horsepower type.	
1902	Glasgow, Scotland; Albion Motor Car Co. begins production of commercial vehicles.	
1902	EXTRA EXTRA, read all about it!!! TEXAS CRUDE OIL PRICES DROP TO THREE CENTS A BARREL!!!	
1902	The first vessel built by the newly formed Manitowoc Dry Dock Company is launched and steams away into Lake Michigan.	
1902	May 18; a tornado strikes Goliad, TX, inflicting tremendous damage, and leaving 114 dead.	
1902	There are now 80,000 coin-operated pay telephones working in the USA.	(see 1905)
1902	Boston, MA; the Reverend Edgar Helms is collecting used household goods and clothing in the more affluent neighborhoods, he then trains and hires poor people and needy immigrants to repair and mend these used items. The refurbished items are then resold or given to the folks who have repaired them. The Reverend's system works quite well and the GOODWILL philosophy of "A hand up, not a handout" is born.	(see 2002)
1902	Twin-City builds and markets their first industrial engines.	

1902	Chicago; this July, the MᴄCᴏʀᴍɪᴄᴋ Hᴀʀᴠᴇsᴛɪɴɢ Mᴀᴄʜɪɴᴇ Cᴏ., and their rival, the Wɪʟʟɪᴀᴍ Dᴇᴇʀɪɴɢ Cᴏ. merge, bringing in three smaller firms with them. The Pʟᴀɴᴏ Mᴀɴᴜꜰᴀᴄᴛᴜʀɪɴɢ Cᴏ., Wᴀʀᴅᴇʀ, Bᴜsʜɴᴇʟʟ & Gʟᴇssɴᴇʀ, and the Mɪʟᴡᴀᴜᴋᴇᴇ Hᴀʀᴠᴇsᴛᴇʀ Mᴀᴄʜɪɴᴇ Cᴏ., this group controls 85% of America's harvester machine business. The new firm is Iɴᴛᴇʀɴᴀᴛɪᴏɴᴀʟ Hᴀʀᴠᴇsᴛᴇʀ Cᴏ., and has assets of $110 million.		
1902	Chicago; the Armstrong Brothers' plant on Austin Avenue burns to the ground on April Fools day. Much of their inventory is salvaged and reconditioned. This plant is rebuilt with twice the floor space.	(see 1905)	
1902	**Glenn Curtiss introduces the V-twin motorcycle engine; the vee configuration gives more power and speed, just what Glenn wants.**		
1902	Mɪɴɴᴇᴀᴘᴏʟɪs offers the first commercially successful cylinder-type corn sheller for farmers.		
1902	Texas; the Tᴇxᴀs Fᴜᴇʟ Cᴏᴍᴘᴀɴʏ opens its first office, in Beaumont. Cᴜʟʟɪɴᴀɴ & Sᴄʜʟᴀᴇᴛ now establish the Tᴇxᴀs Cᴏᴍᴘᴀɴʏ, headquartered in Corsicana; knowing that the Tᴇxᴀs Fᴜᴇʟ Cᴏᴍᴘᴀɴʏ needed more capital to increase operations, the Tᴇxᴀs Cᴏᴍᴘᴀɴʏ takes over the Tᴇxᴀs Fᴜᴇʟ Cᴏᴍᴘᴀɴʏ, inheriting their Beaumont office.	(see 1959)	
1902	From the USA mainland, the laying of the first trans-Pacific communications cable is completed, to Hawaii and on to Guam and on to the Philippines nest year.		
1902	The first steel stanchions are now in use, keeping dairy cows in place while being milked.		
1902	Mr. Levi Strauss passes away this year, while the company bearing his name grosses $1,000,000 this year, a fitting tribute.		
1902	Germany; Opel and Darracq begin producing the French Dᴀʀʀᴀᴄǫ autos under license, branding them "Oᴘᴇʟ-Dᴀʀʀᴀᴄǫ." These are Opel bodies mounted on Darracq chassis, powered by a two-cylinder engine. This autumn, the Opel brothers first design, the 10/12 horsepower model is finished, and debuts at the Hamburg Motor Show. This year sees the first Oᴘᴇʟ motorcycle.	(see 1906)	

No. 768,034. PATENTED AUG. 23, 1904.
I. W. COLBURN.
GLASS WORKING MACHINE.
APPLICATION FILED MAR. 9, 1900.
NO MODEL. 6 SHEETS—SHEET 1.
FIG. 1.
FIG. 2.

	1902	The first patent is issued for a system of "rotary percussion drilling," or "adding percussive blows to regular rotary drilling action."	
	1902	Ohio; in March, Irving W. Colburn patents the "sheet glass drawing machine." The mass production of window panes and such is now possible.	(see 1904)
	1902	Connecticut; the Bʟɪᴄᴋᴇɴsᴅᴇʀꜰᴇʀ Tʏᴘᴇᴡʀɪᴛᴇʀ Cᴏ. of Stamford introduces the first electric powered typewriter.	
	1902	Schenectady, NY; experimental electric, gas, and gas-electric cars are being built by the Gᴇɴᴇʀᴀʟ Eʟᴇᴄᴛʀɪᴄ Cᴏ.	
	1902	USA; a new steam locomotive built for the Mɪssᴏᴜʀɪ Pᴀᴄɪꜰɪᴄ Rᴀɪʟʀᴏᴀᴅ, with engine and tender fully loaded, weighs in at 283,000 pounds (128,336 kg). This is more than 4 times as heavy as the 1851 locomotive.	(see 1904)
	1902	Ohio; the Aᴍᴇʀɪᴄᴀɴ Mᴏᴛᴏʀ Cᴀʀʀɪᴀɢᴇ Cᴏ. of Cleveland builds the "American" horseless carriage through next year.	
	1902	Italy; The first FIAT sportscar, the 24 hp "Corsa" debuts and driven by Vincenzo Lancia, wins the Sassi-Superga race.	(see 1903)

1903	The Mᴀᴄᴋ Bʀᴏᴛʜᴇʀs Cᴏᴍᴘᴀɴʏ is incorporated in New York, John M., Augustus F., and William C. Mack are the directors.		
1903	Cʟᴀʀᴋ Eǫᴜɪᴘᴍᴇɴᴛ Cᴏᴍᴘᴀɴʏ begins operations.		
1903	May 19; Bᴜɪᴄᴋ Mᴏᴛᴏʀ Cᴏᴍᴘᴀɴʏ is incorporated in Detroit, MI. With financing from the Fʟɪɴᴛ Wᴀɢᴏɴ Wᴏʀᴋs, operations are moved from Detroit to Flint, and on September 11, ground is broken for the first Buick engine factory.		

1903	June 16; eight businessmen meet at Alex Malcomson's coal yard, and the FORD MOTOR CO. is founded by the Malcomson group, with Malcomson as the heaviest investor. It is incorporated by Henry Ford, and the first series Model As are produced in a rented plant. Third time's a charm. This year, the Dodge Brothers meet Henry Ford, they then team up and produce his first car for the FORD MOTOR CO., every part, except the wheels and cab for the 1903 FORD Model A Runabout. The DODGE brothers will continue building engines & transmissions for Ford's cars for the next eleven years.	(see 1904) (see 1914)
1903	CLIMAX ENGINE CO. is started.	
1903	Arthur, William and Walter Davidson, and William Harley establish HARLEY-DAVIDSON MOTOR CO. in Milwaukee, WI, their first cycle eventually runs more than 100,000 miles (160,000km), under five owners. This is the beginning of the "Indian and Harley Wars," that will last until 1954.	
1903	December 17; for 59 seconds the Wright Brothers fly their first plane, using IC & SC chains and their own fuel-injected engine.	(see 1909)
1903	England; in May the first VAUXHALL car rolls off the assembly line in South London, it is a one cylinder, five horsepower carriage.	
1903	In a relationship that will last almost 90 years, A. O. SMITH begins supplying frames to CADILLAC for their automobiles.	
1903	William Buchanan's LOUISIANA & ARKANSAS RAILWAY is steaming southward from Texarkana.	
1903	**BUICK builds 16 cars this year.**	
1903	The *OIL & GAS JOURNAL* is founded.	
1903	The US now has 8,000 cars and 144 miles of paved roads.	
1903	In Oklahoma, the SHEEHAN PIPELINE CONSTRUCTION CO. begins digging ditches.	
1903	Joe Joy makes his first sketches (later verified in court by a close friend) of a digging and loading device for coal mines.	
1903	Because of the indifference of BROWN & SHARPE to the project, James Norton leaves BROWN & SHARPE and develops the Norton Abrasive Grinder for metals.	
1903	In Stephen, MN, Richard Russell and C. K. Stockland establish the RUSSELL GRADER MANUFACTURING CO.	
1903	FIRESTONE makes their first solid rubber tires.	
1903	Preston Tucker is born.	
1903	DART TRUCK COMPANY is formed, and begins building "over the road" trucks.	
1903	The first transcontinental automobile trip is started May 23, leaving San Francisco, to August 1, arriving in New York City. WOW, that's 10 weeks to drive across the USA.	(see 1904)
1903	While visiting New York City, from Alabama, Mary Anderson invents windshield wipers after seeing streetcar conductors stick their heads out the side windows to see where they were going. Wipers are soon used on most vehicles with windshields.	
1903	Eighteen year old Albert G. Fuller migrates to Boston and begins at a job selling brushes.	
1903	In Syracuse, NY, L. C. SMITH & BROS. TYPEWRITER COMPANY is established.	
1903	For $3,000 W. C. Coleman buys the original patent rights for the Irby-Gilliland Lamps he has been renting out.	
1903	**BINNEY & SMITH introduce their Crayola brand crayons.**	
1903	In the Benguet Province of the Philippines, the first mine opens for the BENGUET CORPORATION.	
1903	OLDSMOBILE buys its first ever magazine advertising in… the *Ladies' Home Journal*.	(see 1904)
1903	MILLER BREWING COMPANY introduces its Miller High Life beer.	

1903	France; Edmond Fouche and Jean Picard invent the oxy-acetylene welding/cutting torch.	
1903	For the past three years Mr. Parker, an Englishman, has driven a 2 ½ hp car and a 25hp car over 1,000 miles fueled by producer gas; with fairly good results.	
1903	August 25; a patent is issued to the CROWN DRILLING MACHINE CO. for a new "drilling machine," a fairly standard steam-powered unit.	
1903	DANZAS & CO. AG incorporates in Switzerland, now having travel agencies, as well as import and export agencies in each Swiss area, and in France. The Paris office now has 80 employees primarily engaged in importing Swiss fabrics for the Paris fashion trade.	
1903	Having had its initial large crude strike during the 1890s, California is now the leading state in US oil production.	
1903	The STANDARD WHEEL CO. of Terre Haute, IN, expands its bicycle operation to include the OVERLAND AUTOMOTIVE DIVISION, to build motor vehicles, and the OVERLAND "Runabout" debuts.	(see 1908)
1903	In Cleburne, the first automatic telephone exchange in Texas is installed.	
1903	England; BSA builds its first motorcycle.	
1903	Germany; the first fast-running, four-stroke, marine diesel engine is introduced by M. A. N.	
1903	After receiving his chemistry degree from Harvard, L. Valentine Pulsifer, Lawson Valentine's grandson, joins VALENTINE & CO.	
1903	ROYAL DUTCH PETROLEUM CO. and SHELL TRANSPORT & TRADING begin working together to protect themselves from the clout of STANDARD OIL.	(see 1907)
1903	APPLETON ELECTRIC COMPANY is founded.	
1903	Ductile tungsten for use as filament in light bulbs is invented by William Coolidge.	
1903	September 27; "They gave him his orders in Monroe, VA," to speed up and "get her into Spencer on time." The 166 mile run from Monroe, VA, through the rough country down to Spencer, NC was not a racetrack, and engineer Steve Broady was really running too fast and couldn't slow down enough going down onto the Stillhouse Trestle near Danville, VA, and the entire train goes off the tracks and into the ravine. Eleven are killed and the seven survivors are all seriously injured in the "Wreck of Old 97."	
1903	Michigan in November; returning from lunch one cold blustery day, all the coat hooks were taken, and Albert Parkhouse, an employee of the TIMBERLAKE WIRE & NOVELTY CO. could find no place to hang his good coat. Albert finds a piece of heavy wire and twists it into two loops to fit inside his coat and bends the free ends into a hook he could hang someplace. Al earns nothing from his invention, as his employer patents it, and the company attorney put his own name on it. Around this same time, about 80 other garment hangers are patented, but Al Parkhouse's is the basis for the familiar wire clothes hanger that will still be used worldwide more than a century later.	
1903	Texas; the TEXAS COMPANY is saved from bankruptcy, as their third well comes gushing upward, near Sour Lake.	
1903	Chicago; for the next dozen years or so, the BORLAND-GRANNIS CO. is producing 22 mph electric cars powered by G-E motors.	
1903	USA; Congress creates a Department of Commerce and Labor.	(see 1913)
1903	Medina, OH; A. I. Root, a friend of the Wright brothers, publishes the first account of Wilbur and Orville's first flight.	(see 1917)
1903	Oregon passes a law regulating the hours of work for women.	(see 1908)
1903	For another 10 years, the COLUMBUS BUGGY CO. of Columbus, OH, is producing electric and gasoline buggies… uh… er… cars.	

1903	In Europe, the first motorcar race over unrestricted, open roads is the Paris-Madrid race. This event starts with 216 autos and 59 motorcycles, as more than a million spectators line the route. Sadly the race is abandoned in Bordeaux after 5 drivers are killed in a single day.			
1903	William H. Stockham begins his STOCKHAM VALVES & FITTINGS CO. in Birmingham, AL.			

1903	Pennsylvania; the ACME MOTOR CAR CO. of Reading will build and sell the Acme motorcar through 1910.	
1903	Illinois; Michael Owens, a glass worker, is issued a patent for his invention of a machine for glass bottle making.	
1903	California; Webster sells KERN COUNTY FOUNDRY & MACHINE WORKS to the KERN COUNTY BANK.	(see 1906)
1903	Italy; the first FIAT truck, a 4 ton model is introduced, a 5 ton model will follow soon.	(see 1906)
1904	MACK BROS. CO. begins using the "MANHATTAN" trade name for their motorized vehicles, to distinguish them from their horse-drawn products.	

1904	North Carolina; with a $10,000 investment, THOMASVILLE CHAIR CO. is founded, soon turning out 180 chairs each day.	(see 1907)
1904	The US acquires control of the Panama Canal Zone for $10,000,000. The US holds on to it until Jimmy Carter comes along and gives it back to them. Later this year construction starts on the canal. Before it is completed, 225 million cubic yards of dirt will be moved by 77 Bucyrus, 1 Thew, and 24 Marion steam shovels.	
1904	BARFORD & PERKINS adds gasoline and paraffin powered rollers to their steam roller lines.	
1904	BEAN SPRAY PUMP COMPANY is organized.	
1904	**BUICK builds 34 cars this year.**	
1904	**The first STROUD elevating grader is built.**	
1904	PAGE & SCHNABLE, contractors, built the world's first dragline to use on their contract for the Chicago Drainage Canal.	(see 1912)
1904	January; R. E. Olds leaves OLDSMOBILE, and forms REO MOTOR VEHICLES, and for the next two years REO sells more cars than OLDS, but the rest is history. Ransom E. Olds develops the first mechanical "external band" brake system for motorcars.	(see 1905)
1904	Albert Champion moves to Flint, MI, and establishes CHAMPION IGNITION CO. to manufacture spark plugs.	
1904	Clarence Spicer sets up his universal joint manufacturing business in a corner of the Potter Printing Press shop.	
1904	Early this year, H. Royce builds his first motorcar, then in May he meets Charles Rolls, a dealer of quality automobiles in London. They agree that ROYCE LTD. would produce automobiles to be sold exclusively by CHARLES ROLLS & CO, bearing the ROLLS ROYCE nameplate.	(see 1906) (see 2007)
1904	George and Earl Holley begin producing carburetors.	
1904	New York; the DAIMLER MFG. CO. of Long Island City is producing and marketing the "American Mercedes" motorcar, thru 1907.	
1904	BORG & BECK is founded.	
1904	James Buchanan "Diamond Jim" Brady is a gauge salesman for M. M. & M. and a good one he is.	
1904	In Tuscany, Italy, electricity is produced by geothermal energy for the first time.	
1904	J. Garland Pegues establishes CITY GARAGE in Longview, TX.	(see 1915)
1904	Arthur O. Smith incorporates A. O. SMITH CO. in Milwaukee, WI.	
1904	The BESSEMER TRUCK COMPANY is in operation, in Oak Grove, PA.	

1904	DeArment moves CHAMPION BOLT & CLIPPER CO. to Meadville, PA, and begins making wrenches and other hand tools, in addition to their horseshoeing tools.	
1904	C. C. Hobart sells HOBART ELECTRIC MANUFACTURING CO. to his partners—who are mostly Hobart relatives.	
1904	John Harris's first acetylene torch is exhibited at the St. Louis World's Fair this year.	
1904	FORD OF CANADA is chartered by FORD MOTOR COMPANY (FORD).	(see 1905)
1904	BROWN-LIPE sells a progressive type motor car transmission to the H. H. FRANKLIN CO. of Syracuse.	
1904	Billy Durant joins BUICK as general manager.	
1904	Two German glass-blowers form THERMOS Gmbh and begin manufacturing the "vacuum flask," with hand blown glass fillers.	
1904	In their Berwick, PA, Shops, AC&F build the first all steel passenger car ever built; it is the first of 300 sold to the INTERBOROUGH RAPID TRANSIT COMPANY, the beginning of the New York City subway system.	
1904	June; Davis Fletcher of Athens, TX, creates a sandwich of a ground beef patty and onion between two slices of Texas toast and sells it at the St. Louis World's Fair. He calls it a hamburger.	
1904	STANDARD OF CALIFORNIA's Rio Bravo Gathering Station, east of Bakersfield, goes on line.	
1904	Dr. Perley G. Nutting creates and exhibits the first neon sign at the Exposition at St. Louis. The bright red sign spells out: NEON.	
1904	Latrobe, PA; pharmacist David Strickler creates the Banana Split. *OH!! What a day!!!!!*	
1904	This year and for the next four years, CADILLAC offers a van body for its Model A, thus the first CADILLAC truck.	
1904	Carl Fisher organizes the PREST-O-LITE CO. to manufacture the gas tank used for the automobile headlamps.	
1904	**Professor Albert Korn is the first person to send photographs over wires.**	
1904	**Tire chains are invented.**	
1904	In a series of ads placed in trolley cars, the "Campbell Kids" are introduced, to advertise Campbell's soup.	
1904	Oklahoma City; Frank E. Anderson forms a cotton-trading company with his brother-in-law William L. Clayton; Frank invites his brother M. D. Anderson, a banker in Tennessee, to join them in the business. Thus, ANDERSON, CLAYTON & CO. is established.	
1904	The first known dump trucks are built.	
1904	Glenn H. Curtiss, riding a eight-cylinder motorcycle he designed, runs 136 mph at Ormond Beach, FL, earning Curtiss the title of "The Fastest Man on Earth."	
1904	By the end of year, the French DE DION-BOUTON plant has sold over 40,000 petrol (gasoline) powered vehicles, most sold to other vehicle manufacturers.	
1904	In Guildford, near London, England, the Dennis Brothers' well-established bicycle and tricycle factory turns its focus to autos and commercial vehicles.	
1904	Kiev, Ukraine; utilizing a 1600 hp (1177 kw) diesel engine, Germany's M. A. N. installs the world's first large diesel-powered electric power plant.	
1904	The first commercial grapefruit grove in Texas is planted in the Rio Grande Valley.	(see 1980)

1904	HENSCHEL & SON of Germany now earn the First Prize for an aerodynamically streamlined train, the first high speed train of this century.	
1904	Oscar Kjellberg submits a hand-written patent application describing his unique invention; the flux-coated welding electrode.	(see 1906)
1904	Elektriska Svetsnings-Aktiebolaget (ESAB) is founded in Gothenburg, Sweden; primarily focusing on shipyard repairs.	
1904	CLEVELAND TWIST DRILL COMPANY incorporates this year.	(see 1905)
1904	Canada; INTERNATIONAL HARVESTER opens a plant in Hamilton, Ontario, alerting MASSEY-HARRIS that they really do need a US manufacturing presence. However, years of indecision will delay the MASSEY-HARRIS move.	(see 1910)
1904	September 20; at Huffman Prairie, OH, Wilbur Wright makes the world's first ever circling airplane flight.	(see 1905)
1904	USA; the federal government establishes the US Bureau of Public Roads.	
1904	HOLT MFG. CO. starts testing crawler tracks on steam traction engines. Then on Thanksgiving Day, fifty-five-year-old Benjamin Holt first tests his experimental steam-powered, track-type tractor. This machine is heavy and cumbersome, but its endless tracks meet Ben's objective… it will work on soft ground that will not support wheeled tractors. In less than two years, Ben Holt's tractor is in production, and on the market.	(see 1905) (see 1906)
1904	USA; the Savage Brothers of Morrical drill the first oil well in north Louisiana. Business picks up fast and "Oil City" soon becomes a boom town.	(see 1910)
1904	St. Louis; C. H. Summer introduces peanut butter to the world as he sells more than $700 worth at his concession at the 1904 Universal Exposition—it is a hit!!!	
1904	Mr. Ernest R. Kelly of Wilmington, DE, is now building the Acadia automobile, a short-lived venture, it seems.	
1904	USA; August 02; Michael Owen is issued a patent for a "glass shaping machine." The success of this first machine is responsible for all the tremendous production of glass jars, bottles, and other containers.	
1904	The vacuum diode, or Fleming valve, is invented by John A. Fleming.	
1904	California; one thousand six hundred (1,600) motorcars are now cruising the streets of Los Angeles. To "keep 'em in line," the speed limit is six (6) mph in commercial areas, and eight (8) mph in residential locales.	
1904	Ohio; for a few years the CANTONO ELECTRIC TRACTOR CO. of Canton, builds an Italian-designed, but American-built electric auto.	
1904	Iowa; the ADAMS COMPANY of Dubuque will build and market the Adams-Farwell automobile for the next decade or so.	

1904	October, 9th; the New York City Subway system opens for business today and more than 350,000 passengers ride on this first day.	
1904	USA; with loaded engine and tender, the 1904 winner is built for the Baltimore & Ohio Railroad, and weighs 474,000 pounds (215,000 kg)	(see 1911)
1904	Michigan; the BERWICK AUTO CAR CO. of Grand Rapids produces a few of their 2 passenger electric cars, with lots of brass work, but they only go 15 mph.	

1904	The AMERICAN AUTOMOBILE POWER CO. of Lawrence, MA, is building the "American Populaire" motorcar.	
1905	McEVOY is founded to manufacture valves and wellhead equipment.	
1905	January 12; "Tex" Ritter is born in Panola County, deep down in East Texas.	

1905	The MACK BROS. MOTOR CAR COMPANY is founded, and incorporated, with another brother Joseph Mack, now involved. The Mack firm is headquartered in Allentown, PA. They mount a cab directly over the engine of the truck, greatly increasing driver visibility.	
1905	William Pigott, Sr., founds SEATTLE CAR MFG. CO. to build railway and logging equipment, and SEATTLE CAR merges with TWOHY BROS. OF PORTLAND, to become PACIFIC CAR & FOUNDRY (PACCAR).	
1905	KOBE STEEL is founded in Japan.	
1905	January; oil is struck near Humble, TX, population 700, before the year end, the population is 20,000. The first year's production is 15 1/2 million barrels.	
1905	Warren, PA; WALKER'S ICE CREAM discovers how to use an ammonia brine to operate its freezer, eliminating the need for ice.	
1905	AUTOCAR becomes a registered trademark.	
1905	In Newton, IA, the PARSONS COMPANY is founded to build ditching machines.	
1905	THOMAS GREEN & SON, LTD., builds their first fuel engine powered road rollers.	
1905	INGERSOLL RAND is formed.	
1905	Investors take over CHAMPION IGNITION CO., and Albert is out of a job, again.	
1905	Walter Chrysler buys his first car, a LOCOMOBILE Phaeton, at the Chicago Auto Show for $5,000; that's a story in itself.	(see 1911)
1905	AMERICAN ELECTRIC NOVELTY & MANUFACTURING changes its name to AMERICAN EVEREADY.	
1905	Findlay, OH; the INDEPENDENT TORPEDO CO. is formed to shoot oil wells with nitroglycerine, an early form of formation fracturing.	
1905	Frank Phillips and his brother L. E., move from Iowa to Indian Territory, and go into the oil business. Beginning with their fourth well, the Phillips brothers drill 81 consecutive oilers.	
1905	Swiss immigrant K. B. Danuser, in his blacksmith and general repair shop, builds the first piece of DANUSER equipment; a farm wagon.	
1905	DAYTON RUBBER MANUFACTURING COMPANY (DRMC) begins business, one of its first products is the rubber ring used for sealing home canning jars.	
1905	John Harris incorporates HARRIS CALORIFIC in Cleveland.	
1905	In addition to their wagons KNAPHEIDE begins manufacturing bodies for trucks.	
1905	AC&F ship more than 100 rail cars to London for their new "underground" (subway) system.	
1905	Driving a 90 hp Fiat, Louis Chevrolet beats the great race driver, Barney Oldfield in a race in the Bronx, NY.	
1905	More REO vehicles than Oldsmobiles are sold this year.	
1905	OHIO OIL COMPANY moves its headquarters to Findlay, OH.	
1905	In Paris, France, Mata Hari essentially invents the strip tease dance.	
1905	After only three years, the last of the Maxim automobiles is built.	
1905	Wichita, KS; W. C. Coleman begins manufacturing his lamps, where he then lights the field for the first ever night football game.	
1905	The Butt family opens their first grocery store (later to be H. E. B.) in Kerrville, TX.	
1905	The young Amon G. Carter Sr. moves to Ft. Worth, TX and founds the TEXAS ADVERTISING AND MFG. CO., a one-man business. He soon becomes advertising manager for the local Ft. Worth newspaper, while selling peaches from his small farm to make ends meet.	

1905	The FAG symbol is trade-marked and soon becomes a worldwide hallmark of quality and dependability.	

	1905	Germany; Albert Einstein states that solar rays are a combination of electromagnetic waves and corpuscular radiation (photons).	
	1905	The Society of Automotive Engineers (SAE) is formed.	
	1905	Eleven year-old Frank Epperson accidently leaves a glass of lemonade with a spoon in it on the windowsill overnight, where it freezes, making a…?	(see 1924)
	1905	The Durham Furniture Company factory is completely destroyed by fire.	
	1905	August 4; J. E."Gene" Hancock is born in Sherman, TX.	(see 1930)
	1905	Russia; the oilfields in and around Baku are set afire during the Russian Revolution.	
	1905	Houston, TX; Meyer M. Gordon begins offering watches and jewelry in his general merchandise store, thus begins the basis for Gordon's Jewelry.	

1905	Detroit; Henry Ford sets up a plant to begin manufacturing Ford's own engines and transmissions for their cars. Henry believes autos should be available to the "average" man. Ford's major investor, Alex Malcomson, believes autos should be a luxury for the wealthy. Malcomson "hedges his bets," and founds the Aerocar Co. to build large, luxury automobiles.	(see 1906)
1905	March; shortly after Charles Rockwood's second canal opens, an ocean of Colorado River water is forming in the Salton Sink, and causes a huge washout as it exits. The US government steps in to stop it with a $3 million and 2 year project to protect the Colorado River.	
1905	Grant Oil Tools is established.	
1905	Nestlé merges with the Anglo-Swiss Condensed Milk Co., soon their factories are operating in several nations worldwide.	
1905	Cadillac introduces a "high-powered" four-cylinder automobile.	
1905	UK; Mr. Herbert Austin establishes the Austin Motor Co. Ltd.	
1905	**L. Valentine Pulsifer creates Valspar, the world's first clear varnish. Production begins within two years, and the exceptional quality… and promotional stunts, carry Valspar onward.**	
1905	The first patent for a practical turbocharger (a supercharger driven by exhaust gas) for the internal combustion engine, is granted to Dr. Alfred Büchi, a Swiss engineer.	(see 1915)
1905	June-October; the Wrights make more than forty flights at Huffman Prairie, OH. These all are made in the Wright Flyer III, usually considered the world's first practical airplane. Then on October 5th, Wilbur flies almost 25 miles(40 km) while airborne for thirty-eight minutes. The Wrights are the first to make an aircraft usable, by making it steerable while in flight.	(see 1908)
1905	The Mining and Crushing Machine Department of Allis Chalmers, is now building railroad shovels.	
1905	The Glenn Pool oilfield is discovered in Oklahoma.	
1905	Ringling Bros. Circus acquires a partnership with Adam Forepaugh Sells Shows.	
1905	Holt Mfg. Co. of Stockton, CA, continues field-testing Ben's "crawler" tractor prototypes. This March, Holt's photographer, Charlie Clements notes the undulating motion of the upper portion of the track between the drive sprocket and the front idler wheel, and exclaims that it crawls "like a caterpillar." At first Ben doesn't cotton to the idea of comparing his tractor to a worm, but soon he accepts the idea and the "Caterpillar" name is adopted for his crawler tractors. From Thanksgiving 1904 to end-of-year 1906, Holt builds six steam "crawler" tractor prototypes. The third prototype becomes a "production" unit as it is sold to a Louisiana company for use reclaiming wetlands for sugar cane production.	(see 1906)

1905	Ohio; Mr. Addis Emmet Hull establishes HULL POTTERY in Crooksville, to manufacture useful household products.	(see 1920)
1905	**USA; the very first outdoor BELL SYSTEM coin-operated pay phone is installed in Cincinnati, OH.**	
1905	Jacob D. Cox, Sr., retires and Frank F. Prentiss succeeds him as president of CLEVELAND TWIST DRILL COMPANY.	
1905	Chicago; with their business continuing to grow and needing more space, the Armstrong Brothers buy property at 317 N. Francisco Ave, and build a 100, 000 square foot, three-story brick factory. Their only products are the machine tool holders and related machine tool accessories.	(see 1909)
1905	Ohio; Mr. John F. Byers is killed in an accident this year.	(see 1909) (see 1926)
1905	Rhode Island; the "Alco" and "American Berliet" cars are made by AMERICAN LOCOMOTIVE AUTOMOBILE CO. of Providence.	(see 1908)
1905	Germany; a shipyard electrical engineer, Hermann Foettinger of Hamburg, conceives the fluid coupling, or "torque converter" and "torque multiplier." Foettinger is soon applying his invention to ships, to aid in the smooth engagement and higher torque of the driving propeller.	(see 1919)
1905	Texas; the HAWKINS AUTOMOBILE & GAS ENGINE CO. of Houston build the "Hawkins" automobile this year and next.	
1905	From only 300 a decade ago, there are now approximately 78,000 motor vehicles running all around this great nation of ours. A great number of these are "one-off," homemade, and some of these really aren't bad vehicles at all.	
1905	The AMERICAN MOTOR SLEIGH CO. produces the "American Motor Sleigh" during this year.	
1905	Now, the MARION IRON & BRASS BED CO., of Indiana, becomes involved in experimental truck building.	(see 1910)
1905	Miles, WI; after a few years of rough going, the HEIL RAIL JOINT WELDING CO. shows a small profit this year.	(see 1906)
1905	PA; BANKERS BROTHERS CO. of Pittsburgh, builds the Banker Juvenile Electric, a small electric roadster for children.	
1905	UK; in South London, the COMMERCIAL CAR CO. (COMMER) is founded at Lavender Hill to build commercial vehicles. COMMER soon builds a new factory on Biscot Road in Luton.	(see WWI)
05-'06	Oklahoma; GASO begins in business by making a burner in the garage of one of the founders, in Tulsa.	
1906	Stockton, CA; HOLT MANUFACTURING COMPANY sells their FIRST production steam-powered crawler tractor.	
1906	Stockton, CA; the AURORA ENGINE CO. is founded by Benjamin Holt to develop and build gasoline engines.	(see 1908)
1906	Wisconsin; in a small garage in Waukesha, three mechanics start WAUKESHA MOTOR COMPANY, to build natural gas engines. Some of the first viable applications are in the fledgling Texas oil fields.	
1906	Texas; on October first, the ROSCOE, SNYDER & PACIFIC RAILROAD (RS&P) is chartered.	
1906	VAN BUREN, HECK & MARVIN CO., changes their name to the BUCKEYE TRACTION DITCHER CO., due to the machine's success.	

1906	Henry Ford agrees to outfit all FORD CARS & TRUCKS with FIRESTONE TIRES, as original equipment. When Henry Ford orders 10,000 automobile frames, A. O. SMITH develops the world's first mass production process for assembling frames. Alex Malcomson's AEROCAR begins producing air-cooled Model D and the 45hp, 4 cylinder, water-cooled Model F. Ford protests loudly about Alex's competitive automobile venture, leading Malcomson to sell his interest in FORD MOTOR COMPANY to Henry Ford.		
1906	Both LINK-BELT companies are consolidated into the LINK-BELT COMPANY.		
1906	DAIMLER MANUFACTURING COMPANY of New York City produces the first MERCEDES, and it is built in the USA.		
1906	The TERRY STEAM TURBINE COMPANY is founded.		
1906	UK; the ROLLS-ROYCE COMPANY is formed.		
1906	MORSE begins producing automobile drive chain.		
1906	HELIOS ELECTRIC CO. becomes the PHILADELPHIA BATTERY STORAGE COMPANY (PHILCO).		
1906	USA; under the Anti-Trust Act, the federal government files suit against STANDARD OIL CO.		
1906	The EUREKA STONE CRUSHER COMPANY introduces the first jaw crusher with the overhead eccentric principle of pitman construction.		

1906	Massachusetts; the CONCORD MOTOR CAR CO. is building an electric car to show at the 1907 Boston Auto Show, but fail to show up for it.	
1906	Willis Carrier, an employee of BUFFALO FORGE CO., patents his first device, an Apparatus for Treating Air.	
1906	Mark Honeywell starts the HONEYWELL HEATING SPECIALTY COMPANY, Inc.	
1906	**Charles F. Kettering of NATIONAL CASH REGISTER designs the first cash register with an electric motor.**	
1906	Having migrated west from Oklahoma, W. A. Bechtel is contracting railroad jobs up and down the Pacific coast.	
1906	The Great San Francisco Earthquake destroys BJ Machine works, but Byron Jackson soon rebuilds.	
1906	**William Kellogg develops cornflakes.**	
1906	LEIDECKER TOOL CO. of Marietta, OH, advertises the "Marietta Drilling Machine," a crude type of cable tool rig.	
1906	AUERGESELLSCHAFT, a pioneer in the development of the osmium lamp and the tungsten filament, registers the name Osram for its light bulbs.	

1906	The NOVELTY INCANDESCENT LAMP COMPANY (NILCO) is formed in Pennsylvania, to make novelty lights and refill old bulbs.	
1906	Chicago; EXCELSIOR MOTOR MFG. & SUPPLY COMPANY begins building and selling motorcycles.	(see 1911)
1906	The 17 year old Thomas Fawick goes into business designing and building automobiles, a total of 5 Fawick Flyers (the first four-door cars) are built and sold in, and around Sioux Falls, SD.	(see 1914)
1906	E. R. THOMAS CO. buys BROWN-LIPE's first selective type automobile transmission.	
1906	George Roper buys the TRAHERN PUMP COMPANY a established maker of hand operated water well pumps.	
1906	Overtaking OLDS, BUICK and CADILLAC combined, FORD is the number one US automaker, Henry Ford becomes president and majority owner. Also, REO outsells OLDSMOBILE again this year.	(see 1908)
1906	Dr. Lee DeForest develops his "audion tube," or triode, that amplifies electrical signals, thus he becomes a leader in the radio field.	
1906	ALLIS puts their first steam turbine generator into operation.	

1906	French Battery Company is established in Madison, WI.	
1906	The Blaw Collapsible Steel Centering Co. is formed to make and sell reusable steel forms for concrete.	
1906	Beginning this year for the next 8 years, Eclipse is selling a 16' diameter windmill.	
1906	Albert Fuller invests $65 and begins modifying factory made brushes he has bought, and designs a few of his own. In a few years, Albert has salesmen all over the US, and the rest is Fuller Brush history.	
1906	Engineer and inventor, Charles Cotta, establishes Cotta Transmission Company.	
1906	Castrol introduces their first oil specifically for internal combustion engines.	
1906	The world's first successful typewriter is introduced by the Rose Typewriter Company.	
1906	At Ormond Beach, FL, a Stanley Steamer is clocked at 127.6 miles per hour (204.16 kph)… WOW!!!!!!	
1906	South Bend, IN; the South Bend Lathe Works is established to manufacture and market lathes and other associated metal machining equipment.	
1906	Galveston; the Grasso family starts a shrimp fishing and processing business, eventually to be Grasso Oilfield Services, Inc.	
1906	In Alessandria, Italy, Angelo Panelli opens his small electromechanical shop to maintain water pumps and irrigation systems.	
1906	Denver, CO; for a fee of $1, the world's first driver's license is issued.	
1906	Reginald Fessenden broadcasts voice and music of song on radio waves for the first time.	
1906	Germany; physician Aloysius "Alois" Alzheimer describes "Alzheimer's Disease" after extensive treatment, evaluation, and later autopsying of a fifty year old female patient.	
1906	Early 1900s; the Harris Automatic Press Co. introduces many printing innovations such as the first commercially successful offset lithographic press, and the first two-color offset printing press.	
1906	The Federated Boys Clubs originate when the fifty-three independent Boys Clubs now operating determine that a national organization is needed.	
1906	San Francisco; Ruben and Austin Hills, incorporate their business as Hills Bros. Coffee.	(see 1984)
1906	Albany, NY; Dec. 20; a utility holding company, American Gas & Electric Co. is incorporated; they soon acquire their first their first utility company.	
1906	Germany; Opel begins making their own automobiles. Late this year, the 1,000th Opel vehicle is produced.	(see 1909)
1906	Berliet sells license to manufacture his automobile (similar to a Mercedes) to the American Locomotive Company (ALCO)	
1906	Wayne Oil Tank Co. moves from kerosene to gasoline pumps.	
1906	Cadillac now claims to be the world's largest automobile manufacturer, and probably is.	
1906	George Selden, by flexing and twisting US patent laws, is now receiving a royalty of 1.25% of the selling price of almost every automobile built in the US	
1906	Michigan; the "Aerocar" motorcar is being built by the Aerocar Co. of Detroit, this year through 1908.	
1906	Howard Hughes, Sr., now begins experimenting with his idea of a rotary drill bit using two tooth-covered cones. This would pulverize rock formations, instead of scraping them as they drilled.	(see 1908)
1906	The Cullman family establishes the United Cigar Manufacturers Company.	

1906	Young brothers Tom and Jack Loffland go into business together operating a machine shop on Marietta Street in Woodsfield, OH. They soon trade a team of sorrel horses for an interest in their first lease, but the brothers really had more interest in the drilling equipment, than the oil. The LOFFLAND BROTHERS COMPANY is now started.	(see 1909)
1906	Jan 30; livestock rancher members of the AMERICAN STOCK GROWERS ASSN. merge with NATIONAL LIVESTOCK ASSOCIATION creating the AMERICAN NATIONAL LIVESTOCK ASSN., later becoming the AMERICAN CATTLEMAN'S ASSOCIATION.	
1906	The "Big Five" or the "Beef Trust" as it is also known, consisting of Armour, Cudahy, Morris, Swift and Wilson are investigated by the US Federal Trade Commission and are found to "jointly or separately hold controlling interest in 574 companies, minority interest in 95 others, and undetermined interest in another 93. That's a total of 762 firms producing or dealing in 775 different commodities, mostly food and food products.	
1906	A gasoline-powered, self-propelled, fire-pumper is introduced by WATEROUS. This pumper has an engine to power the pump, and another engine to propel the truck.	
1906	Oscar Kjellburg is granted his first patent, a second is soon issued for overhead welding with coated electrodes.	(see 1920)
1906	Coming from Italy, and knowing not one word of English, twelve year old Joseph Zeppa arrives in New York City.	(see 1931)
1906	H. W. Williams, a salesman for HART-PARR is said to have coined the word "tractor;" feeling the phrase "traction engine" is too long and cumbersome.	
1906	Missouri; in St. Louis, the AUTOBUGGY MANUFACTURING CO. is building and selling the A. B. C. motorcar.	(see 1908)
1906	England; the 17,900 ton *HMS Dreadnought* is christened by King Edward III. Built in only 100 days, this is the first ever really true battleship. The steam turbines can drive this monster at 21 knots. The price tag was two million pounds sterling.	
1906	Mishawaka, IN; through 1910, the "American Simplex" motorcar is being built by SIMPLEX MOTOR CAR COMPANY.	
1906	The $200 VICTOR Victrola phonograph is intended only for wealthy customers.	
1906	The first "sonar" like device is invented by Lewis Nixon.	
1906	New Jersey; John M. Landsen and the LANDSEN CO. of Newark, is now producing electric powered wagons (trucks).	(see 1912)
1906	Wisconsin; the HEIL RAIL JOINT WELDING CO. in Miles, experiences more hard times and has to be liquidated to repay investors. Later this year, the HEIL COMPANY is organized.	(see 1910)
1906	California; having recently bought the KERN COUNTY FOUNDRY & MACHINE WORKS, Charles H. Allison, A. J. Crites, Bill Coleman, F. Sprague and C. A. Barlow now operate it as ALLISON MACHINERY.	(see 1907)
1906	New York; in Buffalo, the Babcock, an electric car is built by the BABCOCK ELECTRIC CARRIAGE CO. for the next six years.	
1906	Sweden; Munktell's first piece of road construction equipment is a steam-powered road roller. A very early type of 360-degree-rotating steam-powered excavator is designed and Munktell builds a few.	(see 1913) (see 1914)
1906	The AMERICAN MOTOR CAR CO. of Indianapolis is manufacturing the American Underslung motorcar, on through 1914.	
1906	FIAT now has 2,500 employees, and bring out their 5 ton model truck. FIAT buys the ANSALDI factory, which produces light, four cylinder engines.	(see 1911)

1906	For the next 20 years, George Dorris' DORRIS MOTOR CAR CO. of St. Louis is producing the "Dorris" motorcar, as successor to the "St. Louis" motorcar, as arrived in Dallas back in 1899.	
1906	Philadelphia; the DRAGON AUTOMOBILE/MOTOR CO. produces the "Dragon" motorcar on through 1908.	
1907	January; GULF OIL CORPORATION is formed, as an expansion of the J. M. GUFFEY PETROLEUM CO. and GULF REFINING OF TEXAS.	
1907	Alphonso Plomb & two associates establish PLOMB TOOLS.	
1907	BECKWITH MACHINERY COMPANY is founded in Pennsylvania.	
1907	Steve Briggs and Harry Stratton meet, and almost immediately, BRIGGS & STRATTON is formed.	
1907	**Ole Evinrude (1877-1934) builds the first commercially successful outboard motor.**	
1907	Ruben Baker develops a casing shoe that literally revolutionizes cable tool drilling.	
1907	John's younger brother, James F. Lincoln, joins LINCOLN ELECTRIC, as a salesman.	
1907	THOMASVILLE CHAIR CO. is taken over by T. J. Finch and his brother, D. F. The Finches are timber farmers and lumber dealers, and hold a big chunk of TCC stock they received in payment for lumber, so they buy the remainder, and T. J. is president.	(see 1908)
1907	Ohio; the GALION IRON WORKS CO. is established in Galion by David Charles Boyd.	(see 1911)
1907	ARMINGTON ELECTRIC HOIST COMPANY is formed.	
1907	AUTOCAR is now focusing on trucks, but continues to produce a few cars.	
1907	Sven Wingqvist, a young Swedish engineer, designs the first self-aligning ball bearing; shortly afterward, SKF is founded in Sweden.	
1907	Edward M. Murphy founds the OAKLAND MOTOR CAR CO., in Pontiac, MI.	
1907	Father and son officially become partners, and CHRIS D. SCHRAMM & SON is established.	
1907	The DALLAS-FT. WORTH INTERURBAN transit system starts in business.	
1907	LEE C. MOORE establishes his business.	
1907	June 1; Mr. Robert Driscoll purchases a large tract of land out west of Corpus Christi, TX.	
1907	The WILLIAMS BROTHERS start business in Tulsa, OK.	
1907	F. L. Maytag introduces a wooden tub washing machine, it is so successful that soon he is only building washing machines.	
1907	Halsey W. Taylor, a plant Superintendent for PACKARD MOTOR CAR CO. notices dysentery caused by bad water spreading through the workers. Due to his personal experiences, Taylor is inspired to dedicate his life to providing a safe drink of water in public places.	
1907	THERMOS GmbH sells the Thermos trademark and manufacturing rights to three companies; one is the AMERICAN THERMOS BOTTLE CO. of Brooklyn, NY.	
1907	HENDEE MANUFACTURING CO. introduces the first V-twin engine powered Indian Motocycle.	(see 1913)
1907	Producing 8,820 cars this year, BUICK leads the US auto production.	
1907	Oil is found in great quantity in Persia, or Iran.	
1907	Leo Baekeland invents the first synthetic plastic, called Bakelite.	
1907	Charles M. Hall's aluminum company now has bauxite mines, a refinery and 3 smelters, thus he names it… ALUMINUM COMPANY OF AMERICA (ALCOA).	
1907	Louis Chevrolet begins working with Billy Durant's GM Buick Racing Team.	
1907	For a couple of years, the ALBANY AUTOMOBILE CO. of Albany Indiana is producing the Albany motocar.	

1907	Cleveland, OH; Garrett Morgan opens his own shop repairing sewing machines and such. This is just the first of several businesses Morgan will establish.	
1907	James Beckwith forms BECKWITH MACHINERY COMPANY, in Pennsylvania, as a manufacturers' representative for construction machinery and supplies.	
1907	SHELL TRANSPORT of England merges with ROYAL DUTCH PETROLEUM of the Netherlands, now ROYAL DUTCH SHELL.	
1907	Three young Texas entrepreneurs pass up a chance to buy the Coca-Cola franchise for Missouri, and opt to open a store in Dallas as "a new and exclusive shopping place for fashionable women." Herbert Marcus, his sister Carrie Marcus Neiman, and her husband A. L. Neiman are all only in their twenties.	
1907	Walter A. Sheaffer designs his first writing pen, it has a rubber bladder to hold the ink.	
1907	**The CRESCENT TOOL COMPANY introduces the world's first known adjustable wrench.**	
1907	Hartford, WI; the first Kissel trucks and cars are built by KISSEL KAR CO.	
1907	Seattle, WA; Jim Casey borrows $100 from a friend, then he and Claude Ryan establish AMERICAN MESSENGER CO.	(see 1913)
1907	Germany; Arthur Korn invents the Photo-Telegraph.	
1907	Michigan; PONTIAC SPRING AND WAGON WORKS produces their first motorcars this year.	(see 1908)
1907	M. D. Anderson, financial officer of Anderson Clayton & Co., moves from Tennessee to Houston, to open a branch office.	(see 1939)
1907	July 8; on the roof of the New York Theatre, Florenz Ziegfeld stages his first "Ziegfeld Follies."	

1907	The first electric-powered washing machine is designed by Alva J. Fisher, and manufactured by the HUNLEY MACHINE CORP. of Chicago. Fisher's "Thor" washer is a wooden drum into which clothes and hot water are placed and "tumbled" clean; the drum turns 8 revolutions in one direction, then reverses and turns 8 revolutions in the opposite direction, and so on.	
1907	The FLEXIBLE STEEL LACING COMPANY (Flexco) is founded.	
1907	**The first commercial bus service in Texas begins operating between Colorado City and Snyder.**	
1907	England; BSA produces their first automobile prototype.	
1907	By now LAYNE is incorporated, with branches in four states, and soon to be in nine more.	(see 1912)
1907	Another first for WATEROUS, as they introduce the first single-engine, self-propelled, fire truck.	
1907	December; a group exploring for water in the Comodora Rivadavia area of Argentina accidently discover crude oil.	(see 2007)
1907	Bad investment in oilfields in Texas and in Borneo almost bankrupt SHELL, and although it is about twice the size of ROYAL DUTCH, the two officially merge, with ROYAL DUTCH as 60% owner. SHELL survives and within 12 months, Henri Deterding turns the combination into a profitable business concern.	(see 1919)
1907	Ohio; the AMERICAN METAL WHEEL & AUTO CO. of Toledo is building an electric powered two-seater car for children only.	
1907	Texas; San Marcos Academy, a preparatory school, is established in San Marcos.	
1907	France; brothers Auguste and Louis Lumière invent color photography.	

1907	France; engineer Paul Cornu (1881-1944) builds the first helicopter to perform a manned, free flight. Although Cornu's 24-horsepower twin-rotor machine is very important, this particular design is impractical, and is soon abandoned.	(see 1939)
1907	California; in Bakersfield, ALLISON MACHINERY is now ALLISON & COLEMAN IRON WORKS.	(see 1920)
1907	Massachusetts; S. R. BAILEY & CO. of Amesbury, are producing the Bailey electric auto, and will do so until 1915.	
1907	VACUUM OIL, STANDARD OIL, NEW YORK CENTRAL RR and PENNSYLVANIA RR, are all indicated for violations of Interstate Commerce laws, dealing with unlawful rates while shipping 228 cars of their products.	(see 1911)
1907	New York; through 1909, the Allen-Kingston motorcar is built by the ALLEN-KINGSTON MOTOR CAR CO. of Kingston.	
1908	In Dearborn, MI, Henry Ford invents and utilizes the first "moving" assembly line for automobiles. Ford's line is based on the moving lines that packing plants use for hanging beef. Henry then introduces the Model T, the first automobile ever assembled on a moving assembly line. The Model T is also a "flexible fuel" car: it can run on gasoline, ethanol, or a mixture of both.	
1908	Frank Schwinn is born.	
1908	**J. W. Geiger and W. Muller invent the Geiger counter.**	
1908	Andrews, TX, is founded.	
1908	Under the Finch's management, THOMASVILLE CHAIR CO. makes a profit of $91,522 this year.	(see 1909)
1908	ROLLWAY BEARINGS is founded.	
1908	Baldwin Reinhold and Walter Abegg form the ABEGG & REINHOLD CO.	
1908	The MINNEAPOLIS STEEL & MACHINERY CO. start building the TWIN CITY TRACTORS.	
1908	Texas; June 12; the 31 miles of ROSCOE SNYDER & PACIFIC tracks open from Roscoe to Snyder.	
1908	Robert & Louis Hupp begin producing their own cars in Detroit... HUPMOBILE.	
1908	September; GENERAL MOTORS is organized, incorporating BUICK MOTOR COMPANY; GM then acquires RAPID MOTOR VEHICLE CO. and some other Michigan based automotive firms. With David D. Buick's assistance, Albert Champion founds A-C SPARK PLUG CO. In November, GM buys OLDS MOTOR WORKS. The 52-year-old David Buick severs all ties with the company bearing his name and, with his wife and son, moves back to Detroit. Charles Nash now becomes president and general manager of BUICK MOTOR CAR CO.	
1908	FISHER BODY COMPANY is incorporated by Albert, Fred, and Charles Fisher in Detroit.	
1908	At some earlier date, HALL-SCOTT MOTOR CAR CO. of Berkley, CA, produces its first gasoline engine.	
1908	TERRY STEAM TURBINE COMPANY begins building vertical turbines driving forced-draft fans on US Navy destroyers and the new torpedo boats.	
1908	**Frank Seiberling invents a machine to cut grooves into rubber tires. Previously, all rubber tires were smooth, providing absolutely no traction at all.**	(see 1921)
1908	The 70 year old Count Von Zeppelin's second (first successful) airship debuts, is short-lived, but has a good flight.	
1908	The ACME MOTOR BUGGY MFG. CO. of Columbia Heights Minnesota produces the Acme motor buggy for three years or so.	
1908	Having brought John Secor into their company some years earlier, RUMELY begin building on a prototype oil-burning tractor.	

1908	J. W. Earl establishes the Earl Automobile Works, making customized parts and accessories for cars.	
1908	**Rotary drilling is introduced in California.**	
1908	**Schramm builds their first compressor, a gasoline engine modified to compress air for a customer to use in a marble quarry.**	
1908	Oil is discovered in Persia, soon the Anglo Persian Oil Co. is formed.	(see 1954)

	1908	Diamond Horseshoe Company begins making horseshoes, later it becomes Diamond Tool & Horseshoe Company.	
	1908	J. C. Penny's four "Golden Rule Stores" gross $218,432 this year.	(see 1909)
	1908	Texas; at Goose Creek, Howard Hughes, Sr., first tests his dual-cone rotary bit.	(see 1909)
	1908	**W. H. "Boss" Hoover buys the patent for a "suction sweeper," and starts in the vacuum business.**	
	1908	Marmon Car Co. begins using inline engines, up to now, all Marmons were powered by a air-cooled V-4 engine.	(see 1911)
	1908	Columbus, IN; banker-investor W. G. Irwin hires Clessie L. Cummins to maintain the family automobile, and soon sets him up in his own garage business.	
	1908	*Nathan B. Stubblefield patents his invention to put radios in horseless carriages, making him "the father of the automobile radio."*	(see 1928)

1908	*The gyrocompass is invented by Elmer A. Sperry.*	
1908	In Providence, the Alco automobile is now being built by the American Locomotive Co. (ALCO) and through 1913.	
1908	**On October 30, Ruby Blevins (Patsy Montana) is born in Hope, AR. Ruby grows up with her ten brothers.**	(see 1996)
1908	**In Germany, Rosenbauer introduces the first gasoline engine powered fire-fighting pump.**	
1908	Amon G. Carter Sr. and an investor buy the Ft. Worth Telegram and merge it with the *Star*, making the *Ft. Worth Star-Telegram*.	
1908	Albuquerque, NM; the Galles family opens Galles Motor Company, their first automobile dealership.	
1908	By the end of the year, Alex Malcomson's Aerocar Co. is flat broke, he has lost a small fortune, and he returns to his lucrative coal business.	
1908	Three new 1907 Cadillac Model "K" single-cylinder engine autos are driven 50 miles (80 km), then disassembled. The key parts are mixed up, then reassembled, and driven 50 more miles. Cadillac wins England's Dewar Trophy, rewarding parts interchangeability.	
1908	**Wilbur Wright takes one of his employees along for a ride; this is the world's first airplane passenger flight.**	(see 1909)
1908	Overland Automotive Co. of Indianapolis is bought by John North Willis, who renames it Willys-Overland Motors, Inc. Sales of the "Runabout" grows; Overland then buys the Pope-Toledo auto manufacturing plant in Toledo, moving production of the "Runabout" there.	(see 1940s)
1908	September 17; Orville Wright, while demonstrating the Wright Military Flyer to the US Army at Ft. Myer Virginia, crashes after a propeller splits, wrecking the airplane. Wright's passenger, Lt. Thomas Selfridge (a colleague of Glenn Curtiss' in Alex Graham Bell's Aerial Experiment Association), is killed and Orville is seriously injured. Selfridge is the first known aviation fatality.	(see 1909)
1908	Ringling Bros. Circus buys out the Barnum & Bailey Circus.	
1908	UK; October 16; Mr. Samuel Franklin Cody, of Birdville, TX, makes the first ever sustained flight in Great Britain. Cody has been testing his "powered aeroplane" for several months in this area.	

1908	Illinois; in Springfield, the BAKER MANUFACTURING COMPANY is established.	(see 1918)
1908	Stockton, CA; having converted their "Caterpillar" from steam to gasoline power, HOLT MANUFACTURING CO. is now building and selling track-type tractors powered by their own Aurora gasoline engines. Twenty-eight of these new 40 hp gasoline-powered crawlers go to work on the 233-mile Los Angeles aqueduct water project. HOLT soon introduces a 75 hp crawler tractor.	
1908	Oklahoma; TULSA RIG, REEL & MFG. CO. begin supplying wooden drilling derricks and rigs during the boom.	(see 1911)
1908	The US Congress passes a "employers liability law" giving compensation for certain government employees in case of accidental injury.	
1908	Detroit; as the PONTIAC SPRING & WAGON WORKS merges with OAKLAND, the Pontiac marque is dropped.	(see 1926)
1908	Illinois; Mr. W. S. Darley begins building and selling fire-fighting equipment in Chicago.	(see 2011)
1908	In Muller vs. Oregon, the US Supreme Court upholds the Oregon law regulating women's work hours.	
1908	The five Jonas brothers immigrate from Hungary to the USA and set up three shops, where they master the art of taxidermy and increase its popularity greatly.	
1908	COMMERCIAL CREDIT & INVESTMENT is established.	(see 1915)
1908	In St. Louis, the A. B. C. motorcar is now built by the A. B. C. MOTOR VEHICLE MANUFACTURING CO. and on through 1910.	
1908	Texas; IDECO opens their plant in Beaumont, and begin building and selling oil field drilling and production equipment.	(see 1944)
1908	USA; the "active stabilizer," a gyroscope for use on ships, is created by Elmer Sperry.	(see 1912)
1908	Swiss textile engineer Jacques E. Brandenberger (1872-1954) invents cellophane.	
1908	In Kansas City, MO, the AMERICAN AUTOMOBILE MANUFACTURING CO. is founded.	(see 1910)
1908	Ohio; the BYRIDER ELECTRIC AUTO COMPANY of Cleveland, is producing a small, 2 person, electric car, selling for $1,800.	
1908	A high-wheeler type of horseless carriage, the "Sears Motor Buggy," built by LINCOLN MOTOR CAR WORKS, is now being sold by mail order through the SEARS & ROEBUCK catalog, and delivered to the nearest railroad siding for the buyer.	(see 1912)
1909	January; GENERAL MOTORS buys 50% of OAKLAND MOTOR CAR COMPANY. Edward Murphy dies this summer; then GM acquires full control of OAKLAND.	
1909	*The first pin & box connections are used on a rotary drill string.*	
1909	The Roscoe Snyder & Pacific Railroad opens its short line from Snyder to Fluvanna, TX.	
1909	HOLT MANUFACTURING moves all tractor production from Stockton, CA, to a facility in Peoria, IL.	
1909	The ANGLO-PERSIAN OIL CO. is formed, later to become BRITISH PETROLEUM (BP).	
1909	Texas; out in Callahan county, the *CROSS PLAINS REVIEW* is founded, the only newspaper on the banks of Turkey Creek.	
1909	J. L. Hudson, of department store fame, finances an automobile company. The HUDSON MOTOR CAR CO. acquires the former AEROCAR plant at Beaufait and Mack Streets in Detroit for use as the HUDSON factory, and the first HUDSON auto is assembled there.	
1909	Oil City, LA; Howard R. Hughes Sr. introduces the first roller cutter bit; dramatically improving rotary drilling. SHARP-HUGHES TOOL COMPANY is formed, as Howard Hughes, Sr., partners with Walter B. Sharp.	

1909	Having patented their drill bit, Howard Hughes, Sr., and his partner Walter B. Sharp leave the drilling business, and build their Sharp-Hughes Tool Co. factory in Houston to manufacture the bits. They now lease their drill bits to drilling contractors on a "per hole" basis, at the rate of $30,000 per well.	(see 1912)
1909	Lincoln Electric produces its first electric welding set (motor and generator).	
1909	Having acquired Bard Lumber. & Mfg. Co., the Finch brothers now almost double 1908's profits. They now start their own machine shop, build a three story building for upholstery and wrapping operations, as well as a very large veneer plant. Now that sounds like vertical integration coming on.	(see 1914)
1909	Armington becomes Euclid Crane & Hoist Company.	
1909	*Charles Cotta invents and patents the concept of "constant mesh gearing," to help prevent the grinding of gears when changing.*	
1909	Out in West Texas, the city of Big Spring buys the first motorized fire engine in the entire Lone Star state.	
1909	The Western Auto Company is founded.	
1909	There are now six of J. C. Penny's "Golden Rule Stores," and this year they gross $310,066.	(see 1910)
1909	*Warner Gear produces the first manual automobile transmission.*	
1909	Oklahoma; Williams Brothers is founded.	
1909	**This year 17,771 Model T Fords are sold.**	
1909	Billy Durant tries to buy out Ford for $9. 5 million, but lacks sufficient backing - the bankers turned him down.	
1909	Texas; Ford Motor Co. opens an office with 2 employees in Dallas. In a couple of years they will begin manufacturing cars here.	
1909	Frank Poor and brothers start the Hygrade Incandescent Lamp Co. to manufacture and sell the new carbon filament light bulbs.	
1909	Ohio; the Advance Motor Vehicle Co. of Miamisburg is making and selling the "Advance" motorcar for the next three years.	
1909	June; twenty-two-year-old Alice Ramsey, a housewife and mother from New Jersey, drives across the USA from Manhattan to San Francisco. Alice is the first woman to complete the 3,800 mile trip. Only 152 miles of the route are paved, and it takes her 59 days.	
1909	Kansas; two railroad mechanics in Goodland quit their jobs to work on a rotary-winged aircraft. Their business venture fails, but they patent a predecessor to the helicopter.	
1909	June 4; Austin, TX; the Lone Star Gas Company files for a charter with the state to begin the gamble of becoming the state's first major natural gas distributing company. The charter is granted and Lone Star goes to work building a pipeline from a gas field in Clay County to Ft. Worth and Dallas. Lone Star is pioneering the use of long-distance natural gas pipelines.	(see 1910)
1909	Everett Sawyer joins the Cushmans and production is shifted to farm engines.	
1909	John H. Victor (a career inventor) and brother Joseph, establish the Victor Mfg. & Gasket Co., their copper-asbestos gaskets are superior to all others.	
1909	Copp Bros. Ltd. is reorganized as Arm Co. of Canada, a subsidiary of the American Arm Co.	
1909	Maloney/Crawford starts up in business.	
1909	Timken's first overseas activity is to license Vickers to make bearings under the name British Timken.	
1909	At Santa Ana, CA, Glenn L. Martin flies a plane for the first time. This plane is made of bamboo and silk.	

1909	In July, GM buys CADILLAC AUTOMOBILE CO., Henry Leland and his son Wilfred stay on to run the CADILLAC DIVISION of GM, until 1917. CHAMPION IGNITION COMPANY (later AC Spark Plug) joins GM. GM acquires RELIANCE MOTOR TRUCK COMPANY. After over 16,000 have been sold, the very last CADILLAC single-cylinder engine car is produced.	
1909	Garrett Morgan is now making sewing machines and equipment and has 32 employees in a tailor shop using his machines.	
1909	ROSE TYPEWRITER changes its name to the STANDARD TYPEWRITER COMPANY.	
1909	Schweinfurt, Germany; BALL BEARINGS WORKS GEORG SCHAFER & CO. merges with FIRST AUTOMATIC CAST STEEL BALL FACTORY, formerly known as FRIEDRICH FISCHER COMPANY.	
1909	California; JOHNSTON PUMP CO. begins producing their vertical pumps.	
1909	**USA; the electric toaster is invented.**	
1909	WISCONSIN produces their first air-cooled engines.	
1909	San Antonio; INGRAM ROLLERS is founded; it is closely associated with ACME IRON WORKS CO.; another Ingram family business.	
1909	The HUBLEY MFG. CO. begins making cast iron toys, often models of actual vehicles or equipment.	
1909	The French aviation pioneer, Clément Ader, says, "Whoever will be master of the sky, will be master of the world."	
1909	Tom and Jack Loffland acquire their first complete drilling rig, a steam-powered STARR cable tool rig, capable of drilling to 900 feet. Following the various oil boomtowns, Tom soon moves to Tulsa, and some years later, Jack will move to Ft. Worth, TX.	
1909	SANGER BROS. is the first department store in Texas to install escalators, probably in the Dallas store.	
1909	Canada; WATEROUS ENGINE WORKS acquires the SEAGRAVE FIRE APPLIANCE MFG. CO. of Walkerville, Ontario.	(see 1927)
1909	Berlin, Germany; American aviator Orville Wright lands at Tempelhof Fields, where Prussian Military once exercised.	(see 1912) (see 1923) (see 2008)
1909	Maryland; at College Park, Wilbur Wright establishes ARMY AIRFIELD; a century hence it will still be a going concern.	(see 1910)
1909	Plymouth, OH; J. D. Fate organizes the PLYMOUTH TRUCK CO., to build Plymouth branded motor trucks.	(see 1915)
1909	Texas; the SPOETZL BREWERY begins brewing and marketing their Shiner Beer, right here in Shiner, TX.	
1909	Out on the west coast around Los Angeles, wooden board tracks for car and motorcycle racing first appear. Soon these tracks are springing up all over the country.	
1909	Chicago; ARMSTRONG BROS. builds a forge shop, beginning their own forging operation. They then introduce a line of drop-forged hand wrenches.	(see 1974)
1909	Ohio; BYERS now has a 100 psi, 25 HP steam locomotive powered crane, the Model 328, in production.	(see 1914)
1909	There are about 2,000 tractors working on American farms today, and 25,000,000 horses and mules.	(see 1920)
1909	USA; the first TWIN-CITY farm tractors are now being marketed.	

F. E. SHAILOR.
ELECTRIC HEATER.
APPLICATION FILED JULY 19, 1909.

950,058.   Patented Feb. 22, 1910.

WITNESSES:

INVENTOR
FRANK E. SHAILOR.

1909	USA; due to the Sherman Antitrust Act, the Supreme Court orders the "break up" of the STANDARD OIL trust.		(see 1911)
1909	UK; Welshman David Lloyd George, future Prime Minister, introduces the "Old Age Pension."		(see 1948)
		1909	Indiana; the INDIANAPOLIS MOTOR SPEEDWAY CORP. is founded on the 9th of February. A 2 ½ mile (4 km) asphalt and crushed stone track is built to use for auto testing and racing. On August 19, automotive innovator Louis Schwitzer drives a Stoddard-Dayton car to win the first race (of only two laps) on the new track at its inaugural three-day meet.	(see 1911)
		1909	Germany; selling for less than 4,000 marks (about ½ the price of a luxury auto), OPEL builds and markets the OPEL 4/8, commonly known as the "Doctor's Car," (Doktorwagen) because of its reliability and robustness.	(see 1910)
		1909	The BROC CARRIAGE & WAGON CO. offers several models of electric cars with a 1 HP motor, running up to 24 mph, from their plants in Cleveland, OH, and Saginaw, MI. These are built for several years.	
		1909	Detroit; the ABBOTT-DETROIT MOTOR CAR CO. produces the Abbott-Detroit car for the next half dozen years.	
1909	Illinois; having watched their mother and sisters hand-washing the piles of family clothes, A. W and Silas Altorfer of Roanoke, build a power washing machine. This year the ALTORFER BROS. COMPANY is established to build and market the machines, basically just a wooden tub mounted to a bench with wooden "fingers" or paddles to wash the clothes, powered by a gasoline engine.		(see 1912)
1910	Andreas Stihl puts saw teeth on a roller chain and hooks these to an engine and invents the chain saw, it performs well, but it weighs 147 pounds. *"Yeah Slim, this saw'll make a man of ya!"*		
1910	BUCYRUS acquires VULCAN STEAM SHOVEL CO., then purchases manufacturing rights for the HEYWORTH-NEWMAN dragline excavator.		(see 1912)
1910	N. G. GUIBERSON begins in business.		
1910	Cross Plains, TX, has a population of about six hundred.		
1910	HUDSON is now turning out a good number of cars, all powered by either Atlas engines from Indianapolis, or Buda engines made in Harvey, IL. HUDSON introduces their "fluid clutch," which remains unique to Hudson through 1954.		
1910	February 10; near Hereford, TX, after spending months digging a well, today, D. L. McDonald uses a steam-powered pump to pump water to irrigate land he is wanting to sell. This Pennsylvania native, ex-pharmacist, land speculator, and car salesman, now becomes the "Father of Irrigation" on the Texas high plains.		
1910	Charles Nash takes over when Will Durant loses control of GM.		
1910	Louis and Edward, the Strohacker brothers found STRUCTO TOY CO. in Chicago.		
1910	Detroit; the first FEDERAL trucks are now being built.		
1910	ENERPAC's originator starts by making water pumps for Model Ts, then in the 1920s he brings out the first known hydraulic jacks.		
1910	April 29; LONE STAR GAS COMPANY's pipeline reaches Dallas. The mass marketing of natural gas is working very well, as about 15,000 area customers are on line by end of this year.		
1910	Fred S. Duesenberg designs the MAYTAG-MASON automobile.		
1910	*This year there are 52,500 bales of cotton harvested in Callahan County, TX.*		
1910	The Model B, the first RUMELY OILPULL tractor is introduced. Its guaranteed to burn all grades of kerosene under all conditions, while handling all rated loads.		

1910	*Scientific American* magazine's July issue states, "To affirm that the airplane is going to revolutionize the future, is to be guilty of the wildest exaggeration."	(see 1911)
	"Yeah Slim, thet's tha sci–in–ti–fik explanation!!!"	
1910	PETTERS LTD. is founded in England.	
1910	The first trans-continental horseback trip by a woman, Nan Aspinwall, is made from San Francisco to New York City, leaving on September 1 of this year and arriving on July 8, 1911.	
1910	Mr. Ole Evinrude begins to commercially produce outboard motors.	
1910	HALL-SCOTT MOTOR CAR CO., formed a few years ago, now produces its first gasoline-engine powered rail car.	
1910	California; near Los Angeles, the Lakeview gusher blows out, estimates of rates up to 100,000 BOPD, with a total of about 9 million barrels released before the well is brought under control.	
1910	Steve Briggs patents his "gas engine ignition," and soon BRIGGS & STRATTON is incorporated.	
1910	The UNIVERSAL CRUSHER COMPANY is the successor to the EUREKA STONE CRUSHER CO.	
1910	Byron L. Smith and four friends found ILLINOIS TOOL WORKS (ITW).	
1910	**A. O. SMITH is now the world's largest manufacturer of automobile frames.**	
1910	Twenty-year-old Anthony Fokker builds his first plane, "The Spin," which is actually made from a plane a friend had already built.	
1910	The Longren flyer, the first Kansas built plane is flown.	
1910	**Mechanical domestic refrigeration equipment first appears.**	
1910	BUICK places an order with MOGUL METAL for 10,000 of the replicable die-cast conn rod bearings to be used in the new Buick-10.	
1910	E. D. ETNYRE & CO. introduces its horse-drawn street flusher wagon with riveted tank and engine powered water pump.	
1910	J. C. Penny's fourteen "GOLDEN RULE STORES" gross a total of $662,331 this year.	(see 1911)
1910	MADSEN IRON WORKS begins business in Los Angeles, building asphalt batch plants and other road-building equipment.	
1910	The first talking motion picture is demonstrated by Thomas A. Edison.	(see 1927)
1910	Robert Wood Johnson dies.	
1910	Already successful at processing and marketing salt, MORTON SALT COMPANY is now incorporated in Chicago.	
1910	**There are about 250 different brands of motorcycles now being built in the USA.**	
1910	SEARS, ROEBUCK, & COMPANY purchases the DAVID BRADLEY MANUFACTURING CO.	(see 1931)
1910	Brothers Rodney and Alfred Marchant begin manufacturing mechanical calculators, and soon incorporate into the MARCHANT CALCULATING MACHINE CO.	
1910	Legislation is authorized by the US Congress to set aside land as "Naval Petroleum Reserves."	(see 1912)
1910	KONE begins business as an electrical repair shop in Finland, with a license to import GRAHAM BROTHERS elevators.	
1910	August; ROYAL DUTCH SHELL discovers Malaysia's first crude oil field, and in a few years builds the first refinery there. This year they also begin marketing lubricants in Venezuela.	
1910	The LAYNE PUMPS for irrigation are now widely available, but not cheap.	(see 1912)
1910	KISSEL KAR now begins building and marketing a five ton capacity truck.	
1910	After making an exhaustive study of the industry from 1900 to 1908, *MOTOR MAGAZINE* reports that 502 companies have been started to build automobiles, of which 302 of them have failed.	

Girl Who Crossed U. S. On Horseback

July 13 – 1911
THE KANSAS CITY POST—5 Cents a Week, by Mail or Carrier

NAN J. ASPINWALL

1910	**The first dump-trucks are built, using a hand-cranked winch to raise the bed.**	
1910	Parkersburg, WV; Herbert McGinnis begins publishing the Oil Man's magazine, *The National Oil Journal*. The magazine carries news of the area's petroleum industry activities and technical articles to a nationwide readership.	
1910	Anonima Lombarda Fabbrica Automobili (ALFA) takes over the factory where Alexandre Darracq builds his engines and vehicles.	
1910	US lumber production is now 44.56 BILLION board feet per year.	
1910	Chicago; the AERO SHEET METAL WORKS is established.	
1910	A moving picture is made in Hollywood, California; the start of the Hollywood movie industry. The first ever talking motion picture is made this year, as well.	(see 1920)
1910	With the US Patent Office, HOLT MANUFACTURING CO. registers the CATERPILLAR name as a trade-mark.	
1910	John Endebrock sees the final days of the horse-drawn wagons fast approaching and the future lies in building "truck trailers," an almost unknown concept at this time. So, he concentrates on building a "hauling vehicle" that can be pulled after a Model T car.	(see 1915)
1910	The FRICK CLOCK CO. is sold to F. F. LANDIS, who continues this product line until 1937, as Landis Program Clock Company.	(see 1937)
1910	US farmers are now clearing forests at the rate of 13 ½ square miles (8,640 acres) per day.	
1910	Mexico; this nation's first oil strike first oil strike is near Tampico on the Gulf Coast.	
1910	After a number of owners and name changes of KELLY, MORGAN & CO., it now becomes ARMSTRONG MFG. COMPANY.	
1910	**This year, for the first time, kerosene sales are surpassed by gasoline sales.**	(see 1919)
1910	Having wed in 1901, Alfred Rowe and his wife and four children move back to England to live. He leaves the RO Ranch in the hands of a very capable resident manager. From his acreage, Rowe recently laid out the town site for McLean, TX.	(see 1912)
1910	The US now has 234,000 miles (374,400 km) of railroad track; just replacing the old cross ties requires harvesting 15-20 million acres of trees.	(see 1916) (see 1945)
1910	GENERAL ELECTRIC begins to manufacture turbochargers, for internal combustion engines.	
1910	For the past five decades, the oil fields around Petrolia, Ontario, have furnished 90% of the oil used in Canada.	
1910	Texas; on Eighth Street in Ballinger, a Carnegie library is constructed of native limestone, mined from a quarry out south of town.	(see 2008)

1910	In Oregon, the KLAMATH FALLS IRON WORKS is established and the owners, Elmer Beardsley and Walter Piper, soon develop the Sandslinger, an apparatus to compact foundry sand up against the pattern used to create the mold from which castings are made.	(see 1912)
1910	Now is the heyday of the great railroad circuses and 30 of these are now carrying their entourage to cities and towns all across America.	
1910	Texas; at San Antonio, Lt. Benjamin D. Foulois pilots the first military flight in American history.	

1910	Now, countering the 1904 I-H entry into Canada, MASSEY-HARRIS acquires JOHNSON HARVESTER CO. of Batavia, NY. However, as M-H fails to include their M-H equipment line into the Johnson line, it becomes a perpetual money pit... and a failure.	
1910	California; EDWARD R. BACON COMPANY is founded.	(see 2010)
1910	UK: Harry G. Hawker, having qualified as a pilot, has managed hangers at Brooklands Aerodrome, the center of British aviation. Hawker now becomes the Chief Test Pilot for Tom Sopwith.	(see 1914)

1910	Russia; Frenchman Adolphe Kégresse is employed as technical manager for Czar Nicholas II from 1906 through 1917. About this time, Kégresse invents the Kégresse-drive, using Citroën vehicles. It is a half-track setup, using an endless rubber band of sorts, over a tandem-wheeled bogie, on each side of the rear of the vehicle. Often the front steering wheels had skis mounted under them for steering in snow. Kégresse soon converts several Packard and Rolls-Royce cars for the Czar; in addition to some Austin-Putilov armored cars.	(see 1915)
1910	Texas; CENTRAL TEXAS IRONWORKS is established as a foundry on Webster Street in Waco.	(see 1932)
1910	March 13; Bill Wittber makes a short flight, or hop, often times said to be the first powered and controlled flight down under. March 17; in Bolivar, South Australia, Fred C. Custance flies a Blériot plane for a short ways and ends up with a "very rough landing." This is usually considered the first powered and controlled flight in Australia, as there were several credible witnesses. A short time later, Custance crashes and badly damages the Blériot plane. Eric Weiss, better known as Harry Houdini, came down to Australia in February to demonstrate his Voisin Aeroplane. On March 18 there were many witnesses to his first flight here; very often called the first powered and controlled flight down under. After his three-month stay, Houdini departed, never to return to Australia. Take your choice.	(see WWI)

1910	Fred Lundahl starts the MOLINE PRESS STEEL CO. in East Moline, making various items for truck and farm implement manufacturers. Occasionally Lundhal would make pressed steel toys for his son, Arthur B." Buddy" Lundahl; these high quality well made toys caught the eyes of many locals and soon many were being manufactured for outside sale.	(see 1921)
1910	Louisiana; in Shreveport, Mr. H. C. Brewster and a couple of his friends start up the BREWSTER COMPANY, to manufacture oil well drilling equipment.	(see WWII)

1910	*Seventy-five percent of all towns in America with 2,500 or more population now have a public library.*	
1910	Louisiana; about 25,000 folks now pickup their mail at the Oil City Post Office. Being the first boom town in the ArkLaTex, Oil City is really booming. The ten acre "Reno Hill" red light district and all the regular rowdy folks earn a notorious reputation for Oil City.	
1910	BSA is established this year.	
1910	Nationwide across the US, department store sales have now reached about $700 million each year, and growing.	
1910	Germany; OPEL's first truck, a one-tonner, comes out this year.	(see 1914)
1910	December; having recently acquired the JONZ AUTOMOBILE CO. of Beatrice, NE, the AMERICAN AUTOMOBILE MANUFACTURING CO. now this month moves its offices to Louisville, KY, and sets up manufacturing in an abandoned woolen mill in New Albany, IN.	(see 1912)
1910	Alabama; Orville Wright opens the world's first commercial flight school in Montgomery.	
1910	Texas; the COMMERCIAL MOTOR CAR CO. of San Antonio and Houston is building the "San Antonio" car in… San Antonio.	
1910	Indiana; after several months of building, testing, and rebuilding improvements, the first truck built completely by the MARION IRON & BRASS BED COMPANY is released. Right away it is sold to Mr. O. Gordon, a furniture dealer in Gas City, IN. Some years later, Mr. Gordon sells this first "Indiana" truck to Mr. Charles Stewart, also of Gas City.	(see 1911) (see 1923)
1910	In addition to welding rail joints, the HEIL COMPANY now builds smokestacks and steel tanks. This year they begin building horse-drawn wagons for trash hauling.	(see 1914)
1910	Illinois; the ALBAUGH-DOVER CO. of Chicago, is producing the Aldo car for a couple of years.	
1910	The Alpena Flyer motorcar is built by the ALPENA MOTOR CAR CO. of Alpena, MI, through 1914.	
1910	Kentucky; in Owensboro, the "Ames" motorcar is produced by the CARRIAGE WOODSTOCK CO., this year and next.	(see 1912)

1911	November; Billy Durant and Louis J. Chevrolet establish the CHEVROLET MOTOR COMPANY. The first vehicles are engineered and designed by Louis Chevrolet, and the first Chevrolets are produced before the end of this year.	

	1911	LAPLANT-CHOATE MFG. CO. is founded in Cedar Rapids, IA, building stump pullers and house moving equipment.
	1911	O & K buys out LMG and continue their bucket wheel excavators.
	1911	J. O. Eaton et al form TORBERSEN GEAR & AXLE CO. in New Jersey.
	1911	ARNOLD SCHWINN & CO. buys EXCELSIOR MOTORCYCLE COMPANY.
	1911	STUDEBAKER MFG. CO. joins EVERITT-METZGER-FLANDERS CO., of Detroit, forming STUDEBAKER CORP.; selling automobiles under the E-M-F, and FLANDERS names.
	1911	**Indiana; on May 30th, Louis Chevrolet drives for W. C. Durant in the first INDIANAPOLIS 500. This race is ran for 500 miles (805 km) before 77,000 spectators. Then 32 year old engineer/test driver Ray Harroun drives #32, a single-seater Marmon Wasp, to win this huge event.**

1911	HUDSON introduces the ESSEX automobile, priced just above Ford and Chevrolet.	
1911	The COMPUTING-TABULATING-RECORDING CO. is founded.	
1911	SKF now has thirty-two sales representatives all around the world.	
1911	LINCOLN ELECTRIC produces the first variable-voltage, single-operator portable welding machine in the world.	
1911	DEERE & CO. purchases six various non-competitive farm equipment companies.	
1911	AUTOCAR builds its last cars, will build only trucks from now on.	
1911	Texas; high silica sand begins being shipped from Santa Anna, in Coleman County, to glass plants all around the US	
1911	RUMELY merges with ADVANCE THRESHER CO. forming the ADVANCE-RUMELY CO., building tractors until 1931, when ALLIS-CHALMERS buys 'em out. ADVANCE-RUMELY hooks three of their big "Oil Pull" tractors together to pull a row of fifty plowshares, that's fifty furrows in one pass... this is some publicity stunt.	
1911	HATFIELD MOTOR VEHICLE CO. establishes a truck manufacturing Plant in Cornwall-on-Hudson, NY.	
1911	GENERAL MOTORS hires Walter Chrysler as Works Manager for BUICK.	(see 1917)
1911	DUNN MANUFACTURING CO. starts up in Oxnard, CA, marketing a revolutionary new "casing wrench," the forerunner to present-day casing tongs for drilling rigs.	
1911	HYGRADE LAMP CO. is now marketing tungsten filament bulbs, their BAY STATE bulb renewal operation is now ceased.	
1911	DIXON PAPER COMPANY is established.	
1911	Now they number twenty-two, and a bit over a million dollars is grossed by Penny's "GOLDEN RULE STORES."	(see 1916)
1911	**MAYTAG produces its first electric-powered washing machine.**	
1911	Marshal Ferdinand Foch, the French military strategist and future WWI commander states, "Airplanes are interesting toys, but of no military value."	(see 1910)
1911	The first BROWN-LIPE clutch is shipped to the GRABOWSKY POWER WAGON COMPANY.	
1911	FORD opens its first overseas assembly plant in Manchester, England.	

1911	FAFNIR is founded to serve "the infant automobile industry's need for precision ball bearings."	
1911	The first machine-made glass fillers are used in Thermos "vacuum flasks;" now the Thermos Bottle can be truly mass-produced.	
1911	March 11; backed by Harold McCormick, president of McCormick Reapers, the McCormick-Romme Umbrella plane flies. Mr. Chance Vought works on this plane.	
1911	After fifty years of use by the military, the Gatling Gun is declared obsolete.	
1911	Amon G. Carter, Sr., heads a committee to bring the first airplane to the Ft. Worth area.	
1911	**Edward G. Budd develops an all-steel automobile body.**	
1911	The BREWSTER COMPANY INC. begins manufacturing oilfield equipment in Shreveport, LA.	
1911	John H. Sealy purchases the J. S. CULLINAN CO. and the SECURITY OIL CO. and consolidates the two forming MAGNOLIA PETROLEUM COMPANY.	
1911	**Mr. Garfield Wood, the speedboat racer, invents the hydraulic lift to tilt truck beds to unload coal-hauling trucks.**	
1911	Chicago, IL; the son of a shoemaker, Mr. C. A. Tilt begins building trucks. He chooses the name Diamond T, the diamond stands for quality and the "T" stands for Tilt.	
1911	An export division is formed by GENERAL MOTORS.	
1911	To help promote agriculture, Rudolf Diesel is advocating the use of vegetable oil as a fuel for engines.	
1911	Texas; in Wichita Falls, the WICHITA FALLS MOTOR TRUCK CO. begins building the heavy duty "Wichita" trucks.	(see 1920)
1911	UK; having been fabricated and built in Scotland, the Middlesbrough Transporter Bridge is now installed. It uses a gondola-type carriage.	
1911	Having only recently made his first plane flight, Clyde Cessna now builds a plane near Rago, KS.	
1911	AG & E Co. connects its power plants in Marion and Muncie, IN, 30 miles away, so the plants can support each other and improve customer service.	
1911	Chicago; the AERO SHEET METAL WORKS is incorporated as AUTOMOBILE RADIATOR & PARTS MFG. COMPANY.	
1911	**SPERRY successfully tests its first gyro-compass aboard the USS Delaware. This is the first major improvement in direction-finding since the invention of the magnetic compass, several centuries past.**	
1911	Frank and Ethyl Mars begin making chocolate candy in their kitchen.	
1911	Texas; the LITTLE MOTOR KAR COMPANY builds the "Little Kar" in Arlington. Little also will have a plant in Dallas.	(see 1922)
1911	The first licensed commercial aircraft manufacturer is the BURGESS COMPANY.	
1911	LIMA begins manufacturing locomotives for "Class 1" railroads.	(see 1912)
1911	Mr. Charles Gates, Sr., buys the COLORADO TIRE & LEATHER COMPANY of Denver, for the sum of $3,500. Their sole product is the "Durable Tread," a steel-studded band of leather to fasten around today's flimsy automobile tires to extend their useful mileage.	(see 1917)
1911	Texas; the hat making brothers, Jim and Tom Peters, open PETER BROTHERS HATS in Fort Worth.	
1911	USA; MERCURY MFG. CORP. is established to build the first electric-powered towing tractor, among several other items.	(see 1956)
1911	A tragic fire at the TRIANGLE SHIRTWAIST FACTORY kills 146 workers, mostly immigrant teenage girls, who are usually toiling fourteen hours every day.	

1911	Louisiana; near Oil City, GULF OIL COMPANY has constructed a small platform just off the eastern shore of Caddo Lake. Here GULF drills the first known offshore oil well, and begins producing crude.	
1911	Oklahoma; C. W. Flint Sr. now joins TULSA RIG, REEL & MANUFACTURING COMPANY.	(see 1919)
1911	Brooklyn, NY; the TEXAS COMPANY opens its first filling station, introducing Texaco Auto Gasoline.	
1911	EXCELSIOR MOTOR MFG. is bought by SCHWINN.	(see 1931)
1911	GENERAL MOTORS TRUCK CO. is established to manage the marketing of their Rapid and Reliance trucks.	(see 1912)
1911	Texas; on September 30, the CLEBURNE MOTOR CAR MANUFACTURING COMPANY is established in Cleburne to build and sell motor cars. The first car, a snazzy convertible, is completed and sells quickly on December 20. The various models are the "Luck," "Luck Utility," and the "Chaparral." During the first year of operation, nine cars were completed, and all but one sold rapidly. This business did not do well, mostly because of competition from the larger manufacturers, but continues in operation until 1914.	
	1911 — Alaska; in late September, the first CATERPILLAR ever seen here arrives in Fairbanks. The 60-horsepower, gasoline-powered machine weighs 9 tons. John C. "Jack" Sayers, a local machinist is 1/3 owner and is responsible for getting it finally assembled and running. Sayer's partners are Hanry B. Parkin and Willie T. Pinkerton.	
	1911 — Some sources say there are now 667,000 automobiles registered in the USA.	
1911	October; at Fort Bliss, near El Paso, TX, the first forty-eight star American flag is flown.	
1911	Due to the 1909 Supreme Court ruling, STANDARD OIL is now dissolved into 37 "independent" companies.	
1911	With the STANDARD OIL breakup, VACUUM OIL becomes an independent company again.	(see 1931)
1911	Ohio; the GALION IRON WORKS CO. is now manufacturing a light-duty, horse-drawn road grader.	(see 1929)
1911	November; Billy Durant and Louis J. Chevrolet form the CHEVROLET MOTOR COMPANY. The first vehicles are engineered and designed by Louis Chevrolet. The first Chevrolets are produced before the end of this year.	
1911	Indiana; the MARION IRON & BRASS BED COMPANY changes its name to HARWOOD-BARLEY MFG. COMPANY, devoting itself to truck production, while continuing the manufacture of bedsteads and bedsprings.	(see 1915) (see 1917) (see WWI)
1911	New York; in NYC, the MOTOR CAR CO. OF AMERICA produces the America motor car this year.	
1911	USA; a locomotive built for the CHESAPEAKE & OHIO RAILROAD, with fully loaded engine and tender, weighs In at 493,000 pounds (223,621 kg). This is much more than twice the weight of the 1895 locomotive.	(see 1918)
1911	Sweden; by this time, (AB) Bofors-Gullspång has out-competed, bought, and closed down its Finspang Swedish competitor cannon manufacturer.	(see 1919)
1911	In Detroit, a tiller-steered electric auto is produced by CENTURY MOTOR & ELECTRIC CO., for another four years.	
1911	In Findlay, OH, the "Adams" automobile is being produced by the ADAMS BROS. CO. this year.	
1911	In Elmira, NY, the AMERICAN LAFRANCE FIRE ENGINE CO. produces the "American LaFrance" automobile through 1918.	

1911	Italy; FIAT supplies motor trucks to the Italian forces engaged in the Italian-Turkish conflict; these are probably the first motor vehicles ever used in a war.	(see 1912)
1912	Woodrow Wilson becomes President of the United States of America.	
1912	January 13; the YOUNGSTOWN SHEET & TUBE CO. buys a small supply company owned by former OILWELL SUPPLY CO. employees, W. K. Hughes, W. R. Wilkinson, and W. E. Messenger. Thus is created CONTINENTAL SUPPLY CO. in St. Louis, almost immediately, they open fourteen supply stores in oilfield towns through Oklahoma, Texas, Illinois, Pennsylvania, West Virginia, and Ohio.	
1912	After building draglines for their own use, PAGE ENGINEERING CO., is formed to build and market draglines.	
1912	BUCYRUS buys ATLANTIC EQUIPMENT CO. and introduces the world's first crawler mounted dragline, the BUCYRUS Class 14.	(see 1915)
1912	One thousand five-hundred and seventeen lives are lost as the great TITANIC sinks. Among its fine provisions were 8,000 cigars.	
1912	Great-grandson of the fur baron J. J. Astor, the financier John Jacob Astor (b. 1864), goes down with the Titanic.	
1912	Often returning to Texas to check on his ranching operations, Alfred Rowe makes his final trip this April, as he books passage on the Titanic, and goes down with the ship.	
1912	Ireland; eleven citizens of the little town of Addergoole are lost as the great ship Titanic sinks.	
1912	The GMC nameplate is first introduced.	
1912	**The post offices at Dressy and Dudley, TX, are closed.**	
1912	California; the UNION TOOL CO. establishes its factory in Torrance for manufacturing oil well drilling and production equipment.	(see 1920)
1912	ABEGG AND REINHOLD CO. become active in the oil & gas industry.	
1912	This year there are 276 auto makers in the USA.	
1912	Texas; the TEXAS CENTRAL RAILROAD runs a line from DeLeon through Rising Star, into Cross Plains, TX. This line will be locally known as "The Peanut Special," due to the large amounts of peanuts shipped from the area's farms.	
1912	Leon Leonwood Bean (LL BEAN) opens shop.	
1912	J. I. CASE COMPANY, the world's largest manufacturer of steam engines, is now building some items of road construction equipment, as well.	(see 1919) (see 1922)
1912	The HERCULES BUGGY COMPANY of Evansville, IN, enters the gasoline engine business by buying the HOLMES MACHINE COMPANY of Sparta, MI, and renaming it the HERCULES GAS ENGINE COMPANY.	
1912	STEWART TRUCKS are first produced in Buffalo, NY.	
1912	Diamond Jim Brady becomes a vice-president of MM & M.	
1912	**GRAMM-BERNSTEIN of Lima, OH, build their first trucks.**	
1912	The GADE FARM ENGINE is first built.	
1912	Clarence Birdseye gets the idea for flash-freezing food, during a ice-fishing trip to Labrador, in minus 20° F temperatures.	
1912	For a couple of years, the ARGO ELECTRIC VEHICLE CO. of Saginaw, MI, is producing an electric car using a 60 volt system, and dependable Westinghouse electric motors.	

1912	Halsey W. Taylor develops the Puritan Sanitary Fountain and begins producing it in his plant in Warren, OH.	
1912	The S. S. Kresge Company now has 85 stores.	
1912	**Edgar Rice Burroughs brings his boy Tarzan into the world.**	
1912	Rudolph Diesel's patents expire in the US, some of the companies springing up to build diesel engines are Allis-Chalmers, and Nordberg in Milwaukee, Fairbanks-Morse in Beloit, Worthington-Cudahy, also in Wisconsin, Busch-Sulzer in St. Louis, and Winton in Cleveland.	
1912	As the result of cooperative development between Charles F. Kettering and Electric Storage Battery Co., Cadillac has the very first battery-started car with an internal-combustion engine. This is the first electric "self-starter" to be factory-installed as standard equipment on an automobile.	
1912	Wells Brothers is joined to the Wiley & Russell Company to form Greenfield Tap & Die, with Frank O. Wells as president.	
1912	Conrad Schlumberger conceives the idea of using electrical measurements to map subsurface rock bodies.	(see 1919)
1912	Having recently started Brockway Motor Truck Co. in Cortland, NY, William's son, George Brockway builds his first truck.	
1912	Near Houston; Mr. C. W. Hanslip and one employee start Standco Brake Lining Co., with only had 6 pieces of equipment; (1) a No. 2 washtub, (2) a clothes wringer, (3) two stove pipes, (4) a support to hold the asbestos tape, (5) a hole in the ground and (6) a piece of sheet metal to cover the hole.	
1912	Walter B. Sharp dies, and his partner Howard R. Hughes Sr. buys the Sharp estate's interest of Sharp-Hughes, renaming it Hughes Tool Company.	(see 1924)
1912	Harry W. Morrison and M. H. Knudsen form the Morrison-Knudsen Co. in Boise, ID.	
1912	May 12; the battleship Texas is launched, and is reckoned as the most powerful naval weapon in the world, she will fight in two world wars.	
1912	**Motorized movie cameras are invented, replacing hand-cranked cameras.**	
1912	The Royal Dutch/Shell Group establishes the American Gasoline Co. to sell gasoline along the Pacific coast and Roxanna Petroleum to buy oil properties in Oklahoma.	
1912	Continental Supply Company is founded.	
1912	**Clarence Crane invents Life Savers candy.**	
1912	The first Sheaffer fountain pen factory opens, mass-producing the simple pen that revolutionizes the writing industry.	
1912	Tokyo, Japan; Nippon Kokan (NKK) is founded and begins manufacturing seamless tubular products from day one.	
1912	Termomeccanica Italiana is founded in La Spezia, Italy, primarily building water pumps.	
1912	Depressed, tired, and sickly from fighting off other inventors who are infringing on their patents, Wilbur Wright contracts typhoid fever and dies. Soon, without his brother and partner, Orville loses interest and sells Wright Aircraft Company.	(see 1916)
1912	Indian introduces their 1000 cc, 8 overhead valves, 2 cylinder board track racing motocycle. It is direct-drive with no transmission and no brakes.	
1912	The first parachute jump from a airplane is made this year.	

1912	The STEDMAN FOUNDRY & MACHINE COMPANY is acquired from the Stedman family by three local investors.	
1912	Getting into manufacturing, the very successful THOMAS & BETTS sales agency acquires the STANDARD ELECTRIC FITTINGS CO. of Stamford, CT.	
1912	GLENN L. MARTIN CO. is incorporated in Los Angeles, to manufacture and market airplanes. Some early associates and contributors to Martin's firm are Donald Douglas, James McDonald, Chance Vought, C. A. "Dutch" Van Dusen, Dutch Kindelberger, and Larry Bell!! What a line-up!!! Glenn Martin makes the first-ever flight out over the ocean, thirty-four miles in his own hydroplane.	(see 1913)
1912	CLEVELAND MOTOR PLOW CO. is formed by Roland H. White, head of WHITE MOTOR COMPANY.	(see 1920)
1912	German meteorologist Alfred Wegner first proposes the idea of "continental drift," as the reason for earthquakes.	
1912	As they move from Chicago to Racine, WI, AUTO RADIATOR & PARTS MFG. CO. is renamed PERFEX RADIATOR CO.	
1912	**For the first time, an airplane takes off from a moving warship.**	
1912	Just west of Corpus Christi, the village of Robstown, TX, is incorporated on a few acres of Robert Driscoll's land.	
1912	Allan and Malcolm Loughead form the ALCO HYDRO-AEROPLANE COMPANY.	
1912	Texas; after 20 years, the railroad and port facilities are completed at Aransas Pass, and ready for business.	
1912	Texas; to better facilitate the mining of sulphur, the FREEPORT SULPHUR COMPANY pioneers the technique of using super-heated water.	
1912	Germany; boasting two M. A. N. 1,050 horsepower engines, the *Selandia* is launched. It is the first ocean-going vessel powered by diesel engines.	
1912	With a major project for the Czar's imperial estate in Turkestan, LAYNE goes international.	(see 1913)
1912	Yet another reorganization and LIMA becomes LIMA LOCOMOTIVE CORPORATION (LIMA).	(see 1916)
1912	Lorain, OH; the THEW AUTOMATIC SHOVEL CO. (THEW) is now third in excavator sales in the nation.	(see 1914)
1912	The M. O'NEIL COMPANY of Akron, OH, is acquired by MAY DEPARTMENT STORES, for $1,000,000.	(see 1989)
1912	London; the ANGLO-SWEDISH ELECTRIC WELDING COMPANY LTD. is established.	
1912	Mr. W. H Dangel purchases LOVEJOY TOOL WORKS of Chicago, from Thomas Lovejoy.	
1912	California; Naval Petroleum Reserves No. 1 & 2 are Elk Hills and Buena Vista Hills.	(see 1915) (see 1976)
1912	INGERSOLL-RAND builds their first centrifugal compressor, for air or gas.	
1912	Stockton, CA; a local firm, HOLT MFG. CO. has purchased the second Sandslinger machine from KLAMATH FALLS IRON WORKS. Holt likes the unit and soon is a manufacturer and dealer for the Sandslinger.	(see 1922)
1912	Australia; the teenaged Sidney Cotton designs and builds a light automobile, using a final drive setup similar to some to be used later on by Frazier and also by Nash.	(see 1915)
1912	Texaco Motor Oil is a new product from the TEXAS COMPANY this year.	
1912	Powered by a four cylinder, 20/28 HP Wisconsin engine, through a two-speed transmission, the Nelson Farm Tractor offers four wheel chain drive and four wheel steering.	

1912	Texas; at the Opera House in Nacogdoches, the Marx Brothers are performing as singers when a loud ruckus out in the street distracts their audience. The three brothers turned to comedy snips to re-capture their audience's attention. The rest is history.			
1912	This year J. D. Fate begins producing locomotive cranes.			
1912	Texas; in Cleburne, Slats Rodgers builds an airplane, possibly the first real airplane built in the Lone Star state.			
		1912	Texas; in Houston, furniture retailer, Star Furniture Company, opens for business.	(see 1997)
		1912	Elmer Sperry begins work on his "auto pilot" for the steering of ships, it is called Metal-Mike and behaves as an experienced helmsman. Most major advances in the development of a practical automatic steering of ships have been made, and are being made by the Sperry Gyroscope Company.	(see 1922)
		1912	For the past two years, the American Automobile Mfg. Co. has built their two-stroke "American" engine at the New Albany plant, while also building and selling a very limited number of cars sold as "Jonz," after the "Jonz Tranquil Motor" developed by the three Jones brothers back in Kansas. The company goes bankrupt this year, and Ferdinand N. Kahler buys all the assets. Kahler then forms the Ohio Falls Motor Co., mostly to protect the assets of the Kahler Co., his woodworking business.	
1912	Now having gone to work for GM Truck Company, John M. Landsen is now Manger of the GM Truck Co. Electrical Division. This year GM produces 173 electric trucks, about 40 percent of their total production.			(see 1914)
1912	This is the last year the "Sears Motor Buggy" is sold by Sears Roebuck & Company.			(see 1952)
1912	California; about this time, Frank A. Hopper, Sr. establishes a one-man machine shop on China Grade Loop, out near the Kern River Oilfields. Very shortly, Hopper is mounting a small well-servicing winch (tiny draw-works) on wheeled and crawler tractors. Thus enabling tubing pulling (servicing) a well that has no permanent derrick. Is this the birth of the mobile well servicing business?			(see 1927)
1912	December 31; up to this time, more than 2,900 Chevrolet vehicles have been produced and sold.			
1912	Michigan; the Colonial Electric Car Co. of Detroit, is building closed models and roadsters with tiller steering.			
1912	Illinois; sales of the Altorfer Brothers' "Roanoke Power Machine" is already in the thousands, they now call their company the ABC Washer Company, selling their washing machines are sold by the ABC brand. A new factory is soon built in Peoria, as the old wooden tub is replaced with a metal tub.			(see 1926)
1912	Italy; FIAT founds its own factory for vehicle lubricants, The Fiat Lubricanti. FIAT also builds a factory for cars and their spare parts in Russia this year.			(see WW I)
1912	Kentucky; the "Ames" automobile is now produced by the Ames Motor Car Co. through 1915, in Owensboro.			
1912	This year the first self-contained breathing apparatus for underground mine rescue is used.			
1912	Denver, CO; the American Tri Car Co. is building the "American Tri Car."			
1913	Oscar Martinson designs the world's first walking dragline.			
1913	Monarch Tractor Co. is started in Watertown, WI, to build crawler tractors.			
1913	Brown, Boveri And Company introduces the first supercharged engine, utilizing a mechanically driven air pump.			

1913	All cars built by the STUDEBAKER CORP. are now called… STUDEBAKER.	
1913	Mr. Rudolf Diesel dies.	
1913	Mr. Magnus Hendrickson establishes the HENDRICKSON MOTOR TRUCK COMPANY in Chicago.	
1913	Humphrey & Dudley Pierce found PIERCE MANUFACTURING CO. in Appleton, WI.	
1913	Mr. Byron Jackson dies.	
1913	**The 3300 mile Lincoln Highway is completed across the USA.**	
1913	Henry Ford initiates a moving assembly line to build Model T cars at his Highland Park plant.	
1913	Germany; Hugo Junkers builds a 4 cylinder, lightweight, diesel engine for aircraft. Junkers soon builds a 6 cylinder version producing 368kw @ 2400 rpm.	
1913	Arthur O. Smith dies and his son Lloyd Raymond Smith becomes the 3rd generation of the family to lead A. O. SMITH CO.	
1913	Nebraska; the CUSHMAN MOTOR WORKS is incorporated and a factory is built, and is still in the same location in 2003.	
1913	VICTOR OXY-ACETYLENE WELDING EQUIPMENT COMPANY is founded by L. W. Stettner, a welder who has lost an eye from a welding accident, and wants to design and build better, safer welding equipment.	
1913	UNION TOOL CO. introduces its first rotary table, for well drilling operations.	
1913	California; Allan and Malcolm Loughead (later changed to Lockheed) fly their wood and fabric seaplane, the first LOCKHEED plane out over San Francisco Bay.	
1913	Joe Joy takes a lower paying job with JEFFERY MFG. CO., to have the spare time to work on the development of his loading machine.	
1913	After a dispute, Oscar Hedstrom leaves HENDEE MANUFACTURING CO., and the motorcycle industry, forever.	
1913	**This year, three Indian motocycles are sold for every one Harley Davidson motorcycle.**	
1913	BEST introduces their first track-type tractor, the Best 75 Tracklayer with many significant improvements over previous tracked tractors.	
1913	J. M. Larsen produces a manually operated household refrigeration machine.	
1913	**In a truly uplifting moment, Mary Phelps Jacobs invents the ladies' brassiere.**	
1913	MERCK CHEMICAL COMPANY receives a patent for the chemical we now know as ecstasy.	
1913	CHARLES A. STICKNEY CO. of St. Paul Minnesota ceases to manufacture its engines, but will assemble more from parts stocks during the next few years.	
1913	Max Lillie teaches Chance Vought to fly, using a Wright biplane, Vought is soon an instructor for the MAX LILLIE SCHOOL OF AVIATION.	(see 1915)
1913	ASSOCIATED TELEPHONE UTILITIES, AMERICAN BELL TELEPHONE CO., and other telephone companies sign the Kingsbury Commitment.	
1913	R. J. REYNOLDS TOBACCO CO. introduces "Camel" cigarettes, soon to be the "National Cigarette of the USA." RJR also introduces the "20 pack."	
1913	August; in the Healdton oilfield in Southern Oklahoma, the first successful well is drilled in.	
1913	CORBITT begins manufacturing trucks.	
1913	**The first highway lane markers appear, in Redlands, CA.**	
1913	DONOVAN MARINE is founded.	
1913	December 1; in Pittsburg, PA, GULF OIL COMPANY opens the first true drive-in service station in the United States and begin distributing FREE road maps to their customers.	

1913	Naperville Lounge Factory of Naperville, IL, changes its name to Kroehler Furniture Company.	
1913	Having exclusively delivered on foot and bicycle up to now, American Messenger Co. acquires a Model "T" Ford car as its first motorized delivery vehicle, and changes its name to Merchants Parcel Delivery.	(see 1918)
1913	Ontario, Canada; James "Scotty" Hamilton, delivering lumber and coal with his horse and wagon, establishes Hamilton Cartage Company.	
1913	Ft. Worth, TX; the local Gamer Co. puts out a huge tractor with a 4 cylinder, 10" X 12" engine. Evidently this 'flash-in-the-pan' is only offered this year.	
1913	Houston; one of the first concrete and steel high-rise buildings in town…. the Hotel Cotton opens downtown, advertising "175 fire-proof rooms"' and "a bathroom in every room" *"Yeah Bubba, thay have the turlits inside th' bedrooms."*	
1913	December; the first ever published crossword puzzle appears in the New York World; it has 32 clues.	
1913	For the first time, the count of registered motor vehicles in the US exceeds one million. This year 1,190,000 autos and 67,000 trucks are registered.	
1913	**German engineers design the world's first controlled, or limited-access, highways.**	
1913	Opel is now the largest carmaker in Germany.	
1913	UK; Sidney Slater Guy leaves his upper management job with Sunbeam Motor Car Co., and immediately founds Guy Motors, Ltd., building a new factory at Fallings Park, Wolverhampton, England.	
1913	The first weight limit for trucks on US roads and highways, 18,000 pounds, is enacted by the State of Maine.	
1913	Guildford, England; from now onward, Dennis Brothers concentrates solely on commercial vehicles, continuing this way into the next century.	
1913	UK; after years of producing rugged, reliable, very plain cars, Austin Mfg. Co. begins building trucks. Only 2,000 are built before ceasing production.	

1913	Earlier this year, Chevrolet Motor Co. moves to Flint, MI. In December, Louis Chevrolet leaves his namesake company.	
1913	On the Great Lakes of North America, "the Great Storm" causes the loss of twelve vessels and two-hundred fifty lives.	

1913	Chief engineer of the Russo-Baltic Carriage Factory, a railcar builder, Igor Sikorsky (1889-1972) builds his "Grand." This is the world's first multi-engined airplane. However, while the Grand is sitting parked after a flight, a landing Morane airplane loses its engine, which falls through the Grand, totally wiping it out. *NOTE: In his later years, Sikorsky will state, "In the early days the chief engineer was very often also the chief test pilot (as Sikorsky was), this tended to result in the elimination of poor engineering."*	
1913	The US Congress has eliminated tariffs on low-cost Canadian timber imports, causing a terrible slump in the domestic timber and paper industry.	
1913	Memphis, TN; the local Allen Engineering Company, the world's largest manufacturer of well screens, centrifugal pumps and related water well products, is acquired by Layne Company, Inc.	(see 1922)
1913	This July the temperature reaches 134° F. in Death Valley, CA. In 1922 in the Sahara, at El Aziza in Libya, the temperature was measured at 136.4°, but this measurement was later invalidated due to antiquated equipment. The Death Valley temperature remains the world record.	
1913	Baldwin builds their forty-thousandth railroad locomotive this year.	(see 1916)
1913	USA; in the town of Le Mars, IA, Fred H. Wells starts up a dairy business with $250 and a dream. Wells is soon in the ice cream business.	(see 2009)

1913	**The GEORGE HAISS MFG. CO. invents the bucket loader for coal.**	(see 1946)
1913	Germany; CLAAS is now primarily focused on installing their twine knotters on third-party built hay balers.	(see WWI)
1913	Sweden; ASTRA AB, a small pharmaceutical business is established.	(see 1936)
1913	Pennsylvania; OIL WELL SUPPLY COMPANY of Oil City introduces its "Simplex Pumping Jack," to be used in a rodline and jerker system with a central power source connecting to several wells, each with a "Simplex Pumping Jack."	(see 1925)
1913	USA; every state in this great nation now has an anti-cruelty to animals law, including the Territory of Alaska, preceding statehood by 46 years. However, meaningful enforcement will not come until late this century.	(see 1990)
1913	USA; the Wallis "Cub" is the first farm tractor to successfully work without a chassis, due to using its heavy engine and transmission as a sufficiently rigid structure to handle the strain.	
1913	Michigan; in Bay City, William S. Ramsay and Seth Babcock establish the BAY CITY DREDGE WORKS.	(see 1914)
1913	Along about this time, Henry Leland, himself an excellent machinist, secretly buys a French automobile and when it arrives in Detroit, has his shop disassemble it. Leland mainly wants to see how the only production V-8 engine on earth is put together. He sees that sloppy machining is the reason the V-8 runs so badly. Leland has his shop copy this engine, but machine it to a tolerance of about one one-thousandth of an inch.	(see 1914)
1913	Karl Kinley, an "oil well shooter" decides to use some of his dynamite to blow out a oil well blowout fire; and is successful. Kinley's fifteen year old son, Myron, helps his dad on this job, and in a few years will have his own oil well fire fighting business.	(see 1938)
1913	John D. Rockefeller's wealth is now $900 million, nine times Cornelius Vanderbilt's at his 1877 demise, and twice the worth of Andrew Carnegie when he sold out in 1901.	
1913	USA; separate from the earlier Department of Commerce and Labor, the congress now creates a new Department of Labor, and gives it full cabinet status.	
1913	Welsh coal production peaks with about 61 million tonnes produced in Wales this year.	
1913	Texas; September 3; today it is announced that Southern Select Beer, brewed and bottled in the large MAGNOLIA BREWERY, in the heart of Houston, is Number One!!! At the international competition in Ghent, Belgium, Southern Select Beer outranks 4,067 other beers from around the world. A panel of "…the greatest European scientists, chemists, and brewery experts" judged the competition.	
1913	Ohio; the DOWNING CYCLE CAR CO. of Cleveland, is making the "Downing" motor vehicle through 1915.	
1913	Sweden's first internal-combustion powered agricultural tractor is built by Munktells. This thing weighs 8 tons, the rear wheels are 2. 1 m high, the cooling system holds 400 l of water, it speeds along at 3. 2 kph, powered by the 2 cylinder, 30 hp, crude oil-burning engine. (The 1918 price is 27, 500 SEK {Swedish Krona})	(see 1914)
1913	The A. E. C. motor vehicle is being made and sold by ANGER ENGINEERING CO. of Milwaukee, for a couple of years.	
1913	The Allen motor vehicle is being made and sold by ALLEN IRON & STEEL CO. of Philadelphia, for a couple of years.	
1914	MAYTAG introduces its gasoline "Multi-Motor."	

1914	**Started a decade ago in 1904, the Panama Canal is finally completed.**	
1914	**After several years building cars, and parts, for Ford and others, John and Horace Dodge build the first DODGE motorcars.**	(see 1920)
1914	**HARNISCHFEGER builds the first P&H shovel.**	
1914	TORBERSEN GEAR & AXLE move to Cleveland, OH.	
1914	July 31; ZUMAQUE #1 comes in, the well that starts commercial petroleum production in Venezuela.	
1914	WATERLOO GASOLINE TRACTION ENGINE CO. begins production of the WATERLOO BOY tractor.	
1914	John Murphy of Elgin, IL, invents the motorized street sweeper, the first unit is sold to the city of Boise, ID.	
1914	August; the War to end all Wars starts as Germany declares War on Great Britain.	
1914	Throughout the war, Clessie Cummins operates a machine shop that thrives on government contracts. By now Cummins is convinced that Rudolph Diesel's unproven engine technology holds great promise for economy and endurance.	
1914	**HOLT MFG. CO. pays R. HORNSBY & SONS of England $8,000 for the patent rights to their "chain track" to use on crawler tractors. There are now 2,000 of Holt's CATERPILLAR crawler tractors operating around the world.**	
1914	Having moved to Elmira, NY last year, HATFIELD MOTOR VEHICLE CO. is now shutting down.	
1914	H. Royce designs his first aero engine, the Eagle. ROLLS-ROYCE produces about 1/2 of the total air horsepower used by the Allies in World War One.	
1914	CRAMER FURNITURE CO. is acquired, more than doubling the size of THOMASVILLE CHAIR COMPANY.	(see 1917)
1914	Washington, DC; Having always been horse-drawn, this October the first motorized Post Office vehicles begin picking up the mail.	
1914	In Japan, the first DATSUN automobile is built.	
1914	Brothers-in law John Schaefer and Claude Hart purchase M & M MFG. CO., a maker of tire repair products in Akron, OH.	
1914	EDWARD P. ALLIS CO. (iron castings and steam pumps), FRASER & CHALMERS CO. (rock crushing equipment), GATES IRON WORKS (crushing equipment), and DICKSON MFG. CO. (steam boilers and tanks) merge, have financial distress, and are reorganized as ALLIS-CHALMERS MANUFACTURING COMPANY, with Gen. Otto Faulk, as president and manager. Faulk puts them into agricultural equipment by immediately introducing the 10-18, A-C's first farm tractor.	
1914	A. D. COOK PUMP CO. begins producing fire hydrants after the Ohio river flood of 1913.	
1914	AMERICAN EVEREADY becomes a part of NATIONAL CARBON CO.	
1914	A. O. SMITH introduces the Smith Motor Wheel, intended as a gasoline powered device for bicycles. Smith then introduces the Smith Flyer, America's first sports car.	
1914	Joseph W. Harris, Sr., founds the J. W. HARRIS COMPANY, to distribute and repair automotive and farm equipment parts.	
1914	Waterloo, IA; Thomas Fawick and a friend design a superior tractor and soon receive a contract for 800 units.	(see 1916)
1914	**John Grant invents the first underreamer, for use in oil well drilling.**	
1914	With a cement mixer and a few wheelbarrows, Henry J. Kaiser opens KAISER PAVING CO. as his start in the construction industry.	
1914	The ROGERS BROTHERS CO. sells their first commercial trailer, the Model "A."	
1914	S. C. JOHNSON & SON opens their first overseas subsidiary in Great Britain.	

1914	Texas; up on Buffalo Bayou, the PORT OF HOUSTON opens for business.	
1914	NSK (bearings) is founded.	
1914	**FORD announces the $5 workday at its US plants. FORD MOTOR COMPANY manufactures and markets more automobiles than the combined total of all other makes sold around the entire world. This year, more than 308,000 FORD Model "T" cars are sold.**	
1914	Whitman, an immigrant, starts GREYHOUND with a 7 passenger Hupmobile auto, charging 15 cents from Hibbing to Alice, MN. He will soon get a larger "bus."	
1914	Following the success of its popular Corona model, STANDARD TYPEWRITER renames itself CORONA.	
1914	Oil is discovered at Turner Valley, 30 miles southwest of Calgary, Alberta, Canada as Dingman No. 1 blows in, gushing natural gas.	(see 1924)
1914	George Green of Plainview, TX, creates the right-angle gear-head for pumps, basically using a Model T differential mounted atop the pump.	
1914	**Czar Nicholas II of Russia orders one of each item in the HAMMACHER SCHLEMMER catalog.**	
1914	DESOUTTER is established in the UK as a tool manufacturer.	
1914	Swedish tool maker Oscar Albertson and office boy Harold Jacobson form ALBERTSON & CO., desiring to be the "Best Machine and Tool Shop."	
1914	Ernest Henry Shackleton sails from England, headed for Antarctica.	
1914	UK; GUY MOTORS LTD. produces its first vehicle, a advanced 30 cwt (1 ½ ton) truck, with a governor to control speed of its 15 hp White & Poppe four cylinder engine. Also using a patented three point suspension, and a light pressed steel frame.	
1914	Atlanta, GA; brothers Goodloe H. Yancey, Jr. and B. Earle Yancey open YANCEY HARDWARE COMPANY. They are briskly selling hardware, picks, shovels, and striped prison uniforms to government agencies for road construction work. The Yancey brothers are the first dealer in the nation for the ADAMS mule-drawn grader. This grader requires a team of eight good mules.	(see 1916)

1914	Herbert McGinnis sells *The Oil Man's Magazine* to a national publication that eventually becomes *The Oil & Gas Journal*. McGinnis then founds Tri-State Oil & Gas and Tri-State Tool and Supply company.	
1914	DODGE SALES & ENGINEERING CO. is formed to sell and distribute products from DODGE MFG. CO.	
1914	M. C. Fahey, a prospector, stakes several claims near Questa, in the New Mexico Territory. Speculating that although little is known about molybdenum, it must have some uses, Fahey begins tunneling underground and mining molybdenum.	
1914	Roots patents their Tri-Lobe impeller for blowers.	(see 1929)
1914	In the entire British Empire, there are only about 18,000 hospital beds.	(see 1918)
1914	The GLENN L. MARTIN Co. delivers its first Model TT trainer planes to the US Army Signal Corp.s.	
1914	**The first factory-made tire chains are now being used on automobiles.**	
1914	or 1916.... CADILLAC is the first US manufacturer to produce a V-type, water-cooled, eight cylinder engine. The 314 cid engine produces seventy horsepower at 2400 rpm. This engine is also the first to use a thermostatically controlled cooling system.	
1914	THEW manufactures some of the very earliest gasoline engine powered shovels.	(see WWI)
1914	Brothers E. W. and H. C. Bennett form UTILITY TRAILER MANUFACTURING COMPANY, and build a single-axle trailer that will haul sixty bales of cotton.	(see 1920s)

1914	Returning home for a visit, Harry Hawker demonstrates flying to Australians in a Sopwith Tabloid of his design.	(see WWI)
1914	Antwerp, Belgium; the Belgian-Swedish Electric Welding Co. Ltd. (BSEW) is established.	
1914	Tiffin, OH; Hanson Clutch & Machinery Co. is founded, building cranes and small power shovels.	(see 1966)
1914	Texas; the menagerie started some years ago when George Brackenridge placed deer, elk, and buffalo, as well as caged monkeys, bears, and lions near the south side of San Antonio's Brackenridge Park, is now being moved to a more accessible location nearer the center of the park.	
1914	Ohio; the Byers made steam crane is now branded the "Auto-Crane."	(see 1919)
1914	In Plymouth, MI, the Alter Motor Car Co. builds and sells the Alter motorcar, through 1917.	
1914	Louisiana; as more and more folks are now traveling by roads and highways, at Mooringsport, the Caddo Lake Drawbridge is built, replacing the ferry. Built under the authority of the Caddo Parish Police Jury, the Midland Bridge Company of Kansas City, MO, builds this bridge using the somewhat unique "Vertical-Lift" design of John Alexander Low Waddell of the firm of Waddell & Harrington Bridges.	(see 1941) (see WWII)
1914	Michigan; the Bay City Dredge Works bring out their first product, a heavy, wheeled excavator, riding on a track over the ditch it digs. The BC Land Dredge, comes in ¾, 1, and 1½ cubic yard capacity models. A pontoon model will soon come.	(see 1920)
1914	There are now about 3,000 A & P grocery stores around the United States of America.	
1914	Ohio; the Allen Motor Co. of Fostoria and Bucyrus, and Columbus, will build the Allen motorcar through 1922.	
1914	A portion of the Clayton Anti-Trust Act forbids court injunctions in labor disputes, unless considered necessary "to prevent irreparable injury (damage) to property."	
1914	Michigan; the Morgan & Wright Tire Co. of Detroit, is sold to the Us Tire Company (later Uniroyal).	
1914	Germany; Opel is now the worlds largest manufacturer of motorized vehicles.	(see 1920)
1914	Texas; for the next couple of years, the Hall Cyclecar Manufacturing Co., builds the "Hall Cyclecar," right here in Waco.	

	1914	Nine models from ½ ton to 6 ton capacity are being produced by General Motors Truck Co. This year, about 23% of their production is electric powered.	(see 1915)
	1914	Wisconsin; the Heil Company in Miles has now advanced into building dump bodies for motor trucks.	(see 1929)
	1914	The Colombia Electric Vehicle Co. of Detroit is making electric coupettes and broughams, with wire-spoked wheels.	

1914	During the early years of this century, many sorts of configurations of Ski Kits, chain-driven paddlewheels, and track conversions are appearing on automobiles and motorcycles. This year, in Jackson, MN, Frank and Howard Sawyer build a "snowmo-cycle," with skis and side-by-side seating. The rear wheel is located between the passengers, and it is powered by a twin-cylinder, Excelsior motorcycle engine.	(see 1917)
1914	Sweden; Munktell builds an internal combustion engine powered road roller this year.	(see 1984)
1915	Schuler Axle starts building axles for heavy duty vehicles.	
1915	California; Mr. Edgar Vuilleumiere joins Walter Abegg and Baldwin Reinhold and their company is renamed Vuilleumiere, Abegg & Reinhold Co., and they begin using the "VARCO" trademark this year.	(see 1973)
1915	Hopper, Inc. is formed, and starts building drilling rigs in Bakersfield, CA.	

1915	Moline Plow Co. purchases the Universal Tractor Company.	
1915	P & H starts building ditching machines.	
1915	Michigan; this year the Menominee Electric Mfg. Co. is producing an electric cabriolet automobile.	
1915	Gerlinger Motor Car Co. of Seattle, working in a garage rented from Edgar Worthington, introduce the Gersix, a six cylinder automobile.	(see 1917)
1915	Bucyrus Company start building steam-powered ditchers, some can dig up to 20 feet (6.15 m) deep. Bucyrus introduces the "tower excavator," a close cousin of the dragline, specifically for construction of levees along the Mississippi River. These will be built until 1931.	(see 1925)
1915	**There are 134 tire makers in the USA; of these, 40 are in the fine state of Ohio.**	
1915	Schaefer & Hart acquires the Giant Tire & Rubber Co. of Akron, a tire rebuilding business.	
1915	Williams Bros. begins pipeline work in the USA.	
1915	Wyoming; Naval Petroleum Reserve No. 3 is Teapot Dome.	(see 1916) (see 1924)
1915	Willis Carrier and six friends form Carrier Engineering Co. with $32,600.	
1915	Thompson Products is the largest US manufacturer of engine valves.	
1915	**William Boeing is now taking flying lessons from Mr. Glenn Martin.**	
1915	Eagle Crusher Company is established.	
1915	International Paper is now operating sixteen paper mills across the US.	
1915	Walter Sharp dies, and Howard Hughes Sr. buys his shares, becoming the sole owner of Hughes Tool Co.	
1915	**The one millionth Ford car is built.**	
1915	Arm Co. of Canada is renamed the Dominion Road Machinery Co., and is now more independent of Arm Co. of the USA.	
1915	Frank Donaldson, Sr., develops a simple air cleaner for farm tractors, and Donaldson Engineering Company begins business with a three man shop making the air cleaners. He applies for a patent in 1921.	
1915	Mr. Aben Johnson establishes the Hastings Manufacturing Company in Hastings, MI, to manufacture automotive parts and accessories.	
1915	New York City; Pyrex debuts for public use, sold by Corning Glass Works.	
1915	Los Angeles, CA; only for a few years, the Beardsley Electric Co. builds 12 models of electric cars, all capable of 28 mph.	
1915	**R. J. Reynolds introduces the one piece 10 pack carton of cigarettes.**	
1915	Grant Oil Tool Co. is founded.	
1915	Completed this year, Shell's Martinez Refinery is the first modern continuous-process refinery, for years it will serve as a model for other US refineries.	
1915	Texas, June 18; Houston blacksmith Charles Adair and his wife Mary are the proud parents of a new son, Paul Neal Adair.	(see D-Era)
1915	While working at Mayo Radiator Works, Chance Vought designs and builds his first plane, the Mayo-Vought Simplex. It flies in May this year. The Simplex will be used as a pilot training plane by the British military in WWI.	(see 1917)
1915	Oakland, CA; Thomas Bros. Maps is founded and soon will introduce their "page and grid" system.	

1915	The German drug company BAYER begins selling its aspirin as a powder.	

R. E. OLDS.
POWER LAWN MOWER.
APPLICATION FILED MAY 22, 1914.

1,131,156.

Patented Mar. 9, 1915.

1915	Herman Smith makes his first fishtail drilling bits, these are used in the major oil discovery at Ventura, CA.	
1915	GASO is also manufacturing a "rodline and jerker" pumpjack, and soon will add a line of duplex piston steam pumps and gear-driven power pumps.	
1915	***Ransom E. Olds invents the power lawn mower.***	
1915	December 15; William W. Brian of Woodsboro, TX, files the first patent on the "highway cattle guard."	
1915	Alaska; the ALASKA RAILWAY CORP., needing a construction headquarters, establishes the city of Anchorage.	
1915	KISSEL KAR CO. drops the KAR from their name, as they build the Liberty Trucks for the Allied war effort.	
1915	October 2; "Fiddling" Chubby Wise is born in Lake City, FL.	
1915	Dallas, TX; BILBO TRANSPORT is established.	
1915	France; Paul Langévin invents the first SONAR-type device for detecting submarines called an "echo location to detect submarines," improving on Lewis Nixon's 1906 iceberg detector.	
1915	B. F. AVERY ventures into the motorized tractor business by introducing its "Louisville Motor Plow."	
1915	The use of geology is now becoming widespread in the petroleum industry.	
1915	AHRENS-FOX introduces its Model K fire engine, with some improvements along the way, this will be their standard for the next four decades.	
1915	After years of trials and testing, John Endebrock introduces his "trailer," featuring a iron chassis frame with cross-members, horn-type front spring hangers, a knuckle-type front axle, automobile type springs, artillery type wheels, roller bearings, and a drawbar with housed spring sections. Because it will trail behind an automobile, the name "Trailmobile" is chosen. The good quality trailer is immediately very widely accepted, and thus… SECHLER & COMPANY soon changes its name to the TRAILMOBILE CO.	(see WWII)
1915	Glen L. Martin and his Model T plane star with Mary Pickford in *A Girl of Yesterday;* Glen is trying to drum up interest in his planes.	
1915	In the US, the "average" family's income is $687 this year.	
1915	Switzerland; SULZER BROS. chief research engineer, Dr. Alfred Buchi, proposes and develops the first prototype turbocharged diesel engine. However, it isn't very efficient, being unable to maintain sufficient boost pressure.	
1915	T. Garland Pegues' CITY GARAGE, is now the authorized FORD dealer in Longview, TX.	
1915	Having built about 200 trucks and one car, the PLYMOUTH TRUCK CO., goes out of business. The failure may be partially blamed on the very successful, small yard locomotive that Fate began building some years back… and the truck business suffered.	(see 1919)
1915	Texas; the Stinson School of Flying opens for business in San Antonio, operated by the Stinson family.	
1915	Illinois; the CHICAGO ELECTRIC MOTOR CO. is making 4 and 5 passenger enclosed coupes, for another year or two.	
1915	Missouri; the Alstel motorcar is built for a couple of years by the ALL-STEEL CAR CO. of St. Louis.	
1915	Mr. Alben Johnson establishes HASTINGS MANUFACTURING COMPANY, to make and market automotive aftermarket items, Hastings incorporates on May 11.	(see 1923)
1915	HARWOOD-BARLEY MFG. COMPANY changes its name to the INDIANA TRUCK COMPANY.	(see 1917)

1915	Russia; using the Kégresse drive, Adolph Kégresse converts many Packard trucks to be used as ambulances.	(see 1920)
1915	Illinois; the MOLINE PLOW CO. introduces their "Universal," the first all-purpose tractor having its own complete line of tractor-attached implements, built especially for it. The "Universal" tractor is a really big hit with farmers.	
1915	Australia; having only five hours solo, the twenty-one-year-old Queenslander, Sidney Cotton, becomes a R. N. A. S. pilot and is sent to the front lines in WWI. Cotton soon devises camouflage for aircraft, an upward firing gun mounting, and long-range bombing methods, to name only a few of his accomplishments.	(see WWII)
1915	This year, AJAX MOTORS CO. begins building the Ajax automobile, up in Seattle, WA.	
1915	Electric-powered milking machines come out on the market.	
1915	USA; Mr. W. Baer Ewing attempts to cash in on Henry Ford's well-known, and respected name. Ewing founds the FORD TRACTOR COMPANY, with no connection to Henry Ford; but John Q. Public doesn't realize this. Ewing's Ford Model "B" tractor is so ill-engineered, and after only a short time and a few tractors, the company is in receivership. While Ewing's Ford Tractor Company is still in bankruptcy court, Ewing sets up another Ford company, makes a few more of his tractors, and it is soon in bankruptcy as well. His partner, Robert P. Matcher is convicted of fraud, but the last we heard of Ewing, he is in Canada trying to establish yet another tractor company.	
1915	BAYER "Aspirin" becomes available over-the-counter in tablet form.	(see 1919)
1915	USA; the COMMON SENSE TRACTOR COMPANY introduces a V-8 gasoline engine powered tractor. The full-pressure oiled, 317 cubic inch (5. 2 l) V-8 is 22/40 horsepower at 1200 rpm. The company claims that this engine can be revved up to as much as 70 horse-power in an emergency situation. This beautiful red and yellow machine sells for $2,200.	
1915	The LaFollette Seamen's Act does much to improve the wages and working conditions of men on American merchant vessels.	
1915	This year and next, the TEXAS MOTOR CAR COMPANY builds the Tex automobile in San Antonio.	
1915	In San Antonio, TX, the BLUMBERG MOTOR MANUFACTURING CO. is now building the Blumberg car. Blumberg has a plant in Orange, TX, as well.	(see 1918)
1915	This year, electrics comprise only a dab above 10% of the production of GENERAL MOTORS TRUCK COMPANY.	(see 1916)
1915	Michigan; in Flint, the DORT MOTOR CAR COMPANY produces the "Dort" motorcar through 1924.	
WWI	In August of 1914, the War to end all Wars starts, as Germany declares war on Great Britain.	

WWI	Over the past few years before the war, August Thyssen has expanded internationally into Holland, the UK, France, Russia, the Mediterranean Region and Argentina.	(see 1918)
WWI	In France, General George S. Patton seriously whips the Germans in the first ever truly "mechanized" military battle. The General realizes the main advantages of a tank are firepower, mobility, and shock effect.	

WWI	In 1917, Boeing builds two prototypes of the Model C plane; the US Navy orders fifty of them.
WWI	Citroën is manufacturing armaments for France, after the war, they will begin automobile manufacturing.
WWI	As the US enters the war, the Curtiss Aeroplane Co. is the largest airplane builder in the country... simply because they build the best planes.
WWI	The Ministry of Munitions takes over all vehicle production plants in the United Kingdom.

WWI	Briggs & Stratton are building rifle grenades for the Army, and engines for the Navy.	
WWI	Trailmobile builds 10,000 plus trailer units for dozens of uses by the government; more than all other makes combined.	(see 1919)
WWI	UK; having discontinued autos during the Great War, Dennis Brothers quickly becomes one of the largest manufacturers of military trucks.	
WWI	France; Paul Langévin invents the first SONAR-type device for detecting submarines called an "echo location to detect submarines," improving on Lewis Nixon's 1906 iceberg detector.	
WWI	During the Great War, the US Army uses a modified version of a gas/smoke mask invented by Garrett Morgan.	
WWI	UK; BSA switches back to armaments, producing 10,000 rifles each week and furnishing a total of 145,000 Lewis machine guns. BSA also produce motorcycles and several other military requirements.	
WWI	Throughout WWI, the Allies are using Holt's "Caterpillar" track-type tractors.	
WWI	During the war, due to the efforts of Amon Carter Sr., three military airfields are located in the Ft. Worth, TX, area.	
WWI	In the UK all resources of Humber are focused on producing armament and aeroplane engines.	
WWI	THEW supplies many machines to our armed forces during WWI.	(see 1924)
WWI	German's "U-Boat" fleet demonstrates, too well, the effectiveness of submarines in combat.	
WWI	As pocket watches are impractical during combat, soldiers begin using wrist watches as a viable alternative. Soon after the war, wrist watches will become highly popular world-wide.	
WWI	Fred C. Custance flies BE2Cs in Palestine with the 1st Squadron, creating a flight record from Cairo, Egypt, to Romania in only 40 hours.	(see 1919)
WWI	Kissel Kar Company drops the Kar from their name, as they build the four-wheel-drive Liberty Trucks for the Allied war effort.	
WWI	USA; as one of 15 builders producing the class "B" Liberty Trucks, Indiana Truck Co. sends 475 to our military.	(see 1917)
WWI	Prewar Rolls Royce vehicles are used by the military for ambulances and machine-gun mounted vehicles.	
WWI	France; during 1917, Berliet is building forty trucks each day for the French military forces.	
WWI	UK; Guy Motors Ltd. Ceases all vehicle production, becoming the largest UK manufacturer of depth charge firing mechanisms, as well as producing large numbers of aero engines for the Allies.	
WWI	During "The War to End All Wars," about 210,000 Texans serve in the US military.	

WW I	The Browning Automatic Rifle is first used near the end of the war, but will continue to be in use through the Vietnam War, fifty years later.	
WW I	March 21, 1918; projectiles weighing 264 pounds each are raining down on Paris, France. Propelled by a 400 pound powder charge, each has reached twenty-five miles (40 km) high during its 170-second flight after fired from the Kaiser Wilhelm Geschütz Long Range Guns (Paris Gun), tucked in the forest seventy miles (112 km) from Paris. The FRIEDRICH KRUPP munitions firm builds seven of these guns, each with a 131-foot (40. 31 m) long barrel, with a fifteen-inch (381 mm) bore.	(see 1918) (see 1998)
WW I	Throughout the war, Clessie Cummins' machine shop thrives on government contracts making items for our military.	
WW I	The STINSON SCHOOL OF FLYING opens for business in San Antonio, TX, in 1915.	
WW I	Loughead (Lockheed) makes their first military sale, some Curtiss HS-2L Flying Boats to the US Navy.	
WW I	Germany; the deteriorating quality of available twine during the war pushes August Claas to stringently improve his knotters to cope with even the poorest quality twine.	(see 1920)
WW I	Harry G. Hawker stays busy in England testing hundreds of production aircraft, for the military. After the war, Hawker forms HAWKER ENGINEERING, out of the SOPWITH business.	(see 1919)
WW I	The TAPPAN CO. supplies cooking and kitchen equipment to the US armed forces.	(see WWII)
WW I	This is the first war that depended so much on the control of the petroleum supply, as it is now necessary for planes, ships, and tanks, as well as for surface transport of all sorts. The British capture Baghdad in 1917, and major petroleum production as well.	
WW I	UK; During the war, the COMMERCIAL CAR CO. supplies some 3,000 trucks to the War Office.	(see 1926)
WW I	1914-1918; FIAT supplies very large numbers of trucks to the Allied Forces during the war.	(see 1919)
1916	**GUARDIAN FRIGERATOR CO. is formed to manufacture the first household electric refrigerator.**	
1916	TORBERSEN AXLE CO. of Ohio succeeds the NJ company.	
1916	SKF buys HOFORS BRUK, a high quality Swedish steel plant for their bearing steel.	
1916	**The MAYTAG CO. builds its first little two cycle engine, a series that lasts until 1952.**	
1916	Harry Barber and William Greene found the BARBER-GREENE CO.	
1916	With profits from CHEVROLET MOTOR CO., Billy Durant regains control of GM, and fires Charles Nash for "betraying" him in 1910.	
1916	KELLY-SPRINGFIELD and BUFFALO PITTSBURG merge to form the BUFFALO-SPRINGFIELD ROLLER CO.	
1916	Charles Nash buys the THOMAS B. JEFFERY CO., renaming it NASH MOTORS. The JEFFERY car is renamed RAMBLER, and the Jeffery Truck is now the NASH TRUCK.	
1916	The AMERICAN NATIONAL STANDARDS INSTITUTE (ANSI) is founded.	
1916	Alfred P. Sloan founds UNITED MOTORS CO. and soon acquires BUICK and A-C SPARK PLUG.	
1916	In experiments in Dayton, OH, iodine is successfully uses as an anti-knock additive in kerosene fuel, but is too expensive to be commercially feasible.	
1916	INTERNATIONALE BOHRGESELLSCHAFT AG becomes known as ALFRED WIRTH & CO. They then build their first drilling machines and pumps.	
1916	Wyandotte, MI; electric limousines and commercial electric vehicles are being built by the BELMOUNT ELECTRIC AUTO CO.	

1916	Frank Wheatley begins his business building pumps.	
1916	**Boeing's first plane, a B & W pontoon plane, flies; and William Boeing incorporates PACIFIC AERO PRODUCTS COMPANY.**	
1916	England; Frank Perkins and a partner establish PERKINS ENGINES.	
1916	FOLEY ENGINES is founded in Massachusetts as a engine distributor.	
1916	MHR CO. patents the first electric motor to be approved by UNDERWRITERS LABORATORIES.	
1916	HYGRADE opens a new plant in Salem, MA, that can produce 16,000 light bulbs each day.	
1916	Clyde Cessna moves his aircraft plant to North Wichita, KS.	
1916	Now in Chicago, Thomas Fawick designs and builds a heavy-duty clutch for tractors, soon he has several investors to finance this business.	(see 1918)
1916	James Moore leaves KERR STEAM TURBINE CO. to start up his own business, MOORE STEAM TURBINE CO.	
1916	This year, Naval Oil Shale Reserves are established in Colorado and Utah.	
1916	About 1916, in Milwaukee, WI, LeRoi begins building stationary engines for ice cutters, and such.	
1916	Mr. Harry Sinclair merges eleven different companies to form SINCLAIR OIL CO.	

1916	George Hendee leaves HENDEE MANUFACTURING CO.	
1916	PITTSBURGH STEEL backs Joe Joy, and he eventually builds five units that go to work for them.	
1916	**Sheffield, UK; Harry Brearley (1871-1948) invents "rustless steel," later to be called stainless steel.**	
1916	The first radio tuners, to receive different stations, are invented.	
1916	Unhappy at CHEVROLET MOTORS, Louis Chevrolet leaves, and founds FRONTENAC MOTORS CORP. with his brothers, Andre and Gaston, building Indy 500 race cars.	
1916	**The story goes that while arguing with a maid over the price of milk, Hetty Green, "the Witch of Wall Street," has a stroke and dies, leaving her two children about $50 million each. Her biographer, Charles Stack says this is not exactly the case, as Hetty had already been suffering from a series of strokes for several months.**	

1916	Ohio; WRIGHT CO. of Dayton, merges with GLENN L. MARTIN CO., to form WRIGHT-MARTIN AIRCRAFT CORP.	(see 1948)
1916	The "hobble-skirt" Coca-Cola bottle first comes into use, but it is soon "slimmed down" to facilitate fitting into the bottling machines currently being utilized.	
1916	**Railroading in America reaches its height, with a total of 254,037 miles of track in the nation.**	
1916	**Harleigh Holmes designs a steering-axle drive system and puts it in a three-wheeler. In the next couple of years he will adapt it to Ford's Model "T."**	
1916	California; the first SAFEWAY grocery store is established.	
1916	**The design of the cloverleaf intersection is patented by Arthur Hale of Maryland.**	
1916	Charlie Soderstrom joins MERCHANTS PARCEL DELIVERY, bringing the color brown with him.	
1916	DONALDSON is now selling its air cleaners (made of eider down cloth and a tin can) to Bull Tractor, Hart-Parr, Rumeley, Big Four, and others.	
1916	**The MARKRUM COMPANY builds the first Telex in the USA.**	
1916	**At Madison Square Garden, the amplifying microphone is first tested.**	
1916	YANCEY HARDWARE changes its name to GOODLOE & EARLE YANCEY and moves to quarters with warehouse space behind the store and office.	

1916	North Carolina; the GRAVELY COMPANY is established.	
1916	The TEXAS COMPANY first dabbles in motorsports with a two-man team drives a Maxwell touring car (fueled by Texaco products) from Newark, NJ, to Los Angeles, CA, in 10 days and 16 hours.	
1916	Wisconsin; PERFEX RADIATOR CO. builds a new facility in Racine, they now have over 200 employees, producing four hundred radiators each workday.	
1916	Manual windshield wipers are now standard equipment on all US built automobiles.	
1916	May; showing a young boy pushing a baby buggy while his friends, dressed for baseball, taunt him, Norman Rockwell's first *Saturday Evening Post* cover debuts.	
1916	The Loughead brothers establish LOUGHEAD AIRCRAFT MFG. CO., in Santa Barbara, CA.	
1916	The DAYTON WIRE WHEEL COMPANY is established in Dayton, OH.	
1916	HIGGINBOTHAM BROTHERS CO. of Comanche, TX, builds a new, huge, red brick store building in Cross Plains. At the time of its construction and completion, this fine, block-long edifice is the largest brick building between Ft. Worth and El Paso.	
1916	George J. DeMartini knows he can build a better truck, so, he founds the DEMARTINI TRUCK CO. in San Francisco, mostly making dump trucks.	
1916	Mr. Joel Coffin buys LIMA and renames it again... LIMA LOCOMOTIVE CORPORATION (LIMA).	(see 1947)
1916	Penny's 127 "GOLDEN RULE STORES" undergo an extremely scathing audit. Due to the fanatical and exacting financial accounting and bookkeeping expertise of George H. Bushnell, the team of auditors found "...not one single entry to question."	
1916	The BALDWIN LOCOMOTIVE WORKS now has over 20,000 employees.	
1916	Ohio; the ABBOTT CORP. of Cleveland, makes and markets the Abbott automobile for the next couple of years.	
1916	Suffolk, VA; EXTRA! EXTRA! LOCAL LAD WINS NATIONWIDE CONTEST!!! Drawing a top-hatted peanut with a cane, sixteen-year-old Antonio Gentile of this city wins the five-dollar prize from the Planters Peanut Company.	
1916	Houston; Mr. Ray L. Dudley establishes GULF PUBLISHING COMPANY.	
1916	USA; the Adamson Act puts in place a eight-hour workday for railroad workers across the nation.	
1916	USA; the Keating-Owen Bill forbids interstate shipment of mined products produced by the labor of children under sixteen, and products from factories hiring children under fourteen; however, this bill fails to pass.	(see 1918)
1916	Detroit; this year and next, the ALAND MOTOR CAR CO. is producing the Aland automobile.	
1916	Oklahoma; Mr. H. H. Champlin establishes CHAMPLIN PETROLEUM COMPANY in Enid.	
1916	Chicago; the Drexel motorcar is being built for a couple of years by the DREXEL MOTOR CAR COMPANY.	
1916	The GM TRUCK COMPANY production of electrics is only 3.2% of total production.	(see 1917)
1916	Indiana; through 1920, the "American" and the "American Junior" are built by the AMERICAN MOTOR VEHICLE CO. of Lafayette.	
1916	New Jersey; through 1924, the "American" is produced by AMERICAN MOTORS CORP. of Plainfield, no relation to the Indiana firm.	
1917	JOHN CRANE MECHANICAL SEALS starts up their business.	
1917	REPUBLIC MOTOR TRUCK buys TORBERSEN AXLE COMPANY	

1917	RUMELY CO. brings out their Model H tractor, rated at 14 drawbar and 28 belt horsepower, weighing 9,506 pounds, priced at $2,400, all future RUMELY tractors will keep this same basic design.	
1917	John Pendleton becomes a partner in PLOMB TOOLS, and five years later, his son Morris becomes general manager.	(see 1933)
1917	ARNOLD, SCHWINN & CO. buy the HENDERSON MOTORCYCLE COMPANY.	
1917	Ed Worthington and Capt. Frederick Kent acquire GERLINGER MOTOR CAR CO. and rename it GERSIX MOTOR CO.	(see 1919)
1917	The railroad companies of America order 3,400 new locomotives and 33,000 freight cars. However, the US War Industries Board holds up these orders, while approving 2,300 locomotives to be built for railroads in France for use by our US troops, as well as 300 built for the British and 1,600 for the Russians.	
1917	North Carolina; THOMASVILLE CHAIR CO. sales exceed one million dollars, and T. J. has begun giving key responsibilities to his son T. Austin Finch; grooming the next generation for success.	(see 1919)
1917	The INTERNATIONAL BUSINESS MACHINE DIVISION of the C-T-R-CO. is formed.	
1917	**Oil is discovered at Ranger, TX, on Texas & Pacific Railway land.**	
1917	James F. Lincoln founds the LINCOLN ELECTRIC WELDING SCHOOL, this non-profit school will turn out over 100,000 qualified welders before the end of this century.	
1917	Ira J. Cooper, a auto accessory wholesaler, joins GIANT TIRE CO. as a director. Thus begins the evolution into COOPER TIRE CO.	
1917	OSHKOSH TRUCKS is founded by W. R. Besserdich and B. A. Mosling.	

	1917	**GATES RUBBER CO. designs and produces the first rubber and textile belts.**	(see 1927)
	1917	Osmyn Mowers, a horse and mule trader from Ohio, begins testing a type of pump leather at Saratoga, TX, in RIO BRAVO OIL CO. wells, this evolves into the GUIBERSON swab cups, that will be used world wide in a few years.	
	1917	Count Ferdinand Von Zeppelin dies and is honored as a hero.	
	1917	PACIFIC AERO PRODUCTS changes to BOEING AIRPLANE COMPANY. The B & Ws aren't selling, so Boeing builds two prototypes of the Model "C," then the US Navy orders 50 of 'em.	
	1917	The Pearce family pools their money, abilities, knowledge and machinery, and forms TEXAS IRON WORKS (TIW) at Goose Creek, TX (now Baytown).	
	1917	**G. Sundback patents the modern zipper, but not the first zipper.**	

1917	As the fiscal year ends June 30, the average income per mile of railroad line has risen from $4,250 to $4,850, due to the tremendous surge of war related business.	
1917	**THOMPSON PRODUCTS introduces the one-piece engine valve.**	
1917	The NATIONAL CARBON CO. merges with UNION CARBIDE CO., and begins worldwide expansion.	
1917	BRIGGS & STRATTON (B&S) are building rifle grenades for our military and engines for the USN.	
1917	The several Phillips companies combine into PHILLIPS PETROLEUM CO.	
1917	INDEPENDENT TORPEDO COMPANY establishes a factory in De Leon, TX, servicing the southwestern oil fields.	
1917	Henry and Wilfred Leland leave CADILLAC, and form LINCOLN MOTOR COMPANY.	

1917	DETROIT FUSE & MFG. CO. becomes SQUARE D MFG. CO.	
1917	A tank car leasing operation begins, that eventually becomes SHIPPERS CAR LINE.	
1917	On Long Island, NY, CHANCE VOUGHT AIRCRAFT is founded by Mr. Chance M. Vought. Then, on June 18th, Birdseye Lewis and Chance Vought join forces and form the LEWIS & VOUGHT CORPORATION.	(see 1922)
1917	During WW I, the US ARMY uses a modified version of a gas/smoke mask invented by Garrett Morgan.	
1917	**RAND-MCNALLY introduces its concept of indicating roads by number, first on a road map of Illinois. In time, federal and state authorities adopt this system and it is soon in world-wide use.**	
1917	The first Moon Pies are marketed.	
1917	Texas; due to the efforts of Amon G. Carter Sr., three (3) military airfields are now located in Ft. Worth.	
1917	**The FRANKLIN automobile introduces push-button door locks.**	
1917	Oscar Albertson designs a valve-lathe, a hand tool used to reseat engine valves. This invention will be the basic foundation of Sioux Tools.	
1917	The THOMAS & BETTS COMPANY incorporated and moves all operations under one roof in Elizabeth, NJ. This will be their headquarters until 1993.	
1917	Satisfying Henry Ford's request, the portable, electric, hand drill is invented by Duncan Black and Alonso Decker.	(see 1918)
1917	After seeing so many folks convert their Model "T" cars into trucks of one sort or the other, Henry Ford introduces the Model "TT" or Double "T," one ton chassis for "Heavy Duty" work. Ford's Dearborn factory begins producing Fordson Model "F" farm tractors. FORD also begins building Fordson farm tractors in the UK.	
1917	The CLEVELAND MOTOR PLOW CO. is renamed CLEVELAND TRACTOR COMPANY. (CLETRAC)	
1917	August 29; Robert G. LeTourneau and Evelyn Petersen elope to Tijuana, Mexico, and are married.	
1917	**WALTER KIDDE CO. is founded to produce the first integrated smoke detection and carbon dioxide fire extinguisher system, which has been recently invented by Mr. Walter Kidde (pronounced Kidda).**	
1917	France; Gen. George S. Patton whips the Germans in the first ever "mechanized" military battle. Patton realizes the main advantages of a tank are firepower, mobility, and shock effect.	
1917	On the Ohio River at Wheeling, AG & E's first "super" power plant comes on-line. The largest city to be served by this steam-powered plant is Canton connected by the nation's first 138,000 volt power line. This is the first coal-fired plant to be built at the mouth of a mine.	
1917	BERLIET is now building forty trucks each day for the French military forces.	
1917	With the backing of several Ohio investors, Glenn L. Martin pulls out of the WRIGHT-MARTIN AIRCRAFT CO., and reestablishes the GLENN L. MARTIN COMPANY, this time in Ohio. This is known as the Martin-Wright divorce.	
1917	The UNITED CIGAR COMPANY changes its corporate name to GENERAL CIGAR COMPANY, INC.	
1917	As the US enters WWI, the CURTISS AEROPLANE CO. is the largest airplane builder in the US… simply because they build the best planes.	
1917	ROSS HEAT EXCHANGER COMPANY is established.	
1917	GUY MOTORS LTD. ceases all vehicle production and become the largest manufacturer in the UK of depth charge firing mechanisms and producing large numbers of aero engines, as well.	
1917	USA; as one of 15 builders producing the class "B" Liberty Trucks, INDIANA TRUCK CO., sends 475 to our military.	(see WWI)

C. M. VOUGHT

1917	The Indiana Truck Company reorganizes as Indiana Truck Corporation.	(see 1923) (see 1925)
1917	Buick Motor Car Co., now a division of General Motors, names Walter Chrysler as President and General Manager.	(see 1919)
1917	Since Alfred's death in 1912, the Rowe family has administered the affairs of the RO Ranch, until they now sell the RO to W. J. Lewis, a former top hand on the ranch.	
1917	The first automobile license plates in Texas are issued this year.	
1917	Gates Rubber Company's success is assured when John Gates (Charles' brother) invents the tremendously successful rubber and fabric V-belt.	
1917	Texas; boasting four (yes 4) airplanes, Kelly Field is established near San Antonio.	
1917	Oklahoma; in Enid, Geronimo Motor Company is incorporated this year. Geronimo manufactures farm tractors, roadsters, and full-size five-passenger automobiles, being sold by agents across Oklahoma, Kansas, Nebraska, and West Texas.	(see 1920)
1917	Seeing as Ford is doing so good in the farm tractor business, GM decides to give it a whirl and acquires the Samson "Sieve Grip" tractor line, but financial losses seem inherent.	(see 1922)
1917	Texas; the young Mr. Frank Kent establishes the GMC Truck Co, in Ft. Worth, his first vehicle dealership.	(see 1919)
1917	Minnesota; powered by a Henderson motorcycle motor, Iver Holm of St. Paul builds a snow cycle similar to the Sawyers.	(see 1921)
1917	Texas; in Houston, a pre-fabricated house builder, Houston Ready-Cut House Company is established.	
1917	Ohio; Mr. A. I. Root writes, "I looked up at the stars and stripes that were floating in the wind from the flagpole over our company and said, "The A. I. Root Company, God willing, will last for years after A. I. Root, himself, is gone."	(see 1928)
1917	It appears the "infernal kumbustion" engine has won the battle, at least for the next century. Only one single electric truck is produced this year by General Motors Truck Company, bringing the total to 687 electrics they have built.	
1917	The US government takes control of US railroad carriers, and all are in dire financial straits.	
17-18	Kissel Co. build four-wheel drive trucks under license for the war effort, but switch back to normal pre-war production after the war.	
1918	Albaugh-Dover of Nebraska say their "Square Turn Tractor" could go anywhere and do anything that could be done with a team of horses.	
1918	Fred E. Cooper starts Fred E. Cooper, Inc., later to become Cooper Manufacturing Co., in Tulsa, OK. Soon, Fred signs a contract with Rumely Tractor Co. of La Porte, IN, marking the beginning of the mobile oil-well servicing industry. Fred E. Cooper, Inc. later uses Fordson tractors for his pulling units. Arcadia Refining Co. soon has one of these Fordson's on their Cross Plains production lease, out in Callahan County, TX.	
1918	Iowa; to get started in the tractor business, Deere & Company purchase the Waterloo Gasoline Traction Engine Co. of Waterloo, makers of the Waterloo Boy tractors.	
1918	**Oil is discovered at Burkburnett, and at Breckenridge, TX.**	
1918	SKF now has 12 factories and 12,000 employees, and demand for their bearings still exceeds production.	
1918	Two young wireless radio enthusiasts set up a factory on a kitchen table in Chicago and begin building radio sets for other amateurs; thus begins Zenith.	

ALBAUGH-DOVER "Square Turn"
The Farm Tractor with the "Giant Grip Drive"
Has fewer working parts than any other tractor, having no clutch, no differential and no transmission gears, hence no expensive parts to replace. Every part accessible—easy to get at. Operates successfully on either Gasoline or Kerosene.
Write for FREE Catalog
See for yourself why the "Square-Turn" Tractor will operate most satisfactorily and economically on your farm.
ALBAUGH-DOVER CO.
3020 W. 21st St., Chicago
Factories: Chicago and Norfolk, Nebr.
A One-Man-Two-Way-Square-Turn Tractor. 15 H.P. on the Drawbar. 30 H.P. on the Belt.
3 Plows
NO CLUTCH TO SLIP
NO GEARS TO STRIP
NO EXPENSIVE REPAIR

1918	Ira Cooper forms his own rubber tire company.
1918	ALEMITE introduces the first high-pressure grease fitting.
1918	The B. F. Avery Company introduces the first tractor mounted cultivator.
1918	**HEBB MOTORS CO. of Lincoln, NE, begin producing PATRIOT TRUCKS.**
1918	George E. Failing and Burt Garber found GARBER TOOL & SUPPLY CO. in Tulsa, servicing cable tool and rotary rigs.
1918	Louis Moses opens a tool shop in Paris, France; his first tool was for the FRENCH NATIONAL RAILWAY.
1918	Engineers at A. O. SMITH develop the flux coated welding rod, a breakthrough in arc welding, and they stay in the welding products business until 1965.
1918	**A. H. Petersen develops his "Hole-Shooter," a lightweight, one-handed, electric ¼" drill, at the request of Henry Ford, for use in auto assembly work. This is generally recognized as the first "one-handed" electric drill, and is issued a patent in 1921.**
1918	The TWIN-DISC CLUTCH CO., is incorporated in Racine, WI, with Thomas Fawick as President and General Manager. (see 1928)
1918	Arthur L. Parker establishes the PARKER APPLIANCE COMPANY.
1918	Solomon R. Dresser dies.
1918	NACHI-FUJIKOSHI (NF) is founded in Japan, to manufacture cutting tools and specialty steel.
1918	**KELVINATOR produces the first automatic home refrigerator for the American market, and sells 67 of them, this year.**
1918	CLARK BROTHERS enters the oil field equipment business.
1918	Hoboken, PA, is renamed Blawnox for the BLAW-KNOX COMPANY, which is headquartered there. BLAW was already located there. BLAW-KNOX is created by the merger of BLAW COLLAPSIBLE STEEL CENTERING CO. and the KNOX PRESSED & WELDED STEEL COMPANY.
1918	SOCONY buys out MAGNOLIA OIL COMPANY.
1918	**Charles Jung invents fortune cookies.**
1918	**The superheterodyne radio circuit (still used in EVERY radio and television set) is invented by Edwin H. Armstrong.** (see 1923)
1918	**The first uranium in New Mexico is discovered in the northwestern part of the San Juan Basin by John Wade.**
1918	**The Standard Time Act is passed.**
1918	In Japan, Mr. Kōnosuke Matsushita invents a two-socket electric light fixture; this is the beginning of MATSUSHITA ELECTRICAL INDUSTRIAL CO., LTD.
1918	Frank M. Pool Sr. is born in Grandview, TX. (see 1947)
1918	**The first CHEVROLET trucks are sold, as CHEVROLET is absorbed by GENERAL MOTORS.**
1918	**John Browning's automatic rifle, the BAR, is first used near the end of WWI, and will be in use through the Vietnam War, fifty years later.**
1918	John O'Connell, S. L. Odegard and John Pratt purchase the small Richland, WI, telephone company, and two other local telephone properties.
1918	September; HOG CREEK OIL CO. director Tom Dees strikes oil on land owned by Joe Duke, near Desdemona, TX.
1918	Shreveport, LA; the BAIN-BEAIRD WELDING COMPANY (later BEAIRD INDUSTRIES) is founded with a $500 investment.

DESIGN.
A. H. PETERSEN.
ELECTRIC DRILL.
APPLICATION FILED JUNE 24, 1921.

59,678.

Patented Nov. 15, 1921.

FIG. 1

FIG. 2

1918	Having terminated the GRAHAM BROTHERS' import license last year, KONE starts making and installing its own elevators, as a division of STROMBERG.	
1918	Mike Martinez opens the first EL FENIX restaurant at the corner of Griffin and McKinney in Dallas, TX.	
1918	**General John Thompson invents the Thompson Machine Gun, or "Tommy Gun."**	
1918	Insurance companies NOW realize that workers in the asbestos industry are dying at an earlier age than in other industries.	
1918	December; BOEING has 337 people on its payroll. To keep afloat, after government orders stopped, they are manufacturing furniture and such.	
1918	Orange, TX; the BLUMBERG MOTOR MFG. COMPANY introduces the Blumberg "Steady-Pull" 12-24 tractor. BLUMBERG is also marketing a smaller 9-18 tractor. Blumberg builds their own engines for both tractors.	(see 1924)
1918	**HOLT MFG. CO. awards the very first Caterpillar Tractor dealership to GOODLOE & EARLE YANCEY.** (*This is quite a Yancey story in itself.*)	(see 1925)
1918	PURE OIL COMPANY establishes a refinery at Cabin Creek, WV, near Charleston.	
1918	**WAYNE OIL TANK CO. introduces the Model 276V, the world's first "visible" gasoline pump.**	
1918	As an example of the grand scale of this war, the British Empire now has 630,000 hospital beds.	(see 1914)
1918	The GLENN L. MARTIN COMPANY builds the world's first twin-engine bomber, the MB-2.	
1918	The Loughead F-1 Flying Boat makes its maiden flight, then Loughead makes their first military sale, some Curtiss HS-2L Flying Boats to the US Navy.	
1918	Grapelade, WELCH's first jam is introduced, with the US Army buying the total initial product run, thus when our boys return home, they demand Grapelade for themselves and their families.	(see 1927)
1918	England; the WHITE & POPPE Engine factory is acquired by DENNIS BROTHERS.	

1918	The first production of helium begins in Texas.	
1918	Mr. Billy Durant personally invests in a firm working to build a totally new product, an electric-powered "ice-box"... GUARDIAN FRIGERATOR.	(see 1919)
1918	McLAUGHLIN MOTOR CAR CO. LTD. merges with CHEVROLET MOTOR CO. OF CANADA, forming GENERAL MOTORS OF CANADA.	
1918	October; Clessie Cummins visits the R. M. Hvid Engineering Co. in Chicago, desiring to obtain rights to manufacture the Hvid type oil engine. However the license fee was too much and he returned to Columbus Indiana to convince Mr. Irwin to finance him.	(see 1919)
1918	Dr. Sanford Moss, a G-E engineer, hauls a supercharged 350 horsepower internal combustion engine up to the summit of Pike's Peak in Colorado. Even in the thin air at 14,110 feet (4,341 m), Moss succeeds at boosting the engine up to 356 horsepower.	
1918	Mr. Henry Ford introduces his mass-produced, low-priced FORDSON farm tractor.	(see 1920)
1918	This year, the first fixed, front-mounted backfill blade for wheeled tractors is built by the BAKER MFG. CO.	(see 1924)
1918	INDIAN MOTOCYCLES introduce the first V-twin, 4 valve per cylinder motorcycle engine, about seven decades ahead of their competition.	(see 1923)
1918	In Chicago, *this year and next,* the Amalgamated motorcar is built and sold by the AMALGAMATED MACHINERY CORP.	
1918	August Thyssen, now pushing 80, continues to have sole control of his businesses. He has lost his many foreign companies, and all expansion is ended. His companies are transferred to a new group, Vereinigte Stahlwerke AG.	(see 1926)

1918	The US Supreme Court declares the Keating-Owen Bill to be unconstitutional.	
1918	UNIT CORP. OF AMERICA is founded in West Allis, WI, producing forged steel components for several various industries.	(see WWII) (see 1955)
1918	Texas; the BRIDGES MOTOR CAR & RUBBER CO., of Ft. Worth now builds the Bridges automobile.	
1918	USA; this year's winning locomotive is built for the BALTIMORE & OHIO RAILROAD, and is more than 41 times heavier than the 1837 locomotive. This big fellow weighs 668,000 pounds (303,000 kg) with engine and tender fully loaded. *This is a biiiig steamer!!!*	
1918	Nebraska; for the next four years, the Douglas automobile is built by DOUGLAS MOTORS CORP. of Omaha.	
1919	January 15; two million, three hundred twenty thousand gallons (14,000 tons) of molasses bursts from a ruptured wooden storage tank and sweeps through the streets of Boston, killing 21 and injuring over 150.	
1919	February; CUMMINS ENGINE COMPANY is incorporated (financed by W. G. Irwin), and in a couple of months, Clessie builds his first HVID engines, under a recently acquired license. The first Hvid oil engine from Cummins was a 6 hp model C Thermoil. This engine is very similar to the 6 hp Thermoil engine that HERCULES is building for SEARS & ROEBUCK.	(see 1920)
1919	HERCULES ENGINE CO. builds the 6 and 8 HP Model U Thermoil, oil burning engines, for Sears & Roebuck.	(see 1920)
1919	GENERAL MOTORS purchases GUARDIAN FRIGERATOR COMPANY.	
1919	In Racine, WI, WALLIS TRACTORS CO. and J. I. CASE CO. merge.	(see 1928)
1919	C. L. BEST GAS TRACTION CO. unveils the BEST SIXTY, the first tractor to bear the "CATERPILLAR" name... or is it?	

1919	**RUSSELL GRADER MFG. CO brings out the first self-propelled road grader (maintainer).**	
1919	W-K-M VALVE CO. established in Houston, TX.	
1919	Having run the DAVID BRADLEY CO. for many years, J. Harley Bradley, David Bradley's son, dies.	
1919	Captain F. Kent retires from GERSIX MOTOR CO. and his son Harry Kent becomes Worthington's partner in GERSIX.	(see 1923)
1919	J. O. Eaton, et al, leave REPUBLIC TRUCK and incorporate EATON AXLE COMPANY.	
1919	Nebraska passes the Tractor Test Law, still enforced 90 years later. The first tested and approved tractor is the WATERLOO BOY Model "N," on March 31, 1920.	
1919	**Eastland County, TX, produces over 22 million barrels of oil this year.**	
1919	**In New York City, the AMERICAN PETROLEUM INSTITUTE (API) is established.**	
1919	George and Herman Brown and their bro-in-law Dan Root start BROWN & ROOT COMPANY.	
1919	HERCULES ENGINE CO. is building the 6 and 8 HP Model U Thermoil, oil burning engines, for Sears and Roebuck.	
1919	**Oklahoma; with a wagon, a team of mules, a borrowed pump and $1,500 capital, Erle P. Halliburton starts NEW METHOD OIL WELL CEMENTING COMPANY.**	
1919	MARX TOYS is founded.	
1919	North Carolina; THOMASVILLE CHAIR CO. forms alliances with ST. JOHN'S TABLE CO. of Michigan and buffet builder B. F. HUNTLEY CO. of Winston-Salem to market dining room suites comprised of each other's products. This alliance is the first national sales force in the furniture industry, and it is very successful.	(see 1927)
1919	**NASH is now the largest truck builder in the world.**	

1919	INTERNATIONAL PAPER is now using more than 1,000 horses in their logging woods.	
1919	Albert J. Weatherhead, Jr., starts business with $1,000 capital and his engine priming cups and drain cocks are his only products.	
1919	**Thurber, the principal bituminous coal mining town of Texas, has a population of about 9,000.**	
1919	William Boeing and Eddie Hubbard fly a Boeing C-700 to deliver 60 letters from Vancouver, B. C., to Seattle, WA, the first-ever international air mail flight.	

C. P. STRITE.
BREAD TOASTER.
APPLICATION FILED JUNE 27, 1919.

1,394,450.   Patented Oct. 18, 1921.
5 SHEETS—SHEET 3.

FIG-6

FIG-7

INVENTOR
CHARLES F STRITE
BY
ATTORNEYS

1919	**A new FORD Model "T" costs $500 delivered, a PIERCE-ARROW costs $8,500 plus shipping.**	
1919	From various sources there are now 45 different conversion kits offered to change your FORD Model "T" into a light tractor.	
1919	*Charles Strite invents the pop-up toaster.*	
1919	The original GREY WOLF DRILLING CO. is founded.	
1919	ALEMITE CORPORATION is established.	
1919	In Coffeyville, KS, the JENSEN BROS. start building pumping equipment for oil wells.	
1919	B & S acquires the "Motor wheel" from A. O. SMITH. The BRIGGS & STRATTON Flyer Car is introduced.	
1919	Henry buys out minority stockholders in FORD.	
1919	Three pioneer firms of the electric light, AEG, SIEMENS & HALSKE AG, and AUER-GESELLSCHAFT merge, forming OSRAM.	
1919	Two aircraft factories, The WICHITA AEROPLANE SERVICE CO., and the WICHITA AIRCRAFT CO., are established in Wichita, KS.	
1919	FOKKER builds his first passenger plane, the FII, a four-seater.	
1919	Eugene Cornwell begins producing high quality mechanics' tools in Cuyahoga Falls, OH.	
1919	The complete inventory of PARKER APPLIANCE CO. is lost in a truck wreck. Arthur Parker goes back to work as an engineer, determined to restart soon.	
1919	Marcel Schlumberger joins his brother in Normandy, France, for their first work together, and next year they open their first office… in Paris.	
1919	About this time, Japan begins colonizing the island of Saipan, turning it into a huge sugar cane plantation.	(see WWII) (see 1944)
1919	With financing from his father, Lester Sears founds TOWMOTOR CORP. to build and market tow tractors.	
1919	Joe Joy is issued a patent for his "gathering arm loader." For 5 years the patent is hotly contested, but Joy wins, and JOY MACHINE COMPANY is incorporated.	
1919	HUMBLE OIL & REFINING COMPANY of Houston is bought out by STANDARD OIL COMPANY.	
1919	LAFAYETTE MOTORS CORP. is founded???	
1919	*The short-wave radio is invented, by G. Marconi.*	
1919	**The Desdemona oil field is now the second largest field in the oil belt. Shares in HOG CREEK OIL CO. bought for $100 a short while back, are now being sold for over $10,000. Desdemona's population spurts up to over 15,000 for a short time.** *"Yeah Bubba, 'ats rite, Desdemona really means 'deres de money.'"*	
1919	In France, Marcellin Leroy sets up a business based on producing electric motors and electric generators.	
1919	The BENEDUM-TREES interests now include leases, skimming plants and refineries in five US states and Mexico as well as Colombia. June; TRANSCONTINENTAL OIL CO. is established in Pittsburgh, PA, to consolidate most of BENEDUM-TREES' worldwide holdings.	

1919	Due to prohibition INDEPENDENT BREWERIES CO. introduces IBC Root Beer to help compensate for the lack of real beer.	
1919	**The FT. WORTH *STAR-TELEGRAM* now has the largest circulation of any newspaper in Texas, a lead it maintains into the 1950s.**	
1919	Carruthers Field in Benbrook, TX, is the base of the NATIONAL AIRPLANE CO., the first air freight company in the Ft. Worth area.	
1919	At the Treaty of Versailles, Germany's BAYER loses its trademarks for aspirin in France, the UK, Russia, and the USA, as a bargaining chip.	
1919	Dr. Georg Schäfer joins his father's company, KUGELFISCHER GEORG SCHÄFER & CO. (FAG), he will eventually be responsible for the company's growth far beyond the lines of natural expansion.	
1919	During Prohibition, many brewing companies become ice cream makers, their advertising dollars promote America's interest in ice cream. Also, during Prohibition, about a million gallons of Canadian whiskey makes its way across the border into the "dry" USA. This is about 80% of Canada's total production during this time.	
1919	Amsterdam, the Netherlands; KLM Royal Dutch Airlines is established.	
1919	Henderson, TX; HACKER MACHINE & SUPPLY CO. build their first "oilbath" rotary tables, for use on drilling rigs.	
1919	South America; in Colombia, AVIANCA (Aerovías Nacionales de Colombia SA), a new airline is established.	
1919	Jim Casey and Claude Ryan expand their delivery service to Oakland, CA, and rename again, this time to UNITED PARCEL SERVICE (UPS).	
1919	Houston; the SOUTHERN MOTOR MANUFACTURING ASSOCIATION introduces the Ranger Cultivator, a cultivator powered by a LeRoi engine. This firm will build and market two sizes for the next five years.	
1919	Anaconda, MT; one of the world's tallest free-standing structures is the new smokestack at the ANACONDA COPPER MINING COMPANY smelter. This smokestack is 585 feet (180 m) tall and 86 feet (26. 47 m) diameter at its base. This smokestack will be used through 1980, and will be designated a Montana state monument in 1985.	
1919	Germany; DANZAS & CO. open a Gmbh branch for sea transport from North European ports.	
1919	France; Andre Citroën establishes an automobile factory.	
1919	A US military truck convoy takes 62 days traveling from Washington, DC, to San Francisco, CA. Of course the roads just aren't real good, so they experience quite a few mechanical breakdowns.	
1919	This year about 25 million of the popular 78 rpm phonograph/Victrola records are sold.	
1919	John C. Endebrock builds and patents a "jaw coupled with a spring plunger locking device," mounted on a "lower fifth-wheel." His "fifth-wheel" device locks on to a "king pin" on the underside of the front end of the "semi-trailer." Only one person, the driver, is required to attach and detach the trailer from the towing vehicle. Previously, it took three persons with jacks and tools were for this job. *NOTE: Endebrock's fifth-wheel and king pin setup is very similar to the system used well into the twenty-first century.*	(see 1928)
1919	The first trucks from DEMARTINI finally are produced, marketed, and hit the roads.	
1919	R. G. LeTourneau leaves the auto-repair business and becomes a land-leveling contractor.	
1919	May 27; a Curtiss NC-4 plane, designed in cooperation with the US Navy, makes the first ever airborne trans-Atlantic crossing. SHELL fuel is used in the first Trans-Atlantic airplane flight.	
1919	A world record of 70 mph (112 km) on water is set by Alexander G. Bell's hydrofoil "Hydrodrome IV." The five ton boat has underwater fins to raise the hull and lessen drag.	

1919	In addition to his responsibilities at Buick, Walter Chrysler becomes the first VP of GM, in charge of manufacturing.	(see 1920)
1919	GENERAL MOTORS buys the airplane manufacturer, DAYTON WRIGHT COMPANY.	
1919	The CURTISS-SOUTHWEST AIRPLANE COMPANY is established in Tulsa, OK.	
1919	Along the Colorado River in Arizona, Grand Canyon National Park is created by the US government.	
1919	Plymouth, OH; J. D. Fate joins with the ROOT-HEATH MFG. CO., forming FATE-ROOT-HEATH. F-R-H continues to build clay-working machinery, yard locomotives, and a line of sharpening equipment for reel-type mowers. F-R-H continues to prosper for the next decade, until the crash of '29.	(see 1930s)
1919	The term "white-collar" is coined by writer Upton Sinclair, describing what he calls "the petty underlings of the business world."	
1919	Japan; Mr. Masuo Tadano opens a steel fabrication business in Takamatsu City.	(see 1948)
1919	While attempting to cross the Atlantic in a tri-plane, Hawker goes down, and is rescued by a freighter with no radio. Therefore, it is several days before the public knows if he is dead or alive. However, he does win the 5,000 pound sterling *Daily Mail* Prize.	(see 1921)
1919	Lubbock, TX; moving from Ft. Worth, Frank Kent now owns and manages Kent Buick, a local dealership.	(see 1930)
1919	BROWNHOIST introduces the "Brownhoist Power Scraper Shovel." It is actually a wheeled loader, very likely, the first.	
1919	Australia; after WWI, Fred C. Custance becomes a CATERPILLAR TRACTOR COMPANY dealer. Sadly though, his automobile breaks down in the Australian desert, and he dies of heat exhaustion at age thirty-three.	
1919	Oklahoma; C. W. Flint Sr. and a partner now own TULSA RIG, REEL & MFG. CO. Flint also invests in lumber mills, and expands the construction business.	(see 1924)
1919	Ohio; crawler tracks are now being used under the digging end of the BYERS Auto-Crane, now they are either steam, electric, or gasoline powered.	(see 1926)
1919	The $25,000 Orteig Prize for Aviation is first offered this year. It is to run for 5 years, for the first non-stop solo flight from New York to Paris France, or vice versa. *NOTE: The prize is not awarded and is renewed after the first five-year offering.*	(see 1927)
1919	The Samson "Iron Horse" farm tractor offers four-wheel chain drive, and can turn in its own wheelbase, by the wheels on opposite sides going in opposite directions.	
1919	The second wealthiest man in America dies at age 84. While alive, Andrew Carnegie gave $350 million to various philanthropic, educational, and public advancement items and organizations. His remaining estate assets will now be given to charities, foundations, and pensions.	
1919	England; as the war ends, Mr. Ernest Crump is discharged from the army, as his services as a dispatch rider are no longer required. Carrying everything he owns in a single suitcase, Crump puts a few pounds sterling down on a small shed at Scout Hill, Dewsbury. Within a year, Crump's PELICAN ENGINEERING CO. employs four men, and keeps them very busy converting surplus military vehicles to civilian roadway specifications, and marketing them.	(see 1928)
1919	Michigan; the BATES MACHINE & TRACTOR COMPANY is organized. Their tractors are called "Steel Mules," and half-tracks are the first type built.	(see 1921)
1919	Ohio; the VULCAN IRON WORKS of Toledo develops and builds the first ever electric-powered shovel (or excavator). Using either a remote electric generator or a generator mounted on the shovel, the problems inherent with steam power, i. e., a fireman, fuel-gathering crew, and constant boiler tube repairs (to name a few) are eliminated.	
1919	New York City; the Amco motorcar is built by AMERICAN MOTORS INC., for a couple of years.	

1919	July 7; US Army Colonel Dwight D. Eisenhower joins the First Army's Transcontinental Truck Convoy from "Zero Milestone" near the White House in Washington, DC, along the Lincoln Highway to San Francisco, CA. Averaging only about 58 miles each day, this jaunt takes almost two months, and will definitely shape Ike's thoughts about our need for interstate highways.	(see 1956)
1919	Texas; in San Antonio, at 515 Roosevelt St., the LONE STAR MOTOR CAR CO., also known as LONE STAR TRUCK & TRACTOR ASSOCIATION is established, and will operate through 1922.	
1919	Now, there is no doubt that gasoline has replaced kerosene as the principal product of the American petroleum industry.	
1919	Sweden; this year, (AB) Bofors-Gullspång shortens their company name to AB Bofors.	
1919	Italy; MAGNETI MARELLI is established this year.	
1919	A convoy of 23 FIAT 15 ton trucks cross the Sahara Desert, making the 3,000 km trek with no major mechanical failures.	
1920s	Early 20s, Don Lee, a West Coast Cadillac Dealer, purchases EARL AUTOMOBILE WORKS, becoming DON LEE COACH & BODY WORKS. Harley Earl is the manager.	
1920s	Early 20s, I. H. Grancell invents a "brake dressing" and 'Bestolife (asbestos life) comes into being, to extend the life of brake blocks on drilling rigs at Signal Hill, in California.	
1920s	LEROI is now building 2- and 4- cylinder engines, both air and water cooled, for tractors, compressors and other industrial applications.	
1920s	Sorely needing a portable air compressor for the family business, DAVEY TREE EXPERT CO.; Paul H. Davey Sr. begins development and soon has a workable, portable, relatively lightweight, small air compressor.	
1920s	MISSION SALES COMPANY is founded to market oilfield mud pump pistons for a San Antonio manufacturer.	
1920s	SKAGIT starts up in business in the early 20s.	
1920s	By now, CORBITT MOTOR TRUCK CO. is one of America's leading truck producers, building up to a five ton model.	
1920s	ALLIS CHALMERS will buy the MONARCH TRACTOR CO., the LACROSSE PLOW CO. and STEARNS ENGINE CO. during the roaring twenties.	
1920s	Looking for a practical (and profitable) method to dispose of wood scrap from his auto factory, Henry Ford turns to the recently invented charcoal briquette, and begins manufacturing briquettes in his plant and marketing those, and charcoal grills, through FORD dealers, an instant success. H. G. Kingsford, a relative of Ford's, helps find a good location for the FORD charcoal briquette plant.	
1920s	WOFFORD OIL COMPANY of Atlanta, GA, merges with PURE OIL COMPANY.	
1920s	NESTLÉ first gets into chocolate; soon chocolate is Nestlé's second most important activity.	
1920s	UK; ALBION MOTOR CAR CO. now develops its own engine, after using GARDNER and DORMAN diesels for years. ALBION acquires HALLEY MOTORS LTD., also of Glasgow, Scotland.	
1920s	Valspar is now a common household word, as it is known as "...the varnish that won't turn white."	
1920s	UTILITY TRAILER COMPANY is one of the very first to use aluminum in building their products.	(see 1934)
1920s	ALLIS-CHALMERS' president, Harry Merritt sees a poppy field in full bloom on a visit to California. Merritt is so struck by the bright orange color, he now declares "poppy orange" as the new A-C color. Now another story is that A-C is producing a new tractor for United Tractors & Farm Equipment, a Chicago co-op, whose color is bright orange, and A-C changes their own color just to suit this customer.	

1920	January; Gulf Refining Co. now has almost 900 White Motor Co. brand trucks in its fleet.		
1920	Eaton Axle Co. and Standard Parts Co. merge, with J. O. Eaton as president of Standard Parts Co. Later this year, Standard Parts Company goes into receivership and is liquidated.		
1920	Penn Process is established to manufacture compressors.		
1920	Pauluhn Electric is established in Pearland, TX.		
1920	Cameron Iron Works incorporates in Houston, TX.		
1920	Lovejoy Couplings begins business.		
1920	**Cletrac builds a high sprocket drive crawler, the Model F.**		
1920	Texas; American International Mfg., is established in Ft. Worth, making pump jacks, etc.		
1920	By February, Cummins has already sold 22 of their 6HP oil burning engines; only about 100 or so will be produced.		
1920	Kop-Flex Couplings, etc. starts operations.		
1920	**The end of an era, the last Studebaker Wagon is built, and automobile production is moved to South Bend, IN.**		

	1920	Beckwith Machinery becomes a dealer for C. L. Best Tractors.	
	1920	This year and next, Automotive Products Co. of New York City is making and selling the Alsace motorcar.	
	1920	This year there are about 8,500,000 automobiles and trucks registered in the USA.	
	1920	American Tractor Equipment Co. (ATECO) is formed by the Woodridge family.	

1920	In July the Wall Pump & Compressor Co. is founded, in Quincy, IL.		
1920	Kohler & Silberzhan introduce their cast-iron block engine & generator.		
1920	Chicago Rawhide's primary business now is oil and grease seals.		
1920	**In the past two decades, over 2000 separate companies have built one or more cars.**		
1920	Walter P. Chrysler, age forty-five, retires from General Motors and from the auto industry, a wealthy man. His retirement only lasts a few months. He then is hired to manage and turn about the failing Willis-Overland Co.	(see 1921) (see 1941)	
1920	Amerada Corp. is founded.		
1920	**ITW develops the "shakeproof" toothed lock washer.**		
1920	**DRMC creates the first "airless" automobile tire.**		
1920	E. M. Laird Airplane Co. is formed in Wichita, KS, on the staff are Walter Beech, Clyde Cessna and Lloyd Stearman.		
1920	**Texas Iron Works develops unitized drill pipe slips.**	(see 1932)	
1920	**Briggs & Stratton pioneer overhead valve engine technology.**		
1920	**Timken is producing 90% of the bearings used in the USA.**		
1920	Texas; furniture builder, Olive & Myers Mfg. Co. Inc. at 2220-2222 Young Street in Dallas, is renamed the Mathes Corp.		
1920	**Both of the automobile-building, barroom-brawling Dodge brothers, John and Horace die this year.**	(see 1925)	
1920	The first ever regularly scheduled radio programs are broadcast by KDKA in Pittsburg, PA.		
1920	In New York City there are over a thousand Checker cabs on the streets.		
1920	The first Joy crawler mounted mining loader, the 4B is produced, and sells for $2,800.		

1920	NATIONAL SUPPLY acquires UNION TOOL CO.	
1920	Arthur Pitney and Walter Bowes (PITNEY-BOWES) invent the first postage meter to be approved by the US Postal Dept.	
1920	Garrett Morgan goes into the newspaper business and starts the Cleveland Call. He soon invents the world's first patented traffic signal, and sells the traffic signal rights to GENERAL ELECTRIC for $40,000.	
1920	Dallas, TX; WHARTON MOTORS CO. puts forth their three-wheel-drive, 12-22 tractor, as well as the "Wharton" automobile. Wharton also operates as TEXAS TRUCK & TRACTOR COMPANY, and also have a facility in Kansas City, MO.	(see 1922)
1920	Utilizing a new and unique method (the spring loaded ball and detent) of attaching socket wrenches to their handles, SNAP-ON TOOLS is founded.	
1920	The H. C. SMITH MFG. CO. is founded as Herman adds various types of core bits, underreamers and such in his blacksmith business.	
1920	LEGRAND, SUTCLIFFE & GELL are now focusing on the manufacture of pumping equipment as well as drilling and maintenance of water wells in the UK and Europe.	
1920	METALNA begins in business building water control equipment in Yugoslavia.	
1920	**Neon signs are just beginning to be widely used commercially.**	
1920	Texarkana, TX; the DIXIELAND MOTOR TRUCK CO. introduces the short-lived Dixieland 12-25 row-crop farm tractor, powered by an ERD engine.	
1920	May 17; the first KLM flight is made, in a rented De Havilland DH-16, from London to Amsterdam.	
1920	Mr. Walter and Cordelia Knott begin selling berries and preserves from a roadside berry stand in Buena Park, CA.	
1920	Jan. 15th; Congress enacts the 18th Amendment to the Constitution, prohibiting the manufacture and sale of alcoholic beverages.	
1920	Nantes, France; GEORGES RENAULT is established as a manufacturer of power tools.	
1920	**Laughead (Lockheed of aviation fame) patents a hydraulic brake system for cars; he now sells his patent to BENDIX BRAKES.**	
1920	Ontario, Canada; "Scotty" Hamilton buys his first truck.	
1920	Once again, Billy Durant is forced to resign, and board chairman Pierre S. du Pont, is also named President of GENERAL MOTORS.	
1920	UNION TOOL COMPANY is acquired by NATIONAL SUPPLY CO.	
1920	San Antonio, TX; the STROUD MOTOR MFG. ASSOCIATION brings out its 16-30 "All-In-One," tricycle-type row crop tractor, powered by a four cylinder CLIMAX engine.	
1920	Lloyd C. Douglas' *The Robe* is the first film released in Cinemascope.	(see 1927)
1920	Wichita Falls, TX; the WICHITA FALLS MOTORS CO. introduces their 20-30 "Wichita" tractor, with BEAVER four cylinder engine power.	
1920	January; The National Petroleum News says that GULF REFINING CO. now has 879 WHITE brand motor trucks in its fast-growing fleet.	
1920	November; in Winston, in the Queensland outback of Australia, the QUEENSLAND AND NORTHERN TERRITORIES AIR SERVICE, LTD. (Qantas) is established.	(see 1979)
1920	**The science of reading tree rings is developed by A. E. Douglas.**	
1920	During the past few years, CONTINENTAL SUPPLY CO. has opened forty-seven more stores in and around the oil patch.	

1920	August 26; the 19th Amendment to the Constitution is certified by Secretary of State Bainbridge Colby, granting women the right to vote.		
1920	Radio station KDKA in Pittsburgh, PA, delivers the results of the Harding-Cox election to its audience. This is the first ever regular commercial radio broadcast.		
1920	A turbocharged 12-cylinder Liberty engine is installed in a La Pere biplane for altitude testing. Young John Macready is selected to pilot the plane, and takes it up to 33,113 feet (10,188 m). Macready shortly becomes one of the most experienced high altitude fliers in the world, testing many turbochargers from 1917 through 1923.	(see 1921)	
1920	Dallas; the first radio station in Texas, WWR, is established.		

1920	Australia; about this time, Sydney Josephson sells several new HOLT crawler tractors to local farmers.	(see 1923)
1920	As several small ships have been built using Oscar Kjellberg's welding methods, Lloyds Register now approves his methods.	
1920	In deep south Texas, the first concrete highway in the state is built between San Benito and Harlingen.	
1920	Ohio; INTERNATIONAL DERRICK & EQUIPMENT CO. (IDECO) is established in Columbus, to manufacture steel oil well derricks, derricks and other such towers.	(see 1908)
1920	Germany; in the town of Harsewinkel, August Claas begins the industrial manufacture of hay balers.	(see 1921)
1920	With sales of 67,000 units, FORDSON now claims two-thirds of North America's tractor market, wreaking devastation on its competitors.	(see 1923)

1920	Crooksville, OH; during this decade HULL POTTERY begins to manufacture and market art pottery.	(see 1930s)
1920	France; Andre Citroën begins using a bogie developed by Adolph Kégresse and Jacques Hinstin. Kégresse had returned to France via Finland after the revolution in Russia.	(see 1922)
1920	Oklahoma; the 30,000 square foot GERONIMO MOTOR COMPANY plant in Enid burns to the ground. Having sold more than 1,000 automobiles, in addition to some tractors, they now cease production and go out of business.	
1920	About this time, the LUFKIN COMPANY adds small precision measuring tools to its product line.	(see WWII)
1920	By now, there are more than 246,000 tractors, of all sizes, being used by America's farmers, as well as more animal power than a decade ago… over 26,000,000 horses and mules. *Now, just mull that over for a while.*	
1920	Michigan; the BAY CITY DREDGE WORKS introduce their Model 16 One-Man excavator, a 180 degree swing unit, mounted on a chain drive crawler on front and steel wheels on the rear for steering. This 1/2 cubic yard machine can be set up as dragline, backhoe, skimmer, shovel or clamshell. It is powered by a Hercules gasoline engine or an electric motor.	(see 1923)
1920	In industrialized America, about 40% of the citizens live and work on farms and ranches.	(see 1970)
1920	Germany; early in this decade, OPEL is the first German auto maker to use a moving assembly line to "mass-produce" automobiles. Adam Opel's assembly line and his many other innovations lead the way toward motorized transportation for all classes of folk, not just the wealthy.	(see 1928)
1920	Henry's younger brother, William Ford, has been working in the employment office of FORDSON TRACTOR CO; he now leaves and opens William Ford & Co., the Fordson tractor distributor for Michigan and northern Ohio.	(see 1925)
1920	Fleeing political persecution and other dangers in Muslim Turkey, 19-year-old Alex Manoogian, a Christian Armenian, flees Smyrna and immigrates to the United States of America.	(see 1929)
1920	Oklahoma City; the statewide agent for DOUGLAS TRUCKS, built in Omaha, NE, is the newly formed local firm, CARDWELL-SALES COMPANY. Harland W. Cardwell is president and William J. Lyman is vice-president.	(see 1923)

1920	The Ace motorcar is being built and sold for about three years by the APEX MOTOR CORPORATION of Ypsilanti, MI.	
1920	California; the COLEMAN IRON WORKS is now torn down by owners Arthur S. Crites and George Hay, to make a more profitable use of the real estate.	
1920	Pennsylvania; the WINFIELD BARNES CO. of Philadelphia is building the Adelphia automobile this year.	
1921	MOLYBDENUM CORP. OF AMERICA of Pittsburgh, PA, acquires some claims in the Questa area and begin New Mexico operations with a small underground mine a few miles east.	
1921	A. J. PENOTE CO., a contractor in CLEVELAND builds a small wheeled trencher for their own use.	
1921	Texas; the first ever steel drilling rig derrick is built this year by IDECO, in Beaumont.	
1921	The GENERAL CRUDE OIL COMPANY is formed.	
1921	With a single rig, Lloyd Noble and Art Olsen found the NOBLE-OLSEN DRILLING COMPANY.	
1921	May 13; KOMATSU is established in Tokyo, Japan.	
1921	Texas; about this time LUFKIN FOUNDRY & MACHINE COMPANY begins manufacturing oil well pump jacks.	
1921	UK; BARFORD & PERKINS build their first diesel powered rollers.	
1921	Frank Seiberling resigns from GOODYEAR and starts the SEIBERLING RUBBER CO.	
1921	**Charles Kettering discovers that tetraethyl lead, combined with cleaning agents is found to be an excellent anti-knock additive.**	
1921	MAXWELL-CHALMERS AUTOMOBILE COMPANY hires Walter P. Chrysler to help it out of a bind.	(see 1924)
1921	In south central Oklahoma, Will Haseman, C. Karcher, Irv Perrine and Dan Ohern perform the first experiment using seismic waves to image the subsurface - underground.	
1921	LOCOMOBILE, about to go under, is acquired by HARE'S MOTORS OF NEW YORK.	
1921	WILSON SUPPLY CO. is founded in Houston.	
1921	**The Signal Hill oil discovery is made in California.**	
1921	**THOMPSON PRODUCTS first introduces the highly durable silicon and chrome steel engine valve.**	
1921	A. O. SMITH unveils "the Mechanical Marvel," the world's first fully automated auto frame assembly plant, capable of making one automobile frame every eight seconds.	
1921	HOOVER begins selling their vacuum products worldwide.	
1921	SK TOOLS is founded to manufacture mechanics tools.	
1921	DRMC introduces the first "raw edge" vee belt, same as used today.	
1921	In Huron South Dakota, the SHELDON F. REESE CO. is building the "Aero Car," but it doesn't even try to fly.	
1921	ABEGG & REINHOLD begin making Varco rotary tools.	
1921	**USA; There are twenty-one (21) airplane manufacturers in the state of Kansas.**	
1921	**The five millionth Ford vehicle is built.**	
1921	**W. A. RIDDELL CORP. builds another early motor-powered road grader, their trade name is WARCO.**	
1921	**The first SCAMMELL lorries (trucks) are built in England.**	
1921	LOMBERG, a small auto body manufacturing firm borrows $15,000 from Morris M. Markin, a Russian immigrant clothing manufacturer. LOMBERG soon defaults, and Markin acquires the firm and renames it MARKIN AUTO BODY CORP. They supply bodies to COMMONWEALTH MOTORS, which build MOGUL brand taxicabs.	

1921	Rogers Bros build and sell the first low-boy, heavy-duty trailer, called "the iron wagon." It has a capacity of 40 tons.	
1921	San Angelo, TX; H. G. Wendland establishes Wendland Manufacturing to produce tanks and pressure vessels.	
1921	Louis Chevrolet and C. W. Van Ranst develop an overhead valve cylinder head for the Ford Model T engine, to "soup it up," and that it does.	
1921	Nash Motors president Charles Nash also becomes president of Lafayette Motors Corp.	
1921	Johnson & Johnson employee Earle Dickson invents the "Band-Aid," to help his wife treat cuts and scrapes around the house.	
1921	Texas; brothers Austin and Tom M. Brookshire open the first Brookshire Bros. Grocery store, in the East Texas Piney Woods.	
1921	Lubrikup is established and devoted solely to the design and manufacture of composition cups for pumping crude oil.	
1921	Land O' Lakes food marketing cooperative is established with $1,375 seed money from the US Farm Bureau.	

1921	**Dallas, TX; Hailey's Pig Stand opens; the world's first drive-in restaurant.**	
1921	**This year Hudson is the first auto with adjustable front seats.**	
1921	The makers of Old Grand-Dad bourbon mark their bottles "for medicinal purposes" and continue marketing bourbon during prohibition.	
1921	International Breweries Corp. begins making, bottling and selling "root beer," a new soft drink to help replace their income lost from alcoholic beer.	
1921	July or August; Marrrrrrrrrvin Zindler is born.	
1921	About this time, International Derrick & Equipment Co. of Columbus, Ohio, and Stacey Engineering of Ohio, Indiana, and Pennsylvania, merge to create International Stacey Company.	
1921	Thomas & Betts begins to introduce T & B electric products to the end users, the electrical contractors.	
1921	RKO is formed by the merger of the Radio Corporation of America (RCA) and the Keith-Orpheum theatre chain; hence, Radio-Keith-Orpheum or RKO.	
1921	Jan; Jerry McJunkin and H. B. Wehrle establish McJunkin Supply Company, in Charleston, WV.	
1921	Wichita Falls becomes the first city in Texas to have dial telephone service.	
1921	In the UK, BSA resumes motor car production.	
1921	Michigan; the most modern plant in the industry, GM's Clark Street Cadillac factory in Detroit, goes into production and will continue producing vehicles until 1987.	
1921	September 28; Lt. John Macready takes his open cockpit biplane to his highest at 40,800 feet (12,554 m).	
1921	February; watching a little boy torn between spending his nickel for ice cream or a chocolate bar, Danish immigrant Chris Nelson has an idea for a chocolate covered ice cream bar. With some help from Russell Stover (the candy man), Nelson then creates the Eskimo Pie. The first 250,000 Eskimo Pies sell out within 24 hours, and by springtime, over one million are being sold each and every day.	
1921	Germany; Kjellberg Elektroden & Maschinen GMBH is founded.	
1921	For a couple of years, the Adria Motor Car Corporation of Batavia, NY, builds and sells the Adria motorcar.	

1921	George Washington Carver is called to Washington, DC, to testify before congress, regarding a tariff on peanuts. Carver was granted ten minutes to speak, but his knowledge so impressed congress that he was allowed to speak for 1 1/2 hours.	
1921	Germany; CLAAS receives the first patent on a knotter apparatus which works in a operationally reliable manner. Soon hay balers of many other manufacturers are equipped with CLAAS knotters.	(see 1929)
1921	There are now 186 companies building farm tractors in the United States of America.	(see 1930)
1921	Illinois; MOLINE PRESS STEEL CO. now begins making only "Buddy L" toys in their plant, which will be a popular brand for decades.	
1921	October; in Norway, ME, Charles H. Young files for a patent for a motor-driven sled he developed. It has an endless belt on an independent rear suspended power unit, and a curved front end with skis for steering. Young receives his patent in 1925, preceding Eliason and others.	(see 1924)
1921	In Chicago, the DRAGON MOTOR CORPORATION is producing the Dragon automobile.	
1921	England; practicing for an Aerial Derby, Harry Hawker's plane crashes, and he is killed.	
1921	BATES MACHINE & TRACTOR begins producing the soon to be popular Model "F."	(see 1929)
1921	NY; in Buffalo, a small electric car claiming a 60 mile range and a speed of 25 mph is now being built by the AUTOMATIC ELECTRIC TRANSMISSION COMPANY.	
1921	Mr. Karel Čapek, a science fiction author, invents the robot.	
1921	Texas; the ROBERTSON COMPANY is now building the Robertson motor car in San Antonio.	
1922	Houston; Harry Cameron and the CAMERON Iron Works invent and build the first Blow Out Preventer.	
1922	March 22; Oilman James Abercrombie is constantly worried about well blowouts and fires (his third blowout is now ongoing), and he draws a sketch in the dirt floor of Harry Cameron's Machine Shop in Houston, TX. They have some castings made at Howard Hughes Sr. 's shop, and soon Abercrombie and Cameron have invented the Oil Well Blowout Preventer (BOP). Cameron's little machine shop very soon becomes a multi-million dollar business.	
1922	J. O. Eaton buys his original company, TORBERSEN AXLE CO., back from REPUBLIC MOTOR TRUCK CO. and merges it with EATON AXLE CO.	
1922	AMERICAN APPLIANCE CO. is founded in Cambridge, MA.	
1922	Eddie Wagner & his brothers form the MIXERMOBILE CO. named after their machine. The Wagner brothers soon expand to front end loaders and establish WAGNER TRACTOR COMPANY to manufacture construction equipment.	
1922	**Raymond E. DeWalt perfects the first "radial arm machine" for wood working.**	
1922	INSLEY MANUFACTURING CORPORATION is founded at Indianapolis and start building cable excavators.	
1922	**Mr. Oscar Zerk (not Zert) of ALEMITE develops the first true hydraulic grease fitting, with the "red ball."**	
1922	LINK-BELT now builds a full line of crawler crane shovels.	
1922	George Failing moves his successful business to Enid, OK.	
1922	W. C. Durant acquires LOCOMOBILE CO. OF AMERICA.	
1922	August 31; H. L. Hamilton and Paul Turner incorporate ELECTRO-MOTIVE ENGINEERING in Cleveland, OH.	

1922	Bernard Erskine and partners purchase NILCO and form the NILCO LAMP WORKS.		
1922	A. F. Seibert joins A. H. Petersen and they form the A. H. PETERSEN COMPANY.		
1922	PHILLIPS PETROLEUM forms the predecessor to DUKE ENERGY FIELD SERVICES.		
1922	Morris Markin founds the CHECKER CAB MANUFACTURING COMPANY in Kalamazoo, MI.		
1922	Idaho; at Rigby High School, Philo Farnsworth sketches his first ideas for the electronic transmission of images, for his high school chemistry teacher.		
1922	As their first step into diversification, AC&F acquire CARTER CARBURETOR COMPANY entering the automotive field.		
1922	George Bacon, the chief engineer of DETROIT ELECTRIC VEHICLE COMPANY, designs a new specialty milk delivery truck which can be driven from the front, the rear or either side running board. But battery power can't stand up to the Detroit winters, and his employer doesn't want to build a gasoline-powered truck, so Bacon leaves, and he and his investors form the DETROIT INDUSTRIAL VEHICLE COMPANY (DIVCO), and begin building a LeRoi gasoline-powered prototype truck, as per George's ideas.		
1922	KVÆRNER BRUG begins cooperating with MYRENS VERKSTED and divided the wood pulping and the hydropower works between them.		

	1922	CHANCE VOUGHT AIRCRAFT CO. is formed. The VE-7 Bluebird designed in 1917 was so successful he now starts this company. The first ever takeoff from an aircraft carrier is a CHANCE VOUGHT plane.	(see 1936)
	1922	Texas; in Dallas, the LITTLE MOTOR KAR COMPANY builds the "Texmobile" automobile.	
	1922	GRAY TOOL COMPANY is founded to provide services to a fast growing petroleum industry.	
	1922	**CROSLEY, the world's largest manufacturer of radio receiver sets, now receives license for WLW to broadcast with 100 watts from Chicago.**	
	1922	**The German Shepherd Rin Tin Tin begins in movies, making $1,000 per week, twice his human co-stars.**	
	1922	HOLMES is now changed to American-Coleman, and their steering drive axles are under trucks up to seven tons.	
	1922	MOLYCORP begins New Mexico molybdenum production using an old existing 50-ton gold mill on the Red River near Questa.	

1922	In Ft. Worth, Amon G. Carter Sr. establishes radio station WBAP.		
1922	UK; James Paxman dies.		
1922	In Italy, JAMES MASSARENTI S. P. A. is established as a manufacturer of oil-drilling equipment.		
1922	Angelo Panelli adds the manufacture of centrifugal pumps to his business.		
1922	**The first paid radio commercial ever aired runs in New York City. It promotes an apartment house, costs $100, and runs for 10 minutes.**		
1922	The ACME SPARKLER COMPANY is founded in Chicago, IL.		
1922	UPS purchases a small "common carrier" service in Los Angeles, a move that will influence its growth for the next several decades.		
1922	Temple, TX; the PRAIRIE QUEEN TRACTOR MFG. Co. introduces the Prairie Queen 8-16 tractor, its powered by a Gray-Victory engine. It seems the farm tractor boom has just started going downhill.		
1922	Son Edsel convinces old Henry to buy the technically advanced, although financially troubled, LINCOLN MOTOR CO.		

1922	CAMPBELL PRESERVE CO. is now CAMPBELL SOUP CO., as soup is their main product and biggest income producer.	
1922	The agitator-type clothes washer is invented by Howard Snyder of Newton, IA. This year MAYTAG also introduces a machine that forces water through the clothes by means of an agitator.	
1922	Having developed a very successful line of spudders (cable-tool rigs), ARMSTRONG MFG. CO. introduces self-propelled drilling rigs on traction wheels.	
1922	At the end of this year, there are 563 licensed commercial radio stations in the USA.	
1922	GENERAL MOTORS acquires all outstanding stock of BROWN-LIPE CO., of Syracuse, NY, a maker of vehicle gears and differentials.	
1922	LAYNE INC. de-centralizes into seven affiliates: LAYNE-CENTRAL, LAYNE-TEXAS, LAYNE-OHIO, LAYNE-NORTHERN, LAYNE-WESTERN, LAYNE-ATLANTIC, and LAYNE-NEW YORK.	(see 1927)
1922	Mr. E. W. Marland now controls one-tenth of the world's oil production.	
1922	Texas; it looks as though the WHARTON MOTORS COMPANY of Dallas closes its business this year.	
1922	BEARDSLEY & PIPER, the former Klamath Falls Iron Works, relocates from Oregon to Chicago, now the center of America's foundry industry.	(see 1946)
1922	The Full Crawler Company Department of GEORGE H. SMITH STEEL CASTING COMPANY is established.	(see 1928)
1922	The GM farm tractor business' continual losses bring on the liquidation of the business this year.	
1922	The Trans-Sahara Expedition, delivering mail from Touggourt, Algeria, to Timbuktu, Sudan is completed in twenty days by all five vehicles, and all five are Citroën-Kégresse, half-tracks.	(see 1924)
1922	Chicago; the YELLOW CAB MFG. CO. produces their "Ambassador" automobiles through 1926.	
1922	Canada; this October, the government creates the CANADIAN NATIONAL RAILWAY and its nationalized system.	
1922	Oklahoma; AMERICAN STEEL DERRICK COMPANY is established in Tulsa.	
1922	This, the last year of steam engine production for J. I. CASE COMPANY; they build 153 steamers of all types to finish.	
1922	Michigan; the first fully revolving excavator from BAY CITY is a truck-mounted machine.	
1922	Nicolas Minorsky (1885-1970) attempts to model and analyze an automatic following device. His analysis, Directional Stability of Automatically Steered Bodies, has almost no immediate impact, but it is an achievement showing theoretically that proper automatic steering requires three-term control. However, designing and building apparatus to measure and combine these three terms, and Minorsky is in competition with Sperry as well as with the ANSCHUTZ COMPANY, both having a couple of decades head start.	
1922	Texas; the MCGILL MOTOR CAR COMPANY in Ft. Worth is now building the McGill automobile.	
1922	New York; Mr. Harry Digney becomes General Superintendent of ORBERDORFER PUMPS CORP. and the Digney family will eventually buy the company.	(see 1930s)
1922	Sweden; in Stockholm, Hilding Flygt an engineer, starts a pump and fan sales business.	(see 1929)
1923	R. G. LETOURNEAU builds his 12 yd. electric scraper, the "Mountain Mover," the very first self-propelled dirt scraper. *NOTE: This original machine is now displayed at LeTourneau University in Longview, TX.*	

1923	AMERICAN PUMPS is founded, later REED AMERICAN, and still later a part of BAKER.	
1923	Eaton buys the EATON AXLE CO. plant in Cleveland, PERFECTION SPRING CO., and other assets from the receiver of STANDARD PARTS COMPANY. EATON AXLE now becomes EATON AXLE & SPRING COMPANY.	
1923	**Edgar Worthington & Harry Kent establish KENWORTH MOTOR TRUCK CO. in Seattle.**	(see 1933)
1923	The AUSTIN MACHINERY CO. builds ditchers through the 1920s and '30s.	
1923	Texas; the first Cross Plains Texas oilfield is drilled in. *"Yeah Bubba, thet's thet shaller stuff like out on Old Roy Cowan's place."*	
1923	**38,000 HUPMOBILE cars are produced this year.**	
1923	Howard Hall acquires BERTSCHE ENGINEERING machine shop & renames it IOWA MFG. CO. OF CEDAR RAPIDS, to manufacture crushing, screening, and conveying machinery.	
1923	Five miles north of Cisco, TX, a concrete dam with a zoo inside is completed.	
1923	Charles Kettering forms the GENERAL MOTORS CHEMICAL CORP., jv between GM and STANDARD OIL OF NEW JERSEY, to make "Ethyl," the anti-knock compound, for gasoline. The first "Ethyl" gasoline is sold at a REFINER'S OIL CO. gasoline station in Dayton, OH.	
1923	May 28; after 646 days of cable-tool drilling, averaging less than 5 feet (1.54 m) per day, Santa Rita #1 gushes crude oil out and over the derrick top, outward for 250 yards around the drilling rig. This 3,050 foot (929.64 m) well marks the beginning of Permian Basin oil production.	(see 1990)
1923	Enid, OK; George Franks opens a blacksmith shop to repair oilfield equipment, but is soon designing and building rotary drilling rigs for oil drilling and mining exploration.	
1923	Twenty-two-year-old Mr. Royal Little founds SPECIAL YARNS COMPANY in Boston.	
1923	The PACKARD EIGHTS (straight eight) will run eighty-five mph this year.	(see 1929)
1923	**PEUGEOT is the first auto builder to install diesel engines in their cars.**	
1923	LEIDECKER now catalogs and sells five sizes of "drilling machines" (cable-tool rigs).	
1923	Carl Ingwer founds RIDGE TOOL CO. in North Ridgeville, OH, where he manufactures a new heavy-duty pipe wrench far better than anything else on the market, in fact the Ridgid pipe wrench sets a new standard for pipe working tools.	
1923	**Oil is discovered in the four-corners area, near Farmington, NM.**	
1923	Texas; Ben Laird and his brother S. S. build a new cotton gin in Kilgore, the only other gin in town is Asbury King's.	(see 1925)
1923	July 18; the first CHECKER car is built.	
1923	The extremely rapid growth has led to very serious financial problems for JOY MFG. CO. Joy enters a partnership with COBERN MACHINE CO. for backing.	
1923	Len and Mert Vance build a 750 gallon, hard rubber tired oil distributor, using compressed air to force the oil out, to do "road oiling" jobs. Thus begins VANCE BROTHERS INC.	
1923	The HENDEE MANUFACTURING COMPANY changes its name to the INDIAN MOTOCYCLE CO.	(see 1930)
1923	**Fast freezing of foods for long-term storage is developed by Clarence Birdseye.**	
1923	The LAPLANTE-CHOATE CO. begins commercial production of dozer blades for crawler tractors.	
1923	In an interview, Charles Stuart of Gas City, IN, states, "Almost six years ago I bought my old 'Indiana' truck from Mr. O. Gordon, who had used it for a number of years. I am using this old truck everyday, doing local and long distance hauling. This truck paid for itself the first three months of service. It is very cheap to run and I have absolutely no engine trouble. It starts easily in the morning and keeps running smoothly all day. I consider this old truck equal to any job. This old 'Indiana' certainly is a good one, even though it is 13 years old." At this time this very first "Indiana" truck, made by a bedstead company, has traveled 140,000 miles.	(see 1925)

1923	The first automatic traffic signals in the US are installed in Dallas, TX.	
1923	**BUICK produces 100,000 cars this year.**	
1923	EATON SPRING & AXLE COMPANY acquires COX MANUFACTURING CO, INC. a bumper builder in Albany, NY.	
1923	HASTINGS MFG. CO. introduce their first piston rings in addition to their water pumps, luggage racks, bumpers and other auto accessories.	(see 1935)
1923	ROGERS BROTHERS develops the first goose-neck trailer. *Their old iron wagon looks like one to Old Jim.*	
1923	Using ideas "stolen" from Philo Farnsworth, Vladimir K. Zworykin "invents" the cathode-ray tube.	(see 1927)
1923	John Harwood invents the self-winding watch.	
1923	R. Thomas McDermott and his father J. Ray McDermott win a contract to build 50 wooden derricks for an East Texas wildcatter.	
1923	The PLYMOUTH OIL COMPANY is organized in Pittsburgh, PA, as a holding company for the BIG LAKE OIL CO. of Texas.	
1923	A fold-up, gasoline fired, camp cook stove is introduced by the COLEMAN COMPANY.	
1923	The new president and publisher of the *FT. WORTH STAR-TELEGRAM* is… Amon G. Carter, Sr.	
1923	William D. Shaffer establishes SHAFFER TOOLWORKS, in Brea, CA.	(see 1928)
1923	STEWARTS & LLOYDS LTD. of the UK is the first tubular manufacturer to be licensed by A. P. I.	
1923	There are now 108 manufacturers of automobiles.	(see 1927)
1923	ARCHER-DANIELS LINSEED CO. acquires MIDLAND LINSEED PRODUCTS COMPANY; forming ARCHER-DANIELS-MIDLAND.	
1923	Chicago; G. E. Sellstrom and his wife Ellen establish EXCELL SALES CO. Their first product is a green eyeshade to prevent glare.	
1923	Joe Levit, a former grocer, founds GROCER'S SUPPLY.	
1923	Jamestown, PA; WHARTON MOTORS COMPANY, formerly of Dallas, TX, is now in business here.	
1923	**Frank C. Mars introduces the Milky Way, the world's first filled candy bar.**	
1923	**The Auto-Gyro is invented, but it cannot takeoff or land vertically.**	
1923	**John Logie Baird, a young Scottish engineer, invents the mechanical television transmitter.**	(see 1925)
1923	Corsicana, TX; Charlie L. and brother Arch H. Rowan get their first rig and start drilling east of here in the Powell field.	(see 1924)
1923	In Providence, RI, Henry and Helal Hassenfeld establish HASSENFELD BROTHERS CO. Initially they sell textile remnants, but soon begin manufacturing pencil boxes and other school supplies.	
1923	Texas Technological College is founded, out on the prairie, west of the town of Lubbock.	
1923	January; both of W. H. Dodge's companies are consolidated under the DODGE MANUFACTURING CO. name.	
1923	Slaton, TX; on June 1st, two old family-owned local bakeries consolidate and form the SLATON BAKERY. Some years later the Wilson family takes over the bakery.	
1923	**Power windshield wipers are introduced on several US made cars, this year.**	
1923	Introduced late this year, the 1924 year model Buicks from GM have four-wheel brakes as standard equipment.	
1923	Germany; M. A. N. introduces the first diesel engine for vehicles based on a direct-injection fuel system.	
1923	Girard, OH; YOUNGSTOWN SHEET & TUBE buys the local BRIER HILL STEEL business.	

1923	Australia; due to Josephson's earlier sales, WAUGH & JOSEPHSON is appointed Queensland distributor for the HOLT crawler tractors.		(see WWII)
1923	Oklahoma; Tulsa has a new municipal airport, and the SPARTAN AIRCRAFT COMPANY is established here.		
1923	California; this October, Roy and Walt found the DISNEY BROTHERS STUDIO to produce cartoons. It is later renamed WALT DISNEY COMPANY.		(see 2014)
1923	HASTINGS MFG. CO. introduces their "steel vent" oil control ring; this is the first two-piece piston ring made to control the oil-burning problem of the new high-compression engines, such as the new Ford V8 engines.		(see 1936)
1923	**Mr. O. G. Mandt designs and patents the half-swing wheel loader.**		(see 1951)
1923	Coach Knute Rockne has the members of the Notre Dame football team take dancing lessons to help develop a sense of rhythm, to help with the timing of "shift" plays.		

	1923	The FORDSON now claims 76% of North America's farm tractor business.	(see 1930)
	1923	Kansas; the Baldwin brothers develop the Gleaner grain combine; taking the name from the Jean Francois Millet painting of 1857.	(see 1930s)
	1923	Michigan; BAY CITY's new 16-B is much beefier, and is powered by a CLIMAX engine, or it can be electric powered.	
	1923	The USS Shenandoah, the first American-built, rigid-type airship, makes its maiden flight.	

1923	MM TWIN-CITY puts the first all-steel grain threshers on the American market.		
1923	USA; this December, the country's first diesel locomotive is demonstrated.		(see 1925)
1923	Texas; in Houston, Greek immigrant brothers Tom and James Papadakis flip a coin to see whose name will be used on their new hot dog restaurant. Patterned after the street vendors on the Coney Island Boardwalk in New York, James' Coney Island is soon a roaring success.		(see 2010)
1923	Ohio; about this time in Lisbon, Hal Wright Sr. develops the Wright Hoist, and forms the WRIGHT HOIST CO.		(see 1928)
1923	While looking for useful ways to use smaller versions of the huge circle saws used in sawmills, Edmond Michel invents the worm-drive circular saw. Ed then establishes the MICHEL ELECTRIC HANDSAW CO., later renamed SKILSAW INC.		
1923	GUCCI begins business as a small leather goods firm, making anything from luggage to saddles.		
1923	Texas; owned by W. T. Willis, J. E. Trigg, and H. D. Lewis, the first rotary drilling rig in the Panhandle spuds on S. B Burnett's Four Sixes Ranch. Rotary rigs began replacing cable tool rigs along the Texas coast at the turn of the century, but the lack of a good rotary bit for drilling rock formations kept the old cable tool rigs (or spudders, thumpers, or churn drills), drilling for another two decades up here.		
1923	Kansas; Harland W. Cardwell from Richland, recently of Oklahoma, arrives in Wichita and soon establishes ALLSTEEL PRODUCTS MANUFACTURING COMPANY.		(see 1926)
1923	New York City; founders Briton Hadden and Henry Luce publish the first edition of TIME, the American news magazine.		
1924	GRANT OIL TOOLS is started in Los Angeles.		
1924	FERGUSON-SHERMAN, INC. produces a plow with a "Duplex Hitch" system, invented by Harry Ferguson.		
1924	French brothers, Marcel & Conrad SCHLUMBERGER start a business to provide electronic wireline logging services for oil drilling operations.		(see 1931)
1924	Texas; Roy and Alice Cowan build their Sears-Roebuck "kit" house on their 20 acre truck farm southwest of Cross Plains.		

1924	Raymond E. De Walt forms DEWALT PRODUCTS COMPANY.	
1924	H. B. ZACHRY CO. is founded in Laredo, TX.	
1924	The last BRIGGS & STRATTON "Flyer" car is built.	
1924	Herman Hollerith's C-T-R-Co. changes its name to INTERNATIONAL BUSINESS MACHINES CO. (IBM).	
1924	It seems there has been some political "maneuvering and/or manipulation" by US Secretary of the Interior, Albert Fall, and Secretary of the Navy, Edwin Denby. Both of these men resign during the Teapot Dome Scandal.	
1924	WALL PUMP & COMPRESSOR CO. expands and becomes QUINCY MANUFACTURING CO.	
1924	**ZENITH introduces the first portable radio.**	
1924	**The first API standards are published.**	
1924	**CARRIER installs "human comfort cooling" for the first time in a J. L. HUDSON DEPARTMENT STORE, in Detroit.**	
1924	A new Ford Model T costs $260, and the 1924 SEARS & ROEBUCK catalog offers 5000 + different accessories for the Model T.	
1924	NILCO forms the SYLVANIA PRODUCTS COMPANY to make receiving tubes for radios.	
1924	Arthur Parker restarts PARKER APPLIANCE CO. (later to be PARKER-HANNIFIN)	
1924	HOUSTON ENGINEERS is founded to serve the oil industry.	
1924	**Texas; having earned 75 patents, 54 year old Howard Hughes Sr. passes away, leaving HUGHES TOOL CO. to his 18 year old son, Howard R. Hughes, Jr.**	
1924	A. F. Seibert buys the bankrupt A. H. PETERSEN CO. and establishes the MILWAUKEE ELECTRIC TOOL CO.	
1924	MOGUL METAL CO. merges with FEDERAL BEARING & BUSHING CO. to create FEDERAL MOGUL CORP.	
1924	Franklin, PA; an ex-COBERN plant is reopened, owned by JOY MACHINE CO., and 168 underground mine loaders are produced this year. John L. Lewis calls a national strike against the entire coal industry, with disastrous results.	
1924	ALCO builds their first diesel-electric locomotive, a little 300 hp unit for freight yard work.	
1924	Texas; Louis M. Pearce Sr. founds the PORTABLE ROTARY RIG COMPANY.	
1924	This year 4,000 Checker cars are built.	
1924	Clarence Birdseye launches his frozen seafood company in Gloucester, MA.	
1924	Oklahoma; Glenn T. Braden founds BRADEN WINCH & STEEL CO. producing the popular "Ryan Braden Hub Winch," which is built into the hub of a truck.	
1924	Sweden; Harland Herlin purchases KONE from STROMBERG.	
1924	At Cromwell, OK, WWI vet Myron Kinley of Tulsa offers to extinguish a oil well fire for $500, his offer is finally accepted and he does the job. This is the start of the oil well firefighting industry. Myron brings his brother Floyd Kinley on board and starts his own business.	
1924	SHEAFFER introduces the "white dot" on their pens and pencils to indicate their continuing search for perfection.	
1924	The F. B. LEOPOLD CO. is established to create and maintain public water systems.	
1924	Canada; in Turner Valley, Royalite No. 4 blows in, making 21 million cubic feet of natural gas and more than 600 barrels of white naphtha every day. It will be several weeks before this well can be brought under control.	(see 1937)
1924	KLM makes its first intercontinental flight, from Amsterdam to Batavia (Jakarta) in a Fokker F-VII.	

1924	Walter P. Chrysler launches an automobile bearing his surname.	

Aug. 19, 1924.
F. W. EPPERSON
1,505,592
FROZEN CONFECTIONERY
Original Filed June 11, 1924

Fig. 2.

Fig. 4.

Fig. 1.   Fig. 3.

1924	**Young Frank Epperson patents his 1905 discovery... the Popsicle.**	
1924	**The spiral bound notebook is invented.**	
1924	California; in Los Angeles, UPS builds the first ever conveyor belt system for handling packages.	
1924	It now appears that the BLUMBERG MOTOR MANUFACTURING COMPANY has ceased all business operations.	
1924	Wichita Falls, TX; Morris and William Zale open their first jewelry store.	
1924	A young man from San Antonio, NM, comes to Cisco, TX, to buy a bank. He cannot make that deal, and Conrad Hilton has seen the booming hotel business due the current oil boom, in fact the rooms are rented in three shifts each day. So instead of buying a bank, Hilton buys the hotel where he is staying, the Mobley Hotel. Not a bad choice for him—the beginning of an era.	(see 1925)
1924	USA; paper "handkerchiefs" or facial tissues are invented.	
1924	The Rowan brothers incorporate their business, as they acquire their second drilling rig.	
1924	Paul Blazer becomes manager of the ASHLAND OIL COMPANY, a small refinery.	
1924	CITROËN begins a business relationship with Edward G. Budd, working on a steel auto body.	
1924	The first air-mail service in Alaska is provided by aviator Carl Ben Eielson.	
1924	Thanksgiving Day; spanning the Hudson River in New York, the Bear Mountain Bridge opens to vehicular traffic. This is the world's largest suspension bridge.	
1924	Building small rotary and mechanized wheeled dirt scrapers, the EUCLID ROAD MACHINERY Co. gets going.	(see 1931)
1924	Christmas Eve; Fairfield, MT; at noon today it was 63F, now, at midnight it is -20F, an 84 degree, 12 hr. temperature drop.	
1924	Nevada; John Gee, a convicted murderer dies in only six minutes in the newly introduced gas chamber, a more humane way to dispense justice. *"Yeah Bubba, I'll bet ole John was really happy 'bout thet."*	
1924	The *Little Orphan Annie* cartoons first appear in the newspapers.	
1924	In an eight-month trek traversing Africa, Haardt and Audion-Dubreuill very successfully use Citroën-Kégresse half-track vehicles. Kégresse's concept is now a well-proven success. These vehicles will continue to be manufactured in France and widely used by the French Army, right up to the outbreak of WWII. At least ten other nations use them for their military, as well.	
1924	The completely redesigned excavators from THEW are now rebadged LORAIN.	(see 1964)
1924	Texas; during the '23-'24 winter, the panhandle town of Romero, in Hartley County, records a total of 65 inches of snowfall. This record will stand for many decades for Texas.	
1924	Long Beach, CA; about this time, a young Sam Boyd is working the carnival games on Long Beach Pike Amusement Park, helping support his fatherless family.	(see 1941)
1924	Kansas; H. D. LEE introduces "Lee Cowboy Pants."	(see 1944)
1924	BAKER MANUFACTURING COMPANY puts out the first bulldozer blade for use on a crawler tractor.	(see 1926)
1924	At the request of, and in cooperation with beet growers, MINNEAPOLIS MOLINE designs and begins selling a four-wheeled, towed, beet puller.	
1924	Oklahoma; with a $6,900 investment, C. W. Flint Sr. and K. W. Flint form FLINT RIG COMPANY, headquartered in Tulsa, to build oil well derricks.	(see 1927)

1924	Cellophane is invented this year.	
1924	Germany; M. A. N. brings out the world's first direct injection diesel engine.	
1924	Texas; business is good in Cleburne, as many folks travel there, drawn by Santa Fe RailRoad Central Machine Shops and many such railroad related business. A. J. Wright builds the Liberty Hotel to accommodate these visitors.	(see 1933)
1924	Only sixteen countries participate in the first Winter Olympics, hosted by France.	
1924	UK; Birmingham; William Morris (NUFFIELD ORG.) buys all assets and the marque (badge or brand) of E. G. WRIGLEY & CO., who manufacture and supply axles for OXFORD and the CROWLEY cars, soon changing the name to MORRIS-COMMERCIAL CARS, LTD., and entering the commercial vehicle market.	(see 1930)
1924	BATES MACHINE & TRACTOR CO. now begin producing "more of less" conventional full-crawler farm tractors.	(see 1929)
1924	The synthetic material "artificial silk" now becomes known as rayon.	
1924	Washington; the small tough 5 ton capacity hand winches being made by R. H. Beebe, for his own use, are drawing lots of attention all across Seattle. Taking advantage of that attention, R. H. founds BEEBE BROS, INC. to make and sell the winches.	(see 1938)
1924	Wisconsin; Carl J. E. Eliason of Sayner, begins experimenting with his idea for a motorized toboggan. His vehicle uses a front-mounted, water-cooled outboard motor for power. Eliason will receive a patent in 1927 on "a vehicle for snow travel."	(see 1928) (see 1951)
1925	May; forced by their corporate bankers, the strong competitors BEST and HOLT merge, again, this time forming CATERPILLAR TRACTOR COMPANY.	
1925	Having changed their company name to YANCEY BROS. INC., Goodloe and Earle Yancey are dealers for the new CATERPILLAR tractors in the states of Georgia, Florida, Alabama, and South Carolina.	
1925	DON LEE COACH & BODY is building over 300 custom bodies a year, and shipping them worldwide.	
1925	OWATONNA TOOL CORP. (OTC) is founded on the strength of a soon-to-be patented mechanical gear puller.	
1925	E. E. "Pop" Kelly moves from Missouri to Daytona Beach, FL, as a representative of HOLT MANUFACTURING CO.	
1925	**DODGE BROS. build their one millionth automobile.**	
1925	HUPMOBILE introduces their Straight Eight motor.	
1925	**Oil is discovered in the southwest corner of Eastland County, at Pioneer, TX.**	
1925	TWIN-DISC CLUTCH CO. is established.	
1925	McKISSICK FOUNDRY is established.	
1925	OHMITE is founded.	
1925	BECKWITH MACHINERY becomes one of the very earliest CATERPILLAR dealers in the USA.	
1925	**The State of Texas begins construction of a consolidated highway system, overseen by the State Highway Department. Up to this time, each county was responsible for its highways; that must have been a mess!**	
1925	LAPLANTE-CHOATE MFG. comes out with a hydraulically-operated dozer blade, as an attachment for crawler tractors.	

1925	Electro-Motive Engineering changes its name to Electro-Motive Corporation.	
1925	Manitowoc Drydock Company manufactures their first cranes.	
1925	General Motors buys Vauxhall of Britain.	
1925	AC & F buys Hall-Scott Motor Car Company and primarily uses the engines to power their buses and boats; they also buy Fageol Motors Company.	
1925	England; about this time, the R. A. Lister Co. buys all the patents, designs, and manufacturing rights from the Auto Mower Engineering Co. for the "Auto-Truck," powered by J. A. Prestwich & Co. engines.	
1925	AT&T begins FAX service in the US, calling it Wirephoto, remember A. P. Wirephoto???	(see 1964)
1925	Amerada Petroleum Corp. organizes the Geophysical Research Corp. (GRC) to investigate the possibility of applying geophysical methods to oil exploration.	
1925	Texas; in the best cotton year yet for Gregg county, Laird Bros. Gin in Kilgore is processing an average of 100 bales a day, at five dollars a bale.	
1925	Brown & Williamson buys J. G. Flynt Tobacco Co. makers of "Sir Walter Raleigh" smoking tobacco.	
1925	April; as creditors take over Joy Mfg. Co., Joe Joy resigns as president; broke again… Joe takes a job in Russia in the mines.	
1925	Travel Air Co. is formed by Clyde Cessna, Walter Beech and Lloyd Stearman in Wichita, KS.	
1925	**Sicard invents the snow blower.**	
1925	**Richard Drew, a 3M lab assistant, conceives the idea that leads to masking tape, the first Scotch brand tape.**	
1925	The National Automotive Parts Association (NAPA) is formed in April.	
1925	George Roper dies and his son, Mabon P. Roper, inherits the companies.	
1925	**The very first true pickup truck is introduced, by… Ford.** *"It's a fact Bubba, they made the first, and still make the best!!!"*	
1925	Pratt & Whitney is established.	
1925	Ford establishes itself in Germany.	
1925	Mississippi; Mason Fiber Company (later Masonite Corp.) is formed.	
1925	In Germany, Demag begins building cable excavators.	
1925	Pearce Industries is incorporated in Houston.	
1925	Mr. R. J. Reynolds dies at age sixty-eight.	
1925	August 6; the first of Conrad Hilton's Texas Highrise hotels, the Dallas Hilton opens today. Conrad's marketing is aimed toward the average man.	(see 1931)
1925	William Randolph Hearst sells the *Ft. Worth Record* to Amon G. Carter, Sr., who renames it the *Ft. Worth Record-Telegram*, a morning paper.	
1925	October; Josh Cosden brings in the Connell #1-A, @ 80 bopd, as the first producing well in Ector County, TX.	
1925	Tulsa, OK; Gaso Pump & Burner Company begins manufacturing the "Gaso Walking Beam Pump."	
1925	**John L. Baird builds the first practical television receiving set.**	(see 1927)
1925	Sauder Tank Company is founded in Emporia, KS.	
1925	Magnolia Petroleum purchases the Corsicana Petroleum Company in Corsicana, TX.	
1925	November 28; Uncle Jimmy Thompson, a 77 year old fiddler, is featured on the very first *Grand Old Opry* show.	

1925	**George Washington Carver is granted a patent for a face cream primarily made from peanuts.**	
1925	GENERAL MOTORS establishes its first foreign plant... in Argentina, South America.	
1925	The *USS Constitution* is completely rebuilt, then given a berth in the Charleston Naval Yard.	
1925	**The first portable carbon dioxide fire extinguisher is introduced by the WALTER KIDDE Co.**	
1925	Evansville, IN; W. H. McCurdy sells the HERCULES BUGGY WORKS to SERVEL.	
1925	California; all US movie companies are now headquartered in Hollywood, primarily due to the good weather.	
1925	At this time, BUCYRUS is the industry's leading manufacturer of excavating equipment.	(see 1927)
1925	With 14 factory depots across the US, covering our great nation, INDIANA TRUCK CORPORATION now claims to be "One of the most successful manufacturers of high grade Motor Trucks in the country."	(see 1932)
1925	The movie business is now the fourth largest industry in the United States.	
1925	Even though the Loffland brothers have had very good luck with cable tool rigs, they decide to convert to the modern rotary rigs. This decision was partially due to Grover Simpson, who had been studying rotary rigs in California, and has become a partner with the Loffland Bothers.	
1925	**Early this year, Vernon Dalhart's "Wreck of the Old 97" is hillbilly (country) music's first million-copy record.**	
1925	"Mrs. Stewart's Bluing" is still made today in the original plant in Minneapolis, as well as in Portland, OR, San Francisco, St. Louis, Pasadena, CA, and Winnipeg, Manitoba, Canada.	(see 2007)
1925	A night-time Chicago to New York City flight is the world's first ever, long distance, night time, airmail service.	
1925	In Canada the WATSON JACK CO. is now building portable pumps capable of up to 200 psi. These WaJax pumps, as they are called, are primarily used in fighting forest fires.	(see 1933)

1925	Rome, NY; UTICA FORK & HOE COMPANY establishes its Rome Grader Division.	(see 1930)
1925	Texas; at LUFKIN FOUNDRY & MACHINE Co. in Lufkin, Walter Trout draws his idea for a "counterbalanced oilfield pump jack." Later this year, a prototype is installed and pumping for HUMBLE in their field near Hull, TX.	(see WWII)
1925	USA; factory production of diesel locomotives begins this year.	
1925	Chicago; opened now with 2,000 rooms, the 526 foot (160 meter) MORRISON HOTEL, at the corner of Clark and Madison, is one of the premier hotels of the city. This is the first building outside New York City more than 40 floors tall.	(see 1927)
1925	All assets of the SQUARE TURN TRACTOR COMPANY are sold off at a Sheriff's sale, for only $15K.	
1925	It is about this time that Mack Wooldridge (1890 - 1962) founds a CLETRAC crawler tractor dealership in southern California. Headquartered in Los Angeles, MACK WOOLDRIDGE, INC. has a branch in Birmingham, AL. Wooldridge also builds snowplows for crawlers sold to other CLETRAC dealers up North.	(see 1931)
1925	The POSTUM CEREAL COMPANY of Battle Creek, MI, merges with the JELL-O COMPANY of Leroy, NY, in the first of such transactions that will lead to the formation of GENERAL FOODS CORPORATION.	(see 1926)
1925	Wisconsin; in Racine, the AJAX MOTORS CO. is building the "Ajax-Nash" motorcar, through the end of next year.	

1926	This year the USA's first scheduled air passenger services begins.		
1926	Foster Catheads of Wichita Falls, TX, gets all wrapped up in business.		
1926	Wichita; Allsteel Products Mfg. Co. becomes Cardwell Mfg. Co. and are now building cable tool drilling rigs.	(see 1929)	
1926	**Eaton Axle And Spring produces the first two-speed axle.**		
1926	Elmer Decker is building instruments in California; soon to be Martin-Decker.	(see 1927)	
1926	Minnesota; in Mankato, Kato Engineering is founded by Mr. Jensen & Mr. Wilkerson.		
1926	American Appliance Co. changes its name to Raytheon Mfg. Co. after its successful rectifier tube for battery-powered home radios.		

1926	W. Piggott, Sr., sells controlling interest in Pacific Car & Foundry to AC & F.		
1926	**At the New York Auto Show, the Oakland Automobile Company, a division of General-Motors, introduces their resurrected Pontiac automobile is shown; it bears the Indian head logo and the Pontiac name.**	(see 2009)	
1926	Hendrickson introduces the first successful tandem axle suspension system, a walking beam type.		
1926	**All records are broken when a two-ton GMC truck is driven from New York to San Francisco in five days and thirty minutes.**		
1926	USA; Professor Robert Goddard invents and fires the first liquid fueled rocket. But, it will be a decade before other scientists are interested.		

1926	B & W Tobacco Company buys R. P. Richardson Company.		
1926	The second well drilled on the Cook Ranch near Albany, TX, comes in and flows 1,000 bopd.		
1926	AB Volvo, a subsidiary of SKF, starts production of experimental cars.		
1926	**Zenith builds the first home radio set to operate on house current.**		
1926	Boeing buys Stearman Aircraft of Wichita, KS.		
1926	**Waldo Semon, a B. F. Goodrich scientist invents PVC/Vinyl.**		
1926	The last Patriot Trucks are built.		
1926	Fred Fisher, patriarch of Fisher Bros., (Body by Fisher) gets Harley Earl to come to Detroit to help with LaSalle automobile design problems, and the rest is automotive-styling history. General Motors acquires Fisher Bros. or Fisher Body Works, makers of fine steel automobile bodies.		
1926	Germany; Daimler-Benz is created when Daimler and Benz merge.		
1926	In Japan, Kobe starts building pumps.		
1926	Johnston runs the first commercial drill stem test.		
1926	Halliburton's first field camp outside the US is established in Canada.		
1926	DRMC creates the first "raw edge" cog belt.		
1926	*"Craftsman" brand tools first appear in the Sears, Roebuck & Company mail order catalog.*		
1926	After 25 different prototypes have been operated by the Detroit Creamery, DIVCO begins marketing their truck powered by a 4-cylinder Continental gasoline engine.		
1926	The J. G. Brill Co., a streetcar builder, is acquired by AC & F.		
1926	The Esso brand is first used by Standard Oil, whose initials S. O. spelled phonetically is... Esso.		
1926	Allis-Chalmers establishes a separate tractor division to manufacture and market farm tractors.		

1926	**Louis Chevrolet takes his last laps at Indy as the official pace car driver.**
1926	BELSAW MACHINERY is established in Kansas City, MO, as a manufacturer of saw sharpening machines.
1926	The Wisconsin Group now buys a Long Beach, CA, telephone company and forms ASSOCIATED TELEPHONE UTILITIES as a holding company.
1926	John Moses Browning dies with over 100 patents to his credit; he probably has contributed more to our national security than any other one person.
1926	The H. W. JOHNS-MANVILLE COMPANY is reincorporated as the JOHNS-MANVILLE CORPORATION.
1926	In Springfield, MO, SPRINGFIELD TABLET CO. commences operations and soon begin making their Big Chief writing tablets.
1926	L. C. SMITH & BROS. and CORONA TYPEWRITER both merge with SMITH PREMIER to produce office typewriters and portables.
1926	October 28; TRANSCONTINENTAL's discovery well on the Yates ranch in Reagan County, TX, begins flowing, but it can't save them.
1926	The second generation comes on board as Stanley Marcus starts his career at NIEMAN-MARCUS. Stanley is the one who really gets the company into high gear.
1926	Twenty-nine year old Daniel K. Ludwig buys the very old antiquated oil tanker that starts him in the oil shipping business.
1926	Minneapolis, MN; NORTHWEST AIRLINES is established.
1926	Tulsa, OK; NATIONAL TANK CO. develops the first efficient, high-capacity oil and gas separator.
1926	DAVID & SONS begins roasting and marketing sunflower seeds.
1926	SERVO DELDEN BV, a Dutch chemical company is founded.
1926	November; the 2,400 mile (3,840 km) "Route 66" from Chicago to the Pacific Ocean past Los Angeles opens to traffic.
1926	Norway; Erik Rotheim invents the aerosol spray.
1926	Moving their offices from San Antonio to Ft. Worth, the Rowan brothers now begin drilling in East Texas.
1926	April 4; in Germany, August Thyssen dies, his sons Heinrich and Fritz share his industrial inheritance between them.
1926	Chicago, April 15; a young unknown pilot, (flying for a firm that will grow into American Airlines), heads to St. Louis in a single-engine biplane, carrying the US mail. None can imagine that Charles Lindbergh will one day be famous, or that the small company will someday be the world's largest airline.
1926	England; the first LISTER Auto-Truck is sold; eventually, more than 3,000 different versions will be made and sold.
1926	Hollywood, CA; Alan Loughead's LOUGHEAD AIRCRAFT Co. simplifies their name to LOCKHEED AIRCRAFT Co.
1926	Texas; a oil pipeline from Refugio to Aransas Pass is completed, it goes along the railroad right-of-way and onto Harbor Island, where the crude oil is stored until it is loaded into tanker ships.
1926	Fuzzy's RADIATOR SERVICE is established in Borger, TX.
1926	The 8-hour-a-day, 5-day workweek is adopted by Henry Ford for all his factories.
1926	California; KILLEFER MFG. CORP. introduces a cable-operated loader attachment for HOLT tractors.

(see 1927)

1926	Contractor R. G. LeTourneau has a dirt moving job that is "giving him the dickens." To cure this, he conceives the "rooter," a long tooth on two wheels to be towed by a crawler tractor to break up (or rip up) the hard material. This is the first ripper.		
1926	The US Post Office, as mandated by congress, grants air mail transport contracts to private commercial operators. Previously, the Post Office has been using its own fleet of war surplus Havilland DH-4's with the obsolete 400 horsepower Liberty engines.		
1926	Although a hand-pumped system, the first known hydraulic bulldozer blade comes from BAKER.	(see 1928)	
1926	Ohio; new owners acquire JOHN F. BYERS MACHINE CO. and rename it the BYERS MACHINE CO.		
1926	The makers of SWAN'S DOWN products, as well as IGLEHART BROTHERS and MINUTE TAPIOCA consolidate into the POSTUM CEREAL/JELL-O bunch this year.	(see 1927)	
1926	Jumping into the winch and hoist market, INGERSOLL-RAND introduces their "Classic" winch line.	(see 1950)	
1926	Illinois; ABC produces the industry's first porcelain-lined tub for clothes-washing washing machines.	(see 1928)	

	1926	UK; when HUMBER buys the COMMERCIAL CAR CO. in Luton, and merges with it, COMMER CARS, LTD. is formed.	(see 1928)
	1927	With financial backing from their father, Paul & Tom Braniff start BRANIFF AIRWAYS with a five passenger Stinson, flying between Oklahoma City and Tulsa.	
	1927	TIMBERJACK is founded in Finland to build logging equipment.	
	1927	**Albert Einstein is awarded the Nobel Prize for his discovery of the "photoelectric effect."**	
	1927	**After twenty years and fifteen million Model T's, the last one is built; FORD shuts down for 6 months for retooling, then introduces the second series Model "A." Very shortly, FORD has 50,000 orders for the Model A. FORD begins using shatterproof windshields in its vehicles.**	

1927	BUCYRUS buys the ERIE STEAM SHOVEL, and forms BUCYRUS-ERIE CO., B-E also builds cable tool drilling rigs.	(see 1931)	
1927	C. S. "Punch" Barlow joins THOMAS BARLOW SONS, sells the first Caterpillar tractor in South Africa, TBS then becomes the CATERPILLAR dealer for South Africa.		
1927	MARTIN-DECKER is formed.		
1927	Chicago; the addition of the tower, makes the now 3,400 room MORRISON HOTEL, the "World's Tallest Hotel." It features two huge restaurants, the Boston Oyster House and Terrace Garden Wonder Restaurant, as well as coffee shops, a drug store and barber shop. For decades the Morrison is a popular spot with the Windy City's politicians, as well as with members of the mob.	(see 1965)	
1927	PUROLATOR COMPANY is founded.		
1927	STUDEBAKER CORPORATION purchases PIERCE-ARROW, and begins producing luxury automobiles.		
1927	Juan Trippe starts PAN AMERICAN AIRWAYS, with a rented plane and a short mail hauling contract in Central America, the very first scheduled international mail flight.		
1927	J. Willis Gardner, son of Robert W. negotiates a merger with DENVER ROCK DRILL CO. creating GARDNER-DENVER CO.	(see 1965)	
1927	Having hired their first "in-house" designer, and spurred by the success of the products of their alliance, T. Austin Finch sets it up, and THOMASVILLE CHAIR CO., this year offers a complete line of their own dining room furniture, making THOMASVILLE the most diversified manufacturer in the furniture industry. T. Austin Finch becomes president this year.	(see D'Era)	

1927	At SOUTHLAND ICE CO. in Oak Cliff, TX, an enterprising employee starts offering bread, milk and eggs for sale on Sundays and evenings, when grocery stores are closed. SOUTHLAND soon introduces the TOTE'M Stores, the first "convenience" stores.	
1927	**The Albers brothers of Cherokee, IA, invent a wind-powered generator to recharge a six volt battery, they call it a "Wincharger," it is so successful, that they go into the business.**	
1927	Mar 5; the LaSalle is introduced by Cadillac and is powered by a 90 degree V-8, same as the Cadillac. This LaSalle is the first car designed not by draftsmen and engineers, but by an automobile stylist, in this case, Harley J. Earl.	
1927	March; William W. Grainger establishes his supply company in Chicago, selling from his 8 page "MotorBook" catalog.	
1927	ZENITH RADIO introduces the first push-button radio tuners.	
1927	The City of Odessa, TX, is incorporated.	
1927	Albert Champion dies of a heart attack at age 49. GM buys all his stock from his family, takes over and makes A-C SPARK PLUG CO., a wholly-owned subsidiary of GENERAL MOTORS.	(see 1933)
1927	May; Lindbergh's *Spirit of St. Louis* crosses the Atlantic with A-C spark plugs, and THOMPSON experimental sodium-cooled engine valves. Arthur Parker's company is given a big boost when Lindy chooses PARKER hose fittings exclusively for his plane, due to their great reputation. Ray Simpson builds the compass-indicator for Lindbergh, and TEXACO fuel and lubricants exclusively were used by Lindbergh in his solo crossing. The Spirit of St. Louis has GOODRICH tires mounted on DAYTON wire wheels on its trans-Atlantic flight. Lindy's plane is coated with VALSPAR clear varnish. Lindbergh later states that he carried "only gasoline, sandwiches, a bottle of water, a CRESCENT wrench, and pliers."	
1927	Texas; speaking in Dallas, Charles Lindbergh says, "Keep your airport—it will place you among the commercial leaders of the world."	
1927	Released this year, the first full-length talking movie, *The Jazz Singer*, stars Al Jolson. *"Yeah Slim, I like them talkies."*	
1927	Regarding talking movies, Harry M. Warner of WARNER BROTHERS asks, "Who the hell wants to hear actors talk?"	
1927	**Guy Frazee, a co-founder of IOWA MANUFACTURING CO. develops the one-piece-outfit or OPO, a compact, portable rock crusher to facilitate the many road jobs now starting around the country.**	
1927	AC&F acquires SHIPPERS CAR LINE.	
1927	Philo T. Farnsworth is the first to develop a complete working electronic television apparatus.	(see 1928)
1927	**The first well over a mile (1.6 km) deep is drilled by NOBLE-OLSEN DRILLING CO.**	
1927	**GRC introduces the reflective seismic technique.**	
1927	**The first flight between the continental US and Hawaii is powered by Phillips Aviation Fuel.**	
1927	WRIGHT TOOL COMPANY is established in Barberton, OH.	
1927	After leaving TRAVEL AIR last year, Lloyd Stearman formed his own company in California, now he moves it to Wichita.	
1927	After leaving TRAVEL AIR last year, now Clyde Cessna forms CESSNA AIRCRAFT COMPANY.	
1927	Wichita, KS, now bills itself as the "Air Capital of the US."	
1927	WERKSPOOR (later STORK) builds the "Jumbo" for KLM, who use it until it is destroyed in the very early days of WWII.	
1927	The first state to require automobile insurance is Massachusetts.	

1927	To escape the perils of "Uncle Joe" Stalin, Joe Joy "commandeers" a railroad locomotive and escapes to Poland with his staff.		
1927	The first automatic refrigerated air-conditioning for buildings is introduced.		
1927	GEARENCH MFG. CO. is founded in Houston by J. A. Peterson and C. E. "Pat" Olsen.		
1927	The AUBURN AUTOMOBILE COMPANY purchases the LYCOMING MANUFACTURING COMPANY.		
1927	Albert Luce, the FORD dealer in Perry, GA, builds the first school bus body in his shop and mounts it on a Model "T" truck chassis; also, this is the first Blue Bird Bus.		
1927	**The world's first underwater color pictures are published by... *NATIONAL GEOGRAPHIC*.**		
1927	Frank E. Hutchison founds HUTCHISON MANUFACTURING COMPANY.		
1927	London based BRITISH AMERICAN TOBACCO acquires BROWN & WILLIAMSON.		
1927	The ACADEMY OF MOTION PICTURE ARTS & SCIENCES is formed by Louis B. Mayer.		
1927	CHEVROLET outsells FORD for the first time.		
1927	LOVEJOY TOOL WORKS buys the patent for the "jaw coupling" from Louis Ricefield, thus these couplings will be called LR couplings for many decades.		
1927	In Fresno, CA, BAILEY begins business, producing valves.		
1927	This year, copper tubing is first used on a widespread basis.		
1927	The Holland Tunnel in New York City officially opens to traffic.		
1927	The COLUMBIA BROADCASTING SYSTEM (CBS) is established.		
1927	George Souders wins the Indianapolis 500 with a speed of 97.545 mph (156.072 kph).		
1927	The Savoy Big Five, an all-black basketball team, go to Hinckley, IL, and play their first game outside of Chicago. They will soon become famous as the Harlem Globetrotters.		
1927	Commercial telephone service is introduced between New York and London, and a three minute call costs only seventy-five dollars ($75).		
1927	JOHNSTON invents the formation testing tool for drilling. With a single formation testing tool, JOHNSON TESTERS is established.		
1927	Now there are only 44 automobile manufacturers.	(see 2000)	
1927	Hastings, NE; Edwin Perkins creates Kool-Aid.		
1927	**Philip Drinker and Louis A. Shaw build the first iron lung, using two vacuum cleaners; it is known as the Drinker respirator.**		
1927	August; Capt. Eddie Rickenbacker closes the deal to buy the Indianapolis Motor Speedway from Carl Fisher for $700,000.		
1927	John Riggs, Sr., establishes the ARKANSAS ROAD EQUIPMENT COMPANY in Little Rock.	(see 1928)	

1927	New York City; design and planning begins for the George Washington Bridge.	
1927	The Mississippi River Basin floods as 145 levees give way to the big river, resulting from the rains which began in the summer of 1926. These floods claim more than 300 lives as millions of acres are inundated. Due to the federal government's rapid and positive response to this situation, many US citizens will begin depending on Washington to bail them out after any serious natural disaster.	

1927	**WAYNE introduces the first power driven pumps for gasoline.**	(see 1928)	
1927	PEABODY HOLMES begins manufacturing rotary positive displacement air blowers.		
1927	The LOFFLAND BROTHERS COMPANY incorporates.		

1927	WELCH's first non-grape product is introduced: Welch's Homogenized Tomato Juice.	(see WWII)
1927	To advance from the old wooden rigs, ARMSTRONG MFG. CO. begins building steel-framed, cable-tool, drilling rigs.	
1927	Ten years having passed since John Gates invented the V-belt and GATES RUBBER has established itself as the world's largest manufacturer of quality V-belts. GATES RUBBER will retain this title well into the next century.	
1927	With the death of Mahlon E. Layne, leadership of LAYNE passes to his son Louis Layne.	(see 1928)
1927	Canada; now producing a wide range of items, WATEROUS ENGINE WORKS is renamed WATEROUS LTD.	(see 1944)
1927	W. A. Morrison builds the first quartz clock, it combines an electronic oscillator with a quartz crystal, to maintain exact time.	
1927	The Orteig Prize for Aviation is awarded to Charles Lindbergh this year.	
1927	With teams of Brits leading the way, the land speed record is now just a bit past 200 miles per hour.	(see 1928)
1927	FLINT RIG incorporates in Oklahoma. Wooden derricks are now being replaced by steel.	(see 1934)
1927	At this time 98% of the farm tractors in the Soviet Union are American imports. During the past four years, 27,000 farm tractors have been exported from the USA to the USSR.	
1927	Johnny Weissmuller sets the 100 yard, free-style swim record of 51.0 seconds.	
1927	Germany; DEUTZ offers a 14-horsepower air-cooled diesel engine powered farm tractor this year.	
1927	Joining the POSTUM CEREAL/JELL-O bunch this year are FRANKLIN BAKER COCONUT COMPANY, WALTER BAKER CHOCOLATE CO. and LOG CABIN SYRUP.	(see 1928)
1927	Colorado; sitting at the kitchen table in his home in Denver, Carl Norgren draws the first lubrication system for compressed air piping.	
1927	The Rheem brothers, Richard and Donald, establish RHEEM.	(see 1987)
1927	Henry J. Kaiser has a contract to build highways in Cuba, and LeTourneau builds several dirt scrapers for Kaiser's job.	
1927	LYCOMING, the engine manufacturer in Pennsylvania, is acquired by E. L. Cord.	
1927	Africa; in the Anglo-Egyptian Sudan, out in a cotton field, a tractor powered by a German-built BENZ diesel engine seriously beats a gasoline-powered CATERPILLAR tractor in a plowing contest. Humiliated by the loss, CATERPILLAR buys a Benz diesel engine and ships it to their research department in San Leandro, CA. They also buy Atlas, Buda and Coho diesel engines, and examine all of them thoroughly. Hiring consulting engineer Carl G. Arthur "Art" Rosen is a big step, as he is determined to build a better diesel engine than the Benz, or the others, and in the process will go on to create the tough and durable Cat D-9900 four banger diesel.	(see 1930)
1927	The Bakersfield *Californian* states that Frank Hopper, Sr. has "secured a site and will be erecting a new and modern foundry and machine works." The newspaper goes on saying that products made by HOPPER MACHINE WORKS, presently out on the Kern River are "being shipped to companies all over the world."	
1928	Herbert Hoover is the new President of the United States of America.	
1928	Alaska; the first CATERPILLAR dealer in the state is SAMSON HARDWARE CO. of Fairbanks.	(see 1929)
1928	KATO master electrician, Cecil Jones invents a device to operate AC appliances from DC storage batteries, for use in rural areas, called the KATO rotary converter, it is a huge success.	
1928	VAN DOORNE BROS. open a small engineering & machine shop in Eindhoven, Netherlands, primarily building trailers.	

1928	March; C. L. Best meets with Carl George Arthur Rosen and they discuss the possibility of installing a diesel engine in a CATERPILLAR Sixty tractor. Prior to this, Henry J. Kaiser has installed 60 horsepower ATLAS IMPERIAL diesel engines in two CATERPILLAR Sixty tractors. Due to the heavy weight of the ATLAS stationary diesels, the project met with very little success.	
1928	**R. G. LeTourneau invents the first reliable Power Control Unit, a winch driven from the tractor PTO.**	
1928	Allis-Chalmers buys MONARCH TRACTOR COMPANY. However, the MONARCH name will continue being used for several more years.	
1928	DRESSER is acquired by the W. A. Harriman investment banking firm.	
1928	MASSEY-HARRIS buys J. I. CASE PLOW WORKS including all rights to the names CASE and J. I. CASE THRESHING MACHINES.	(see 1937)
1928	Many TOTE'M Stores now began selling gasoline.	
1928	BEAN SPRAY PUMP CO. is renamed JOHN BEAN MFG. CO., after acquiring ANDERSON-BARNGROVER CO. and SPRAGUE-SELLS, both are makers of canning machinery, making Bean the worlds largest manufacturer of food machinery. In a contest for a name, FOOD MACHINERY CORP. wins. Later to be called, simply, FMC.	
1928	MANNING, MAXWELL & MOORE acquire AMERICAN SCHAFER and BUDENBURG CO. for a complete line of industrial temperature instruments.	

	1928	The COSDEN refinery opens in Big Spring, TX.	
	1928	CHICAGO RAWHIDE introduces the first integrated, self-contained shaft seal.	
	1928	May 22; T. Boone Pickens is born in Holdenville, OK.	
	1928	**The last FALCON-KNIGHT autos are built.**	
	1928	**In the largest cash transaction ever, Walter P. Chrysler acquires the Dodge Bros. Co.**	(see 1930)
	1928	CHRYSLER CORP. introduces the 1929 model DeSoto to compete with Oldsmobile, Pontiac, and Nash.	(see 1960)

1928	BORGWARNER CORP. is formed by the merger of BORG & BECK, MARVEL-SCHEBLER, WARNER GEAR, and MECHANICS UNIVERSAL JOINT CO.	
1928	ELECTRO-MOTIVE CORP. and WINTON produce an eight cylinder, 400 horsepower gasoline engine, and install two in an 800 horse-power locomotive.	
1928	**MAGIC CHEF builds the first gas cook stove.**	
1928	NATIONAL SUPPLY buys SUPERIOR ENGINE CO; NATIONAL also opens their first overseas store, in the UK.	
1928	EAGLE CRUSHER CO. builds its first portable hard-rock crusher.	
1928	**GRC introduces the first bottomhole pressure gauge, known as the Amerada Bomb.**	
1928	BRIGGS & STRATTON buys EVINRUDE MOTORS.	
1928	INDEPENDENT TORPEDO CO. merges with EASTERN TORPEDO CO.	
1928	FOKKER is the world's largest airplane builder, but will soon start losing ground to BOEING and DOUGLAS, with their aluminum structures.	
1928	**PHILLIPS PETROLEUM introduces the first specialty trucks for aviation refueling.**	
1928	Thomas Fawick sells his part of TWIN-DISC CLUTCH and leaves to pursue other interests.	(see 1930)
1928	**Spang, Chalfant, & Co. pioneers the "Magna-Glo" inspection system, to locate cracks in pipe.**	
1928	**Lonely, impoverished, and forgotten, radio pioneer Nathan B. Stubblefield starves to death in a shack and is buried in an unmarked grave in his hometown of Murray, KY.**	
1928	SHAFFER TOOL WORKS in Brea, CA, starts making well control items.	(see 1955)
1928	Paul V. Galvin founds the GALVIN MFG. CORP. in Chicago.	

1928	WORTHINGTON PUMP & MACHINE COMPANY introduces the first angle engine and compressor.	
1928	CENTRAL TRACTOR CO. of Greenwich, OH, now becomes CENTAUR TRACTOR CORPORATION, and they use LeRoi engines in their products.	
1928	GENERAL ELECTRIC introduces their "Monitor Top," the first "hermetic" or sealed (motor & compressor) refrigeration unit.	
1928	In Lima, OH, the OHIO POWER SHOVEL CO. is founded (LIMA LOCOMOTIVE WORKS).	
1928	Late 20s, MARLAND OIL CO. purchases CONTINENTAL OIL CO., but continues using the Continental name, later to be CONOCO.	
1928	BLAW-KNOX acquires A. W. FRENCH & CO., a manufacturer of concrete related equipment.	
1928	NATIONAL SUPPLY purchases a 50% interest in OILWELL ENGINEERING.	
1928	East Texas; there are now eight Brookshire brothers and sisters involved in the several stores of the BROOKSHIRE BROS. grocery business.	
1928	Amon G. Carter, Sr., is a director and partial owner of the AVIATION CORPORATION; later a component of AMERICAN AIRLINES.	
1928	H. C. SMITH MFG. CO. moves to Los Nietos, CA, and builds a new plant.	
1928	**A-C develops the mechanical fuel pump for cars.**	
1928	Indiana; Reverend Ira Weaver starts growing and selling popcorn. Before long he is selling his popcorn nationwide. Ira's grandson and great-grandson will take "Pop Weaver's" popcorn into the next millennium.	
1928	**The first home television set is demonstrated, with a screen measuring 3 inches by 4 inches.**	(see 1940)
1928	**The world's first known cloverleaf highway intersection is built at Woodbridge, NJ.**	
1928	**La-Z-Boy introduces their first reclining chair, the recliner.**	
1928	**Otto Rohwedder invents the bread slicing machine.**	(see WWII) (see 1943)
1928	Now renamed STANDARD CARTAGE, Hamilton Cartage gets its first major contract… with KROEHLER FURNITURE CO.	
1928	Having recovered after the 1905 fire, DURHAM FURNITURE with its 180 employees in the 100,000 square foot factory, using 3,000,000 board feet of lumber each year, now produce a railroad boxcar load of fine furniture every 11 hours.	
1928	Lima cable-type excavators are introduced, after LIMA LOCOMOTIVE WORKS buys the OHIO POWER SHOVEL COMPANY.	
1928	The radio parts distributing branch of COLUMBIA RADIO CORPORATION is henceforth called ALLIED RADIO.	
1928	November 24; CATERPILLAR buys the RUSSELL GRADER MFG. CO. and awards John Riggs, Sr. the CAT dealership for 45 counties of Arkansas, Riggs changes his company name to ARKANSAS TRACTOR & EQUIPMENT, and is the first CAT dealer in Arkansas.	
1928	RUGGLES MOTOR TRUCK CO. of Saginaw, MI, builders of 3/4 to 2 1/2 ton trucks and sightseeing buses, goes out of business.	
1928	Two former school teachers found PLAY-SKOOL COMPANY in Milwaukee, WI.	
1928	France; CITROËN introduces the first all-steel automobile body in Europe.	
1928	Corsicana, TX; William Orville (it's no wonder they call him "Lefty") Frizzell is born on March 31.	

1928	Wayne Oil Tank Company is renamed Wayne Pump Company, they introduce the first metered pump.	
1928	The Trailer Company of America is the new moniker, as Trailmobile merges with the Lapeer Co. of Lapeer, MI, a maker of "automatic" trailers.	(see 1929)
1928	The Glen L. Martin Co. opens a aircraft manufacturing plant near Baltimore, in Middle River Maryland. This plant will remain active well into the 21st century.	

CITY PARK AT WEST PALM BEACH, WITH TREES WHIPPED BY THE WIND & UPROOTED

PHOTO MADE AT WEST PALM BEACH AT HEIGHT OF HURRICANE

1928	The first trans-continental flight is made in a Lockheed Vega, a four-passenger wooden monoplane, in only nineteen hours.	
1928	Without a doubt, Dennis Brothers is now Britain's most successful truck manufacturer.	
1928	Monahans, TX; the Shell Oil Co. builds the world's first one-million barrel (42 million-gallon) capacity oil storage tank.	
1928	Texas Air Transport starts Texas's first regularly scheduled passenger flights.	
1928	UK; Guy Motors Ltd. takes over the near bankrupt Star Vehicle Co., continuing to produce Star vehicles until 1932, then ceasing due to lack of sales.	
1928	The Okeechobee Hurricane hits Florida, leaving four thousand (4,000) persons dead in its trail.	

1928	Having just taken the reins of Layne just last year, Louis Layne now passes away.	(see 1934)
1928	Named for the nearby JAL Ranch, the town of Jal, NM, is incorporated, calling itself the "Natural Gas Capital of the World."	
1928	France; after selling the small bicycle and parts store he had bought with his savings, Faustin Potain founds the Potain Co. while submitting patents for construction of buildings and roadworks. Soon, Potain is making small pieces of construction equipment, such as wheelbarrows, troughs, scaffolding, and the like.	
1928	The Minnesota Canning Company introduces the Jolly Green Giant.	
1928	Robbins establishes a Chevrolet dealership in Humble, TX.	
1928	The Oklahoma City oilfield is discovered, and soon is producing tremendous quantities of crude oil.	
1928	National Biscuit Co. acquires the Shredded Wheat Co., and is now in the "ready-to-eat" cereal business.	
1928	Farmers Insurance Company is founded.	
1928	The Full Crawler Company Division of George H. Smith Steel Co. becomes the Trackson Co.	(see 1936)
1928	Daytona Beach, FL; British driver H. O. D. Segrave reaches 231 mph in his Golden Arrow. This narrow, twelve-cylinder-powered vehicle, looks more like a plane than a car.	(see 1960)
1928	CASE buys the farm implement manufacturing business of Emerson-Brantingham.	(see 1937)
1928	Canada; Jeffrey Mfg. Co. Ltd. is established in LaSalle, Québec, and is soon producing power transmission equipment, sprockets, chains, mining machinery, and all such items.	(see 1929)
1928	Texas; Gifford-Hill is the contractor building the St. Louis Southwestern rail line from Tyler northward to Mt. Pleasant, which should take a couple of years to complete, providing gainful employment to many East Texans.	
1928	Ohio; Hal Wright Sr. sells the Wright Hoist Co., and the new owners soon move the business to York, PA.	(see 1942)
1928	The first known powered hydraulically operated bulldozer blade is introduced by the Baker Mfg. Co.	(see 1930)
1928	Michigan; ending USA production, Henry builds the last of the Fordson Model "F" tractors in Dearborn. About 750,000 have been built here; now they will all be manufactured in Cork, Ireland.	

1928	Ohio; at the request of a local priest in Medina, the A. I. Root Company turns to candle making, a natural connection to the beeswax and honey business.	(see 2009)
1928	And now, MAXWELL HOUSE COFFEE, LA FRANCE Laundry Products , and CALUMET BAKING POWDER join the POSTUM-JELL-O bunch.	(see 1929)
1928	On a course near Russelsheim, Germany, the OPEL RAK-2, propelled by 24 solid propellant rockets, runs 238 kph (147.56 mph). This event is witnessed by many of Berlin's citizens, giving Opel another boost.	(see 1929)
1928	England; Ernest Crump's PELICAN ENGINEERING CO. moves to larger facilities on Pepper Road in Hunslet, Leeds, as they have really outgrown the original Scout Hill shops.	(see 1931)
1928	Louisiana; ROBIN MOTOR COMPANY opens as the FORD dealership in the town of Jeanerette.	
1928	Late in this decade, motorcycle riders (bikers) begin to wear leather riding garb.	(see 1953)
1928	California; as partners, ice cream maker William Dreyer and candy maker Joseph Edy open a neighborhood ice cream parlor.	
1928	The INDIANA TRUCK CORPORATION is acquired by BROCKWAY. The INDIANA marque will be continued into 1939.	
1928	Olean, NY; local engine manufacturer, CLARK BROS. COMPANY, is now a leading builder of oil drilling rig engines, now has a factory branch in Tulsa, OK, as well as warehouses in McCamey and Sweetwater, TX, and Artesia, NM. Out on the West Coast, Clark Bros. is represented by SMITH BOOTH USHER COMPANY of Los Angeles and San Francisco.	
1928	Illinois; the Altorfer brothers' ABC takes over the FEDERAL WASHING MACHINE COMPANY of Chicago, which was producing washing machines for Samuel Insull's INSULL UTILITIES COMPANY. ABC becomes INSULL's supplier, making washing machines for them exclusively under the "Fedelco" brand.	(see 1952)
1928	Little America, Antarctica; at one point, Admiral Richard E. Byrd leaves his base on the Bay of Whales in a converted Ford Model T. But it was abandoned about 75 miles from his Camp.	(see 1939)
1928	UK; the ROOTES Group takes over HUMBER LTD. and the COMMERCIAL CAR COMPANY.	(see 1952)
1929	INTERNATIONAL HARVESTER CORP. builds its first crawler tractor.	
1929	The first COMPOSITE CATALOG of oilfield goods and services is published.	
1929	Working as a hotel clerk, David D. Buick dies of cancer, impoverished… and forgotten for the most part.	
1929	E. BOYDELL & CO. of England introduces its cable operated front loader attachment called the MUIR-HILL Loader, first on a 28 hp FORDSON.	
1929	The MOLINE IMPLEMENT CO., the MINNEAPOLIS THRESHING MACHINE CO., and the MINNEAPOLIS STEEL & MACHINERY CO. all three merge to form the MINNEAPOLIS-MOLINE POWER IMPLEMENT CO.	
1929	COOPER FOUNDRY merges with the BESSEMER GAS ENGINE COMPANY. BESSEMER is now also producing diesel engines.	
1929	WILLAMETTE ERSTED COMPANY begins making winches and lifting equipment for the logging industry, in Portland, OR.	
1929	Niels Miller (1899-1962) builds the first MILLER WELDING machine in his basement, out of scrap materials. This is the world's first "cracker box" welder.	
1929	INTERNATIONAL DERRICK & EQUIPMENT CO. (IDECO) and LEIDECKER are selling cable tool rigs under the IDECO-LEIDECKER brand name.	

1929	**HUDSON is third in auto sales in the US, behind FORD and GM.**	
1929	UNITED AIRCRAFT & TRANSPORTATION buys STEARMAN AIRCRAFT CO.	(see 1934)
1929	**CEDARAPIDS introduces one of the very first hot-mix asphalt plants.**	
1929	KOEHRING CO. buys the PARSONS COMPANY.	
1929	BORGWARNER acquires MORSE CHAIN COMPANY.	
1929	Born in 1844, the son of a German locomotive engineer, Carl Benz dies this year.	
1929	In Norfolk, England, CHARLES BURRELL & SONS, a pioneer steam roller builder, shut their doors for good.	
1929	In April, a merger of the AMERICAN SEEDING MACHINE COMPANY, HART-PARR TRACTOR COMPANY, NICHOLS & SHEPARD COMPANY, and the OLIVER CHILLED PLOW WORKS forms the OLIVER FARM EQUIPMENT COMPANY.	
1929	**PHILLIPS PETROLEUM CO. is the first to market propane for home use.**	
1929	**Joseph B. Wood develops the Controlled Vertical Drilling Instrument, and forms TECHNICAL OIL TOOL CORP. (TOTCO) to market it. Manufacturing of the instruments is being carried out in Wood's home in Hollywood, CA.**	
1929	R. A. LISTER & CO. produce their first diesel engines in Dursley, England.	
1929	MARTIN-DECKER CORP. is formed as Elmer Decker and Frosty Martin buy out the LOOMIS OILWELL CONTROL CO. business in Long Beach, CA.	
1929	**Clessie Cummins fits his 6.25 liter diesel engine into a PACKARD automobile and drives from Indianapolis to New York City for the Auto Show; he gets a cool reception, but executives from both FORD and GENERAL MOTORS ask for private demonstrations.**	(see 1932)
1929	MISSION SALES CO. is developing its own line of fluid-end parts, for rotary drilling mud pumps.	
1929	BJ acquires the PACIFIC CEMENTING CO., and begins oil well cementing operations in the Los Angeles Basin.	
1929	BESSEMER GAS ENGINE CO. of Oak Grove, PA, and C & G COOPER of Mt. Vernon, OH, merge to form COOPER-BESSEMER CORP.	
1929	Walter Beech, the last original partner, sells TRAVEL AIR COMPANY to CURTISS-WRIGHT.	
1929	Art and Al Mooney form MOONEY AIRCRAFT COMPANY, in Wichita, KS.	
1929	June 17; using "Travel Air" five passenger planes, DELTA AIR SERVICE inaugurates its first passenger service between Jackson, Mississippi, and Dallas, with stops in Shreveport and Monroe, LA.	
1929	SQUARE D MFG. CO. merges with INDUSTRIAL CONTROLLER CO.	
1929	**This year 4.5 million cars are produced in the USA.**	
1929	SPICER acquires BROWN-LIPE. *"Naw Bubba, it ain't Brown Light."*	
1929	OILWELL acquires WILSON-SNYDER MFG. CORP. of Pittsburgh, PA.	
1929	Tulsa, OK; Harley Pray builds his first winches using the gears from Ford Model "T" truck rear ends, thus begins TULSA WINCH CO.	
1929	The DAVEY COMPRESSOR COMPANY is formed to market Mr. Paul Davey's popular compressor. It is the first portable, air-cooled air compressor, using aluminum for the first time to further reduce weight.	
1929	The luxurious LOCOMOBILE automobile comes to its end. Also, two other Durant cars, the Flint and the Star, meet their demise.	
1929	Soon after the stock market crash, BJ acquires DUNN MANUFACTURING CO. and others, to establish BYRON JACKSON OIL TOOL DIVISION.	

1929	Mr. Castor Oyl asks a question: "Hey there! Are you a sailor?" and Popeye "the sailor-man" says his first words… "ja think I'm a cowboy?" Oyl replies "Okay, you're hired." … and thus a long-running popular cartoon begins.	
1929	The ARM Co. is experiencing financial difficulty (who isn't?) and is sold, leaving the Goderich, Ontario, plant as the sole producer of Champion graders.	
1929	Spurred by the innumerable crop fires each year caused by sparks from tractor's exhausts, DONALDSON develops the first practical exhaust spark arrestors.	
1929	MID-CONTINENT SUPPLY starts as an oilfield supply company with small warehouses in Ft. Worth and Houston, TX.	
1929	**The first diesel-electric passenger locomotive is built by ALCO for New York Central.**	
1929	ALCO buys MCINTOSH & SEYMOUR's diesel engine plant in Auburn, NY.	
1929	**"Bib-Label Lithiated Lemon-Lime Soda" is introduced; it will later be called simply… Seven-Up.**	
1929	Texas; contractor Jerry Garvin is constructing US highway 380 from near Clairemont down to Post, in Garza County.	
1929	The small town of Andrews, TX, is given a "shot in the arm" by the DEEP ROCK OIL COMPANY's first strike.	
1929	E. L. Cord founds the CORD CORP. and introduces many automotive innovations, including streamlined design, front-wheel drive, and hidden headlights.	
1929	Birdseye sells his frozen seafood company for the tremendous sum of $22 million.	
1929	The first fire engine to carry its own water hits the streets this year.	
1929	Putting out a oil well fire near Gladewater, TX, Myron Kinley is seriously injured.	(see 1938)
1929	MANSFIELD SANITARY POTTERY of Fredericksburg, OH, is incorporated.	
1929	H. C. Smith sells out and retires.	
1929	The new radio sensation is the "Amos and Andy" show… and neither was black.	
1929	Toronto, Ontario, Canada; celebrated by four simultaneous ongoing balls, the British Empire's largest hotel, The Royal York, debuts.	
1929	USA; the first gyroscopic well survey instrument is built, its copyrighted name is "Surwell."	
1929	The first hydraulic operated landing gear for planes is developed.	
1929	Houston, TX; Meyer M. Gordon opens his first jewelry store, and introduces the practice of selling jewelry on credit.	
1929	Marble Falls, TX; the BLUE BONNET CAFÉ opens for business.	
1929	**The first miniature golf course in America, the THUMB GOLF COURSE, is built in Chattanooga, TN.**	
1929	November 19; a $100,000 business for manufacturing equipment and contracting dirt work is incorporated as R. G. LETOURNEAU, INC. of Stockton, CA.	
1929	December 12; Charles Goodnight dies in Tucson, AZ, and is brought to his home in Goodnight, TX, for burial.	
1929	GENERAL MOTORS buys 80% of OPEL of Germany.	
1929	WAYNE introduces hydraulic lifts for servicing automobiles.	
1929	ROOTS & CONNERSVILLE BLOWER is purchased by STACEY ENGINEERING. Stacey centrifugal pumps are combined with Roots Engineering to produce Roots Centrifugal air blowers.	(see 1941)
1929	TRAILMOBILE introduces the first trailer specifically for piggy-back usage.	(see 1932)
1929	LOCKHEED AIRCRAFT becomes a division of DETROIT AIRCRAFT.	

1929	RADIO CORPORATION OF AMERICA (RCA), acquires VICTOR, and Nipper is now the RCA VICTOR dog, and soon a fascinating assortment of "Nipperie" collectables are readily available.	(see 2007)
1929	Today's farmer with a new '29 John Deere GP, pulling a 10' disc, takes about 5½ hours to disc 40 acres.	(see 1936)
1929	The nation's two largest aircraft makers, CURTISS and WRIGHT, merge, forming CURTISS-WRIGHT CORP. with combined stock of $220 million. Walter Beech, the last original partner, sells TRAVEL AIR COMPANY to the newly formed CURTISS-WRIGHT CORP.	
1929	FOKKER AIRCRAFT CORP. buys all assets of DAYTON WRIGHT COMPANY from GM.	
1929	Faustin Potain applies for a patent on a scaffold connector he invents; the Indestructible Ties are a huge success.	

GULF BUILDING, HOUSTON, TEXAS

ERECTED BY JESSE H. JONES

1929	WATEROUS produces their last complete pumper truck, and, from now onward, will concentrate on manufacturing fire hydrants, fire pumps, and water system valves.	
1929	Houston, TX; the art deco masterpiece, the 36 story Gulf Building opens; it's the tallest building West of the Mississippi.	
1929	SHELL, with 11% of the world's crude production and 10% of the tanker capacity, is the world's leading oil company.	
1929	Texas; the fourteen-story, 450-room Spanish-Renaissance BAKER HOTEL is constructed in Mineral Wells. The Baker also has a swimming pool, indoor spas, steam rooms, and a private bowling alley.	
1929	Alaska; the local CATERPILLAR dealership of SAMSON HARDWARE CO. is taken over by NORTHERN COMMERCIAL CO.	
1929	California; in North Hollywood, the CLYDE W. WOOD MFG. CO. is established.	(see 1940)
1929	Texas; a long and illustrious career begins as Murvaul native, Woodward M."Tex" Ritter, begins singing on radio station KPRC in Houston.	(see 1974)
1929	Dirt moving equipment maker A. W. FRENCH & COMPANY is now acquired by BLAW-KNOX.	
1929	Germany; this year CLAAS builds 2,960 hay balers, their highest production ever.	(see 1931)
1929	Cedar Rapids, IA; the local major manufacturer of aggregate crushers and the like, IOWA MANUFACTURING CO., now adds asphalt plants to their line of fine products.	
1929	**October 24; "Black Thursday" on Wall Street ushers in more than a decade of hard times.... the Great Depression!!!**	
1929	Galion, OH; the local GALION IRON WORKS is acquired by the JEFFREY MFG. CO., of Columbus.	(see 1973)
1929	Michigan; over in Bay City, the BAY CITY DREDGE WORKS is renamed BAY CITY SHOVELS, INC.	
1929	The first known "tractor pulls" are taking place in Bowling Green, MO, and Vaughnsville, OH. Usually they pull very heavily loaded skidpans (sleds) over a 10 yard (9.1 m) course. Very often the winner is the tractor that does not break in two.	
1929	GENERAL FOODS CORPORATION is the new moniker for the group that began with the POSTUM CEREAL and JELL-O merger. Over the next few years BIRDSEYE FOODS, GAINES DOG FOOD, KOOL-AID, GOOD SEASONS, as well as S. O. S. will join this very tasty conglomerate.	(see 1965)
1929	Germany; the firm of OPEL AG is taken over by GENERAL MOTORS of the United States.	(see 1931)
1929	The FOOTE GEAR CO. buys out BATES MACHINE & TRACTOR CO.	(see 1937)

1929	Ft. Worth; Kenneth W. Davis Sr. joins MID-CONTINENT SUPPLY, and invests heavily in the oilfield supply business. Davis has boldness and good judgment, and he trusts that this is the future… although within a couple of years, crude oil drops to a dime a barrel (42 gallons) and most other investors are really running scared.	(see 1930s) (see 1930)
1929	Kansas; November; H. W. CARDWELL MFG. CO. begins construction of their new facility at 801 S. Wichita St. in Wichita.	(see 1956)
1929	Wisconsin; the HEIL COMPANY has now developed their "Collecto" line of garbage bodies for trucks, and will soon begin building concrete mixers and tank trailers.	(see 1938)
1929	Sweden; Hilding Flygt and the Stenbergs were brought together by a newspaper advertisement, and the Stenbergs now begin making Flygt pumps in the city of Lindås.	(see 1956)
20s–30s	USA; during the late 1920s and early 1930s the nationwide rise in school consolidations causes a tremendous demand for school student transportation vehicles.	
1930s	As orders for the expensive Plymouth yard locomotives slow severely, F-R-H searches for a less expensive product, that more folks can afford. Plymouth, OH, is surrounded by prime farm land, and it's decided to build a farm tractor.	(see 1935)
1930s	Milwaukee, WI; Alfred Woelbing invents Carmex lip balm; he hand pours the mixture into the tiny glass jars with metal lids, and sells to drug stores from the trunk of his car.	(see 2009)
1930s	GLEANER BALDWIN COMBINES goes into receivership; William James Brace and his son-in-law buy Gleaner out of bankruptcy.	(see 1955)
1930s	Designer Raymond Loewy joins INTERNATIONAL HARVESTER to help "slick-up" their tractors.	(see 1939)
1930s	Ohio; cookie jars and piggy banks are now coming from HULL POTTERY in Crooksville.	(see 1950)
1930s	Throughout this decade of Great Depression, MID-CONTINENT SUPPLY CO. opens stores in such places as Turnertown, Refugio, Kermit and Odessa, all in Texas, as well as Rodessa, LA, and Magnolia, AR.	(see 1930) (see 1933)
1930s	In the early part of the decade, Robert Pott invents the electric impact wrench, and calls it the IMPACTOOL.	
1930s	During this decade, crawler tractors of any make can be made a very versatile piece of equipment by using LeTourneau's attachments; such as bulldozer blade, rear-mounted 1 or 2 drum cable control unit, as well as a towed rooter, also known as a ripper.	
1930s	HOBART BROS. ventures into the steel house construction business in and around Troy, OH.	
1930s	**Richard Drew notes that a specific tape is needed to seal the popular material, cellophane, thus is born Scotch brand cellophane tape from 3M.**	
1930s	The GALVIN CORPORATION begins making and selling car radios under the Motorola name.	
1930s	**THOMAS & BETTS introduces the first cast solderless lugs for wire and cable connections.**	
1930s	**The automatic safety and relief valve is invented for use on home water heaters.**	
1930s	By mid-decade, both BARBER-GREENE and ADNUN have developed the first, formless, free-traveling asphalt pavers.	
1930s	Late this decade, Ned S. Woolley founds WOOLLEY TOOL COMPANY, in Monahans, TX.	

1930	January 1; having joined the firm last year, Ken W. Davis, Sr., becomes president and general manager of MID-CONTINENT SUPPLY CO.		
1930	BROWN OIL TOOLS, INC., is founded in Houston.		
1930	BETTIS RUBBER PRODUCTS begins in Whittier, CA.		
1930	In Callahan County, TX, the Admiral Post Office is closed.		
1930	BAROID COMPANY is established.		
1930	VAN GORP pulleys, conveyors, etc., begins business in Pella, IA.		

1930	September 8; Dad Joiner brings in the "Daisy Bradford No. 3;" starting the East Texas Oil Field. This well was drilled at the spot where the rig was stopped during skidding to a new location and one of the major wooden skid beams broke. Unable to afford to buy a new wooden skid beam, Joiner decided to drill right where it sat, and… the rest is oilfield history.	
1930	Arthur M. Young (1905-95) builds and demonstrates a flyable helicopter.	(see 1941)
1930	May 6; today is one of the very worst days ever for tornados in Texas. Austin, Abilene, and Spur are hit in the morning. Ennis, Bynum, Irene, and Frost suffer damage and deaths during the afternoon. Before midnight, Kennedy, Runge, Nordheim, Bronson, San Antonio, and Gonzales are struck. The sad total is eighty-two deaths, and two and a half million dollars in damages.	
1930	May 27; the Chrysler Building opens. At 1048 ft. (322.46 m) and 77 stories, it's the tallest building on earth for only a few months.	(see 1933)

1930	New York City; at 1,250 feet (384.61 m) tall, the Empire State Building opens.		
1930	Ira Cooper's COOPER CORPORATION and the GIANT TIRE COMPANY merge with the FALLS RUBBER CO. to form MASTER TIRE & RUBBER CO.		
1930	**The last of the GRAMM-BERNSTEIN trucks are made.**		
1930	George Failing mounts a small steam rig on a 1927 Ford truck, modifies it to run off the PTO, and has the first truly portable drilling rig, George patents it and starts the GEORGE E. FAILING CO., a driller for shot holes and core holes.		
1930	July 3; CATERPILLAR test runs its first precombustion-chambered test engine. As there is no actual "diesel" fuel available, it must be able to run on any of various distillates of varying composition and quality. Any engine put into production must be able to operate on whatever fuel happens to be available locally. An overhead-cam direct-injection engine is also tested, but is not put into production due to its intolerance to many of the presently available fuels.		
1930	June; GENERAL MOTORS buys WINTON ENGINES, then buys ELECTRO-MOTIVE CORPORATION. of Cleveland this December.		
1930	NOBLE DRILLING COMPANY is formed.		
1930	TOYODA MACHINE WORKS is established in Japan.		
1930	Now in its third generation, the WACKER name is trusted, WACKER introduces the "electric ramm."		
1930	During the Great Depression, MARMON CAR CO. joins forces with ex-military engineer Col. Arthur Herrington, who is involved in the design of four wheel-drive vehicles, resulting in the MARMON-HERRINGTON COMPANY.	(see 1960)	
1930	The ELECTRIC STORAGE BATTERY COMPANY has evolved into EXIDE CORP.		
1930	**FOKKER planes are now being manufactured in 22 countries around the world, and are in use by 54 airlines.**		

1930	FRANKS MACHINE WORKS is established in Enid, OK.	
1930	All various manufacturers in the USA produce 1.1 million cars this year.	
1930	UNITED STATES STEEL (USS) acquires OILWELL, now OILWELL DIVISION OF US STEEL.	
1930	This winter, R. G. LeTourneau builds his second plant, in northeast Stockton, CA. This facility is considered to be the first building in the world of all-welded steel construction.	
1930	**R. G. LeTourneau pioneers the unitized wheel tractor and scraper.**	
1930	**Powel Crosley makes the first commercial radio broadcast from an airplane.**	
1930	Harry Barber sketches out the first travel mixer and asphalt paver.	
1930	GREYHOUND BUS LINES now has 1,800 buses on the roads of America.	(see 1950)
1930	The aircraft industry loses one of its pioneers, as Chance M. Vought dies of blood poisoning at the young age of 40.	
1930	Wisconsin; Thomas Fawick and Clearance Eason establish INDUSTRIAL CLUTCH CORPORATION in Waukesha.	(see 1936)
1930	Around this time, James and Harold's dad, Walter Mueller, starts his business building fine quality metal water cisterns for farmers and ranchers out around Ballinger, TX.	
1930	TRANSCONTINENTAL OIL CO. is no more, as Michael Benedum trades all its assets, including 376 MARATHON stations, for OHIO OIL CO. stock.	
1930	**The first large, land-based desalination plant is erected at Aruba, in the Netherlands Antilles.**	
1930	OTIS ENGINEERING CO. is established.	
1930	E. Paul duPont begins running the INDIAN MOTOCYCLE COMPANY, a job he stays with for fifteen years, setting the standard for Indian and introducing their streamlined, art-deco style.	(see 1933)
1930	The Mars family introduces a new candy bar, named after their daughter's horse… Snickers.	
1930	**The vortex tube is invented by Georges Ranque.**	
1930	At this time IDECO is building airplane hangars, airport equipment, and fire-watch towers for the US Forest Service.	
1930	The Grand Saline, TX, native, Wylie Post is now working as a test pilot, airplane racer, and cross-country flier.	
1930	Mr. Addison Holton forms the ESSEX WIRE CORP. in Detroit. Essex soon has 700 employees making Model "A" Ford wiring harnesses and battery cables. Essex soon acquires RBM MANUFACTURING CO., a maker of automotive electrical switches.	
1930	Texas; at this time, US highway 287 is being extended from Carmona to Woodville.	
1930	Gene Hancock and his wife Eileen move to Lubbock, TX. Gene works odd jobs while earning his degree from Texas Tech. He will teach school at several area towns before moving back to Lubbock to farm for a living.	(see 1947)
1930	The XP-900, Lockheed's first fighter plane is a trend-setter. It's the first fighter to depart from the traditional configuration of externally braced, open cockpit biplanes, as well as having a new 600 horsepower engine.	
1930	Airing on the radio, Painted Lives by Irna Phillips, although short-lived, is usually considered to be the first radio "soap opera."	(see 1932) (see 1934)
1930	France; a Frenchman, Georges Bataille founds POCLAIN; for the manufacture of agricultural machinery.	
1930	Neoprene is invented by Wallace Carothers working at DuPont Laboratories.	

1930	Minneapolis Moline is now marketing the first "Quick-on-Quick-Off" tractor implements, using a square tool bar.	
1930	Chevrolet purchases the Martin-Parry Corp., allowing Chevrolet to offer a variety of bodies on their trucks.	
1930	Valspar & Company acquires Con-Ferro Paint & Varnish Co., as well as Detroit Graphite Co.	
1930	EMSCO develops a line of duplex, double-acting, slush (mud) pumps for rotary drilling operations.	

1930	The planet Pluto is discovered by Clyde Tombaugh of New Mexico, working at Lowell Observatory in Flagstaff, AZ.	(see 2006)
1930	The first roadside park in Texas is built along highway 71, in Fayette county.	
1930	After more oil discoveries locally, Tulsa, OK, is now well-known as the "Oil Capital of the Nation."	
1930	The Rome Grader Division introduces its first motor grader, and as most are, it's built on a farm tractor chassis.	(see 1951)
1930	The Kellogg Company cuts their employees' work week to thirty hours, with NO loss of productivity.	
1930	USA; the first portable irrigation sprinkler system is developed.	
1930	North America now has only thirty-eight manufacturers of farm tractors.	
1930	Texas; returning to Ft. Worth from Lubbock, Frank Kent buys Earl North's part of Webb-North Buick dealership, thus Kent becomes VP of Webb-Kent Buick Company.	(see 1935)
1930	May 15; Iowa farm girl and registered nurse, twenty-five year old Ellen Church loves aviation. She takes flying lessons and works on aircraft engines in her spare time. After being turned down cold when she asked to be hired as a pilot by Boeing Air Transport (United), Church suggested that the airline hire registered nurses to attend passengers in flight. Also helping reassure nervous passengers. Today, Ellen Church crews the first airliner ever to carry a flight attendant, a Boeing 80A trimotor.	
1930	This year, Baker Manufacturing Co. brings out the first balcrank or indirect lift bulldozer blade, as well as the first hydraulic bulldozer blade with twin cylinders mounted on the track roller frames.	(see 1932)
1930	A. B. DuMont has experimented with mechanical television broadcasting, with no success, and is now even more convinced that the cathode ray tubes are the way to go. One problem is that the present day cathode ray tubes only last about a day or so. Lee DeForest disagrees and refuses to finance further C-R-T research by DuMont. DuMont resigns about the same time DeForest sells his radio manufacturing business to David Sarnoff over at RCA.	(see 1931)
1930	There are now more or less two billion persons on earth, and the real population explosion now begins…	
1930	Bill Lear takes his profits from Galvin and other interests and establishes Lear Developments (later Lear Inc., and still later Lear Siegler), specializing in aircraft and later aerospace instrumentation and electronics.	(see 1935)
1930	UK; now having a successful 15 cwt. Military truck for the British Army, Morris-Commercial this year takes over the old Wolseley vehicle works in Adderley Park, expanding their range of trucks.	(see 1951)
1930	October 1; Transcontinental Air Transport (TAT) merges with Western Air Express, forming Transcontinental & Western Air, Inc. (T&WA).	
1930	Boston, MA; at MIT, Vannevar Bush invents the analog computer, or "differential analyzer."	

1930	There are about 920,000 tractors residing on farms across the USA.	
1930	Pennsylvania; the AMERICAN AUSTIN CAR CO. of Butler produces the "American Austin" on through 1934.	
1930	California; the TUCKER MOTOR COMPANY has developed a most unique method of over-the-snow propulsion—an auger!! The "Spiral Over-Snow Vehicle" is sixteen feet long and steers with a single ski. Some day POLARIS will also try the auger idea, but with little success.	(see 1954)
1931	ALLIS-CHALMERS buys the ADVANCE-RUMELY THRESHER CO., bringing a sorely needed dealer network to A-C. The last RUMELY OIL PULL tractor leaves the factory. ALLIS-CHALMERS also acquires RYAN MFG. CORP., a builder of road graders.	
1931	EUCLID ROAD MACHINERY COMPANY is incorporated.	
1931	In the early '30s, REDA PUMP CO., is established.	
1931	QUAKER STATE OIL & REFINING CO. is formed, but PHINNEY BROS., a predecessor, sold a Quaker State branded oil as early as 1913, or perhaps even earlier.	
1931	Selling refinery leftovers (resids) to hotels, from the backend of a heated tank truck, Leon Hess begins HESS OIL CO.	
1931	BROWN-LIPE moves to Toledo, OH.	
1931	**FORD builds its 20 millionth automobile, a (second series) Model "A."**	
1931	W. A. Bechtel helps put together the six-company consortium that wins the contract to build Boulder/Hoover Dam, for $48.9 million. This is the largest single contract the US government has ever awarded. This is equal to $577 million in 2006 dollars.	
1931	HALL-SCOTT introduces its famous six-cylinder marine Invader engine, with overhead cam, aluminum pistons, chrome-nickel iron block and head, twin ignition and seven main bearings.	
1931	Piccard and Kipfer ascend to 52,493 feet in a balloon, while testing stratosphere rays.	
1931	HYGRADE, NILCO and SYLVANIA merge to form HYGRADE SYLVANIA CORP., selling Hygrade light bulbs and Sylvania radio tubes.	
1931	FERRETERIA E. LANZAROTE a general industrial supply store is established in Mexico, the beginnings of an empire.	
1931	A few truckers and fleet operators begin to repower their vehicles with diesels after the Cummins team sets a 13,535 mile endurance record at Indianapolis Motor Speedway.	
1931	The first true Bedford truck rolls off the line of VAUXHALL's Luton plant.	
1931	Architects Marion Fooshee and James Cheek begin planning and soon start construction of a shopping center in the classy Highland Park area of Dallas.	
1931	The INDIAN OIL CO. of New York City is bought by the TEXAS COMPANY, and for the next decade or so, Indian is TEXACO's lowest priced grade of gasoline.	
1931	Shojiro Ishibashi founds BRIDGESTONE TIRE COMPANY. Ishibashi literally translates to "stone bridge" in English.	
1931	I. H. Grancell develops a superior tool joint dope, and "Bestolife 270" is invented.	
1931	Work begins on the 1600 foot long dam across the Pecan Bayou, a few miles north of Brownwood, TX.	
1931	Allan S. Vinnell establishes the VINNELL CONSTRUCTION COMPANY, in California.	
1931	California; SHELL CHEMICAL opens its Shell Point synthetic ammonia plant; the first plant ever to make ammonia from natural gas.	

1931	**At the Cowboy's Reunion at Stamford, TX, the world's first Barrel Racing contest gets underway.**		
1931	Clessie L. Cummins drives coast-to-coast in a Cummins diesel powered truck, using only $11.22 in fuel.		
1931	The first walk-behind garden tractor is introduced, the David Bradley Handiman.	(see 1938)	
1931	October; Caterpillar introduces their first production diesel engine, the D 9900, weighing 5,175 pounds and producing all of 89 horse-power. *NOTE: This very first original production engine off the assembly line is now resting in the Smithsonian. It was ran in the 1970s for critical emissions testing… which it passed. Caterpillar's first diesel-powered tractor, the Model Sixty is introduced, powered by Cat's very own new D 9900 diesel engine.*		
1931	Cashman Equipment begins business as the Caterpillar dealer in Las Vegas, NV. Good deal, as there's a really big dam being build just down the road a few miles.		
1931	Through the Depression, Conrad Hilton loses four of his hotels… but manages to keep five of them!	(see 1949)	
1931	Myron and Floyd Kinley recognize that Houston is becoming the global oil industry headquarters, and move their company there from Tulsa. Floyd dies shortly afterward.		
1931	Speedstar builds its first rotary drilling rig.		
1931	R. G. LeTourneau, Inc. completes the Boulder Dam highway, and nets a $100,000 loss.		
1931	Reda Pump is founded and begins manufacturing submersible electric pumps.		
1931	Dallas; Security Engineering begins manufacturing tools for the drilling industry.		
1931	**Nevada is the only state to exercise its state's rights and legalize gambling casinos.**		
1931	Dec; Mr. C. F. Richter establishes the "Richter Scale" for measuring the magnitude of earthquakes.		
1931	Immigrant brothers Joe and Phillip Drago, invest $2,000 and open Drago Hardware, as a retail business in Port Arthur, TX.		
1931	October; eight months early and $1,000,000 *under* budget, the George Washington Bridge opens to traffic.		

1931	Lou Gehrig matches Babe Ruth for baseball honors.	
1931	W. Lee "Pappy" O'Daniel, the president of Burrus Mill & Elevator Co., of Ft. Worth, hires Bob Wills and his "hillbilly" band to promote Light Crust Flour on a morning radio show; and the Light Crust Doughboys are born.	
1931	March; in Germany, Ernst Ruska and Max Knott co-develop the electron microscope.	
1931	September 12; George Jones is born in Saratoga, Hardin County, TX.	
1931	The last 20% of Opel is bought by GM; the Opel family is a total of $ 33,300,000 richer, and GM is sole owner of Opel.	
1931	The first electric can-opener debuts.	

1931	Stacey Engineering merges with International Derrick & Equipment Co. (IDECO).		
1931	Ruby Blevins, singing, wins a talent contest, and now known as Patsy Montana, makes her first recording, for RCA.		
1931	On its silver anniversary, Loffland Brothers has 37 rotary rigs, and high hopes for the future, but the first Golden Era is over.		
1931	Bad timing… this is the last year of major production for DeMartini Trucks, but they will continue to manufacture dump beds for three more years.		

1931	Ft. Worth, TX; April 15; Abilene restaurateur Mr. Plennie L. Wingo, has lost his restaurant in this "Great Depression," and he says "As the whole world is going backwards, The only way to see it is to turn around." Thus Wingo heads out for New York City on the first leg of his around the world trip, walking backwards all the way.	
1931	RUSTON BUCYRUS is formed as the excavating interests of RUSTON & HORNSBY of England, are allied with those of BUCYRUS ERIE of the United States.	(see 1933) (see 2007)
1931	Race driver Barney Oldfield gets a speeding citation for driving a pneumatic-tired farm tractor at 10 to 15 mph through a small rural Indiana town.	
1931	Florida; millionaire philanthropist Charles Stewart acquires the bankrupt SOUTHERN SUGAR COMPANY; thus founding US SUGAR, and eventually growing sugar cane on 187,000 acres of the Everglades.	
1931	Born in 1928, Miss Shirley Temple begins her acting career. The little cutie now appears in *The Red-Haired Alibi*.	
1931	Germany; CLAAS begins building straw presses; because of demand for higher bale density and uniform sized bales. CLAAS will produce these for the next four decades or so.	(see 1934)
1931	November 20; the first commercial teletype service is inaugurated today.	
1931	BROWNHOIST merges with INDUSTRIAL WORKS, forming INDUSTRIAL BROWNHOIST.	
1931	In his basement, Allen DuMont starts his own business building somewhat longer lasting cathode ray tubes, he soon sells two C-R-Ts to two college science labs for $35 each.	(see 1932)
1931	Under the direction of the federal CCC, Mack Wooldridge opens a school for bulldozer operators, making him one of the first equipment manufacturers offering a training program for operators of the equipment.	(see 1934)
1931	Germany; OPEL establishes a truck factory at Brandenburg and the 2 1/2 ton OPEL "Blitz" soon comes on the scene.	(see 1935)
1931	Finland; SISU begins production of a hooded, three-ton truck.	(see 1943)
1931	England; commencing a partnership that will last six decades, PELICAN ENGINEERING CO. is now the licensed agent for GARDNER oil (diesel) engines.	(see 1934)
1931	SCHWINN drops the EXCELSIOR name from its motorcycle line.	
1931	The Schlumberger boys successfully identify the presence of petroleum in a underground formation by measuring resistivity.	(see 1934)
1931	As our government gives up on preventing it; VACUUM OIL and STANDARD OIL OF NEW YORK (SOCONY) merge. This merger makes SOCONY-VACUUM CORP., the third largest oil company on earth… with Charles Everest as salaried president.	(see WWII)
1931	Texas; November 17; in Longview, four immigrants and a native Texan manage to borrow $22,000, buy two old junk drilling rigs and found a drilling company. Houston-born Robert Stacy, an experienced salesman, and Joseph Zeppa, who had worked up to executive positions with ARKANSAS NATURAL GAS and McMILLIAN PETROLEUM CO, teamed with three Jewish refugees from pogroms in Czarist Russia: Simon Goldman, Sam Sklar and Sam Y. Dorftman. The partnership was in thirds, Zeppa, Stacy, and Dorfman-Goldman-Sklar, thus the triangular Greek letter "delta" is used in the green company logo, as DELTA DRILLING CO. is established.	
D'Era	During the Depression LOFFLAND BROTHERS CO. takes drilling contracts at cost, and sometimes below, to keep their tool pushers and crews.	

D'Era	By unveiling many new products, and acquiring other paint and varnish companies, VALSPAR & COMPANY successfully weather the Depression.	
D'Era	Around Texas, the armadillo is currently known as a "Hoover hog."	
D'Era	Texas; cold, hard, cash as everyone knows, is very scarce, but chickens ain't. Thus, Miss Jessie Williams, Madame of a brothel near La Grange, has posted this sign… ONE CHICKEN, ONE SCREW. From this time onward, this place will be known as the Chicken Ranch.	
D'Era	USA; HOMER LAUGHLIN's "Fiesta" dinnerware is begun as Mr. Wells tells his potters "We (Americans) need something bright and colorful to brighten our day, and cheap so we can afford it." Thus, Fiesta Ware is born.	
D'Era	North Carolina; rather than cutting back and laying off employees, T. A. Finch sets THOMASVILLE CHAIR CO. up to produce higher grades of furniture, aimed at the folks who aren't quite so "depressed." To this end, in 1937 conveyor equipment and some automated equipment is installed. Thus, when the economy picks up, THOMASVILLE is all ready and going strong.	(see 1943)
D'Era	Texas; Paul Neal Adair, now known as Red, drops out of high school and goes to work helping his family make ends meet.	(see WWII)
1932	The first CATERPILLAR Diesel Engine for use by another manufacturer is sold to the THEW SHOVEL CO. of Lorain, OH, a D-9900, for a 1½ yard shovel. The D-9900 weighs 5,175 pounds, and produces 89 HP @ 700 rpm. Also, CATERPILLAR changes from GREY with RED trim to its famous "HIGHWAY YELLOW" paint color.	

	1932	Walt Durst founds DURST.	
	1932	MONIGHAN MACHINE CO. is bought out by BUCYRUS.	
	1932	February 25; Faron Young is born in Shreveport, LA.	
	1932	EATON AXLE & SPRING is renamed EATON MANUFACTURING CO.	
	1932	Walt Wells, president of PACIFIC OIL TOOL CO., LTD., and Bill Lane form LANE-WELLS , which soon includes PACIFIC OIL TOOL CO., LTD., in Los Angeles.	
	1932	Harvey Firestone introduces the first practical pneumatic farm tire, and this year ALLIS-CHALMERS introduces their tractors with pneumatic tires. A-C then hire race drivers Barney Oldfield and Ab Jenkins to take the rubber-tired A-C Model "U" tractors to county fairs all over America, and have tractor races. R. G. LeTourneau replaces steel wheels with pneumatic tired wheels on his machines this year.	(see 1933)
	1932	USA; Karl Jansky invents the radio-telescope.	

1932	Arthur Taubman buys a chain of three home and auto stores in Virginia, naming them ADVANCE STORES, later to become ADVANCE AUTO PARTS.	
1932	The last of W. C. Durant's automobiles, the DURANT, closes shop forever.	
1932	MANNING, MAXWELL & MOORE acquire BOX CRANE & HOIST CO., and combine it with SHAW ELECTRIC CRANE COMPANY, resulting in SHAW-BOX CRANE & HOIST CO.	
1932	April 14; as if we weren't depressed enough already, a real dust storm hits… the beginning of the "Dust Bowl."	
1932	June 7; during this worldwide Depression, Frank Perkins, now an engineer, founds F. PERKINS LIMITED in Peterborough, England, with his old friend and cohort Charles Chapman as the technical manager. They hire six employees and this autumn turn out the first PERKINS diesel engine. The little four-banger is hand-cranked from cold and starts as combustion caps heated red-hot in a coke stove are rapidly fitted back into the combustion chamber… it fires and runs, but is quickly shut down when it reaches 4,000 rpm, as it has no speed governor fitted.	(see 1937)

1932	Having given up on finding oil on the mainland of the Arabian peninsula, the Brits discover oil on the island of Bahrain, only a mere eighteen miles away. *"Yeah Bubba, Ah kin tell ya why them Limeys couldn't find eny all in Saudi Raby."*	
1932	PHELPS-DODGE CORP. forms PHELPS-DODGE INDUSTRIES, to serve as a built-in market for the raw copper being produced by the PHELPS-DODGE mining operations.	
1932	The CHEMICAL PROCESS CO. sets up shop in Breckenridge, TX, specializing in oil well acidizing and successfully acidizes the first wells in Texas.	
1932	Amelia Earhart, the first woman to fly across the Atlantic solo, lands her Lockheed Vega in Ireland.	
1932	Three immigrant craftsmen establish MODERN TOOL & DIE CO., (MTD) in Cleveland, OH.	
1932	Walter Beech and wife Olive Ann, found BEECH AIRCRAFT CO., in Wichita, KS.	
1932	Through reorganization of the fledgling company, the modern LOCKHEED CORP. is formed.	
1932	AMERICAN CYANAMID and IP formed ARIZONA CHEMICAL, as a joint venture, to refine crude liquor turpentine.	
1932	FORD of England introduces its Model Y.	
1932	The OAKLAND marque is dropped and this GENERAL MOTORS division is renamed PONTIAC.	(see 1955)
1932	HARLEY-DAVIDSON introduces the three-wheeled Servi-Car motorcycle.	
1932	**TEXAS IRON WORKS (TIW) manufactures the first unitized draw-works for drilling rigs.**	(see 1941)
1932	FORD introduces its "flathead" V-8 engine with 221 cubic inches of displacement.	
1932	LeTourneau becomes a supplier of bulldozer blades to the ALLIS-CHALMERS COMPANY.	
1932	SINCLAIR REFINING CO. of Chicago registers a brontosaurus as their company logo.	
1932	The FOOTE CO. introduces the Adnun Black Top paver, the first self-propelled, non-form-riding asphalt finisher.	
1932	July 3; although deliberate impoundment of water is due in July 1933, heavy downpours on the Jim Ned Creek and Pecan Bayou of central Texas mostly fill Lake Brownwood in six hours.	
1932	DOWELL is formed as a division by the DOW CHEMICAL COMPANY.	
1932	In California, the Knott family business cultivates a luscious new fruit, the boysenberry.	
1932	Charles Elmer Doolin, a San Antonio promoter, borrows $100 from his mother, and buys the recipe and seven sales outlets of a corn chip he has tasted and evidently liked. He makes the chips in Mom's kitchen and sells them out of the back of his Ford Model "T" car.	(see 1933)
1932	Enid, OK; Harold C. Groendyke establishes GROENDYKE TRANSPORT CO. More than seven decades later GROENDYKE is still a family owned business.	
1932	Leland Stanford founds the STANFORD FINANCIAL GROUP.	
1932	The *Autocar*, a British magazine, clocks a Lincoln KB at 95.74 mph, a speed only exceeded by a "supercharged" Alfa Romeo at 106 mph. The Lincoln KB weighs in at 5,535 pounds.	
1932	The first 3 Musketeers candy bars are marketed by Mars.	
1932	One of the first to sell electronics by mail, ALLIED RADIO begins their first marketing of radio parts and kits to home hobbyists. This year, ALLIED RADIO opens their first retail stores to sell to ham radio operators, electronic tinkers, etc.	
1932	The world's fastest bomber is the Martin YB-10 plane.	
1932	Mr. Ariens and his son Mike start the ARIENS COMPANY.	
1932	TRAILER CO. OF AMERICA acquires HIGHLAND BODY MFG. CO., and begins producing trailers with bodies.	(see 1939)

1932	A group of investors buys LOCKHEED AIRCRAFT from DETROIT AIR.	
1932	"Just Plain Bill" is the radio program creating the cultural rocket, that will soon be nicknamed for the sponsoring product-soap.	
1932	The first self-propelled drilling rig on crawler tracks appears from ARMSTRONG MANUFACTURING COMPANY.	
1932	ROSS HEAT EXCHANGER COMPANY is acquired by AMERICAN STANDARD.	
1932	After struggling with declining business for more than a decade, DE DION-BOUTON builds its final car, an 11 hp model. They'll build trucks for another decade, and the marque will last be seen in the 1950s, on motorcycles.	
1932	PACKARD ELECTRIC COMPANY, a maker of automotive electrical items, "joins" GENERAL MOTORS.	(see 1939)
1932	MINNEAPOLIS MOLINE introduces the first farm tractors with factory-installed pneumatic tires.	

1932	Germany; M. A. N. introduces their 160 horsepower (118 kw) truck engine; it is the most powerful truck engine on earth.	
1932	INDIANA TRUCK CORP. becomes a subsidiary of WHITE CORP., initiating another name change, the new moniker is INDIANA MOTORS CORP. On December 12, WHITE CORP. announces it will move production of the "Indiana" trucks from the Marion, IN, plant to Cleveland, OH.	(see 1939)
1932	VALSPAR & COMPANY begins operations as a subsidiary of the newly-formed VALSPAR CORPORATION.	
1932	Spain; ESAB-IBERIA S. A. is established in Madrid. ESAB S. A. BRUSSELS is established, as is PEAS in Prague.	
1932	June 24th; Texas's first jackrabbit roping contest is held at Odessa.	
1932	In a Democratic landslide, Franklin Delano Roosevelt is elected President of the United States.	
1932	Agricultural (off-road) diesel fuel sells for 4-7 cents a gallon, while agricultural gasoline is selling for 14-16 cents. During these extremely depressed times farmers are certainly looking for less expensive alternatives for everything they need to continue in business.	
1932	Troy, OH; the local MIAMI TRAILER-SCRAPER COMPANY builds wheeled, pull-scrapers, but manufactures loader attachments for CATERPILLAR 15, 20 and 25 crawler tractors, as well.	
1932	Texas; expanding on the foundry business, CENTRAL TEXAS IRONWORKS, is now fabricating steel.	(see 1953)
1932	BAKER is first again, this year with a direct lift, positive down-pressure twin-cylinder bulldozer blade.	(see 1937)
1932	Having an octane rating higher than the federal government requires for fire engine fuel, TEXACO Fire Chief Gasoline now replaces TEXACO New & Better Gasoline.	
1932	Allen DuMont proposes a "ship finder" device he has invented to the US Army Signal Corp.s. His device uses radio wave distortions to locate objects on a C-R-T screen; he has essentially invented radar. The US military asks DuMont to keep his invention secret, not taking out a patent. Thus, in the future, DuMont will rarely be mentioned as a radar pioneer.	(see 1937)
1932	Presently, only about 11% of the farms across the USA have electricity.	(see 1942)
ca1933	Morris Pendleton of PLOMB TOOLS, introduces the first line of combination wrenches to the market.	
1933	USA; January; Franklin Delano Roosevelt is inaugurated President of this great nation.	

1933	February; BOEING introduces the ten passenger Boeing 247, the first truly modern passenger airliner. UNITED orders 59 of these; that's at least a year or more production for Boeing.	
1933	February; as the Boeing 247 first flies this month, DOUGLAS is building their Douglas Commercial-1 (DC-1), a modern twelve passenger airliner. But before production begins next year, the DC-1 is stretched to accommodate another row of seats, becoming the fourteen passenger DC-2 airliner.	
1933	Pop Kelly buys CLEWISTON MOTOR CO. to form KELLY TRACTOR CO. and becoming the first CATERPILLAR dealer in southern Florida.	
1933	October 17; fleeing Nazi Germany, Albert Einstein migrates to the USA, and arrives today.	
1933	ARNOLD, SCHWINN & CO. introduce the 26" x 2.125" balloon bicycle tire.	
1933	STUDEBAKER CORPORATION goes into receivership.	
1933	KENWORTH was the first truck manufacturer to install diesel engines as standard equipment in their vehicles. KW is also the first to install factory sleeper cabs, KW sells its first sleeper cab truck to CENTRAL GROCERY of Yakima, WA.	(see 1936)
1933	Harry Ferguson and David Brown found FERGUSON-BROWN CO. and begin producing the Model A farm tractor, with a hydraulic system, 1,300 are produced in all.	
1933	San Antonio, TX; Bill Holt forms WILLIAM K. HOLT MACHINERY CO. as a South Texas CATERPILLAR Dealer.	
1933	**CATERPILLAR has the first and the world's only moving assembly line producing diesel engines. This year, the CATERPILLAR diesel engine production exceeds the TOTAL US production of all manufacturers for last year.**	
1933	Texas; the MKT abandons the railroad line to Cross Plains from DeLeon. The "Peanut Special" runs no more!!	
1933	NISSAN MOTOR COMPANY is founded in Japan.	
1933	The CALIFORNIA ARABIAN STANDARD OIL COMPANY (CASOC), affiliated with STANDARD OF CALIFORNIA, now begins searching for oil along the east coast of Saudi Arabia.	(see 1944)
1933	**HUGHES TOOL COMPANY introduces the first tri-cone bit, previously all rotary cone bits only had two cones.**	
1933	GENERAL MOTORS research laboratory produces the first prototype two-cycle diesel engine, an eight cylinder, 201 series engine.	
1933	HYDRIL CO. is established by Frank Seaver (he is a story himself) who develops the first hydraulically operated blowout preventer, then soon, the first annular BOP.	
1933	In the doldrums of the Great Depression, engineers J. C. Gorman and H. E. Rupp ante up $1,500 and with a handshake, start a pump business in a barn near Mansfield, OH. GORMAN-RUPP soon manufactures the first self-priming pump with no valves or orifices.	
1933	RAY-O-VAC patents the first wearable vacuum tube hearing aid.	
1933	Ft. Worth; Dixon T. Harbison and Charles A. Fischer pool their oil tools, knowledge of steel, their experience, and found HARBISON-FISCHER MFG. COMPANY, with a furnace, and a belt-driven machine shop, powered by a old Cadillac engine.	
1933	FORD is left in third place in sales by GM and CHRYSLER; as the CHRYSLER "Airflow" is introduced—just before its time.	(see 1937)
1933	Henry Salvatori founds WESTERN GEOPHYSICAL CO. a pioneer in seismic surveying.	
1933	To strengthen their line of turbine driven centrifugal pumps, INGERSOLL-RAND acquires a line from GENERAL ELECTRIC.	

1933	Lester Sears designs the first cantilevered forklift, and TOWMOTOR sells many of these to various stevedore companies.	
1933	GM subsidiary, AC SPARK PLUG COMPANY, now becomes a full division of GENERAL MOTORS.	
1933	INDIAN motocycles introduces their three-wheeled Dispatch-Tow.	(see 1953)
1933	HAMMERMILL introduces the 8 hour workday throughout its paper business.	
1933	Louis M. Pearce, Sr., gets the Texas distributorship for Waukesha engines for his PORTABLE ROTARY RIG CO. and it now becomes WAUKESHA-PEARCE INDUSTRIES, Inc. and opens its first branch in Greggton, TX, (western Longview).	

	1933	**The first Soap Box Derby is held in Akron, OH.**	
	1933	April 1; the US Congress approves legislation creating FDR's "Tree Army"; the Civilian Conservation Corps is the first government "relief measure" passed during the Depression. On April 7th, Henry Rich of Virginia signs up as the first CCC enrollee. April 17th; the first CCC camp, Camp Roosevelt opens in George Washington National Forest in Virginia. Across our nation, 25,000 have enrolled in the next two weeks. By July 1st, more than 1,300 CCC camps are opened, and over 274 thousand men have enrolled. Every state has at least one camp, as well as Alaska, Hawaii, Puerto Rico, and the Virgin Islands."Big Labor" organizations decry the low pay of one dollar a day, but it is a lot more than the zero dollars most were earning before enrolling.	(see 1935)
	1933	Another wild and crazy idea from Powel Crosley, as he introduces the Crosley Shelvador refrigerator. *"Can you believe it, shelves in the door???"*	

1933	June 6; supposedly inspired by complaints from his "very healthy" (Rubenesque) mother, about the miniscule size of theatre seats, Richard Hollingshead and his partner, Willis W. Smith, open the CAMDEN DRIVE-IN THEATRE, in Pennsauken, NJ. The movie showing this first evening in the world's very first drive-in theatre is *Wives Beware*.	
1933	Because of financial problems from 1929 and before, ASSOCIATED TELEPHONE UTILITIES goes into receivership.	
1933	USA; KOOL, the first menthol cigarette, is introduced by BROWN & WILLIAMSON.	
1933	Near Zavalla, TX, XACT CLAYS (later a division of MAGCOBAR) begins to process local clays for use in drilling mud for the petroleum drilling industry.	
1933	The COLEMAN COMPANY is surviving the Depression by producing natural gas floor furnaces and oil fired space heaters.	
1933	The BOSTON & MAINE AIRWAYS (sponsored by the BOSTON & MAINE and the CENTRAL VERMONT RAILROAD), makes its maiden flight.	
1933	June; with two of the five passenger, single-engine Bellancas, Carleton Putnam organizes PACIFIC SEABOARD AIRLINES, to serve Los Angeles and San Francisco.	
1933	Kentucky; Bill Weaver decides that telescopic rifle sights are too expensive, so he invents a modest-priced scope and forms the W. R. WEAVER COMPANY.	
1933	USA; the first chocolate chip cookies are now baked.	
1933	MANSFIELD SANITARY POTTERY purchases the Perrysville, OH, plant of OHIO POTTERY.	
1933	In California, the first "impact sprinkler" is being manufactured and sold by RAIN BIRD.	
1933	Paris, France; AIR FRANCE is established.	
1933	P & H build the last of their ditching machines.	

1933	Germany; this January, Adolph Hitler becomes chancellor. As Hitler comes to power, he adopts the idea of controlled or limited access highways as his own.	
1933	Holland; a KLM Fokker F-VIII "Pelican" sets a new record for Amsterdam to Batavia of 4 days, 4 hours, 35 minutes on what will remain the longest scheduled flight in the world until the second world war.	
1933	Leighton A. Wilkie invents the metal-cutting band saw, leading to the creation of the DoAll Company.	
1933	After some "tinkering" with the corn chips to "get 'em just right," Elmer Doolin moves his company to Dallas, where his Fritos are still being made, some eighty years onward.	(see 1959)
1933	December 5th; Federal Prohibition (of alcoholic beverages) ends in the Unites States.	
1933	Nine year old Chet Atkins, already a ukulele and fiddle player, trades his older brother Lowell a pistol and some chores for a guitar, and from here on, it is just beautiful history!!!	
1933	Bucyrus-Erie acquires the line of cable tool drilling rigs (churn drills, also known as stompers) from Armstrong Drill Co. For the next decade the Armstrong rigs will be sold as Bucyrus-Armstrong, then change over to the Bucyrus-Erie name.	(see WWII)
1933	April; President Franklin D. Roosevelt removes the United States of America from the gold standard. *"Yeah Bubba, I'll bet every liberal in our great nation pulls a week-long drunk to celebrate."*	
1933	Continental Supply Company moves to Dallas from St. Louis.	
1933	Grand Saline, TX; EXTRA!! EXTRA!! The first around-the-world solo airplane flight is made in 7 days and 19 hours by local native Wylie Post in "Winnie Mae," his Lockheed Vega airplane.	
1933	The federal government of the United States announces the National Recovery Association.	
1933	Although there is considerable variation, all states now have maximum weight limits for trucks on their highways.	
1933	W. A. Bechtel dies, and his son Steven takes over half way through the construction of the Hoover Dam.	
1933	Oklahoma; the town of Goodwell is barraged by seventy (yes, 70) severe dust storms this year.	
1933	Banks foreclose on 200,000 farms this year, most of them in the "Dust Bowl."	
1933	The Watson Jack Co. first begins officially using the acronym WAJAX, as their pumps are nicknamed.	(see 1965)
1933	March; the United States government creates the Farm Credit Administration.	
1933	The first Walden Book Store is opened for business.	
1933	Ab Jenkins sets a new speed record of 67.877 mph (119.237 kph) on a rubber-tired Allis Chalmers Model "U" tractor.	
1933	The US Congress establishes the Tennessee Valley Authority (TVA), kicking off a wave of dam construction across the southeast US. *NOTE: The TVA's modus operandi remains controversial for its lifetime, even though it did create a heck of a lot of very sorely-needed employment.*	
1933	Texas; Canadian Lawrence Welk and his Hotsy-Totsy Boys perform at the Liberty Hotel in Cleburne.	
1933	Ken W. Davis, Sr., establishes the Diesel Division of Mid-Continent Supply Co. and begins selling and repairing engines built by Cummins Engine Co. of Columbus, IN.	(see 1962)
1933	Another casualty of these hard times. The Marmon Car Company goes into receivership.	
1933	The Texas Company has the first submersible drilling barge working in Lake Pelto, LA.	(see 1934)

1934	Euclid Road Machinery Co. introduces the first ever haul truck specifically designed for off-highway usage.	(see 1939)
1934	Dodge selects the Bighorn Ram as its "mascot." The Dodge 1½ ton military 4x4 truck is the first vehicle ever that can be shifted out of, or into, four-wheel drive using a lever inside the cab.	
1934	Thornhill-Craver is established to manufacture chokes and couplings.	
1934	Austin Mfg. Co. merges with the Western Wheeled Scraper Co., creating Austin-Western Co.	
1934	P. Piggott, son of Will, buys a major interest in Pacific Car & Foundry from American Car & Foundry. Pacific Car & Foundry introduces its line of Carco winches for mounting on crawler tractors for the logging industry.	
1934	Fram Co. starts making oil filters… by hand… at the rate of ten filters each day.	
1934	The first drilling rig with diesel engines is put out in the oil patch.	
1934	Franklin Motor Car Company of Syracuse, NY ceases production of cars, but a variation of the Franklin engine will used in the Tucker automobile in the late 1940s.	
1934	For years, loggers have cried "hoist'er" to the winch operators; this cry eventually became "hyster," and Hyster is now used by the W. Ersted Company as their equipment brand.	

Oct. 22, 1935. G. W. PETTENGILL ET AL 2,018,569
RADIO SIGNALING APPARATUS
Filed June 17, 1933 3 Sheets-Sheet 3

Fig. 5.

Fig. 6.

Fig. 7.

INVENTORS:
Carleton D. Haigis,
George W. Pettengill
BY R.L.Goldsborough
THEIR ATTORNEY

1934	Tioga, TX, native, Gene Autry's first "singing cowboy" film, *Tumbling Tumbleweeds* hits the theatres.	
1934	Ingersoll-Rand acquires rights from Pott, and makes its first pneumatic Impactool, a ¾" drive impact wrench.	
1934	**An Illinois farmer, Gifford C. Parker comes to work in the Oklahoma and Texas oil fields, and soon establishes Parker Drilling Company in Tulsa.**	(see 1935)
1934	Aveling & Porter merges with Barford & Perkins to form Aveling-Barford, Ltd.; soon to become one of Europe's top equipment builders.	
1934	May; in this month's issue, *Popular Science Monthly* magazine states, "Only a handful of men in the world have the strange power to make a bit, rotating a mile below ground at the end of a steel drill pipe, snake its way in a curve or around a dog-leg angle, to reach a desired objective." George Failing and John Eastman, working in the Conroe, TX, oil field are two of these very few men.	
1934	**The first commercial "walkie-talkie" is introduced as a "portable superregenerative receiver and transmitter."**	
1934	Canada; the Dionne quintuplets are born.	
1934	The diesel-electric locomotive era begins on April 7th, as GM's EMD's first diesel-electric streamlined train rolls out of the Budd Mfg. plant in Philadelphia.	
1934	Due to a anti-trust ruling, Boeing is being broken into three companies, United Airlines, United Aircraft (later to be United Technology), and Boeing Airplane Co. William Boeing loses interest, leaves the aviation industry, goes out and raises horses.	(see 1935)
1934	**DRMC manufactures the first synthetic rubber car tires.**	
1934	Spencer-Harris Machine Co. is established in Gladewater, TX, by brothers Fred and Lee Spencer.	
1934	June; Carleton Putnam moves Pacific Seaboard Airlines to Memphis, TN, to haul air-mail between New Orleans and Chicago.	
1934	Amana Company is founded to build beverage coolers.	
1934	The Easy Mfg. Company, owned by John and Charles Ammon, merges with the Cushman Motor Works.	

1934	Houston; Schlumberger Well Surveying Corp. (later known as SCHLUMBERGER WELL SVCS.) is founded.	(see 1940)
1934	McQUAY-NORRIS builds six Tear-Drop test cars, on 1932 and 1933 Ford V8 chassis and engines.	
1934	Beginning a forty year reign, J. Irwin Miller, W. G.'s great-nephew becomes General Manager of CUMMINS ENGINE CO.	
1934	SHELL OIL COMPANY's research lab comes up with the first 100 octane fuel, it is to be used as a aviation gasoline.	
1934	WAUKESHA-PEARCE IND. forms WAUKESHA SALES & SERVICE and soon has several branches around Texas and Louisiana.	
1934	In Cincinnati, OH, the most powerful radio station in the world (ever), Powel Crosley's WLW is now on the air with 500,000 watts. WLW begins broadcasting daytime dramas sponsored by PROCTER & GAMBLE, these dramas are soon called "soap operas."	
1934	FOLEY MANUFACTURING begins business making sharpening equipment.	
1934	George Blaisdell moves his ZIPPO manufacturing works to expanded facilities, upstairs over a gas station.	
1934	July; the third drive-in theatre in the US opens in Galveston, TX.	
1934	Cartoonist (Gerald Caplin) Al Capp introduces his hillbilly boy, Li'l Abner, in eight newspapers, but soon he will be in more than 250 newspapers.	
1934	Texas; MERLA TOOL CO. begins business in Garland. MERLA will be a pioneer in gas lift technology for oil production.	
1934	CITROËN, the French auto maker, shocks the world as they mass-produce the world's first production front-wheel drive vehicle! The Citroën Traction Avant also has a unitary (unitized) body (no separate frame), and front-wheel independent suspension. Then debt, probably due to the rapid development of the Traction Avant, forces Citroën into foreclosure and it is taken over by the largest creditor, Michelin.	
1934	Started in 1932, the 1150 mile Kirkuk to Tripoli pipeline is now completed by IRAQ PETROLEUM COMPANY, LTD.	
1934	EVINRUDE introduces the Lawn Boy mower, with Briggs & Stratton's engines. It's the first powered reel mower made in the US.	(see 1950)
1934	Artie Baker, a banker in Lockney, TX, has the AMARILLO MACHINE SHOP to turn out a right-angle gear head, compatible with old Ford and Chevy engine speeds. Used auto engines are readily available and real cheap. Thus the Amarillo Gear-Head is born, putting affordable irrigation into more farmer's hands.	
1934	The Lockheed Model 10 Electra is the first all-metal transport plane, and the first to be pressurized.	
1934	William Lightfoot Schultz establishes the SHULTON CO. and soon introduces the Old Spice line of men's colognes.	
1934	Cy Bell joins with Loffland Bros, forming BELL & LOFFLAND INC. to drill in California. They pioneer the chemical treating of drilling fluids (mud).	
1934	LAYNE is now under the leadership of J. I. Seay, who arranges for the LAYNE affiliate firms to buy the Layne estates stock.	(see 1950)
1934	ESAB operating companies are set up in England, Denmark, and Italy.	
1934	CLAAS, in Germany, builds the first pickup and loading balers, used primarily for harvesting food crops. The finished bale is loaded via chute directly onto a wagon or truck.	
1934	June 9; with only a bit part in *The Wise Little Hen*, Mr. Donald Duck makes his movie debut. In his original role, Duck is somewhat smaller, and his bill is rounded, but his almost unintelligible voice and his short temper remains the same forever.	

1934	A young Cyrus R. Smith becomes president of AMERICAN AIRLINES. Smith will consolidate American's jigsaw of routes into a sensible network of routes, while standardizing their very peculiar collection of airplanes with a fleet of the new DC-3 planes over the next five years. C. R. will pilot AMERICAN AIRLINES for the next 34 years, thus helping shape the entire airline industry.	(see 1936)
1934	USA; the debut of the diesel-electric locomotive is made by BURLINGTON NORTHERN'S Pioneer Zephyr, as well as UNION PACIFIC RAILROAD'S M-10,000 City of Salina.	
1934	Oklahoma; as steel fabricated derricks are becoming more the norm, FLINT RIG forms AMERICAN STEEL DERRICK CO. FLINT then acquires TULSA BOILER & MACHINERY CO., for boilers and pressure valves, as well.	(see WW II)
1934	Mack Wooldridge is issued a patent for a pulled (towed) dirt scraper. Soon Mack's company is building several sizes of these scrapers.	(see 1938)
1934	England; PELICAN ENGINEERING CO. becomes involved with FODEN TRUCKS of Sandbach, Cheshire... the number of Foden's on the roads is rapidly increasing. This year, PELICAN officially becomes the FODEN TRUCK agent for Yorkshire. Dating back to steam engines of the 1800s, Foden, like Pelican Engineering is a family owned and managed business.	(see 1940) (see WWII)
1934	Mr. Joseph Begun invents the first tape recorder for broadcasting, thus the first magnetic recording takes place.	
1935	An oil field equipment salesman, Hugh S. Chancey has an idea for a rotary drilling rig that he believes will be a winner, thus, UNIT RIG & EQUIPMENT COMPANY is established in Tulsa, primarily to build draw-works and related equipment for oil field drilling and workover rigs.	
1935	SEALMASTER BEARINGS start building mounted (pillow block) bearings in Aurora, IL.	
1935	The GMC Suburban is introduced.	
1935	DODGE acquires GRAHAM TRUCK COMPANY, which had been building all of the DODGE trucks, anyhow.	(see WWII)
1935	**The first streamlined locomotive, the "Hiawatha" is built by ALCO.**	
1935	According to some sources, the DETROIT DIESEL ENGINE DIVISION of GM is founded this year.	
1935	FAIRBANKS-MORSE builds their first opposed piston diesel engine.	
1935	Tyler, TX; TYLER IRON & FOUNDRY is founded.	
1935	July 19th; the first parking meters in the world are installed in Oklahoma City. *"...an' 'em Okies brag about that!"*	
1935	PARKER DRILLING pioneers the use of diesel-electric drilling rigs.	(see 1945)
1935	WINCHARGER incorporates, and moves its plant to Sioux City, later this year, ZENITH RADIO CORP. buys control of WINCHARGER and in a couple of more years, will also offer their units in 12, 32, and 110 volts, and the WINCHARGER is soon world famous.	
1935	MONO PUMPS LTD. began manufacturing the "progressive cavity pump," utilizing a new pumping concept.	
1935	AB VOLVO becomes independent of SKF.	
1935	BUFFALO-SPRINGFIELD builds its last "steamroller," although the word becomes generic for all steel-wheel rollers.	
1935	Lawrence D. "Larry" Bell establishes BELL AIRCRAFT CORPORATION with 56 employees.	
1935	The FRENCH BATTERY COMPANY is renamed the RAY-O-VAC CO.	
1935	DANIEL ORIFICE FITTING COMPANY is established in Los Angeles to manufacture natural gas measuring instruments.	

1935	**CATERPILLAR introduces the RD-8 designation for its largest crawler tractor. (RD for Rudolf Diesel)** *NOTE: It will be another twenty years before CATERPILLAR will introduce a larger crawler tractor. CAT also introduces the Vee configured, eight-cylindered D-17000, their first engine not designed for any particular piece of CAT equipment. This popular engine is used in many varied applications, will be produced for twenty years, and many will be in use for four decades. It also has its own pony motor, used nowhere else.*	(see 1955)
1935	The one-cylinder "oil test" engines that Cat builds for their own use to test various brands and types of engine oils, are now made available to petroleum manufacturers to test their oils. CATERPILLAR continues building and using these one-cylinder test engines and making them available to the petroleum industry, well into the next century.	
1935	In Uncle Joe's Russia, the huge Tupolev ANT-20 MAXIM GORKY airplane lives its short lifespan.	
1935	Lincoln, NE; a youngster has powered his sidewalk scooter with an old CUSHMAN washing machine engine, and comes to the CUSHMAN plant looking for spare parts. Charles Ammon, the owner of CUSHMAN sees this and has the idea that a motor scooter might be a good product.	(see 1936)
1935	SQUARE D introduces the first circuit breaker for residential use.	
1935	FORD introduces its first medium-priced car, the Lincoln Zephyr.	
1935	The now successful PACIFIC SEABOARD AIRLINES is renamed CHICAGO & SOUTHERN AIR LINES, to better reflect its new region of operation.	
1935	In mid-Depression, PARKER APPLIANCE CO. buys a 450,000 sq. ft. building from the HUPP MOTORCAR CO. for its thirty-eight employees and plant.	
1935	EATON SPRING & AXLE COMPANY acquires engine valve maker, DETROIT MOTOR VALVE COMPANY.	
1935	An automatic refrigeration system for long haul trucks is introduced.	
1935	CABOT CORPORATION now begins drilling for oil out in West Texas.	
1935	Darryl F. Zanuck founds TWENTIETH CENTURY FOX movie studio.	(see 1946)
1935	The original FALCON SEABOARD starts up as a true independent in the oil and gas industry.	
1935	CHANCE VOUGHT AIRCRAFT, SIKORSKY, PRATT & WHITNEY, and HAMILTON-STANDARD all now become subsidiaries of the new UNITED AIRCRAFT CORPORATION.	(see 1974)
1935	AMERICAN TELEPHONE UTILITIES emerges from receivership and is reorganized as GENERAL TELEPHONE CORP.	(see 1955)
1935	**George R. Dempster dreams the idea of the Dempster-Dumpster to facilitate waste disposal on construction sites.**	
1935	USA; in the midst of the Great Depression, PARKER BROS. brings out their biggest game hit ever... Monopoly!!!	
1935	In Dallas, Julius Schepps establishes JULIUS SCHEPPES WHOLESALE LIQUORS INC.	
1935	BRANIFF AIRWAYS acquires LONG & HARMON AIRLINES, now BRANIFF AIRWAYS routes stretch "From the Great Lakes to the Gulf."	
1935	Bill Weaver moves the W. R. WEAVER COMPANY from Newport Kentucky to El Paso, TX.	
1935	OILFIELD MACHINE & SUPPLY COMPANY (OMSCO) is founded as a manufacturer of oilfield equipment.	
1935	Bell Garden, CA; the C. D. SPRACHER CO. INC. is founded to manufacture protection switches for engines.	
1935	Texas; a purebred Hereford bull, Ike Domino, is bought and will serve as the foundation for the PITCHFORK RANCH's new Hereford breeding program.	(see 1963)

1935	The US Congress passes the Federal Motor Carrier Act of 1935, it has a profound effect on the trucking industry.			
1935	This spring, R. G. LeTourneau, Inc. builds a plant in Peoria, IL, to be near his largest customer, Caterpillar Tractor Co.			

1935	Rowan Drilling's first diesel-electric rig goes to work near Hobbs, NM.	
1935	May 19; the first stretch of the Autobahn is opened, but only 1 of every 75 Germans even own a car.	
1935	The Ft. Worth Well Machinery & Supply Co. is now building eight different sizes of cable-tool rigs, rated from 200' to 4,000' capabilities. Any of these may be either steam or internal combustion engine powered.	
1935	Frank Lloyd Wright designs "Falling Water," located on a Western Pennsylvania stream, probably his best known residential home design.	
1935	About this time, John W. Chamberlain invents a device touted as one of the most significant of all washing machine improvements. His device washes, rinses, and extracts the water from clothes in a single operation.	
1935	Monarch Industries is founded, manufacturing hydraulic components.	

1935	Pan Am's "China Clipper," as they call the Martin M-130, makes the first ever scheduled trans-Pacific flight.	
1935	Utility Trailers' success enables the Bennetts to buy their own steel foundry, in Southgate, CA.	(see 1942-WWII)
1935	The Red Cross sets up a half-dozen emergency hospitals across Oklahoma, Colorado, and the Texas panhandle, to accommodate persons with "dust pneumonia"—actually it is silicosis, caused by the dust breathed in by folks.	
1935	This year, the first 326 Plymouth "Silver King" farm tractors are built by Fate-Root-Heath.	(see 1954)
1935	UK; London; Allen Lane, Esq., establishes Penguin Books, as one of the earliest mass-producers and vendors of paperbacks. This helps put affordable reading in the hands of many more people.	(see 1936) (see 1939)
1935	Ft. Worth, TX; Frank establishes and runs the Ford and Lincoln-Mercury dealership, Frank Kent Motor Co.	(see 1953)
1935	McDonnell-Douglas Aircraft introduces a new bigger, safer, and more comfortable airliner, the DC-3. Then on December 17th, the 32nd anniversary of the Wright brothers historic flight, the Douglas DC-3 first flies. This is the plane that will put the stumbling airline industry up on solid footing.	
1935	Illinois; General Motors purchases a huge cornfield on a railroad line, near La Grange, for the new Electro-Motive facility, having many acres left over for expansion. Much more will be utilized during the upcoming war.	
1935	USA; the first factory-built farm tractor with high a compression head for burning regular gasoline is the new MM KTA.	
1935	On its maiden voyage, the *S. S. Normandie* crosses the Atlantic from Le Havre, France, to New York City in four days, 11 hours and 42 minutes, a new world record. NOTE: Some sources state 4 days, 3 hours and 14 minutes.	
1935	April; Patsy Montana (nee Ruby Blevins) records "I Want to be a Cowboy's Sweetheart." This recording is the first million-seller for a female country singer.	
1935	August; the CCC is now at its peak enrollment of 520,000 men. Although segregated, the Negro CCC has 200,000 total men working throughout the program. The American Indian CCC has 80,000 men taking advantage of earning, learning, and helping their nation.	(see 1942)

1935	Bill Lear invents the Lear-O-Scope, one of the very first commercial radio compasses.		(see 1940)
1935	Germany; the first manufacturer to produce more than 100,000 vehicles per year is OPEL. This is primarily due to the little OPEL "P4" car, selling for 1,650 DM with a 1.1 liter, 4 cylinder, 23 horsepower engine, and a top speed of 85 kph (52.7 mph). This year OPEL introduces their "Olympia," the first mass-produced vehicle with a self-supporting all-steel body (no separate frame). Light weight with good aerodynamics, good performing and good fuel economy as well, Opel's patent on the "Olympia" is considered one of the most important innovations in automotive history.		(see 1939)
	1935	Nylon (polymer 6.6) is invented by Wallace Carothers and DuPont Labs.	
	1935	Robert Watson-Watt is issued a patent for radar.	
	1935	Texas; in Lubbock, a singing family has no money to buy medicine for their sick daughter, Effie. So Dave Carter, another daughter Lola, and son Ernest go over to radio station KFYO asking for a live singing job on radio, to be able to buy medicine for Effie. They get the job; soon Effie is well and rejoins them and the Carter Quartet remain at KFYO for about a year. Please note that Dave Carter's family is not related the Carter Family in Bristol, VA.	(see 1937)
	1936	LINK-BELT introduces the "Speed-o-Matic" hydraulic control system, it soon becomes the standard of the industry.	
1936	Raymond Loewy begins his association with STUDEBAKER CORP., an alliance that will last 'til '55. The STUDEBAKER PRESIDENT is the first new car sold with an engine oil filter as standard equipment, a FRAM filter.		
1936	KENWORTH introduces their COE (cab over engine or just cab-over), the "BubbleNose."		(see 1938)
1936	J. A. Baldwin founds his filter manufacturing business in Kearney, NE.		
1936	B & W introduces the cork-tipped Viceroy cigarette.		
1936	February; the first ever true stock car race is ran, and Bill France comes in fifth. A few years hence, Bill will be an organizer of NASCAR.		
1936	The TEXAS COMPANY acquires 50% interest in SOCAL's concession in Saudi Arabia.		
1936	The first production CORD automobiles rolls off the assembly line, in the midst of the Great Depression.		(see 1937)
1936	A. O. SMITH founds its water products division.		
1936	CUSHMAN introduces its first motor scooter.		
1936	May 25; Tom T. Hall is born in Olive Hill, KY.		
1936	**SQUARE D introduces the first residential circuit-breaker, the Multi-Breaker.**		
1936	Working with a major builder of gears for the USN, Thomas Fawick develops the Airflex Clutch. The Airflex design will be in thousands of Allied Naval vessels in WWII.		(see 1938)
1936	While many have experimented with hydraulic controls, CHAMPION introduces its first fully hydraulic maintainer… and the first truly reliable hydraulic system.		
1936	Charles Nash more or less retires.		(see 1937)
1936	BRADEN separates into two unique companies, BRADEN STEEL COMPANY and BRADEN WINCH COMPANY.		
1936	June 30; in New York City, Margaret Mitchell's *Gone with the Wind* is first published.		
1936	November 23; the first weekly issue of *Life Magazine*, America's first photo-magazine, is published.		

1936	The tung orchards of China can't supply the world's demand for tung oil, so, near Zavalla, the only tung orchard in Texas now begins producing tung oil.	
1936	D. K. Ludwig buys several WWI government surplus cargo vessels, converts them to tankers, and consolidates them as National Bulk Carriers. *NOTE: Mr. Ludwig will someday become the first billionaire in the USA.*	
1936	Herman C. Smith un-retires and opens the H. C. Smith Oil Tool Co. in Compton, California.	
1936	Mid-Continent Supply builds its first power drilling rig.	
1936	Germany; the Volkswagen "Beetle" is designed by Ferdinand Porsche and introduced this year.	

1936	Robbins & Myers begin manufacturing the Robbins & Myers Moyno Pump.	
1936	Nylon, the first synthetic from petrochemicals, is invented.	
1936	January; the first issue of *Western Horseman* magazine is published.	
1936	Germany; Heinrich Focke builds a twin-rotor helicopter.	
1936	Mr. Edsel Ford establishes the Ford Foundation.	

1936	The concept of the self-contained drilling barge for the South Louisiana marshes is pioneered by Rowan, Inc.	
1936	**Bill and Charlie, the Monroe brothers, make their (and the) first "bluegrass" recording. It's called *Hillbilly Music*, and it's great!!! Bill gives their music the "bluegrass" tag, after their home state of Kentucky.**	
1936	In South Texas, the 750-square-mile Pearsall field is discovered, but drilling is minimal for the next few decades.	
1936	Essex Wire Corp. buys the old Dudlo Mfg. Co. in Ft. Wayne, IN, and begins producing magnet wire. Dudlo originates modern magnet wire enameling.	
1936	October; the Boulder (Hoover) dam generators produce their first electric power, more than two years ahead of schedule. This Powerhouse utilizes seventeen dynamos (generators) in ten acres of floor space to produce over four billion kwh.	
1936	July; extremely high temperatures this summer, such as the 120s in the Dakotas, spur on the dust bowl of America's Great Plains.	
1936	This farmer using a new Farmall F-20, pulling the single moldboard "sulky" plow, will take about 25 hours to plow 40 acres.	(see 1956)
1936	Utility Trailer Company invents the first shockless air-operated pintle hook for doubles operation.	
1936	The "Tough Guy" character of Hastings Mfg. Co. is born, he will appear in their ads for many decades.	(see 1939)
1936	August 12; the temperature reaches 120 degrees Fahrenheit today in Seymour, TX. *"Yeah, Bubba, 'at's HOT!"*	
1936	Sweden; Astraab develops the first sulfonamide antibiotic used in the routine treatment of infections. They develop an anti-malarial as well.	(see 1941)
1936	Dale Carnegie's influential book, *How to Win Friends and Influence People,* is the first ever paperback million-seller.	
1936	The Trackson Company begins working with Caterpillar, producing various attachments for Cat.	(see 1951)
1936	Built to American Airline's specifications, the most famous, prop-driven, transport plane in history, the DC-3 makes its maiden commercial flight.	(see 1944)
1936	Conley-Lott-Nichols is founded.	

1936	Florida; the first stock car race here at Daytona Beach… loses money.	(see 1946)
1936	June; Henry Luce and the management at TIME INC. are looking, fighting, scrambling, spending, and spending some more, trying to put out a new "picture magazine." On November 19, the first copies of the first issue of *LIFE, The Picture Magazine,* are placed on sale… and are sucked up like a vacuum cleaner hit the newsstands. In December, *Time* dumps many thousands more copies in a test of selected newsstands - they all sell immediately!!!	
1936	This year's Miss Hungary is young Miss Zsa-Zsa Gabor; this achievement puts her on the road to stardom.	
1936	After the slowdown during the Depression, TB WOOD'S SONS business picks up considerably under FDR's New Deal.	(see WWII)
1936	California; having acquired the business of ROBINSON TRACTOR, Howard Peterson establishes PETERSON TRACTOR & EQUIPMENT COMPANY, with stores and shops in San Francisco and Oakland.	
1936	A voice recognition machine is invented by Bell Labs.	
1936	As farmers are seeing and hearing more and more about the success of diesel power, CATERPILLAR sells more diesel engines this year, than they sold in the last four years combined.	
1936	A thin, black and white, advertisement-free magazine, *Consumer Reports,* begins publication to help consumers.	
1936	In Saudi Arabia, TEXACO takes a 50% share of CASOC.	(see 1938)
1937	McGILL PRECISION BEARINGS is originated in Valparaiso, IN.	
1937	KRISPY KREME punches the holes in their first donuts.	
1937	Old Charles Nash buys KELVINATOR CO., to get its president, George Mason, as his successor; this produces NASH-KELVINATOR CO.	
1937	PURE OIL CO. and SUPERIOR OIL, both independents, take the plunge and move away from the shoreline, hiring BROWN & ROOT to build the first freestanding structure in the ocean, anywhere. They built it in Gulf of Mexico State Lease No. 1; 13 miles from Cameron, LA, in 14 feet of water, 1½ miles offshore. Prior to this, all "offshore" wells were at the end of a wooden dock.	(see 1938)
1937	TOYOTA MOTOR CO. LTD. is established as a spin-off of TOYODA AUTOMATIC LOOM WORKS.	
1937	The large engine division of WINTON ENGINE is renamed CLEVELAND DIESEL DIVISION of GENERAL MOTORS.	
1937	**B. F. GOODRICH scientists produce the first synthetic rubber.**	
1937	The CHRYSLER Airflow is discontinued; it is a great design, but simply a few years before its time.	(see 1940)
1937	March 18; in an explosion caused by a natural gas leak at the New London High School, 293 lives are lost. A horrible catastrophe for this small East Texas, Piney Woods town.	
1937	The NISSAN "Type 5" is the first mass-produced motor vehicle in Japan.	
1937	RAY-O-VAC receives patents for the first portable, high fidelity, radio.	
1937	CUMMINS ENGINE CO. earns its first profits.	
1937	Harold Howard opens HOWARD SUPPLY CO. in Los Angeles.	
1937	THOMASVILLE CHAIR installs conveyors and some automated machines, so when the economy picks up, they will be up and going.	
1937	G. F. LeBus originates the LeBus Wire Groove Bar principle, to aid in spooling wire rope onto drums, then founds LEBUS, INC. in Longview, TX.	
1937	J. W. Harris formulates his Stay-Clean soldering flux, which he sells by mail order to the refrigeration industry until he retires in 1956.	

1937	A. R. Long and his son John B. Long found the LONG SUPER MINE CAR COMPANY (LONG).	
1937	**May 6; the Hindenburg airship crashes at Lakehurst, NJ. This disaster effectively ends the era of commercial airship travel.**	
1937	WORTHINGTON buys MOORE STEAM TURBINE CO.	
1937	The twenty-five millionth FORD is built.	
1937	San Francisco, CA; the new $35 million GOLDEN GATE BRIDGE opens to vehicular traffic on May 28th.	
1937	June 3; extra, extra, read all about it!!! Today in London, Edward VIII, who abdicated the throne, marries Mrs. Wallis Warfield Simpson, an American commoner… and a divorcée. Imagine that, American… commoner… and a divorcée, Wow!!	
1937	June 15; in Littlefield, TX, Waylon Jennings is born.	(see 1959)
1937	August 7; the last CORD automobile leaves the assembly line.	
1937	CABOT CORPORATION builds their first gas-processing plant in West Texas.	(see 1957)
1937	CASE buys the ROCK ISLAND PLOW COMPANY, primarily to get its unused factory facility.	
1937	**BARBER-GREENE brings out the first continuous mix asphalt plant, having a unitized aggregate dryer.**	
1937	CASE opens its Burlington, IA, plant.	
1937	By now, most farm tractor builders are introducing the first mechanical "power-lifts" for their cultivators and planters.	
1937	DART TRUCK CO. build their first, heavy-duty, off-road haul trucks.	
1937	QUINCY introduces its QR-25 reciprocal compressors, a successful line that will be a force well into the next century.	
1937	SOONER PIPE & SUPPLY is founded by Henry Zarrow in Tulsa, OK.	
1937	BETHLEHEM STEEL CORP. buys WILLIAMSPORT WIRE ROPE, and it becomes BETHLEHEM WIRE ROPE DIV.	
1937	The JOHN N. MARTIN CO. is founded as a maker of subsurface oil well pumps.	
1937	Buffalo, NY; R. P. ADAMS CO. begins manufacturing water filters.	
1937	GOODALL RUBBER CO. introduces the "Barney" hose coupling, the only coupling stronger than the high-pressure hose.	
1937	Sylvan Goldman invents the shopping cart and revolutionizes the grocery business.	
1937	SOUTHERN MAID DONUT FLOUR CO. is founded.	
1937	Waco, TX; Grover C. Thomson and R. H. Roark invent "Sun Tang Red Cream Soda," marketed exclusively in Central and South Texas, and in Louisville, KY.	
1937	Arlington, TX; W. T. "Hooker" Vandergriff opens a Chevrolet dealership at the corner of Division (US80) and Central.	
1937	Mason, MI; DART MANUFACTURING CO. begins business as a small machine shop originally making small plastic and metal items.	
1937	Pennsylvania; Bob and Ray Cleveland start a landscaping company.	
1937	Corpus Christi, TX; Joseph Swiff and his son-in-law Herbert Train begin operations reprocessing loose cotton. They soon expand into import and export of steel products, chemicals, and other agricultural products.	
1937	In its centennial year, JOHN DEERE introduces the Model "G," the biggest and best of all the "poppin' Johnnies."	
1937	**The jet engine is invented by Frank Whittle of England and Hans Van Ohain of Germany.**	

1937	MARTIN AIRCRAFT develops the first power-operated revolving gun turret. It will be used on many Allied aircraft during WWII.	
1937	The US Army Air Force awards LOCKHEED the contract for delivery of the first P-38 "Lightning," multi-engine planes. Ten thousand are eventually produced.	
1937	October; Chester Carlson files for patents for his unsubstantiated ideas for electrophotography, later to be called xerography.	(see 1938)
1937	F. F. LANDIS becomes a part of the CINCINNATI TIME RECORDING COMPANY.	
1937	At the Dollar Mountain Resort in Sun Valley, ID, UPRR engineers (not the train drivers), build the world's first chair-lift. Six more chair-lifts are immediately ordered.	
1937	Tulsa; the first Unit Rig U-10 draw-works is built, powered by three Caterpillar diesel engines. It is used by Portable Drilling Co. to drill their first well. On a location near Oklahoma City, they drill to 5,500 feet with 4½" drill pipe, a great success as the U-10 is only rated for 4,000 feet deep.	
1937	TUBOSCOPE is now established, effectively founding the business of oilfield tubular inspection.	
1937	Belt-driven and mounting between the carburetor and the standard intake manifold, MCCULLOCH MOTORS' first super chargers are built for the flathead FORD V-8 engine.	(see 1942)
1937	The submerged arc welding method is invented.	
1937	The AMERICAN TRUCKING ASSC. (ATA) creates and sponsors the first National Truck Roadeo to "draw attention to safety and professionalism" in the trucking industry.	(see 1976)
1937	The average power of today's "modern" farm tractors is about 35 horsepower.	
1937	ROCK ISLAND PLOW COMPANY is purchased by CASE, giving CASE a full line of farm implements.	(see 1953)
1937	The WESTERN ELECTRIC CO. markets the first commercial radio altimeter, the more accurate nomenclature of "radar altimeter" will come into use after WWII, as RADAR stands for "RAdio Detection And Ranging."	
1937	The innovative BAKER MFG. CO. now introduces the first inside push beam bulldozer blade.	(see 1946)
1937	This year's SEARS & ROEBUCK catalog offers a farm tractor. The two plow Bradley GP is noted for its adjustable tread and engine-driven pto.	
1937	USA; knocking out James Braddock, Joe Louis wins the World's Heavyweight Title.	
1937	In the USA, STERLING introduces the tilt-cab on some of its highway trucks.	
1937	The "magic eye tube," used as a tuning accessory in radios, and as an inexpensive level meter in reel-to-reel tape recorders is invented by Allen DuMont.	(see 1938) (see WWII)
1937	Calgary, Canada; WESTERN EXPLOSIVES LTD. is founded to furnish specialized explosives for the mining and petroleum industries.	
1937	Michigan; BATES MACHINE & TRACTOR ceases all production this year, the Model "F" is produced until the very end.	
1937	England; the Perkins P6 diesel engine is designed, and prototypes are out and running only six months after the first blueprints are made. Developing 83 bhp at 2,400 rpm, the P6 firmly establishes Perkins in the diesel engine market.	(see 1938)
1937	Texas; President Franklin D. Roosevelt goes fishing off Aransas Pass in a local built FARLEY BOAT, and lands an 80 pound Tarpon.	
1937	In Illinois, in 1937, 447 wells are drilled searching for crude oil, and 285 are drilled with rotary rigs. By end-of-year a total of more than 20,000 oil wells have been drilled, almost all with cable tool rigs, but that is changing rapidly as this past January, the first rotary well was the "duster" in the Patoka field.	

1937	Having had overwhelming response in Lubbock, Dave Carter has now moved to the big city, Ft. Worth. They auditioned for several radio stations, and were hired by 50,000 watt WBAP, the local giant. Now they were given the *Chuck Wagon Gang*, by their sponsor, BEWLEY MILLS. The *Chuck Wagon Gang* quickly becomes very popular and BEWLEY MILLSoffers a picture of the group for some coupon from their flour sacks. In short order, more than 100,000 requests for pictures are received.		
1938	Ventura, CA; VENTURA TOOL COMPANY (VETCO) forms its inspection division.		
1938	PHILCO-YORK introduces the first air conditioner window unit.		
1938	**CATERPILLAR introduces its No. 12 maintainer, the 9K series, and Jim Cowan has worked on Serial # 9K 36, which Mr. Dan Cooley delivered new to the US Forest Service this year. CATERPILLAR, working with LOUIS-ALLIS Co. introduces a line of self-regulated generators, powered of course, by Caterpillar diesel engines. Although up to this time, many Caterpillar engines have been installed in trucks, CATERPILLAR also introduces the D468, their first true truck engine, as well as a line of marine engines.**		
1938	Harry Ferguson and Henry Ford meet, and with a handshake, begin producing FERGUSON SYSTEM TRACTORS.		
1938	February 28; David B. Lack opens a small auto supply store in Beeville, TX, and soon begins carrying some furniture lines.		
1938	GENERAL MOTORS DIESEL DIVISION is formed.		
1938	STEWART & STEVENSON become distributors of diesel engines by GENERAL MOTORS.		

		1938	ALLIS-CHALMERS starts developing its diesel tractor line, using GENERAL MOTORS diesels.	
		1938	England; Neville Chamberlin returns from meetings in Germany babbling about "…peace in our time."	
		1938	March; in the Gulf of Mexico, the first ever offshore oil is produced, from a well on the first offshore platform ever built. This is the first well in what is called the Creole Field is a huge step for the petroleum industry.	
		1938	SHAW-BOX CRANE & HOIST introduce the Budget line, the first successful electrically operated line of chain hoists.	
		1938	**USA; the 40-hour work week is more widely established, more or less as a standard.**	
		1938	Texas, March 12; Floyd Kinley (b. 1904), Myron's brother, dies from injuries suffered fighting an oil well fire near Goliad.	(see 1978)

1938	March; the government of Mexico nationalizes its oil industry, the first nation to do so.		
1938	**Texas; the RAINBOW BRIDGE opens over the Neches River between Port Arthur and Orange, for a while it is the highest bridge in the southern US.**		
1938	EMD begins building its own engines, generators, electric motors and introduces the 567 series diesel engine. That's 567 cubic inches per cylinder. Having developed its own electrical transmission equipment, EMD quits buying generators and traction motors from GENERAL ELECTRIC, and begins using its own.		
1938	The LISTER-WISCONSIN "kit" engine is being sold in the UK, the kits are imported from WISCONSIN in the USA.		
1938	**March; Saudi Arabia's first commercial oil field is discovered at Dhahran by Standard of California, the oil is being exported by barge across to Bahrain.**		
1938	This year oil is discovered in Kuwait.		

1938	Marvin Baird establishes BAIRD TIRE CO. in Kilgore, TX.	
1938	On the orders of Adolph Hitler, the VOLKSWAGEN "beetle" is created, to give every German family a car, but aren't mass-produced until after WWII. Speaking of Hitler, the beginning of WWII in Europe causes serious dislocations of exports from many industries in North America.	
1938	Cadillac Motor Car Division introduces the "flat" V-16 engine, so called because it has 135 degrees between the cylinder banks, WOW!	
1938	England; Sunday, July 3rd, the LONDON & NORTH EASTERN RAILROAD's system 4 class "Mallard" streamlined steam locomotive, on a special run to test braking, sets the steam record of 126 mph (202.8 kph), at milepost 90¼, going south from Grantham toward Peterborough. This record is never beaten by a steam locomotive.	(see 1990)
1938	Harvey Firestone dies.	
1938	July 17; at 5:15 am, in a very blinding fog, Galveston, TX, native Douglas Corrigan is required by authorities to take off eastward from Floyd Bennett Field in Brooklyn, NY, (there are many tall skyscrapers to the west) headed for California. Corrigan's homemade fuel tanks stand so tall in front of him, he cannot see directly forward, and he claims he has trouble with his compass. Only 28 hours and 13 minutes later, Corrigan lands his second-hand, patched-up, and overloaded 1929 Curtiss-Robin monoplane at Baldonnel Airport in Dublin, Ireland. Thus he becomes known as "Wrong Way" Corrigan. Most Americans figure, and, probably correctly, that Corrigan's trans-Atlantic flight was a prank, as he has been trying to get a flight plan to Ireland approved for over a year, but it is denied twice due to the age and condition of his aircraft. He was permitted to legally fly back and forth across America.	
1938	BJ builds a plant in Houston, TX.	
1938	The 10,000th LISTER Auto-Truck is built.	
1938	EXIDE acquires the GRANT STORAGE BATTERY COMPANY.	
1938	HYGRADE SYLVANIA markets its first fluorescent lamp bulb.	
1938	December; the FAWICK GENERAL CO. is formed, Fawick and GENERAL TIRE & RUBBER are primarily concerned with industrial clutch applications.	(see 1941)
1938	MUDCO VALVE COMPANY of Tulsa is producing a successful damper-type butterfly valve for controlling drilling mud. They are soon purchased by the W. C. Norris Company.	
1938	Mr. Frank Mosing begins stabbing and running with FRANK'S CASING CREWS.	
1938	JOY introduces their first "shuttle car" for mining.	
1938	OILFIELD MACHINE & SUPPLY CO. (OMSCO) is founded.	
1938	CLARK BROS. COMPANY merges with S. R. DRESSER MFG. COMPANY.	(see 1956)
1938	March; the very first self-propelled, rubber-tired earth moving scraper is introduced. The LETOURNEAU Model "A" Tournapull is powered by Caterpillar's Model D-17000 V-8 diesel engine and runs on tires molded by Firestone, to R. G's exact specifications.	
1938	J. J. Swanson and W. A. Norris establish the CATERPILLAR dealership of NEBRASKA MACHINERY CO.	
1938	The little newly introduced Crosley car gets 50 mpg... but no one cares.	(see 1939)
1938	The GRAHAM-BRADLEY farm tractor is introduced by DAVID BRADLEY MFG. CO.	(see 1940)
1938	Frank Hutchison coins the phrases "shale shaker" and "rumba action" and HUTCHISON MFG. introducess the "Rumba" shale shaker.	

| 1938 | October 22; Chester Carlson discovers the xerography method of copying, but its almost a decade before he can sell the idea or obtain financing. | |
| 1938 | The young Roy Acuff auditions for the GRAND OLD OPRY, singing his recently recorded "The Great Speckled Bird." | |

	1938	In Illinois, a father and son team develop "soft-serve" ice cream.	
	1938	Kirchdorf, Germany; Hans Liebherr takes over the family construction business.	
	1938	Arkansas Tractor & Equipment is renamed J. A. RIGGS TRACTOR CO. as CATERPILLAR expands their territory to sixty-six counties.	
	1938	As LeTourneau's Peoria plant is seriously overloaded, R. G. decides to build another plant, down in Toccoa, GA.	
	1938	USA; *The War of the Worlds,* a radio sketch by Orson Wells, causes wide spread panic	
	1938	Germany; only 300 Volkswagens are completed before Hitler orders the plant closed for WWII.	
	1938	The use of the inland drilling barge is pioneered by LOFFLAND BROTHERS, in South Louisiana's bayous.	

1938	Curtis L. Carlson borrows $55 from his landlord; and pays a department store employee $10 for a copy of the Security Red Stamp master contract, then goes and founds the GOLD BOND STAMP COMPANY.	
1938	The government of Mexico nationalizes all foreign oil companies there, placing all their assets under PEMEX control.	
1938	Columbia, SC; a local automobile dealer goes to a livestock auction and wonders if autos could be sold the same way. He gives it a try, and with good results; the automobile auction industry has begun.	(see 1953)
1938	President Franklin Roosevelt establishes the first minimum wage and the 44-hour work week.	
1938	In Longview, TX, Mr. Leroy Rader establishes the first RADER FUNERAL HOME.	
1938	USA; KENWORTH introduces the first "torsion-bar" suspension on its trucks this year.	(see 1944)
1938	Two 1934 electrical engineering graduates, Bill Hewlett and Dave Packard, build their 200A audio oscillator, and market it for $55, while some inferior units made by the "big boys" are selling for as much as $200.	(see 1939)
1938	USA; Minneapolis-Moline introduces their very streamlined Comfortractor, with many items for operator comfort.	
1938	DuMont is the first company to manufacture television receiver sets for use in the home.	(see 1940)
1938	Sunnyvale, CA; Mack Wooldridge is joined by Harold Guzman in forming Wooldridge Manufacturing Company. They open a new plant here, building blades, rippers and scrapers. . . up to a 25 cubic yard scraper with six rear wheels. This is the first one in their Terra Clipper line.	(see 1942)
1938	California; a Hollywood studio opens for shooting underwater film footage; it's named MARINE STUDIOS, later MARINELAND.	
1938	England; the PERKINS engine family now includes the Wolf, Lynx, Leopard I and II diesel engines, in vehicular, industrial, agricultural, and marine versions with specifications covering 650 different applications. Frank has already acquired land at Eastfield for expansion with his vision of becoming a world leader of diesel engine manufacturing.	
1938	Roy J. Plunkett invents tetrafluoroethylene polymers, better known as "Teflon."	
1938	Miles, WI; hearing that the CLEVELAND TRACTOR CO., having streamlined their crawler tractors, they have been looking for a full-line dozer manufacturer, the HEIL COMPANY steps up, and does a fine job of "filling the bill."	

1938	The BEEBE BROS product line now goes up to 30 ton capacity, hand operated, winches.	(see 1941-45) (see WWII)
1939	January 1; Hewlett and Packard officially begin in business as partners. The firm name is decided by a coin toss, HP wins over PH.	(see 1947)
1939	MIXERMOBILE MFG., INC. of Portland, OR, introduces its SCOOPMOBILE line of loaders.	
1939	FRANK G. HOUGH CO. markets its first rubber-tired wheel loader, the model HS (Hough Small); not just a farm tractor with attachments the HS is the world's first integrated wheel loader.	
1939	Hinderliter Tool Corp. is now making gun barrels for the Allied Forces in Europe.	
1939	ANSUL, INC. begins operations making fire fighting equipment.	
1939	DELCO division of GENERAL MOTORS puts its first AC generator in service.	
1939	KATO gets government contracts to supply various sizes generators for the military.	
1939	LANE-WELLS introduces the Gamma-Ray log, moving into open hole logging with their Electrolog Service.	
1939	May; about 1,800 miles of the German Autobahn have now been completed.	
1939	MARION STEAM SHOVEL CO. build their first walking dragline.	
1939	LUFKIN FOUNDRY & MACH CO. buys MARTIN WAGON & TRAILER MFG. COMPANY. LUFKIN also begins building industrial gearboxes for various industries.	
1939	Production begins on the FORD 9N tractor.	
1939	The first factory equipped air conditioned car… is a PACKARD. (see 1954)	
1939	AVELING-BARFORD builds its first off-road dump truck.	
1939	LINK-BELT buys SPEEDER MACHINERY CO. and merges Speeder's smaller machines into their line, this forms the LINK-BELT SPEEDER CORPORATION, a wholly-owned subsidiary of LINK-BELT CORPORATION.	
1939	WILLIAMS BROTHERS begins its first international pipeline job, in Venezuela.	
1939	NF begins production of bearings.	
1939	B & W is founded to manufacture cementing tools for oil well casing.	
1939	JOSEPH REID GAS ENGINE CO. ceases operations.	
1939	WIX is founded by J. D. "Jack" Wicks and Paul Crawshaw with the idea of making filter replacements that would simplify the process of filter changing.	
1939	Oklahoma; Frank W. "Pat" Murphy, the sales manager for a major equipment outfit develops the Murphy Swichgage to counter the problem of the great number of "burned-up" engines he was seeing. This year Murphy begins making the Swichgages in Tulsa.	
1939	LEE C. MOORE designs and builds the very first cantilever mast for a drilling rig.	
1939	Douglas Herrick, a Wyoming taxidermist screws antelope horns into a mounted jackrabbit, and the "jackalope" is born.	
1939	Zygmunt Zukowski founds EUCLID INDUSTRIES, INC. in Cleveland, OH, the Truck Parts People.	
1939	The world's first leak-proof "sealed in steel" dry cell battery is introduced by RAY-O-VAC.	
1939	In Seagraves, TX, H. E. "Eddie" Chiles and Robert Wood found the WESTERN COMPANY.	
1939	BB&C builds the first combustion gas turbine for generating electricity.	
1939	Production begins of the Lincoln-Zephyr Continental.	

1939	**During the Depression-era 30s, 3M Co. expands sales, employment and facilities… and pays dividends every year, thanks to sound fiscal policies.**	
1939	A lumberman from the northwest, Theodore Alfred Peterman, buys Fageol Truck and Coach Co. of Oakland, CA, and then starts Peterbilt. Alfred wants to build trucks that will stand up to the "out in the woods" rigors of the lumber industry.	
1939	Casite Automotive Chemicals joins the Hastings family and soon Casite Motor Honey is sold around the world, as the most accepted oil additive.	(see 1944)
1939	Delta Drilling opens an office in Evansville, IN, to better cover the "tri-state" area.	
1939	Introduced last year, the world's first compact economy car, the Crosley is now the first car with 4-wheel disc brakes.	
1939	Frank Sears calls the first ever safety conference to set some standards for school buses, one standard was the new color of "school bus yellow."	
1939	Igor Ivanovich Sikorsky's (1889-1972) Vought-Sikorsky VS-300 becomes America's first successful helicopter.	
1939	Mr. Wood T. Brookshire splits off from Brookshire Bros., taking three stores in Tyler, TX, and renaming them Brookshire's Food Stores. There are now only four of the Brookshire family members remaining in the Brookshire Bros. grocery business.	
1939	H. C. Smith Oil Tool Co. expands and adds a long-tooth cross-sector rock bit to its line of oil drilling bits.	
1939	Hillman-Kelly develops the first commercial power tubing tongs and will soon introduce the first power rod wrench.	
1939	Louisiana; Tom Scott and his wife Mayme, and eight employees, open Scott Truck & Tractor in Monroe.	(see 2014)
1939	Bariod makes "on-location" mud logging available to the drilling industry.	
1939	**The first commercially produced western style shirts with snaps are marketed.**	
1939	Idaho; Joe Albertson opens his first grocery store.	
1939	The theme of the New York World's Fair is "The World of Tomorrow."	
1939	Gordon E. Steed, Sr., joins Hamilton Cartage.	
1939	In Shreveport, James W. Morton establishes United Tool & Valve Repair Co., specializing in the repair of oilfield equipment across Northern Louisiana.	
1939	Mercury Outboards is founded by Carl Kiekhaefer.	
1939	Henry J. Kaiser founds Permanente, the largest cement plant on planet earth.	
1939	At age 66, Mr. M. D. Anderson dies; his foundation receives about $20,000,000 from his estate. Anderson, a life-long bachelor, was probably the most desirable in Texas, or maybe anywhere.	
1939	Krueger Brewing introduces the first canned beverages.	
1939	April; Detective Comics No. 29 hits the newsstands, selling for a dime; this is Batman's debut.	(see 2004)
1939	Like many other companies, Trailer Company of America begins shifting to war materials production.	(see WWII)
1939	Euclid begins designing its first scraper prototypes.	(see 1940)
1939	A really good one "bites the dust," as the last trucks bearing the "Indiana" marque are produced.	
1939	Major E. H. Armstrong demonstrates his system of radio frequency modulation, or FM radio.	
1939	May 5; an asset for our entire nation, the McDonald Observatory is dedicated today, near Ft. Davis in West Texas.	
1939	Texas; having worked several years on drilling rigs, as a roustabout, floor hand, and driller, William P. "Bill" Clements graduates from SMU.	(see 1942)

1939	Deep in the Piney Woods of East Texas, Kilgore College president Mr. B. E. Masters tells Miss Gussie Nell Davis, "Find a way to keep people in their seats at half-time." Miss Davis does so by forming the Kilgore Rangerettes, the first "high-kicking" drill team to ever complement a football team.	
1939	USA; Robert F. De Graff, with support from Dick Simon and Lincoln Schuster of SIMON & SCHUSTER, launches POCKET BOOKS, a paperback to sell for a quarter each. Many folks are paying $5 a week for rent, and a good quality hardback is $4 - $5, so there's a real market for good twenty-five cent books.	
1939	A ship docked at Mobile, AL, discharges some stowaways from the Paraguay River's floodplain in Southern Brazil… and those little stowaway fire ants will be one of the most bothersome of all illegal aliens, and they have staying power.	
1939	October; Ralph Lifshitz is born in the Bronx, NY. (see 1957)	
1939	The US Navy installs its first commercial radar in the battleship TEXAS, and next year the TEXAS will be designated the flagship of the US Atlantic fleet.	
1939	USA; usually considered "fly-by-night" businesses, trucking companies often have great problems with financing. This year, US TRUCK LINES is the first trucking company ever to have a public stock offering. (see 1951)	
1939	JOHN DEERE calls on designer Henry Dreyfuss to help "spruce up" their tractors. OLIVER does this stylist-designer job in-house, and comes out looking as good as the others.	
1939	**September 1; Hitler's German army invades Poland. England and France now declare war on Germany; the beginning of WWII.**	
1939	Germany; OPEL's highly successful "Captain" debuts, with its six cylinder, 2. 5 lt. engine, all-steel body, independent front suspension, hydraulic shock absorbers, hot water heating with an electric blower, as well as a good speedometer. More than 25,300 will be built before Hitler's government orders all civilian auto manufacturing to cease before WWII.	(see 1945)
1939	Composer Irving Berlin writes his wonderful "White Christmas."	(see 1942)
1939	In Antarctica again, Admiral Byrd is using a Snow Cruiser, a large, twin-tracked vehicle, especially made for Arctic and Antarctic travel. Evidently it fared no better than his Model T in '28, as it was also abandoned away from base.	
1940s	Perry, OK; GERONIMO MANUFACTURING COMPANY is established, building safety escape devices for drilling rig derricks.	
1940s	The first Compressed Air Foam Systems (CAFS) appear on the fire-fighting scene.	
1940s	The LeRoi small engine division in Milwaukee is sold to WAUKESHA.	
1940s	COTTA TRANSMISSION CO. shifts from automotive transmissions to industrial and off-highway transmissions and gearboxes.	
1940s	FLINT is a pioneer in oil field waterflood operation and technology, with some of the first systems in Illinois.	(see 1947)
1940s	1941-1945; GEORGE E. FAILING CO., supplies Allied troops with portable drilling equipment and supplies to drill for water wherever they need.	

1940	Illinois; PLOMB TOOLS buys CRAGIN TOOL of Chicago.	
1940	January; REO MOTOR VEHICLES reorganizes as REO MOTORS INC.	
1940	Texas; out on Turkey Creek, in Callahan County, the population of Cross Plains is 1,229 this year.	
1940	EUCLID introduces the world's first continuous excavator, the model BV.	(see 1953)
1940	In July, the movie *A Wild Hare* introduces a new star, Mr. Bugs Bunny.	

	1940	August 18; CHRYSLER CORPORATION founder and chairman Walter Percy Chrysler dies at age 65.	(see WWII) (see 1947)
	1940	*"The Most Powerful Truck Engine Built,"* the HALL-SCOTT 400 produces 295 hp @ 2000rpm, 940 lb. ft. torque @ 2200 RPM, has 1090 cid, weighs one ton, and burns either gasoline or LPG.	
	1940	NATIONAL SUPPLY acquires CENTRAL TUBE COMPANY.	
	1940	England; Neville Chamberlin resigns and Winston Churchill takes the reins as British Prime Minister.	
	1940	CATHAY PACIFIC of Hong Kong begins flying.	

1940	A. O. SMITH acquires SAWYER ELECTRIC of Los Angeles, and gets into the electric motor business.	
1940	BAKER OIL TOOLS, SCHLUMBERGER, BJ, and DOWELL, consolidate all assets, forming INTERNATIONAL CEMENTERS INC.	(see 1952)
1940	The AMERICAN ASSOCIATION OF OILWELL DRILLING CONTRACTORS (AAODC) is founded.	
1940	England; RUSTON & HORNSBY LTD., gain controlling interest in DAVEY, PAXMAN & CO. LTD. (PAX).	
1940	WARNER GEAR begins manufacturing transfer (gearboxes) cases.	
1940	The railroads sell their interest in BOSTON & MAINE AIRWAYS to ATLAS CORPORATION, and the company is renamed NORTHEAST AIRLINES.	
1940	The AGAR MANUFACTURING CO., a maker of corrugated cardboard is acquired by IP.	
1940	CUMMINS offers the diesel engine industry's first 100,000 mile warranty.	
1940	**Ray Ferwerda builds a machine with telescoping boom, and a oscillating bucket, for more flexible work.**	(see 1946)
1940	DAVID BRADLEY MFG. CO. converts to wartime production, making submarine net floats, parts for army tank engines and the 4.2 mortar shells.	(see WWII)
1940	In Holdenville, OK, Frank and Hugh Drane sell DRANE TANK COMPANY to BLACK, SIVALLS & BRYSON.	
1940	In Southern California, JOHNSON MACHINERY is established as a dealer for CATERPILLAR.	
1940	The HALTOM-TREANOR partnership is a CATERPILLAR dealer based in Visalia, CA.	
1940	The Civil Aeronautics Board determines that railroad companies should not be allowed to control air transportation service.	
1940	Joliet, IL; on July 22, Mr. Sherb Noble opens very first DAIRY QUEEN, specializing in the recently developed "soft-serve" ice cream. To call it an instant success is understating.	(see 1947)
1940	SALT WATER CONTROL INC. is founded.	
1940	Auger mining machines are first being used in surface mines.	
1940	As France, Holland, Belgium, Denmark, and Norway fall to Germany, Hitler's Panzer troops enter Paris.	
1940	Marvin R. Jones begins development of blowout preventers (BOP) for protection during the drilling of oil and gas wells.	
1940	The GEOLOGRAPH COMPANY is founded in Oklahoma City.	

1940	PARKERSBURG RIG & REEL CO. buys OIL COUNTRY SPECIALTIES (OCS), this brings PARKERSBURG to Coffeyville, KS.	
1940	January; HUGHES TOOL CO. begins its weekly rotary drilling rig count, being released each Monday morning.	
1940	FONTAINE TRAILER COMPANY is founded by Mr. John P. K. Fontaine.	
1940	GILDEMEISTER S. A. C. becomes the CATERPILLAR dealer for the nation of Chile.	
1940	Mr. John Walters, Sr., establishes AMERICAN TORCH TIP CO. in Pittsburgh, PA.	
1940	Jackson, MS; a young German aeronautical engineer has manufacturing rights to two new products. In an abandoned milk processing plant, he establishes AEROQUIP CORPORATION to make reusable hose fittings, and self-sealing, quick-disconnect couplings.	
1940	January; LOFFLAND BROTHERS CO. puts its first submersible drilling barge in operation. Eventually Loffland has nine barges drilling in Louisiana.	
1940	August 19; today is the first flight of NORTH AMERICAN AVIATION's "Mitchell B-25" medium range bomber. Almost 10,000 will eventually be built (6,000 in one plant) and used by most Allies during WWII. It will be four decades before the last B-25 is retired.	(see 1942)
1940	Texas; the Crenwelge family opens a Chevrolet dealership.	
1940	Butler, PA; Karl K. Pabst, with the BANTAM CAR COMPANY, builds a four-wheel drive vehicle that will become famous as the JEEP.	
1940	January 11; GENERAL MOTORS produces its twenty-five millionth US built vehicle.	
1940	The Great Lakes' "Storm of '40" causes the loss of two ships and one hundred lives.	
1940	The UNITED STATES RUBBER COMPANY purchases the GILLETTE SAFETY TIRE COMPANY.	(see 1967)
1940	ESAB WELDING CORPORATION is established in the United States of America.	
1940	California; CLYDE W. WOOD, General Contractor, now begins to build road-mixer machinery.	(see 1953)
1940	Mississippi; on radio station WGRM, Mr. B. B. King makes his first live broadcast.	
1940	J. I. RODALE publishes "Organic Farming & Gardening," championing sustainable practices.	
1940	DuMont is licensed to operate its first experimental television station, W2XWV in New York City.	(see 1944)
1940	The Frank M. Hawks Award is presented to Bill Lear for his designing the Learmatic Aircraft Navigator.	(see 1962)
1940	***Only ten years old, and covering a bit over 200 square miles, the East Texas Oil Field now has more than 25,000 producing wells.***	
1940	England; over the past decade, PELICAN ENGINEERING CO. has made more than 800 truck and bus conversions, removing the petrol (gasoline) engines and replacing them with GARDNER DIESEL engines.	
1940	Tennessee; an employee of radio station KDEF in Chattanooga is having a flat fixed when a man's voice comes over the tire shop's PA system and really impresses him. He confronts the "voice on the PA," twenty year old Luther Masingill, and offers him a job in radio; Luther accepts and begins work at KDEF.	(see 2012)
1940	The Gross National Product of the USA is $200 Billion this year.	(see 1950)
1940	Paul J. Foley, a finance department employee of CATERPILLAR TRACTOR CO. joins a newly formed dealership in Wichita, KS, and the KARCHER-WOLTER-FOLEY COMPANY is established.	(see 1942)
1941	Using $50,000 borrowed money, a young Robert O. Anderson becomes a ⅓ owner of MALCO REFINING of Artesia, NM.	(see 1942)

1941	The "general purpose" vehicle (G. P. or Jeep) is first being produced by the WILLIS-OVERLAND CO.	(see 1942)
1941	Due to the small capacity of WILLIS-OVERLAND's plant, FORD builds G. P.s at Dearborn, and B-24s at Willow Run.	
1941	LeBus is founded in Longview, TX.	
1941	The demise of the HUPMOBILE automobile.	
1941	Louis Chevrolet dies.	
1941	FORD signs their first UAW contract.	
1941	The R S & P abandons its 17 mile line between Snyder & Fluvanna, TX.	
1941	PLOMB TOOLS buys P & C TOOLS of Oregon.	(see 1942)
1941	**Alfred LeTourneur sets a record of 108.92 mph on a SCHWINN Paramount bicycle, drafting behind a race car.**	
1941	The word earthmover first appears in dictionaries.	
1941	Lawrence D. "Larry" Bell sets up a shop for Arthur Young, a youthful inventor.	
1941	The last of the STEWART TRUCKS are built in Buffalo, NY.	
1941	WEATHERFORD SPRING COMPANY is founded.	
1941	AMERADA merges with HESS PETROLEUM & CHEMICAL CO. forming AMERADA PETROLEUM CORP.	
1941	In the hot, sweltering, humid summer of 1941, while preparing soldiers for war, the US Army holds maneuvers in the Mooringsport, LA, area. Generals Dwight D. Eisenhower and George S. Patton are in Mooringsport leading the Red and Blue Armies in the "capture" of the Caddo Lake Drawbridge, which is "bombed" with sacks of flour.	(see WWII) (see 1989)
1941	At DANUSER MACHINE CO., Henry Danuser builds the first rear-mounted blade for a tractor.	
1941	As America enters WWII, many price controls (effected during the Depression) are lessened, or even lifted, giving a double-boost to American industry.	

1941	FAWICK GENERAL CO. becomes FAWICK AIRFLEX CO.	(see 1942)
1941	**TIW is granted a patent on the first automatic bottom-hole packer.**	(see 1987)
1941	**The first commercial FM (frequency modulation) broadcast service for sound programs starts.**	
1941	Commercial television broadcasting is adopted, but is largely ignored until after the war in 1945.	(see 1946)
1941	**The FRANK G. HOUGH CO. introduces the model HL (Hough Large), the first wheel loader designed with the operator seated at the front of the unit.**	
1941	Jr. High dropout Henry J. Kaiser puts the assembly line method to work building freighter ships for the military, taking months off the production time required; these are the Liberty Ships with triple expansion steam engines.	

1941	SHELL scientists invent a method to synthesize 100 octane gasoline needed for the new aviation engines. Early in WWII, SHELL produces a quarter of all 100 octane aviation gasoline used by our military.	
1941	GM's "Parade of Progress," featuring the 12 specially built Futurliners, tours small cities and towns across the nation, until halted by WWII.	
1941	ANDEROL INC. is established as a manufacturer of specialty lubricants.	
1941	MINNEAPOLIS-MOLINE introduces the first ever factory produced farm tractor equipped for burning LP gas; their Model "U."	
1941	Furniture maker KROEHLER of Canada is established.	

1941	Willard M. Johnson (1906-2000) establishes the MAGNET COVE BARIUM CORP. (MAGCOBAR) in Magnet Cove, Arkansas.	
1941	THE WILTON TOOL CO. is founded, soon becoming famous for their vises, they will later expand into woodworking tools and equipment.	
1941	The American chemist Lyle D. Goodhue develops and patents the aerosol dispenser. It is first used for insecticides.	
1941	The first Texas "Farm-to Market" road is opened; FM 1 runs three miles into the Piney Woods to the TEMPLE LUMBER COMPANY sawmill at Pineland.	
1941	July 2; NBC's first commercial television show, Ralph Edward's *Truth or Consequences*, is broadcast. The first-ever commercial television advertisement features BULOVA watches. A ten-second commercial costs $9.00.	(see 1946)
1941	Ansel Keys, a nutritionist, develops a portable, healthy, almost tasteless preserved food: the "K-Ration," soon used extensively by the military.	(see 2004)
1941	October 31; commissioned in 1920, the *USS Reuben James* is sunk near Iceland by a German U-551 while protecting a convoy of freight from Britain coming to North America.	
1941	In their twelve jewelry stores in Texas and Oklahoma, ZALES introduces the credit plan of "a penny down and a dollar a week," a revolutionary marketing strategy.	
1941	On Labor Day, with $80 cash, Mr. and Mrs. Sam Boyd and their small son, William, arrive in Las Vegas, NV. Sam works as a dealer, and manages his money well.	(see 1950s)
1941	**The Photovoltaic (solar) cell is developed.**	
1941	ROOTS furnishes the US Navy submarines and large surface craft with special screw compressor to blow ballast.	(see WWII)
1941	Earnest Tubb first records "Walking the Floor Over You," eventually to become his trademark song.	(see 1942)
1941	Using chocolate from HERSHEY, MARS introduces M & Ms.	
1941	Germany; M. A. N. begins production of diesel-powered tractors.	
1941	Sweden; the first stable liquid multivitamin is developed by ASTRA AB.	(see 1950s)
1941	EOY; with sales of $41 million, LETOURNEAU is now a well established player in the earthmoving equipment business.	
1941	At this time, Texas produces 40% of all American crude oil, and 25% of the world's overall crude oil production.	
1941	Near Baku, in the Bayil area, a slant well is drilled to about 2,000 meters by drillmaster Agha Neymatulla and his team, using the turbodrill method.	
1941	The first computer controlled by software is the Z3, built by Konrad Zuse.	
1941	December 7; as Japan bombs Pearl Harbor, the US, finally joins the war with the Allies. This greatly accelerates the sluggish economic recovery that the US has been experiencing since the end of the "Great Depression."	
1941	December 8; this Monday, all across Texas, large groups of men line up at all recruiting stations. The Lone Star State has five percent of America's population, and furnishes seven percent of the nation's military personnel.	
1941	As America goes to war after Pearl Harbor, PACIFIC CAR & FOUNDRY's Renton Washington plant begins building Sherman tanks and tank recovery vehicles for our military. This plant builds steel tugboats and dry docks for the military during the war.	(see 1962)
1941-1945	Over the next four years, more than 1,000 water landing craft are equipped with BEEBE BROS. two-ton hand winches for ramp handling, for our Military's war effort.	(see WWII) (see 1959)

| 1942 | January; Robert O. Anderson and his wife and little daughter pack everything they own into their car and make the 1,200 mile trek from Chicago to the wild western town of Artesia, NM. Bob will be running the MALCO refinery, of which he now owns one-third. | |

	1942	February; all civilian automobile production is curtailed in the USA diverting all efforts to support war materials production.	
	1942	February 8; Congress advises President Roosevelt that Americans of Japanese descent should be locked up "en masse," so they don't oppose the US war effort. Eleven days later, FDR orders detention and internment of West Coast Japanese-Americans.	
	1942	February 10; the first-ever "Gold Disc" is awarded to Glenn Miller for selling a million platters of "Chattanooga Choo Choo."	
	1942	February 11; the first *Archie* comic book hits the stands.	
	1942	February 16; an oil refinery on Aruba is shelled by a German submarine.	
	1942	February 20; over in the Pacific Theatre of War, Lt. E. H. O'Hare single-handedly shoots down five (5) Japanese heavy bombers.	

1942	February 23; the Japanese submarine I-17 shells the Ellwood oil field a dozen miles north of Santa Barbara, CA. The only damage is a wooden pier and an old Lufkin pump-jack, but it causes some panic of a Japanese invasion of America.	
1942	**BELL AIRCRAFT tests the first US jet plane.**	
1942	SPECIAL YARNS CO. is booming, (now called ATLANTIC RAYON COMPANY) primarily by supplying materials for parachutes for the Allied Forces.	
1942	PENENS TOOL CO. of Cleveland, OH, is bought out by PLOMB TOOLS.	(see 1947)
1942	Japan invades Indonesia in 1942, primarily for their crude oil reserves.	
1942	BOEING is now building sixty planes per month.	(see 1944)
1942	April 18; four months after Pearl Harbor, Jimmy Doolittle uses sixteen "Mitchell B-25" bombers in his raid on Tokyo and other cities in Japan. Jimmy Doolittle and company spend about "30 Seconds Over Tokyo." *I think the Japanese now realize they are going to be in for a fight. They just don't know how much of a fight!!!*	(see 1979)
1942	BRANIFF AIRWAYS move their headquarters to the Dallas-Ft. Worth area.	
1942	FORD 9N farm tractor production ends & FORD 2N production begins.	
1942	**Henry Ford patents the construction of plastic automobile, but it is never put into production.**	
1942	RAYTHEON invents microwave Sea-Going (SG) Radar, the world's first submarine detection system.	
1942	UNIVERSAL ENGINEERING CORP. is formed and acquires all of the UNIVERSAL CRUSHER CO.	
1942	For the next three years BRIGGS & STRATTON will be building water-cooled engines for the US military.	
1942	HYGRADE SYLVANIA changes its name to SYLVANIA CORPORATION and debuted the "flashing S" logo.	
1942	Thomas Fawick develops the "Golf Pride" grip for golf clubs. The "Golf Pride" is the best selling golf grip in the world, well into the twenty-first century.	(see WWII) (see 2003)
1942	Mabon P. Roper dies, ending the family line, he is succeeded by Stanley Hobson, who continues the fine Roper tradition.	
1942	Ft. Worth, TX; CONVAIR begins producing the B-24 "Liberator" bombers.	

1942	Texas; Reece Albert quits his job with the city of San Angelo and goes into business with a truck, a tractor and a pull-behind "pony" blade as his only equipment.	
1942	Captain Eddie Rickenbacker and his companions spend 24 days adrift in the Pacific Ocean, before being rescued.	
1942	MARTIN introduces the Mars, a huge seaplane, this flying boat will be the world's largest airplane for almost 30 years, until the Boeing 747 comes along.	
1942	SMITH CORONA suspends typewriter production and begin making rifles for the war effort.	
1942	As well as modifying over 1,000 planes for military uses, DELTA AIRLINES also trains pilots, aircraft mechanics, and rebuilds engines for the military.	
1942	England; JOHN ALLEN & SONS (Oxford) Ltd. Begins building BAY CITY truck and crawler cranes under license, and will continue doing so for the next couple of years.	
1942	B. F. AVERY introduces his little Model "A" tractor.	
1942	The Japanese occupation of the Aleutian Islands spurs the US military to construct the Alaska Highway. Across mountains and through muskeg valleys, the 1,523 mile roadway is completed in less than twelve months.	
1942	Germany; the roadway system known since 1933 as "Adolph Hitler's Road" now becomes known as the Autobahn.	
1942	Manchuria, China; in the worst mine disaster in history (and hopefully forever) 1,549 coal miners are killed.	
1942	In Nashville, TN, Ernest Tubb, native of Crisp, Texas (Ellis County), strolls on the stage at the Ryman Auditorium and sings "I'm Walking the Floor Over You," in the distinctive baritone voice that will thrill fans for the next four decades.	
1942	McCulloch Motors sales are $3 million this year, only General Motors builds more superchargers.	(see 1943)
1942	About now, ESAB builds a welding machine factory in Laxå, Sweden.	
1942	About this time, Mr. Roy O. Billings, president of MILWAUKEE HYDRAULICS CORP. realizes that a small, lower-priced mobile crane is needed. Billings soon designs and builds a truck-mounted hydraulic, telescopic boom crane with hydraulic operated outriggers.	(see 1946)
1942	This summer, due to high wartime employment, Congress ends funding for the C. C. C., which had been approved every six months for the past decade. A few of the notable C. C. C. enrollees were Raymond Burr, Robert Mitchum, as well as Doyle and E. L. Cowan. More than 40,000 C. C. C. men learned to read and write in the after hours education program in many camps.	
1942	By now, all Wooldridge equipment is cable operated; they soon add a line of one, two, three and even four drum cable control units. The Wooldridge Terra Clipper line of scrapers now range from six to twenty-eight cubic yards.	(see WWII)
1942	Ohio; following Hal Sr. into the hoist business, Hal Wright Jr. establishes the CHESTER MANUFACTURING CO. Producing hoists designed similar to old Hal's, using the brand name Chester.	(see 1986)
1942	Texas; construction begins in August on the 24" diameter "Big Inch" crude oil pipeline from Longview across 1,254 miles to Phoenixville, PA. WILLIAMS BROTHERS is the principal contractor, and the job is finished next February.	(see 1943)
1942	Orson Welles wins an Oscar for his starring role in *Citizen Kane* last year.	(see 2011)
1942	Kansas; Paul Foley buys out his partners in Karcher-Wolter-Foley Co. and FOLEY TRACTOR CO. is born. Throughout this decade, increasing opportunities in the oil fields and agricultural fields cause Foley to open stores in Great Bend and Pratt.	(see 1958)

1942	The first electronic digital computer is built by John Atanasoff and Clifford Berry. The "Information Age" has begun.	
	1942	Now, almost 50% of the farms across America have electricity.	(see 1932)
	1942	Bing Crosby first records Irving Berlin's beautiful song, "White Christmas."	
	1942	Texas; in the oil patch, a producer can hire a "pulling unit" or light "well service" or small "workover" rig, with a skilled three man crew for about fifty dollars for an eight hour day.	
	1943	January; WILLIAMS BROTHERS, the principal contractor, starts on the 20" Little Big Inch pipeline for refined petroleum products from the refinery complex between Houston and Port Arthur up to Linden, NJ, and will be completed in March of 1944.	
1943	January 18; the US Secretary of Agriculture bans the sale of sliced bread for the duration, as the metal from bread slicing machines is needed for the war effort.	
1943	FOOD MACHINERY CORPORATION gets into the chemical business, with the purchase of NIAGARA.	
1943	DRMC makes tank treads, oxygen hoses, rubber rafts, among other rubber goods for the military during the war.	
1943	Mr. Royal Little vertically integrates ATLANTIC RAYON CO., & renames it TEXTRON (TEXTile & RayON).	
1943	The RADIO CORPORATION OF AMERICA (RCA) completes the sale of the NBC Blue radio network to Ed Noble for eight million dollars, he renames it the AMERICAN BROADCASTING CO. (ABC).	
1943	**DANUSER MACHINE develops the rear-mounted post-hole digger for tractors.**	
1943	Arthur L. Parker dies, but his widow determinedly continues running PARKER APPLIANCE CO.	
1943	General Dwight D. Eisenhower is named to command the US invasion of Europe, hopefully to remove the German scourge.	
1943	Edsel Ford dies of cancer; old Henry is elected president of FORD; grandson Henry the second (Henry II) gets out of the US Navy to help run FORD MOTOR CO.	
1943	The various KAISER SHIPYARDS with their 1.3 million employees are launching three Liberty Ships each day. Some have been completed from start to finish in as little as 80 hours. *"Yeah Bubba, 'at's a buildin' sum boats."*	
1943	VULTEE AIRCRAFT CO. acquires CONSOLIDATED AIRCRAFT CORP., making CONSOLIDATED-VULTEE AIRCRAFT CORP., soon called CONVAIR.	
1943	North Carolina; Mr. T. Austin Finch dies, and his younger brother Doak Finch, who has had a growing management role for several years, carries on the lineage of Finch presidents of THOMASVILLE CHAIR COMPANY.	(see WWII)
1943	HALTOM TRACTOR gets its own territory as a CATERPILLAR dealership in Merced, CA.	
1943	MINNEAPOLIS-MOLINE manufactures about 1,000 different vital parts for the US Army and Navy Bofors anti-aircraft guns.	
1943	May 20; J. C. Trees dies, ending the 48 year partnership of BENEDUM-TREES in petroleum exploration and production.	
1943	While trying to develop a rubber substitute for military tires and boots, James Wright accidently invents "Silly Putty."	
1943	The Alabama-Mississippi Talent Contest is won by a young Elvis Aaron Presley.	

1943	The first of the all-US air raids over Germany begin.	
1943	R. G. LeTourneau develops a line of four large, rubber-tired dozers, up to 750 HP, and mechanically propelled. Production is delayed by the war. These are the first rubber-tired dozers ever to be made.	
1943	**Jacques Cousteau and Emile Gagnan invent the aqualung for breathing underwater; so now our US Navy frogmen can attach mines under enemy ships.**	
1943	**Texas; at Bryan Field, near Galveston, Lt. Joseph Duckworth takes a dare; flies his plane into a hurricane… and Hurricane Hunting is born.**	
1943	In their first foray outside the US, LOFFLAND BROS. takes their rig #48 to Hillsborough Bay, P. E. I., Canada, for SOCONY-VACUUM, (later MAGNOLIA, later MOBIL). They drill past 14,000 feet before abandoning in a stratum of salt.	
1943	GENERAL MOTORS TRUCK & COACH DIVISION is now formed as GM acquires all assets of YELLOW TRUCK & COACH CO.	
1943	SHELL produces a quarter of all 100 octane aviation gasoline used by our military.	
1943	Texas; the small Lee County town of Dime Box is the first "municipality" in the nation to have 100% of its residents contribute to the March of Dimes.	
1943	Restless and wanting to try other things, Robert McCulloch sells MCCULLOCH MOTORS to BORG WARNER, for one million dollars which McCulloch invests in American Airways stock. Six months later, McCulloch sets up MCCULLOCH AVIATION, Inc. to manufacture six thousand drone planes for the US Army Air Force.	(see 1946)
1943	Texas; at Medina Lake, Mr. H. R. Magee lands a thirteen and one-half pound largemouth bass.	
1943	Wally Fowler and the Georgia Clodhoppers form, and Wally soon renames the group the Oak Ridge Quartet.	(see 1957)
1943	USA; First Lady Eleanor Roosevelt plants a White House "Victory Garden," thus inspiring the nation to grow veggies at home.	
1943	Watching her father Edwin, take photos, three year old Jennifer Land asks, "Why can't I see the pictures now?"	(see 1948)
1943	Finland; truck builder SISU joins with VANAJAN AUTOTEHDAS OY, concentrating on military vehicles, under the Yhteissisu marque.	(see 1948)
1943	Canada; the Nodwell brothers, Bruce and Jack, establish NODWELL BROTHERS, a contracting business in Calgary. Previously the brothers invented a pipe-wrapping machine for the pipeline contracting industry. They have been experimenting with various ideas for off-road vehicles, and have decided a tracked vehicle would be best for the purposes they have in mind.	(see 1952)
1943	Louisiana; in Lafayette, HUB CITY FORD is established as the local dealership.	
WWII	Worldwide, the Allied and Axis forces are comprised of 50 million military personnel.	
WWII	About 1937, MARTIN develops the first power-operated revolving gun turret. It'll be used on many Allied war planes.	
WWII	Only 300 Volkswagens are built before Hitler orders the plant closed for the war in 1938.	
WWII	By May of 1939, about 1800 miles of the German Autobahn are complete.	(see 1942)
WWII	The start of WWII in Europe causes serious dislocations of many exports from North American industries.	

Sow the seeds of Victory!
plant & raise your own vegetables

WRITE TO THE NATIONAL WAR GARDEN COMMISSION — WASHINGTON, D.C. for free books on gardening, canning & drying

"Every Garden a Munition Plant"
Charles Lathrop Pack, President

WWII	Early on, SHELL scientists invent a method of synthesizing 100 octane gasoline required for the new aviation engines. Throughout the war, SHELL produces a quarter of all 100 octane aviation gasoline used by our military.	
WWII	Among many items STUDEBAKER builds for the war effort are the engines for the B-17 "Flying Fortress"......and DODGE builds B-29 aircraft engines.	(see 1946)
WWII	During the early years of the war, Allen DuMont receives a US government contract to provide some large, three foot wide cathode ray tubes to be used by Manhattan Project scientists to study the actions of accelerated electrons.	(see 1944) (see 1950s)
WWII	KATO gets US government contracts to supply various sizes generators for the military.	
WWII	GEORGE E. FAILING CO. supplies Allied forces with portable drilling equipment and supplies to drill for water wherever needed.	
WWII	KAISER SHIPYARDS will build over 1,500 cargo ships during the war.	
WWII	Oklahoma; From 1939 onward, HINDERLITER TOOL CORP. is making gun barrels for the Allied forces in Europe.	
WWII	1940, DAVID BRADLEY goes to war production, making submarine net floats, tank engine parts, and 4.2" mortars.	(see 1953)
WWII	SMITH CORONA suspends typewriter production and begin making rifles for the war effort.	
WWII	ROOTS furnishes the US Navy submarines and large ships with special screw compressors to blow ballast rapidly.	(see 1944)
WWII	In 1941, Texas produces 40% of all American crude oil, and 25% of the world's overall crude oil production.	

WWII	The "general purpose" vehicle (GP or Jeep) is first being built by the WILLIS-OVERLAND COMPANY in 1941.	
WWII	The FORD MOTOR COMPANY plant in Dallas Texas produces more than 100,000 Jeeps and Army trucks for our Military.	
WWII	In the hot, sweltering humid summer of 1941, while preparing soldiers for war, the US Army holds maneuvers in the Mooringsport, Louisiana area. Generals Dwight D. Eisenhower and George S. Patton are in Mooringsport leading the Red and Blue Armies in the capture of the Caddo Lake Drawbridge, which is "bombed" with sacks of flour.	(see 1989)

WWII	During the years of 1941-1945, ALLIED RADIO focuses on the war effort with government contracts and war-related private industry sales.	
WWII	As the US enters WWII, many Depression-era price controls are lifted, giving a double-boost to American industry.	
WWII	1942; as the Japanese occupy the Aleutian Islands, the US Military is spurred into action and constructs the Alaska Highway, for 1,523 miles, across mountains and through muskeg valleys, finishing in less than a year.	
WWII	From 1942 -1945, BRIGGS & STRATTON will be building water-cooled engines for US military applications.	
WWII	In 1942, CONVAIR in Fort Worth, TX, begins building the B-24 Liberator bombers.	
WWII	Japan invades Indonesia in 1942, primarily for their crude oil reserves.	
WWII	Allen B. DuMont has developed long-range, precision radar for use of the US and the Allies.	
WWII	In 1942, Captain Eddie Rickenbacker and his companions spend 24 days adrift in the Pacific Ocean, before survivors are rescued.	
WWII	Jimmy Doolittle and company spend about "30 Seconds Over Tokyo," in 1942.	

WWII	USA; in February of '42, all civilian auto production is curtailed, diverting all efforts to support war materials production.	
WWII	Texas; all able-bodied men are needed in our country's military, and travel restrictions are… well… very restrictive. Although the Texas League (minor league baseball) played in 1942, there are no minor league games in Texas until after this war, in 1946.	
WWII	From 1942 onwards the US government gets 85% of CATERPILLAR'S production; the remaining 15% goes to contractors working on high-priority government projects. Until government orders begin to slack off in late 1944, CAT dealers have almost no new machines to sell, and must survive by parts sales and sometimes labor to repair and overhaul older machines.	
WWII	Texas; February, 1942, in Longview, Harmon General Hospital is established by the US Army as a major medical center. Soon the 156 acre site south of town has over 200 buildings on it, almost 3,000 hospital beds, and a staff of 1,500 during peak times. The last patients leave in December of 1945, and in January of 1946, the facility is deactivated.	(see 1946)
WWII	Henry J. Kaiser puts the assembly-line method to use building freighter ships with triple-expansion steam engines for the military. This takes months off the usual production time of these Liberty Ships.	
WWII	In 1942, BOEING is now building sixty planes per month.	
WWII	RAYTHEON invents Microwave Sea-Going (SG) Radar in 1942, the world's first submarine detection system.	
WWII	1942; a Japanese submarine shells an oilfield on the California coast. The worst result is mass panic, as casualties were only a LUFKIN pump jack and a wooden dock.	
WWII	January 1943; the USDA bans the sale of sliced bread for the duration, as metal from the slicing machines is needed for war effort.	
WWII	The Allies control of the oil supply from Baku and the Middle East, from 1939-1943, plays a tremendous role in the events of this war, and the ultimate Allied victory. Japan is seriously weakened by cutting off the oil supply in the latter portion of the war.	
WWII	In 1943, General Dwight D. Eisenhower is named to command the US invasion of Europe to remove the German scourge.	
WWII	1943; Robert McCulloch establishes MCCULLOCH AVIATION to build 6,000 drone planes for the US Army Air Force.	
WWII	1943; the first of the all-US air raids over Germany begin.	
WWII	By 1944, America is producing two times the combined totals of ALL the Axis (enemy) nations. This includes planes, tanks, ships and all other tools of war. Our war production is 44% of GNP for 1944. Almost 19 million more Americans are working than five years ago, and of these additional workers, 35% are women. Twelve million Americans are in the military services in 1944.	
WWII	DRMC makes tank treads, oxygen hoses, rubber rafts, and many other rubber goods for our military during the war.	
WWII	Texas; with gasoline rationed, most Texans are limited to 3 gallons per week. Governor Coke Stevenson certainly doth protest, saying gasoline is as important to Texans as "…the saddle, the rifle, the axe, and the Bible."	
WWII	Texas; the Corpus Christi Naval Air Station is commissioned.	
WWII	USA; to conserve gasoline and tire rubber, the wartime speed limit is a sleepy 35 miles per hour.	
WWII	The various KAISER SHIPYARDS and their 1. 3 million workers are launching three Liberty Ships each day. Some have been completed from start to finish in as little as eighty hours.	
WWII	IBM introduces the Mark I, its first calculator/computer.	

WWII	Jacques Cousteau and Emile Gagnan invent the aqualung, for breathing underwater; enabling our US Navy "frogmen" to attach mines directly under enemy ship hulls.	
WWII	In 1944, Boeing is now building 362 planes per month, about 12 planes per day.	
WWII	Myron D. Stepath conceives the idea of combining a carbon arc to melt metal and compressed air to blast away the molten metal. Myron's idea works, but it is a two man operation.	
WWII	June 6, 1944; the Allied forces assault of Normandy beach in France will stand as the largest seaborne invasion in history; it is D-Day.	(see 1944)

| | WWII | During WWII, Hobart Bros. Co. is chosen as the chief supplier of gasoline engine driven welders for the armed forces. Hobart earns such an international reputation, that in some countries, Turkey for one, to this day all welding machines are called Hobarts. | |
| | WWII | Throughout the war, 65% of Thomasville Chair Co.'s production is government orders for the war effort. A few of their items are double bunk beds, tent stakes, wooden spatulas and wooden plugs for bombs. | (see 1950) |

WWII	1944; the Liberty Ships are replaced with the Victory Ships, more streamlined, with a 6,000 hp or 8,500 hp steam turbine engine; these can outrun the German U-boats.	
WWII	Ford builds 8,485 B-24 bombers for our military.	
WWII	In 1944, Minneapolis-Moline works in close cooperation with US Army; manufactures and supplies vital parts for the secret amphibious Sherman Tank... important in saving thousands of lives on D-Day.	
WWII	Germany begins robot bomb attacks on England in 1944.	
WWII	At mid-year 1944, there are 25,000 Japanese settlers living on Saipan; additionally there are 1,000s of Okinawans, Koreans and natives of other Pacific islands, all of whom are brutalized and utilized as slaves, harvesting sugar cane for Japan. As a portion of Japan's "regime of enforced prostitution" there are a couple of thousand young Korean women forced to service the Japanese military as sex slaves.	
WWII	In 1944, the Texas Interconnected System (later to become the Electric Reliability Council of Texas) is created to be sure that the many plants and factories in Texas would continue to receive sufficient electricity to continue to operate, making their full contribution to the war effort. This is the beginning of the Texas Interconnection power grid, that covers 85% of Texas' electrical needs, and is not interdependent on neighboring states or countries.	
WWII	Iowa Manufacturing Company builds 1,700 rock crushers to supply the allied forces in every theatre of war.	
WWII	Europe; LeGrand Sutcliffe & Gell switch their emphasis to the manufacture of oil production equipment, due the inability of producers to obtain such equipment from the USA.	
WWII	The prefabricated Quonset Huts are introduced, being manufactured in... Quonset, Rhode Island, of course.	
WWII	The Euclid Road Machinery Co., like CAT and LeTOURNEAU, is allowed by the US government to continue manufacturing its standard products, during the war. However, almost all production goes to the military.	
WWII	Thousands of Allied Naval vessels use Thomas Fawick's Airflex Clutch on their gear drive trains.	(see 1968)
WWII	While concentrating on the war effort, the Thomas & Betts plant in Elizabeth, New Jersey, is declared one of the twelve most critical plants in the nation during the war.	
WWII	Throughout WWII, 60% of Bucyrus-Erie's production goes to the US government for the allied war effort.	(see 1948)

WWII	**During the war, improved forklift trucks are developed in both Australia and America.**	
WWII	The only NFL team playing in Pennsylvania is the STEAGLES. The Steelers and the Eagles merge for the duration while many players from both teams are serving in the armed forces overseas.	
WWII	ESSEX WIRE produces the wire used to make millions of transformers used by the Allied forces, also making 1,000s of miles of field telephone wire for the Army Signal Corp.s, as well as wiring harnesses for our B-24 bombers.	
WWII	The all-male military college, Texas A & M, puts about 20,000 men into the US Armed Forces, of which 14,000 are officers. No other school in the nation, not even the Military Academy at West Point, places this number of men into our military.	
WWII	UK; DENNIS BROS. builds 700 of the 35 ton Churchill tanks and 7,000 trailer pumps and 1,000s of other trucks and specialized vehicles for the Allied military forces.	
WWII	Products from AEROQUIP become Military Standards on all US aircraft. This establishes Aeroquip's reputation as a quality manufacturer and supplier.	
WWII	INTERNATIONAL HARVESTER produces crawler tractors, half-tracks, gun carriages, ammunition, and much other varied war material, in addition to 122,000 trucks for the war effort.	
WWII	During tank warfare, the British develop the idea of radiators with individually replaceable tubes.	
WWII	NESTLÉ, having their business reduced by 75% during the depression, begins to recoup as their newest product, "Nescafe," becomes a staple drink of the US military… leading to Nestlé's economic recovery.	
WWII	Texas; TODD SHIPBUILDING CORP. has shipyards in Galveston and Houston. BROWN SHIPBUILDING CORP. has a shipyard in Houston, as well. These Houston and Galveston shipyards employee 35,000 men and women. Destroyer escorts, wood-hulled mine-sweepers, and amphibious landing craft are being built in three shipyards in Orange Texas. Liberty Ships are being built in Beaumont at the Pennsylvania Shipyard.	
WWII	TRAILMOBILE furnishes about 40,000 trailers for use by our armed forces.	(see 1944)
WWII	Texas; among the 830,000 Texans serving in the US Military are 12,000 women. Of these Texans, 23,000 give their lives for our nation during this war.	
WWII	1945-47; more than $3.4 billion value of military equipment including 500,000 Dodge trucks, are supplied to US and Allied forces by CHRYSLER, whose M4 tank is the primary combat vehicle of the US and its Allies.	(see 1946)
WWII	USA; while five star General Dwight E. Eisenhower fights in Europe, five other future presidents of the USA, John F. Kennedy, Lyndon B. Johnson, Richard M. Nixon, Gerald Ford, and George H. W. Bush are serving the US military in the Pacific Theatre. Ronald Reagan serves in the military as a training instructor.	
WWII	UK; ALBION MOTOR CAR CO. supplies military vehicles throughout the war.	
WWII	CORBITT produces military and civilian trucks including heavy 6X4 truck tractor units.	
WWII	SAVAGE ARMS makes over 2,500,000 aircraft-type machine guns, sub-machine guns, and infantry rifles for our military.	
WWII	Most WELCH'S production goes to our military, and WELCH'S takes out magazine ads explaining the shortage in grocery stores.	(see 1952)
WWII	More than 425,000 Axis POWs are incarcerated in 650 POW camps across America.	
WWII	UK; the AUSTIN MOTOR CO. produces large numbers of trucks for military use.	
WWII	All of the standard products of T. B. WOOD'S SONS help the war effort; they also are making machine gun mounts and steel turret rings for tanks.	(see 1953)

WWII	UK; BSA, with 67 factories, carries on with civilian production, but furnishes 126,000 M20 military trucks for the Allies.	
WWII	CHEVROLET furnishes 150,000 1½ ton trucks to the US and its Allies, the most of any manufacturer of 1½ ton trucks.	
WWII	Tulsa; the young and successful UNIT RIG & EQUIPMENT CO. slows production of oilfield equipment and builds anchor windlasses and marine transmissions for the USN. Later in the war, they produce 155mm artillery shells for our military.	
WWII	Manufacturers in the US build more than 2,600,000 trucks of various sizes and types for the Allied war effort.	
WWII	France; in a solo chase of a Nazi Messerschmitt Bf109G fighter plane, US AAF pilot William Overstreet, Jr. (1921-2014), flies under the arches of the lower legs of the Eiffel Tower to keep close on his prey.	
WWII	During the war years, the full strength of blowers and turbochargers is well tested. The B-17, B-29, P-38, and P-51 are outfitted with turbos and controls. The B-36 bomber has 6 of the 28 cylinder engines. The B-36 flight engineer's handbook states, "…the B-36 would require 90 cylinders (instead of 28) per engine to achieve the same performance as the turbo-supercharged design."	
WWII	WOOLDRIDGE MFG. CO. produces dozer blades, pull scrapers and rippers for the US military during the war.	(see 1945)
WWII	More than three thousand trailers for the Allied war effort are built by UTILITY TRAILER COMPANY.	(see 1951)
WWII	A line of heavy-duty, rotary, gear pumps are produced for use on military ships as liquid cargo pumps, and ballast tank pumps, in addition to other wartime necessities from WATEROUS.	
WWII	Texas; during the war, about forty-thousand naval aviators are trained at the Corpus Christi Naval Air Station.	
WWII	USA; before the war, HERCULES MOTORS had a huge market share of the military market. Now they rapidly expand their plants, as well as the facilities of their shared suppliers. During the war, HERCULES produces three-quarters of a million engines for powering an endless supply of our military needs, including vehicles, generators, and marine usage includes PT boats, landing craft, as well as amphibious tractors.	
WWII	Australia; mostly for the war effort, WAUGH & JOSEPHSON manufacture, under license, CATERPILLAR No. 12 motor graders as well as other items.	(see 1989)
WWII	Red Adair, the blacksmith's son from Houston, proudly serves in the US Army in the 139th Bomb Disposal Squadron.	(see 1947)
WWII	The Australian Sidney Cotton is a friend of Ian Fleming. It is often thought that Cotton was the model for Fleming's James Bond, as well as the inspiration for some of "Q's" gadgets, in the Bond series.	
WWII	Our US military services are furnished with kitchen and cooking equipment by the TAPPAN COMPANY of Ohio.	(see 1955)
WWII	Five different times during the war, the LUFKIN RULE CO. is presented with the Army-Navy "E" Awards for production excellence and efficiency. Of the total number of plants performing war-related work, only about 5% ever receive this award.	
WWII	The British government commandeers all eighty-seven oil tankers in the SHELL fleet.	
WWII	CATERPILLAR, and LETOURNEAU are the largest suppliers of earthmoving items to our military. After the war, Mr. R. G. claims his company was the largest wartime supplier of earthmoving equipment to the military; and that might have been the case volume-wise, but the CATERPILLAR dollar volume was considerably larger.	

WWII	At peak wartime production, LeTourneau is shipping 70-80 Tournapulls per month, to the US Army. By the war's end, LeTourneau now has more practical experience building rubber-tired earthmovers than all his competitors combined.	
WWII	Flint Rig builds US Army camps, and with well service equipment acquired from Cities Service Co., Flint further expands their services.	(see 1940s)
WWII	General Motors division, Fisher Body is building the US Navy designed 5 inch multi-purpose gun, for the US military.	
WWII	Under license from Oerlikon AG of Switzerland, Pontiac Motor division of GM, is producing the 20 mm Oerlikon anti-aircraft cannon for US Navy.	
WWII	Louisiana; in Shreveport, the Brewster Company suspends production of drilling equipment and manufactures materials for the war effort. Five times, the Army-Navy "E" Award is awarded to the Brewster Company.	
WWII	Minneapolis-Moline manufactures about 1,000 different vital parts for the US Army and Navy Bofors anti-aircraft guns.	
WWII	During war production, Minneapolis-Moline is the first and maybe the only company to win all these awards, (1) the Victory Fleet Flag, (2) Maritime "M" pennant with three gold stars, (3) the Army-Navy "E" pennant w/ two gold stars, and (4) the Army Ordnance Banner.	
WWII	Universal Unit Power Shovel Corp. builds cranes and excavators, as well as anti-aircraft gun mounts for our military.	
WWII	By the end of the war, 350 million barrels of oil and products have been shipped via the "Big Inch" and the "Little Big Inch" pipelines. That's more than 300,000 barrels each day since their completion.	
WWII	About 50,000 Sherman tanks are built in the US, mostly by locomotive builders Electro-Motive, Lima, Baldwin, and Alco.	
WWII	England; primarily preparing and re-furbishing army trucks, Pelican Engineering Co. works almost exclusively for the British Ministry of Defense, and the firm continues growing throughout the war.	(see 1946)
WWII	For our war effort, more than 1,000 water landing craft are equipped with Beebe two ton hand winches for ramp handling.	(see 1959)
WWII	Vacuum Oil facilities in Poland are captured and operated by the German Nazis, using forced labor from the Tschechowitz I & II sub-camps of Auschwitz.	(see 1955)
WWII	The US Marines land on Iwo Jima, and soon the US ends Japan's barbaric ambitions for the world. **July 16;** during the past 3 years the US government has spent more than $2 billion on the Manhattan Project, employing over 120,000 people, in 37 different facilities, to build three atomic bombs. Today the first atomic bomb is exploded in a successful test in New Mexico. **August 6;** this week the other two atomic bombs are exploded, one each on Hiroshima and Nagasaki, Japan, effectively ending WWII in the Pacific.	
WWII	**The second World War ends with the collapse of the regimes of Japan and Germany in 1945.**	
WWII	**As the war ends, Boeing has to lay off seventy thousand employees.** *"Yeah, Bubba...at's rite, 70,000 laid off."*	
WWII	After the war, Manitowoc begins producing food service equipment.	
1944	Pacific Car & Foundry acquires Kenworth Motor Truck Co. as a wholly owned subsidiary.	(see 1951)
1944	Frank G. Hough has the first hydraulic bucket tilt system on a front end loader.	

1944	Oliver Corporation buys the Cleveland Tractor Company, makers of Cletrac crawler tractors.	
1944	Dresser acquires Ideco, including the plant in Beaumont, TX.	
1944	Alabama; H. L. Hunt drills in the Jackson #1 on February 17th, bringing in the Gilbertown oil field as the first commercially usable oil well in the state after 350 dusters.	
1944	Dresser Industries acquires control of Roots Blowers.	(see 1999)
1944	W. Ersted Co. officially becomes Hyster Co.	
1944	March; at Flour Bluff, just south of Corpus Christi, Corpus Christi Naval Air Station is commissioned.	
1944	Hughes Tool Co. compiles & makes available for publication the first weekly tally of rotary rigs drilling in the US and Canada, still uninterrupted in 2004.	

1944	April 4th; Wendell Willkie drops out of the race for President. Willkie dies this October 8th.	
1944	Rolls-Royce begins development of the aero gas turbine, pioneered by Sir Frank Whittle.	
1944	**Wix manufactures the first "can type" filter refills.**	
1944	Casoc changes its name to the Arabian American Oil Company (ARAMCO).	
1944	**Of the 300 commercial airliners flying in the US, 275 are DC-3s.**	
1944	**Phillips Petroleum is the first to produce "cold" synthetic rubber that is superior to natural rubber.**	

1944	Oilwell Division acquires Witte Engine Works.	
1944	About this time, the Texas Interconnected System (later to become the Electric Reliability Council of Texas) is created to be sure that the many plants and factories in Texas would continue to receive sufficient electricity to continue to operate, making their full contribution to the war effort. This is the beginning of the Texas Interconnection power grid, that covers 85% of Texas' electrical requirements, and is not interdependent on neighboring states or countries.	
1944	Cancer claims the life of T. A. Peterman, and his widow takes over ownership of the Peterbilt Company.	
1944	Worthington acquires the Electric Machine Mfg. Company.	
1944	T. H. "Tandy" Hamilton opens the first Piccadilly Cafeteria in Baton Rouge, LA.	
1944	Hastings enters the oil filter business beginning R & D work for the high compression engines that are still on the drawing boards.	(see 1995)
1944	Replacing the Liberty Ships, the Victory Ships are introduced; more streamlined and with a 6,000 or 8,500 hp steam turbine engine, it outruns the German U-boats.	
1944	Delta Drilling's "foreign" experience begins with the drilling of some wells for Lion Oil Co. on Cape Breton Island, off Nova Scotia, Canada.	
1944	June 6; beginning today, the Allied forces assault Normandy beach in France. Sixty years onward, this action still stands as the largest seaborne invasion in the history of the world; D-Day.	
1944	June 10; at 6 ft, 3 in tall, at the age of fifteen years, ten months and eleven days, Joe Nuxhall steps in as a Cincinnati Reds relief pitcher. Joe's parents allowed him to join the Reds when school was out this spring. A few weeks earlier, Joe was pitching to 13 and 14 year olds. Now Joe looks up and there is Stan Musial and his like. The youngest pro pitcher ever, Nuxhall retires in 1966, then goes on to be the "Voice of the Reds" until 2004.	
1944	June 10; Canada; in Ontario, the Brantford Exposition highlights the centennial of Waterous Ltd.	(see 1953)
1944	On a 8,600 acre site, in the mountains, west of Phoenix, AZ, Caterpillar Tractor Co. establishes its proving ground and technical center.	

1944	Both the ALASKA JUNEAU and the TREADWAY mines close; since 1880, they have often produced as much as 20,000 tons of gold ore daily.	
1944	The International Bretton Woods Conference establishes US currency at a value of US $35 per ounce of gold. Other nations soon adjust their rates according to the US dollar, effectively recognizing America as the world's central economy.	
1944	The TRAILER COMPANY OF AMERICA changes its name back to TRAILMOBILE, because of the respect it had gained during the three decades its semi-trailers were branded thusly.	(see 1982)
1944	The GENERAL CIGAR CO. introduces the "Cigarillo."	
1944	TIG welding (heliarc) is invented.	
1944	Kansas; the LEE denim cowboy pants are officially renamed "Lee Riders," by the H. D. Lee Company.	
1944	USA; utilizing its DC-3 Flagship Air Freighter, AMERICAN AIRLINES introduces the world's first transcontinental, all-cargo service.	(see 1953)
1944	MINNEAPOLIS-MOLINE works in close cooperation with US Army; manufactures and supplies vital parts for the secret amphibious Sherman Tank… important in saving thousands of lives on D-Day.	
1944	Germany begins robot bomb attacks on England.	
1944	At this time there are 25,000 Japanese settlers living on Saipan; additionally there are thousands of Okinawans, Koreans and natives of other Pacific islands, all of whom are brutalized and utilized as slaves, harvesting sugar cane for Japan. As a portion of Japan's "regime of enforced prostitution" there are a couple of thousand young Korean women forced to service the Japanese military as sex slaves.	
1944	DuMont's experimental television station W2XWV, now becomes a commercial station WABD (DuMont's initials), and will someday become WNYW.	(see 1940s) (see 1950s)
1945	January; FDR begins his fourth term, but dies on April 12th. Harry S. Truman takes the reins of the US presidency.	
1945	TRACTOMOTIVE CORP. is established in Findlay, OH.	
1945	The first ARROW model "C" gas fueled "hit & miss" engines are built.	(see 1946)
1945	With a melted candy bar in a shirt pocket, RAYTHEON accidentally discovers microwave cooking.	
1945	The JIFFY TOOTH EXCAVATING COMPANY (soon shortened to JETCO) is formed in Alhambra, CA.	
1945	In San Francisco, the first United Nations parlay takes place.	
1945	**Mr. R. G. LeTourneau moves to Longview, TX, and begins preparations to build a plant there.**	(see 1946)
1945	TYLER IRON & FOUNDRY becomes TYLER PIPE & FOUNDRY COMPANY.	
1945	PARKER DRILLING starts up their Venezuelan operations.	(see 1947)
1945	Minnesota; Gordon Jensen and Leo Grzesowski establish GRESEN HYDRAULICS in St. Paul.	
1945	TEXAS MILL SUPPLY is founded.	
1945	Saudi Arabia; on the East Coast, ARAMCO's huge Ras Tanura refinery begins operations.	
1945	TRI-STATE OIL TOOLS is formed with stores in Kilgore, TX, Bossier City, LA, and Magnolia, AR.	
1945	**BJ develops the power slip, for more efficient rotary drilling operations.**	
1945	**RIDGE TOOL CO. develops the first power drive to use with hand tools.**	
1945	Texas; Ramsey C. Armstrong forms WELL EXPLOSIVES CO. in Ft. Worth, to do down-hole perforating, later to become WELEX JET SERVICES.	

1945	**July 16;** during the past three years the US government has spent more than $2 billion on the Manhattan Project, employing over 120 thousand people, in 37 different facilities, to build three atomic bombs. Today the first atomic bomb is exploded in a successful test in New Mexico. **August 6;** this week the other two atomic bombs are exploded, one each on Hiroshima and Nagasaki, Japan, effectively ending WWII in the Pacific.
1945	August 10; this morning at 03:00 hours, Japanese Emperor Hirohito, without consent of his cabinet, announces his concession of surrender, thus ending the war in the Pacific.

	1945	Texas; south of Daingerfield, the US government builds an integrated steel mill, DAINGERFIELD STEEL, to have an inland, protected source of wartime steel.
	1945	The second World War ends this year with the collapse of both Japan and Germany.
	1945	As WWII ends and Germany is occupied by the Allies… they begin the break-up of the GHH Group, breaking off the steel-producing companies. GHH and M. A. N. in Germany suffered heavy war damage, and lost all their foreign operations.
	1945	OILWELL DIVISION acquires NEILSEN PUMP COMPANY.
	1945	FORD resumes civilian production, and Henry II is elected president.
	1945	Petroleum producer W. H. BARBER & Co. is purchased by Pure Oil Co.; both companies are in Chicago.

1945	UNITED TOOL and VALVE REPAIR (UNITED ENGINES) gets the distributorship of Detroit Diesel engines from GENERAL MOTORS.	
1945	FAIRBANKS, MORSE & Co. introduce their Model 45 or Eclipse 45, the last windmill they will produce, it will be marketed into the mid 1950s.	
1945	Texas; in Fort Worth, the AMON G. CARTER FOUNDATION is founded.	
1945	The CROSLEY CORPORATION sells out to AVCO.	
1945	Jeannie C. Riley is born in Anson, TX.	
1945	OMSCO invents the OMSCO Kelly Valve.	
1945	**The first eddy current brakes are now being used to retard speeds on rotary drilling rig draw-works.**	
1945	Tony Hulman buys the INDIANAPOLIS MOTOR SPEEDWAY from Rickenbacker for $750,000. Being closed during the war years, it is really a wreck.	
1945	New York City; the additional lanes on the main level of the George Washington Bridge are now paved.	
1945	Germany; the Allied governments order the liquidation of the Zeppelin Co. All their hangars and airship construction facilities were destroyed by Allied bombing.	
1945	LOFFLAND BROTHERS' second foreign contract is off the Northern coast of Cuba, near Coco Island. Later this year they start their first contract outside North America, as they start drilling operations in Venezuela.	
1945	The trading stamp industry, having "hibernated" during WWII, begins over a decade of fairly steady expansion.	
1945	USA; although he is blind from a childhood disease, Ralph Teetor invents cruise control for motor vehicles.	(see 1957)
1945	HANAB is founded.	
1945	The world's first pneumatically controlled power drilling rigs are introduced by NATIONAL SUPPLY CO.	

1945	From now through 1966, PETTIBONE-MULLIKEN is producing a good line of buckets for cable backhoes, shovel dippers, clamshell and dragline buckets and larger dipper buckets for stripping shovels.	(see 1946)
1945	I don't know what a "kum-pewter" is, but the one at Harvard University broke down. The culprit is found to be a moth that has gotten into one of its circuits; thus begins the saying, "It has a bug in it."	
1945	August 15; the US government lifts rationing of gasoline and fuel oil.	
1945	Ernest Chan, Howard Florey and Alexander Fleming win the Nobel Prize for the world's first antibiotic: penicillin.	
1945	And, speaking of bugs… the insecticide DDT is first commercially available this year.	
1945	Beginning this year and for the next three years, LINK-BELT-SPEEDER builds an unusual loader attachment; the TF-4 TractoLoader for the CATERPILLAR D-4 tractor. The fully hydraulic unit swivels 180 degrees (90 to the right and 90 to the left), mounted atop the tractor, to dump its loaded bucket. Only 40 units will be made throughout its 3-year lifespan.	
1945	The Terra Cobra Model TCY, WOOLDRIDGE MFG. CO.'s first motor scraper, is introduced this year.	
1945	Reconstruction begins on the almost completely leveled OPEL factory at Russelsheim, Germany.	(see 1946)
1945	Physics professor Isidor Rabi of Columbia University suggests a clock can be made a technique he developed during the past decade, called atomic beam magnetic resonance.	(see 1949)
1945	Oklahoma City; A couple of local entrepreneurs establish DRILLING EQUIPMENT MANUFACTURING CO.	(see 1965)
1945	Although steel on steel is the most efficient method of freight transportation, the US railroads are now in decline. This is due to the expansion of trucks and the better highways for them to operate them upon. And no small part is due to the B of RT and other unions.	
1946	**Ray Ferwerda, a Cleveland, OH, contractor, has invented the GRADALL, and finally gets WARNER & SWASEY to produce the equipment.**	
1946	January 19; Dolly Parton is born near Sevierville, TN.	
1946	The last patients left last month, and this January, the Harmon General Hospital in Longview, TX, is deactivated, and for sale. R. G. LeTourneau buys the old Harmon army camp in Longview and founds LeTourneau Technical Institute.	
1946	TOTE'M changes its name to 7-ELEVEN.	
1946	BERGEN DIESEL COMPANY is founded in Norway.	
1946	The first King Midget cars are built.	
1946	**BJ introduces the first 10,000 psi cementing pump.**	
1946	CHRISTENSEN DIAMOND BITS is founded in Salt Lake City, UT, with one product; diamond rotary drill bits.	
1946	Oklahoma; Don R. Hinderliter founds DON R. HINDERLITER INC. in Tulsa.	
1946	March 1, UK; after 252 years, the British government takes control of the BANK OF ENGLAND.	
1946	The BADGER MACHINE COMPANY is established and introduces the "HOPTO."	
1946	USA; March 5; in Fenton, MO, Winston Churchill delivers his "Iron Curtain" speech. This term is used throughout the Cold War.	
1946	After receiving awards for military production during WWII, MASTER TIRE & RUBBER CO. changes its name to COOPER TIRE & RUBBER CO.	
1946	WEBB starts manufacturing hubs and spoked wheels in Cullman, AL.	

1946	SPICER CORPORATION acquires AUBURN CLUTCH CO., then because of the various companies in SPICER CORP. decides to rename itself. DANA CORPORATION is the chosen name, to honor Charles Dana's 32 years of service to SPICER.
1946	March; a BELL MODEL 47 receives the world's first commercial helicopter license, signaling the start of a new industry.
1946	As WWII ends, BOEING AIRPLANE COMPANY has to lay off 70,000 employees.
1946	April 1; in the USA the WEIGHT WATCHERS group is initially formed.
1946	A. D. COOK PUMP COMPANY is sold to BYRON JACKSON PUMP COMPANY.
1946	Following the American model, FACOM brings tool demonstration trucks to France.
1946	May 9; the television industry's first variety show, *Hour Glass*, premiers on NBC-TV.
1946	Oklahoma; CRANE CARRIER CORP. (CCC) begins, in Tulsa, as a small company buying surplus military vehicles and modifying, reinforcing and often re-manufacturing them for the petroleum and construction markets.
1946	DRMC changes its name to DAYTON RUBBER CO. (DRC).
1946	Darryl F. Zanuck, head of 20th Century Fox, says, "Television won't be able to hold on to any market it captures after the first six months. People will soon get tired of staring at a plywood box every night." *"Wal, Ah guess we showed him."*
1946	Five PETERBILT employees get together and buy the PETERBILT COMPANY from Mrs. Peterman.
1946	With the war ending and product demand dropping considerably, PARKER APPLIANCE toughs it out, with Mrs. Parker's very efficient leadership.
1946	The first Dodge Power Wagon for civilian use is introduced. (see 1968)
1946	NORMAR is established in Oslo, Norway, to build offshore platforms, derricks, etc.
1946	MARTIN-DECKER and NATIONAL SUPPLY collaborates on a new type of drill line anchor and weight indicator combination, finalized after over a year of work; this type of unit continues to be the most common used system sixty years later.
1946	EATON SPRING & AXLE acquires DYNAMATIC CORP. of Kenosha, WI.
1946	Glenn Stahl begins his business in Kansas, STAHL SPECIALTY COMPANY, specializing in aluminum castings.
1946	SERVCO is formed as a downhole tool company.
1946	VINNELL begins its transition from general contractor to government services contractor.
1946	Oklahoma; Harley Pray sells TULSA WINCH COMPANY to VICKERS INC. of Detroit, MI.
1946	In Vancouver, BC, Canada, Frank Lawrence founds GEARMATIC, to build air-shift transmissions for yarders.
1946	Under Japan's postwar policy of decentralizing industries, MITSUBISHI splits itself into many independent companies.
1946	After the war the CAB grants BRANIFF nearly 8,000 miles of routes, some as far south as Santiago, Chile, and Buenos Aires, Argentina.
1946	Denver; ELDER TRAILER & BODY CO. is formed as a builder of quality transport trailers.
1946	KLM launches its scheduled air passenger service between Amsterdam, Holland, and New York City.

1946	ZALES JEWELERS moves their headquarters from Wichita Falls to Houston, TX.	

	1946	USA; Mr. Delmer Harder develops or invents robot automation.
	1946	Shreveport, LA; UNITED VALVE & TOOL CO. (UNITED ENGINE) becomes a dealer for DETROIT DIESEL DIVISION of GM.
	1946	Chet Atkins makes his first GRAND OLD OPRY appearance as a part of Red Foley's band.
	1946	Paul Brown organizes the CLEVELAND BROWNS as an AFL franchise, naming the team after himself.
	1946	Meteorologist Harold Taft takes a job with American Airlines.
	1946	Van Dobeus perfects all-hydraulic loaders for installation and use on crawler tractors.
	1946	Bill Rosenberg founds INDUSTRIAL LUNCHEON SERVICES.

1946	Although Tom and Jack have the largest drilling rig fleet on earth, they decide to sell their interest in LOFFLAND BROTHERS to MID-CONTINENT SUPPLY, under the management of Kenneth W. Davis, Senior.	
1946	Ken Davis buys HARRISBURG INC.; maker and distributor of diamond hard products for drilling rig centrifugal and mud pumps. Davis then opens a MID-CONTINENT Export sales office in New York City to deal with rapidly expanding international drilling operations.	(see 1948)
1946	February; reporting on his own 1946 Ford, Tom McCahill sells his first article to *Mechanix Illustrated* (MI) magazine, establishing a relationship to last many years.	
1946	The "Hit and Miss" AJAX engines are now being primarily used by petroleum companies; often powering pump jacks individually, or powering the powerhouse for a "Rodline and Jerker" pumping system for several wells.	
1946	*As the war ends and its welding machines are in much less demand, HOBART BROS. does not lay off anyone, but helps many employees find work in the Troy area, such as in a cabinet shop and some were picking fruit in orchards, and HOBART BROS. pays these employees the difference, up to equal their regular wages.*	
1946	MCCULLOCH AVIATION moves from Milwaukee to Los Angeles. There they buy fifteen acres and build a new one million dollar factory, and change the name to MCCULLOCH MOTORS CORPORATION.	(see 1947)
1946	Orange, CA; UNION OIL OF CALIFORNIA (UNOCAL) decides to sell its drilling department and get out of the drilling business. A group of senior management from the drilling department has the idea for drilling department employees to but the drilling operations and equipment… and they do so. Thus, SANTA FE DRILLING is initially formed as an employee-owned land drilling company, head quartered at Santa Fe Springs, CA.	
1946	PETTIBONE acquires BEARDSLEY & PIPER of Chicago, Illinois. PETTIBONE MULLIKEN also acquires GEORGE HAISS MFG. CO. of New York City, but will continue to operate under the Haiss name until 1971.	(see 1948)
1946	Texas; in Houston, Mr. Len Eldridge establishes L. C. ELDRIDGE SALES CO. the exclusive agent for HARTZELL FAN, INC.	
1946	Iowa; in Davenport, Marion "Bud" Murray and his family begin operations of their family-owned trucking company.	
1946	ALLIS-CHALMERS brings out the world's largest crawler tractor, the HD-19 powered by a Detroit 6-110 developing 163 horsepower. The new ALLIS-CHALMERS HD19 has the first ever hydraulic dozer cylinders mounted on the engine housing or frame, this of course comes from BAKER, which has provided A-C with attachments for a good many years.	(see 1955)

1946	Greenville, SC; today's race has drawn 20,000 fans, promoter Big Bill France will later call it, "the start of NASCAR."	
1946	Billing's H-2 Hydrocrane is introduced. It is immediately successful, selling 200 by end-of-year. This successful machine draws the attention of Bucyrus-Erie in nearby South Milwaukee, WI.	(see 1948)
1946	La Mesa Park opens at Raton, the first horse racing track in New Mexico.	(see 1992)
1946	Each of the seven thousand (7,000) TV receiver sets in the US is tuned in to one, or maybe two, of the ten (yes only 10) television broadcasting stations around the country.	
1946	As rebuilding continues, OPEL "Lightning" trucks are rolling off the assembly line at the Russelsheim, Germany, plant.	(see 1948)
1946	England; Ernest Crump's PELICAN ENGINEERING CO. has now outgrown their Pepper Road facilities and move once more, this time to the old tram workshops at Bell Hill, Rothwell.	(see 1952)
1946	Canada; EQUIPMENT SALES & SERVICE COMPANY is founded in Edmonton, Alberta.	(see 2012)
1946	CATERPILLAR TRACTOR COMPANY introduces their first self-propelled scraper, the DW-10.	
1946	Texas; at Goose Creek (Baytown), Mr. Frank Inman is building the "Inman" automobile.	
1946	Texas; the "Roadable" marque motor car is built by the SOUTHERN AIRCRAFT COMPANY of Garland.	
1947	Arthur Leman (1903-1985) begins SOUTHWEST OILFIELD PRODUCTS in Houston, with a new idea for a pump piston.	
1947	**LeTourneau begins marketing the first large rubber tired dozers.**	
1947	Texas A&M graduate, Frank M. Pool starts POOL WELL SERVICE, with only a underfunded roustabout service out in San Angelo.	
1947	April 16; while docked and being loaded with ammonium nitrate and other volatile cargo, the French ship *Grandcamp* explodes at Texas City, TX, killing at least 580 and injuring about 3,500; the ship burns for almost a week.	
1947	PLOMB TOOLS purchases J. P. DANIELSON Co. of Jamestown, NY.	(see 1951)
1947	UNIT RIG is reorganized.	
1947	**A UFO lands near Roswell, NM... or does it??**	
1947	UK; Leslie Smith and Rodney Smith (not related) found LESNEY PRODUCTS, making die-cast industrial parts and pieces.	
1947	Roy Furr (1904-1973) opens the first FURR'S CAFETERIA, in Odessa, TX.	
1947	**BROWN & ROOT build the first offshore platform.**	
1947	Japan; TOYOTA builds their first small car.	
1947	Texas; having left LAMB CHEVROLET in Snyder, Lee Bishop founds BISHOP CHEVROLET in Cross Plains.	
1947	The FORD 8N farm tractor is introduced, as the 2N tractor era ends.	
1947	Guy F. Atkinson begins construction of the McNary Dam, on the Columbia river.	
1947	New Mexico; DALE BELLAMAH begins building houses in Northeast Heights of Albuquerque.	
1947	HALOID agrees to develop the xerographic machine invented by Chester Carlson.	
1947	**The first wells drilled out of the sight of land are drilled by PHILLIPS, in the Gulf of Mexico.**	

1947	Gwinner, ND; local man, Edward G. Melroe, invents the windrow pickup machine for farmers, and starts up the family-owned MELROE MFG. COMPANY, building agricultural equipment, here in town.	
1947	In Longview, TX, Frank L. LeBus, Sr., comes up with what will be known as the LeBus Counterbalanced Spooling System, utilizing grooves on the drum for the wire rope.	
1947	In Shady Grove, PA, Mr. John L. Grove's company, GROVE starts building cranes.	
1947	October 14; dropped from a B-29 bomber, Air Force test pilot Chuck Yeager breaks the sound barrier flying the experimental Bell XS-1 rocket plane (with straight, unswept wings) over Edwards AFB, CA.	
1947	INTERNATIONAL HARVESTER introduces the TD-24, of 180 horsepower, eclipsing the world's largest crawler tractor title from the recently released Allis-Chalmers HD-19.	
1947	The GALVIN MFG. CORP. changes its name to MOTOROLA, INC.	
1947	**Henry Ford and Billy Durant both die this year, talk about the end of an era.**	
1947	A young Texan, David Pace, creates a new hot sauce, and coins English use of the word *picante,* which means "stinging" or "biting" in Spanish.	
1947	Elmer's Glue-All is introduced by BORDENS.	
1947	Daniel W. Varel establishes VAREL MANUFACTURING COMPANY to make and market oil well drill bits.	
1947	**INGERSOLL-RAND & CLARK design the first centrifugal compressor for natural gas.**	
1947	Texas; with a couple of old drilling rigs and borrowed money, William P. "Bill" Clements, Jr., and I. P. Larue found SEDCO.	(see 1955)
1947	In Sweden, HIAB introduces the Hiab-19, the first ever regular production vehicle-crane.	
1947	On Guadalupe Street in Austin, the first DAIRY QUEEN in Texas opens for business.	(see 1951)
1947	FORD MOTOR CO. seriously considers buying the VOLKSWAGEN CO., but decides against doing so.	
1947	Ed B. Williams, Jr., establishes WILLIAMS BIT & TOOL COMPANY to provide the oil industry with new diamond bits and new drilling techniques.	
1947	In Wichita Falls, TX, WICHITA CLUTCH is founded to be the sole supplier of clutches for WILSON MFG. COMPANY for their oil-well service and drilling rigs.	
1947	Former RCMP John B. Denison and his brother buy a ex-military Marmon-Herrington all-wheel drive truck and begin trucking through the snow and across the frozen lakes of the Northwest Territories of Canada, becoming the first "Ice Road Truckers."	
1947	Gifford Parker's son Robert L. Parker joins PARKER DRILLING COMPANY.	(see 1949)
1947	March; the REYNOLDS, WILLIAM, & NOONAN CONST. COMPANY begins work on the Town Bluff Dam (Dam B) in Tyler and Jasper counties of East Texas.	
1947	February 13; after a string of 133 "dusters," costing some $23 million , Vern "Dryhole" Hunter brings in the Leduc No. 1 for IMPERIAL OIL COMPANY, subsidiary of STANDARD OIL OF NEW JERSEY. Producing 1,000 bpd from the Devonian reef, the Leduc No. 1 opens the oil boom in Alberta, Canada.	
1947	Dutch businessman Ben Pon travels to Minden, Germany, to look into the possibility of importing Volkswagens to the Netherlands. While in Germany, Pon sketches an idea he has for a transport vehicle, "an oblong box on wheels," rear-engined, same as the VOLKSWAGEN beetle. Someone did pay attention to him.	(see 1950)
1947	Netherlands; the artificial kidney machine is invented by Willem Kolff.	

1947	Texas; Gordon McLendon and his father form Liberty Broadcasting System, and establish radio station KLIF in the Oak Cliff subdivision of Dallas.	
1947	Belgium; Bernard Van Hool establishes Van Hool NV company at Koningshooikt; someday to be one of the major bus and truck builders of Europe.	
1947	Soon after being discharged from the Army, Red Adair goes to work for Myron Kinley, putting out oil well fires.	(see 1951)
1947	Mound, MN; the Mound Metalcraft Co. makes and sells their first Tonka Toys.	
1947	Farny and Weidmann establish Farymann Diesel in Germany.	
1947	By now, Rolls Royce autos and commercial vehicles are equipped with radiators utilizing individually replaceable cooling tubes.	
1947	Nestlé merges with Maggi, a large maker of seasonings and soups.	
1947	Edward Lowe asks his cat-loving neighbor to try a dried, granulated clay (used to soak up oil spills in shops) as litter for his housecat. Thus the oil-absorbing material becomes cat litter.	

1947	Texas; J. E. Hancock has always looked for better ways to do his farming and earth-tending, now, while farming near Lubbock, he has invented the "Elevating-Terracer." This year Hancock establishes the Hancock Manufacturing Co. to build the scrapers.	(see 1953)
1947	September; the US Army Air Force separates from the army and becomes the US Air Force.	
1947	The first "Jim's" restaurant opens in San Antonio, TX.	

1947	Japan; in post-WWII Tokyo, in a bombed out building, Sony begins business as a radio repair shop.	
1947	The Duck Inn restaurant on the waterfront in Rockport, TX, opens for business; GREAT service, serving GREAT food.	(see 2007)
1947	The US Government sells the "Big Inch and Little Inch" pipelines to Texas Eastern Transmission Company. Texas Eastern immediately converts both to natural gas pipelines.	
1947	Chrysler increases output and puts eleven new plants in production from now through 1950.	(see 1950)
1947	Lima merges with General Machine Corporation of Hamilton, OH; thus we now have Lima-Hamilton.	
1947	South Korea; the original Hyundai Company is founded as a construction company.	
1947	Lovejoy purchases the Variable Speed Pulley Line.	
1947	Robert's chainsaws are catching on; McCulloch Motors sales are one million dollars.	(see 1950)
1947	Hammermills, Inc. is founded in Chicago, IL, USA.	(see 1965)
1947	Hewlett Packard incorporates this year.	(see 1958)
1947	Texas; on Robstown's Avenue "A," or FM 665, Joe Cotten opens his beer joint and gambling hall, tossing in some of his barbecue to keep 'em from going hungry.	(see 1969)
1947	December 14; Nascar is founded as Big Bill France meets with a group of 35 drivers, owners, and mechanics at Daytona Beach's Streamline Hotel.	
1947	The first producing oil well on the Outer Continental Shelf off Louisiana is brought in by Kerr McGee.	
1947	The first real Nascar race is run... and a bootlegger's car wins.	
1947	Shell Oil awards a $100,000 contract to Flint Rig for waterflood systems in oil fields around Benton, IL.	(see 1949)
1947	France; Samiia is founded to manufacture and market hoists primarily for mining use.	(see 1990)

1948	McClure Machinery (Dub McClure) is now the Allis-Chalmers heavy equipment dealer in Abilene, TX.	
1948	Bucyrus Corp. buys Milwaukee Hydraulics Corp.	
1948	In spite of the over-confidence of Republicans, and some newspapers, Democrat Harry Truman is elected to his first full term as President, defeating Thomas Dewey.	
1948	Gary Vermeer establishes Vermeer Manufacturing Co. to build his modified farm wagon with a mechanical hoist.	
1948	**Oil is discovered just North of Snyder, TX, and the town of 4,000 grows to 12,000 in just a few weeks.**	
1948	Holmes Thurmond of Marshall, TX, builds what is to become known as the first "bass boat." It is a small wooden boat, and because it "zips around like a mosquito," it is called a "skeeter." The first ones built to sell, are sold by a boat dealer in Shreveport, LA. This evolves into the Skeeter Boat Company.	
1948	Santa Fe International drills its first international well… in Venezuela.	
1948	**March; at Tinker Air Force Base, OK, the first tornado warning siren is heard.**	
1948	Parker Hoses is founded.	
1948	Mooney Aircraft is established.	
1948	**Lesney Products make their first Matchbox die-cast toy, an Aveling-Barford road roller.**	
1948	June; discharged from the US Navy, a 24 year old George H. W. Bush begins his "oilfield career" working in Ideco's Odessa store.	
1948	Influenced by Lockheed's P-38 Lightning fighter plane, Harley Earl places some small tail fins on the '48 Cadillacs, starting a trend to last more than a decade.	
1948	Oklahoma; George E. Failing's monthly payroll in Enid is over $80,000. A little Failing 914, the first rotary drilling rig in Saudi Arabia, goes to work drilling water wells.	
1948	At about 80 Billion barrels, estimated to be the largest conventional oil field on earth, the Ghawar Field is discovered in Saudi Arabia.	
1948	Pettibone-Mulliken Co. buys Universal Crusher Co., in a parallel deal P-M is buying Hammermills, Inc., which is merged into Universal Crushers.	(see 1949)
1948	Standard Oil of New Jersey and Socony-Vacuum Oil join SoCal and Texaco as owners of Aramco.	
1948	Howard Hughes, Jr., flies his $18 million birch wood plane, the "Spruce Goose" for about a mile, 30 feet over the water, then puts it in mothballs.	
1948	Maytag introduces the automatic washer.	
1948	**The Western Co. introduces hydraulic fracturing, a new well stimulation technique.**	
1948	UK; after service in the Royal Air Force, John Cooper and his father, Charles, form John Cooper Works, home of the "Mini."	
1948	The war over, the US government privatizes Daingerfield Steel, (the underutilized steel mill in East Texas). A group of Dallas businessmen buy it and rename it Lone Star Steel.	
1948	Loral Corp. is formed by William Lorenz and Leon Albert, as a small defense electronics manufacturer.	
1948	Centaur Tractor is deep in debt, and is taken over by LeRoi and becomes the Centaur Division of LeRoi.	
1948	June; the transistor is invented at Bell Telephone Laboratories.	

1948	DELTA DRILLING CO. of Tyler, TX, begins drilling in the Rocky Mountain region and opens a regional office in Denver.	
1948	BLAW-KNOX acquires the FOOTE CO. developer of the ADNUN paver.	
1948	The FRANK G. HOUGH CO. introduces its model HM, the first known 4-wheel-drive, rubber-tired loader.	
1948	**New York; ALCO builds its last steam locomotive at its Schenectady plant.**	
1948	**GARLOCK begins experimenting with PTFE (Teflon), as a bearing material.**	
1948	John T. Hayward, chief engineer for BARNSDALL OIL CO., has an idea and designs the submersible Breton rig 20, the world's first movable offshore drilling barge for protected waters. Rig 20 is designed to operable in 20 feet of water and does so for two decades.	
1948	**ALCOA introduces the first forged aluminum wheel for trucks.**	
1948	At age 84, Charles W. Nash dies in Beverly Hills, CA.	
1948	The Soviet's "Berlin Blockade" is overcome by America's Airlift of foodstuffs and medical necessities to Berlin.	
1948	The FLUKE CORPORATION is founded.	
1948	**The PORSCHE automobile is introduced this year.**	
1948	**FORD MOTOR COMPANY introduces the F-series pickup truck.**	
1948	MUSTANG DRILLING is established in Henderson, TX.	
1948	KERR-MCGEE drills the first well to strike oil in the Gulf of Mexico, using a combination of platform and drilling barge.	
1948	Kilgore, TX; Dayton Walkup, son of the founder of AMERICAN SUPPLY CORP., et al, establish KILGORE CERAMICS.	

1948	The first Lightin' mud mixers go to work, blending drilling fluids.	
1948	Houston; STONEBOR, INC. is founded as a manufacturer of hard trim and hard-surfaced flame sprayed parts.	
1948	June 3; self-taught sculptor Korczak Ziolkowski begins chippin' on a mountain near Custer, SD, carving Chief Crazy Horse.	
1948	PARKER-HANNIFIN branches out into the hose making business.	

1948	Weatherford, TX; WEATHERFORD OIL TOOLS, INC. is established, as is WEATHERFORD OIL TOOLS OF CANADA.	
1948	Houston, TX; OTECO is founded to manufacture oilfield valves.	
1948	Quincy, MA; Bill Rosenberg founds the OPEN KETTLE eatery; it is soon known as the first DUNKIN DONUTS store.	(see 1950)
1948	Ohio; aircraft pioneer Orville Wright dies at his home in Dayton.	
1948	CLEVELAND BROTHERS INC. is formed as Bob and Ray Cleveland take over the CATERPILLAR dealership in central Pennsylvania.	
1948	The color-coded system of wire and cable connectors is introduced by THOMAS & BETTS.	
1948	Canada; Gordon E. Steed Sr. and his wife Helene become owners of STANDARD CARTAGE, thus becoming STEED'S STANDARD CARTAGE LTD.	
1948	Rowan reorganizes, with Charlie over ROWAN DRILLING INC. and Arch over ROWAN OIL COMPANY, the production arm.	(see 1950)
1948	Ted Mack, formerly with Major Bowes' *Amateur Original Hour* on radio, begins hosting Ted Mack's *Original Amateur Hour* on four TV networks.	

1948	Arthur Godfrey's *Talent Scouts* moves from radio to CBS television.	(see Nov. 1948)
1948	July; LeTourneau introduces the world's first rubber-tired dozer, the 750 hp Model A-dozer. Although not a commercial success, it is soon followed by successful units from LeTourneau and many more from other heavy equipment manufacturers.	
1948	Minneapolis-Moline introduces their "Powerflow" hydraulic and pneumatic transmission; providing many advantages on their self-propelled harvester.	
1948	October; the first-ever known "thermal inversion" causes 21 deaths in Donora, PA, a small industrial town of 14,000.	
1948	Dallas; Ed McLemore's Sportatorium, at the corner of Cadiz and Industrial begins hosting the *Big "D" Jamboree,* on Saturday nights, to supplement the Tuesday night pro wrestling program.	
1948	All cars running at the Indianapolis 500 this year are running on Dayton wire wheels.	
1948	The first automobile manufacturing plant in Venezuela is a new GENERAL MOTORS facility in Caracas.	
1948	Shreveport, LA; this spring, radio station KWKH launches a new weekly radio program, *The Louisiana Hayride.*	
1948	**The first electric guitar is introduced by Leo Fender, as he debuts his "Broadcaster" solid-bodied electric guitar; later it's renamed the "Telecaster."**	
1948	HEEREMA is established as a construction business in Venezuela.	
1948	Germany; Berlin's Templehof Airport is now being used as a landing field for US aircraft bringing food and coal to the local people, as the USSR has now sealed off West Berlin, compliments of good old "Uncle Joe" Stalin.	(see 2008)
1948	November 13; in Tuckerman, AR, Jim Davidson organizes the first cable television program, the Tennessee and Mississippi college football game. This is just a one program deal, but in a few more weeks Davidson goes farther.	(see Nov. 25th)
1948	November 25; Ed Parsons of Astoria, OR, has just bought a television set. But to receive the signal from KRSC-TV in Seattle, he rigs a large antenna on the roof of the Astoria Hotel, and runs a coaxial cable across the street to his apartment. Ed gets it working today, and soon people are about to crowd him and his wife out of their home, so he runs another cable down into the lobby to another TV set. Before long, the crush of folks in the lobby is creating havoc for the hotel's operations. To solve that problem, Ed begins running cable to various folks' houses around Astoria. And, the community antenna television (CATV) is born. His local system in Astoria is the first in the US to use coaxial cable, amplifiers, and a community antenna to deliver signals to an area that is otherwise unable to receive broadcast television signals. Thus, Ed Parsons is considered to be the "inventor" of cable TV.	(see 1949)
1948	France; in the town of Le Plessis-Belleville, Georges Bataille builds his first hydraulic truck-mounted loader.	(see 1951)
1948	Japan; TADANO IRON WORKS LTD. is founded in Takamatsu to manufacture cargo handling equipment.	(see 1950)
1948	Florida; February 15; on Daytona's "beach-and-road" course, Red Byron, a WWII wounded veteran wins the first NASCAR "sanctioned" race. February 21; NASCAR is incorporated by Big Bill France; he gives himself 50% of the stock.	
1948	Mostly due to the Hydrocrane H-2, BUCYRUS-ERIE purchases the MILWAUKEE HYDRAULICS CORP. and develops the Hydrocrane into larger machines.	(see 1951)
1948	The Welshman Aneurin Bevan establishes a National Health Service for Great Britain.	
1948	The POLAROID CORP., headed by Edwin Land, begins marketing their instant cameras (Polaroid Land Camera) and film; and young Jennifer can see the photos now!!!	(see 1972)

1948	Postwar, GENERAL MOTORS is re-established at Russelsheim, Germany, at Opel.	(see 1950)
1948	About this time, UNIT RIG builds about a dozen very large bucket-wheel type, hydraulic drive, crawler ditching machines, called the "Big Incher" for CRUTCHER, ROLF & CUMMINGS (CRC) This machine is a big hit at the 1949 IPE show here in town.	
1948	Finland; SISU and VANEJA become independent companies as Yhteissisu "un-merges."	(see 1958)
1948	STRATOFLEX, INC., is founded by Ken Davis to manufacture and market flexible hoses and fittings for various industries.	(see 1951)
1948	The "Aerocar," an automobile that really does fly, is built and sold by AEROCAR INC. of Longview, WA, through 1962.	

1949	BALDERSON Inc. is established, building attachments for crawler tractors.
1949	Seventy-five year old J. O. Eaton dies in Cleveland, OH.
1949	Holland; VAN DOORNE builds the first DAF truck.
1949	JOHN DEERE purchases LINDEMAN POWER EQUIPMENT CO. for their line of crawler tractors.
1949	Elmer WAGNER invents the 4wd, articulated tractor.
1949	Oklahoma; Charlie's son, Edwin Malzahn, builds the first DITCH WITCH trencher, and shortly afterwards, he establishes the CHARLES MACHINE WORKS in the town of Perry to build more.

1949	Forecasting the future of computer technology, *Popular Mechanics* magazine predicts that "Computers in the future may perhaps only weigh one and one-half tons."	
1949	PARKER DRILLING opens a Canadian division, with Jim Nabors from Oklahoma as superintendent.	(see 1957)
1949	TEXTRON sales are $68 million this year.	
1949	**AMANA introduces the "side-by-side" refrigerator/freezer.**	
1949	RAY-O-VAC introduces their famous steel Sportsman flashlight.	
1949	JET-LUBE, INC. is formed and creates its specialized drill pipe dope, for rotary drilling operations.	
1949	A. O. SMITH introduces the Harvestore structure of glass-lined steel, for storage of forage for dairy and livestock operations.	
1949	In a hanger in Wichita, KS, Art and Al, the Mooney brothers and two financiers launch MOONEY AIRCRAFT CORP.	
1949	The Hayward-Barnsdall submersible drilling barge goes to work, good for depths to 45 feet, its the only offshore mobile rig in existence for the next few years.	
1949	June 19; Charlotte, NC; no pre-war modified cars are allowed in the first ever NASCAR "strictly stock" race. Eleven-year-old Richard Petty attends with his dad, Lee, who races a borrowed 1946 Buick Roadmaster, and wrecks it. They have to hitch a ride home with some friends.	
1949	After perfecting his air carbon arc torch into a hand-held efficient tool, Myron D. Stepath and some associates found the ARCAIR COMPANY.	
1949	At Rock Springs, WY, a rig using NATIONAL drilling equipment drills to a record depth of 20,521 feet.	
1949	INA develops its breakthrough caged needle bearing to meet the demand for small light bearings in compact German cars.	
1949	Alfred Bloomingdale and a wealthy friend have lunch at an elite restaurant, and neither have enough cash to pay out. This event starts Bloomingdale to begin to set in motion the beginnings of DINER'S CLUB, the first credit card company, at first primarily for wealthy businessmen in NYC. *NOTE: Bloomingdale's wife came to the rescue and bailed them out.*	

1949	In China, defeated Chiang Kai-Shek and his army flee to the island of Formosa (Taiwan). The Communists now take over on the Chinese mainland. Shortly, Mao Tse-tung meets with "Uncle Joe" Stalin in Moscow, promising 100% support of the Soviet's International Communist Policies. Communists worldwide celebrate Stalin's 70th birthday, paying tribute to him as "Champion of Peace," although his every move is warlike and aggressive.	
1949	Texas, October 30; today's "record-setting" four hundred and eighty page *Fort Worth Star-Telegram* weighs seven pounds.	
1949	Washington DC; having heard about Ed Parsons' cable TV system in Astoria, the FCC sends him a letter asking for an explanation of his CATV system. Ed responds in great detail what he has done and how it functions. This is the first known FCC investigation involving cable TV. After a time, an FCC attorney decides that CATV is a common carrier, subject to FCC jurisdiction. However, it will be another sixteen years before the FCC decides to regulate cable TV.	(see 1950)
1949	In Germany, Hans Liebherr builds a tower crane, the first LIEBHERR crane.	
1949	In Shady Grove, PA, Mr. John L. Grove builds a two-ton crane.	(see 1959)
1949	JOHNSON & JOHNSON break off their suture manufacturing business, and name it ETHICON.	
1949	Texas; DELTA DRILLING Co.'s Chapel Hill gas plant (between Tyler and Kilgore) goes on line. Spending $3 million, Joe Zeppa bails out J. C. and acquires the 22 rigs and substantial oil reserves of J. C. HAWKINS DRILLING Co., thus creating DELTA GULF DRILLING COMPANY, and having effectively doubled Delta's size.	
1949	October; with Harold Taft's inaugural five-minute weathercast, he becomes the first TV meteorologist west of the Mississippi, and one of only three in the entire US.	
1949	Seismographs in the USA record atomic explosions in Russia as an A-bomb is tested.	
1949	The US Congress approves to raise the minimum wage to 75 cents an hour, up from 40 cents an hour.	
1949	New York City; Conrad Hilton purchases the famed Waldorf Astoria Hotel.	(see 1979)
1949	EASTMAN KODAK, a division of KODAK, decides to locate a polyethylene plant in Longview, TX.	(see 1950) (see 1976)
1949	The EMSCO DERRICK & EQUIPMENT Co. moves their plant from Dallas, to their large, new modern, facility thirteen miles north, out in the sticks, in Garland, TX.	
1949	USA; the National Bureau of Standards announces the first atomic clock that uses the ammonia molecule as the source of vibration; this clock is built using techniques developed by Isidor Rabi of Columbia University.	(see 1952)
1949	George Balkwill, majority owner, sells his shares of CLEVELAND FROG & CROSSING Co. to PETTIBONE-MULLIKEN, and the firm is soon renamed PETTIBONE OHIO CORPORATION.	(see 1950)
1949	L'Anse, MI; Mr. Phil LaTendresse of LATENDRESSE MFG. Co. develops the Cary-Lift, the world's first extended-reach rough-terrain forklift.	(see 1951)
1949	EUCLID ROAD MACHINERY COMPANY introduces the world's first wheel tractor-scraper having a separate engine powering the scraper wheels. The Euclid 51FTD/13SH is feasible technically by using the Allison "Torqmatic" automatic transmission introduced last year. Each of the Jimmy 6-71's has this transmission behind it… this is the birth of the Euclid Twin Power Concept.	(see 1950)
1949	Azerbaijan; just offshore, at Oil Rocks (Neft Daşları), out in the Caspian Sea, the first oil drilling takes place. This eventually brings about a small city built on pylons out in the sea.	

1949	Across America this year, fifty-one lives are lost as tornadoes, blizzards, and sub-zero cold sweeps across the Midwest. Many cattle are saved from starvation as baled hay is airlifted and dropped on ice-covered fields for feed.	
1949	Entering the Canadian market, FLINT opens an office in Edmonton, Alberta, with sales of $117,000 this year.	(see 1950s)
1949	Los Angeles, CA; the BOULEVARD MACHINE WORKS is now producing small electric "mini-cars," called the BMW.	(see 1966)
1949	Meanwhile, down in San Diego, the T. P. HALL ENGINEERING CO. builds the "Airway," a flying automobile, for a couple of years.	
1949	Richard Nixon's friend, Robert Abplanalp, invents the aerosol valve.	
1949	November 25; the one millionth Cadillac rolls off the assembly line today. Cadillac introduces their first "hardtop," the Coupe de Ville.	
1949	December 3; KRLD-TV goes on the air as Dallas' second TV station. The premier program is the Notre Dame-SMU football game. The new 586 foot KRLD-TV broadcasting tower is the tallest communications tower in the world.	(see 1950)
1950s	During this decade, the TEXAS COMPANY makes several good acquisitions, including SEABOARD OIL CO., PARAGON OIL CO., THE TXL OIL CORPORATION, and the SUPERIOR OIL COMPANY.	
1950s	During the Korean War, the WAYNE PUMP CO. manufactures 60 caliber machine guns and 20mm shells.	
1950s	Throughout this decade, there are more than 1,000 producing oil wells within the city limits of Kilgore, TX.	
1950s	Having worked his way up from dealer to pit boss to shift supervisor, by the early fifties, Sam Boyd has raised enough money to buy an interest in the SAHARA HOTEL in Las Vegas. Sam soon moves on to the MINT in downtown Vegas. Here Sam introduces many new innovations to the business.	(see 1973)
1950s	Sweden; the first chewable multivitamin, the first capsule shaped tablet, the first effervescent laxative formula, and the first instant liquid vitamin mix are only some of the products developed by ASTRA AB during the 1950s. They also develop the first synthetic arterial graft made of tube-knitted Dacron.	(see 1961)
1950s	FLINT RIG adds locations in Colorado, Nebraska, and Kansas, while closing some in Oklahoma and Illinois. Flint's oil field lumber yards are all closed by end of year.	(see 1955)
1950s	Throughout the 1940s and 1950s, DuMont black and white televisions are regarded as the very highest quality; these sets often include built-in AM/FM radios and three-speed phonographs.	
1950s	During the 1940s CONTINENTAL AIRLINES expands its fleet as well as its profits greatly, by participating in WWII by the transporting of military personnel, and continuing on through this decade doing likewise.	(see 1959)
1950s	California; the AUTOETTE ELECTRIC CAR CO. of Long Beach is producing the Autoette, a small electric car used in retirement villages.	
1950s	USA; most coal produced here is now being used by industry, however, many, many, homes continue to be heated by coal.	

Fig. 3   Fig. 4

Fig. 5

INVENTOR
Robert H. Abplanalp
BY
AGENT

1950	Texas; WOOLLEY TOOL CO. expands to Snyder, but after only a short time, both operations are closed as Ned Woolley decides to relocate to the larger oilfield town of Odessa.	
1950	INTERNATIONAL HARVESTER begins selling the four-in-one loader bucket, from Drott Mfg. Co.	
1950	YALE & TOWNE starts building wheel-type front end loaders, using the "YALE" and "TROJAN" brand names.	
1950	CEDARAPIDS purchases the major agricultural equipment manufacturer, NEW HOLLAND EQUIPMENT.	
1950	**Two farmers in Dallas County, AL, conceive the idea of the Bush Hog rotary cutter.**	
1950	BORGWARNER introduces the "Ford-O-Matic" automatic transmission, as well as the Sprag Clutch.	
1950	Longview, TX; LEBUS, INC. now has over 200 patents.	
1950	SCHRAMM introduces the Pneumatractor, a wheeled tractor and air compressor combination unit.	
1950	**BRIGGS & STRATTON introduces the first vertical shaft, aluminum block lawn mower engine.**	(see 1958)
1950	AMERICAN STEEL FOUNDRIES, INC. acquires DIAMOND CHAIN (IC & SC).	
1950	**FORD overtakes CHRYSLER for second place, in the new vehicle sales race. CHRYSLER introduces ignition key-turn starting… no more starter buttons.**	
1950	**CATERPILLAR builds its first overseas plant, in Leicester, England.**	
1950	After 6 years of R & D, HASTINGS begins marketing their oil filters; due to Hastings' Densite filtering media, the successful filters are a good seller.	
1950	In the first 5 years after the end of WWII, Americans have bought an astonishing 14,000,000 automobiles, for a total of 40 million now in use across the country. The "average" American family car travels 12,500 miles each year.	
1950	LeRoi drops the Centaur name for its tractors and introduces the LeRoi "Tractair 125," a 42 hp tractor and 125 CFM air compressor combination unit.	
1950	AETNA OIL CO. of Louisville, is bought out by ASHLAND OIL CO. of Ashland, KY.	
1950	Texas; young Paul C. Koomey starts working for STEWART & STEVENSON in Houston.	
1950	**Paddy Martinez accidently discovers uranium in the Haystack Butte area just west of Ambrosia Lake and Grants, NM.**	
1950	US TIME CORP. introduces the Timex wrist watch, soon news commentator John Cameron Swayze is extolling its virtues, as it "takes a licking and keeps on ticking."	
1950	GREYHOUND now has 6,200 buses on the highways of America, hauling us around.	
1950	"Basically, I'm honest," says Preston Tucker as he is acquitted of charges of mail fraud and such. *"Wal Slim, I dunno, but ah think Tucker is OK, but tha Big Three jest want him outta tha way!"*	(see 1956)
1950	EMPIRE MACHINERY is established as a CATERPILLAR dealer in Arizona.	
1950	Texas; LONE STAR STEEL adds a cast iron pressure pipe factory and expands their operation into a fully integrated steel mill, at a cost of $87 million.	
1950	With all USA domestic industries experiencing a strong economic recovery, THOMASVILLE CHAIR CO. has a very prominent share of the furniture market all across the south.	(see 1958)
1950	PAYNE begins specializing in the manufacture of control systems for blowout preventers.	
1950	Quincy, MA; Bill Rosenberg opens the first DUNKIN DONUTS store.	
1950	The first VOLKSWAGEN Transporter, or Microbus, arrives in the United States.	

1950	Minden, LA; Mr. Lamar Clement and Byron Braswell establish Clement Braswell Trailers, producing dump trailers for carrying sand and gravel from the nearby pits on Dorcheat Bayou.	
1950	Corpus Christi, TX; In a small, portable "box" at 2609 Ayers Street, Mr. Harmon Dobson opens the very first What-A-Burger drive-in hamburger stand; the first What-A Burger patty hits the grill, and the great-tasting legend begins.	
1950	Baldwin-Lima-Hamilton (B-L-H) is the new name of the Lima Locomotive Works.	(see 1951)
1950	Construction begins on the Eastman chemical plant near Longview, TX.	
1950	**The Rowan companies initiate a policy of paid annual vacations for field personnel, heretofore this type of benefit is pretty much *unheard of with drilling contractors in the oilpatch… and it is very slow catching on!!!***	(see 1957)

1950	There are now over 200 active iron foundries in Central Scotland.	
1950	The Sperry Rand Corporation builds Univac 1, the world's first data processing machine.	
1950	September 27; WPAB-TV's remote unit covers a speech by President Harry Truman in downtown Ft. Worth. This is the first remote television broadcast in Texas, and probably the first in the southern US.	
1950	The Southern Pacific Railroad now has 14,000 miles of track, across twelve states.	
1950	In a small two-story building, Radiation Inc. is formed with 4 employees at a former Naval Air Station, in Florida.	
1950	The world's population is approximately 2.33 billion, having essentially doubled during the past century.	
1950	June; Monarch Airlines, flying routes over Colorado, and Challenger Airlines flying over Colorado and Wyoming, as well as Arizona Airways flying over Arizona, all merge to form Frontier Airlines. By the end of the year, Frontier will also have established routes over Missouri, Montana, North Dakota, and Nebraska.	(see 1965)
1950	US natural gas consumption rises to 2.5 trillion cubic feet, more than twice the 1946 usage.	
1950	Culminating decades of controversy, the US Supreme Court declares "…the offshore waters the province of the federal government."	
1950	October; Delta Gulf Drilling Company brings in the H. W. Thompson, kicking off the Hulldale Field, often described as the "best oilfield in the country."	
1950	The 800,000 acre Matador Ranch on the Texas Plains, has been grossing about a million dollars each year. The ranch now sells to non-ranching, New York speculators, for nineteen million dollars.	
1950	USA; James S. Robbins & Associates invents the model 910-101 tunnel boring machine (Mittry's Mole). This 26-foot diameter machine is used to bore a series of tunnels for the Oahe Dam project in South Dakota.	
1950	Layne acquires General Filter, thus expanding into the water treatment business.	(see 1992)
1950	The cardiac pacemaker is invented by Canadian electrical engineer John Hopps. It is an external pacemaker, as it is too large to be implanted in a human body.	
1950	Edgar Rice Burroughs, the creator of Tarzan, dies this year.	
1950	Hull Pottery of Crooksville, OH, suffers a bad flood, followed by a worse fire, but recovers and continues.	(see 1986)
1950	Germany; Opel's annual production again climbs to over 100,000 vehicles, for the first time since the war.	(see 1958)
1950	USA; the American "white-collar" workforce has tripled during the first half of this century.	

1950	There are now about four million television receivers (TV sets) in homes in the United States of America.	(see 1952)
1950	May 1; Robert McCulloch sets up Paxton Engineering to research new product lines. MCCULLOCH MOTORS effects a $2.5 million plant expansion.	(see 1951)
1950	Texas; more from the Piney Woods: the editorial in the first issue of the *Kountze News* states, "Hello Folks, the *Kountze News* is just one day old. It's small, but give it time and it will grow, especially if you subscribe to it quickly. (Only $2 a year) Archer Fullingim, editor." *NOTE: The* Kountze News *succeeds and publishes for the next twenty-five years.*	
1950	WARNER & SWASEY purchase an existing facility in New Philadelphia, OH, equipping the facility for producing Gradalls. They then establish a separate Gradall Division.	(see 1980)
1950	JOHNSTON & JENNINGS is acquired by PETTIBONE-MULLIKEN and will operate as JOHNSTON & JENNINGS DIVISION for the next three decades.	(see 1951) (see 2008)
1950	The Cold War heats up as fighting breaks out in Korea.	
1950	Meanwhile, back at the U. N., "free-world" members are trying to organize against oppression. The "Champion of Peace," Joe Stalin's boy (UN delegate) Vyshinsky fights this organizing, tooth and nail.	
1950	In the May issue, *Popular Mechanics* reports on engineers claiming that they could start building a lunar spacecraft, "…if (only) some agency would finance the project."	(see 1958)
1950	Rock-crusher manufacturer PIONEER ENGINEERING WORKS now builds a 6,000# capacity forklift attachment for the CATERPILLAR D-4, and the INTERNATIONAL HARVESTER T9, TD9, T14, and TD14 crawler tractors.	
1950	August 19; ABC becomes the first television network to air Saturday morning programming aimed specifically at children, with the introduction of *Animal Clinic* and *Acrobat Ranch*.	
1950	Motor City, USA; the population of Detroit, MI, now stands at 1,849,568 persons.	(see 1960)
1950	Japan; TADANO invents and patents a railroad track maintenance machine, starts production, and delivers some units to the JAPAN NATIONAL RAILWAYS.	(see 1955)
1950	EUCLID establishes a British manufacturing subsidiary.	(see 1953)
1950	In the past 120 years, since 1830, 175,000 steam locomotives have been manufactured in the USA. About 37,000, or just over 20% were built specifically for export.	
1950	US President Harry S. Truman awards Bill Lear the 1949 Collier Trophy for his development of the F-5 Autopilot, the first ever for jet planes.	
1950	The Uni-Harvester, a self-propelled combine that can be quickly converted to a self-propelled corn picker/husker, is now introduced by MINNEAPOLIS-MOLINE.	
1950	September 4; Darlington, SC; twenty-five thousand fans attend the inaugural Southern 500 here on the first US asphalt superspeedway.	
1950	This year aspirin is included in the *Guinness Book of World Records* as the best selling painkiller, ever.	
1950	About 228,000 guitars are sold this year in the US.	(see 1971)
1950	Canada; the Calgary Board of Trade is now renamed the Calgary Chamber of Commerce.	
1950	MORRISON-KNUDSEN CO. acquires a financial interest in WOOLDRIDGE MFG. COMPANY.	(see 1958)
1950	For school children, the *Hopalong Cassidy* metal lunchbox from ALADDIN INDUSTRIES debuts this year.	
1950	The Gross National Product of the USA is $300 Billion this year.	(see 1960)
1950	INGERSOLL-RAND now offers a wide range of air hoists for industrial applications.	(see 2010)

1950	The use of central power (rodline and jerker) pumping systems (each system pumping several wells) are now declining and trending toward a "unit pumping" system on each producing crude oil well.	(see 1980)

1950	Connecticut; the "Airphibian" car, is built by CONTINENTAL INC. in Danbury, for the next half dozen years. Does it drive, fly, or swim?	
1951	CAMERON IRON WORKS OF CANADA is established in Edmonton, Alberta.	
1951	**FRAM introduces the dry-type air cleaner to replace the oil-bath type.**	
1951	New York; in Buffalo, H. William Derrick, Jr. founds the DERRICK CORPORATION, building solids control equipment. *"Hey Slim… why doan' he build derricks?"* *"Yeah Bubba, Derrick Derricks has a good sound to it."*	
1951	Texas; over in Arlington, Joe Martin Sr. gears up and opens the first MARTIN SPROCKET & GEAR plant.	
1951	Americans are singing "Old Soldiers Never Die, They Just Fade Away," as President Truman relieves General Douglas MacArthur of his command in the Far East.	
1951	CATERPILLAR purchases the TRACKSON CO., and thus begins CATs line of "Traxcavators" wheeled and tracked loaders.	
1951	BALDWIN-LIMA-HOWARD takes over AUSTIN-WESTERN.	(see 1954)
1951	SANTA FE INTERNATIONAL begins drilling in the Middle East.	
1951	WILLIAMS BROS. completes the last 450 miles of the Tapline (Trans-Arabian pipeline) through Jordan, Syria, and Lebanon.	
1951	January; Ken W. Davis Sr. (later KENDAVIS INDUSTRIES) buys UNIT RIG & EQUIPMENT of Tulsa, OK, from William C. Guier and Ray E. Carter, the two remaining original partners, for $2,000,000. Davis buys Jack and Tom Loffland's substantial interest, and now owns 100% of LOFFLAND BROTHERS DRILLING (the world's largest drilling contractor) as well as Cummins Sales and Service, and several other companies.	(see 1952)
1951	NORTHERN ORDANCE is sold to QUAKER STATE Oil Company.	
1951	US President Harry Truman asks Congress for a tax increase of ten billion (yes B) dollars this year.	
1951	TEXTRON buys HOMELITE (maybe??).	(see 1953)
1951	The 126 year old firm of B. F. AVERY & SONS COMPANY merges with the 86 year old MINNEAPOLIS-MOLINE COMPANY.	
1951	PLUMB HAMMER CO. files suit against PLOMB TOOL CO., after PLOMB introduces a ball peen hammer into their line. PLOMB then has a contest to come up with a new company name, and a lady employee comes up with "PRO-TO," for "Professional Tools"… thus PLOMB becomes… PROTO. *"Yeah Bubba, 'ats all fer them ole PLOMB tools."*	
1951	BELL AIRCRAFT creates a separate helicopter division, headquartered in Ft. Worth, TX.	
1951	**EMD delivers its 10,000th diesel locomotive to the WABASH RAILROAD.**	
1951	BRIGGS & STRATTON introduce the "rewind" starter for its little air-cooled engines.	
1951	**KENWORTH designs the 40 ton model 853 truck for ARABIAN AMERICAN OIL CO., it is so successful, that eventually 1,700 of the 853s are ordered.**	(see 1956)
1951	AMERICAN TRACTOR EQUIPMENT CO., (ATECO) begins building a small line of crawler tractors, known as "TerraTracs."	
1951	Four businessmen in Selma, AL, buy the manufacturing and marketing rights to the BUSH HOG rotary cutter, and begin manufacturing and selling this new machine throughout the southeast US.	

1951	**CHRYSLER introduces the engine with hemispherical heads, their 354 cubic inch "Hemi."**	(see 1952)
1951	BJ buys out the partners in INTERNATIONAL CEMENTING, and renames it BJ SERVICES.	
1951	**PHILLIPS PETROLEUM invents polyethylene plastics.**	
1951	**The B-47, the world's first jet bomber rolls off BOEING assembly lines in Wichita, KS.**	
1951	The first Mooney plane, the M18 is certified in July.	
1951	Dallas, TX; after two decades and being interrupted by the Great Depression and WWII, HIGHLAND PARK VILLAGE, the first real shopping center in the US, is finally opened.	
1951	New Mexico; flying geologists discover the uranium lode on Laguna Indian Reservation land between Grants and Albuquerque that will soon be the ANACONDA Jackpile Mine.	
1951	MILWAUKEE ELECTRIC TOOL CO. introduces the Sawzall.	
1951	About this time KAISER-FRAZER CORP. franchises SEARS, ROEBUCK & CO. to sell the Henry J compact car as the SEARS Allstate Automobile.	
1951	Early in the 1950s HOMESTAKE diversifies into uranium mining and production.	(see 1958)
1951	A new DAIRY QUEEN opens in Henderson, TX. It is still going strong in 2016, the oldest DAIRY QUEEN in continuous operation in Texas.	(see 1953)
1951	Red Adair hires Boots Hansen to work with him and Myron Kinley.	
1951	The first microbes begin appearing that are resistant to penicillin. *". . at didn't take long, did it Bubba????"*	
1951	Texas; WEATHERFORD OIL TOOLS INC. move their general offices to Houston leaving only the manufacturing plant in Weatherford.	
1951	Kilgore, TX; Gore Kemp and Mr. Davis establish the DAVIS-KEMP TOOL CO. INC.	
1951	Texas; Neches River water is deliberately impounded at the unfinished Town Bluff Dam, or Dam "B."	
1951	July 10; in Kaesong Korea, truce talks begin…	
1951	Texas; down in Corpus Christi, twenty-seven year old Oscar Wyatt forms HARDLY ABLE OIL CO., with a $800 loan, using his 1949 Ford car as partial collateral. This is the foundation of COASTAL STATES GAS PRODUCING COMPANY.	(see 1985)
1951	Sweden; the waxed cardboard milk cartons with "pull-out" spouts are invented by Ruben Rausing.	
1951	The first IKEA catalog is mailed out to prospective buyers.	
1951	Texas; LONE STAR INDUSTRIES puts its new cement plant online at Maryneal, in Nolan County.	
1951	WAYNE PUMP CO. merges with MARTIN & SCHWARTZ and moves to Salisbury, MD.	
1951	May; twenty-six-year-old Mac Wiseman celebrates his birthday by recording his first sides for DOT RECORDS in Nashville.	
1951	DART TRUCK CO. introduces the world's largest truck, a 600 hp, 75-ton capacity, off-road haul truck, powered by a pair of 300 horsepower BUDA diesel engines.	
1951	The RAPIER CO. of the UK sets a size record with its W1400 walking dragline, with a 15. 3 m³ bucket and 85. 9 m long boom. *NOTE: The tubular framework of its lattice boom is pressurized, thus any drop in pressure indicates the presence of hairline cracks.*	
1951	France; POCLAIN's Georges Bataille carries out the world's first trials of a towed, fully-hydraulic excavator/loader, developed primarily for farm use. The POCLAIN model TU is powered by the towing tractors hydraulic system.	(see 1960)
1951	UK; BRITISH MOTOR COMPANY (BMC) is formed as AUSTIN merges with NUFFIELD, the producer of Morris-Commercial trucks.	

1951	This spring, oilman Sid Richardson flies to Paris, France, to try to talk Four Star General Dwight Eisenhower into running for President; Sid even pledges three million dollars to Ike's campaign. This July, Ike resigns from the US Army and runs for the office of President of the United States of America.	
1951	Texas; Le Tourneau's own steel mill goes on-line. Steel plates from ¾" to 8" thickness are rolled out right here in Longview.	
1951	LEYLAND MOTORS LTD. takes over ALBION MOTORS, and right away begin phasing out most of Albion's heavy truck production.	
1951	UK; the BSA Group purchases TRIUMPH MOTORCYCLES, making BSA the world's largest producer of motorcycles.	

1951	The use of polyurethane insulation in refrigerated trailers is pioneered by UTILITY TRAILER CO.	
1951	McCULLOCH MOTORS' four million dollars in sales is mostly due the chainsaw's success.	(see 1954)
1951	ESAB sets up in France, and begins production in a new electrode plant in Perstorp, Sweden.	
1951	October 20; today on television, the COLOMBIA BROADCASTING SYSTEM (CBS) eye logo is first shown.	
1951	**Marion Donovan patents the disposable baby diaper.**	
1951	On the Brazos River in Central Texas, the newly constructed Whitney Reservoir is slowly filling with water, inundating the little town of Towash and other villages.	
1951	Because of the hard maple wood in Maine's northern forests, the LUFKIN RULE COMPANY purchases the ANSON STICK CO. of North Anson, ME.	(see 1955)
1951	PACIFIC INTERMOUNTAIN EXPRESS (PIE) has their IPO, making a total of only five truck lines ever having done so.	(see 1956)
1951	BUCYRUS-ERIE introduces the H-3 Hydrocrane, a three ton crane which can also be set up as a truck-mounted backhoe, the Hydrohoe.	
1951	UK; as AUSTIN-MORRIS merges with MORRIS COMMERCIAL LTD. (the BMC Bunch). Their trucks start developing along very similar lines.	(see 1956)
1951	Wisconsin; Eliason has evolved from their wooden, front-engine toboggans, to rear-engine steel models, strongly influencing later snow vehicle manufacturers.	
1951	Michigan; PETTIBONE Co. is founded in L'Anse. PETTIBONE then acquires the ROME GRADER DIVISION from UTICA FORK & HOE CORPORATION. PETTIBONE also acquires manufacturing and marketing rights to the LaTendresse extended reach, rough terrain forklift, production will remain in L'Anse until 1967, when it is moved to Baraga, MI. As MANDT MANUFACTURING is acquired by PETTIBONE-MULLIKEN. The Mandt line of loaders gives rise to Pettibone's "Speed Swing" wheel loader line, as well as the "Speedall" line of loaders.	(see 1953)
1952	January; EMSCO DERRICK & EQUIPMENT COMPANY changes its name to EMSCO MANUFACTURING COMPANY. In September, EMSCO MFG. CO. acquires the swivel joint line from RASMUSSEN MFG. COMPANY.	
1952	Max Cline leaves DART and forms CLINE TRUCK MFG. CO.	
1952	FRANK G. HOUGH CO. merges with INTERNATIONAL HARVESTER COMPANY.	
1952	The W. W. GRAINGER *MotorBook* now has 104 pages.	
1952	Peter Bawden establishes BAWDEN DRILLING LTD.	

1952	About this time, Robert O. Anderson and MALCO purchase the old WILSHIRE OIL CO. refinery in Los Angeles, with help from GULF OIL, after reaching an agreement with GULF to refine about 20,000 bpd of Kuwait imported oil for them.	
1952	The SCHWEITZER turbocharger is introduced at the Indy 500, as AG KKK is developing turbochargers in Germany.	
1952	This year and next, the "Allstate," a re-badged version of KAISER FRAZER's "Henry J American" automobile is being offered for sale through the SEARS, ROEBUCK & CO. CATALOG. A primary drawback is that Sears doesn't accept trade-ins.	
1952	Ben Alexander establishes DA & S OIL WELL SERVICING in Hobbs, NM.	
1952	March; the first products are shipped from the EASTMAN CHEMICAL plant at Longview, in the East Texas piney woods.	
1952	March 21; Cleveland, OH; fueled and strengthened by the strange new sound of rock and roll, frenzied young fans storm the arena and Alan Freed's Moondog Coronation Ball ends in a riot. This event is considered by many to be the "Birth of Rock and Roll."	(see 1986)
1952	NATIONAL CASH REGISTER acquires CRC, of Hawthorne, CA.	
1952	**Tex Johnston makes the first test flight in a BOEING B-52 bomber.**	
1952	STAR DRILLING MACHINE COMPANY and KEYSTONE PORTABLE STEAM DRILLER COMPANY merge to form STARDRILL-KEYSTONE COMPANY.	
1952	SCHLUMBERGER buys 50% of FOREX DRILLING.	
1952	ROBERT BOSCH GmbH and REXROTH both get into hydraulics manufacturing in 1952 and 1953.	
1952	ALLIS-CHALMERS MFG. CO. acquires LAPLANTE-CHOATE MFG. CO.; but maintain LaP-C model designations.	
1952	CLARK EQUIPMENT CO. sets up its Construction Machinery Division.	
1952	Houston; Otis Massey, Frank Turner and Earl Calkins found MUSTANG TRACTOR & EQUIPMENT CO. as a CATERPILLAR dealer.	
1952	CATERPILLAR introduces its No. 6 shovel, the first integrated-design track-type, front-end loader.	
1952	STEWART & STEVENSON introduce their BOP control system, the first modern system.	
1952	BRANIFF's domestic route expansion is accomplished with their merger with MID-CONTINENT AIRLINES.	
1952	H. C. SMITH OIL TOOL COMPANY initiates its forge plant operation.	
1952	France; SOGETRAM is established as a underwater contractor and before long it will be the world's largest.	
1952	Houston; in a rented warehouse Paul C. Koomey with two other S & S employees to help him begin the first operations of STEWART & STEVENSON OILTOOLS.	
1952	CHURCH's starts cooking chicken.	
1952	**BUCYRUS-ERIE introduces the first commercially successful pneumatic rotary blast-hole drill.**	(see 1969)
1952	**JUSTICE BROTHERS originate the world's first transmission stop-leak additive for automotive transmissions.**	
1952	Granbury, TX; the BRAZOS DRIVE-IN THEATRE opens, it will continuously operate well into the next century.	
1952	**The hydrogen bomb (H-bomb) is developed in the USA.**	
1952	With 450 affiliated stations, Gordon McLendon's LIBERTY BROADCASTING SYSTEM is the second largest radio network in America.	
1952	The first television commercial to sell a toy hits the airwaves, advertising Hasbro's Mr. Potato Head.	

1952	In Canada, Volkswagen of Canada is established.	
1952	Canada; off-road haul trucks in Labrador are now equipped with the radiators with individually replaceable cooling tubes.	
1952	The Nineteen Hundred Corporation (later Whirlpool) introduces the first top-loading automatic washing machine.	
1952	Gold Bond Stamp revenue reaches a million dollars this year.	(see 1968)
1952	Electric steam irons are in wider use about this time.	
1952	June 30; the radio soap opera, *The Guiding Light*, debuts on CBS television.	
1952	Lacks now has five stores committed to marketing furniture and appliances, but still carrying some auto supplies and hardware items.	
1952	The National Grape Cooperative Association, Inc. acquires Welch's.	
1952	Kewanee Ross is the new name of the Ross Heat Exchanger Company.	
1952	Jupiter space exploration missiles for the US Army, are being built by the Chrysler Corp.	
1952	Founder Richard Corbitt retires, and Corbitt ceases volume production of trucks.	
1952	Trucks are now moving 16% of all land-moved freight across the US, indicating steady growth of trucking and increased competition for the railroads.	
1952	The truce talks continue in Kaesong, Korea…	
1952	Rev. Rex Humbard has the first weekly nationwide television evangelistic program in the USA.	(see 1953)
1952	Scientist Albert Einstein is offered the presidency of Israel when President Chaim Weizmann dies, but Einstein declines.	
1952	Mid-year, R. G. LeTourneau, Inc. and Dempster Brothers introduce the TournaDiggster attachment for LeTourneau's Super "C" tractor. This unit uses hydraulics for the lift and crowd, but hydraulic problems soon doom the project. All of R. G. 's future wheel loaders will have electric motors and rack and pinion movements.	
1952	One of the world's first jetliners, Comet I cruises at 500 miles per hour, halving the flight time between London and Johannesburg, South Africa, to about 23 hours. Most piston-powered commercial planes now top out about 300 mph, while the Comet I has four gas-turbines that can output 20,000 horsepower total, the most powerful piston aero engines can only make about 14,000 horsepower.	
1952	LeTourneau dealer Joseph L. Rozier Machinery Company relocates its operations from the Midwest to Orlando, as the Caterpillar Tractor Company dealer for central Florida.	(see 1970s)
1952	**Having handily whupped Adlai Stevenson, General Dwight D. Eisenhower is elected President of the United States.**	
1952	IH brings out their Farmall Super MTA, based on the old Farmall M, the MTA boasts a "torque amplifier." This two-speed planetary transmission in front of the 5 speed transmission. This is the first "shift-on-the-go" tractor transmission ever, and it is a real hit!!! In thirty-six months time, about 22,000 new Super MTA tractors are sold.	
1952	England; Ernest Crump's only son, twenty-two year old Bob has finished his British military obligation, and joins Pelican Engineering Co. as the firm's first ever salesman. Bob's focus is putting more Foden trucks on the roads; and he does just that. Due in no small part to Bob Crump, Foden will someday be the UK's foremost supplier of trucks to the construction industry.	(see 1968)
1952	Grand Old Opry star and hillbilly fiddler Uncle Dave Macon passes away.	

1952	Ken Davis forms PIONEER WELL SERVICES LTD., providing well completion and workover services all across the Permian Basin.	
1952	Canada; desiring to broaden the exploration season in the far north, IMPERIAL OIL LTD. has designed a wide-tracked vehicle for hauling men and supplies, and Imperial gets Bruce Nodwell to build it. The vehicle doesn't work very well and neither do its successor vehicles, so Imperial shuts down the project, although Bruce is certain the basic concept is good.	(see 1954)
1952	The US National Bureau of Standards announces the first atomic clock using cesium atoms as the vibration source (this clock is known as NBS-1).	(see 1954)
1952	Illinois; the ALTORFER BROTHERS COMPANY (ABC) is bought by NASH-KELVINATOR, and begin manufacturing products under the "Kelvinator" brand as well as the others.	(see 1957)
1952	UK; having outgrown its Biscot Road plant, COMMER moves to a new factory in Dunstable, west of Luton.	(see 1992)
1953	January; twenty-nine-year-old hillbilly singer Hank Williams, Sr., dies.	
1953	January; Dwight David Eisenhower is sworn in as America's 34th President. Ike is the first president to be a licensed airplane pilot.	
1953	**MIXERMOBILE introduces the world's first ever articulated frame wheel loader, the SCOOPMOBILE LD-5.**	
1953	GENERAL MOTORS takes over EUCLID EQUIPMENT.	(see 1959)
1953	LeTourneau sells his earthmoving equipment business to WABCO, thus comes LETOURNEAU-WESTINGHOUSE equipment.	
1953	Evangelist Dr. Billy Graham asks his friend R. G. LeTourneau to design and build a structure capable of being assembled and disassembled for transport, for a crusade series around England. R. G. did; the prototype (300'dia X 85'high w/capacity of 12,000) is built in Longview, TX, to be first used in a Michigan Crusade, however Michigan's building inspector nixed it, and England soon follows suit. R. G. keeps it and builds four more, all in use at LeTourneau's Longview, TX, plant. *"Bubba, these aluminum domes are the now familiar 'Tourneau Titties.'"*	
1953	April; Mr. Charles Deere Wiman, president of DEERE & CO. has his engineers begin working on a new generation of tractors to replace the extremely reliable old "Poppin' Johnny" two-bangers. He stresses they need only carry over the green and yellow paint.	(see 1956)
1953	WHITE MOTOR CAR COMPANY buys AUTOCAR and moves it to Exton, PA.	
1953	May 11; an old Indian legend tells that the Waco, TX, area will never be hit by a tornado. Today a monster twister tears through five miles of Waco, including two miles of the downtown area, almost two hundred commercial buildings are leveled, one hundred and fifty homes are demolished, one thousand and ninety-seven persons are injured and one hundred and fourteen are killed. The total damage exceeds fifty million dollars. *"Yeah Slim, 'at's right, so much fer old Injun legends!"*	
1953	Carter and Ralph, the bluegrass singing Stanley Brothers, sign to record for Mercury Records, Carter Stanley dies later this year.	
1953	CATERPILLAR TRACTOR CO. creates a separate sales and marketing group for their engines.	
1953	ROLLS-ROYCE enters the civil aviation market.	
1953	Michigan; CLARK EQUIPMENT COMPANY acquires the MICHIGAN POWER SHOVEL CO. and at Benton Harbor establishes its CONSTRUCTION MACHINERY DIVISION.	

1953	Once the Rolls Royce of motorcycles; INDIAN MOTOCYCLES folds its teepee, giving in to HARLEY DAVIDSON. This is the end of the classic Indian Motocycles; as well as the end of the Harley and Indian war.	(see 1954)
1953	KAISER-WILLIS is now the firm building jeeps.	
1953	DELTA DRILLING COMPANY, headquartered in Tyler, TX, moves their Rocky Mountain regional office from Denver, CO, to Casper, WY. DELTA begins drilling in Spain this year, and young Joe Hendrix is a truck driver over there for them.	
1953	ALLIS-CHALMERS CORPORATION buys BUDA CORPORATION, an old industrial engine manufacturer. BUDA will be operated as a division for a few years, during which some engines will be branded Allis-Chalmers-Buda.	
1953	April 3rd; the first issue of *TV Guide* magazine hits the shelves, on the cover is Lucille Ball's new baby, Desi Arnaz IV. *TV Guide* will soon become the most popular weekly magazine in America.	(see 1953)
1953	TEXTRON buys its first non-textile business, BURKART MANUFACTURING COMPANY of St. Louis, MO.	
1953	Starting a new profession, Roger Jensen begins storm chasing.	
1953	WIX manufactures the first "750" type oil filter housing with a "T" handle, to facilitate changing an oil filter without tools.	
1953	**MAYTAG introduces its first electric clothes dryer.** *"Humm, 'lectric clothes, ya better be careful 'bout getting' 'em wet ennie how!"*	
1953	Laguna Indian Reservation, NM; ANACONDA starts operations of what will someday be one of the largest open-pit uranium mines in the world, the JACKPILE MINE.	
1953	Mr. George Failing, with over 300 patents to his credit, all retained by his company, sells GEORGE E. FAILING CO. to WESTINGHOUSE AIR BRAKE COMPANY (WABCO).	
1953	Based in Dallas, Hal Darr acquires a CATERPILLAR franchise, and establishes DARR EQUIPMENT CO. as the CATERPILLAR dealer, covering a very large portion of northeast Texas.	
1953	ASEA invents synthetic diamonds.	
1953	NATIONAL CASH REGISTER establishes an electronics division.	

	1953	CRANE CARRIER CORPORATION begin building their own specialized heavy-duty mobile equipment, trucks and chassis.	
	1953	Hugh and Bill, the Liedtke brothers, and George H. W. Bush found ZAPATA PETROLEUM.	
	1953	MOONEY AIRCRAFT CORPORATION moves to Kerrville, TX, to be near the family's dairy operations.	
	1953	**BOEING begins production of the soon-to-be famous B-52 bomber.**	

1953	ROCKET CHEMICAL CO. is trying to create a line of rust-preventers and degreasers for the aerospace industry. Their 40th attempt yields what they call WD-40, which stands for Water Displacement perfected on the 40th try. An early user is CONVAIR to protect the outer skin of the Atlas missile.	
1953	McNEIL LABORATORIES is acquired by JOHNSON & JOHNSON.	
1953	The record depth of 21,482 feet is drilled in the Paloma Field of California.	
1953	HUMBLE OIL CO. grants a license to MARTIN-DECKER to manufacture and market a revolutionary diaphragm which becomes part of the "sensator," replacing a piston load cell.	
1953	Tulsa; MID-CONTINENT SUPPLY (a KENDAVIS Co.) introduces the Golden Driller, the world's largest free-standing statue, at the International Petroleum Exposition.	
1953	In October, PETROBRAS (Petroleum Brasil) is established in Brazil.	

1953	**The Baron Bich of France introduces the first inexpensive, mass-produced ball-point pens, branded the BIC.**	
1953	MASSEY-HARRIS merges with old Harry Ferguson to form MASSEY-FERGUSON.	
1953	GM's Parade of Progress resumes (until mid 1956) across the US. Ten of the twelve Futureliners are still in existence fifty years later.	
1953	June; Mr. and Mrs. Lewis Ackers of Abilene, TX, buys the construction permit from REPORTER BROADCASTING CO. (RBC) for a television station for Abilene. Mid-August; KRBC TV begins its broadcasting from temporary quarters in Cedar Gap, south of Abilene.	
1953	After 121 years, farm implements are no longer built by DAVID BRADLEY, although Sears will continue to sell implements with the David Bradley name.	(see 1966)
1953	RAMEY MANUFACTURING CO. of Two Harbors, MN, now produces a direct-copy of the free-swing log jammers being built a decade ago. RAMEY is building the first truck mounted, all-cable, self-loader, using seven winches in all. Soon RAMEY is replacing various winches on their equipment with hydraulic cylinders.	
1953	CHICAGO & SOUTHERN AIR LINES merges with DELTA AIRLINES.	
1953	Texas; GREATER FT. WORTH INTERNATIONAL AIRPORT (Amon Carter Field) opens for business.	
1953	WINTERS THERMOGAUGES, LTD. is established.	
1953	James Watson and Francis Crick discover the unique double-spiral structure of DNA.	
1953	CADILLAC and OLDSMOBILE introduce 12 volt automotive electrical systems to the US.	
1953	Deep in East Texas in the edge of the Big Thicket, Dam "B" and Lake Steinhagen are finally completed.	
1953	The first DANNY'S DONUT SHOP is opened, soon there will be fifteen of those shops.	(see 1959)
1953	With 14,000 employees, SERVEL is the largest employer in Evansville, IN.	
1953	France; Citroën and Panhard automobiles merge their sales networks.	
1953	The first dual sided gasoline pump is introduced by WAYNE PUMP COMPANY.	
1953	**For the first time, sales of automatic washing machines surpasses sales of wringer-type machines.**	
1953	From their Lubbock, TX, plant, HANCOCK MFG. CO. will produce several newer, larger, more efficient scrapers over the next three decades.	(see 1966)
1953	CBS launches the EPIC record label.	
1953	Their first hydraulic excavator for construction digging use is introduced by POCLAIN.	
1953	In Winters, TX, Charles R. "Pinky" Pinkerton opens WINTERS WELDING WORKS.	(see 1982)
1953	Augsburg, Germany; the M. A. N. WORKS Museum is founded for M. A. N. diesel engine and printing press activities.	
1953	Canada; having been recently bought by the KOEHRING CO. of Milwaukee, WATEROUS LTD. is now known as KOEHRING-WATEROUS.	(see 1988)
1953	Brazil; ESAB-BRAZIL is now established.	
1953	Art Wooly and T. C. Pierce pull a 302 pound, 7½ foot long alligator gar from the Nueces River, near Cotulla, TX. *"Yeah Bubba, thet 'uns big enuf tuh be a reel gater, not jest a gar!!"*	
1953	**Affiliated with the University of Houston, the first television station in the nation to present educational programming is station KUHT-TV in Houston, TX.**	

1953	The National Auto Auction Association (NAAA) is organized.	(see 1995)
1953	Pettibone acquires Wood Manufacturing Company, calling it their Road Machinery Division.	(see 1956)
1953	The first Canadian Dairy Queen opens in Estevan, Saskatchewan.	(see 2009)
1953	Using its four prop-engine DC-7 planes, American Airlines inaugurates the first non-stop transcontinental service, coast-to-coast, in both directions.	(see 1961)
1953	Euclid is now a $33 million business, with 1,600 employees turning out 170 off-highway vehicles each month, making this company the market leader in bottom-dumps and off-highway trucks. Also this year, General Motors buys Euclid from the founding Armington family for $22 million in GM stock… this "takeover" immediately attracts the attention of the US. Department of Justice.	
1953	Although combines (combined harvesters) have now been around for three decades, Case finally builds their last threshing machine.	
1953	**The Harley Earl-designed Chevrolet "Corvette," debuts at the MotoRama.**	
1953	Texas; relinquishing the Ford and Lincoln-Mercury franchise, Frank Kent gets the local Cadillac distributorship, continuing business as Frank Kent Motor Co., now the Cadillac dealer in Ft. Worth.	(see 1967)
1953	Texas; Having acquired plants in Midland and Abilene, in addition to the Waco plant, Central Texas Ironworks now incorporates.	(see 1958)
1953	Pennsylvania; TB Wood's Sons begin marketing their mechanical variable speed-belted drives as well as its "Sure-Flex" couplings.	(see 1968)
1954	Jan; when Tom Braniff tragically dies in a private plane crash, Fred Jones of OKC becomes CEO of Braniff Airways.	
1954	Lockheed Aircraft introduces the C-130.	
1954	Dresser-Atlas acquires the Lane-Wells Company.	
1954	Cameron Iron Works buys the British Oilfield Equipment Co. of London and Leeds.	
1954	**In Chicago, James Robbins invents the tunnel boring machine.**	
1954	**The 1954 Packard is the first car ever to be sold with factory-installed tubeless tires as standard equipment. Packard merges with Studebaker, but it doesn't really help either of them, it just prolongs their agony.**	(see 1956)
1954	Hudson merges with Nash, to form American Motors Corp.	
1954	Link-Belt introduces the LS-98, one of the most successful pieces of construction equipment ever built, as during the next forty-two years, more than 7,000 LS-98s will be built and sold.	
1954	December; REO Motors Inc. becomes REO Holding Corp.	
1954	Lister begins producing a line of one and two cylinder, air-cooled diesel engines, the LD1 and the LD2.	
1954	The Anglo Persian Oil Company is renamed British Petroleum (BP).	
1954	Stewart & Stevenson develops the Koomey bop control system, named for Paul C. Koomey, head of their oilfield equipment division.	

Aug. 16, 1955   J. S. ROBBINS   2,715,524
BORING HEAD FOR CONTINUOUS MINING MACHINE
Filed June 1, 1954   2 Sheets—Sheet 2

Fig. 2

Fig. 3

INVENTOR.
James S. Robbins
BY
Murray A. Gleason
ATTORNEY

1954	Due to their wide diversification, AMERICAN CAR & FOUNDRY changes its name to ACF INDUSTRIES, INC. (ACF).	
1954	The last all-new HALL-SCOTT engine, the 590 is introduced; it's a great gasoline engine, but can't compete with diesel, so ACF now "spins-off" HALL-SCOTT.	
1954	Recently retired from CUMMINS ENGINES, Clessie Cummins invents the engine brake, and after getting the "cold-shoulder" from the company bearing his own name, he gets JACOBS of drill chuck fame, to manufacture it. Thus, the "Jake Brake" is born.	
1954	**AMANA builds the first window-mounted air conditioner.**	
1954	DAVEY COMPRESSOR CO. introduces their Rotary Drill Division.	
1954	George H. W. Bush buys ZAPATA OFFSHORE from his partners.	
1954	DAYTON RUBBER CORPORATION introduces the famous Dayton Thoroughbred tubeless tire.	
1954	INDIAN is selling the Corgi folding motorcycles, calling them the Indian Papoose. (see 1959)	
1954	About this time, LeRoi is purchased by WABCO, and moved to Sydney, OH.	
1954	**The '55 Thunderbird debuts. Automotive writer Tom McCahill purchases the first one off the assembly line, then races it successfully in the 1955 Daytona Speed Trials.** (see 1975)	
1954	The OFFSHORE CO., a joint venture of SOUTHERN PRODUCTION (later SONAT), J. RAY MCDERMOTT, and DELONG launch the first self-elevating offshore drilling rig, Offshore Rig 51. Using the Delong jacking system, it has 10 legs, each 6' in diameter and 160' tall, standing on large spud cans.	
1954	This year Americans are purchasing 7,000,000 tankfuls of gasoline each day. The truly booming demand for gasoline and other oil products catches all oil companies by surprise. They expected a good boom after the war, but expected nothing like this.	
1954	*Mr. Gus is a Bethlehem designed, self-elevating unit (jack-up drilling rig) built this year for C. G. GLASSCOCK DRILLING CO. intended for operating in up to 100 feet of water.*	
1954	CUMMINS introduces their revolutionary PT (pressure-time) fuel system.	
1954	January 6; Texas; the BUICK-OLDSMOBILE-PONTIAC DIVISION of GENERAL MOTORS Arlington Plant, builds its first vehicle, out "South of Town." Better known as GM Arlington, this plant (46 acres under the roof) will turn out seven and one-half million vehicles by its 50th anniversary.	
1954	DEMAG brings out their first hydraulic excavator.	
1954	PUREMCO is established in Waco, TX, producing dominoes and other games.	
1954	Over the next year or so, ALGORD OIL CO. and CREEK OIL CO. are both "absorbed" into DELTA GULF DRLG. CO.	
1954	RJR TOBACCO introduces Winston cigarettes.	
1954	BLAW-KNOX acquires ALL-PURPOSE SPREADER COMPANY, known as APSCO.	
1954	California; fifty-two-year-old Ray Kroc discovers the McDonald brothers hamburger joint in San Bernadino, and convinces them to let him franchise their system.	
1954	Abilene, TX; contrary to other statements, KRBC TV becomes affiliated with NBC later this year.	(see 1955)
1954	WICHITA CLUTCH is incorporated and becomes a division of WILSON MANUFACTURING CO.	
1954	**The three-barreled Vulcan machine gun is developed, using many ideas from the Gatling Gun.**	
1954	Brazil; SIDERCA S. A. I. C. begins producing oil country tubular goods.	

1954	LeGrand, Ltd. moves some of its manufacturing works to Calgary to take advantage of the booming Canadian oil industry.	
1954	Kroehler Manufacturing, the world's largest furniture maker, acquires Durham Furniture Company of North Carolina.	
1954	USA; the female contraceptive pill is developed by Gregory Pincus and John Rock.	
1954	Phillip Morris buys Benson & Hedges.	
1954	Finally, polyethylene production is started at the Eastman Chemical plant in Longview, TX.	
1954	Briggs & Stratton introduces the aluminum block engine, not cast-iron.	
1954	Vicksburg, MI; on November 11, work commences on LeTourneau's three-legged jack-up rig, the "Scorpion."	(see 1955)
1954	Hickory, NC; Superior Cable Corp. is founded to make plastic-insulated twisted-pair wire, copper cable and wire for the phone industry.	
1954	Caterpillar Tractor Co. introduces their first new crawler in two decades. The 286 horsepower, 58,000 pound, D9 is 40% bigger than any other crawler around. In fact, many construction folks are saying it is too big to sell successfully. Having the first turbo-charged engine ever used in earthmoving equipment, the D-9 easily displaces the A-C improved HD-20, which with its predecessor HD-19 have since 1947 held sway as "the world's largest crawler tractor."	(see 1956)
1954	**Wix patents the "spin-on" oil filter.**	
1954	Wayne Pump Co. acquires Schirmer-Dombriel, and introduces several new products.	
1954	Touting Southern Maid Doughnuts, Elvis Presley makes his one and only ever television commercial.	(see 1955)
1954	Chrysler Corporation begins its revolutionary program of gas turbine engine vehicles.	
1954	Lima-Hamilton merges with Baldwin Locomotive Works, giving us Baldwin-Lima-Hamilton (BLH).	(see 1958)
1954	The McCulloch VS57 supercharger is standard equipment on the Kaiser Manhattan's six cylinder, 226 cid engine this year. During the next few years, the VS57 will be marketed on various Fords, Studebakers and Packards, as well as Kaisers. They will be "aftermarketed" on many other marques.	(see 1957)
1954	Plymouth, OH; after building only 8,717 units, F-R-H finishes the Plymouth "Silver King" farm tractors.	
1956	Jim Cowan sees his first BIG (probably a double) rotary drilling rig in operation, from Hack Drilling Co., of Abilene, TX.	
1954	In South Texas, uranium is discovered in Karnes County.	
1954	After Bell Labs recent invention of the silicon photovoltaic (PV) cell, and AT&T publicity film touts, "It is stern work to thrust your hand into the sun and pull out a spark of immortal flame to warm the hearts of men, yet in this modern age, men have at last harnessed the power of the sun." *"Naw Bubba, it doan ketch on all thet fast."*	(see 1962)
1954	Omaha, NE. one of several firms now building dozer-loader attachments for small Cat and A-C crawlers is our local Teale & Company.	
1954	Montana; folks around Rogers Pass just thought they had been cold before, but this morning the temperature dropped to -69 degrees Fahrenheit. This is the lowest ever recorded in the forty-eight contiguous states. (This record still stands in 2016.)	
1954	Texas; on the Brazos River not far west of Hillsboro, water begins to be impounded behind the new dam at Lake Whitney.	

1954	Canada; with ideas gained by previous experiments, Bruce establishes BRUCE NODWELL, LTD., with the idea to develop and build a six-ton crawler transporter vehicle (truck). About this time his 4' wide track system of rubber belts and steel bars debuts, only exerting +/- 2 psi ground pressure.	(see 1959)
1954	SCHWINN introduces their Jaguar bicycle for $74.95. (You can buy a fairly good used car for that today.) This deluxe bike has a horn, rear carrier, tank, and stainless steel fenders; it is a beauty!	
1954	The clock NBS-1, is moved to NIST's new lab in Boulder, CO.	(see 1955)
1954	Minnesota; HATTEEN HOIST & DERRICK CO. of Roseau, now becomes POLARIS INDUSTRIES working on their own rear-engine snow vehicle. A decade or so in the future, the poorly conceived, front-engine "Comet," almost bankrupts the company.	
1954	Boston; Dr. Joseph Murray performs the first successful internal organ transplant. Identical twins and WWII vets, Richard and Ronald Herrick, are 23 years old, and Richard's kidneys are failing. Ronald donates one of his kidneys in this successful transplant. Richard lives a good life for another eight years, and the donor Ronald lives to age 79, passing in 2010.	
1955	BJ and BORG-WARNER merge.	
1955	KAISER-FRASIER shuts down after selling 2,700,000 cars, and losing $62,000,000… the last WILLIS was in May and the last KAISER is built in June. The KAISER-FRAZER shutdown also marks the end of the Allstate car for SEARS & ROEBUCK.	
1955	In April, BAKER MANUFACTURING is acquired by ALLIS-CHALMERS.	
1955	INTERNATIONAL PARTS DEPOT (IPD) is founded to manufacture "may-fit" aftermarket parts for CATERPILLAR, DETROIT DIESEL, and other diesel engine manufacturers.	
1955	REO HOLDING CORPORATION merges into the NUCLEAR CORPORATION OF AMERICA, INC.	
1955	The Laborde family and other investors build the EBB TIDE, and TIDEWATER MARINE SERVICE is off and running.	(see 1958)
1955	The first major pipeline system in Alaska (625 miles) is completed by WILLIAMS BROTHERS.	
1955	DELTA MARINE DRILLING is established as DELTA's offshore drilling arm.	
1955	SCHRAMM introduces their Rotadrill, proving to be a great success. They also builds their first top head drive rotary drilling rig.	
1955	March 3; Johnny Cash receives his first royalty check ($2.41) today; it from Sam Phillips at Sun Records for "Hey Porter."	
1955	JOY MANUFACTURING is founded in Buffalo, NY.	
1955	LETOURNEAU builds the first practical, usable jack-up rig, the Scorpion (forerunner of modern jack-up) for ZAPATA. Future US. President, George H. W. Bush is president of ZAPATA DRILLING and the Scorpion is only the sixth jack-up rig on earth.	(see 1957)
1955	PHILLIPS drills past 25,300 ft. near Ft. Stockton, TX, a record that will stand for twelve years. PHILLIPS also drills the first wells ever drilled out of sight of land, drilling 40 miles offshore in the Gulf of Mexico, the farthest out yet.	
1955	FORD MOTOR COMPANY introduces the 1956 Continental Mark II. FORD debuts their THUNDERBIRD; it's sort of thrown together to compete with the CHEVROLET CORVETTE. The "T-Bird" sells 14,000 this year, compared to 700 Corvettes sold.	(see 2005)
1955	Ft. Worth, TX, loses its real-life hero when Amon G. Carter, Sr. dies.	
1955	Tom Brown and Joe Roper form TOM BROWN DRILLING CO., INC.	
1955	Texas; Mr. Ashbury Parks starts PARKS EQUIPMENT, in his garage in Odessa.	

1955	Jim Wilden develops the air-operated double diaphragm pump and forms the WILDEN PUMP & ENGINEERING CO.
1955	Houston; PORTA-KAMP starts in business, building… portable camps.
1955	FEDERAL MOGUL merges with BOWER ROLLER BEARING to form FEDERAL MOGUL BOWER BEARINGS, INC.
1955	MARTIN-DECKER receives a patent for a torque-indicating apparatus with a weight sensing attachment for cable anchors.
1955	READING & BATES enters the offshore drilling business.
1955	Edward G. Melroe dies and his sons and son-in-law take over the business.
1955	Because of diversification, ALCO changes its name to ALCO PRODUCTS, INC.
1955	Billy Pugh develops his Billy Pugh Net to safely transfer personnel between boats and platforms and/or rigs.
1955	WAUKESHA-PEARCE INDUSTRIES (WPI) form their construction equipment division.
1955	**Dr. Norman F. Ramsey, a physicist, invents the first atomic clock, accurate to within one second in 300 years.**

1955	**GREYHOUND introduces the Scenicruiser double-decker, the first 40 foot long bus, also the first bus with rest rooms.**	
1955	In Tulsa, OK, the ARROW SPECIALTY COMPANY is founded.	
1955	Having grown very large through acquisitions, THEODORE GARY & CO. and GENERAL TELEPHONE CORP. are the two largest independents in the US, and they merge this year under the GENERAL TELEPHONE COMPANY name.	(see 1959)

1955	The 8th-largest coal company, PEABODY, and the 3rd-largest, SINCLAIR COAL merge and retain the PEABODY name.
1955	Mid-year, there are now estimated to be 60,640 good folks, and a couple of old grouches, living in Abilene, TX.
1955	MALCO WILSHIRE is now the largest independent refiner and marketer in California, grossing $70 million this year.
1955	**There are now over 400 drive-in movie theatres in Texas. Many of these were built, and terraced up, by Denver Watkins of Ballinger.**
1955	SMITH CORONA begins production of the first electric office typewriter and in two more years will produce the first portable electric typewriter.
1955	The Swedish made HIAB knuckle boom loader is introduced to the US. through fab shop owner Bob Larsen of Ely, MN. By late this year Larsen introduces his Hiabob knuckle boom, built on a basic Hiab unit with a few additions of his own.
1955	*Time Magazine* names the Oak Ridge Quartet as "The Largest Drawing Gospel Group" ever.
1955	KERR-MCGEE begins searching for uranium in the Ambrosia Lake area, west of Grants, NM.
1955	Kirchdorf, Germany; LIEBHERR introduces the L-300, a hydraulic wheeled excavator weighing ten tons, with a 3/8 cubic yard bucket.
1955	BUTLER MACHINERY CO. is formed as Francis J. Butler, a former contractor of Grand Forks, ND, becomes a CATERPILLAR dealer.
1955	SELLSTROM (formerly Excell Sales Co.) expands and moves to Palatine, IL.
1955	England; Christopher Cockerell invents the hovercraft.
1955	USA; President Dwight D. Eisenhower suffers a heart attack, and the stock market drops to its lowest since the crash of 1929.

1955	England; Dr. Narinder Kapany invents optical fibers.	
1955	Fifty-eight thousand imported cars are sold in the US this year.	
1955	Houston; Jim Petersen teaches electric motor design at Rice University, and also works nights at the GENERAL ELECTRIC Motor Repair Center to get "hands-on "experience. Jim also starts his own business in his mother's garage; it soon grows into GULF ELECTROQUIP. Yes, before long he quits both his "day jobs."	
1955	Tinley Park, IL; in this Chicago suburb, PANDUIT CORPORATION is established.	
1955	Steelworker's son and steel broker John H. McConnell, borrows $500 against his 1952 Oldsmobile and finances WORTHINGTON STEEL COMPANY.	
1955	Joe Rodgers Jr. and Tom Forkner open the first WAFFLE HOUSE restaurant.	
1955	ZENITH engineer Eugene Polley invents the "flash-matic," a wireless remote control for television.	(see 1956)
1955	December; LeTourneau's 4,500 ton "Scorpion" jack-up rig is launched in the Mississippi River at Vicksburg.	(see 1956)
1955	KEWANEE ROSS becomes ROSS HEAT EXCHANGER DIVISION of AMERICAN STANDARD CORPORATION.	
1955	This is the best sales year ever for PONTIAC.	(see 1962)
1955	**This year for the first time ever, seven-inch 45 rpm singles outsell the old standard ten-inch 78 rpm platters. This is the last year of major production of the 10-inch, 78 rpm recorded disc.**	
1955	Germany; the M. A. N. truck works opens in Munich.	
1955	Texas; APPLIED RESEARCH & DEVELOPMENT COMPANY (ARDCO) is founded, in Addicks, as a manufacturer of all-terrain drill carriers.	(see 1989)
1955	During this decade, UNIT CRANE & SHOVEL introduces the quickly popular Unit Mariner pedestal crane for offshore oil and gas production platforms as well as offshore drilling rigs.	(see 1960s)
1955	MIXERMOBILE MANUFACTURERS introduce the first articulated-frame wheel loaders, their LD-5 and LD-10 models. However this idea doesn't really catch on until later.	(see 1959)
1955	Wisconsin; BELIOT TOOL COMPANY is incorporated by Kenyon Y. Taylor, while he is working from his home, with three friends. Within six months, Taylor moves his business to an abandoned roller rink.	(see 1957)
1955	Smethport, PA; Jim Herzog is grinding magnets for the family toy-making business, SMETHPORT SPECIALTY CO., and he conceives the idea for Wooly Willy. After several month of unsuccessful peddling, a reluctant buyer for G. C. MURPHY CO. agrees to take six dozen for a trial in Murphy's Indianapolis store. The buyer commented that they would probably still have them all after the trial period. A few days later the Murphy buyer calls and orders 1,000 dozen of them.	
1955	Japan; TADANO introduces Japan's first hydraulic truck crane, the OC-2, with a lifting capacity of 2 tons.	(see 1960)
1955	ALLIS-CHALMERS have been building the Gleaner combines for several years; this year, A-C acquires the GLEANER CORP. of grain combine fame. The BAKER MANUFACTURING CO. of Springfield Illinois is also acquired for Baker's attachments for crawler tractors.	
1955	With their 1,400 employees, this is the peak employment year for the LUFKIN RULE COMPANY.	(see 1966)
1955	FLINT RIG enters the well service business in Canada. FLINT moves their US headquarters to Billings, MT.	(see 1957)
1955	November 19; the first issue of William F. Buckley's *National Review* hits the streets.	
1955	FIRESTONE brings out the first tubeless tires for trucks.	

1955	Mr. I. P. Larue sells his portion of SEDCO to his partner Bill Clements for $1. 2 million.	(see 1984)
1955	England; the National Physics Laboratory builds the first cesium-beam clock used as a calibration source.	(see 1958)
1955	TAPPAN introduces the microwave oven, and it will someday revolutionize our cooking.	(see 1960)
1955	The world's first rotary vane air hoist is debuted by ARO EQUIPMENT CORPORATION.	(see 1990)
1955	SOCONY-VACUUM now becomes SOCONY MOBIL OIL COMPANY.	(see 1963)
1955	SHAFFER TOOL WORKS develops the first subsea well completion system, for TEXACO and UNION OIL CO.	(see 1968)
1956	LeBus of Longview, TX, joins the CROSBY GROUP.	
1956	The Strategic Air Command's Dyess Air Force Base begins operating near Abilene, TX.	
1956	STUDEBAKER-PACKARD CORP. loses $43,000,000 and that ain't hay!! June 25th, the last Packard rolls off the assembly line.	

1956	January; Dwight David Eisenhower begins his second term as US President. Ike soon signs into law the Federal-Aid Highway Act of 1956, authorizing the National System of Interstate Highways and creating the Federal Highway Trust Fund.	
1956	The innovative and unappreciated auto builder, Preston Tucker dies.	
1956	AMANA acquires the DEEP-FREEZE CO.	
1956	BEAIRD INDUSTRIES begins fabricating rail cars.	
1956	CEDARAPIDS introduces its first asphalt paver (lay down machine).	
1956	BOEING begins production of the 707 jet passenger plane.	

1956	VOLKSWAGEN introduces the little KARMANM-GHIA sports car.	
1956	GUIBERSON becomes a part of DRESSER INDUSTRIES.	
1956	TECHNICAL OIL TOOL COMPANY (TOTCO) introduces the first practical multi-pen drilling recorder.	
1956	The KENWORTH CORPORATION comes to an end, as it is acquired by PACIFIC CAR AND FOUNDRY (PACCAR), now to be KENWORTH MOTOR TRUCK COMPANY, a division of PACCAR.	(see 1960)
1956	FRAM CORP. introduces the first "Spin-On" oil filter.	
1956	COSDEN PETROLEUM COMPANY and W. R. GRACE CO. merge in a $55 million deal.	
1956	**Andrews County, TX, is the largest crude oil producing county in the US, at 164,400 bopd or 60,000,000 barrels this year.**	
1956	SANTA FE INTERNATIONAL gets into the offshore drilling business; they put a land drilling rig on a barge, send it to Trinidad, and start drilling.	
1956	June; young Jim Cowan sees his first Caterpillar D-9 dozer at a roadside park in Colorado.	
1956	June 25; the last true PACKARD automobiles are built, a high-quality tradition since 1899. STUDEBAKER-PACKARD will produce some "so-called" Packards until 1958, but they are actually only "fancied up" Studes.	(see 1958)
1956	CHEMICAL PROCESS buys INTERNATIONAL/EASTERN TORPEDO CO., and BJ-BORG WARNER acquires CHEMICAL PROCESS.	
1956	EVEREADY BATTERY COMPANY introduces the first 9-volt battery (for little transistor radios).	
1956	A specialized tin-silver solder is introduced by J. W. HARRIS.	

1956	This summer Zapata Drilling's LeTourneau built "Scorpion" begins drilling for Standard of Texas, off Port Aransas.
1956	July 26; Gamal A. Nasser, the president/dictator of Egypt, nationalizes the SUEZ CANAL CO. This firm, owned by British and French shareholders, has operated the canal since its opening 90 years ago. The company's concession was due to expire in 1968.
1956	New Mexico; Lonnie and Barbara Allsup open their first "convenience" store, over in Curry County, in Clovis.
1956	CESSNA introduces the 172, and it sets world sales records.
1956	A new depth record well is drilled to 22,570 feet.
1956	SCHLUMBERGER acquires JOHNSON TESTERS.
1956	Trying to diversify, INTERNATIONAL PAPER acquires LONG-BELL LUMBER COMPANY.
1956	ARROW OIL TOOLS is started in Tulsa, OK.
1956	FEDERAL MOGUL BOWER acquires NATIONAL SEAL DIVISION from NATIONAL MOTOR BEARING CO.
1956	The firm created by the 1938 merger of CLARK BROS. and DRESSER is finally incorporated as DRESSER INDUSTRIES.
1956	An idea and product that will lead the industry for decades, HASTINGS introduces its Flex-Vent oil control ring.
1956	The number one song in the US this year is Elvis Presley's "Heartbreak Hotel."
1956	DELTA GULF DRILLING CO. is now "absorbed" into DELTA DRILLING CO.
1956	CUMMINS opens their first foreign plant in Shotts, Scotland.
1956	NYERFOR, a division of NYERPIC begins producing turbodrills for the petroleum drilling industry.
1956	The wealthy old "commie" Armand Hammer retires in California, buys lethargic OCCIDENTAL PETROLEUM (OXY) as a tax write-off, OXY then makes its first profits in decades.
1956	After replacing all his winches with hydraulic cylinders, RAMEY introduces the first all-hydraulic knuckle boom loader (for pulpwood) built in the US.
1956	WEATHERFORD OIL TOOLS OF MEXICO is established.
1956	STEWART & STEVENSON OILTOOLS develops the first BOP closing unit with a remote operation station for blowout prevention.
1956	A twenty-four-mile-long, two-lane causeway bridge opens, carrying traffic across Lake Pontchartrain, from New Orleans.
1956	This year a record number of 13,082 oil wells are drilled in Texas.
1956	Houston; Monty Levine is promoting a monorail for mass transit; a monorail "test line" is set up at Hobby Airport.
1956	HART-CARTER sells its LAUSON Division to the TECUMSEH PRODUCTS COMPANY.
1956	PACIFIC INTERMOUNTAIN EXPRESS (P. I. E.) is now the largest freight trucking company on the planet.
1956	PURE OIL COMPANY merges with UNION OIL COMPANY.
1956	France; the very last CITROËN "Traction Avant" automobile rolls off the assembly line.
1956	Robert Adler, a ZENITH engineer, introduces high-frequency sound to make the television remote control more efficient; the Zenith "Space Command" remote. — (see 1957)
1956	Our farmer's son, using a new Farmall 450, only takes 16½ hours to plow his 40 acres with a single moldboard "sulky" plow. — (see 1997)

1956	Ross Heat Exchanger Division develops the world's first "off-the-shelf" heat exchangers.	
1956	During this entire year, only 1.76" of rain falls in Wink, TX.	
1956	Venezuela; in Lake Maracaibo, Heerema is now constructing small offshore platforms, using prestressed concrete pilings. *"Yessir Bubba, they are REALLY small platforms"*	
1956	Investing $2,500, T. Boone Pickens and two partners form what will become Mesa Petroleum.	

1956	Esab-Austria is established.	
1956	Pettibone purchases Mercury Manufacturing Corporation.	(see 1957)
1956	Cedar Rapids, IA; the local Cedarapids Inc. introduces their first asphalt pavers, this year.	
1956	The gross revenue of PIE is $52 million, the top of the heap for the 2,939 "Class I carriers" in the USA, splitting total revenues of more than $5 billion. *NOTE: An ICC "Class I carrier" must gross a minimum of $200,000 to qualify as "Class I."*	(see 1957)
1956	October; Mack buys Brockway Motor Co.	
1956	Curtiss-Wright Corp. takes over the Studebaker Corporation.	(see 1958)
1956	In the post-war decade just past, 14,100,000 new residential houses are built across the United States.	
1956	UK; from now onward, all Austin and all Morris trucks will be badged as Morris; as the Morris-Commercial name is dropped.	
1956	Africa; oil is discovered in Algeria and Nigeria this year.	
1956	Arnold Neustadter and Hildaur Neilsen invent the Rolodex, a handy little device for storing printed business contact information in a small desktop rotating file.	(see 2011)
1956	Unit Crane & Shovel Corporation is the new moniker of Universal Unit Power Shovel Corporation.	
1956	Deere & Co. begin field-testing their "New Generation" tractors; the prototype OX (later 4010) and OY (later 3010), while hoping to introduce them to their dealers in 1958.	(see 1958)
1956	Sweden; having invented the first submersible drainage pump back in 1947, Sixten Englesson, chief engineer of Flygt, now invents the first submersible sewage pump.	(see 2012)
1957	White Motor Corp. acquires REO Motors of Lansing, MI.	
1957	Oil Industrial Machine & Equipment (OIME) is started in Odessa, TX.	
1957	The Hudson automobile nameplate passes into history.	
1957	**J. I. Case Co. builds the first integrated tractor loader/backhoe combination, the model 320. Case then purchases ATECO for their crawler tractor lines.**	(see 1966)
1957	**Ford introduces the 1958 Edsel.**	
1957	Harley Earl retires, after thirty-one years as chief of styling and design at General Motors.	
1957	**Esso makes the first oil strike in Libya.**	
1957	USA; Germany's Wacker opens its first international office, in Hartford, WI.	
1957	Mathes Corp. renames to Curtis Mathes Mfg. and enters the Hi-Fi audio and television marketplace.	(see 1958)
1957	Huber Mfg. acquires the W. A. Riddell Corporation, a old motor grader builder. This brings about the Huber-Warco graders.	

1957	**BOPPARDER MASCHINENBAU-GESELLSCHAFT MBH (BOMAG) is founded in Boppard on the Rhine, Germany, and soon build the world's first double-drum vibratory roller with all-drum drive, the BW-60.**	
1957	ROPER PUMP CO. sells the original ECLIPSE STOVE CO.	
1957	EXIDE acquires RAY-O-VAC.	
1957	OMC acquires all CUSHMAN MOTOR CO. stock.	
1957	Earle P. Halliburton dies.	
1957	PARKER APPLIANCE CO. acquires HANNIFIN and becomes PARKER HANNIFIN CORPORATION.	
1957	With 190 patents to his name, Joseph F. Joy dies, having made the underground mining industry a much safer, more productive business, worldwide.	
1957	DIVCO purchases WAYNE WORKS, a school bus builder, and renames the company, DIVCO-WAYNE CORP.	
1957	So pleased was he with the LeTourneau-built Scorpion, George H. W. Bush orders the Vinnegaroon, ZAPATA's second jack-up, and the seventh in a worldwide count of eight. Early this year, LeTourneau's second jack-up, the "Vinnagaroon," goes to work for ZAPATA in the Gulf of Mexico.	
1957	PYRAMID CO. is founded.	
1957	**The WHAM-O CO. creates the "Frisbee," naming it after the Frisbee Pie tins that college students spin through the air.**	
1957	The F & M NATIONAL BANK changes its name to the FIRST NATIONAL BANK of Abilene, TX.	
1957	The privately owned BEAIRD INDUSTRIES of Shreveport is acquired by AMF CORPORATION of New York City.	
1957	Having powered the D-9 since its birth, CATERPILLAR now introduces the first of its 6 ¼" bore industrial and generator engines, the six-cylinder, inline D-353. This line will be produced for the next 33 years, until 1990.	
1957	The SCHURZ CORPORATION is founded to manufacture controls for use on water purification systems.	
1957	LeGRAND, LTD. is acquired by STONE-PLATT INDUSTRIES.	
1957	**October 4; Russia uses a kerosene fueled rocket to launch SPUTNIK I, small and useless as it is, it gets the "Race for Space" underway. Sputnik is the first earth-orbiting satellite.**	
1957	Oil is discovered on Alaska's Kenai Peninsula, as ROWAN drills Alaska's first wildcat well for HUMBLE OIL CO.	(see 1958)
1957	In the Canadian wilderness, the "motorized toboggan" (snowmobile) makes its debut.	
1957	**Electronic "cruise control" is first introduced on automobiles.**	
1957	DYNA-DRIL runs the first positive displacement mud motor on a drill string.	
1957	STEWART & STEVENSON OILTOOLS introduces the 3000 psi BOP closing system. It is soon the standard of the industry and before long the term "Koomey Unit" is used a generic term for any BOP closing accumulator system.	
1957	Robert L. Parker buys PARKER DRILLING COMPANY from its founder, his father Gifford C. Parker.	(see 1965)
1957	FOLEY INC. becomes the CATERPILLAR dealer for the state of New Jersey.	
1957	This year 225,000 imported autos are sold in the Good Old USA.	(see 1958)

1957	Arkansas Louisiana Gas Company (ARKLA) buys several facilities from Servel.	
1957	Chrysler replaces their 354 Hemi with a new 392 Hemi, with larger valves and ports, a beefier block and crankshaft and improved bearings. This 392 Hemi is only available in Chrysler and Imperial models.	(see 1958)
1957	Harris-Seybold (formerly Harris Automatic Press Co.) merges with Intertype Corp., forming Harris-Intertype Corp., they soon acquire Gates Radio of Quincy, IL, calling it Harris Broadcast Division.	

1957	L & M Radiator acquires the rights to the concept of individually replaceable tubes in radiators. They bring this concept to the Mesabi Iron Ore Range in Minnesota. L & M's "Mesabi" Radiator gains rapid acceptance.	
1957	Continental Supply weds Emsco Mfg. Co. and this union produces Continental-Emsco Co. a division of Youngstown Sheet & Tube Company.	
1957	Floydada, TX; native Don Williams grew up and resides in Portland, TX, and now, makes $25 for his first paying gig… at a gas station grand opening in nearby Taft, TX.	
1957	Young Ralph Lifshitz has stated in his high school yearbook, that his "Ambition" is to be a millionaire.	(see 2014)
1957	Union Carbide patents the first nozzles for plasma cutting.	
1957	The Dallas-Fort Worth Turnpike opens, the first toll turnpike in Texas. Austin politicos promise the tolls will be removed whenever the thirty mile pike has paid for itself. This sounds too good to be true, but we will see.	(see 1977)
1957	Using a "build-on-order" system, Corbitt attempts to revive its truck business, but it doesn't work out.	
1957	Having used several McCulloch superchargers in the past few years, the Granatelli Brothers sell out in Chicago and move their racing operations to Los Angeles, just to be near McCulloch. The Granatellis and John Thompson continue using these superchargers into the mid-1970s.	(see 1958)
1957	Pettibone buys Transitler Truck, a forklift manufacturing concern. Pettibone then moves to Baraga, MI.	(see 1958)
1957	To repay a gambling debt, Wally Fowler sells the Oak Ridge Quartet name to group member Smitty Gatlin.	(see 1961)
1957	Beloit, WI; Kenyon Y. Taylor now acquires the cutting tool manufacturer, Crest Tool Industries.	(see 1963)
1957	Mr. Christian Dior designs (who knew it was designed?) the sack dress.	
1957	USA; a new ICC requirement is that a truck line must now gross $1 million to qualify as a "class I carrier."	
1957	Flint Rig's operations are moved to Calgary, Alberta, and renamed Flint Engineering & Const.	(see 1963)
1957	Loffland Brothers Company is now the largest drilling contractor on planet Earth.	
1957	Peter J. Bily with the Chiksan Corp. greatly improves on the Chiksan swivel pipe joints having been produced since being invented in 1940 by the Chiksan Tool Company.	
1957	Alfred Fielding and Marc Chavannes are trying to make plastic wallpaper with a paper backing. After several failures, they find they have invented… Bubble Wrap, a new packing material.	
1957	Texas; Mr. Hudson L. Anderson establishes Anderson Machinery Company in Corpus Christi.	
1957	Canada; in Sudbury, Ontario, Howard Schraeder produces his rear-engine, single ski, "Snowbug" snow vehicle.	(see 1958)

1957	Illinois; February 4th; having sold the family washing machine business in 1952, Edward J. Altorfer has been introduced to Caterpillar by his friend Mr. Buck Swords, owner of PEORIA TRACTOR & EQUIPMENT CO., the local Cat dealer. Today, Ed Altorfer signs the Caterpillar sales and service contract with CATERPILLAR TRACTOR CO. Initially, ALTORFER MACHINERY COMPANY has stores in Cedar Rapids and Davenport, IA, and Hannibal, MO, employing about 100 people.	
1958	EATON MFG. buys FULLER MFG. CO. (transmissions) and its subsidiaries, SHULER AXLE CO. and UNIT DROP FORGE of Kalamazoo, MI.	
1958	**The last PACKARD named automobiles are built; but for the last couple of years they have only been a "fancied-up" Studebaker.**	
1958	June; PACCAR buys PETERBUILT, and then shortly afterwards buys the DART TRUCK COMPANY.	
1958	Brothers Cy and Louis Keller, blacksmiths in Rothsay, MN, build a little self-propelled, three-wheeled, loader to help a turkey farmer clean the tight areas in his pens. Later this year the Kellers move to North Dakota and go to work for E. G. MELROE COMPANY, and the rest is "Bobcat" history.	
1958	*My Little Truck Salesman* magazine is founded.	
1958	Eddie Wagner develops the rubber tired, trackless front end loader for underground mining for PHILLIPS PETROLEUM COMPANY. It is the WAGNER MS-1, the world's first underground articulated mining scoop.	
1958	The NASH name is dropped and all AMERICAN MOTORS cars are now... RAMBLERS.	
1958	THOMPSON PRODUCTS merges with RAMO-WOOLDRIDGE to form THOMPSON-RAMO-WOOLDRIDGE or TRW.	
1958	TIDEWATER MARINE SERVICES begins their first international operations, on Lake Maracaibo, in Venezuela, and they're still here in 2003.	(see 1966)
1958	MAKITA introduces their first electric tools.	
1958	**The first Japanese cars are imported into the US and 83 new DATSUNS are sold here this year.**	(see 1959)
1958	Noted for their excellent gasoline engines, HALL-SCOTT is purchased by HERCULES MOTOR CORPORATION.	
1958	The A. O. SMITH automobile frame-making "Mechanical Marvel," operating since 1921 is shutdown; replaced by newer technology.	
1958	EXIDE acquires the WISCONSIN BATTERY CO. of Racine, and renames it WISCO COMPANY.	
1958	FOKKER introduces their F-27 "Friendship," a very successful small plane.	(see 2003)
1958	WD-40 is now put in aerosol cans and first appears in stores in San Diego, CA.	
1958	The BROCKWAY Huskie truck is introduced.	
1958	A-Z INTERNATIONAL is established.	
1958	MTD builds their first lawnmowers.	
1958	FORD has a late introduction of the 4-seater '58 Thunderbird. *"Yeah Bubba, that's my favorite T–Bird of 'em all."*	
1958	Still under contract to, and still working with Colin Chapman, Duckworth joins Costain and on September 30, COSWORTH ENGINEERING LTD. is formed.	
1958	"Red" Booker of BOOKER DRILLING designs some of the first self-erecting platform rigs in the Gulf of Mexico, using box-on-box substructures, are the first of the "bootstrap rigs."	
1958	During October, MADSEN IRON WORKS is acquired by BALDWIN-LIMA-HAMILTON, of Lima, OH, changing the name to MADSEN WORKS.	

1958	Bic (of France) buys 60% of New York-based Waterman Pens.	
1958	Massey-Ferguson acquires F. Perkins Ltd., England's leading diesel engine producer; giving M-F a ready source for engines.	
1958	In the Groningen Field in the Netherlands, natural gas is discovered.	
1958	Homestake opens their uranium mill at Ambrosia Lake, just a few miles north of Milan, NM.	(see 1960)
1958	Ambrosia Lake, NM; Kerr-McGee spends $18 million building the largest yellowcake mill of its type in the nation, to process the uranium ore coming from their mines in the area.	
1958	Johns-Manville purchases L. O. F. Glass Fibers and gets into the fiberglass insulation business.	
1958	In a step to diversify from typewriters, Smith Corona Co. acquires Marchant Calculating Machine Co. The firm soon becomes Smith-Corona-Marchant (SMC).	
1958	Leo Heikkinen of Heikkinen Machine Works in Prentice, WI, introduces his knuckle boom loader. Soon the name of his company and product will be changed to Prentice.	
1958	Ex-Halliburton hand Coots Matthews joins Myron Kinley and the boys. Near Ahvaz, Iran, Myron Kinley finds the first fire he can't put out, and calls Red Adair to come and help him… on the fifth try Red gets it extinguished.	
1958	Whittier, CA; H. C. Smith Oil Tool Company becomes Smith Tool Company.	
1958	Klampon Crop. is founded in California to serve the oil industry.	
1958	Ft. Worth; SPM is founded.	
1958	September 12; Mr. Jack Kilby demos his new invention, the integrated circuit, to his superiors, the management at Texas Instruments.	
1958	Harold Jansing, president of the San Antonio Bottling Co. plant renames "Sun Tang Red Cream Soda," simply… "Big Red."	
1958	About this time, Dart Manufacturing Co. begins to manufacture "insulated foam" (Styrofoam) cups. This family-owned firm soon becomes Dart Container Corporation, and fifty-five years later the Dart family still owns it.	
1958	Sioux Tools produces its first air-powered tools.	
1958	Toluca Lake, CA; The first International House Of Pancakes (IHOP) opens for business.	
1958	October 10; Tanya Tucker is born in Seminole, TX.	
1958	The Malco Wilshire refinery operation is sold to Gulf Oil Corp.; Robert O Anderson and Malco walk off with a tidy profit.	
1958	The plastic "Ty-Rap" is introduced by Thomas & Betts, the first month's sales of this product is $350.	
1958	Peter Chivers of England invents the sailboard.	
1958	Rowan Oil Company (not Rowan Drilling) sells out to Texas-Pacific Coal & Oil Company.	(see 1963)
1958	North Carolina; Thomasville Chair Co. opens a massive four story showroom that dwarfs those of most competitors.	(see 1961)
1958	Arthur Godfrey's *Talent Scouts* finishes its decade long TV run. Some of the amateurs on were Patsy Cline, Tony Bennett, Don Knotts and Roy Clark.	(see 1960)
1958	Although it will be a legend well into the next century, this is the last year of production of the Chrysler 392 Hemi engine.	(see 1960)
1958	Another Wayne Pump Company merger brings about Symington Wayne.	

Sept. 4, 1962   J. S. KILBY   3,052,822
MODULAR ELECTRICAL UNIT
Filed May 28, 1958   3 Sheets-Sheet 2

FIG. 4

FIG. 5

INVENTOR
JACK S. KILBY
BY John W. Michael
ATTORNEY

1958	Las Vegas, NV; the world's largest hotel, the STARDUST RESORT & CASINO opens on July second. The Stardust has six dollar room rates, on-site car rental, nine eateries, a spa, a fitness center, and wedding chapel. It will exceed all others, and more than hold its own for almost three decades.	(see 2006)
1958	As VALSPAR CORP. merges with the ROCKCOTE PAINT CO., and their headquarters is moved to Rockford, IL. ROCKCOTE is a 26-year-old firm with COLOR CORP. OF AMERICA and MIDWEST SYNTHETICS as subsidiaries.	
1958	AJAX introduces the DPC-230, its first integral engine/compressor, specifically designed for infield gas-gathering operations.	
1958	France; POTAIN ships their first exports... to the UK, Germany, and Holland.	
1958	NATIONAL SUPPLY COMPANY merges with ARMCO STEEL CORPORATION.	
1958	Robert P. McCulloch sells PAXTON PRODUCTS and expands MCCULLOCH MOTORS to building outboard motors. He buys land on Lake Havasu, in Arizona, to be able to test run his outboards on the lake.	(see 1962)
1958	The new ESAB manufacturing plants in Canada and Brazil go online.	
1958	NATIONAL IRON COMPANY is acquired by PETTIBONE, making iron ore handling equipment and some products will continue to be branded "NICO."	(see 1961)
1958	The USA government forms the NATIONAL AERONAUTICS AND SPACE ADMINISTRATION (NASA). President Eisenhower commissions Dr. T. Keith Glennan as the first administrator for NASA and Dr. Hugh L. Dryden as deputy administrator, swearing them in on August 19, 1958.	(see 1969)
1958	CA; HEWLETT PACKARD's first acquisition is F. L. MOSELY CO. of Pasadena, a maker of top quality graphic recorders.	(see 1982)
1958	SAAB offers a seatbelt/harness combination on its cars in the US However, NASH, FORD, and CHRYSLER have offered lap belts in past years.	
1958	Algeria; this January after ten years of searching, oil is finally discovered at Hassi Messaoud, out in the Sahara. The first oil flows to France this month.	
1958	Texas; CENTRAL TEXAS IRONWORKS now builds their fourth plant in West Waco.	(see 1960)
1958	Indiana; CURTISS-WRIGHT CORP. of South Bend buys the WOOLDRIDGE DIVISION from MORRISON-KNUDSEN CO. They then dedicate 400 acres of land adjacent to their Studebaker plant for a scraper proving ground.	
1958	In Germany, OPEL introduces the 4.8 meter (15.6 ft.) long Captain, with its radical body style and two-color lacquer paint job. By mid-1959, more than 35,000 Captain P series will have been produced.	(see 1965)
1958	Finland; SISU now uses LEYLAND engines as its standard diesel truck engine. In a couple of years SISU introduces their tilt-cab, forward control trucks.	(see 1967)
1958	Commercially-made cesium clocks are now available for about $20,000.	(see 1960)
1958	FOLEY TRACTOR CO. acquires ROBERTS TRACTOR CO. and OEHLERT TRACTOR CO., other CAT dealers.	(see 1973)
1958	Due to be introduced this year, DEERE's "New Gen" tractors have so very many new systems (8 forward, 3 reverse speed transmissions, shift on the fly under full torque load by the power shift torque converter, and on and on) and their grueling testing, correcting, and continual improving hold up introduction to the public.	(see 1960)
1958	China; TONGHUA PETRO-CHEMICAL MACHINERY is established, and soon produces the first Chinese built oil well workover rig.	

1958	San Diego, CA; for the next couple of years, the STINSON AIRCRAFT TOOL & ENGINEERING Co. will produce an electric car, the "Charles Town-About," looking very similar to the current VW Karmann Ghia.			
1958	Québec; Hus-Ski of Point Claire begins testing an unusual designed snow vehicle. The twin-tracked front-power unit tows a passenger sled behind it. Production will not begin until 1962.			(see 1962) (see 1965)
1958	Texas; in Odessa, Emery L. Eckel grabs some chalk and draws out his design for a hydraulic power tong on the floor of the shop. That is essentially the beginning of ECKEL MANUFACTURING COMPANY.			
1959	For a good number of years, TRACTOMOTIVE has built loaders and other attachments for ALLIS-CHALMERS. Now A-C buys the TRACTOMOTIVE CORPORATION.			
1959	McKISSICK joins the CROSBY GROUP.			

1959	LINCOLN ELECTRIC founder John C. Lincoln dies.	
1959	**CATERPILLAR introduces its first wheel loader, the rigid frame, front-wheel steer, Continental gasoline engine powered 944A.**	
1959	Iowa; in February, a small single-engine plane crash in a ice-covered corn field near Clear Lake, claims the lives of twenty-two-year-old "Buddy" Holly from Lubbock, TX, Richie Valens, and J. P. "Big Bopper" Richardson from Beaumont, TX. This tragedy, on February 13th, leaves a huge void in the Rock and Roll world. Littlefield, TX, native Waylon Jennings had given up his seat for Richardson, and will live for many more years.	(see 2002)

1959	February 22; Lee Petty (Richard's dad) wins the inaugural Daytona 500 on the new superspeedway. Many drivers consider this track to be very unsafe.	
1959	**The last FEDERAL trucks leave the factory.**	
1959	The KOEHRING COMPANY purchases the STARDRILL-KEYSTONE Co.	
1959	SYLVANIA ELECTRIC PRODUCTS merges with GENERAL TELEPHONE to create GENERAL TELEPHONE & ELECTRONICS (GTE).	
1959	**NISSAN introduces the first compact pickup into America, a DATSUN.**	
1959	The E & P subsidiary of PANHANDLE EASTERN CORP. is given the name ANADARKO, after the Anadarko Indians, part of the Caddo nation.	
1959	ROPER PUMP Co. acquires O. E. SZEKELY & Co., pump specialists in Georgia, soon known as ROPER UNIQUE & RELIABLE STAINLESS STEEL PRODUCTS.	
1959	FORD discontinues the Edsel; FORD's 50,000,000th car is produced, a Ford Galaxie.	
1959	**ACF builds their very last railroad passenger car.**	
1959	The INDIAN SALES CORP. brings out a new Indian Chief motocycle, but it is actually an imported Enfield Meteor 700.	(see 1960)
1959	GROVE introduces their first truck crane and their first rough terrain crane.	
1959	Twenty-one years after Carlson's discovery, HALOID XEROX debuts the first ever xerographic machine, their model 914, the world's first plain paper copier.	
1959	Paul N. "Red" Adair leaves Myron Kinley, taking Boots Matthews with him, and founds RED ADAIR Co. INC. to fight oil well fires and Red is soon known world-wide as the "hellfighter."	
1959	Robert Noyce of FAIRCHILD SEMICONDUCTOR also invents an integrated circuit, somewhat different from Kilby's, and gets it patented six months later.	
1959	The Father of Fritos, Elmer Doolin, dies.	

1959	Having added sandwiches and other menu items, DANNY'S DONUT SHOPS becomes... DENNY'S.	
1959	Corpus Christi, TX; SWIFF-TRAIN gets into the floor covering business.	
1959	Thirteen-year-old Dolly Parton first appears on the Grand Old Opry.	
1959	The Drago Brothers part ways; Phillip stays in Port Arthur and opens DRAGO SUPPLY, fulfilling his dream of a wholesale industrial hardware supplier.	
1959	Having completed and opened to traffic the lower second deck, the George Washington Bridge is now the busiest bridge in the world. Fifty years later it will still be the busiest.	(see 2009)
1959	In the United States this year, 614,000 imported cars are sold.	
1959	Middle East; one of the hottest wildcat drilling areas in the world now is Libya, and LOFFLAND BROS. sends a new Mid-Continent U-36 specially built desert drilling rig there to drill for ESSO STANDARD LIBYA. And in Venezuela, having added a new drilling barge for SIGNAL OIL & GAS CO., LOFFLAND BROS now has seven barges drilling on Lake Maracaibo.	
1959	Acknowledging the power of its brand name, the directors of the TEXAS COMPANY officially change the firm's name to TEXACO INC.	
1959	The *Fibber McGee and Molly Show* ends its twenty-five year run of fine radio comedy entertainment.	
1959	HARRIS-INTERTYPE acquires RADIATION INC. of Melbourne, FL, near Cape Canaveral.	
1959	Tom McCahill conducts and reports on the first road test of Chevrolet's Corvair. Tom reports that the Corvair handles better than the '59 Porsche. *Note: Character, agitator, and political wannabe Ralph Nader ("Unsafe at Any Speed") will soon argue otherwise.*	
1959	JAMES CAMPBELL SMITH INC. patents a steering mechanism for forklift trucks.	(see 1966)
1959	CONTINENTAL-EMSCO purchases the entire inventory of BETHELEM SUPPLY CO., which is then sold as C-E "B" Line equipment.	
1959	MERCURY MANUFACTURING is merged into PETTIBONE, making PETTIBONE-MERCURY.	
1959	EUCLID introduces their line of articulated-frame wheel loaders. The concept seems to catch on, and soon will be more or less the standard design for all future wheel loaders.	(see 1968)
1959	VOLKSWAGEN OF AMERICA is established.	
1959	April 25; the new ice-breaker, *D'Iberville*, sails through the just completed St. Lawrence Seaway, on its maiden voyage. This summer, President Eisenhower and Queen Elizabeth II will officially celebrate the grand opening of this joint US and Canadian project.	
1959	USA; forty-six percent of all the trucks on the planet are now operating in our great nation.	
1959	April 27; the American Football League (AFL) is born. Because of the NFL's reluctance to expand to Dallas and Houston, Lamar Hunt joins team owners in seven other cities and announces the birth of the AMERICAN FOOTBALL LEAGUE (AFL). Mid-May; now, since the AFL is in, the NFL finally decides to expand into Dallas and Houston.	
1959	VOLVO patents the three-point seatbelt and offers it in Sweden.	(see 1963)
1959	California; in Butte County, the Bureau of Reclamation's 80-million-cubic-yard, 774-foot-tall, earth-filled Oroville Dam is completed. This is the highest earth-filled dam in the world, and the highest dam of any sort in our nation. It is a definite irrigation aid to the farms of the state's Central Valley, and also houses the third-largest hydroelectric plant in our nation.	

1959	Edmonton, Alberta; FLINT RIG's sales this year in Canada are $2,500,000, and will double over the next decade.	
1959	THOMPSON-RAMO-WOOLDRIDGE introduces the transistor-based RAMO-WOOLDRIDGE R-W 300 computer as a process control machine.	(see 1965)
1959	By the end of the decade, CONTINENTAL AIRLINES has routes to Chicago and Los Angeles, and flies seven days a week.	(see 1962)

	1959	BEEBE BROS, INC. introduces their hand-operated ratchet hoists, or come-alongs.	(see 1962)
	1959	Egypt; at the Arab Oil Congress held in Cairo, a "gentlemen's agreement" is made for oil producing countries to have greater influence on crude oil production and marketing.	(see 1960)
	1959	UNIT RIG is the first to use the G-E motorized wheel drive system in a mining haul truck.	(see 1963)

1959	STUDEBAKER rebounds financially by introducing the LARK, which proves to be a popular mid-size automobile.	
1960s	TIDEWATER OIL COMPANY becomes GETTY OIL COMPANY.	
1960s	Mid-Decade; R. J. REYNOLDS TOBACCO begins diversifying into foods and other non-tobacco businesses, forming R. J. REYNOLDS INDUSTRIES, INC. *"Naw Bubba, that don't smell as much like tobacco."*	
1960s	Throughout this decade, UNIT CRANE & SHOVEL CORP. builds many specialized material handlers, such as some used for placing the Titan missiles into their underground silos.	(see 1967)
1960s	Late 60s; the SUN OIL COMPANY and SUNRAY DX COMPANY merge.	
1960s	After several decades of derision from most geologists and scientists, Alfred Wegner's idea of "continental drift" is now supported by plausible evidence. However, it is now called "plate tectonics."	
1960s	Canada; experiments are initiated to efficiently recover usable petroleum from oil shale and tar sands.	

1960	January 1; having driven their old Ford pickup straight through from Minnesota, Wilbur and Fern Atwood arrive in Enid, OK. They come to Enid to start a business in a community they like, and there they establish ATWOOD DISTRIBUTING COMPANY.	
1960	January; the first prototype of UNIT RIG & EQUIPMENT's "Lectrahaul," diesel-electric drive, off-road truck is put to work.	
1960	PACIFIC CAR founds KENMEX (Kenworth of Mexico).	(see 1969)
1960	February 14; Junior Johnson wins the Daytona 500 as he discovers "drafting," running close behind another car, so he could go faster.	
1960	March; this month UNIT CRANE & SHOVEL buys all assets of BAY CITY SHOVELS, INC. of Bay City, MI. Inc.luded are all manufacturing rights and the Bay City manufacturing facility.	
1960	May 1; John L. Rust founds RUST TRACTOR CO., buying the northern N. M. Caterpillar franchise, of R. L. HARRISON COMPANY, a dealership which predates CATERPILLAR TRACTOR COMPANY, going back to the BEST and HOLT days.	
1960	May 1; Major Francis Gary Powers is shot down in his U-2 plane over the USSR, and the Cold War heats up a little more.	
1960	EATON acquires DEARBORN MARINE ENGINES, INC., and operates it as EATON MARINE DIVISION.	
1960	Harry Ferguson dies, with many patents to his credit.	
1960	WAGNER introduces the MT-10, the first 4wd rear-dump truck for underground mining.	
1960	WEATHERFORD OIL TOOLS establishes an affiliated company in Hanover, Germany.	
1960	JETCO moves to Dallas, TX, and soon changes their name to DALLAS JETCO.	
1960	TEXTRON buys BELL HELICOPTER CORP., and they also buy E-Z GO golf carts.	
1960	The 2,175 mile MID-AMERICA PIPELINE from a salt cavern west of Seminole, TX, to International Falls, MN, is built by WILLIAMS BROTHERS.	
1960	KOLLMANN, maker of power drain cleaning tools (snakes) is acquired by RIDGE TOOL CO.	
1960	**The "dieselization" of the American Railroad is complete; now, 60,000 steam locomotives have been replaced by 28,000 diesel-electric locomotives.**	
1960	WHITE MOTOR CORP. acquires DIAMOND-T MOTOR TRUCK CO. of Chicago. In November, WHITE buys OLIVER CORP.	(see 1960-61)
1960	Steven Bechtel, Jr. becomes president of BECHTEL CORP.	
1960	DAYTON RUBBER CO. becomes DAYTON CORPORATION.	
1960	Having doubled in size to 7 employees, WD-40 is now selling 45 cases per day from the trunks of their cars to hardware, sporting goods, and auto parts stores.	
1960	DOWELL-SCHLUMBERGER (50% Schlumberger and 50% Dow Chemical) is created, to provide complete service to the oil industry throughout the free world.	
1960	MARMON-HERRINGTON buys LONG and merges it with CARDOX, forming LONG-AIRDOX, with John B. Long as president and CEO.	
1960	CHRYSLER's problems in the 1950s now result in the DeSoto being merged with Plymouth. Late this year, the 1961 model DeSoto is unveiled; the last ever to be built, after thirty-two years of production.	(see 1961)
1960	ASSOCIATE MOTORCYCLES (AM) of Britain acquires rights to the INDIAN name and renames the dealers, AMC/INDIAN.	(see 1963)

1960	**Ray Kroc buys out the McDonald brothers, and the rest is fast food history.**	
1960	BIC buys the remainder of WATERMAN PEN CO.	
1960	ALCO is acquired by WORTHINGTON.	
1960	Ballinger, TX; Walter Mueller's sons, James and Harold, are running the old cistern making business. Now they are into sheet metal building construction related products and supplies.	
1960	Lead and zinc producing is added to HOMESTAKE's buffet.	(see 1980)
1960	GEARMATIC introduces the first hydraulic planetary winches and immediately GROVE CRANE orders them for their crane winches.	
1960	After forty-four years of using their special shaped bottle, the Coca-Cola bottle finally becomes a legal trademark.	
1960	GULF OIL acquires WILSHIRE OIL CO. OF CALIFORNIA.	
1960	ELDER TRAILER & BODY COMPANY (ELDER) expands its operations to Houston.	
1960	LEGRAND, LTD. has now expanded into the design and production of oil and gas processing equipment.	
1960	LOR, INC. begins manufacturing downhole drilling tools.	
1960	**Responding to the "pregnant peanuts," or imported foreign cars, the Big Three introduce the Plymouth Valiant, the Chevrolet Corvair, and the Ford Falcon.** *"Yessir Slim, now there's a trio of real winners…"*	

	1960	About this time, Robert A. Moog invents the music synthesizer.	
	1960	The GLEN MARTIN COMPANY ceases aircraft production, to focus on missiles.	
	1960	**Lasers are invented in the USA.**	
	1960	The publisher HENRY HOLT & COMPANY merges to become HOLT, RINEHART & WINSTON.	
	1960	Due to a heart condition, Carroll Shelby retires from racing. He immediately begins building Cobras.	

1960	Michigan; Bruce Halle stocks the shelves of an old store building in Ann Arbor with two new tires, four recaps, and a small assortment of incidental auto supplies. Bruce names his little store… DISCOUNT TIRE COMPANY.	
1960	NESTLÉ acquires CROSSE & BLACKWELL of the UK.	
1960	**The first commercial geothermal power plant in the United States goes on line at the Geysers, a 40 square mile steaming valley, near San Francisco.**	
1960	CONTINENTAL-EMSCO buys all assets of WIN-WEL MFG. CO. and adds the Win-Wel Rotary Selector Valve to the fast growing line of "Green Triangle" products. They are built in Garland, and Win-Wel is soon dropped from the name.	
1960	With television and "rock and roll" taking their toll, the popularity of *The Louisiana Hayride* on the radio wanes.	(see 1969)
1960	The "average" new US built automobile contains sixty-three pounds of aluminum.	(see 2007)
1960	Dallas, TX, is chosen as the "field of battle," as the NFL decides to expand in its effort to stymie the new American Football League. Although Dallas has the AFL team "Texans," belonging to Lamar Hunt, the NFL now awards a new franchise to Clint Murchison, Jr., and Bedford Wynne. They choose "Cowboys" as their team's name, and select Mission, TX, native Tom Landry of the University of Texas as the head coach. The Cowboys lose the first ten games they play. Murchison and Wynne pay $500,000 for the Dallas NFL franchise.	(see 1984)
1960	France; POCLAIN introduces their model TY45, the machine that really introduces the POCLAIN name to the international excavator market. Eventually more than 30,000 TY45 units will be sold.	(see 1970)

1960	Alaska; bush pilot Don Sheldon lands his small single engine plane at 13,400 feet altitude on Mt. McKinley for a rescue mission. This high altitude landing begins the "glacier landings" for hunters and such.	
1960	Houston; Dr. Denton A. Cooley establishes the TEXAS HEART INSTITUTE.	
1960	Guided by Ralph and F. J. Baudhuin, VALSPAR has a great period of growth. From 1958 throughout this decade, VALSPAR averages two good acquisitions each year. Some acquisitions are NORO PLASTICS, MCMURTY MFG., KEYSTONE PAINT & VARNISH, as well as the trade sales division of MOBIL CORPORATION.	(see 1970)
1960	Meeting in Baghdad, the countries of Saudi Arabia, Venezuela, Kuwait, Iraq, and Iran, found the ORGANIZATION OF PETROLEUM EXPORTING COUNTRIES (OPEC).	(see 1973)
1960	Japan; TADANO's first exports are some hydraulic truck cranes to Indonesia.	(see 1970)
1960	US automobile production has increased sixty percent during the decade and half since 1945. This year's census reveals that Detroit, MI, the Motor City, has started losing people, it population is now 1,670,144. Go figure!!!	(see 1970)
1960	Having worked on it for more than two years, William Chardack, Andrew Gage, and Wilson Greatbatch invent the implantable cardiac pacemaker.	

1960	Dallas; August 30; today (D-Day) DEERE & CO. host almost 6,000 dealers and spouses to the "NEW GEN" introduction show at the Cotton Bowl. Deere president Bill Hewitt finishes the introduction, and still the guests have only seen the New Gens from their stadium seats. As it has truly been a well-kept secret, most were surprised at the multi-cylinder news. Then as they are directed out the rear door of the stadium, they are met with 15 acres of Cotton Bowl parking lot holding 136 tractors and 324 other John Deere New Gen machines, and they can get "up close and personal" with this amazing display. Deere's seven years of designing, building, testing, rebuilding, as well as flat-out denials of anything ever having more than two cylinders, plus an all-day introduction party was a fantastic success. Some years later, Hewitt recalls that no one complained about anything that day.	
1960	California; September 8; the Torrance Herald contains this article: **Two National Supply Co. Executives Ending Careers** "Forest I. Young, chief engineer, and Lloyd C. Warthan, supervisor of factory sales, have retired after 43 years service at the Torrance plant of the National Supply Co. Starting in 1917, when cable tool drilling was predominant and the deepest well was around 7,000 feet deep, the men have witnessed the change in preference to rotary drilling, with an increase in drilling depths to below 25,000 feet. The Torrance plant, established in 1912 by the Union Tool Co., was acquired by National Supply in 1920. Young's earliest experience was in the development of tools for cable tool drilling. Later, he contributed many of the designs and features included in National's rotary drilling equipment. He has served as chief engineer since 1945, during which time National rigs drilled eight successive world's depth record wells, from 10,655 feet to 25,340 feet. Warthan started as a clerk in the sales order department. He is regarded as having an encyclopedic memory of all plant products, including their part numbers, produced since 1917. After considerable field experience, he was appointed supervisor of factory sales in 1949."	
1960	Bonneville Salt Flats, UT; aiming for 500 mph in his jet-propelled "Flying Caduceus," Nathan Ostich hits only 331 mph, 63 mph short of the 1947 record of 394 miles per hour.	(see 1965)
1960	Texas; CENTRAL TEXAS IRONWORKS begins furnishing customers with structural steel, and exporting some through the PORT OF HOUSTON.	(see 1963)

1960	Loretta Lynn, a young mother of four, cuts her first record, "I'm a Honky Tonk Girl," for Zero Records in Nashville.	
1960	December 16; about 5,000 feet over New York City, a United Airlines DC-8 jetliner collides with a TWA prop-driven Constellation airliner, killing all 128 aboard as well as six persons on the ground. This is the first time the "black boxes" or flight recorders are used extensively in investigating the pre-crash details. This disaster spurs the FAA to institute many new procedures and rules, and begin the long-term modernization of the Air Traffic Control System.	(see 1985)
1960	The population of planet earth is now about three billion persons, give or take a couple of dozen folks.	
1960	A new atomic clock, the NBS-2, is introduced at the NIST lab in Bolder. This new clock can run for long periods unattended, and is used to calibrate secondary standards.	
1960	Voss Trucking sells out to Western-Gillette Transportation.	(see 1977)
1960	The Tappan Company invents and introduces the electronic ignition for gas cook stoves.	(see 1979)
1960	The Gross National Product of the USA is $500 Billion this year.	
1960	Zimmerman International is founded to build equipment systems that assist in ergonomic handling operations.	(see 1996)
1960-61	Cyrus V. Helm founds International Air Drilling Co. (INTAIRDRIL), with a borrowed $8,000.	(see 1978) (see 1991)
1960-61	IH dealer Dan Johnston in Cross Plains, TX, is selling more new International trucks than the factory branch dealership in Lubbock.	
1961	Dodge City, KS; Roy C. Broce (Marvin's dad) forms Broce Manufacturing Company, and builds the first self-propelled road sweeper broom, the "Broce Broom."	(see 1982)
1961	B. D. Holt and Mark Hulings form B. D. Holt Co., a Caterpillar dealership with headquarters in Corpus Christi, TX.	
1961	Intercontinental Engineering & Manufacturing Corp. of Parkville, MO, start building the largest, most powerful dozer ever to be built.	(see 1963)

The Huntsville Times — Man Enters Space

1961	Texas; in February this year, the first "Six Flags Over Texas" amusement park opens on US highway 80 in Arlington.	
1961	The Cleveland Diesel Division is consolidated into E-M-D.	(see 2011)
1961	March; after a year long buying and leasing spree, the ranchland holdings of Robert O. Anderson of Roswell now comprise almost 600,000 acres of New Mexico.	
1961	The Ringhaver family of central Florida first becomes associated with Caterpillar Tractor Co. as a dealer based in Tampa.	
1961	April 12; Russian Yuri Gagarin is the man in the first ever First Manned Space Flight.	(see 1968)

1961	LeTourneau introduces its K-205, a huge, 1260 hp, five wheel dozer powered by three 12V-71 Detroit Diesel engines.	
1961	Williams Brothers acquires MSI Energy Services of Alberta, Canada, to get a foothold in the tar sands.	
1961	**Bob Lilly is the first player ever drafted by the Dallas Cowboys. Bob will later be known as "Mr. Cowboy;" Bob eventually plays in eleven Pro-Bowls, more than anyone else as of 2006.**	
1961	**The 1961 year model DeSoto from Chrysler Corporation is the last, after 32 years of production.**	(see 1970)

1961	In Savannah, GA, optometrist Stanley Pearle opens his first office location.	
1961	The GLENN L. MARTIN CO. merges with AMERICAN-MARIETTA CORP. to establish MARTIN-MARIETTA CORPORATION.	
1961	SOLARTRON of the UK, an electrical instrumentation company, is acquired by SCHLUMBERGER.	(see 1971)
1961	WARNER GEAR introduces the first aluminum automatic transmission, the Model 35.	
1961	April; all Madsen operations are moved to BLH's Lima, OH, facilities, renaming it "LIMA WORKS," but using the Madsen name on products.	
1961	Sweden; Mylanta is launched by ASTRA AB.	(see 1978)
1961	IOWA MOLDING TOOL CO. (IMT) begins business providing new tread designs for tire recappers.	
1961	OCCIDENTAL PETROLEUM makes its first major discovery, by drilling deep in the Sacramento Basin of California.	
1961	FRITOS merges with the LAY COMPANY, to become FRITO-LAY.	(see 1965)
1961	LIEBHERR of Germany establishes a subsidiary company in France.	
1961	FORD MOTOR CO. introduces its own "oblong box on wheels," the Econoline van.	
1961	May; naval Commander Alan B. Shepard is the first American in space. After his 15 minute flight, Shepard comments, "Boy! What a ride!"	
1961	Inspired by science fiction, George Devol and Joseph Engelberger invent Unimate, the first industrial robot, which goes to work for GENERAL MOTORS.	
1961	**GM introduces the first American V-6 passenger car engine.**	
1961	**The first WHAT-A-BURGER A-frame building makes its debut. The idea is from Harmon Dobson's napkin sketches. Its height and visibility make it virtually impossible not to be seen… day or night.**	
1961	Texas; on November 7th, agricultural leaders from all across East Texas meet with Texas A&M officials at Tyler's Blackstone Hotel. They're discussing the possibility of building a consolidated agricultural research center in the area.	(see 1965)
1961	North Carolina; THOMASVILLE CHAIR merges with B. F. HUNTLEY, carrying on their 35-year alliance marketing complete furniture packages. The new firm is named THOMASVILLE FURNITURE INDUSTRIES, and it goes public next year.	(see 1968)
1961	Houston; Rice University donates most of the land to NASA needed for construction of the Manned Spacecraft Center, near here.	
1961	The size of the Shredded Wheat Juniors Biscuits is made even smaller, and reintroduced as Spoon Size Shredded Wheat.	
1961	PETTIBONE establishes PETTRAC CORPORATION as a manufacturer of crawler tractor "after-market" parts. In Greenville, AL, PETTIBONE ALABAMA is established, building log skidders and some other equipment.	(see 1962)
1961	Said to be the world's first articulated wheel-dozer, the D-500 Paydozer is introduced by FRANK G. HOUGH CO.	
1961	After recording for four different labels, the OAK RIDGE QUARTET becomes the OAK RIDGE BOYS.	(see 1974)
1961	AMERICAN AIRLINES is the first airline to fly fanjets in their "turbofan" engines, of their BOEING 707 planes.	(see 1971)
1961-62	Hess buys AMERADA PETROLEUM, making AMERADA-HESS.	
1961-62	Morris Pendleton sells PROTO to INGERSOLL-RAND.	

1961-62	The Melroe Bobcat, little skid steer, rubber tired loader is being seen everywhere now.	
1961-62	Texas; in Corpus Christi, Marine Drilling is founded by James Clay "Jimmy" Storm.	
1961-62	Thibodaux, LA; the Cane Machinery & Engineering Co. (CAMECO) is established to design and build modern field machinery for the sugar cane farmers.	
1962	AGIP USA is formed to market petroleum drilling and production equipment worldwide.	
1962	LeBus, Inc. of Longview, TX, establishes a plant in the UK.	(see 1963)
1962	In Garden City, MI, S. S. Kresge Co. opens its first K-Mart store. This same store is still going fifty years later.	
1962	White Motor Co. buys Canada's Cockshutt Farm Equipment Co., and will begin selling some Oliver products under the Cockshutt name.	
1962	Boeing builds the last new B-52 bomber, but this military workhorse will be rebuilt and updated and used continuously well into the next century.	
1962	Millers Falls Company becomes the Millers Falls Division, of Ingersoll-Rand.	
1962	March 14; GM's seventy-fifth million US made vehicle, a Pontiac Bonneville convertible, rolls off the assembly line.	(see 1964)
1962	Philco goes bankrupt and its remaining assets are sold to Ford Motor Company, thus creating Ford-Philco.	
1962	**EMD's 25,000th diesel locomotive is delivered to the Louisville & Nashville Railroad.**	
1962	Texas; Kelly-Springfield's Tyler plant opens, producing 6,500 tires per day.	
1962	After Herman Brown's death, Halliburton buys Brown & Root Construction Company.	
1962	BJ releases their famous Pacemaker Triplex Pump line.	
1962	Nitrogen Oilwell Service Company (NOWSCO) is formed in Red Deer, Alberta, Canada.	
1962	American Steel Foundries becomes Amsted Industries.	
1962	Venezuela; began in 1959, the five-mile-long General Rafael Urdaneta Bridge over the outlet of Lake Maracaibo is now completed as one of the world's longest bridges.	
1962	Designed by Thomas W. "Bill" Kellogg, the sporty Studebaker Avanti is introduced, but sadly, the classy, beautiful, little sports coupe won't be enough to save Studebaker.	
1962	The Pritzker family buys Marmon-Herrington.	
1962	Cushman Motors becomes a division of Outboard Marine Corporation (OMC).	
1962	Molycorp. begins its surface strip mining operations East of Questa, NM.	(see 1965)
1962	Texas; Dover Corporation acquires Parks Equipment Co. of Odessa.	
1962	Texas; Permian Engineering & Manufacturing Co. (PEMCO) begins building masts for workover rigs in its Odessa facility.	
1962	David Bradley Mfg. Co. becomes a part of the Newark Ohio Company, also owned by Sears, Roebuck & Company.	
1962	Smith Corona changes its name to the SCM (Smith-Corona-Marchant) Corporation.	
1962	Ohio Oil Co. is renamed Marathon Oil Co., and soon Plymouth Oil Company directors agree to sell virtually all assets to Marathon Oil Company.	
1962	Howard Hughes, Jr., buys controlling interest in Northeast Airlines.	
1962	After almost 40 years of fighting oil well fires, sixty-six year old Myron Kinley retires.	

1962	GREATER FT. WORTH INTERNATIONAL AIRPORT is renamed GREATER SOUTHWEST INTERNATIONAL AIRPORT-DALLAS-FT. WORTH, but the City of Dallas, haughtily, refuses to be involved with this project.	
1962	In Algeria; the oil well blowout, the Devil's Cigarette Lighter, burns for six months, before Red Adair puts it out this April.	
1962	**The first kelly spinners are introduced by the INTERNATIONAL TOOL CO. of Houston, as an aid to rotary drilling.**	
1962	The ALLIED RADIO subsidiary, ALLIED ELECTRONICS, puts out their first industrial catalog.	
1962	Washington; the steel for construction of the Space Needle at the World's Fair is fabricated by PACCAR.	
1962	Roy Acuff is inducted into the Country Music Hall of Fame, the first living performer ever to be inducted.	
1962	GOLD BOND STAMP acquires much prime Minneapolis real estate, including the downtown Radisson Hotel. Carlson will soon expand it into a chain of 350 hotels.	
1962	GENERAL MOTORS sells ETHYL CORPORATION to the ALBEMARLE PAPER MANUFACTURING COMPANY.	
1962	GOOSENECK TRAILER MANUFACTURING COMPANY is established in Bryan, TX.	
1962	HEREEMA now begins operations on the North Sea continental shelf.	
1962	Robert McCulloch, known in Europe as "the Mad American," thinking he is buying London's Tower Bridge, pays $2.5 million for the famed London Bridge. He dismantles the bridge, ships it to Lake Havasu City, AZ, and has it rebuilt across a portion of the lake. The reassembly is completed in 1971.	(see 1977)
1962	A plant for making oxy-acetylene cutting equipment is opened by ESAB, in Rodheim, Germany.	
1962	Canada; Mr. Richard Piche establishes RICHARD PICHE INC., concentrating primarily on production of heavy-duty industrial snow removal machinery.	(see 1986)
1962	Illinois; REPLACEMENT PARTS COMPANY, is founded by PETTIBONE in Aurora.	(see 1963)
1962	The first ever communications satellite, Telstar, is powered by the Bell Solar Battery, or PV cell.	
1962	USA; New York and Wisconsin pass laws requiring seatbelt anchors for the front seats of vehicles.	(see 1965)
1962	The man who put the WHITE name on cars, trucks, and tractors, Rollin H. White dies this year.	
1962	With headquarters in Santa Monica, Bill Lear's company has plants in California, Michigan, Ohio, as well as in Germany. Lear has about 5,000 employees overall locations. However, Bill and his management have a falling out and he sells his part for $14.3 million, and goes forward on his own.	(see 1967)
1962	Ken W. Davis, Sr., forms DIESEL INTERNATIONAL, INC., as a distributor of PERKINS diesels, and CHRYSLER marine and industrial engines, among other brands.	(see 1968)
1962	About this time, CONTINENTAL AIRLINES moves their HQ to Los Angeles and are providing transport for US military personnel involved in the Vietnam War. CONTINENTAL soon forms AIR MICRONESIA, getting routes between Saipan and Honolulu.	(see 1982)
1962	BEEBE BROS, INC. sales reach to one million dollars this year.	(see 1987)
1962	Québec; in La Pocatière, Bouchard starts his Moto-Ski business and produces 10 machines.	(see 1963)
1963	The largest, most powerful dozer ever built, is completed for the WESTERN CONTRACTING CO., it weighs 170 tons, on four huge rubber tires. *NOTE: This record will stand for several decades.*	
1963	AJAX ENGINE CO. and PENN PROCESS are both acquired by COOPER INDUSTRIES.	

1963	The unusual LONGHORN TRENCHERS are now being built in Roswell, NM (from experience, it is a very poorly designed trencher).	
1963	EATON acquires YALE & TOWNE, and also DOLE VALVES; EATON FULLER introduces the ROAD RANGER truck transmission.	
1963	Tulsa, OK; UNIT RIG enters the off highway truck field, in a BIG way! They begin production of their off-road dump trucks, several of the first trucks go to the MOLYCORP. mine, out east of Questa, NM.	

1963	Debuted last year, the futuristically-designed, fiberglass-bodied Avanti from STUDEBAKER has sold only 4,600. Bye-Bye Avanti.	
1963	STUDEBAKER CORP. closes their South Bend plant, leaving only the Canadian plant in production.	(see 1966)
1963	CATERPILLAR TRACTOR CO. and MITSUBISHI HEAVY INDUSTRIES, LTD. form a joint-venture, the first in Japan with a US firm as a major partner.	
1963	BARKO HYDRAULICS is established in Duluth, MN, to build knuckle-boom loaders.	
1963	DANA CORPORATION acquires the old, esteemed, piston ring maker; PERFECT CIRCLE.	
1963	STEWART & STEVENSON manufacture the first gas turbine-powered oilfield cementing unit.	
1963	**CATERPILLAR introduces the 988, its first articulated-frame wheel loader, sporting a six cubic yard bucket as standard.**	
1963	GRESEN HYDRAULICS sells out to TOR CORP.	
1963	May 1; Jim Whittaker of Port Townsend, WA, arrives at the summit of Mount Everest, the first American to make the journey and the climb.	
1963	TEXTRON sells its last textile operations plant.	
1963	LEBUS, INC. of Longview, TX, establishes a plant in Germany.	
1963	PENNZOIL CORP. is formed by a merger of SOUTH PENN OIL, ZAPATA PETROLEUM and STETCO PETROLEUM.	
1963	July 1; Postmaster General J. Edward Day inaugurates the Zoning Improvement Plan (ZIP) code system, to streamline mail deliveries. Unlike most federal government "improvement" projects, the ZIP actually works.	
1963	NATIONAL CRANE begins building their truck-mounted cranes, in Waverly, NE. 40 years later, 90% ever sold are still working.	
1963	MARMON TRUCKS is founded in Garland, TX, as a continuation of MARMON-HERRINGTON.	(see 1974)
1963	CONTINENTAL-EMSCO introduces the Electrohoist II draw-works. The draw-works is the primary hoist on drilling rigs.	
1963	BERLINER MOTOR CORP. takes over distribution of AMC bikes and drops the Indian name altogether.	(see 1968)
1963	As an industry trend, CUMMINS attempts a consolidation with WHITE MOTORS, but in the end CUMMINS remains independent. Now, WHITE MOTOR COMPANY purchases MINNEAPOLIS-MOLINE COMPANY.	
1963	On August 5th, 26-year-old Craig Breedlove drives the jet-powered tricycle car, "Spirit of America" 407.45 mph at Bonneville Salt Flats.	(see 2006)
1963	PACCAR purchases GEARMATIC.	
1963	October; the first flight in a Learjet is made.	
1963	The oilfield supply firm, OILTOOLS INTERNATIONAL, is founded by Cyrus V. Helm.	
1963	**This year the average (median) salary in America passes $100 per week for the first time ever.**	

1963	A former MARCHANT engineer Carl Friden who had started his own company introduces the first all-transistor electronic desktop calculator.	
1963	King Kircher and Don Bodard buy the three rig operation of UNIT DRILLING from WOOLAROC OIL CO. and soon buy four rigs from FALCON-SEABOARD.	
1963	The first CVS (Customer Value Store) opens in Lowell, MA, selling health and beauty products.	(see 1967)
1963	Texas; the PITCHFORK RANCH holds its first horse sale.	
1963	ROWAN DRILLING COMPANY move their Ft. Worth headquarters to Houston, TX.	(see 1967)
1963	KENNER PRODUCTS CO. introduces the Easy-Bake Oven for children.	
1963	The US government inaugurates the Emergency Broadcasting System (EBS). During this "cold war" era, Uncle Sam wants a way to easily reach most homes.	
1963	The first aluminum beverage cans are introduced.	
1963	Trying something VERY different, CONTINENTAL-EMSCO acquires majority interest in TIMBERLINE EQUIPMENT CO. maker of the Buschcombine, a mobile pulpwood harvesting and handling machine. About 150 of these are built before C-E realizes it is cheaper to hire sawyers and chain saws to cut pine, than to maintain a Buschcombine machine.	
1963	Three-year-old Marie Osmond makes her television debut on *The Andy Griffith Show*.	(see 1966)
1963	**The "J619," the first of a long line of Cat elevating, self-loading scrapers, is developed by teamwork between CATERPILLAR of Peoria Illinois, and JOHNSON of Lubbock, TX.**	
1963	ITT acquires BELL & GOSSETT.	
1963	After 150 years of using the eleven locks in the Forth and Clyde Canal, and the Union Canal, construction begins on a huge river water carousel.	(see 2007)
1963	The world's first ship converted to a crane vessel is launched. HEEREMA's *Global Adventurer* has a 300 ton lifting capacity.	
1963	Duluth, MN; BARKO HYDRAULICS is founded when the Bartells acquire the bankrupt pulpwood loader builder, RAMEY MFG. & ENGINEERING COMPANY, combining it with their custom truck body building business, LAKESHORE BODY COMPANY.	(see 1975)
1963	Mexico; PETTIBONE S. A. de C. V. is founded. Pettibone is ⅔ owner. This division builds rock-crushers and such, for distribution throughout Mexico, Central and South America. Also, MULTIHOE, of Mundelein, IL, a local company building loaders and back-hoes, is acquired by PETTIBONE.	(see 1966)
1963	HYDRAULIC POWER EQUIPMENT CORPORATION is founded in Milwaukee, WI.	(see 1968)
1963	USA; the jet ski is invented by Clayton Jacobson, though he doesn't apply for a patent until 1966.	
1963	Kenyon Taylor moves BELIOT TOOL CO. headquarters to a new location, in an old farmhouse, and acquires the historic DURST FOUNDRY & MACHINE WORKS, of Shopiere, WI, Walter Durst stays on as a consultant.	(see 1973)
1963	All VOLVO cars now sold in the United States have three-point seatbelts as standard equipment.	
1963	Texas; CENTRAL TEXAS IRONWORKS, INC. of Waco is acquired by the HERRICK CORP. of California.	(see 1990)
1963	Selling more than 648,000 units, this is the greatest year ever for the FORD Galaxie.	
1963	FLINT acquires KENT WELL SERVICES in Kansas. FLINT is now providing plant maintenance and production services throughout Alberta, Canada.	(see 1973)
1963	September 2; CBS doubles its network news time, with Walter Cronkite, from 15 minutes to thirty minutes. NBC follows soon suit. In these early years of television, this is a tremendous step to take.	

Feb. 20, 1968   C. J. JACOBSON   3,369,518
AQUATIC VEHICLE
Filed Nov. 3, 1966

FIG.1   FIG. 2   FIG. 3   FIG.4   FIG.5

INVENTOR
CLAYTON J. JACOBSON
BY
ATTORNEY

1963	Socony Mobil Oil Co. now becomes Mobilgas, and before long, it will be just Mobil.	
1963	The first to build and sell a fleet of diesel-electric mining Haul trucks is Unit Rig of Tulsa, OK.	(see 1965)
1963	Rejean Houle of Wickham, Québec, produces twenty "Skiroules" snow vehicles this year.	(see 1964)
1964	To get into the excavator business, P & H acquires rights to two small excavators designed by Cabot Machinery Corporation.	
1964	The windmill maker Aermotor moves its manufacturing facility from San Angelo, TX, to Broken Bow, OK.	(see 1969)
1964	January; with $46 in his pocket, Tom T. Hall takes his guitar and moves to Nashville, TN.	
1964	Ray-Go, Inc. is founded.	
1964	Borgwarner and NSK Ltd. form a joint venture, NSK-Warner.	
1964	Dresser Industries of Dallas buys the worldwide assets of Manning, Maxwell & Moore, to form the Instrument Division of Dresser.	
1964	Neptune Drilling is created of 50% Forex and 50% Languedocienne.	

	1964	Introduced at the New York World's Fair, the first "pony car," Lee Iacocca's Mustang, is brought out by Ford. WOW! About 60,000 Mustangs are sold on the first day of sales!!! The first year's sales are four times Ford's expectations!!!
	1964	Kemper Valve & Fittings Co. is founded in Wauconda, IL, to manufacture forged steel pipe unions and fittings.
	1964	J. Ray McDermott & Company move their corporate headquarters to New Orleans from Houston.
	1964	**At the Anchor Bar in Buffalo, New York, Teressa Bellissimo concocts a special recipe for chicken wings… soon to be called… Buffalo Wings.**
	1964	After forty years of research and trials, Orville Redenbacher finally succeeds with the development of his "signature hybrid corn," for superior popping.

1964	Elder acquires Oilfield Truck Equipment Co., and is soon renamed Elder Oilfield Inc.	
1964	AT&T introduces its "picture-phone" at the World's Fair; to be fair, it is the flop of the fair.	(see 1991)
1964	Cat dealer Butler Machinery Co. expands into western North Dakota; buying Schultz Machinery Co. and its two stores.	
1964	June 1; in search of a recording contract, young Dolly Parton moves to Nashville, TN.	
1964	After eighty years in the business, Sargent & Company sell their last woodworking planes this year.	
1964	**Pontiac Division of General Motors introduces the GTO….. and the great Muscle Car craze begins.**	(see 2009)
1964	Superior Cable Corp. builds their Brownwood Texas telephone cable plant to better serve the southwestern states.	
1964	Mr. Robert Soloff receives the first patent for ultrasonic plastic welding.	
1964	Sales of Thew have declined and now Thew becomes the Thew-Lorain Division of the Koehring Co.	(see 1987)
1964	Forty percent Shell-owned Conch International Methane delivers the first tanker of liquefied natural gas (LNG) from Algeria to the UK.	
1964	Royal Crown Cola (RC) is the first beverage maker to market soda in aluminum cans.	
1964	Texas; for a couple of years, Vanguard Motors Corporation of Dallas is building the "VettaVenture" automobile.	

1964	Unable to withstand competition from more advance synthetic-fiber ropes, and declaring bankruptcy, the PLYMOUTH CORDAGE COMPANY closes down after 140 years of continuous operation. For many years it was the largest employer in the area; and next year COLUMBIAN ROPE COMPANY will buy its assets. Some parts of the original equipment is displayed at Mystic Seaport, CT.	
1964	Sno-Jet makes 25 of their snow vehicles in Thetford Mines, Québec, Canada.	
1965	RUST TRACTOR CO. buys the CATERPILLAR franchise, formerly HAAG TRACTOR CO., covering the southern half of New Mexico, plus El Paso, and three other counties in far west Texas. This gives Rust the largest area-wise Cat dealership in the lower forty-eight. To get this franchise, Jack Rust has to agree to build new facilities in both El Paso, TX, and Hobbs, NM. After selling his CATERPILLAR dealership, Al Haag goes into real estate development full time.	
1965	About this time, HYDRIL CORP. buys BETTIS RUBBER PRODUCTS.	
1965	January; the Bruce McMillan, Jr. Foundation and Texas A&M, under university President Earl Redden, agree for the new EAST TEXAS AGRICULTURAL RESEARCH & EXTENSION CENTER to be built at Overton. Initially the foundation grant totals $300,000, plus 150 head of Hereford cattle, as well as 22 acres of land deeded to A&M for the station headquarters, plus three 25-year leases on 1,221 acres for the experimental work.	
1965	GENERAL MOTORS DIESEL becomes DETROIT DIESEL ENGINE DIVISION of General Motors.	
1965	COOPER INDUSTRIES begins major diversification into electrical, automotive, tools, and hardware fields.	
1965	RAYTHEON acquires AMANA CO. of Iowa.	
1965	The real power behind LINCOLN ELECTRIC for many decades, James F. Lincoln dies.	
1965	Texas; Andrews County produces its billionth barrel of crude oil.	
1965	PARKER DRILLING drills past 18,000 feet for GULF OIL, in Pecos County, TX.	(see 1972)
1965	**HOLLEY CARBURETOR Co. builds its 100 millionth carburetor.**	
1965	OLIVER builds the last of its OC (Oliver-Cletrac) crawler tractors.	
1965	SULLAIR CORP. is founded, concentrating solely on rotary screw compressors.	
1965	ELECTRO-MOTIVE DIESEL introduces its 645 Series Engines. That is 645 cubic inches displacement PER cylinder.	
1965	UK; R. A. LISTER & COMPANY is sold by the Lister family to the HAWKER SIDDELEY GROUP, however, some of the Lister family continue working for the new owners.	
1965	Sam Bonham of Sulphur Springs, TX, discovers the "tougher than steel" epoxy, and names it J-B WELD.	
1965	Chicago; the old MORRISON HOTEL is demolished to clear the location for the FIRST NATIONAL BANK building, later to be known as Bank One Plaza. The Morrison Hotel demolition job is the tallest building on earth ever purposely razed.	
1965	In Germany, WIRTH builds their first tunnel boring machine.	
1965	The BLUEWATER No. 2, SANTA FE's first semi-submersible drilling rig, goes to work.	
1965	VICTOR EQUIPMENT COMPANY moves from its original home in San Francisco to Denton, TX, and in a few years, opens a new plant in Abilene, TX.	

MORRISON HOTEL
Chicago

1965	In its first major foray outside the Anadarko Basin, ANADARKO buys the assets of AMBASSADOR OIL for twelve million dollars.	
1965	FORD introduces their '66 Bronco, the world's second SUV. *"Yeah Bubba, tha Cornbinders Scout wuz furst."*	
1965	FEDERAL MOGUL BOWER BEARING again becomes FEDERAL MOGUL CORPORATION.	
1965	Elmer Decker sells MARTIN-DECKER to GARDNER DENVER, including a newly completed plant in Santa Ana, CA.	(see 1979)
1965	In Houston, TX, PRIDE PETROLEUM SERVICES is formed, as a domestic well service company.	
1965	Having outgrown the little Cotton Bowl, Clint Murchison is looking for a new home stadium for his Dallas Cowboys.	
1965	Mr. Delmar Wright is the superintendent for LOFFLAND BROS. as they drill the very first half-dozen oil wells in the rain forest of the Oriente del Ecuador.	
1965	**TRANSOCEAN builds the first jack-up rig to work in the North Sea's rugged climate.**	
1965	Most of the assets of ALCO are purchased by the WORTHINGTON CORP.	
1965	E. D. ETNYRE & CO. acquires WYLIE MANUFACTURING, a maker and marketer of asphalt plants.	
1965	The first "red light camera" to catch light-runners and speeders is installed in the Netherlands.	
1965	In Kearney, NE, AG-TRONIC, a farm supply manufacturer begins making portable gasoline powered generators.	
1965	Michael Dell is born.	
1965	A crude oil refinery is built on the Kenai Peninsula of Alaska.	
1965	**The federal government of the United States of America passes the Motor Vehicle Air Pollution Act. This will haunt us forever.**	
1965	**Oldsmobile Division of GM introduces its front-wheel-drive Toronado, the first front-wheel-drive car built and sold in the US since the 1930s.**	(see 1973)
1965	GarWood Industries purchases CLEMENT BRASWELL TRAILERS, and begin nationwide sales and marketing.	
1965	Jim Hall revolutionizes auto racing with his Winged Chaparral racing cars. Jim's aerodynamic innovations transform auto racing, as well as the safety and fuel efficiency of our everyday passenger cars.	

1965	**The first Slurpees are made and sold at SEVEN-ELEVEN stores.**	
1965	Houston, TX; the 8th man-made "wonder of the world," the Astrodome, the first domed stadium opens. Of necessity, AstroTurf is soon invented.	
1965	FRITO-LAY merges with PEPSI-COLA, becoming the gigantic PEPSICO.	
1965	New Mexico; this spring MOLYBDENUM CORP. OF AMERICA (MOLYCORP.) officially opens its new $40 million mine and mill, 5 miles east of Questa.	
1965	France; CITROËN takes over the operations of PANHARD.	
1965	After eight decades of family ownership, the Waterous family sells their company to AMERICAN HOIST & DERRICK, right in their neighborhood.	
1965	Canada; one of the final portions of the 401 freeway between Toronto and Montréal is completed by a contractor utilizing several Le Tourneau SL-40, low-profile, rubber-tired, articulated, mining loaders... supplied by WAJAX.	
1965	HAMMERMILLS, INC. is somehow joined with UNIVERSAL ENGINEERING for the next decade and half.	

1965	USA; in Washington, DC, a Senate subcommittee predicts that automation will lead to a 21st century work week of only fourteen (14) hours. *"Naw Bubba, I ain't seed it yit."*	(see 2009)
1965	YE OLDE PEPPER CANDY COMPANY is now owned and operated by George Burkinshaw's son, who is making the candy in his basement. This year they open a retail store near where Mrs. Spencer first launched her "Gibralter" candy business.	(see 2009)
1965	Working full-time designing nuclear reactors for GE, nuclear physicist Frank Buck puts up $1,000, with his friend Fred DeLuca, to open the first SUBWAY SANDWICH SHOP.	(see 2009)
1965	Driving the "Spirit of America-Sonic 1," Craig Breedlove breaks the 600 mph land speed record.	(see 1970)
1965	All US auto-makers are now providing two front seat lap belts in every automobile.	(see 1967)
1965	Brazil; the government of Brazil begins inviting private development of its tremendous iron ore reserves.	

1965	The construction of America's interstate highway system is now at its peak. In a bit less than a decade, just over 21,000 miles, or about fifty-two percent of the system is now in everyday use. These projects have been a real bonanza to the road construction industry and therefore to the construction equipment industry.	(see 1976)
1965	KUBOTA introduces the first Japanese farm tractor to the US market. However, neither the nine-horsepower gasoline Kubota RV or the 20-horsepower diesel D20 make a big splash. Kubota will eventually do better over here, though.	
1965	THOMPSON-RAMO-WOOLDRIDGE officially change names to T-R-W INC. and they also cease marketing computers commercially.	
1965	For the fiscal year ending March 31, GENERAL FOODS net sales were $1. 5 billion. This marks the thirteenth straight year with an increase in net sales and net earnings, as well as the 43rd year this firm has paid a dividend every quarter to their stockholders. GENERAL FOODS now has about 30,000 employees in 60 plants, warehouses, and offices, and 77,000 shareholders in the US and 17 foreign countries. They make and sell more than 200 products under 30 well-known brand names.	
1965	FRONTIER AIRLINES is now moving over half-million passengers annually. They have grown from their DC-3s to CONVAIR 580 and are moving on to BOEING 727s. Soon they will merge with CENTRAL AIRLINES, bringing routes in the Midwest and Southwest.	(see 1975)
1965	September; OPEL, of Germany, reveals their "Experimental GT," to be used primarily "for R & D purposes."	(see 1968)
1965	Oklahoma City; DRILLING EQUIPMENT MFG. CO. becomes DEMCO, INC.	
1965	UNIT RIG has now built the first gas turbine-engine powered open-pit mining truck.	(see 1970)
1966	STUDEBAKER CORP. closes their plant at Hamilton, Ontario, Canada, ending 114 years of vehicle production by STUDEBAKER.	
1966	EATON now is EATON YALE & TOWNE, INC.	
1966	**LeTourneau, Inc. builds the LT-360, the largest dirt scraper ever built... this triple-pan unit still is not topped 50 years later.**	
1966	**Longview, TX; now holding more than 300 patents for equipment and related improvements, Mr. R. G. LeTourneau officially retires from his position as CEO and Chief Engineer of LeTourneau, Inc.**	(see 1969)
1966	WIX is now producing all AUTO-LITE filters for FORD.	

1966	James D. Abrams founds J. D. Abrams Const. Co. of El Paso, TX.	
	"Bubba, J. D. is just a workin' man."	
1966	The Koehring Co. acquires the world-famous Franks Machine Co. of Enid, OK, they soon create the Speedstar Division.	
1966	Tidewater now has more than 200 vessels at work on the water around the world.	(see 1968)
1966	Daniel Orfice Fitting Co. becomes Daniel Industries, Inc.	
1966	The English Electric Co. Ltd., acquires Ruston & Hornsby and Davey Paxman.	
1966	The Ariel Corporation is formed in Mt. Vernon Ohio, to produce and market direct drive compressors.	
1966	Victor Mfg. & Gaskets joins the Dana family of companies.	

1966	Case establishes the first construction equipment rental system.	(see 1968)
1966	The George D. Roper Corp. purchases the Newark Ohio Co., ending fifty-six years of Sears' ownership of David Bradley.	(see 1968)
1966	Gulf Oil acquires a large portion of the distribution and retail outlets of Cities Service Oil Co. putting Gulf service stations in each of the lower 48 states.	
1966	The last of the James motorcycles are produced in the UK.	

1966	Dallas; Bill Grisgby and J. T. Watson finance a new Cat 955H with Darr and begin excavating construction sites, part time; thus B & J Excavating is born.	(see 1967)
1966	Northeast Airlines is purchased by Storer Broadcasting Company of Miami, FL.	
1966	Kelly Plow Company of Longview, TX, ceases its business operations.	
1966	The world-wide operations of Mannesmann AG now employ about 74,000 people.	
1966	Halliburton acquires Otis Engineering Corp. of Carrollton, TX.	
1966	W. R. Grace Co. buys 53% of Miller Brewing Company.	
1966	Mr. Carter Stanley passes away, leaving the singing here on earth to his brother Ralph and others.	
1966	Walter Kidde & Co. acquires Fenwal, Inc. of Ashland, MA; making Kidde-Fenwal.	
1966	September 8th; the first episode of *Star Trek* airs on television.	(see 1967)
	"Yeah Bubba, thet Captain Kirk looks like a young Denny Crane."	
1966	July; Clark Equipment Corp. acquires the Hancock Manufacturing Co. of Lubbock, TX.	(see 1971) (see 2004)
1966	Ross Heat Exchanger Division of American Standard is acquired by ITT.	
1966	Ringwood, OK; with only a single bobtail truck, Harold Hamm starts in business as Harold Hamm Tank Truck Services. The business grows, and soon becomes Hamm & Phillips Service Company.	
1966	Introduced in 1963, the Studebaker Wagonaire is now being cancelled, after selling only 940 units. It seems most folks prefer either a Ford Ranchero or Chevrolet El Camino, to the Wagonaire's "hybrid" pickup/station wagon design.	
1966	Tiffin, OH; this June, Pettibone acquires Hanson Machinery Co., renaming it Pettibone Tiffin. Pettibone also acquires James Campbell Smith Inc.	(see 1968)
1966	The Lufkin Rule Co. discontinues its precision tool operations and sells that operation to Pratt & Whitney Machine Tool Company of Colt Industries.	(see 1967)
1966	Texas; Anheuser-Busch begins brewing in a new 136 acre complex over on the east side of Houston.	
1966	This year the Boulevard Machine Works produces a 60 mph electric roadster.	

1967	January 1; ARNOLD, SCHWINN & COMPANY, becomes the SCHWINN BICYCLE COMPANY.	
1967	CATERPILLAR TRACTOR CO. buys TOWMOTOR & gives them a lift. Some years earlier, TOWMOTOR had bought GERLINGER, of Oregon, who made mostly straddle-lift carriers.	
1967	COOPER INDUSTRIES moves headquarters to Houston.	
1967	RAYTHEON introduces the "Amana Radar-Range," the first successful microwave oven for home use.	
1967	WHITE MOTORS merges REO and DIAMOND-T to form DIAMOND REO, a division of WHITE MOTOR CORPORATION.	
1967	**As a way to use his integrated circuit in a consumer product, Jack Kilby co-invents the hand-held electronic calculator.**	
1967	REGAL-BELIOT acquires DURST.	
1967	EY&T acquires TIMBERJACK MACHINES, LTD., of Ontario, Canada.	
1967	FMC buys LINK-BELT CO. soon LINK-BELT SPEEDER is spun-off to become the CONSTRUCTION EQUIPMENT GROUP of FMC.	
1967	Texas; TYLER PIPE & FOUNDRY becomes TYLER PIPE INDUSTRIES.	
1967	April 21; GM produces its 100,000,000th US made vehicle.	
1967	MAYTAG creates the "Lonely Repairman" advertising campaign.	
1967	April; "Float like a butterfly, sting like a bee," being afraid to serve and refusing military service, Muhammad Ali is banned from the sport of boxing for about three years.	
1967	FORD OF EUROPE is formed.	
1967	CONTINENTAL-EMSCO introduces the HUGE 37½" rotary table.	(see 1973)
1967	Even though he left school at 13, to help support his family, Henry J. Kaiser didn't do too bad by them. Henry J. Kaiser dies this year.	
1967	DAEWOO INDUSTRIAL CO. LTD. is established in Seoul.	
1967	June 5; in just six days, the nation of Israel demonstrates its superiority at warfare to its war-mongering Arab neighbors.	
1967	**HIAB introduces the stowable knuckle boom (Napoleon's Arm). Later this will be copied by almost every knuckle boom crane builder.**	
1967	Dallas; J. T. Watson dies suddenly and Bill Grigsby's brother, J. W., buys J. T.'s portion of B & J EXCAVATING CO. from Mrs. Watson.	
1967	TWENTIETH CENTURY TOOL CO. is established in Houston by the consolidation of several persons with years of experience in the design and manufacture of industrial and oilfield specialties.	
1967	The BOP closing unit maker PAYNE MANUFACTURING COMPANY is acquired by CAMERON.	
1967	DETROIT DIESEL introduces its largest 2 cycle engine yet, the 149 series, up to 2200 horsepower.	
1967	**Opening its bitumen mine, GREAT CANADIAN OIL SANDS LTD., later to be SUNCOR, starts the oil sands industry in Alberta province of Canada.**	
1967	CVS opens its first stores with pharmacies.	(see 1985)
1967	ERA HELICOPTERS, INC. of Alaska is acquired by Rowan Drilling Company.	(see 1973)
1967	DODGE MFG. CO. merges with RELIANCE ELECTRIC COMPANY.	
1967	Now, HARRIS-INTERTYPE merges with its subsidiary, RADIATION INC.	

1967	Continental Telephone acquires Superior Cable and merges it with similar plants already owned.	

Oct. 31, 1967   O. L. BROWN ETAL   3,349,949
RING-SHAPED TAB FOR TEAR STRIPS OF CONTAINERS
Filed July 6, 1965   3 Sheets-Sheet 1

1967	France; Panhard ceases building vehicles.	
1967	France; Berliet is acquired by Citroën.	
1967	The first NFL Super Bowl is simulcast over several television networks.	(see 1969)
1967	October 1; Richard Petty wins his tenth consecutive race, earning him the nickname of… "The King."	
1967	October; a pull tab to open aluminum beverage cans, or steel cans with aluminum tops, is patented by Omar L. Brown and Don B. Peters.	
1967	Houston; disgusted with poor garbage collection service, two residents of Willowbrook Subdivision buy a used garbage truck and form American Refuse Systems (ARS).	
1967	The United States Rubber Company changes its corporate name to Uniroyal.	(see 1986)
1967	Mr. Irwin Feld purchases the Ringling Bros. and Barnum & Bailey Circus.	(see 1979)
1967	April; having built 146 Learjets, Bill is $13 million in debt, and sells Learjet to Gates Rubber Company of Denver. However, Bill Lear eventually realizes about $18 million from this sale.	(see 1968)
1967	In its two-season life, the AMC (Rambler) Marlin has sold only 17,000 units. The Marlin is now "dead in the water." NOTE: The sporty Marlin precedes the Dodge Charger by about a year.	
1967	USA; lap belts are now required for all seating positions in all new automobiles.	(see 1968)
1967	Texas; in Fort Worth, Frank Kent Cadillac Inc., succeeds Frank Kent Motor Co. as the primary Cadillac dealership, with Frank Kent as chairman, John Ludington as president, and Kent's grand-daughter, Wendy K. Churchill, as vice-president and treasurer.	(see 1987)
1967	Cooper Industries buys the Lufkin Rule Co. adding Lufkin to their Hand Tools Division. Cooper only offers Lufkin products to industrial distributors and users.	(see 1998)
1967	Finland; Sisu takes over Vaneja and the two companies are united once again, after a two decade separation.	(see 1974)
1967	This year Unit Crane & Shovel Corporation moves to New Berlin, WI.	(see 1982)
1967	December; Clint Murchison announces the Dallas Cowboys will be leaving the Cotton Bowl for a new $35,000,000 stadium to be located a few miles west, in Irving, TX.	(see 1971) (see 2009)
1967	December 31; Gulf Oil with assets of $ 6. 5 billion and 163,000 shareholders, has 58,000 employees in 50 countries and processes 1,300,000 barrels of crude oil every day.	
1967	Bill Lear has a bit part in the movie In Like Flint, (starring James Coburn) in which Lear looks after Flint's Learjet. Lear's single line is, "The ashtrays were full so I got you a new airplane, Mr. Flint."	
1968	January 1; Case takes over the Drott excavator line. Soon, Case purchases the Davis Manufacturing Co., for the Davis line of small trenchers.	(see 1999)
1968	The Scoopmobile line of wheel loaders is merged into the Construction Equip. Div. of Westinghouse Air Brake Co., and the machines are marketed under the Wabco name.	
1968	Eaton, Yale & Towne buys Fawick (clutches), also American Monorail.	(see 2003)
1968	Tidewater acquires Twenty Grand Marine's fleet of 150 vessels.	(see 1969)
1968	Dixie-Narco is acquired by Magic Chef.	
1968	Lane-Wells merges with Pan Geo Atlas Corporation, to form Dresser-Atlas.	
1968	San Antonio, TX; Fiber Glass Systems Inc. is established.	

1968	US Justice dept. rules that GM must divest itself of the EUCLID name, and discontinue the manufacture and sale of off-road trucks in the US for four years. Thus EUCLID becomes a subsidiary of WHITE MOTOR CORPORATION.	(see 1977)
1968	G. M.'s Scotland plant continues building off-road trucks, and G. M. begins using the TEREX name worldwide. *NOTE: The word Terex comes from "Terra," meaning earth, and "Rex," meaning King. Thus Terex is "King of the Earth"... And a caterpillar is just a worm that crawls around... some wild imagination, huh?*	
1968	TOTCO sells to BAKER OIL TOOLS, to get more financial backing.	
1968	TOM BROWN DRILLING acquires and merges into GOLD METAL CONSOLIDATED MINING CO.	
1968	UNITED GAS merges with PENNZOIL CORPORATION.	
1968	**The last Dodge Power Wagons are sold domestically in the US, although they will be exported for another 10 years.**	
1968	Tulsa, OK; Wayne Rumley and partners form R & R ENGINEERING to design and manufacture cooling equipment, primarily for air and gas compressors. R & R soon earns a name known worldwide as a manufacturer of superior quality air cooled heat exchangers.	
1968	DIVCO-WAYNE CORP. is acquired by BOISE-CASCADE CORP., who soon spin-off the delivery truck business to HIGHWAY PRODUCTS, INC., located in the old TWIN COACH plant in Kent, OH. HIGHWAY PRODUCTS quickly sells DIVCO to TRANSAIRCO, later CORRECT MFG., owned by Glenn Way.	
1968	The Davey family sells the DAVEY COMPRESSOR COMPANY to ALCO STANDARD, an industrial holding company.	
1968	THOMASVILLE FURNITURE INC. becomes a subsidiary of ARMSTRONG CORK CO., and soon ARMSTRONG CORK CO. becomes ARMSTRONG WORLD INDUSTRIES.	(see 1987)
1968	The long-time Indian dealer and enthusiast, Floyd Clymer (well-known author and gearhead) obtains rights to the Indian name and he tries to produce a new model Indian Motocycle, but runs into legal difficulties. While Clymer did import a few and rebadge them as the Indian Velo 500, this will soon end as he dies in 1970.	(see 1970)
1968	KV delivers their first KG2 gas turbine as emergency power to Norway's NATIONAL POWER SYSTEM.	
1968	**The last DAVID BRADLEY two-wheeled garden tractor is built.**	(see 1983)

1968	BETHLEHEM WIRE ROPE installs a planetary stranding machine capable of making up to 5½ inch diameter wire rope.	
1968	ALLIED PRODUCTS CORP. buys BUSH HOG.	
1968	OCCIDENTAL PETROLEUM gets into the chemical business with the acquisition of HOOKER CHEMICALS.	
1968	HAZARD WIRE ROPE CO. is now a division of AMERICAN CHAIN & CABLE CO. (ACCO)	
1968	Oil is discovered at Prudhoe Bay on the North Slope, or Arctic coast, of Alaska, initiating the construction of the Alaska Pipeline from Prudhoe Bay south to Valdez.	
1968	Being "squeezed out" of Cleveland and the Browns, Paul Brown organizes the CINCINNATI BENGALS, as another AFL franchise.	
1968	HARBOR FREIGHT is established to sell low-priced tools and shop equipment.	
1968	Houston; about this time, the Hotel Cotton becomes the Montagu Hotel.	
1968	J. D. Power III establishes J. D. POWER & ASSOCIATES, soon to become the leader of auto rating companies.	
1968	SYMINGTON WAYNE is taken over by DRESSER INDUSTRIES, making DRESSER WAYNE.	

1968	This year, GOLD BOND STAMPS revenue reaches one hundred million dollars… $100,000,000. But Curtis Carlson sees that the future doesn't bode well for the trading stamp business, and it is screeching to a halt as Curtis Carlson begins diversification of GOLD BOND STAMPS.	(see 1976)
1968	August 29; seventy-two-year-old Pennsylvania native, Kenneth William Davis, Sr., dies at his home here in Ft. Worth, having lived here since 1929. An Army Air Corps veteran of WWI, Second Lieutenant Davis served as a pilot and instructor at several airfields. Davis is also the primary owner and the driving force behind KENDAVIS INDUSTRIES, comprised of more than 80 companies.	
1968	At this time, there are about 2,000 truck stops scattered around the United States.	
1968	**Jim Drake modifies, redesigns, and patents the sailboard.**	
1968	UK; all Austin and Morris trucks now carry the BMC marque, or badge.	
1968	Bill Lear buys the old STEAD AFB at Reno Nevada for $1. 3 million, and establishes LEAR MOTOR CORPORATION and LEARAVIA CORPORATION.	
1968	The "First Man in Space," Russian Yuri Gagarin, dies in an airplane crash.	
1968	SHINGLE BELTING COMPANY acquires the century old HARRINGRON HOIST COMPANY.	(see 1978)
1968	As RUCKER CORPORATION acquires SHAFFER TOOL WORKS… RUCKER SHAFFER comes into being.	(see 1972)
1968	USA; in new cars, lap and shoulder belts must now be provided for front outboard seating positions.	(see 1969)
1968	UK; Mr. Ernest Crump dies, leaving PELICAN ENGINEERING COMPANY to his son Bob.	(see 1980)
1968	PETTIBONE now offers two lines of pedestal cranes, for offshore drilling rigs and platforms. The six models cover from 10 to 80 tons capacity. In another PETTIBONE drama, PETTRAC, as well as REPLACEMENT PARTS COMPANY, is merged into WESTRAC. This year, PETTIBONE-MULLIKEN acquires HYDRAULIC POWER CORP. and will run it as a P-M company for a few years.	(see 1970)
1968	This autumn, OPEL debuts two versions of the OPEL GT.	(see 1973)
1968	Germany; POTAIN GMBH is established.	
1968	TB WOOD'S SONS now enters the electronic drives market, introducing the new "Ultracon" line.	(see 1986)
1968	Texas; the BUSHMASTER COMPANY is established at 6615 N. Lamar in Austin, building the "Bushmaster" vehicle.	
1968	The "Paisano Dune Buggy" is being built on a VW base by the VWC SPECIALTY COMPANY of Kermit, TX.	
1969	**R. G. LeTourneau dies this year and is buried on the campus of LeTourneau University in Longview, TX.**	
1969	Dallas; VEHICLE CONSTRUCTORS DIV. (V-CON) of PEERLESS MFG. COMPANY is formed, intent on building the world's largest mining truck.	
1969	AERMOTOR moves its headquarters from Broken Bow, OK, to Conway, AR.	(see 1986)
1969	*Big Muskie, the greatest dragline ever, goes into service for MUSKINGHAM COAL CO. The BUCYRUS-ERIE 4240-W swings a 220 cubic yard bucket weighing 550 tons, from a 310 foot boom. The entire machine weighs about 15,000 tons, has taken three years to build, and cost $25 million.*	(see 1982) (see 1991)
1969	EY&T sells DEARBORN MARINE, and buys McQUAY-NORRIS MFG., and also buys TROY TOOL PRODUCTS CO.	

1969	Laguna, NM; due to modern processing methods, most of the uranium ore now being produced from the ANACONDA JACKPILE MINE is from the old tailings dump.	
1969	INGERSOLL-RAND buys TORRINGTON BEARINGS.	
1969	Corpus Christie, TX; B. D. Holt & Mark Huling form ENERGY INDUSTRIES, manufacturing, packaging, and marketing gas compressors.	
1969	WHITE MOTOR buys MINNEAPOLIS-MOLINE, and begins selling some OLIVER models under the M-M tag.	(see 1977)
1969	TIDEWATER MARINE acquires SOUTH COAST GAS COMPRESSION and creates TIDEWATER COMPRESSION SERVICE, INC.	(see 1977)
1969	After a run of 53 years, the last RAMBLER automobile is produced.	
1969	KENWORTH AUSTRALIA is founded as a subsidiary of PACCAR.	(see 1972)
1969	GENERAL MOTORS CHILE is established.	
1969	April; automobile designer Harley Earl dies of a stroke at age 75.	
1969	**AMANA introduces the first commercial microwave oven.**	
1969	PHILLIPS discovers oil in the North Sea, beginning a tremendous petroleum extraction project.	
1969	RYAN EQUIPMENT is established in St. Paul, MN.	
1969	ROCKET CHEMICAL CO. renames itself after its only product, to WD-40 CO., INC.	
1969	USA; the government NASA puts a man on the moon. Astronaut Neil Armstrong walks on the moon wearing space boots with soles made by 3M.	
1969	Houston, TX; Mr. Ross Hill establishes ROSS HILL CONTROLS.	
1969	AMERICAN PETROLEUM INSTITUTE (API) moves its headquarters to Washington, DC.	
1969	The TRANSOCEAN Mercury jack-up drilling rig is delivered to work in the Gulf of Suez.	(see 2002)
1969	Henry II is now chairman of FORD, and Lee Iacocca, "the Daddy of the Mustang," is president of North American Automotive Operations.	
1969	LONG-AIRDOX is now the world's largest manufacturer of underground mining equipment.	
1969	CUMMINS ENGINE COMPANY now has plants in half-dozen foreign countries, and 2,500 dealers in 98 countries.	
1969	The old ALCO plant in Schenectady is closed and is soon leased to GENERAL ELECTRIC for turbine generator production.	
1969	MELROE is acquired and becomes a division of CLARK EQUIPMENT COMPANY.	
1969	NEIMAN-MARCUS is sold to CARTER HAWLEY HALE STORES, INC.	
1969	ALBERTSON'S grocery stores merges with SKAGGS' drug stores of Salt Lake City, making SKAGGS-ALBERTSONS.	
1969	Belle Chasse, LA; MARSH BUGGIES INC. is established.	
1969	September 14; the largest and fastest motorsports oval on earth, the Talladega Speedway is opened by NASCAR. Thirty-seven drivers consider it unsafe and walk off today.	
1969	Eighteen-year-old Tommy Hilfiger starts selling blue jeans in New York City. Who knows, maybe the kid will make a name for himself.	

1969	Louisiana; the second two-lane bridge across Lake Pontchartrain is completed and is opened to traffic.	
1969	The Phillip Morris Company buys Miller Brewing Company.	
1969	The first Doubletree Hotel opens.	
1969	Lebanon, TN, September; Dan Evins and his friend Tommy Lowe open the first Cracker Barrel Old Country Store.	
1969	November 10; puppeteer Jim Henson first puts his Muppets in front of the television cameras.	
1969	Parker Bros. introduces the first indoor ball, the Nerf-Ball: "it won't break windows, or hurt people."	
1969	Another "Muscle Car," the 1970 model Dodge Challenger is introduced this fall.	

1969	Houston; ARS, wanting to be quick-listed on the NYSE, acquires controlling interest in listed Browning-Ferris Machinery Co. ARS merges with Browning-Ferris and is renamed Browning-Ferris Industries (BFI).	
1969	December; the US Air Force "closes the book" on Project Blue Book, and essentially "washes its hands" of "flying saucers."	
1969	The Chevrolet Vega is introduced.	
1969	After a primary run of twenty-one years, the *Louisiana Hayride* hangs it up.	(see 1973)
1969	**Ted Hoff invents the first microprocessor.**	
1969	Continental-Emsco introduces their one thousand horsepower F-1000 triplex (three cylinder) mud pump for drilling.	
1969	Muammar Gaddafi launches a coup, takes over the government of Libya, cuts crude oil production, closes all the bars, and raises crude oil prices. Libya provides about a fourth of all oil exported to Europe.	
1969	USA; federal regulators "propose" that all new cars have positive restraints (automatic seatbelts or airbags), starting in 1972. Implementation will be delayed repeatedly. Volvo and Mercedes Benz now make 3 point seatbelts standard in the rear outboard seating positions.	(see 1972)
1969	December; the first production model Boeing 747 "Jumbo Jet" is delivered to Pan-American World Airways.	
1969	Texas; established back when gambling was only a misdemeanor, Joe Cotton "goes straight" when it became a federal offense. Joe turned his Robstown joint and his attention to barbecue. He takes eight years to perfect the sauce as he wanted it. This year he builds a plain, new, wooden building on the outskirts of town on US 77, it can and sometimes does, seat 360 people.	
1969-70	**The last Hall-Scott engine leaves the Hercules plant in Ohio, no one seems to know exactly when this era ended. Hall-Scotts are really great old gasoline burners, but they can't compete with the diesels. Hall-Scott built a few diesels, but they just weren't commercially successful.**	
1970s	Lacks phases out auto parts and hardware, emphasizing only home furnishings.	
1970s	While the recession has the entire world in its grip, in the UK, Humber is quietly fading away.	(see 1867)
1970s	Zales grows to 1,700 jewelry stores and now sometimes post single-day sales of $10 million.	
1970s	In the early 1970s, Hanab merges with Visser & Smit.	
1970s	In the 1970s, Mr. Joseph L. Rozier passes on and his son-in-law G. Robert Blanchard takes the helm at Joseph L. Rozier Machinery Company.	(see 1982)

1970	**CATERPILLAR ceases making and selling equipment with gasoline starting engines. The "pony motor" is no longer available, even as an option. However, young Jim Cowan converts a new #12E maintainer to gasoline start for Quay County, NM, by ordering each of the separate parts, building and installing a pony motor to fulfill the terms of the purchase contract.**	
1970	January; PAXMAN becomes a part of RUSTON PAXMAN DIESELS LTD.	(see 1998)
1970	EY&T acquires CHAR-LYNN CO., a manufacturer of hydraulic motors.	
1970	GENERAL MOTORS merges DETROIT DIESEL ENGINE DIVISION with the transmission and gas turbine operations of the ALLISON DIVISION of Indianapolis, forming the DETROIT DIESEL ALLISON DIVISION.	
1970	April; LONE STAR STEEL purchases certain production equipment, patents, etc, used in the manufacture of the highly respected A. O. SMITH line of high strength steel casing.	
1970	Starting this year, AMERICAN MOTORS CORP. takes over manufacture of the jeep.	
1970	A recent government ruling forbids non-profit foundations from owning more than a small percentage of a corporation. The LETOURNEAU FOUNDATION must divest itself of LETOURNEAU, INC. It is finally sold to MARATHON MFG. CO., becoming MARATHON LETOURNEAU COMPANY. The foundation has been the primary support for LETOURNEAU UNIVERSITY, and a large supporter of several other Christian charities.	
1970	HUBER MFG. CO. becomes a subsidiary of A-T-O INC.	
1970	EMERSON ELECTRIC acquires BROOK INSTRUMENTS.	
1970	German bearing manufacturer SKF now has 68 factories and 67,000 employees around the world.	
1970	Germany; the fifth generation of the Wacker family is now at the helm of the family business.	
1970	PENNZOIL UNITED, INC. spins-off its retail gas distribution assets into ENTEX CORP.	
1970	USA; this June 21st the PENN CENTRAL RAILROAD is bankrupt; the largest corporate bankruptcy in US history up to this time.	
1970	Wisconsin; BOMAG is acquired by the KOEHRING COMPANY of Milwaukee.	
1970	South Africa; BARLOW RAND is formed when THOMAS BARLOW & SONS acquires RAND MINES, LTD.	
1970	Texas; the end of an era, there'll be no more "Made in Texas by Texans" decals on Fords, as the outdated Dallas plant is closed.	
1970	Lee Iacocca becomes president of FORD, and soon the "subcompact" FORD Pinto is introduced. The Pinto is to compete directly with the recently introduced CHEVROLET Vega. *"Bubba, there's sumpin' to really brag about!"*	
1970	**The Environmental Protection Agency is created by the US government.**	
1970	On the Kola Peninsula, the Soviets begin drilling the Kola Borehole.	
1970	June; privately held MINNESOTA PAINTS, of Minneapolis, with annual sales of $24 million, merges with VALSPAR CORP., and the headquarters is moved to Minneapolis. In short order, PHELAN FAUST PAINT, SPEED-O-LAC CHEMICAL, CONCHEMCO'S DETROIT CHEMICAL COATING, and ELLIOT PAINT & VARNISH, are all joined together in "one big happy family."	
1970	A California attorney buys the Indian name to put on minibikes from Taiwan, but this venture will go bankrupt in 1976.	(see 1998)
1970	Certain assets of ROEBLING WIRE ROPE are acquired by BETHLEHEM WIRE ROPE DIVISION.	
1970	Japan becomes the world's second-largest producer of passenger cars. *"Hey Bubba, ya notice I didn't say automobiles."*	
1970	GENERAL MOTORS is leading the conversion to the use of unleaded gasoline.	

1970	Servo Delden of the Netherlands is acquired by HULS A. G. of Marl, Germany.	

	1970	Chrysler begins importing and marketing small passenger cars and light trucks built by Mitsubishi Motor Corp. (MMC) These vehicles from MMC will be branded and sold as Dodge and Plymouth brand names.	(see 1976)
	1970	Liebherr of Germany establishes a subsidiary company in Newport News, VA, USA.	
	1970	B-L-H Corporation becomes a part of the Clark Equipment organization.	
	1970	The headquarters of Allied Electronics is moved to Fort Worth, TX, from Chicago, IL.	
	1970	**For digital information storage, the 8 inch "floppy disc" is invented at IBM by a team reporting to Alan Shugart.**	
	1970	**The first game of the National Football League's *Monday Night Football* is broadcast on ABC-TV. ABC will carry this program for the next thirty-six years.**	(see 1974)
	1970	After a twenty-two-year television run and discovering Pat Boone, Ann-Margaret, and Gladys Knight, to name a few, Ted Mack's *Original Amateur Hour* is cancelled.	(see 1974)

1970	Carl Kiekhafer departs Mercury Marine Co.	
1970	By this time, over four million imported cars have been sold in the United States.	
1970	UK; from here on out, all Austin and all Morris trucks will carry the Leyland nameplate.	
1970	Heerema acquires the controlling interest in Wilbros.	
1970	North Carolina; fifteen-year-old Stephen Smith begins making pottery in the basement of his parents home.	(see 1977)
1970	Since being introduced in 1966, the AMX from AMC has only sold 19,000 cars, so don't expect to see a 1971 AMX.	
1970	Having been in production since '53, the last of the Pettibone motor graders are built this year.	(see 1972)
1970	France; at the Paris Intermat exposition, Poclain introduces the world's largest hydraulic excavator, their model EC 1000, with a 10 yd^3 bucket, powered by three GM 8V-71s for 840 horsepower, for this 150 ton machine. *NOTE: A competitors representative is overheard to say, "What a monster, why would anyone want a hydraulic backhoe that size."*	(see 1977)
1970	Lee Riders shifts its focus from work wear to fashion wear.	
1970	October; Muhammad Ali returns to boxing and shortly afterwards KO's Jerry Quarry.	
1970	Michigan; it is sliding on downwards… the population of Detroit is now 1,511,482 people.	(see 1980)
1970	Japan's first hydraulic "rough terrain" crane is introduced by Tadano, their TR-150, with a 15 ton capacity.	(see 1990)
1970	Bonneville Salt Flats, UT; a former delivery driver, Gary Gabelich, reaches 622.4 miles per hour in his rocket-powered vehicle, "Blue Flame."	(see 1983)
1970	Diesel/trolley power is first used for a fleet of large open-pit mining haul trucks.	(see 1972)
1970	Caterpillar Tractor Co. establishes the Cat Reman (parts and component remanufacturing) business.	
1970	In December, Lone Star Steel purchases the Ft. Collins plant of Southwestern Pipe of Colorado, Inc.	
1970	December 3; R. J. Reynolds Tobacco contracts to sponsor Nascar's premium division, now the Winston Cup Series.	
1970	Now only approximately five percent of Americans live and work on farms and ranches.	

1970	December 31; in the USA, today is the final day for cigarette advertising on television.	(see 1974)
1970-72	WILLIAMS BROS. builds the 315-mile, 20-to-26 inch, Trans-Ecuadorean Pipeline to carry crude oil from the oilfields in the Oriente del Ecuador, across the Andes. It is considered the most logistically difficult pipeline project ever built up to this time.	(see 1986)
1971	WOOLLEY TOOL CO. is acquired by CHROMALLOY AMERICAN CORP.	
1971	EATON YALE AND TOWNE, INC., changes its name to EATON CORPORATION.	
1971	Olathe, KS; RIMPULL CORP. is established to build mechanical-drive, off-road, dump trucks.	
1971	DIAMOND REO DIVISION is sold and re-registered as DIAMOND REO TRUCKS, INC.	
1971	Dallas; SOUTHWEST AIRLINES is founded by Rollin King and Herb Kelleher, with Lamar Muse as president.	
1971	UNITED MOTOR SERVICE is renamed UNITED DELCO DIVISION OF GENERAL MOTORS.	
1971	TOM BROWN DRLG, INC., changes its name to TOM BROWN INC. (TMBR)	
1971	July; the entire PAYNE organization, all personnel and manufacturing facilities become a part of CAMERON IRON WORKS, INC.	
1971	RAY-O-VAC is awarded patents for the silver oxide "button cell battery."	
1971	Tulsa businessmen catch GRC as it is spun-off from AMERADA-HESS.	
1971	SCHLUMBERGER acquires FLOPETROL, then acquire the other 50% of FOREX, creating Forex Neptune Drilling Co.	(see 1981)
1971	Canada; with financial backing of the New Brunswick government, Malcolm Bricklin starts producing his "safety" sports car, bearing the Bricklin name, of course.	(see 1974)
1971	In Longview, TX, CAPACITY OF TEXAS begins business building the terminal tractors, aptly called "Trailer Jockey."	
1971	MARITIME HYDRAULICS A/S is founded in Norway.	
1971	Developed by VERMEER, the first hay baler for large round bales is introduced.	
1971	USA; the AMTRAK railroad system is born.	
1971	The WEDC (Water Engineering for Developing Countries) organization becomes active.	
1971	KOPP AG is founded as a international pipeline service and testing business in Germany.	
1971	December 29; NUCLEAR CORP. OF AMERICA recapitalizes as NUCOR CORP., and they still are connected to REO, but don't ask me how.	
1971	Orlando, FL; WALT DISNEY WORLD opens to the public.	
1971	The LIMA CO. is purchased by CLARK EQUIPMENT COMPANY and its products are known as Clark-Lima. AUSTIN-WESTERN becomes a part of CLARK EQUIPMENT CO.	(see 1972)
1971	Albuquerque, NM; the first International (Hot Air) Balloon Fiesta is launched. *"And believe me, Bubba, I was there, and it is impressive."*	
1971	The LOUISVILLE & NASHVILLE RAILROAD with its 6,575 miles (10,520km) of track is bought by the SEABOARD COASTLINE RAILROAD. (SCInd)	
1971	**Beating the Giants 20-13, the Dallas Cowboys play their last game in the Cotton Bowl. Two weeks later the Cowboys beat the Patriots 44-21 in their inaugural game in Texas Stadium, their new home field in Irving.**	(see 2010)
1971	After 106 years, the UNION STOCKYARDS in Chicago cease operations.	

Florida Welcomes Walt Disney

WALT DISNEY — GOV. HAYDON BURNS — ROY DISNEY

1971	General Motors buys a one-third stake in Isuzu Motors of Japan; soon GM will buy up to a 49% interest.	
1971	Using Dassault Falcon planes, recently discharged Marine Captain Fred Smith establishes Federal Express Corp.	
1971	Utah Construction changes its name to Utah International, Inc.	
1971	Nestlé acquires Libbys foodstuffs company of the USA.	
	Missouri; operating from the basement from his father's warehouse in Springfield, John L. Morris opens the first Bass Pro Shop. John soon expands his Bass Pro Shop to include a full-line mail-order service, with a 180-page catalog.	
1971	Zambia; this African nation's federal government takes control of all major mines in Zambia's "copper belt."	
1971	Hancock GMBH is founded in Dörnigheim, Germany, by some leading employees who departed Esab-Kebe.	(see 1981)
1971	"Wide-body" DC-10 service is first introduced to the USA by American Airlines flights between Los Angeles and Chicago.	(see 1984)
1971	Chile; a few years ago, Anaconda, as well as Kennecott Copper agreed to "co-production" arrangements with the "middle-of-the-road" Frei government here. This year the far-left Allende government nationalizes completely Anaconda's Chuquicamata and El Salvador mines, as well as Kennecott's El Teniente mine.	
1971	This year in America, 2.3 million new guitars are sold. *"Yeah Bubba, that sounds really good to me."*	
1971	The OPEC countries begin nationalizing their oil assets, usually from foreign companies. Libya nationalizes the BP concession.	
1972	Kenworth's 50th Anniversary, and the first-ever year with unit sales volume in five figures.	(see 1975)
1972	**Echo manufactures the first leaf blower.**	
1972	Paccar buys Wagner Mining Equipment, Inc.	
1972	Westinghouse Air Brake sells George E. Failing Co., and the Failing name to Azcon Corporation.	
1972	Delta Drilling hires Claudine Shapley as "the first lady roughneck in the western world."	
1972	Howard Hughes, Jr., sells all his shares of Hughes Tool Co. and the company goes public.	
1972	Parker Drilling breaks its own record with a 20,500 foot (6,308 m) well in Pecos County, TX.	(see 1975)
1972	Pan Eastern Exploration Co. (later APX Corp.) is created as parent company of Anandarko.	
1972	Donaldson enters the dust collection business with the acquisition of Torit Corp.	
1972	Pampa, TX; Pupco is created by E. L. Hudson, C. Richards, and E. M. Keeler when they buy all the rights to Cabot Corporation pumping units.	
1972	Standard Oil replaces their Esso brand with Exxon, in most areas. Enco also becomes Exxon.	
1972	July; Clark Equipment Co. acquires BLH, and renames it Clark Equipment-Lima Div., producing "Clark-Madsen" equipment.	
1972	August; Northeast Airlines merges into Delta, giving Delta Air Lines more than 33,000 unduplicated route miles.	
1972	Texas; Pearce Industries Inc. is formed as the parent company of Waukesha-Pearce Industries and Texas Iron Works.	

1972	The AAODC is renamed the INTERNATIONAL ASSOCIATION OF DRILLING CONTRACTORS (IADC), to better reflect the true scope of their international operations.	
1972	Mansfield, TX; AZTEC TRAILERS is founded.	
1972	Pasadena, TX; GROVES INDUSTRIAL SUPPLY is founded as a distributor of EXXON Paint as well as EXXON Chemical Products.	
1972	TRI-STATE OIL TOOL INDUSTRIES, INC. is now the world's largest international fishing service company.	
1972	Already having two stores in East Texas, DAVIS-KEMP TOOL CO. buys the 50 year old RUSSELL TOOL & SUPPLY COMPANY of Monahans, TX.	
1972	Kentucky has now became America's leading coal-producing state.	(see 1988)
1972	Wearing hot pants, cleavage-revealing tops, and white boots, the transformed DALLAS COWBOYS CHEERLEADERS make their season debut.	
1972	UK; the HESTAIR GROUP, owners of Yorkshire Vehicles and of Eagle Engineering, takes over DENNIS BROTHERS.	
1972	The first FIESTA MART ethnic grocery stores are opened for business.	
1972	Houston, TX; a new "World-Class" indoor shopping mall, the GALLERIA, complete with ice-skating rink, opens for business.	
1972	The TSS Mardi Gras, CARNIVAL CRUISE LINE's first ship, runs aground on a sandbar on its maiden voyage.	
1972	USA; oil-digesting microbes are created by Dr. Ananda Mohan Chakrabarty.	
1972	According to one source, there are only three billionaires living in the entire world today.	
1972	CATERPILLAR's primary radiator supplier, PERFEX of Milwaukee, is now being represented by EDWARD D. NEWELL CO. (ENCO) of Kenosha, WI.	
1972	UK; LEYLAND MOTORS LTD. ceases production of all Albion trucks, dropping the Albion name.	
1972	In just the past four years, the number of truck stops in the US has almost doubled, from 2,000 to 3,800.	(see 2008)
1972	Europe; once again, interest is stirred regarding a tunnel between England and France, under the English Channel.	
1972	ESAB INC. is established in the USA.	
1972	PETTIBONE relocates its Road Machinery Div. to Ft. Worth, it then becomes a part of PETTIBONE TEXAS.	(see 1975)
1972	Since its 1958 introduction, the CHEVROLET Impala has sold ten million units, and that ain't hay!	
1972	LEE, as in LEE RIDERS, is the first to introduce the "leisure suit." *"Naw Slim, I shore wouldn't have told that!"*	
1972	USA; "FASTEN SEAT BELTS" warning lights and buzzers now nag drivers to buckle up.	(see 1974)
1972	CATERPILLAR introduces their first excavator, the hydraulic model 225. Having several evolutions of prototypes during the past ten years or so, the 225 is a very good machine. The 225 almost immediately eclipses the competition world-wide, some of whom are in their second or third generation.	
1972	Having spent the past decade and a quarter of a billion dollars on development, almost ruining POLAROID CORP., they now release the iconic Polaroid SX-70, and it seems to catch on, really catch on!!!	(see 1974)
1972	Wichita, KS, July 18; Harland W. Cardwell, Sr., dies at age 91. Born in Richland, KS, the retired owner and founder of CARDWELL MANUFACTURING Co. came to Wichita in 1923.	

1972	Wichita, KS; this summer, all operations are ceased at the CARDWELL MANUFACTURING facility at 801 S. Wichita Street.		
1972	RUCKER SHAFFER develops the first spherical blow-out preventer (BOP).	(see 1975)	
1972	UNIT RIG is the first manufacturer to build a 200 ton capacity, two-axle, rear dump truck for mining.	(see 1974)	
1972	The government of Iraq nationalizes the Iraq Petroleum Concession.		
1973	ABEGG & REINHOLD change their name to VARCO INTERNATIONAL.	(see 2004)	
1973	MARION POWER SHOVEL CO. purchases V-CON from PEERLESS MFG.		

1973	Out Snyder way, Scurry County, TX, produces its billionth barrel of crude oil.	
1973	GM manufactures the first production car equipped with an optional air cushion restraint system. The Oldsmobile Toronado is the first production car with safety air bags.	(see 1975)
1973	November 24th, George Failing gets in his car, drives to the hospital, and dies at the age of 87.	
1973	OILWELL SUPPLY introduces the "Really Huge" 49½" rotary table.	(see 1998)
1973	BORGWARNER develops a modern "full time" 4WD transfer case.	
1973	**One of the first personal computers is the Xerox Alto, with a whopping 128K of memory.**	
1973	The original Fuller Brush Man, Albert G. Fuller dies. There are now more women "Fullerettes" than Fuller Brush men, selling Fuller brushes.	

1973	In Everett, WA, EVERETT PAD & PAPER COMPANY is founded.		
1973	The RILEY CORPORATION acquires BEAIRD INDUSTRIES of Shreveport, LA.		
1973	Texas; the GREATER SOUTHWEST INTERNATIONAL AIRPORT closes as the DALLAS/FT. WORTH REGIONAL AIRPORT opens only a few miles North.		
1973	In the UK, Godfrey N. Houndsfield's CT Scanner is first used.		
1973	SMITH TOOL COMPANY becomes simply SMITH TOOL.		
1973	ROWAN DRILLING acquires the air-taxi operator MERRIC, INC. of Anchorage, AK.	(see 1975)	
1973	LISTER Auto-Truck production is transferred to CROMPTON of Tredegar, or somewhere like that.		
1973	STOUFFERS is acquired by NESTLÉ.		
1973	Now that GOLD BOND STAMPS is quite diversified, Carlson changes its name to the CARLSON COMPANIES.		
1973	During the past four years, BFI has acquired more than 150 local waste companies around the US; BFI is now the world's largest trash collector.		
1973	Don Williams is the first Country singer to make a video to support release of a song, with his "Come Early Morning."		
1973	On KWKH radio in Shreveport, a "resurrected" *Louisiana Hayride* takes off for another run.	(see 1987)	
1973	December 1; in Pasadena, TX, Larry N. Forehand opens the first CASA OLE Mexican food restaurant.		
1973	After fifteen years, William "Bill" Boyd leaves his law practice, and joins full-time his dad Sam, and they buy the ELDORADO CLUB in Henderson, NV.	(see 1975)	

1973	BELIOT TOOLS's name is changed to REGAL-BELIOT by Kenyon Taylor.	(see 1978)
1973	Galion, OH; the local GALION IRON WORKS is renamed GALION MFG. CO., a division of JEFFREY GALION INC.	(see 1974)
1973	This year, the five FLINT companies are combined into FLINT INDUSTRIES.	(see 1993)
1973	Germany; in August production of the OPEL GT ceases, after more than 103,400 are produced and sold.	
1973	The Saudi Arabian government acquires a 25% interest in ARAMCO, as Iran nationalizes its petroleum reserves.	
1973	Paul Foley's son, Paul J. (Skip) Foley, Jr., becomes president of FOLEY TRACTOR COMPANY.	(see 1997)
1973	The Yom Kippur War, as Egypt and Syria attack Israel. The US sides with and supports Israel. Crude oil prices go from $2.90 up to $11.65 a barrel, as the Arabs embargo oil exports to the US for siding with Israel.	
1973	Egypt, retaliating against Britain's support of Israel in the Yom Kippur War, seizes all SHELL assets here… OPEC raises oil prices from three dollars to twelve dollars per barrel.	

1974	Manufacturing rights for SCOOPMOBILE loaders are purchased by EAGLE CRUSHER of Galion, OH, but they will build fewer and fewer of them.	
1974	FIAT SpA of Italy purchases a majority of ALLIS-CHALMERS' shares, and the FIAT-ALLIS joint venture was born.	
1974	Columbus, OH; as DRESSER INDUSTRIES buys the JEFFREY GALION CO. so GALION IRON WORKS & MFG. of Galion, OH, now becomes a division of DRESSER CORPORATION.	(see 1976) (see 1977)
1974	UNITED DELCO DIVISION and A-C SPARK PLUG DIVISION combine, forming A-C DELCO.	
1974	NATIONAL CASH REGISTER CO. changes its name to NCR CORP.	
1974	HUGHES TOOL acquires BJ SERVICES from BORG-WARNER, and soon changes the name to BJ-HUGHES.	
1974	The Black Butte Mine, near Rocksprings, WY, is established, it will eventually cover over seventy square miles.	
1974	UNITED GAS PIPELINE is restructured as UNITED ENERGY RESOURCES, INC.	
1974	REPUBLIC STEEL buys MOONEY from BUTLER AVIATION.	
1974	March; the Arab oil embargo on exports to the US is lifted.	
1974	Texas; ANADARKO petroleum moves their headquarters from Ft. Worth to Houston.	
1974	MARMON introduces a new generation of highway trucks.	(see 1976)
1974	**VOLKSWAGEN builds the last KARMAN-GHIA.**	
1974	CCC introduces the first complete vehicle specifically designed for waste management (garbage truck). Previously the special compacting bodies were mounted on a standard truck chassis.	
1974	MOTOROLA sells its television business, Quasar, to MATSUSHITA ELECTRONICS of Japan.	(see 1978)
1974	ALCO STANDARD sells DAVEY COMPRESSOR CO. to the RAZETTE BROS.	
1974	CHICAGO PNEUMATIC buys ALLIED CONSTRUCTION PRODUCTS, INC.	
1974	The "Taser" is invented by Jack Cover and named for the book *Thomas A. Swift and his Electric Rifle*.	
1974	A machine to make wire rope up to 7 inches in diameter is installed by BETHLEHEM WIRE ROPE.	
1974	In San Diego, CA, Tom Hawthorne (chairman of the CAT dealer HAWTHORNE MACHINERY) starts the first CATERPILLAR "Rent-to-Rent" business.	
1974	UNIT DRILLING CO. buys four rigs from LEABEN DRILLING CO.	
1974	USA; thanks to the oil embargo "crisis," a nationwide 55 mph speed limit goes into effect.	

1974	Lone Star Production drills the Bertha Rogers # 1-27 to a depth of 31,441 feet (9,583 meter) in Washita County, OK. Drilling is stopped when they strike molten sulphur.	
1974	The bearing manufacturer, FAG now have over 31,000 employees working in over 100 countries.	
1974	Panex Corp. is founded in Sugarland, TX.	
1974	Stewart & Stevenson Uk, Ltd., is established in the UK.	
1974	Harris-Intertype, now renamed Harris Corp., moves from Cleveland, OH, to Melbourne, FL.	
1974	Essex Wire merges with a subsidiary of United Aircraft, later to be named United Technologies.	
1974	With the acquisition of L'Oréal, Nestlé diversifies from their strictly food-related products.	
1974	Texas; the "Weed Eater," invented by George Ballas of Houston, is first marketed.	
1974	Having introduced American audiences to so many timeless legends, such as Nat "King" Cole, Ella Fitzgerald, Elvis Presley, the Rolling Stones, Itzhak Perlman, and the Beatles, the stone-faced Ed Sullivan dies. He had so very many "really good shews."	

1974	GM introduces the catalytic converter, a technology it developed in the 1960s, on its passenger vehicles. All 1975 year model passenger cars sold in the US and Canada are equipped with catalytic converters, to comply with provisions of the US Federal Clean Air Act.
1974	UK; BMC's Scammel truck tractors are now being assembled at the old Guy Motor Works facility.
1974	Texas; Panola County native "Tex" Ritter dies, having acted in 85 movies and recorded hundreds of songs. A few of his best-known and most successful were "Rye Whiskey," "You are My Sunshine," "The Boll Weevil Song," "High Noon," and "Wayward Wind." Ritter will be buried in Port Neches, TX.
1974	The Ford Motor Company introduces its F-150 (⅝ ton) pickup truck.

1974	About this time, the Oak Ridge Boys crossover from gospel to country music and immediately become major league chart-toppers. The next 15 years will see about 50 hits from them, including 17 that reach #1 on the charts.	(see 2009)
1974	On cars built in the USA, ignition-interlocks prevent the engine starting unless the driver's seatbelt is buckled. Tremendous public outrage prompts Congress to rescind the ignition-interlock feature this October.	(see 1975)
1974	May 8; a fire today severely damages a 700-foot section of the "Great Bridge" at Poughkeepsie, NY. The eighty-five-year-old railroad bridge is now closed to all traffic.	(see 2009)
1974	China; new steam locomotives are still being built in several plants here, at the rate of about one per day, for use on the nation's railroads. The "Steam Age" has long since past in North America, Britain, and mainland Europe, but is still going strong in much of Asia.	
1974	Armstrong Bros. Tool Co. builds a second manufacturing facility in Fayetteville, AR. It features one of the most modern drop forge shops in the world, among all the other modern equipment.	(see 1994)
1974	I guess it did catch on: Polaroid's SX-70 cameras spit out about a billion photos this year.	
1974	Finland; Saab-Scania and Leyland each had 10% of Sisu stock, but this year Sisu returns to 100% Finnish state ownership.	(see 1998)
1974	Now get this... Unit Rig is the first to develop and operate a fleet of "Driverless Trucks" working in an open-pit mine.	

ca. 1975	BREWSTER EQUIPMENT CO. of Shreveport, is bought by SKYTOP DRILLING EQUIP. of Victoria, Texas; now SKYTOP BREWSTER.	
1975	About this time, GETTY OIL and SKELLY merge.	
1975	DIAMOND REO TRUCKS, INC. goes into receivership. In late 1975, DIAMOND REO sells to CONSOLIDATED INDUSTRIES of Columbus, OH. Vehicle production is discontinued & manufacturing rights for conventional models is acquired by former DIAMOND-T distributor, OSTERLAND, INC. of Harrisburg, PA.	
1975	Texas; PARKER DRILLING buys OIME, in Odessa, and creates PARTECH.	(see 1981)
1975	UK; MARSHALL & SONS, LTD., merges with AVELING-BARFORD, to form AVELING-MARSHALL.	
1975	Dr. Tetsuya Fujita explains "microbursts" of wind.	
1975	Ray Brazzel and his wife Ann found BANDERA DRILLING in Abilene, TX.	
1975	Houston; Ellis Williams founds his company with the idea to subcontract manufacturing of pumps for other factories.	
1975	PHILLIPS PETROLEUM CO. receives its 10,000th US patent.	
1975	Both the DIAMOND IRON WORKS and the legendary AUSTIN-WESTERN CRUSHER COMPANY are acquired by EAGLE CRUSHER COMPANY.	
1975	CHAMPION unveils the largest production road grader ever, their 100-T, weighing… 100 tons. It will be produced until 1989.	
1975	NATIONAL SUPPLY buys the remaining 50% of OILWELL ENGINEERING.	
1975	TOTCO acquires CALCO INSTRUMENTS of Oklahoma City.	
1975	Canada; after producing 2062 cars and with 12 still on the assembly line, BRICKLIN MOTORS goes into receivership, over one-half of all the cars BRICKLIN produced, are still in use 30 years later.	(see 2005)
1975	The first "longwall shearer" for mines is introduced by JOY.	
1975	I-R purchases WALCO LORAIN of Okmulgee, OK.	
1975	The renamed TIMEX CORP. sells one of every two watches sold in the US, due in no small part to the 250,000 sales outlets.	
1975	Joe Bowden, Sr. starts WILD WELL CONTROL CO.	
1975	USA; UPS forges the "Golden Link," becoming the first package delivery company to serve every address in the "Lower 48."	
1975	CAMECO is now a multi-national company, distributing their specialized sugar cane machinery.	
1975	ROWAN DRILLING COMPANY acquires LIVINGSTON COPTERS, INC. of Juneau, AK.	(see 1985)
1975	Texas; serious drilling is now beginning in the Austin Chalk formation of the Pearsall field of South Texas.	
1975	As DRESSER WAYNE acquires SPENCO SYSTEMS, they also introduce the first electronic computing fuel dispenser.	
1975	Sadly for all of us "gearheads," renowned automotive journalist Tom McCahill dies at home at age sixty-eight. McCahill is credited with creation of the "Zero to Sixty" acceleration measurement, now universally accepted in automotive testing.	
1975	KOOMEY CONTROL SYSTEMS is acquired by RUCKER SHAFFER CORPORATION.	(see 1978)
1975	USA; the Volkswagen "Rabbit" is the first car to have passive (automatic) seatbelts (shoulder belts only).	(see 1981)

1975	Scientists develop a featherless chicken, however, it is not commercially viable. They find it is more expensive to heat the chicken houses more often and to warmer temperatures than it is to pluck the feathers from the chickens.	
1975	Los Angeles; after they saw a man die after a fall into a vat of cleaning chemicals, Bruce FaBrizio and his father, a chemical salesman, decided to create a safe, environmental-friendly cleaning fluid, made in America. This year, their "Simple Green" general purpose cleaning fluid is first marketed.	

1975	Duluth, MN; the Bartell family sells Barko Hydraulics Inc. to Pettibone, then the Bartells stay on to manage Barko. Barko continues to operate as a division of Pettibone well into the twenty-first century.	(see 1980)
1975	Twenty-nine lives are lost when the *Edmund Fitzgerald* is the only vessel lost in yet another bad Great Lakes storm.	
1975	Nevada; Sam and Bill Boyd open the California Hotel & Casino in downtown Las Vegas. Soon they create the revolutionary Sam's Town in nearby Boulder, starting what will be known as the Boulder Strip, the third major gaming area for Las Vegas. Sam's Town is built on 13 acres of desert land at the "quiet" intersection of Boulder highway and Nellis (AFB) Boulevard as a resort to cater to locals, and the Boyd's gamble pays off very well.	(see 1993)
1975	The Oldsmobile Cutlass is the "Best Selling Mid-Size" auto in the United States of America.	
1975	During the decade 1966 to now, Caterpillar has doubled its manufacturing space to almost 32 million square feet. In line with that, their long-term debt has risen from $123 million in 1965 to $851 million this year. On the other hand, Cat has tripled its business over this past decade. This year Caterpillar almost reaches the $5 Billion mark.	(see 1976)
1975	Springfield, MO; Ozark Kenworth opens for business with only three persons, no parts, or service department. In the future Murphy-Hoffman Co. will be an extension of Ozark Kenworth.	(see 2005)
1975	The Venezuelan oil industry is nationalized.	
1975	Due to market slump, and more taxes, Frontier Airlines is now experiencing record revenue losses. Now Frank Lorenzo's Peoples Express Airlines buys Frontier for only $24 a share.	(see 1986)
1975	The first crude oil is produced from the North Sea.	
1976	**The United States Of America CELEBRATES its bicentennial.** *"Yeah Bubba, our great republic is 200 years old."*	
1976	New Mexico; moving from the old facilities built forty-odd years ago by Col. R. L. Harrison, Caterpillar dealer Rust Tractor Company moves into a new, truly world class facility on Osuna Rd NE, just off I-25, in northeast Albuquerque.	
1976	Koehring divides and sells Parsons; Seaman-Maxe takes the small trenchers and Trenchliner buys the larger ones.	
1976	Eaton Corp. sells McQuay-Norris.	
1976	Goodbary starts building off-road, bottom dump, electric drive trucks.	
1976	CCC introduce their "Corsair" line of oil well pulling and workover rigs.	
1976	**The last Oliver name-plated tractor is produced.**	
1976	Mannesmann AG makes a 100% takeover of Rexroth.	
1976	Cedarapids buys El Jay, Inc., for its famous RollerCone Crushers.	
1976	Don Branham sells his interest in Pyramid Derrick & Equip. and founds Branham Industries in Conroe, TX.	

1976	MARMON installs its first sleeper cabs on its hand-made trucks, the trade press is touting MARMON as "The Cadillac of the Industry."	(see 1998)
1976	DRESSER-CLARK tests the highest air or gas compressor pressure ever, 10,500 psi.	
1976	GRAY TOOL CO. becomes a division of COMBUSTION ENGINEERING.	
1976	The digital vernier caliper is invented by BROWN & SHARPE.	
1976	MANSFIELD SANITARY POTTERY becomes MANSFIELD PLUMBING PRODUCTS, INC.	
1976	SWACO is spun off as a separate division of DRESSER INDUSTRIES.	
1976	In the piney woods of East Texas, LONE STAR STEEL completes a $81 million expansion program.	(see 1977)
1976	**The AUTOMOTIVE HALL OF FAME opens in Midland Michigan, 130 miles north of Detroit.**	
1976	W. Glen Hicks buys CLEMENT TRAILERS from GARWOOD INDUSTRIES, and renames it CLEMENT INDUSTRIES, INC. During the next two decades, trailer production will be increased 500% and the products will be sold world-wide.	
1976	AMSTAR acquires MILWAUKEE ELECTRIC TOOL CORPORATION.	
1976	Americus, GA; Millard Fuller founds HABITAT FOR HUMANITY... self-help, homebuilding organization.	
1976	The digital camera is invented by Steven J. Sasson, an engineer at EASTMAN KODAK COMPANY.	(see 2011)
1976	Red (he could make a mule cry) Sovine's tear-jerking narration of "Teddy Bear" climbs to #1 on the charts faster than any other song in recording history. The song's record speed to #1 remains intact for decades.	
1976	SUPERIOR CABLE is divested by CONTINENTAL TELEPHONE, but will soon be acquired by SIECOR CORP.	
1976	UTAH INTERNATIONAL effects a $2.3 billion merger with GENERAL ELECTRIC.	
1976	The now-diversified GENERAL CIGAR COMPANY, changes its name to CULBRO CORPORATION.	
1976	LYKES-YOUNGSTOWN CORP. name is shortened to LYKES CORPORATION.	
1976	The CARLSON COMPANIES' revenue climbs to one BILLION dollars this year.	(see 1993)
1976	Columbus, OH; JEFFERY MINING & MANUFACTURING sells to DRESSER INDUSTRIES, closing the local facility.	
1976	CHRYSLER CORP. gets a $4 billion US Army contract to build XM-1 tanks.	(see 1978)
1976	April; CADILLAC produces the last American convertible, for almost a decade, anyhow.	
1976	The first National Bus Roadeo, similar to the Truck Roadeo, is held this year.	
1976	This year CATERPILLAR surpasses the $5 billion mark as they gross $5.4 billion. They must be doing something right!!	
1976	USA; twenty years after its initiation, 38,000 miles (60,800km) of the 42,500 mile (68,000km) Interstate Highway system are completed are completed and open to traffic.	(see 1981)
1976	Canada; VERSATILE has made some big 400-500 hp tractors, and this year, their "Big Roy," a 25 ton, 8 wheeled (2 on each axle shaft), monster is powered by a CUMMINS turbocharged/ intercooled six cylinder job, putting out 600 horsepower @2100 rpm. Sporting a 463-gallon fuel tank, only one is ever built, as the recession hits about this time.	
1976	The Elk Hills Naval Petroleum Reserve in California is opened up for commercial production.	
1977	January; for the first time known, snow falls in Miami, FL. This same storm pushes snow as far south as the Bahamas.	

U.S. Patent   Dec. 26, 1978   Sheet 1 of 2   4,131,919

FIG.1
FIG.3
FIG. 4
PRIOR ART

1977	February 25; working to the end on the continuing development of Lake Havasu City, AZ, Robert Paxton McCulloch dies.	
1977	February; Page R. Lewis is the first toolpusher on the first SCR land rig in Venezuela, LOFFLAND Rig 68. It's a UNIT 1220, with a Lee C. Moore derrick.	
1977	TIDEWATER, INC. acquires HILLARD OIL & GAS, a drilling and production firm.	(see 1979)
1977	B & S introduces the "Farymann" air-cooled diesel engine, to the US	
1977	DAIMLER-BENZ acquires EUCLID from WHITE MOTOR CORPORATION.	(see 1984)
1977	S. S. KRESGE is now K-MART CORP.	
1977	The BOLER COMPANY purchases HENDRICKSON.	
1977	April; LONE STAR STEEL begins a $100 million expansion program, soon an additional $13.5 million plan is added.	
1977	May; the 48-inch, 800-mile, $8 billion Trans-Alaska pipeline is completed. After three years work, costing $7.7 Billion, it is the most expensive private engineering and construction project in history. The fleet of equipment is sold at auction, and although the many used track-type pipe layers will glut the world market for the next decade, overall, the general "purpose machines" are absorbed with minimal impact on new equipment sales. There are a total of 720 tracked machines. *"Bubba, 'at's ten mil-yun dollars a mahl!"*	(see 1987)

1977	June 5; the first Apple II computer goes on sale. With a list price of $1,298, more than five million will be sold.
1977	Kenneth Olsen, founder and president of DIGITAL EQUIPMENT CORP., firmly states, "There is no reason for any individual to have a computer in their home." Decades later, Olsen says that is not "exactly" what he said.
1977	DOMINION ROAD MACHINERY CO. has prospered through the years with its Champion graders, so now it's renamed CHAMPION ROAD MACHINERY COMPANY.

1977	REPUBLIC STEEL purchases HOWARD SUPPLY CO. and makes it a division of REPUBLIC SUPPLY.	
1977	**BROCKWAY MOTOR TRUCK CO. is shut down permanently by MACK, its parent company.**	
1977	Chester Posey buys PUPCO.	(see 1978)
1977	Oklahoma; PACCAR purchases BRADEN WINCH COMPANY.	
1977	DANA CORP. acquires WEATHERHEAD.	
1977	KENNECOTT sells PEABODY COAL CO. and other entities, and PEABODY HOLDING COMPANY is created.	
1977	There are now thirteen Cracker Barrel Old Country stores.	
1977	Oklahoma City; Robert R. Willis, who started mudlogging with HYCALOG in 1950, departs DRESSER, and establishes TECHNICAL DRILLING SERVICES.	
1977	BFI gets the garbage contract in Oklahoma City, as it is one of the first cities to privatize waste collection.	
1977	Even though it is just a revamped gasoline engine, GM offers the first domestic diesel automobile engine in some of its 1978 model year Oldsmobile passenger cars.	
1977	Canada; KREMCO completes its first "in-house" designed workover rigs.	
1977	North Carolina; realizing that pottery making will be his career, Stephen Smith now founds TUMBLEWEED POTTERY.	
1977	DRESSER INDUSTRIES acquires the MARION POWER SHOVEL CO., the second largest shovel builder after BUCYRUS-ERIE.	(see 1982)

1977	TENNECO CORPORATION becomes a major stockholder in POCLAIN, and will over the next few years, merge the POCLAIN excavators and TENNECO's existing Case-Drott excavators into a single product line.
1977	WESTERN-GILLETTE TRANSPORTATION sells out to ROADWAY EXPRESS.
1977	December 31; at midnight tonight, the tolls stop and the 30-mile Dallas-Fort Worth Turnpike is officially transferred to the Texas Department of Highways and Public Transportation. Removal of the toll booths will begin in a few days.
1978	ENSEARCH CORPORATION purchases all INTAIRDRIL Companies, (except Sholas Schall, Oiltools, International, & Intairdril Switzerland) from Cyrus V. Helm, for US $140,000,000 PLUS other considerations. Many other considerations. POOL ARABIA is merged with INTAIRDRIL SAUDI, creating such a mess as few of us have ever seen. *"Yessir, Alvie, you and I will see it again."*
1978	EATON acquires CUTLER-HAMMER.
1978	February; the film soundtrack to *Grease,* starring John Travolta and Olivia Newton-John, hits number one this month.
1978	SCHWINN introduces the "AIRDYNE" stationary bicycle for exercise.
1978	BAYLOR ELECTRIC of Sugarland, TX, buys the rights to the DELCO AC generators from GENERAL MOTORS CORP.
1978	**The fastest production "stock" vehicle sold in the US is the DODGE LIL' RED WAGON, a pickup truck.**
1978	Knowing his high standing in the industry, Ellis Williams is pressured into building his own EWCO brand mud pumps.
1978	Born June 26, 1902, William P. "Bill" Lear dies of leukemia on May 14, having earned over 150 patents during his lifetime. Lear had been currently working on the Model 2400 Learfan, a "…somewhat radical" seven-passenger plane powered by two turboprop engines also powering a prop on the plane's tail. Lear's estimated wealth is about $75 million. His widow, Maya, continues to run LEAR AVIA, as well as LEARENO, and she sits on the board of LEAR FAN.
1978	COOPER ROLLS, a joint venture, is formed to market gas turbines.
1978	EAGLE CRUSHER buys MADSEN ASPHALT.
1978	INGERSOLL-RAND shuts down the few remaining operations of MILLERS FALLS MFG.
1978	KATO ENGINEERING becomes a subsidiary of RELIANCE ELECTRIC.
1978	CURTIS MATHES is now known as "The most expensive television in America, and darn well worth it."
1978	NATIONAL SUPPLY acquires PAR INDUSTRIES, then acquires DERRICK SERVICE INT'L and COMPRESSOR PUMP & SERVICE.
1978	PHOENIX-SEADRILL is formed when Mr. Hargrove and his wife sit at their kitchen table in Houston and decide to get into the off-shore drilling business.
1978	**After years of prototype testing, CAT introduces the elevated sprocket "high drive," 700 hp D10, weighing 88 tons with dozer blade.**
1978	TOTCO acquires the Visulogger line from METRODATA, of Norman, OK. Later this year TOTCO division headquarters move from Glendale, CA, to Norman, OK.
1978	Chester Posey buys GEARENCH, including facilities in Houston and Clifton, TX.
1978	J. RAY MCDERMOTT acquires BABCOCK & WILCOX.

(see 1999)

(see 2015)

(see 1979)

WILLIAM P. LEAR WITH TURBINE ENGINE

1978	EAGLE CRUSHER of Galion, OH, buys the batch plant line from CLARK EQUIPMENT, and now only makes parts for existing plants, building no new units.		
1978	July 13; Henry the second fires Lee Iacocca as president of FORD MOTOR COMPANY; bad mistake Hank (I have always thought he was afraid of Iacocca's potential). This year the 150,000,000th FORD motor vehicle is built. Shortly afterward, Lee Iacocca arrives at CHRYSLER CORPORATION... and did they ever need him!!!		
1978	"Mr. Zippo," George Blaisdell dies.		
1978	Ron Shore and his wife Grace found TEC WELL SERVICE in Kilgore, TX.		
1978	Houston; Boots Hansen and Coots Matthews abruptly leave RED ADAIR, forming BOOTS & COOTS INTERNATIONAL.		
1978	Snyder, TX; PATTERSON DRILLING is founded by A. Glenn Patterson.		
1978	**Janet Guthrie, driving the Texaco Star, becomes the first female driver to complete the Indy 500.**		
1978	In the past three years, over 1,000 wells have been drilled in the Pearsall field in South Texas.		
1978	Canada; in the oil sands of the province of Alberta, SYNCRUDE opens its bitumen mine.		
1978	UK; all vehicle production has ceased at the old GUY MOTOR WORKS plant, and before long this facility will be demolished.		

		1978	The HARRINGTON HOIST business is taken over by the ARBEE CORPORATION.	(see 1990)
		1978	HEEREMA introduces the world's first two semi-submersible crane vessels; the Balder and the Hermod each have a 2,000 ton as well as a 3,000-ton crane.	
		1978	US auto supplier, the BUDD COMPANY, is acquired by the THYSSEN GROUP of Germany.	
		1978	Texas; Bob Ryan is the first to call the Dallas Cowboys, "America's Team," and the idea spreads like wildfire.	

1978	Having acquired several smaller players, such as EMPIRE GAGE, WALTER T. COLE, STALWORTH TOOL, M. E. C. CORPORATION, CALEDEC GAGE, PREMIUM CUTTING TOOLS, and GLENBARD MFG., over the past few years, Kenyon Taylor now buys ORBMARK COMPANY, and soon brings James Packard from FRITO-LAY, as his General Manager of REGAL-BELIOT.		
1978	September; Tommy Corder and Leroy Belcher organize RAMCO WELL SERVICE, based in Ballinger, TX.		
1978	ASTRA-ZENECA launches their Patient Assistance Program, to provide A-Z medicines to many folks who otherwise could not afford their medication.		
1978	At BIG BUD TRACTORS, Ron Harmon builds the world's first 1000-horsepower farm tractor. The Big Bud 16V-747 is a big articulated brute with a Detroit Diesel 16V-92 power plant. This 1464-cubic-inch (24 L) engine is rated at 760 hp, but easily can be turned up to 1,000 horsepower. Only one Big Bud is ever built; its owner claims it paid for itself in only two years, due to its prodigious amount of work.		
1978	December 6; JONES & LAUGHLIN SUPPLY CO. is merged into CONTINENTAL-EMSCO (C-E) as part of the new C-E under LTV Corp. C-E now has 108 supply stores, as well as manufacturing plants in Garland and Houston, TX, and Sand Springs, OK.	(see 1981)
1978	NL INDUSTRIES (formerly National Lead) acquires RUCKER SHAFFER.	(see 1992)
1979	McGRAW-EDISON purchases STUDEBAKER-WORTHINGTON, making TURBODYNE a part of a major international company.		

1979	February 15; Paul C. Koomey founds KOOMEY, INC., in Houston. Previously Paul Koomey has been head of STEWART & STEVENSON's oil field division.	
1979	February 18; today's Daytona 500 is the first 500 mile race in history to be telecast live, flag-to-flag.	
1979	March; the near catastrophe at Three Mile Island nuclear power plant in New York.	
1979	ZENITH acquires HEATH, of Heathkit fame.	
1979	WHITE CONSOLIDATED INDUSTRIES buys FRIGIDAIRE from GM.	
1979	COOPER INDUSTRIES acquires GARDNER-DENVER CO. and its various divisions.	(see 1993)
1979	The fluid filter manufacturer WIX merges into DANA CORPORATION.	
1979	DRESSER-ATLAS introduces their Computerized Logging Services.	
1979	THOMAS BARLOW & SONS acquires WRENN BROTHERS and moves some operations into the US.	
1979	TRI-FLO INDUSTRIES begins operations in Conroe, TX.	
1979	TIDEWATER MARINE adds an additional twenty-six vessels to its fleet.	(see 1983)
1979	NORGE and ADMIRAL are acquired by MAGIC CHEF this year.	
1979	NATIONAL acquires BAYLOR ELECTRIC, then acquires a small oilfield services company in Oklahoma, and renames it NATIONAL CHEMICALS.	
1979	ANADARKO discovers the High Island A-376 oilfield just off the Texas coast.	
1979	The old boy from the flatlands of New Mexico, Conrad Hilton dies.	(see 2008)
1979	The WALWORTH COMPANY (valves, etc.) is acquired by LANZAGORTA of Mexico.	
1979	FORD acquires twenty-five percent of TOYO KOGYO (MAZDA) of Japan.	
1979	MARATHON MFG. including Marathon LeTourneau becomes a wholly-owned subsidiary of PENN CENTRAL CORP.	
1979	FALCON SEABOARD merges with DIAMOND SHAMROCK.	
1979	The first AUTO SHACK store opens in Forrest City, AR, with Doc Crain as manager.	
1979	The RILEY CORPORATION sells BEAIRD INDUSTRIES to UNITED STATES FILTER CORPORATION.	(see 1981)
1979	Adding exploration and production to its drilling business, UNIT DRILLING changes its name to UNIT DRILLING & EXPLORATION COMPANY.	
1979	TARO INDUSTRIES, LTD. acquires LEGRAND, LTD.	
1979	SKAGGS and ALBERTSON's have an amicable divorce, thus dissolving SKAGGS-ALBERTSON's.	
1979	Durham, NC; STRATHERN HOUSE GROUP acquires the old DURHAM FURNITURE COMPANY factory.	
1979	The great-grandson of a freed slave, Robert Johnson founds BLACK ENTERTAINMENT TELEVISION (BET).	(see 1982)
1979	**The Australian airline QANTAS becomes the world's first all-747 airline, as they phase out the last of their 707 planes. QANTAS also introduces the world's first Business Class, between coach and first-class service.**	
1979	As IEA is developing its own line of various types of industrial flat-tube radiators, its representation of the PERFEX RADIATOR line now ceases.	
1979	Louisiana; HUNT ENGINE COMPANY is established as a Detroit Diesel Dealer.	
1979	VISSER & SMIT HANAB is formed by the combined merger earlier this decade.	
1979	INTERCONTINENTAL TRUCK BODY establishes a facility in Conrad, MT.	

1979	The Iran-Iraq War combined with the Iranian Revolution further restricts crude oil supplies. Over the next two years this sends prices from $13 up to $37 a barrel.	
1979	This year, the *Ice Follies* are acquired by Irwin Feld, who also acquires Holiday On Ice.	
1979	Sometime back, Indonesia had acquired several old "Mitchell B-25" bombers from the Netherlands. Indonesia retires the last of these planes this year; marking the end of the B-25's working life.	
1979	The Tappan Company now becomes SJC Corporation.	(see 1998)
1979	USA; there are now about 20,000,000 folks employed in manufacturing jobs in this country.	
1980	National buys all assets of Grenco Corporation.	
1980	**Dreco introduces their "Slingshot" substructure, for rotary drilling rigs.**	
1980	**Motorola develops the first electronic engine control module.**	
1980	Warner Gear introduces the T4 & T5 manual trannies for cars and pickups.	

1980	**Italy; Umberto ACCO builds the largest maintainer (road grader) ever, it will probably remain so forever.**	
1980	Texas; in Houston, Henry A. Lee founds Halco, Inc., manufacturing centrifugal pumps and such.	
1980	Exxon purchases Reliance Electric, including Kato.	
1980	Beech Aircraft becomes a subsidiary of Raytheon Corp. of Lexington, MA.	
1980	Koehring is acquired by Amca International.	

1980	Louisiana; America's last operating steam-powered water works, the McNeill Street Pumping Station in Shreveport is retired, and will someday be a National Historic Civil Engineering Landmark.	
1980	Goodbary ceases making off-road trucks.	
1980	June 1; "Captain Outrageous," Ted Turner starts Cable News Network. Initially, CNN is a laughingstock; but not for long.	
1980	August; Ingersoll-Rand Oilfield Products Co. is born as Ingersoll-Rand purchases the Machinery Division of Cabot Corp., which produces the Cabot/Franks line of well servicing and workover rigs in Pampa, TX.	
1980	Bronco Mfg., Inc. (and their subsidiary Hi-Tech Ltd.) is founded in Tulsa by three former officers of Cooper Mfg. Corp.	
1980	I-R buys Knight Industries, Inc. of Broken Arrow, OK.	
1980	Homestake gets into oil and gas projects in a big way in this decade.	(see 1990)
1980	Blue Circle Industries buys Armitage-Shanks Co. UK.	
1980	**In Bangladesh, the inclined, hand-operated, "rower pump" for water wells is developed.**	
1980	With Lee Iacocca's guidance and US government loan guarantees, Chrysler Corporation avoids bankruptcy.	(see 1982)
1980	Retsco Ltd. Begins business supplying and servicing mud relief valves, mud gauges, etc., to the drilling industry.	
1980	American Torch Tip Co. moves south to Bradenton, FL.	
1980	Chevrolet discontinues its heavy-duty trucks, but will continue on with its light truck line.	
1980	Denmark; M. A. N. of Germany takes over the local diesel engine operations of Burmeister & Wain (B&W Diesel AS).	

1980	CATERPILLAR TRACTOR COMPANY introduces the Challenger, the first farm tractor with flexible rubber tracks.	
1980	PACCAR, INC. acquires FODEN TRUCKS, UK.	
1980	Texas now ranks second in grapefruit production in the United States.	
1980	The little village of Tulsa, OK, now has a population of 361,000 citizens.	
1980	About this time, PETTIBONE introduces an 18-ton crawler-mounted hydraulic crane; its tracks can be extended from eight to ten feet across, powered by a Jimmy 6V-53 diesel engine.	(see 1989)
1980	BENDIX CORPORATION acquires WARNER & SWASEY, including its Gradall division.	(see 1983)
1980	The population of Detroit, MI, has slid down to 1,203,399. I doubt if any UAW fat cats are hurting though.	(see 1990)
1980	USA; President Jimmy Carter signs the Staggers Rail Act on October 14; thus deregulating railroads and leading to the divesture of several thousand miles of unprofitable rail lines.	
1980	Throughout this year, country singer Kenny Rogers sells about 35,000 albums each day; or about 12,775,000 total for the year.	
1980	England; Bob Crump's PELICAN ENGINEERING CO. now employs fifty people. The GARDNER engine reconditioning business is really declining and PELICAN is now manufacturing specialized marine generator sets for trawlers and small ships - initially using GARDNER diesels, they are now changing to mostly utilize CATERPILLAR and CUMMINS diesel engines for power. Also, FODEN goes into receivership and is bought by the American parent company of KENWORTH and PETERBILT; PACCAR, which now invests heavily in FODEN, allaying fears stemming from a "foreign takeover."	(see 1989)
1980	Worldwide, the unit pumping of oil wells has almost entirely replaced central power, or rodline and jerker, systems.	
1980	Saudi Arabia buys the balance of ARAMCO from the US oil companies who built it up and owned it.	
1981	January 1; Stephen G. Shank, the president of TONKA, announces the sale of GRESEN MANUFACTURING CO. to DANA CORP. of Toledo.	
1981	The TEREX DIVISION OF GENERAL MOTORS is sold to IBH, of Germany, but GM keeps the diesel-electric product line, calling it the "TITAN."	
1981	The TRENCHER CORPORATION OF AMERICA is founded in Grand Prairie, TX (TRENCOR).	
1981	February; DART & KRAFT INC. acquire Hobart Corporation for $460 million.	
1981	VOLVO buys WHITE, and retains the AUTOCAR name.	
1981	**The world's first 50,000-foot rated drilling rig is completed, PARKER DRILLING No. 201.**	(see 1983)
1981	W. W. Grainger's *MotorBook* has 1,000 pages this year.	
1981	B & W merges with TRICO.	
1981	KUWAIT PETROLEUM CORP. acquires SANTA FE INTERNATIONAL, as a wholly-owned subsidiary.	
1981	HARDWICK STOVE COMPANY is acquired by MAYTAG.	
1981	DUPONT acquires CONOCO for $7 billion.	
1981	CLARK EQUIPMENT closes their Lubbock, TX, plant, where cranes and AUSTIN-WESTERN maintainers have been built. This facility was Gene Hancock's old HANCOCK scraper plant.	
1981	HANCOCK GMBH is acquired by ESAB.	

1981	Texas, May; a completely new line of extruded seamless steel tubulars for the oil and gas industry is introduced by Lone Star Steel.		
1981	National Supply (Armco) acquires Equipetrol, S. A.		
		1981	GTE Corp. sells its electronics holdings to North American Phillips, a subsidiary of N. V. Philips, Europe's largest electronics company.
		1981	Schlumberger acquires Applicon and Balteau.	(see 1999)
		1981	David H. Dewhurst reestablishes Falcon Seaboard, after obtaining naming rights from Diamond Shamrock.
		1981	The USA launches the first space shuttle.	(see 2011)
		1981	Johns-Manville is reorganized as Manville Corp., and next year will file Chapter 11 for protection against asbestos health related claims.
		1981	Ashland Oil acquires the Beaird Industries operations in Shreveport, LA; from US Filter Corporation.
		1981	**Japanese and Dutch scientists invent the compact disc (CD) for recording.**
1981	Taro Gear, a division of Taro Industries, moves from England to Calgary, then acquires Fresno-Legrand of Fresno, TX.		
1981	EOY; the 4,520 active petroleum drilling rigs in the US is a historical high that won't be seen again soon.		(see 1992)
1981	THE BOOM IS ON!!! Continental-Emsco now has 118 stores. C-E buys the Wilson line of mobile well servicing and drilling rigs, then she purchases the old Bucyrus-Erie plant in Evansville, IN, converting it to the manufacture of drilling machinery.		
1981	GM's Delco Air Conditioning Div. and their Harrison Radiator Division are merged. GM acquires Hughes Aircraft Company, a leading defense electronics firm.		
1981	Dreco introduces the first 4,000 horsepower draw-works for land rigs, as well as the first 1,250 ton rated traveling block.		
1981	Regal-Beliot initiates the low-inventory technique that will later be known as "just-in-time-delivery."		(see 1985)
1981	Caterpillar Financial Services is established by Caterpillar, Inc.		
1981	The Mercedes Benz S-Class cars have the first seatbelt pre-tensioners, to take up slack in a crash. In the USA seatbelt usage is now running about 11%. The NHTSA rescinds the "passive restraint" rule this year.		(see 1983)
1981	USA; twenty-five years after beginning construction, 40,250 miles of the 42,500 mile Interstate Highway system are open to traffic; a gain of only 2,250 miles in the past five years. The basic Interstate Highway plan is now pretty much complete, however, many changes will be made to existing Interstate routes, and new Interstate routes will be added throughout future decades.		
1982	January 13; immediately after takeoff from Washington National Airport in Washington, DC, in a strong nor'easter and terrible snowstorm, Air Florida flight 90 crashes into a bridge and falls into the Potomac River. This crash leads to numerous changes in foul weather crew training, procedures, aircraft maintenance, and such.		(see 1985)
1982	**Varco introduces the first viable top drive drilling system.**		
1982	Dodge City, KS; inventor and manufacturer of the Broce Broom, Roy C. Broce, dies.		
1982	**After 64 years, the last Zenith radio is made.**		

1982	**The last uranium ore is removed from the ANACONDA JACKPILE MINE, Old Jim put in many hours working on Cats in that pit, also.** *"Yeah Bubba, you kin ask him about the JACKPILE name."*	
1982	**May; Gary Kehrer of Rockwall, TX, sets a new world water speed record of 184 mph, on the Brazos River in a supercharged, alcohol-burning, hydroplane boat.**	
1982	MAYTAG acquires JENN-AIRE.	
1982	In Marysville, OH, HONDA builds the first "foreign car" plant on American soil. Ask old Jim Cowan about the first Honda car ride he ever took, back in 1965 or 1966.	
1982	Winters, TX; Pinky Pinkerton and partners build a new facility for WINTERS OILFIELD SUPPLY. However, a tornado very severely damages the new facility only a few days before the Grand Opening is to take place.	
1982	GRADALL acquires LOED.	
1982	About now, W. R. GRACE CORPORATION acquires BOOKER DRILLING, operations continue under the GRACE OFFSHORE name.	
1982	**The last CHECKER car rolls off the assembly line on June 12th, ending a run of sixty years.**	(see 1999)
1982	In Russia, the enormous Antonov 124 cargo plane is introduced. At 224 feet and 3 inches (69 m) long, with a wingspan of 237 feet and 3 inches (73 m), it is big.	
1982	J. RAY MCDERMOTT & COMPANY becomes MCDERMOTT, INC.	
1982	US STEEL acquires MARATHON OIL CO.	
1982	In Cardin, OK, the small WEISDA COMPANY begins building giant diesel-electric haul trucks.	
1982	VINNELL CORP. moves their HQ from California to Virginia. This will be very handy for the government contracts they often seek.	
1982	BLODGETT acquires PITCO-FRIALATOR.	
1982	The two largest manufacturers of saw-filing equipment, FOLEY UNITED and BELSAW MACHINERY merge their firms.	
1982	In Santa Fe, NM, the SANTA FE NATURAL TOBACCO COMPANY is established.	
1982	Thanks to Lee Iacocca's management, CHRYSLER posts record profits and repays the government loans, seven years early. This repayment sounds good on the surface, but it goes deeper than that…	(see 1985)
1982	September; Merv Griffin's *The Wheel of Fortune*, soon to be hosted by Pat Sajak and Vanna White, debuts on television.	
1982	The GREAT PETROLEUM DRILLING DEPRESSION begins, it will last fourteen years.	
1982	The LOUISVILLE & NASHVILLE RR COMPANY officially merges into the SEABOARD SYSTEM RAILROAD.	
1982	Ziolkowski dies, but his wife and children carry on with the Crazy Horse sculpture.	
1982	As part of the govt. bailout deal, CHRYSLER sells its Marine Division to WELLCRAFT MARINE CORPORATION.	
1982	GRAVELY becomes a wholly owned subsidiary of the ARIENS COMPANY, now headquartered in Brillion, WI.	
1982	On television, The Weather Channel is launched; most folks doubt it will catch on.	(see 1997) (see 2007)
1982	Germany; M. A. N. introduces the first-ever two-cycle diesel engine with more than a fifty percent efficiency rating.	
1982	TRAILMOBILE introduces the usage of "panel foam" as insulation in its trailer bodies.	
1982	USA; the "average" CEO earns (is paid) about 42 times as much as the "average" worker.	(see 1990)

1982	USA; unemployment climbs to 10.8%, the highest since the Great Depression.		
1982	Compaq Computer Corp. is founded in Houston by three former Texas Instrument executives, Rod Canion, Jim Harris, and Bill Murto.		
1982	Appleton Electric Co. becomes a wholly owned subsidiary of Emerson Electric Co. (Emerson & SPX = EGS Electrical Group)		
1982	November; I-H is in terrible financial straits, and Dresser Industries gets the bargain, DI buys the company for $82 million cash, about 25% of book value. A Swag is that the parts inventory and new machines on hand alone are worth that amount. Dresser also gets the rights to the "International," "Payline," Payloader" and "Hough" names.	(see 1984)	
1982	Mr. G. Robert Blanchard establishes Blanchard Machinery Co. as a Caterpillar dealer in South Carolina.		
1982	Sea Recovery Corp. starts as a manufacturer of compact, economic desalination systems, primarily for use in the marine industry.		
1982	The last excavator rolls off the line at Unit Crane & Shovel Co. However the Unit Mariner cranes and some cranes specifically for scrap metal handling continue to be built.	(see 1988)	

	1982	Continental Airlines merges with Texas International Airline under Frank Lorenzo's management. Although Continental now has over 100 planes and routes over South America, Asia, and Australia, they have a very tumultuous time.
	1983	IBH of Germany fails and Terex is returned to General Motors.
	1983	Caterpillar acquires Eder, a German manufacturer of excavators.
	1983	Wix acquires Air Refiners of Oklahoma City.

(see 1983 — appears in top-right of Continental Airlines cell)

1983	February 28; this evening, almost 106 million folks watch the final episode of M*A*S*H. (More than a quarter of a century later, no other single program has ever had this viewer count, until Super Bowl XLIV in 2010 hits 106.5 viewers.)		
1983	In the Anadarko Basin of Oklahoma, Parker Drilling rig No. 182 drills to 29,312 feet. *"Slim, 'at's mor'n fiv' naf molls deep!"*	(see 1991)	
1983	April; Unit Rig buys the Dart product line of wheeled loaders and mechanical drive mining trucks.		
1983	**Conrail begins to phase out their cabooses, others rail companies soon follow suit.**		
1983	...and this year, Tidewater Marine builds fifty-nine additional vessels for its fleet.	(see 1985)	
1983	**The 50,000th EMD powered locomotive is produced.**		
1983	ACMA's new Drilling equipment Division includes Speedstar and the Morgan petroleum pumping units.		
1983	Republic Steel merges with LTV Steel, with LTV Steel as the surviving name.		
1983	Wire rope (cable) manufacturer, Broderick & Bascom is acquired by MacWhyte Company.		
1983	Greenwood Valve & Machine Co. is purchased by Kemper, greatly increasing Kemper's line.		
1983	There are now only 80 breweries in the entire United States.		
1983	**Maytag ceases production of its wringer-type washers.**		
1983	Southern Pacific Company sells the small long-distance carrier US Sprint to GTE Corp.		
1983	Summer; due to labor disputes, Roper operations at Bradley, IL, now come to an end, marking the end of the David Bradley name, after 150 years. Another good name comes to an end...		

1983	Autumn; SKEETER PRODUCTS INC. is acquired by the COLEMAN COMPANY.	
1983	GM restructures, announces SATURN CORP., and the disbanding of FISHER BODY WORKS.	
1983	**BUCYRUS-ERIE introduces the first 400 foot dragline boom; on their 2570W machine.**	(see 1984)
1983	**This year, for the first time, audio cassettes outsell Long-Play 33⅓ rpm records.**	
1983	HARRIS CORP. sells its printing equipment business, then acquires LANIER BUSINESS PRODUCTS of Atlanta, GA.	
1983	FORD replaces its once-popular F-100 with the new F-150 pickup.	
1983	ALLIED CORPORATION acquires Gradall from BENDIX, but soon sells Gradall to GBKS.	(see 1985)
1983	**The first "robot-making" robot is invented.**	
1983	With losses of nearly $.25 Billion, CONTINENTAL AIRLINES files for bankruptcy and restructuring.	(see 1984)
1983	Bonneville Salt Flats, UT; returning the record to British hands, Richard Noble, in his jet-powered "Thrust 2" edges slightly past Gary Gabelich to a record 633½ miles (1,013.6 km) per hour.	(see 1997)
1983	USA; STATE FARM INSURANCE successfully sues, forcing the NHTSA to reinstate the "passive restraint" rule, taking effect next year.	(see 1984)
1983	Oklahoma City; specializing in oilfield, construction, and industrial hoses, Harvey Sparkman establishes MIDWEST HOSE & SPECIALTY CO.	
1983	During this year alone, more than six trillion dollars goes into the US Treasury from offshore petroleum and gas leases.	
1984	BUCYRUS-ERIE sells all of its construction equipment business to NORTHWEST ENGINEERING CO., also B-E hydraulic excavators are discontinued. The last BUCYRUS "churn-drill" (spudder, cable-tool rig) is produced. Over the decades, more than 11,600 of these rigs have been sent out to drill all around the world.	(see 1988)
1984	KERR-MCGEE CORP. buys ALL production and production related facilities of DELTA DRILLING CO. for only $145,000,000.	
1984	March 5; after a bidding war with ARCO, GULF is acquired by, and merged into, CHEVRON (SOCAL) in a $13.2 billion deal, the largest merger ever in corporate history.	
1984	SANTA FE INTERNATIONAL buys KEYDRILL, INC.	
1984	Deregulation forces the RS&P RR to scrap its line from Roscoe to Snyder, leaving only +/- 2 miles of storage tracks near the car rebuild shops in Roscoe, TX.	
1984	STANLEY TOOL WORKS purchases PROTO from INGERSOLL-RAND, and forms STANLEY-PROTO INDUSTRIAL TOOLS.	
1984	Texas; TRENCOR buys DALLAS JETCO and it becomes TRENCOR JETCO.	
1984	DAIMLER-BENZ sells EUCLID to the CLARK-MICHIGAN CO.	(see 1992)
1984	Texas; Peter M. Holt becomes CEO of the HOLT COMPANIES, the CATERPILLAR dealerships, and other businesses.	
1984	SUNDSTRAND CORP. acquires SULLAIR CORP.	
1984	ZENITH RADIO CORP. becomes ZENITH ELECTRONICS CORP.	
1984	Mr. H. B. Zachary dies.	
1984	EMD introduces its 710 series engine. *"Yeah Bubba, 'ats 710 cubic inches displacement in each cylinder."*	
1984	RALSTON PURINA CO. purchases the EVEREADY BATTERY CO.	

1984	John B. Long and his son Armisted establish JOHN B. LONG CO. (JBLCO), to manufacture and market underground mining equipment and systems.	
1984	Longview, TX; COLLINS INDUSTRIES, INC., of Hutchinson, KS, acquires privately owned CAPACITY OF TEXAS.	
1984	The MELROE CO. becomes a division of CLARK EQUIPMENT COMPANY.	
1984	McDERMOTT, Inc. is renamed McDERMOTT INTERNATIONAL.	
1984	At age 57, Norman Petty succumbs to leukemia in Clovis, NM.	
1984	ARMCO sells its West Virginia coal mines to PEABODY.	
1984	The BURLY CORP., owned by the Davenport family, buys MUELLER SUPPLY COMPANY of Ballinger, TX, from James and Harold Mueller.	
1984	Young Michael Dell starts his own company.	
1984	Thanks to its Sable and Taurus sedans, FORD earnings surpass GENERAL MOTORS for the first time since 1924.	
1984	SMITH INTERNATIONAL launches its weekly rig count, adding whether oil or gas is each rig's goal.	
1984	HASBRO, of Pawtucket, RI, purchases the MILTON BRADLEY CO., making HASBRO the world's largest toymaker. Later this year, HASBRO acquires the PLAY-SKOOL COMPANY, giving way to more international expansion.	
1984	ARKLA sells its Evansville facility to PREWAY.	(see 1987)
1984	CARNATION a leading maker of condensed milk, dried milk, and other milk-related foodstuffs is acquired by NESTLÉ.	(see 1985)
1984	Bill Monroe opens the Bluegrass Hall of Fame and Museum in Nashville, TN.	
1984	HILLS BROS. COFFEE buys the name and facilities of CHASE & SANBORN COFFEE COMPANY.	(see 1985)

1984	The first Dirt Devil vacuum cleaners are marketed.	
1984	After a dry spell of a few years, convertible automobiles are reintroduced in the US.	
1984	Having recorded more than 250 songs, and selling more than thirty million records, Country Music Hall of Fame member Ernest Tubb dies. Tubb was born February 9, 1914 in Crisp, TX.	
1984	Texas; the twenty-four year old NFL franchise in Dallas is sold for $50,000,000.	
1984	USA; New York is the first state to absolutely mandate seatbelt usage. The automatic seatbelts begin to appear, either attached to the door, or on a motorized track. People despise them, and many folks then neglect to fasten the manual lap belt, defeating the purpose.	(see 1988)
1984	USA; the American Eagle System, a network of regional airlines, is now fully integrated into AMERICAN AIRLINES' domestic route system.	
1984	DRESSER INDUSTRIES now picks up WABCO for $66 million plus, probably another bargain. Dresser then combines WABCO, International-Hough, Marion, as well as Jeffrey Galion, and mold that into the Mining and Construction Equipment Division of Dresser.	(see 1999)
1984	SEDCO merges with SCHLUMBERGER LTD. with Bill Clements as board chairman; but he retires next year.	
1984	By the end of year, CONTINENTAL AIRLINES is once again showing a profit.	(see 1986)
1984	Sweden; after seven decades, and declining profitability, the last agricultural tractor rolls out of the old Munktell factory.	
ca. 1985	**Eugene Eisenberg, et. al., buy NABORS DRILLING of Canada, starting the behemoth on its way.**	(see 1987)

1985	**DELTA DRILLING'S motto is "STAY ALIVE IN '85."** Everyone just knows things will get better any day!	
1985	KENWORTH introduces the T-600, with the sloped nose cab, changing the look of highway trucks forever.	
1985	The CLARK-MICHIGAN CO. enters into a JV with VOLVO AB of Sweden, and the VME (Volvo-Michigan-Euclid) name is started.	
1985	GENERAL MOTORS sells its TITAN DIVISION to MARATHON-LETOURNEAU CO. of Longview, TX.	
1985	TORRINGTON BEARING CO. and FAFNIR BEARINGS merge.	
1985	CMI Corp. purchases RayGo, Inc.	
1985	Peter M. Holt establishes a CATERPILLAR dealership in OHIO.	
1985	SPX CORPORATION acquires OTC CORPORATION, the old Owatonna Tool Company.	
1985	Rudolph Lenz purchases the NORTHWEST ENGINEERING COMPANY.	
1985	GENERAL GAS LIGHT CO. is renamed HUMPHREY PRODUCTS.	
1985	ALLIS-CHALMERS farm equipment operations are sold to KLOCKNER-HUMBOLDT-DEUTZ and DEUTZ-ALLIS tractors will be made until 1989.	
1985	TIDEWATER records its first loss in its history, and sells HILLARD OIL & GAS while adding 40 vessels costing $104 million.	(see 1992)
1985	The KENDAVIS GROUP goes into Chapter 11 bankruptcy for a $750 million restructuring.	
1985	TITAN SERVICES, a subsidiary of DRESSER INDUSTRIES forms a partnership with HUGHES TOOL CO. (BJ TITAN SERVICES CO.)	
1985	C. F. MARTIN & CO. now comes under the sixth generation of family ownership/management, as C. F. Martin, IV, takes the helm of the guitar company.	
1985	LTV sells the REPUBLIC SUPPLY CO. holdings to Mr. F. M. Late, of Dallas (Mr. Frank Late is a story in himself).	
1985	FEDERAL MOGUL acquires the MATHER COMPANY, a leader in PTFE technology.	
1985	Put together by Bob Geldorf, the first "Live Aid Concert" raises $283 million to feed the starving in drought-stricken Ethiopia.	
1985	August 2; in late afternoon, approaching DFW airport from the north, after clearance for landing, DELTA AIRLINES Flight 191 from Fort Lauderdale, FL, encounters a "microburst" wind shear and crashes. Only 21 survive and 134 perish in the crash of the L-1011 plane. This crash and the subsequent NTSB investigation will lead to a great many safety upgrades, including the installation of the new technology "Doppler" radar at forty-five US airports.	
1985	August 7; today's announcement that the IDECO plant in Beaumont, TX, is closing in a few months, means 350 employees losing their jobs. The closing is due to the formation of a new company, IRI INTERNATIONAL CORP., jointly owned by DRESSER INDUSTRIES, INGERSOLL-RAND CO. and a management group. The new firm will base its oil field manufacturing operations in the old CABOT plant in Pampa, TX. Additionally, workers in Service Centers in Odessa, TX, Oklahoma City, OK, and Casper, WY, will be terminated.	
1985	Iowa; to honor the high reputation of its trademark name, IOWA MANUFACTURING CO. becomes CEDARAPIDS INC.	
1985	The Kola Borehole is now past 40,000 feet deep, per Larry Gedney.	

1985	Dresser Industries buys 50% of KV Gas Turbine Division, making Kongsberg Dresser Power.	
1985	The Korean industrial empire, Hyundai, establishes an organization for developing construction equipment.	
1985	RJR acquires Nabisco Brands, next year the parent company will be renamed RJR Nabisco, Inc.	
1985	The investment banking firm of Geinor of Switzerland buys the Sheaffer Pen Co.	
1985	CVS Drugstores reach $1 billion in sales.	(see 1990)
1985	Bruce J. Zoldan buys Acme Sparkler Co., renames it Diamond Sparkler Co., and moves it to Youngstown, OH.	
1985	Nestlé buys the Hills Bros. coffee brand.	(see 1999)
1985	Dallas; this October, the first Blockbuster video rental store opens with an inventory of 8,000 VHS movie tapes.	(see 2014)
1985	New Iberia, LA; Access Oil Tools is founded.	
1985	**At Nikon University in Japan, a soap-less, ultrasonic washer is invented.**	
1985	Europe; the crane business of Boilot-Pingon Richier is taken over by Potain.	
1985	GBKS sells the Gradall business to ICM Industries.	(see 1996)
1985	In its 30th year, Regal-Beliot now employs 1,250 in its 18 manufacturing and service facilities.	(see 1990)
1985	IBM has 406,000 employees. *"Naw Bubba, I doan know how many workers they have."*	
1985	After being towed from the North Atlantic, the Rowan Gorilla III jack-up drilling rig is outfitted with a record-setting 604 feet of legs, for Gulf of Mexico deepwater drilling.	(see 1994)

Windows breaks down walls.

	1985	Parker Hannifin acquires Racor Filters.	
	1985	Microsoft finally releases Windows 1.0, two years past Bill Gates' original promise.	
	1985	Farymann Diesel becomes a independent German GMBH, or limited liability company.	
	1985	Oscar Wyatt teams with Michael Milken, the junk bond king, for a hostile takeover of American Natural Resources (ANR). Coastal's $2.5 billion takeover of ANR is the first time junk bonds are used in a successful takeover.	(see 1991)
	1985	Siecor dumps Superior Cable.	
	1985	About this time, it is discovered that 30 to 40% of our nation's underground gasoline storage tanks leak (well, imagine that, as many steel tanks have now been buried for fifty years and more). That's about 200,000 tanks leaking gasoline into the ground. As per the EPA, the gasoline marketing companies are given until 1998 to upgrade or remove all of these tanks.	
	1985	Chrysler and MMC (Mitsubishi) form the Diamond-Star Motors Corporation.	(see 1986)

1985	Only 5,000 new cars are sold in China to the 1,070,200,000 citizens this year.	(see 2011)
1986	In a leveraged buyout, Reliance Electric purchases the company (itself) back from Exxon.	
1986	January; the Rock and Roll Hall of Fame inducts its first members. Among the inductees are Little Richard, Ray Charles, and Elvis Presley. The Hall will later be moved to Cleveland, site of the first rock and roll concert in 1952.	

1986	January 28; the Space Shuttle Challenger tragically explodes 73 seconds after launch. Astronauts Christa McAuliffe, Gregory Jarvis, Judith A. Resnik, Francis R. (Dick) Scobee, Ronald E. McNair, Mike J. Smith, and Ellison S. Onizuka are lost.	
1986	**The very last TEREX crawler tractor is built.** *"Yeah Bubba, so much for King of the Earth..."*	
1986	**Early on, the price of crude falls from $32 a barrel (42 gallons) down to less than $12.**	
1986	MAYTAG acquires MAGIC CHEF.	
1986	Late July, Glen Patterson, et. al., buy the repossessed Bethlehem jack-up, Bigfoot II, for $365,000. It is freshly USCG approved and ready to work, except for a string of drill pipe.	
1986	BLODGETT acquires MAGIKITCH'N.	
1986	STARRETT purchases the EVANS RULE COMPANY.	
1986	AB ELECTROLUX buys WHITE CONSOLIDATED INDUSTRIES, thus FRIGIDAIRE now becomes a part of AB ELECTROLUX.	
1986	TAYLOR MACHINE WORKS buys M-R-S MANUFACTURING CO. (MISSISSIPPI ROAD SERVICES).	
1986	PACCAR buys TRICO IND. INC. makers of oilfield pumps, etc.	
1986	An Investors Group buys AERMOTOR and moves it back to San Angelo, TX, and the Argentina plant is closed down.	(see 1998)
1986	NORTHWEST ENGINEERING takes over TEREX from GENERAL MOTORS.	
1986	INSLEY is purchased by BADGER CONST. EQUIPMENT COMPANY.	
1986	A joint venture between FMC CORP. and SUMITOMO HEAVY INDUSTRIES creates LINK-BELT CONSTRUCTION EQUIPMENT CO.	
1986	After almost 80 years, IDECO's Beaumont, TX, plant is closed.	
1986	This year is the 100th Anniversary of the automobile, and of MERCEDES-BENZ!!!	
1986	CHRYSLER CORP. now builds the Jeep.	(see 1987)
1986	**After more than a century B. F. GOODRICH exits the tire business.**	
1986	SKF acquires MRC bearings of the USA.	
1986	UK; the R. A. LISTER CO. and PETTERS LTD. merge to form LISTER-PETTER LTD.	
1986	A. O. SMITH acquires the small motor business of WESTINGHOUSE ELECTRIC CO.	
1986	PREMARK INTERNATIONAL (PMI) is created by the separation of DART & KRAFT's operating units and HOBART becomes a part of PMI's food equipment group.	
1986	**CESSNA halts production of the 172, after 30 years and 35,000 planes, due to soaring product liability costs. GENERAL DYNAMICS buys out CESSNA AIRCRAFT this year.**	
1986	IP acquires HAMMERMILL PAPER COMPANY.	
1986	After selling 1,000 D10s, CAT replaces it with the 770 hp D11N, soon to be the D11R with a 22-foot-wide dozer blade.	
1986	INGRAM PETROLEUM SERVICES merges with CACTUS WELLHEAD, to form INGRAM CACTUS COMPANY.	
1986	FEDERAL MOGUL acquires CARTER AUTOMOTIVE CO., INC. (carburetors, fuel pumps, etc) and also SIGNAL-STAT DIVISION (auto lighting and safety).	

1986	Due to product liability suits against Skyworker cranes, also built by Correct Mfg., the company goes into bankruptcy, and the very last Divco trucks are produced under authority of bankruptcy trustee in January. Sad way for Divco to go after sixty years.	
1986	October; Baker merges Totco with their Exlog division.	

	1986	Razette Bros is bought out by Purvin Industries.
	1986	Barber-Greene is purchased by Astec Industries.
	1986	WPI acquires all the assets of Plains Machinery Company.
	1986	Development begins on the V-22 Osprey, the tiltable twin engines turn its rotors (propellers) up for VTOL, similar to a helicopter.

1986	**After 111 years of mail-order service, Montgomery Ward & Company discontinues their catalog order department.**	
1986	Vickers, Inc. sells Tulsa Winch Company to an investor group.	
1986	December; Magcobar Group of Dresser Industries now merges with IMCO Services Division of Halliburton, to form M-I Drilling Fluids.	
1986	Unit Corporation is formed as the parent company of Unit Drilling & Exploration Company.	
1986	The Coleman Company wanting a line of small generators, purchases AG-Tronic.	
1986	SPM of Ft. Worth acquires Geoquip Pumps. SPM also acquires the high-pressure valve line from Wheatley Pump & Valve Co. of Tulsa, OK.	
1986	Southland Corp. (7-11) sells fifty percent interest in its Citgo marketing chain to PDVSA of Venezuela.	
1986	The Chessie System becomes CSX Transportation.	
1986	In a leveraged buyout, Zales Jewelers is taken over by Peoples Jewelers of Canada, and Swarovski International of Austria. Zales then buys the 469 store chain of Gordons Jewelers.	
1986	As Harcourt Brace Jovanovich Inc. acquires Holt Rinehart & Winston from CBS; Henry Holt & Company is separated and sold to the German publisher, Holtzbrinck.	
1986	The two great American soft drink makers Dr. Pepper and Seven-Up merge their companies.	
1986	American Standard is "swallowed up" by ITT Industries.	
1986	France and the UK sign an agreement to join forces to build a tunnel under the English Channel. Once the tremendous haggling is over, a consortium of five British and five French companies is selected to build the tunnel. The concession to own and operate the tunnel is awarded to Anglo-French Company Eurotunnel for fifty-five years. Ten more years are later added to their contract.	
1986	Germany; M. A. N. and GHH merge to form MAN AG, with headquarters relocated to Munich. Their diesel engine operations are separated as MAN B&W Diesel.	
1986	Uniroyal merges with the B. F. Goodrich Co. becoming Uniroyal Goodrich Tire Co.	(see 1990)
1986	The Boeing "Condor" plane sets an altitude record for reciprocating engines at 66,980' or 12.68 miles, or 20.28 kilometers.	
1986	Fiat and Hitachi Construction Machinery form the Fiat-Hitachi joint venture, to manufacture excavators and the former Fiat-Allis product line. The Fiat-Allis brand will continue to be used in the USA.	
1986	Canada; Richard Piche Inc. acquires Blanchet Equipments, Ltd.	(see 1987)

1986	USA; the Federal Truth in Mileage Act (TIMA) is enacted, as another small step to help keep the used car business "in line." This act requires vehicle the readings on vehicle title documents, to be printed on secure paper.	
1986	Ohio; after eighty-one years, and plenty of ups and downs, Hull Pottery of Crooksville, ceases operations and shuts down.	
1986	Ohio; Chester Hoist Co. buys the Coffing Worm Drive Electric Wire Rope hoist line from Duff-Norton, they will manufacture these in Lisbon, branding them Chester.	(see 1989)
1986	Still not able to improve its financial situation by much, Frontier Airlines tries to merge with United Airlines, but when the UA employees learn that the FA employees are to be absorbed by United, the deal goes sour. Unable to find a good buyer, Frontier files bankruptcy, and shuts down. Continental Airlines shows up, buys all Frontier holdings and begins flying its routes. The Frontier buyout should give Continental the boost it needs.	(see 1990)
1986	Pennsylvania, USA; Thomas E. Foley buys TB Wood's Sons Inc. of Chambersburg.	(see 1991)
1986	Oklahoma; Albert Equipment Co. Inc. of Tulsa acquires most of the assets of Boecking Machinery Inc., of Oklahoma City, the dealer for Caterpillar in western Oklahoma. This makes Albert Equipment the state's sole Caterpillar dealer.	
1987	January 1; Nabors Industries Ltd. comes into being and soon buys the worldwide operations of Westburne Drilling.	
1987	January; the legendary B. B. King donates his collection of 7,000 record albums to the University of Mississippi.	
1987	Dresser Industries and Ingersoll-Rand Co. form a joint venture of their common businesses to create Dresser-Rand Co.	
1987	Texas; Richard Rainwater forms Ensco Drilling by merging Blocker Drilling and Penrod Drilling, to make the world's largest drilling business. Then old John Blocker goes down the street in the big city of Alice (pop 10,000) and starts up again.	
1987	Mobilized and starting work within 2 weeks after the devastating Andean earthquake, Williams Bros. rebuilds 25 miles of the Trans-Ecuadorian pipeline across the Andes Mountains, and completes the job in 6 months.	(see 1991)
1987	Howard Supply Company is "spun-off" from Republic Supply Corporation.	
1987	Litton Industries, forms a joint venture with Dresser Industries, and they combine Western Geophysical, Dresser Atlas, and other firms to form Western Atlas International Inc.	
1987	In a plant in the UK, the last Motorola brand car radio is produced, after 55 years.	
1987	Ford acquires Hertz Corporation, and a partnership.	
1987	Grandson of old Henry and son of Edsel, Henry Ford II dies.	
1987	Exide buys General Battery Corporation.	
1987	Texas Iron Works (TIW) is acquired by the Drexel Group.	(see 1995)
1987	Thomasville Furniture acquires the Westchester Group of Companies.	(see 1995)
1987	Carter-Day, another leader in the dust collection industry is acquired by Donaldson.	
1987	The Auto Shack company changes its name to Auto Zone.	
1987	Peabody acquires large coal properties from Eastern Gas & Fuel Associates.	
1987	General Cinema Corp. acquires a majority share in Carter Hawley Hale's specialty store division, including Bergdorf Goodman and the Neiman Marcus stores. This will be known as the Neiman Marcus Group.	

1987	Swaco merges with Geolograph Pioneer.	
1987	Shreveport; after a fourteen year second run on KWKH, *The Louisiana Hayride* once again hangs it up.	
1987	Finally, construction is actually started on the thirty-one mile tunnel from Cheriton, England to Sangatte, Calais, France.	
1987	Detroit Diesel Allison Division of GM introduces the Series 60, a four cycle engine, primarily for trucks.	
1987	Joy Industrial Compressor Group, now CTC, is acquired by Cooper Industries, as well as W-K-M, and the Demco companies.	
1987	Baker International and Hughes Tool Company merge to form Baker Hughes, Inc.	
1987	Chrysler Corporation buys American Motors; also buys Lamborghini, reentering the European vehicle marketplace. Chrysler Corporation introduces the Eagle, its first new marque since 1928.	
1987	Borgwarner becomes a private company.	
1987	Raygo rights are passed from CMI to Caterpillar.	
1987	Preway goes bankrupt.	
1987	Chicago Pneumatic is acquired by Atlas Copco, however, both trademark brand names are continued.	
1987	**Ink made from soybeans is first introduced, and is used to print some newspapers**	
1987	Terex Corporation acquires Koehring, including all remnants of the Thew-Lorain Division.	(see 1988)
1987	S. C. I. P. J. Legrts & Company takes over the Potain Company.	
1987	In the Piney Woods of East Texas, little old Gregg County has now produced more crude oil than any other county in the state.	
1987	Heerema commissions the world's largest launch barge, their H851.	
1987	EXTRA!! EXTRA!! Wedding of the year!! After decades as "bed partners," National Supply Company and USS Oilwell do finally take the big step and wed… uh… er… merge.	
1987	Canada; Richard Piche Inc. renames itself R. P. M. Tech Inc., then acquires TOR TRUCK INC.	(see 1999)
1987	Active in his business to the end, local Ft. Worth icon and automobile dealer, Mr. Frank Kent, passes away September 18, only two days before his 92nd birthday. Now, John Ludington moves to chairman, and Mrs. Churchill is a major owner and board member.	(see 1989)
1987	Paloma Industries of Nagoya, Japan, purchases Rheem.	
1987	Washington; as Ingersoll-Rand establishes a Material Handling Division, they acquire Beebe Bros. Inc. of Seattle.	(see 2010)
1987	USA; the Naval Oil Shale Reserve is transferred to the Ute Indian Tribe.	
1988	January 1; Detroit Diesel Corp., a joint venture of Penske Corp. and General Motors begins operations as the successor to Detroit Diesel Allison Division.	
1988	Terex Corporation buys O&K Mining, then soon after buys Unit Rig & Equipment and merges the two, forming Terex Mining.	
1988	Enterprise Engineering, an aftermarket services business is acquired by Cooper Industries.	
1988	Woolley Tool Co. is bought by employees and investors.	

1988	Caterpillar dealers B. D. HOLT and HOLT MACHINERY merge to form HOLT COMPANY OF TEXAS.	
1988	EATON acquires CESSNA's fluid power division.	
1988	KOMATSU LTD. and DRESSER INDUSTRIES begin a joint venture, establishing the KOMATSU-DRESSER CO. (KDC), to market lines of both companies. DRESSER INDUSTRIES acquires M. W. KELLOGG COMPANY.	
1988	BUCYRUS CORPORATION acquires RANSOMES & RAPIER, LTD., of England. BUCYRUS-ERIE forms MINSERCO.	(see 1996)
1988	HARNISCHFEGER CORPORATION buys PAGE ENGINEERING COMPANY for the PAGE draglines.	
1988	GUNNEBO CORPORATION of Sweden purchases JOHNSON MANUFACTURING COMPANY.	
1988	OTC becomes a separate operating unit of SPX CORPORATION.	
1988	EVI and WEATHERFORD-ENTERRA merge, to form WEATHERFORD INTERNATIONAL.	
1988	TEREX supersedes NORTHWEST ENGINEERING as parent company of the group.	
1988	**RAY-O-VAC invents a computer clock battery to power the real time clock in personal computers.**	
1988	BAKER HUGHES acquires WESTERN ATLAS.	
1988	ASEA, with 71,000 employees, and BROWN BOVERI COMPANY, with 97,000 employees, merge to form ABB LTD., one of the world's largest electrical engineering companies.	(see 1989)
1988	MARK IV INDUSTRIES buys DAYTON CORPORATION.	
1988	ARCAIR CO. is bought by THERMADYNE INDUSTRIES, and soon combined with TWECO.	
1988	Texas; RHODES, WOLTERS & ASSOCIATES of San Antonio change their name to SKYTEX INTERNATIONAL, and close on the purchase of SKYTOP BREWSTER of Victoria.	
1988	INTERNATIONAL PAPER acquires MASONITE CORPORATION.	
1988	NOBLE acquires PETER BAWDEN DRILLING COMPANY.	
1988	ASTEC INDUSTRIES purchases TRENCOR JETCO.	
1988	MANSFIELD PLUMBING PRODUCTS acquires the ARMITAGE-SHANKS plant in Kilgore, TX.	
1988	England; the last SCAMMELL trucks are built as the plant closes forever.	
1988	EXLOG and TOTCO both move their main offices to Houston.	
1988	**CATERPILLAR builds its twenty-five thousandth crawler tractor. It is a D-9N... more than one per week since starting in 1925.**	
1988	CHICAGO PNEUMATIC sells ALLIED to DANAHER CORP.	
1988	In a record 1,350 feet (415.4 m) of water in the Gulf of Mexico, SHELL installs the Bullwinkle platform.	

"I saw it on the bank, Bubba, an' it's BiiiiiiGGGG!!!"

1988	GTE sells controlling interest in GTE SPRINT to UNITED TELECOMMUNICATIONS, United will buy the remainder in a few years.	
1988	NEYRFOR-WEIR LTD. is formed by the merger of the turbodrilling business of NEYRFOR DRILLING SRVCS and WEIR DRILLING.	
1988	The CATERPILLAR dealer BUTLER MACHINERY acquires the assets of KEARN MACHINERY COMPANY. BUTLER now serves all of North and South Dakota, and a part of Minnesota.	
1988	HARRIS CORPORATION acquires GE's semiconductor line, to merge with their own existing line.	
1988	A 50/50 joint venture of MAN DIESEL and MTU is to operate SEMT PIELSTICK in France.	

1988	About this time, Koehring-Waterous is sold to Timberjack, Inc.	(see 1992)
1988	All Allis Chalmers manufacturing operations are sold. The Fiat-Allis crushing equipment lines are sold to Svedala Industries of Sweden.	
1988	Single mother of three, Jean Daum of Winnipeg, having previously failed with two community newspapers, now has the idea to start *Coffee News,* to be distributed free in restaurants. The little single sheet brown paper is a huge success.	(see 2007)
1988	Only 126 years after President Abraham Lincoln signed the Homestead Act, and two years after its repeal, Alaskan Ken Deardoff receives a homestead land title from the government, making him America's last official homesteader.	
1988	USA; Chrysler announces that all its cars will be equipped with driver's side air bags, by 1990. Other automakers rapidly follow Chrysler's lead. This makes automatic seatbelts obsolete.	(see 1990) (see 1991)
1988	New Orleans, LA; the local Offshore Crane Co. buys the remaining crane business of Unit Crane & Shovel of New Berlin, WI.	(see 2005)
1988	Wyoming is now our leading coal producing state, putting Kentucky in the no. 2 slot…	
1989	Cameron Iron Works is acquired by Cooper Industries, and renamed Cooper Oil Tools.	
1989	With the Cobey family still at the helm, Eagle Crusher Works builds the last Scoopmobile loader. It's a model HP, only slightly different from when it was born, 32 years ago. Eagle Crusher also acquires Stedman Machine Co. of Indiana.	(see 1990)
1989	The Kola Borehole is now 39,851 feet deep???? …	(see 1985)
1989	Atlas Copco AB buys Wagner Mining Equipment Co. from Paccar.	
1989	After a century of destruction and $14 billion of losses in cotton crops, the Cotton Boll Weevil is finally essentially eradicated.	
1989	Nacco Corp. purchases the family-owned Hyster Co.	
1989	March 24; the two year old supertanker Exxon Valdez runs aground, spilling more than 11 million gallons of crude oil into Prince William Sound, off western Canada. March 24, 12:04 am; radio quote, "The Exxon Valdez is… hard aground." The 200,000 cwt., 980 feet (300 m) long tanker is on Bligh Reef.	
1989	Cedarapids Inc. acquires Standard-Havens Inc. for their line of high-tech hot-mix asphalt plants.	
1989	April; the Kohlberg Kravis Roberts & Co's merger/takeover of RJR Nabisco is completed.	
1989	K-H-D sells Allis-Chalmers, and it is renamed AGCO.	
1989	Sam Bonham dies. Mary, his wife and partner continues to run the J-B Weld Company in Sulphur Springs, TX.	
1989	ABB acquires forty companies in its first full year, including the power transmission business of Westinghouse Electric Co.	
1989	The little hot pink Energizer bunny first appears.	
1989	National Oilwell acquires Mission, manufacturer of high quality centrifugal pumps.	
1989	General Motors buys SAAB of Sweden.	
1989	BJ Titan is dissolved to become a part of Baker-Hughes.	
1989	Maytag acquires Chicago-Pacific, including the Hoover company.	
1989	European companies, Zanders Feinpapiere AG of Germany, and Aussedat-Rey of France are acquired by IP.	

LARVA   PUPA   ADULT

1989	FORD acquires the ASSOCIATES financial services company and JAGUAR CARS, and sells ROUGE STEEL COMPANY.	
1989	Addicks, TX; ARDCO is acquired by PETTIBONE.	(see 1995) (see 2008)
1989	WILLIAMSPORT WIREROPE WORKS (WWW) is formed as the manufacturer of Bethlehem brand wire rope.	
1989	WILLIAMS HOLDINGS, of Great Britain acquire all operations of FENWAL and all KIDDE fire protection companies.	
1989	Since 1970, the US government has received $55 trillion from offshore petroleum leases.	
1989	W. W. WILLIAMS is acquired by WPI.	
1989	UK; the DENNIS BROTHERS manufacturing firm is now acquired by TRINITY HOLDINGS.	
1989	With further mergers, the M. O'NEIL name is now dropped from the MAY/KAUFMAN'S STORES in Ohio.	
1989	HEEREMA and McDERMOTT form the HEEREMAC joint venture operating four semi-submersible crane vessels for offshore installation work. HEEREMA also acquires controlling interest in WIJSMULLER TRANSPORT GROUP, owner and operator of self-propelled semi-submersible heavy-lift vessels.	
1989	The DREXEL GROUP acquires BRANDT solids control business.	
1989	DRESSER-RAND buys the other 50% of KV and renames this division DRESSER-RAND AS.	
1989	AMERICAN CAST IRON PIPE CO. buys the WATEROUS Co. from AMERICAN HOIST & DERRICK.	
1989	Australia; the 66-year-old WAUGH & JOSEPHSON CAT dealership is acquired by Robert Holmes a Court, then by the Bond Group, who then decide a CAT dealership is a non-core asset, and will be divested. Mr. Harcourt Gough and Tony Gilmour acquire the CAT dealership operations of WAUGH & JOSEPHSON in New South Wales and ACT; they will operate thus until April of 2004.	
1989	November 9; the Berlin Wall, separating East and West Berlin in Germany, falls, making way for the reunification of Germany in October, 1990.	
1989	Midland, MI; the late Mr. Frank Kent, automobile dealer of Fort Worth, TX, is posthumously inducted into the Automotive Hall of Fame.	(see 1995)
1989	Louisiana; a new two-lane bridge is built, replacing the landmark Caddo Lake Drawbridge at Mooringsport. The old drawbridge is now being used as a pedestrian walkway and tourist attraction.	(see 1996)
1989	In their Lisbon, OH, plant, CHESTER HOIST Co. begins manufacturing "low headroom" electric and manual chain hoists. This early step soon puts CHESTER way out in front in the close-headroom hoist business.	(see 1995)
1989	England; ending a very good decade for PACCAR, FODEN has a record setting sales of 350 FODEN trucks this year.	(see 1991)
1990s	Three more dust collection/filtration firms are acquired by DONALDSON during this decade... AERCOLOGY, AIRMAZE, and DCE CORP.	

1990	Fairbanks-Morse introduces their Envior-Design co-generation engines.	
1990	Texas; the population of Cross Plains is now 1,063.	
1990	Steven Bechtel Jr. retires and his son, Riley P. Bechtel becomes president of Bechtel Corporation.	
1990	Marathon Oil Company moves its headquarters from Findlay, OH, to Houston, TX.	
1990	Susanne Cobey becomes president of Eagle Crusher which has recently acquired Stedman Machine Company.	
1990	November; Varco International finalizes the purchase of Totco from Baker-Hughes and forms a new company by merging the two great names in oil well drilling instrumentation, Martin-Decker, Inc. and Totco… it is now… M/D Totco.	

1990	SKF buys Chicago Rawhide, to keep the oil in their bearings.	
1990	Mark IV acquires Anchor Swan.	
1990	Bombardier purchases Learjet Inc.	
1990	November; Nabors Industries acquires Loffland Drilling, previously one of the Kendavis companies.	
1990	Federal Mogul acquires the auto lighting business of R. E. Dietz & Co.	
1990	The Lockheed-built Hubble Space Telescope is deployed.	
1990	The 1991 Ford Explorer SUV is introduced.	
1990	The Fuller Co. of Bethlehem PA, buys the assets of Davey Compressor Co., making Fuller-Davey Compressor Co.	

1990	Bridgestone USA merges with Firestone Tire & Rubber Co., creating Bridgestone Americas Holding, Inc., with 38 facilities, the largest subsidiary of Japan's Bridgestone Corp.	
1990	There are almost 300 items in the Caterpillar product line this year. *"Yeah Bubba, that's a lotta yeller arn!!"*	
1990	WPI acquires the assets of Houston Heavy Equipment Company.	
1990	New Mexico; Homestake closes their Ambrosia Lake uranium yellowcake mill.	(see 1992)
1990	Oiltools International, an old Cy Helm business, is once again reborn as a independent company, Oiltools.	
1990	By mid-year, Hanson PLC has acquired 100% of Peabody Holding Company.	
1990	Shreveport; Beaird Industries is acquired by Trinity Industries of Dallas.	
1990	**Timken now produces about one-third of all the world's bearings.**	
1990	Lincoln Electric buys Harris Calorific.	
1990	**The well that birthed Permian Basin crude production, the famous Santa Rita #1 near Big Lake, TX, is plugged and abandoned, or P & A'd.**	
1990	Mansfield acquires Norris Plumbing Products.	
1990	The name of the Armitage-Shanks Group is changed to Blue Circle Plumbing Fixtures.	
1990	PDVSA (the national oil company of Venezuela) purchases the remaining 50% of Citgo from the Southland Corp.	
1990	Foley Pressure Inc. of Jennings Louisiana is acquired by Quality Oilfield Products Inc. (QOP).	
1990	CVS acquires the 500 stores of People's Drugs.	(see 1997)

1990	Mostly due to loading up with untimely acquisitions, PACIFIC INTERMOUNTAIN EXPRESS goes into receivership.	
1990	PROCTOR & GAMBLE purchase the Old Spice line of men's toiletries from SHULTON.	
1990	PEABODY HOLMES is acquired by DRESSER INDUSTRIES.	
1990	Edward Lowe sells his "cat litter" business for $200,000,000.	
1990	**BFI now collects the trash from more than three million households.**	
1990	MICHELIN of France takes over the UNIROYAL GOODRICH TIRE COMPANY.	
1990	HARRINGTON HOISTS now becomes a wholly owned subsidiary of KITO CORPORATION, thus becoming the sole source for HARRINGTON/KITO crane and hoist products in the USA.	
1990	HEEREMA acquires GROOTINT, a steel construction yard and offshore contractor. HEEREMA FABRICATION GROUP BV is founded to manage all of the Heerema manufacturing activities.	
1990	France, May 18; the French National Railway (SNCF) sets a new high-speed train record 319.5 mph (515.3 kph).	(see 2007)
1990	The "average" American CEO NOW is paid +/- 107 times as much as today's "average" 1990 employee.	(see 2007)
1990	During the past decade, REGAL-BELIOT paid cash, not stock, for 12 firms it purchased. Thus offering a much faster recovery of their expenditures.	(see 2004)
1990	Michigan; Detroit's population continues to drop all through the 1980s... now down to 1,027,974 folks.	(see 2000)
1990	TADANO acquires the Crane and Vehicle Divisions of FAUN AG, creating FAUN GmbH, a wholly-owned subsidiary. A 360 ton lifting capacity truck crane, the TG-3600 is introduced by TADANO.	(see 1993)
1990	Seat-anchored belts appear in MERCEDES BENZ SL roadsters this year.	(see 1995)
1990	Texas; during the past couple of decades, the all the older CENTRAL TEXAS IRONWORKS plants are sold off, and completed this year is a expansion project tripling the size of and modernizing of the West Waco plant.	
1990	USA; in the first known case of this type, a Massachusetts citizen is jailed for abusing an individual animal.	
1990	Late this year, CONTINENTAL AIRLINES files bankruptcy again; perhaps it's a Lorenzo ploy to try to break up the unions.	(see 1993)
1990	On Christmas Day, British computer scientist Tim Berners-Lee, demonstrates the workings of his new creation, the World Wide Web, over the internet.	
	Eat your heart out, Al Gore!!!	
1990	The digital camera is introduced.	(see 2009)
1990	INGERSOLL-RAND acquires SAMIIA of France, expanding I-R's manufacturing and geographic market base. I-R also acquires ARO EQUIPMENT CORP. of Bryan, OH, a manufacturer of air hoists up to two ton capacity.	(see 2010)
1990	USA; oil production in the state of Pennsylvania has dropped to a bit over 2 million barrels annually; about the 1865 production.	
1991	January; the Gulf War (the first) ensues with Operation Desert Storm, and Iraqis set the Kuwait oil fields afire as they retreat back home.	
1991	INTAIRDRIL founder, Cyrus Vincent Helm dies of heart attack at age 63, and Cy was somewhat of a health nut!!!	
1991	Texas; HARRISBURG COMPANY, of Houston, buys WOOLLEY TOOL COMPANY, of Odessa.	

1991	Pan American World Airways is now gone.	
1991	Keeping the ditchers, Astec sells rights to all Barber-Greene paving products to Caterpillar.	
1991	After 22 years, Big Muskie is shut down and parked; but it is still the biggest dragline ever built.	(see 1999)
1991	Agco purchases White Tractors (including Minneapolis-Moline and Oliver).	
1991	Parker Drilling builds a track mounted rig for the North Slope of Alaska, No. 245.	(see 1996)
1991	**Texas; Trencor Jetco builds the largest chain driven trencher ever, for John D. Stephens Inc. of Georgia, to use laying the 156-mile water pipeline from Lake O. H. Ivie to the Midland-Odessa area.**	(see 1997)

		1991	After reorganization, Fuller-Davey is a part of Fuller-Kovako Corp., a division of Flsmidth Ind., the largest industrial group in Denmark.	
		1991	Corpus Christi, TX; Jimmy Storm, founder of Marine Drilling dies.	
		1991	NCR Corp. is acquired by AT&T.	
		1991	Fiat-Allis discontinues sales of construction equipment in North America.	
		1991	*Texas Monthly* magazine profiles "rags to riches" Houston oilman Oscar Wyatt as "meaner than a junkyard dog."	(see 1997)
		1991	Apple introduces the PowerBook, a laptop model computer with up to 8 MB of memory and a maximum 80 MB SCSI harddrive.	
		1991	USA; recyclable vinyl beverage bottles are first introduced.	

1991	USA; Hasbro acquires Tonka and its Kenner and Parker Bros. divisions.	
1991	August 1; after 41 years and 10 months forecasting North Texas weather, Harold Taft, "The World's Greatest Weatherman," makes his last broadcast. In September, stomach cancer claims the life of Harold Taft.	
1991	Ferrante Auto Court of the UK is acquired by Dresser Wayne.	
1991	Chrysler sells its equity in Mitsubishi Motors Corporation.	(see 1992)
1991	UK; BSA is merged with yet another "buy-out" company, and Mike Jackson's Andover Norton International Ltd., thus is formed as a new BSA group.	
1991	Pieter H. Heerema becomes the sole owner of the Heerema Group.	
1991	England; Pelican now gets a Seddon Atkinson main dealership, operating it as a separate business unit - Knottingley Trucks, in a facility in Knottingley Village.	(see 1996)
1991	Succeeding five generations of Wood family presidents, Michael L. Hurt becomes president of TB Wood's Corp.	
1992	VME teams up with Hitachi to form Euclid-Hitachi Heavy Equip., Inc.	(see 1994)
1992	Caterpillar sells manufacturing rights to most of their forklifts to Mitsubishi, but Caterpillar maintains a 20% interest in Mitsubishi/Caterpillar Forklifts of America. The forklift manufacturing facility is then moved to Houston, TX.	
1992	Humphrey Fluid Power opens in Canada.	
1992	Clark Equipment Co. sells its forklift truck division to Terex Corp.	
1992	Spencer Heads of Gladewater is sold to Preventive Maintenance of New Iberia, LA.	
1992	Textron acquires Cessna from General Dynamics.	
1992	Vinnell Corporation is acquired by BDM.	

1992	TIDEWATER, INC. completes its merger with ZAPATA GULF MARINE, doubling the size of its fleet; they then buy nineteen more offshore construction vessels from McDERMOTT.	(see 1994)
1992	FORD introduces their first minivan, the Mercury Villager. FORD also forms a joint venture with NISSAN this year.	
1992	The helicopter divisions of AEROSPATIALE-MATRA (France) and DAIMLER CHRYSLER AEROSPACE (Germany) merge to form EUROCOPTER group.	(see 1994)
1992	CORONA CORPORATION, a large Canadian gold producer is acquired by HOMESTAKE.	(see 2001)
1992	July 2; the one millionth CHEVROLET Corvette rolls off the assembly line today.	
1992	AT&T introduces their "Videophone 2500," it is not "exactly" a success.	
1992	The active US drilling rig count has now dropped to 621 rigs. *"Hey Slim, 'member the 4,500 plus, 'bout a decade ago?"*	
1992	Durham, NC; a group of local investors buys the Durham plant and reopens it as DURHAM FURNITURE INC. after STRATHERN HOUSE goes broke.	
1992	LAYNE becomes a publicly-held company for the first time.	(see 2005)
1992	HEEREMA sells its controlling interest in WILBROS.	
1992	VARCO INTERNATIONAL acquires RUCKER SHAFFER, maker of blowout preventers and related oilfield equipment.	(see 2005)
1992	October; after 148 years, the WATEROUS ENGINE WORKS is shut-down, closed forever. Another dead one!!	
1992	The "friction stir welding process" is invented by the Welding Institute (TWI).	
1992	At age 92, singer Roy Acuff dies.	
1992	New Mexico; after forty-six years, La Mesa Park in Raton, the oldest horse track in the state, closes its gates forever.	
1992	UK; the ROOTES GROUP just sort of fades away, as do the COMMER badged vehicles, but they are in use all around the world.	

1993	COOPER INDUSTRIES spins-off GARDNER-DENVER COMPANY.	(see 1996)
1993	SNAP-ON TOOL COMPANY buys the 110 year old hand tool maker, J. H. WILLIAMS COMPANY, of Columbus, GA.	
1993	RAYTHEON CORP. acquires the line of HAWKER jets from BRITISH AEROSPACE SYSTEMS, and forms RAYTHEON CORPORATE JETS.	
1993	SCHWINN BICYCLE CO. files for bankruptcy protection. New management takes over, stating, "We fell, we got up! End of apology."	
1993	HOLT COMPANY OF TEXAS celebrates sixty years as a CATERPILLAR dealer; HOLT OF TEXAS sells ENERGY INDUSTRIES.	
1993	Drilling and workover rig builder, HOPPER of Bakersfield, California, goes "belly-up." WATSON TRUCK & SUPPLY of Hobbs, NM, a HOPPER dealer for several decades, buys all assets of HOPPER, moves it to Hobbs, and forms WATSON-HOPPER, a wholly owned subsidiary of WATSON TRUCK & SUPPLY.	
1993	RAY-O-VAC Introduces The Renewal, A Reusable, Long-Life, Alkaline Battery.	
1993	Texas; NABORS INDUSTRIES buys HENLEY DRILLING of Mt. Pleasant, in June.	
1993	OSRAM GmbH acquires SYLVANIA lighting from GTE, making OSRAM SYLVANIA.	
1993	VICTOR merges with German gasket maker Reinz to form VICTOR-REINZ.	
1993	MARK IV buys PIRELLI's rubber belt business.	

1993	Offshore Rigs LLC acquires Grace Offshore, including the 50 acre yard and first class facilities at Houma, LA.	
1993	Danaher Corp. sells Allied Steel & Tractor Products, Inc. to Pubco Corp.; who then change the name to Allied Construction Products Co.	
1993	September; the 1,000th Boeing 747 flies out the door, just short of 24 years after the first 747 was sold.	
1993	In Chile; Caterpillar dealer Gildemeister S. A. C. is acquired by Finning.	
1993	Martin-Marietta acquires the aerospace division of General Dynamics.	

1993	The UP acquires the Southern Pacific and names all their routes, Union Pacific.	
1993	The Carlson Companies' revenue is ten billion dollars this year.	
1993	Dockwise is founded as Wijsmuller Transport merges with Dock Express Shipping.	
1993	Old Sam Boyd passes away, and his son Bill continues to oversee Boyd Gaming Corporation.	
1993	Tadano establishes Tadano America Corporation in the USA.	(see 1996)

1993	Probably the greatest aviator ever, ninety-six year old James Harold "Jimmy" Doolittle dies this year.	
1993	Flint Industries is now renamed Flint Canada, Incorporated.	(see 1998)
1993	Continental Airlines buys 90 new Boeing aircraft; consisting of 737, 757, 767 and 777s, using financial input of Air Canada and Air Partners. President Gordon Bethune seems to be on the right track.	(see 2012)
1994	Rockwell International Corp. acquires Reliance Electric, including Kato Engineering.	
1994	VME drops the Michigan name from its heavy equipment line, in favor of the Volvo name. After 40 years, no more Michigans.	
1994	Axelson merges with Guiberson, and becomes a part of Dresser Industries.	
1994	February; Pride Petroleum Services acquires Hydrodrill, S. A., a four rig Argentine operation. In June Pride acquires all assets of Offshore Rigs LLC.	
1994	**Terex discontinues their front-end loader production.** *NOTE: The "King of the Earth" bites the dust again.*	
1994	Schwinn moves from Chicago to Denver.	
1994	After 43 years, Textron sells Homelite Corporation.	
1994	Raytheon Aircraft is formed by the merger of Beech Aircraft and Raytheon Corporate Jets.	
1994	Astec Industries acquires Capitol Trenchers, merges it with Trencor Jetco and forms Trencor, Inc.	
1994	The tunnel and rail connection between England and France under the English Channel, the "Chunnel," is completed, and opens for rail traffic. Queen Elizabeth II and French President Mitterrand officiate at the opening.	
1994	Euclid-Hitachi Heavy Equipment Inc. is established in the USA. Sorry Euclid, no more Eucs!!!	
1994	Cash strapped Chrysler sells Lamborghini to Mega-Tech.	(see 1999)

1994	TIDEWATER COMPRESSION acquires BRAZOS GAS COMPRESSOR CORPORATION, and also buys a compression division from HALLIBURTON.	(see 1996)
1994	NABORS INDUSTRIES acquires the land drilling operations of GRACE DRILLING CORPORATION. Then in October, they acquire MND Drilling Company.	
1994	NOBLE DRILLING acquires TRITON ENGINEERING SVCS CO., then completes the merger of CHILES OFFSHORE.	
1994	FIGGE INTERNATIONAL (formerly A-T-O Inc.) sells its HUBER MANUFACTURING DIVISION to ENTERPRISE FABRICATIONS, INC., and the business returns to Galion, OH.	
1994	Mid-90s; after a business relationship of over thirty years, FORD acquires COSWORTH ENGINEERING, LTD.	
1994	JOY MANUFACTURING becomes associated with HARNISCHFEGER INDUSTRIES, INC.	
1994	DRESSER's 64% of M-I DRILLING FLUIDS (soon to be M-I LLC) is acquired by A. SMITH INTERNATIONAL, INC.	
1994	KONE completes the acquisition of MONTGOMERY ELEVATOR COMPANY of the US.	
1994	MANSFIELD becomes a part of FALCON BUILDING PRODUCTS INC. of Chicago.	
1994	GROVES INDUSTRIAL SUPPLY acquires the GLOVE COMPANY and merge the two companies.	
1994	USA; in new automobile air conditioners, R-134 refrigerant replaces CFC-12 Freon.	
1994	February; ROWAN completes the purchase of the net assets of the MARATHON LETOURNEAU COMPANY, from GENERAL CABLE.	
1994	**Texas; the largest wheel loader ever built and operated, now debuts; the 50 ton bucket capacity LeTourneau L-1800.**	(see 2000)
1994	**In trials, the (LeTourneau-built) Rowan Gorilla II is raised to a world record air-gap of 429 feet, then goes to work in the GOM, offshore Louisiana, drilling in 400 feet of water.**	
1994	The CMOS image sensor, also called the "camera on a chip," is invented by a team at the Jet Propulsion Lab, led by Dr. Eric R. Fossum. This sensor leads to the development of DSLR cameras, smartphone cameras, "pill" cameras, and many other applications.	
1994	Louisiana; HUNT ENGINE buys PEMCO of New Orleans.	
1994	UK; December; a newly formed BSA REGAL GROUP, takes over the COLQUHOUN and the JACKSON's BSA GROUP.	
1994	THULE RIGTECH is acquired by VARCO INTERNATIONAL.	
1994	ESAB is purchased by CHARTER PLC of the UK.	
1994	The USA government lifts its ban on liquor auctions.	(see 2008)
1994	TEXAS STATE UNIVERSITY buys Aquarena Springs in San Marcos; numbering the days of "Ralph the Swimming Pig."	
1994	December; after 105 years of Armstrong family ownership, ARMSTRONG BROS. TOOLS is acquired by the DANAHER CORP. They continue the strict adherence to Armstrong's high standards of quality, and continue to make all Armstrong tools in the USA.	
1994	California; HUCK INTERNATIONAL INC. a division of THIOKOL of Ogden, UT, buys most assets of DEUTSCH FASTENER CORP. of Lakewood. Deutsch runs about $15 million annually, making and marketing a variety of special nuts and bolts used in building commercial aircraft. Some Deutsch products are used in the oil patch, as well.	
1995	TEREX CORP. builds the last DART loader, end of another long line of good machines.	
1995	PRIDECO, INC., merges with GRANT TIW to form GRANT PRIDECO.	

1995	SCHWINN BICYCLE's second century begins with the introduction of a high-tech line of mountain bikes, and production is moved back to the USA.	
1995	Texas; TYLER PIPE INDUSTRIES is purchased by RANSOM INDUSTRIES, INC.	
1995	SKF now has 90 factories, and 44,000 employees, 84% are outside Sweden.	
1995	ROLLS-ROYCE acquires ALLISON ENGINE COMPANY of Indianapolis, IN.	
1995	PRIDE acquires X-PERT ENTERPRISES (well service) of New Mexico, and their 35 rigs. Then in October, PRIDE purchases MARLIN COLOMBIA DRILLING CO. from SHELL OIL.	
1995	**BELL HELICOPTER celebrates fifty years and 34,000 choppers.**	
1995	January; NABORS INDUSTRIES buys EXETER Drilling Company.	
1995	UNIVERSAL CRUSHERS is sold by PETTIBONE to SVEDALA INDUSTRIES of Sweden.	(see 1998)
1995	**MAYTAG is the first in the home appliance firm in the industry to eliminate CFCs from all its products.**	
1995	ATLAS COPCO purchases AMSTAR CORP.	

1995	B. J. SERVICES acquires the WESTERN CO. OF NORTH AMERICA.	
1995	MARK IV acquires PUROLATOR CORP., then moves DAYCO Aftermarket from Dayton, OH, to Tulsa, OK.	
1995	July; Jeff Bezos brings Amazon.Com online and they sell their first book: Douglas Hofstadter's *Fluid Concepts and Creative Analogies: Computer Models of the Fundamental Mechanisms of Thought.*	
1995	LOCKHEED MARTIN CORP. is formed by the merger of LOCKHEED CORP. and MARTIN MARIETTA CORP.	
1995	This year THOMASVILLE FURNITURE INDUSTRIES is bought by FURNITURE BRANDS INTERNATIONAL INC.	

1995	REECE ALBERT, INC., of San Angelo buys SOUTH TEXAS CONSTRUCTION CO. of Midland, expanding Albert's territory into the Permian Basin.	
1995	WD-40 COMPANY acquires the 100 year old brand 3-IN-1 oil from RECKITT & COLEMAN.	
1995	To concentrate on their core products (piston rings and Casite products) HASTINGS sells its filter operations to CLARCOR.	
1995	LIEBHERR-AMERICA INC., acquires WISEDA, for their line of giant, off-road trucks.	
1995	The J. RAY MCDERMOTT name is revived and given to McDermott's marine operations, as a subsidiary of MCDERMOTT INTERNATIONAL.	
1995	BRYAN STEAM CORP. of Indiana buys WENDLAND MFG. COMPANY and renames it WENDLAND MANUFACTURING CORP.	
1995	KKR completes its divesture of RJR NABISCO.	
1995	ALLIED ELECTRONICS puts out the first electronics catalog in a CD-ROM format.	(see 1999)
1995	October 3; former NFL great, O. J. Simpson, is today acquitted of murdering his ex-wife and her boyfriend.	(see 2008)
1995	Having been closed for several years, LETOURNEAU's Vicksburg, MS, yard is reopened… and that's a good sign!!!	
1995	Rowan's ERA purchases Anchorage-based ALASKA HELICOPTER COMPANY.	(see 2000)
1995	Celebrating its centennial year, HARRIS Corporation is now a $3.5 billion annual grossing business with 27,000 employees.	
1995	TEREX acquires PPM CRANES.	
1995	Texas; Mr. John Ludington retires and Mrs. Wendy Kent Churchill (old Frank's granddaughter) becomes major owner and president of FRANK KENT CADILLAC CO., in Fort Worth.	(see 1999)

1995	USA; the 252 NAAA member auctions provided services for more than fifteen million wholesale vehicle transactions; this year the total sale prices of these transactions exceeds sixty billion dollars ($60,000,000,000).	
1995	USA; New Hampshire is now the only state without mandatory seatbelt usage laws.	
1995	The DVD format is perfected.	
1995	It is no secret that, for some time now, Coca-Cola has been the most recognized brand name on earth.	
1995	CHESTER HOIST COMPANY becomes a part of the COLUMBUS MCKINNON industrial family. COLUMBUS MCKINNON has 3,400 employees at 76 locations in 14 countries as well as 11,000 distributors around the globe.	(see 2010)
1996	ITW buys the family-owned (since 1897) HOBART BROS. COMPANY of Troy, OH.	
1996	GARDNER-DENVER merges with LAMSON of Syracuse, NY, becoming the world's largest manufacturer of blowers.	(see 1997)
1996	The government oil company, YPF of Argentina, buys all assets of MAXUS of Dallas, TX.	
1996	AT&T spins-off NCR CORP.	
1996	BUCYRUS-ERIE CO. changes its name to BUCYRUS INTERNATIONAL, INC.	
1996	PACCAR buys DAF TRUCKS of the Netherlands.	
1996	PARKER DRILLING buys MALLARD DRILLING.	(see 1997)
1996	BORGWARNER buys HOLLEY CARBURETOR and other firms from COLTEC.	
1996	HORNBECK OFFSHORE SERVICES is acquired, bringing TIDEWATER's vessel count to over 600.	(see 1997)
1996	NABORS INDUSTRIES buys SUNDOWNER OFFSHORE.	
1996	THOMAS H. LEE COMPANY acquires RAY-O-VAC and plans to take it public.	
1996	BJ SERVICES acquires NOWSCO WELL SERVICE LTD., of Canada.	
1996	A new $100 bill is issued by the US Treasury, featuring an enlarged image of Ben Franklin and a new color-shifting ink used as a security measure.	
1996	ENSCO acquires DUAL DRILLING CO.	
1996	COOPER-CAMERON CORPORATION and INGRAM-CACTUS merge.	
1996	MAYTAG acquires BLODGETT CORPORATION.	
1996	FACOM of France buys SK TOOLS of the US	
1996	CATERPILLAR INC. acquires MaK MOTOREN of Germany, creating the CM series of Caterpillar diesel engines.	
1996	NABORS buys DELTA DRILLING of Tyler, TX, immediately laying off all maintenance, materials, and transportation personnel.	
1996	**Ford builds its 250,000,000th vehicle.** *"Yeah Slim; 'at's uh quarter uf a billyun Fords!!!"*	
1996	HASTINGS moves its Tennessee piston ring and related operations back to Hastings, MI.	
1996	CALENERGY buys the following cogeneration plants from FALCON SEABOARD; Power Resources, Inc., in Big Spring, TX, also Northern Consolidated Power in Northeast Pennsylvania, and Saranac Energy, Inc., of Plattsburgh, NY.	
1996	TULSA WINCH CO. is acquired by DOVER RESOURCES division of DOVER CORPORATION.	
1996	After 86 years FOKKER folds, but STORK carries on a portion of their aircraft production.	
1996	SELLSTROM completes acquiring RTC, a fall protection company, now known as SELLSTROM/RTC CUSTOM SOLUTIONS.	

1996	There are now 260 Cracker Barrel Old Country Stores.	
1996	Lockheed Martin spins-off Martin-Marietta Materials, as a separate and independent entity.	
1996	May 3; Country music loses a true pioneer, with the death of 87-year-old Patsy Montana.	
1996	Having fallen on hard times, Pabst Brewing Co. shuts down mid-shift, with canning and bottling lines going. They just close up, padlock the twenty-two-acre plant, and walk away.	

1996	Winters, TX; local businessman Charles R. "Pinky" Pinkerton dies.	
1996	The company's founder, T. Boone Pickens, is forced out of Mesa Petroleum.	
1996	Tuboscope Vetco acquires Drexel Oilfield Services.	
1996	The 12.4 million Chevrolet Impalas sold since its 1958 birth is good, very good.	
1996	Morgan, Lewis, Githens & Ahn acquire Gradall from ICM Industries, then soon turn around and sell Gradall to JLG Industries.	(see 1999) (see 2006)
1996	Carl Sagan, noted astronomer and astrophysicist, and host of the *Cosmos* television show on PBS, dies in December this year.	
1996	Clark Material Handling is dumped by Terex.	
1996	Japan; including all types of cranes, Tadano produces their 300,000th unit this year.	(see 1998)
1996	Louisiana; this year the Historic Caddo Lake Drawbridge, on Hwy 538, just north of downtown Mooringsport, is officially entered into the National Register of Historic Places.	
1996	England; Bob Crump retires and passes the Pelican reins to his son Richard.	(see 2001)
1996	Michigan; Zimmerman International of Madison Heights is acquired by Ingersoll-Rand.	(see 2010)
1997	A merger of American Yard Products Co., Frigidaire, and Poulan/Weedeater forms the Electrolux Group.	
1997	Caterpillar, Inc. buys Perkins Engines of England and becomes the world's leading diesel engine manufacturer.	
1997	Bucyrus Corp. buys Marion Power Shovel Co., ending 113 years of competition.	
1997	Eaton buys Dana's worldwide Spicer Truck Clutch business.	
1997	Wabash National buys all assets of Fruehauf Trailers.	
1997	About this time, Kerr McGee buys Oryx.	
1997	February; Pride sells its entire US domestic workover rig fleet, to concentrate on international contracts. This month Pride also completes the acquisition of Forasol-Foramer N. V. of France. May; Pride acquires Noble's twelve rig mat-supported jack-up fleet in the GOM.	
1997	Continental Emsco merges Skagit and Smatco Industries, Inc., to form CE Marine Products.	
1997	Gardner-Denver acquires Tamrotor, of Finland, a pump and compressor manufacturer, also acquires Champion Pneumatic Machinery Company.	
1997	Parker Drilling buys Bollifax SA of Boliva, and also Hercules Offshore.	(see 1999)
1997	Champion Road Machinery, Ltd., is acquired by Volvo Construction Equipment Group.	
1997	Borgwarner acquires ownership of AG KKK.	
1997	B. F. Goodrich merges with Rohr Co.	

1997	KUWAIT PETROLEUM CO. sells most of SANTA FE INTERNATIONAL.	
1997	Louisiana; JUSTISS OIL COMPANY of Jena, sells 12 of its 13 drilling rigs to GREY WOLF DRILLING COMPANY.	
1997	TIDEWATER MARINE now has over 700 vessels, after buying O. I. L. Ltd.	(see 2003)
1997	NABORS INDUSTRIES buys the remainder of the NOBLE DRILLING land rig fleet.	
1997	GOODMAN acquires AMANA.	
1997	Texas; Lucien Flournoy retires and sells FLOURNOY DRILLING of Alice to GREY WOLF for $30 million.	
1997	March; Sky Tower opens in Auckland, New Zealand, as the tallest structure in the Southern Hemisphere. It took two and a half years to build.	
1997	After more than 90 years, A. O. SMITH leaves the automotive industry by selling their Automotive Products Co. to TOWER AUTOMOTIVE.	
1997	The only HUBER grader now being built (M-850-A) a small hydrostatically-driven machine is a direct descendent of the first HUBER maintainer (road grader) built in 1943, and has been in continuous production for fifty-four years.	
1997	NATIONAL OILWELL acquires ROSS HILL CONTROLS, then DRECO of Canada, and PEP, INC.	
1997	FORD sells its heavy duty truck business to FREIGHTLINER.	
1997	LINCOLN-MERCURY division of FORD, moves its headquarters to Irvine, CA.	
1997	TEREX Corp. purchases the German Orenstein & Koppel's mining division, including its fine hydraulic excavators.	
1997	Talk about diversification… GEARENCH purchases PUREMCO, INC., of Waco.	
1997	July; READING & BATES merges with FALCON DRILLING; creating R&B FALCON DRILLING CO.	
1997	July; ASPHALT EQUIP. & SERV. CO. (AESCO) of Auburn, WA, acquires the entire Madsen line from EAGLE, including all BLH/CLARK/EAGLE equipment, and everything from day one of Madsen; all new equipment is being branded as "Aesco Madsen."	
1997	TRW acquires VINNELL from BDM.	
1997	July; after 51 years, the Ackers family of Abilene, TX, sells KRBC TV to SUNRISE TELEVISION CO.	
1997	GTE acquires BBN in a $616 million transaction.	
1997	FEDERAL SUMMIT is established.	
1997	COLFAX PT GROUP acquires INDUSTRIAL CLUTCH CORP. from the Eason family.	
1997	A private investment firm buys RAND-McNALLY CO. from the McNally family.	
1997	The AUTOMOTIVE HALL OF FAME leaves Midland, MI, to a new home next to the Henry Ford Museum in greater Detroit.	
1997	CVS Drugstores acquires REVCO and its 2,552 stores.	(see 1998)
1997	COASTAL STATES (old Oscar is still a strong player) Gas sells to EL PASO CORP. for $24 billion, making the largest natural gas pipeline system in the US	(see 2001)
1997	CULBRO CORPORATION splits in two… GENERAL CIGAR HOLDINGS, and GRIFFIN LAND & NURSERIES.	
1997	Our old farmer's grandson, maybe great-grandson, using a new JD 8100 and a 25 foot disc, takes only 1.1 hours (66 minutes) to disc his 40 acres.	(see 2005)

1997	Volker Vessels merges with Visser & Smit Hanab.	
1997	The Heerema Group acquires the semi-submersible crane vessel, Thialf, the world's largest, with a lifting capacity of 14,000 tons. The Heeremac joint venture is terminated this year.	
1997	BP Energy Fund is formed by T. Boone Pickens. It will be called BP Capital Management, in a few years.	
1997	Gerlach, NV, October 15; out here in the Black Rock Desert, Andy Greene drives Richard Noble's twin-engine "Thrust SSC" up to 763.035 miles (1,221 km) per hour, crushing Noble's own old 1983 record.	
1997	Texas; Warren Buffet's Berkshire Hathaway Inc. buys Star Furniture Co. of Houston.	(see 2012)
1997	USA; this year 41% of all new clothing sold here is made here.	(see 2012)
1997	Continential-Emsco acquires Gregory Rig Service of Odessa in December.	
1997	Ann Konecny, Skip Foley's daughter, becomes president of Foley Tractor Co. and soon opens their Cat Rental Store.	(see 2007)
1997	December; Paccar sells Trico Industries, Inc., to EVI of Houston.	
1998	January; Curtis Mathes Holding Corp. has changed its name to Uniview Technologies Corporation.	
1998	G-D acquires Wittig, of Germany.	
1998	Paccar buys Leyland, (British Leyland).	
1998	British Petroleum buys Amoco to make BP-Amoco.	
1998	Ingersoll-Rand International buys Bowen Tools from Air Liquide America.	
1998	February 15; on his 20th try, seven time cup series champion Dale Earnhardt finally wins the Daytona 500. Today's race ends in a fist fight involving the Allison brothers, and Cale Yarbrough.	
1998	Quaker State Corporation is merged into Pennzoil Products Group, making the new company of Pennzoil-Quaker State Company.	
1998	A joint venture between Sumitomo Heavy Industries and Case Corp. forms LBX, to market and sell Link-Belt excavators, leaving Link-Belt Cranes as a part of Link-Belt Construction Equipment Co.	
1998	Schwinn Bicycle Co. acquires Hebb Industries, thus becoming a major player in the exercise and fitness industry.	
1998	Eaton sells its worldwide axle & brake business to Dana Corp. & sells its leaf spring business to Oxford Automotive of Troy, MI.	
1998	April; Snap-On Tools buys Hein-Werner, a old manufacturer of high quality hydraulic jacks and body repair equipment.	
1998	Total, of France, acquires Petrofina of Belgium, making Total Fina.	
1998	After 45 years out of business, Indian Motocycles re-emerges, on a very small scale, with hand-made machines.	(see 1999)
1998	After almost a century, Marmon trucks goes out of business. Another old, real good one dies.	(see 2003)
1998	Advance Auto Parts buys Western Auto from Sears, Roebuck & Co.	
1998	EMD enters into an alliance with Caterpillar and MPI, for design, marketing and selling a new low horsepower branch line and switching engine.	
1998	Mega-Tech sells Lamborghini to, now get this… the Volkswagen Group.	

1998	TULSA RIG IRON, INC. purchases the old rig-builder SPENCER-HARRIS MACHINE of Gladewater, TX.	
1998	NATIONAL-OILWELL acquires privately-held CONTINENTAL-EMSCO (a privately held co.) for $65 million. C-E's products mostly consist of EMSCO drilling machinery and WILSON mobile rigs. C-E's revenue last year was $100 million. NAT-OIL then purchases PHOENIX ENERGY SERVICES. NAT-OIL acquires DOSCO, a Canadian supply company, from WESTBOURNE, INC.; and wrap the deal for ROBERDS-JOHNSON INDUSTRIES, then acquire SPECIALTY TOOLS. NAT-OIL also acquires VERSATECH of Canada, then PHOENIX ENERGY SERVICES which includes HARRISBURG, WOOLLEY, M&W, as well as CDI.	
1998	DAWSON PRODUCTION SERVICES (and their 500 or so riglets) is now acquired by KEY ENERGY SERVICES.	
1998	A. SMITH INTERNATIONAL acquires the remaining part of M-I DRILLING FLUIDS.	
1998	TEREX acquires two European tower crane manufacturers, PEINER HTS of Germany and GRU COMEDIL SPA of Italy.	
1998	**PHILLIPS PETROLEUM receives its 15,000th US patent.**	
1998	INDUSTRIAL HOLDINGS, INC. acquires BEAIRD INDUSTRIES of Shreveport, LA.	
1998	BAKER HUGHES acquires WESTERN ATLAS INTERNATIONAL creating the third-largest oilfield services company.	
1998	**The world's largest off-highway truck, ever, the CATERPILLAR 797 debuts at the Caterpillar proving grounds in Arizona.**	
1998	**CONTINENTAL-EMSCO brings out the world's first 60½" rotary table, primarily for offshore rigs to handle large diameter riser pipe.**	
1998	Through a series of recent acquisitions, ALSTOM ENGINES now controls RUSTON PAXMAN, and PAXMAN becomes ALSTOM ENGINES-PAXMAN DIVISION.	
1998	FEDERAL MOGUL acquires FEL-PRO, a leading maker of gaskets, then completely acquires COOPER AUTOMOTIVE.	
1998	FULLER-KOVAKO sells DAVEY COMPRESSOR COMPANY to JENNY PRODUCTS, INC., of "Steam Jenny" fame.	
1998	JOY MFG. acquires the mine bolting products firm, CRAM of Australia.	
1998	Kees Verheul buys AERMOTOR COMPANY, the old windmill builder of San Angelo, TX, where it first began.	
1998	December; BRYAN STEAM CORP. and WENDLAND MANUFACTURING CORP. become members of BURNHAM HOLDINGS, INC.	
1998	SCF PARTNERS acquire SOONER INC.	
1998	AVAQ GROUP buys MOONEY AIRCRAFT CORP.	
1998	WEATHERFORD ENTERRA merges with EVI, INC., to form WEATHERFORD INTERNATIONAL, LTD.	
1998	CVS acquires the 207 stores of ARBOR DRUGS of Michigan.	(see 2004)
1998	VOLKSWAGEN acquires BUGATTI, an old French automaker.	
1998	DANZAS is acquired by DEUTSCHE POST of Germany.	
1998	DRESSER INDUSTRIES merges with, or is acquired by, HALLIBURTON.	
1998	On the 50th anniversary of Ziolkowski starting work, Crazy Horse's face is dedicated; his head is 87½ feet high.	

1998	UK; now, the MAYFLOWER GROUP acquires the DENNIS BROTHERS FIRM.		
1998	ESAB acquires ALCO TEC WIRE COMPANY of the USA, the world's largest producer of aluminum wire.		
1998	North Anson, ME; due to whatever factors, COOPER INDUSTRIES sells the local Anson plant to the Meisner family. Along with the plant, the Meisners have acquired all of Edward T. Lufkin's original product lines. The Meisners primarily wanted the sawmill and kilns at the Anson plant, but all the equipment and the processes to produce the original Lufkin products are now their property. Many distributors and customers are asking the Meisners to produce the old Lufkin line of wood rulers and "L" squares. These many requests are accommodated as the Meisners now found the SKOWHEGAN WOODEN RULE CO., INC., producing LUFKIN products and never relaxing Lufkin's standards, even rehiring some of the locals who have crafted these wooden measuring tools for several generations.		

	1998	Chicago; BEARDSLEY & PIPER is acquired by SIMPSON TECHNOLOGIES CORP. from PETTIBONE, to create the SIMPSON GROUP... continuing as a manufacturer of foundry equipment well into the twenty-first century.	(see 2008)
	1998	STEWART & STEVENSON acquire all rights from DETROIT DIESEL ALLISON, to the Allison HT-70 and Allison CL(B)T 4460. S&S is now the OEM for new parts and rebuilt units for these two transmission lines.	
	1998	Two students at Stanford University, Larry Page and Sergey Brin, incorporate Google.	
	1998	TADANO brings out Japan's largest "all-terrain" crane, their AR-5500, having a 550-ton lifting capacity.	
	1998	Late in year, EXXON buys MOBIL OIL to form EXXON-MOBIL.	
	1998	Under license from WHITE-WESTINGHOUSE, the NORDYNE GROUP revives the TAPPAN name.	
1998	FLINT ENERGY SERVICES, LTD. is incorporated, and acquisitions include the HMW Group, BRAIDNOR, and REID'S CONSTRUCTION.		(see 2000)
1998	December; NEW HOLLAND N. V. buys German excavator manufacturer ORENSTEIN & KOPPEL AG (O & K) from FRIED KRUPP AG HOESCH KRUPP.		(see 1999)
1998	Finland; production of the SISU XA-184 and similar type armored vehicles is moved from SISU to PATRIA VEHICLES OY.		
98-99	RAYTHEON CORP. sells CEDARAPIDS to TEREX CORP. *"Hey Brother, remember the Peter Rabbit Pugmill?"*		
1999	TOTAL FINA acquires ELF AQUITANE making TOTAL FINA ELF.		
1999	BP-AMOCO buys ARCO.		
1999	February; Curtis L. Carlson, founder of GOLD BOND STAMPS and the CARLSON COMPANIES, dies at age 84. Marilyn Nelson, the eldest daughter of Carlson, succeeds him running the family-owned businesses.		
1999	KERR MCGEE completes the buyout of ORYX.		
1999	LINCOLN ELECTRIC sells its electric motor division to MARATHON ELECTRIC, but assures ~~guaranteed employment for ALL LINCOLN employees in the deal.		
	...UTH LOCOMOTIVE WORKS merges with OHIO LOCOMOTIVE CRANE COMPANY, thus ...ng OHIO INDUSTRIES.		

1999	During this year, NATIONAL-OILWELL buys all assets of bankrupt SKYTOP-BREWSTER, and the drilling equipment business of CONTINENTAL-EMSCO, also the DUPRÉ COMPANIES, and DRECO ENGINEERING SERVICES LTD. of Canada, then they sell their tubular goods business to SOONER, INC. Then, NATIONAL-OILWELL buys MARITIME HYDRAULICS of Canada, as well.	
1999	EATON CORP. acquires AEROQUIP-VICKERS, INC., then sells its FLUID POWER DIV. to BORG-WARNER AUTOMOTIVE CORP.	
1999	SOUTHLAND CORPORATION changes its name to 7-ELEVEN, INC.	
1999	EMERSON ELECTRIC of St. Louis, buys KATO; then merges KATO with Emerson's three other generator manufacturing plants. EMERSON is now one of the largest manufacturers of generators in the world.	
1999	GARDNER-DENVER acquires GEOQUIP, ALLEN-STUART, AIR RELIEF, and BUTTERWORTH JETTING SYSTEMS.	(see 2000)
1999	GRADALL is purchased by JLG INDUSTRIES.	(see 2006)
1999	The EC approves the acquisition of CASE CORP. of Racine, WI, by NEW HOLLAND NV. Then CASE and NEW HOLLAND join to form CNH GLOBAL. The formation of CNH merges the interests of CASE and farm machinery giant NEW HOLLAND. This merger brings the CASE-POCLAIN machines, now designed by SUMITOMO, under the same umbrella as several other well-known excavator names already in the NH empire. These include FIAT-ALLIS excavators, as well as O&Ks construction sized hydraulic excavator line.	(see 2002)
1999	UNIT DRILLING buys almost all of PARKER DRILLING's land rigs in the lower forty-eight states.	
1999	ZENITH ELECTRONIC CORP. becomes a subsidiary of LG ELECTRONICS of Korea.	
1999	TRW purchases LUCAS/VARITY PLC for seven billion dollars.	
1999	B. F. GOODRICH merges with COLTEC INDUSTRIES.	
1999	WEATHERFORD INTERNATIONAL acquires DAILEY INTERNATIONAL, another manufacturer of oilfield drilling tools.	
1999	In the largest locomotive purchase ever, UNION PACIFIC RAILROAD orders one thousand of the new SD 70M locomotives from EMD locomotive division.	
1999	March; GALION IRON WORKS is acquired by KOMATSU of Japan.	
1999	BJ SERVICES acquires FRACMASTER and consolidates it into NOWSCO-FRACMASTER.	
1999	April; DANZAS acquires NEDLLOYD of Holland and SWEDEN ASG AB, both large logistics firms. Then they soon acquire AIR EXPRESS INTERNATIONAL of the US.	
1999	May 2-8; in the space of one week, 154 tornadoes touch down in the Midwest, with the peak of activity hitting Oklahoma, Kansas, Nebraska, Texas, and Arkansas. More than $1.5B of damage is done in and around Oklahoma City, and 36 people lose their lives.	
1999	EMERSON ELECTRIC acquires DANIEL INDUSTRIES, INC.	
1999	RAY-O-VAC acquires ROV, LTD.	
1999	May 20; the 5" diameter cables holding the boom of BIG MUSKIE are severed by explosives, and the boom craters, the end of an era, as the behemoth is scrapped out. During its 22 working years, BIG MUSKIE moved over 608 million cubic yards of overburden, much more than twice the amount moved in building the entire Panama Canal.	
1999	FACOM becomes a subsidiary of FIMALAC.	

1999	*Initially touted as a merger, Daimler-Benz buys out Chrysler Corp., and it is a buyout, plain and simple!*	(see 2000)
1999	Conoco becomes independent after Dupont "spins it off."	
1999	In A. O. Smith's largest acquisition ever, they purchase the world-wide electric motor operations of Magnetek.	
1999	WD-40 acquires Lava hand soap from Block Drug Company.	
1999	A $30 million merger of several motorcycle companies creates the (new) Indian Motorcycle Corp., in Gilroy, CA, and sells eleven hundred bikes this year.	
1999	Philadelphia based Rohm & Haas Co. acquires the Morton Salt Company.	
1999	Sara Lee buys the Hills Bros. Coffee brand from Nestlé.	(see 2005)
1999	Ford acquires Volvo Cars and the Think electric cars.	
1999	Sooner Inc. acquires the tubular divisions of Continental-Emsco, National-Oilwell and Wilson Supply.	
1999	Schlumberger Ltd. acquires 40% of M-I LLC from A. Smith International; Camco International merges into Schlumberger.	
1999	GTE is taken over by Verizon.	
1999	Rand-McNally Co. acquires Thomas Bros. Maps.	
1999	Ideal Standard of the US buys the bathroom fixtures division of Blue Circle.	

1999	NASA launches the Chandra X-Ray Observatory, which joins the Hubble Telescope in orbit as one of the "Great Observatories." The world's largest X-Ray telescope, Chandra is the largest and heaviest payload ever launched by the Space Shuttle by this time. The device's mission was expected to last only 5 years, but is still sending data to Earth today.	
1999	October; the German materials giant Dyckerhoff AG buys Lone Star Industries for $1.2 billion.	
1999	French automaker Renault takes controlling interest in Japanese carmaker Nissan, which is facing possible bankruptcy.	
1999	Dow Chemical Company acquires Union Carbide.	
1999	Although the petroleum industry has been in a slow rebound, the 488 active drilling rigs in the US is the lowest since drilling became a viable industry.	
1999	Allied Radio & Electronics is acquired by Electrocomponents of the United Kingdom.	
1999	With headquarters in Little Rock and eight branches around the state, Arkansas' sole Caterpillar dealer is now being operated by four generations of the Riggs family.	
1999	General Motors spins-off Delphi, one of its major auto parts suppliers.	
1999	Having 36 facilities in 11 nations, employing 8,000 people, Aeroquip now becomes the Aeroquip Division of Eaton.	
	and DMD Division of Dresser Equipment Group, Inc., are combined.	
	tronics merges with LG Electronics of Korea.	
	Allied Waste Industries.	
	uires PMI, including Hobart.	
	in New York City is retired, seventeen years after the last Checker	
	ch Inc. acquires Tor Truck USA, Inc., located in Pennsylvania.	(see 2006)

1999	NATIONAL-OILWELL collaborates with HITEC to design and build the first AC driven "Active Heave Compensating Draw-works."	
1999	Milwaukee, WI; after 152 years, the last employee turns the lights off, closes the doors, and leaves forever, from the old, historically important, ALLIS-CHALMERS home offices.	
1999	Germany; THYSSEN and KRUPP merge, creating one of the world's largest technology companies.	(see 2006)
1999	There are now 434 nuclear power plants in use in 31 countries around the world. About 365 of these are in the "Western" world. In 18 of these nations, nuclear energy provides at least 25% of the energy for power generation.	
1999	Since its 1961 debut, almost twelve million OLDSMOBILE Cutlass cars have been sold. And that is great!!!	(see 2004)
1999	Texas; in Ft. Worth, FRANK KENT AUTO GROUP and FRANK KENT CADILLAC, are merged into one company; once again it is FRANK KENT MOTOR COMPANY, now with Mrs. Churchill as owner and president.	(see 2005)
1999	November 24; NABORS INDUSTRIES buys POOL ENERGY SERVICES, including ALL Pool and Intairdril Companies, worldwide, but guarantees nothing to the POOL employees.	
1999	December; WILSON INDUSTRIES, a subsidiary of SMITH INTERNATIONAL INC. acquires TEXAS MILL SUPPLY & MFG., INC.	
1999	December 31; TRANSOCEAN OFFSHORE, INC. merges with SEDCO FOREX HOLDINGS LTD.; forming TRANSOCEAN SEDCO FOREX (TSFX) the world's largest offshore drilling company, with a total of more than 70 Mobile Offshore Drilling Units.	
2000	January; NATIONAL-OILWELL acquires I. P. S., SCR systems, etc.; then in September, acquires BAYLOR ELECTRIC from BOOTS & COOTS INTERNATIONAL. NAT-OIL then buys WHEATLEY-GASO and OMEGA pump lines from HALLIBURTON; they also acquire HITEC USA, a manufacturer of electronic control equipment. Then NAT-OIL buys REPUBLIC SUPPLY CORP. as well.	
2000	LeTOURNEAU, a wholly-owned subsidiary of ROWAN COMPANIES, completes its purchase of ELLIS WILLIAMS CO., INC., and EWCO, INC.	
2000	February; WEATHERFORD INTERNATIONAL merges WEATHERFORD GLOBAL COMPRESSION SERVICES with UNIVERSAL COMPRESSION HOLDINGS. Then, in April, WEATHERFORD INTERNATIONAL spins off GRANT-PRIDECO as a separate entity, and acquires ALPINE OIL SERVICES of Calgary, Alberta, Canada.	
2000	Beginning early this year, T-3 ENERGY SERVICES acquires and merges with COR-VAL INC. and PREFERRED INDUSTRIES, both of Houma, LA.	(see 2010)
2000	February; INGERSOLL-RAND buys HALLIBURTON's share of the DRESSER-RAND joint venture.	
2000	March; EVERETT PAD & PAPER COMPANY acquires the SPRINGFIELD TABLET COMPANY.	
2000	JOHNSON SCREENS, INTERNATIONAL NITROGEN SERVICES, and CAC are all acquired by WEATHERFORD INTERNATIONAL this year.	
2000	GARDNER-DENVER acquires AIRFLOW SYSTEMS, JETTING SYSTEMS & ACCESSORIES, and CRS POWER FLOW, INC.	
2000	June; PARKER-HANNIFIN acquires COMMERCIAL INTERTECH hydraulics.	
2000	JOHN DEERE purchases TIMBERJACK from METSO CORP. of Finland.	
2000	WILBROS acquires ROGERS & PHILLIPS, a pipeline construction company. After 91 years in Tulsa, WILLIAMS BROTHERS (WILBROS) moves to Houston.	(see 2001)
2000	As the DE SOTO was in 1957, PLYMOUTH automobiles are being phased out by CHRYSLER.	

2000	DAIMLERCHRYSLER AG acquires ALL outstanding shares of DETROIT DIESEL CORP., including a 48.6% ownership share of PENSKE CORP., DAIMLERCHRYSLER then consolidates various engine and powertrain activities, including DETROIT DIESEL CO., MTU FRIEDRICHSHAFEN and MERCEDES BENZ industrial engines into a new business, named DAIMLERCHRYSLER POWERTRAINS. Thus, DETROIT DIESEL, or Jimmy Diesel, if you will, is now a subsidiary of DAIMLERCHRYSLER AG of Germany.	(see 2002)
2000	SKF builds a 44 foot diameter, 154,000 pound roller bearing (a crane slewing bearing). *"Bubba, 'at's a biiig bear'n!!"*	
2000	The world's largest Ferris Wheel, the "London Eye," opens in the UK.	
2000	Tokyo, Japan; the 20,000th 7-ELEVEN convenience store opens.	
2000	Petroleum marketing pioneer Leon Hess dies.	
2000	PARKER DRILLING sells its last US land rig, the big rig 245, to NABORS ALASKA, ending PARKER'S sixty-six years of US domestic land drilling activity.	(see 2001)
2000	**There are about 23 large companies around the world manufacturing automobiles.**	(see 1923) (see 1927)
2000	**An international "jury" names the FORD MODEL T, as the Car of the Century.** *"Bubba, I agree 100 purcint!"*	
2000	April; ENERGIZER (EVEREADY) is spun-off from RALSTON PURINA CO.	
2000	PHILLIPS PETROLEUM buys ARCO ALASKA INC. in the largest acquisition of their history.	
2000	PFIZER and WARNER-LAMBERT merge their drug operations.	
2000	CHEVRON PHILLIPS CHEMICAL CORP. is a joint venture for plastics and chemicals.	
2000	EXIDE acquires GNB TECHNOLOGIES, thus becoming EXIDE TECHNOLOGIES.	
2000	MOTOROLA and GENERAL INSTRUMENT CORP. merge.	
2000	ANADARKO merges with UNION PACIFIC RESOURCES of Ft. Worth, doubling ANADARKO'S reserves.	
2000	June; PAXMAN becomes a part of MAN B&W DIESEL AG, Augsburg, as MAN acquires ALSTOM ENGINES LTD; also includes Ruston and Mirrlees Blackstone.	
2000	July; ALLIED PRODUCTS sells BUSH HOG to CROWN CO. INDUSTRIES; who rename it BUSH HOG, LLC.	
2000	July; INGERSOLL-RAND CO. sells its reciprocating gas compressor packaging and rental operations to HANOVER COMPRESSOR COMPANY.	
2000	FORD acquires LAND ROVER from BMW, then FORD spins-off VISTEON, its parts-making branch.	
2000	July; the CARLYLE GROUP acquires VOUGHT AIRCRAFT INDUSTRIES, INC.	
2000	ALCOA spends $5.8 billion to acquire REYNOLDS ALUMINUM.	
2000	GENERAL MOTORS buys 20% of FIAT'S automotive works.	
2000	August; in an $8.8 billion deal, TRANSOCEAN SEDCO-FOREX is planning a merger with R&B FALCON.	
2000	TULSA WINCH CO. acquires PULLMASTER WINCH of Surrey, BC, Canada.	
2000	September; US GEARMOTORS joins the EMERSON POWER TRANSMISSION group of companies.	
2000	Consummating two years of negotiations, GTE and BELL ATLANTIC merge to form a $60 billion company… VERIZON.	
2000	**OCCIDENTAL is now the largest gas producer in California, and the largest oil producer in Texas.**	

2000	October; the LeTourneau L-2350, a rubber-tired (70/70-57 each bare tire weighing 7.7 tons) front-end loader is first shown to the public. The L-2350 sports a 53 cubic yard rock bucket and the bare machine weighs in at 270 tons. The spirit of R. G. still reigns, as these are the largest tires ever made for any application.	(see 2001)
2000	There are now only 945 million acres of farmland in the USA.	(see 2006)
2000	MANSFIELD PLUMBING PRODUCTS is acquired by the STAMFORD CAPITAL GROUP.	
2000	Now marketing products of over 300,000 farmers and ranchers, LAND O' LAKES is the top marketer of butter, butter blends and deli cheeses in the US.	
2000	October; CATERPILLAR purchases 15% of ASV GROUP with plans to jointly manufacture "multi-terrain" loaders.	
2000	November; J. D. ABRAMS, INC. now becomes J. D. ABRAMS, LP.	
2000	The BUCYRUS 2570WS (lot 2) is commissioned. It is the world's largest operating dragline since the retirement of "Big Muskie."	(see 2004)
2000	USA; YANCEY BROS. INC. of the state of Georgia is recognized as the nation's oldest Caterpillar dealer.	
2000	It is estimated that there are now not more than 100 forging plants in England.	(see 1900)
2000	There are now approximately only 4,500 operating sawmills in the USA.	(see 1840)
2000	SWEDISH MATCH buys over sixty percent of GENERAL CIGAR HOLDINGS.	
2000	DRESSER MEASUREMENT is formed as the newly combined division joins with the Dresser Instrument Division.	
2000	LOCKHEED MARRIETA introduces the C-130 J, a stretched version of the 46-year-old workhorse, uh, er, airplane.	
2000	HEEREMA acquires INTEC Engineering Company.	
2000	TUBOSCOPE CORPORATION merges with VARCO INTERNATIONAL.	
2000	Canada; up to now, the Petrolia, Ontario, region has produced an estimated ten billion barrels of crude oil.	
2000	… and as the rust and corruption has really eaten away at Detroit, finally got it below a million… now 951,270. Somewhat less than half of its 1950 population, and the UAW deserves most of the credit. Once the 4th largest city in the US, Detroit is now the 11th.	
2000	TITAN ELECTRIC & CONTROLS, PROCALL MANAGEMENT, and KLINGER'S OILFIELD SERVICES are among the acquisitions of FLINT ENERGY SERVICES this year.	(see 2001)
2000	Texas; Houston-based WEATHERFORD INTERNATIONAL announces it has acquired OIL COUNTRY MANUFACTURING of Ventura, CA, a leading producer of well servicing and workover equipment.	
	Well folks, so much for the twentieth century—as Porky Pig says, "Tha-tha-tha… that's all folks!!!"	
2001	After 80 years, the SPRINGFIELD TABLET COMPANY plant is closed, and the Big Chief tablet is no longer made.	
2001	After sixty-seven years in Tulsa, PARKER DRILLING moves its corporate offices to Houston.	
2001	February 18; running third, Dale Earnhardt is killed in a crash in the final turn of today's Daytona 500.	

2001	CHAMPION (of Canada) is now VOLVO MOTOR GRADERS, after 126 years. Another good name in earthmoving bites the dust.	
2001	NATIONAL-OILWELL buys IRI, which includes all of GARDNER-DENVER, except for pumps; buys BOWEN, buys TECH-POWER CONTROLS. NAT-OIL then acquires RYE SUPPLY COMPANY of West Texas and New Mexico.	
2001	The Oklahoma City National Memorial and Museum opens in memory of the 168 victims of the 1995 bombing.	
2001	This spring, DARR EQUIPMENT is bought out, partially by WEST TEXAS EQUIPMENT and partially by HOLT MACHINERY. This now gives WEST TEXAS EQUIPMENT the largest area-wise CATERPILLAR dealership in the lower forty-eight states.	
2001	May; PATTERSON DRILLING merges with UTI ENERGY, making PATTERSON-UTI.	
2001	June; TIME-LIFE ceases weekly publication of *Life Magazine* after 65 years.	
2001	MARINE DRILLING and PRIDE INTERNATIONAL merge in June, continuing as PRIDE INTERNATIONAL around the world.	
2001	July; GRAND VEHICLE WORKS HOLDINGS, LLC (GVW) buys the Xpeditor truck line from VOLVO TRUCKS NORTH AMERICA, this includes the AUTOCAR name. GVW names its new subsidiary AUTOCAR, LLC., based in Union City, IN.	
2001	GLOBAL MARINE, started as UNION OIL's first offshore drilling operation, and now merges with SANTA FE, making GLOBAL-SANTA FE the second largest drilling company on earth. They have now come full circle.	(see 1946)
2001	METSO CORP. of Finland acquires SVEDALA, including UNIVERSAL CRUSHERS.	
2001	LETOURNEAU buys ELLIS WILLIAMS CORP., they will be building and marketing LEWCO (LETOURNEAU ELLIS WILLIAMS CO.), formerly EWCO triplex and quintuplex mud pumps.	
2001	PHILLIP MORRIS, INC. changes its name to ALTRIA GROUP; maybe that won't smell so much like tobacco.	
2001	MAERSK DRILLING is selling its land rigs, supposedly getting out of the land drilling business. (It didn't happen, though.)	
2001	CHEVRON buys TEXACO, forming CHEVRON TEXACO.	
2001	ENI GROUP (AGIP) acquires LASMO.	
2001	FMC CORP. spins-off all its non-chemical related companies into FMC TECHNOLOGIES (machinery), including FMC LINK-BELT.	
2001	B. F. GOODRICH becomes GOODRICH CORPORATION.	
2001	GOODMAN sells AMANA to MAYTAG.	
2001	This year AMERADA-HESS buys TRITON ENERGY LTD.	
2001	September; UNIVIEW TECHNOLOGIES sells its Curtis Mathes brand name to CM ROYALTIES of Minneapolis, MN.	
2001	Texas, Sept 10; Herman Mayhew, Jr., age 86 dies in Corpus Christi, survived by a son, Herman Mayhew, III, of Dallas.	
2001	USA; September 11; the Al Qaida-instigated terrorist attacks kill thousands today. This event forever changes the way Americans look at their nation's security.	
2001	October; ABBOT GROUP acquires DEUTAG DRILLING; then merges it with KCA DRILLING to form KCA DEUTAG, a wholly-owned subsidiary of ABBOT GRP. PLC.	
2001	Texas; CAMERON DIVISION acquires RETSCO INTERNATIONAL LP of Tomball, makers of motion compensator equipment.	

2001	A. O. SMITH acquires STATE INDUSTRIES nearly doubling the size of its water heater business.	
2001	BRIGGS & STRATTON buys GENERAC portable generator products.	
2001	PHILLIPS PETROLEUM acquires TOSCO, a very large refiner.	
2001	In October, CMI merges with TEREX.	
2001	SPX CORPORATION of Charlotte, NC, acquires BOMAG.	
2001	ANADARKO finishes the billion-dollar acquisition of BERKLEY PETROLEUM of Canada, then acquires GULFSTREAM RESOURCES, mainly operating in the Middle East, then near the year's end, ANADARKO forms a joint venture with EL PASO ENERGY to develop deepwater pay zones in the Gulf of Mexico.	
2001	Bill Ford, Jr., becomes CEO, the 4th generation of the founding Ford family to have an active management role in FORD.	
2001	Texas; LETOURNEAU begins marketing the L-2350 rubber-tired loader for mining operations, This is definitely the largest machine of its kind on earth, running on the largest tires on earth. *"Yessir Bubba, R. G. 's Longview boys do it again!!!"*	
2001	GOODRICH, the owner of GARLOCK BEARINGS, acquires GIB, and forms GLACIER GARLOCK BEARINGS.	
2001	NABORS INDUSTRIES acquires COMMAND DRILLING CORP.	
2001	The London Stock Exchange goes public this year.	
2001	AKER and KVAERNER OILFIELD PRODUCTS merge in late November.	
2001	SOONER, INC. is acquired by OIL STATES INTERNATIONAL, INC.	
2001	BARRICK GOLD CORP. of Toronto buys the 125 year old HOMESTAKE CORP.	
2001	December; BEAIRD INDUSTRIES of Shreveport, LA, is under private ownership for the first time since 1957 as it is acquired by some private investors.	
2001	FEDERAL SUMMIT merges with M-I LLC and becomes M-I HDD Mining & Waterwell.	
2001	ACCESS OIL TOOLS moves to new facilities in Broussard, LA.	
2001	COASTAL CORP. (remember Oscar Wyatt's Hardly Able Oil Co.) is sold to EL PASO CORPORATION for $22 Billion, thus giving El Paso Corporation the largest network of pipelines in North America.	(see 1951)
2001	MARTIN-MARIETTA MATERIALS acquires MATERIAL PRODUCERS, INC., of Oklahoma. Then in two more separate acquisitions, MARTIN-MARIETTA buys BRAUNTEX MATERIALS' limestone facility at the chemical lime quarry near New Braunfels, TX. They also acquire the POWELL GRAVEL & TOPSOIL assets in Cincinnati, OH.	
2001	The DRESSER EQUIPMENT GROUP separates from HALLIBURTON, through a management buyout; to form DRESSER, INC.	
2001	MANITOWOC (the world's leading manufacturer of high-capacity lattice-boom crawler cranes) acquires POTAIN S. A. of France.	
2001	Texas companies CHAPPARAL EQUIPMENT & SERVICES and SAFETY HAWK SERVICES are acquired by FLINT, which also acquires IPEC LTD. and goes public as FLINT ENERGY SERVICES, with headquarters in Calgary.	(see 2002)
2001	San Antonio, TX; after more than a century, PEARL ceases brewing its beer.	
2001	England; after fifty-five years in South Leeds at their Rothwell facility, PELICAN, of necessity, relocates to a newly-built, for their purpose, facility at Wakefield, Europort. Next year, the Knottingley dealership joins the FODEN business at this facility.	(see 2003)

2002	NATIONAL-OILWELL purchases HALCO. Additionally, NATIONAL-OILWELL also acquires HYDRALIFT ASA.
	"Yeah Bubba, I'm surprised that old Henry Lee sold out."
2002	March; ADVANCED AERODYNAMICS & STRUCTURES (AASI) of Long Beach, CA, buys MOONEY AIRCRAFT out of bankruptcy.
2002	GOODRICH acquires TRW Aeronautical Systems, then spins off its industrial businesses creating ENPRO INDUSTRIES, INC. One of its offspring is GLACIER GARLOCK BEARINGS. Then in June, ENPRO purchases the QUINCY MANUFACTURING COMPANY.
2002	Two old originally Oklahoma companies, PHILLIPS PETROLEUM and CONOCO, are working on a merger.
2002	SHELL US buys PENNZOIL-QUAKER STATE.
2002	June; ENSCO DRILLING buys CHILES OFFSHORE.
2002	Kentucky; LINK-BELT CONSTRUCTION EQUIPMENT CO. of Lexington is now a wholly-owned subsidiary of SUMITOMO HEAVY INDUSTRIES.
2002	July 1; NORTHRUP GRUMMAN purchases TRW CORP., including VINNELL for almost $8 billion… anyone remember the parts maker, THOMPSON, RAMO, WOOLRIDGE?
2002	July; SIEMENS sells DEMAG CRANES to the investors, KOLBERG, KRAVIS, ROBERTS.
2002	PETROBRAS acquires PEREZ-COMPANC.
2002	This spring DRESSER-RAND becomes wholly-owned by INGERSOLL-RAND of Woodcliff Lake, NJ.
2002	DAIMLERCHRYSLER, the world's first and largest volume truck builder, buys a chunk of MITSUBISHI's line of FUSO trucks. (see 2004)
2002	Texas, October; Boyd Spencer, co-founder with his father C. O. Spencer, of SPENCER HEADS, dies in Gladewater, Boyd's brothers, Fred and Lee Spencer were the founders of SPENCER-HARRIS, in Gladewater.

2002	A century later, GOODWILL INDUSTRIES is now located in thirty-four countries. In North America there are 181 independent member organizations, with more than 1,700 retail stores. Ninety-eight percent of all goods donated to GOODWILL are sold in some manner, and eighty-four percent of the revenue goes directly to programs to help people to have better lives.
2002	FLUOR spins off A. T. MASSEY COAL mining operations to be separate from its engineering and construction business.
2002	BRIGGS & STRATTON receive their 770th patent from the US patent office.
2002	GORMAN-RUPP acquires AMERICAN MACHINE & TOOL, a centrifugal pump manufacturer.
2002	Key management personnel of UNIVERSAL form UNIVERSAL ENGINEERING CORP. to again provide high quality US engineered and US built rock crushers.
2002	AGCO buys SUNFLOWER MFG. CO., a maker of farm equipment; then AGCO buys the ag-equipment business of CATERPILLAR, including the popular Challenger tractor line.
2002	WACKER becomes WACKER CONSTRUCTION EQUIPMENT A. G.
2002	ANADARKO acquires HOWELL CORP., including the Wyoming Salt Creek Field.
2002	This year BUICK MOTOR DIVISION's 20,000 employees produce 350,000 vehicles on the 300 acre complex near Detroit.
2002	*After thirty-three years, the TRANSOCEAN Mercury jack-up rig continues to drill in the Gulf of Suez.*
2002	BJ SERVICES acquires OSCA, INC.
2002	NABORS INDUSTRIES acquires ENERSCO ENERGY SERVICE COMPANY, and also RYAN ENERGY TECHNOLOGIES.

2002	R. J. REYNOLDS TOBACCO HOLDINGS INC. acquires SANTA FE NATURAL TOBACCO COMPANY.		
2002	WWW purchases PAULSEN WIRE ROPE out of bankruptcy, and restarts operations as a new company, SUNBURY WIREOPE WORKS, INC.		

2002	July; the SOUTH AFRICAN BREWING CO. buys MILLER BREWING CO. making SABMILLER, with facilities in forty countries, and hundreds of brands selling 130 million barrels of beer each year. *"Bubba...'atsa lotta beer, a lotta beer."*	
2002	The EASTMAN CHEMICAL plant in Longview, TX, now has about 1,800 employees.	
2002	Struggling, restructuring GENERAL MOTORS is selling down its stake in ISUZU, but the companies will continue to work together on diesel engines and mid-size trucks.	
2002	New Mexico; this October, after 42½ years, John L. "Jack" Rust retires and sells RUST TRACTOR CO. to WAGNER, the CATERPILLAR dealer in Colorado. This gives WAGNER all of Colorado and New Mexico, as well as El Paso and three other far west Texas counties.	
2002	Robert Johnson sells BLACK ENTERTAINMENT TELEVISION to VIACOM… for $3 billion.	
2002	BROWNING-FERRIS INDUSTRIES is now serving more than seven million households with trash collection.	

2002	Scotland; near the town of Falkirk, Queen Elizabeth opens the Falkirk Wheel Boat Lift, connecting the Union Canal with the Forth and Clyde Canal.		
2002	NESTLÉ acquires RALSTON PURINA, makers of pet and livestock feeds, DREYERS ice cream, and the $2.6 billion acquisition of CHEF AMERICA INC.		
2002	LACKS now have thirty-eight home furnishings stores.		
2002	CHARLES MACHINE WORKS in Perry, OK, now has more than 1,300 employees, under 30 acres of roof, building Ditch Witch equipment.		
2002	New headquarters for ESAB are established in London, England.		
2002	Despite the much-ballyhooed debut in 1999, Plymouth's retro sporty Prowler has sold only 8,100 cars, and won't be around next year.		
2002	Selling only 3,300 units in two seasons, the $50,000 plus LINCOLN Blackwood "super-fancy" pickup truck, is doomed.		
2002	A new agreement between CASE-NEW HOLLAND (CNH) and Japan's KOBELCO introduces the Fiat-Kobelco range of excavators replacing the long heritage influenced by POCLAIN designs.		
2002	FLINT ENERGY SERVICES acquires the CANTU Lease in Texas.	(see 2004)	
2003	January; VARCO purchases the WOOD GROUP.		
2003	January; two specialty lubricant makers, ANDEROL INC. and ROYAL LUBRICANTS, merge under the ANDEROL name.		
2003	January; taxidermist Douglas Herrick, father of the "jackalope," dies this month.		
2003	February; TIMKEN acquires the old US needle and bearing manufacturer, TORRINGTON, from INGERSOLL-RAND.		
2003	ENSCO sells their 28 service vessels in the Gulf of Mexico to TIDEWATER MARINE.		
2003	Arizona; the PHELPS-DODGE MORENCI MINE is still producing and is the largest copper mine in North America.		

2003	On June 16th, Ford Motor Co. celebrates its 100th birthday.	
2003	June 30th; after almost 50 years in operation, the last plant building the Volkswagen "beetle" closes up in Puebla, Mexico.	
2003	Tom Brown Inc. (TMBR) acquires Matador Petroleum Corp.	
2003	Several hundred of the old, tough and dependable Douglas DC-3 planes are still in everyday use all around the globe.	
2003	The Marmon Group now consists of over 100 companies, a far cry from the old Marmon Car Co. of 1900.	
2003	Morrison-Knudsen merges with Dennis Washington's Washington Group.	
2003	June, the Eurofighter, an air-to-air fighter plane is introduced, billions of euros and 17 years after its initial planning. Each unit costs an estimated $140 million. It is also probably the greatest white elephant ever built. This plane is the single most expensive industrial project ever undertaken in Europe.	

2003	National Oilwell buys Monoflo, Inc. and the Mono Group. Also acquired is Grey Mekaniske Verksted AS of Norway.	
2003	Ford introduces the redesigned F-150 pickup.	
2003	JBLCO becomes a wholly-owned subsidiary of Compro Systems.	
2003	Patterson-UTI's fleet is increased to 358 drilling rigs by their acquisition of TMBR/Sharp Drilling.	

2003	June 19; Nextel agrees to a decade-long $700 million sponsorship of Nascar's Cup Series.	
2003	August; Mooney Aircraft goes into Chapter 11 bankruptcy.	
2003	It appears that by year end, Paxman engines will be no more, all will carry the Man B&W brand; after 138 years of engine building… another dead one.	
2003	The Fokker F-27 "Friendship" continues to be the world's largest selling turboprop airplane.	
2003	August; having forever sold their baked goods only in Texas, the old Texas bakery Mrs Baird's Bread begins wholesale distribution of its products in El Paso and portions of Eastern New Mexico.	
2003	Six decades later, Thomas Fawick's "Golf Pride" is still the best selling golf grip in the world.	
2003	Dresser Wayne acquires certain North American assets of Tokheim Corporation.	
2003	Ingram Compaction LLC (formerly Ingram Rollers) is now headed by Ko Kryger, and based in Racine, WI.	
2003	Introduced back in '81, the little Ford Escort has sold 5.4 million units up to this time.	
2003	Caterpillar and Blount International have joint-ventured to produce and market products globally, under the Cat and Timberking brands. Caterpillar has gross revenues of $22.75 billion this year.	(see 2007)
2003	England; Richard Crump's Pelican buys all property and assets of Linpac DAF at Sherburn-in-Elmet; then moves this business to their Casteford location, making this the largest single site truck business in Yorkshire.	(see 2005)
2004	January; now commanding 11% of the world market, Toyota unseats Ford as number two automaker of the world. Only GM and Ford of the top 4 are US automakers, since for all practical purposes, Chrysler is now German-owned.	
2004	March; Precision Drilling Co. of Canada acquires all the worldwide land rig operations of Global-Santa Fe (GSF).	
2004	March; convenience store operator Seven-Eleven sells its Dallas headquarters for $124 million.	

2004	March 3; at age 98, holding 18 patents for machinery design, J. E. "Gene" Hancock dies in Lubbock, TX. Mr. Hancock and his wife were among the top supporters of Lubbock Christian University. He served on the LCU board for 37 years, and was the largest single donor ever in the school's history.	
2004	March; GREY WOLF buys NEW PATRIOT DRILLING, a twelve rig company of Casper, WY.	
2004	April; ABER DIAMONDS acquires controlling interest in HARRY WINSTON, the very upscale jewelry retailer.	
2004	April 7; the very last Oldsmobile is produced as the final Alero rolls off the assembly line in Lansing, MI. Truly, a sad day.	
2004	Since H&P started their FlexRig program in 1998, they build their 50th FlexRig this spring, each rig now costs $10.75 million.	
2004	May 6; after over 65 years on radio and television, Harry Holt, the Dean of West Texas farm and ranch news reporting, dies in Abilene this April. At 90 years old, Holt lived on his ranch south of Cisco in Eastland county.	(see 2007)
2004	May; in California, HAWTHORNE MACHINERY purchases PACIFIC MACHINERY, INC.	
2004	June 21; the first privately-funded non-governmental space flight (just by 400 ft.), is successful.	
2004	Two old family owned brewers, ADOLPH COORS of Colorado, USA, and MOLSON of Australia, merge to help stave off outside takeover attempts.	
2004	USA; every 20 minutes a new BLUE BIRD bus rolls out the factory door in Georgia.	
2004	**The highest bridge on the planet, the Viaduc de Millau, is now carrying traffic across the River Tarn in Southern France. One point in the 1.5 mile span is 1,125 feet high.**	
2004	A local entrepreneur buys WWW and the old Paulsen plant and forms a new company, WIREROPE WORKS, INC.	
2004	PRESSTEK plans to buy the bankrupt A. B. DICK COMPANY.	
2004	NATIONAL-OILWELL and VARCO merge, the result is NATIONAL OILWELL VARCO. *Oh, what a mess!!!*	(see 2013)
2004	RJR TOBACCO CO. merges with the US operations of BROWN & WILLIAMSON TOBACCO forming REYNOLDS AMERICA, INC., as the parent company.	
2004	November; K-MART CORPORATION buys SEARS ROEBUCK & COMPANY; ain't that a kicker!	
2004	November 23; Mr. Ansel Keys (the K in "K-Ration") dies at age 100.	
2004	CANRIG buys the remaining assets and manufacturing rights of MID-CONTINENT SUPPLY CO.	
2004	KLM Royal Dutch Airlines and AIR FRANCE merge, forming Europe's largest airline group.	
2004	ECKERD DRUGS and its 1,260 stores are acquired by CVS.	(see 2008)
2004	Texas; GROCER'S SUPPLY COMPANY acquires the FIESTA MART grocery stores.	
2004	BUCYRUS builds their 8750, the first dragline to be totally powered with a Siemens AC static drive system, and the first direct (gearless) drive system for hoist and drag motions. This machine is sold to a customer in China.	(see 2007)
2004	AIRBUS, the consortium of Europe, passes BOEING as the world's leading producer of passenger planes… of course, being backed by two European federal governments doesn't hurt AIRBUS financially.	
2004	An original, single copy of Batman's debut comic book, now 65 years old, is valued at more than half a million dollars.	
2004	DRESSER WAYNE buys certain distribution businesses of NUOVO PIGNONE.	
2004	INGERSOLL-RAND sells its rock-drill manufacturing operations to Atlas Copco.	

2004	In the Piney Woods of East Texas, a TEMPLE-INLAND sawmill still operates on the same site of Mr. T. L. L. Temple's original sawmill of 1894. This Angelina County location has been the site of a continuous operating sawmill site for Temple.	
2004	Effectively doubling its size, REGAL-BELIOT has acquired two companies from General Electric.	
2004	Mercury Division of FORD has sold only 11,000 Mercury Marauders in their two years of life, so I don't expect to see the Marauder around next year.	(see 2011)
2004	FLINT ENERGY SERVICES acquires WESTERN SLOPE OILFIELD SERVICES in Colorado.	(see 2005)
2004	Nevada; during the boom in building and housing in Las Vegas, a new house is completed every twenty minutes here or out in the suburbs.	
2004	December 31; having bought a thirty rig drilling operation in Colorado, PATTERSON-UTI now has 361 land drilling rigs, making them the second largest land rig owner after NABORS INDUSTRIES.	
2005	January; MCDONALDS now serves 47 million customers daily in its so-called "restaurants" located in 119 nations around the world.	
2005	January; PATTERSON UTI completes its acquisition of the US land drilling assets of KEY ENERGY SERVICES.	

2005	Former *Tonight Show* host Johnny Carson passes away. As host of *The Tonight Show,* Carson delivered 4,531 opening monologues.
2005	Japan; the 16.4 mile long Hakkōda Tunnel is completed as part of a new bullet-train line.
2005	April; CHEVRON/TEXACO CORP. will acquire UNOCAL (UNION OIL OF CALIFORNIA) in a $18 billion deal. CHEVRON/TEXACO then changes its corporate name to the CHEVRON CORPORATION. Just easing the old TEXAS COMPANY name into the grave.
2005	Now, there are 537 CRACKER BARREL OLD COUNTRY STORES in forty-one states.
2005	Sadly, there are now only a few working iron foundries in central Scotland.
2005	McGRAW HILL acquires J. D. POWER & ASSOCIATES.

2005	Texas; after several years of battling illness, Wendy Kent Churchill passes away on May 27. Her children (great-grand-children of Frank Kent), Will and Corrie Churchill, are dealers, and oversee the operation of FRANK KENT MOTOR CO.	
2005	PROCTOR & GAMBLE and GILLETTE merge into one huge company.	
2005	After thirty-six years of *Monday Night Football* on ABC, the NFL moves it to ESPN.	
2005	FEDERATED DEPARTMENT STORES buys MAY DEPARTMENT STORES.	
2005	July 1; after fifty years, the very last FORD THUNDERBIRD rolls off the assembly line of a FORD plant in Wixom, MI.	
2005	August 29; portions of the Gulf Coast are devastated by Hurricane Katrina.	
2005	September 22; Hurricane Rita hits and destroys portions of the coast to the west of Katrina's devastation, in the Cameron, Port Arthur, and Beaumont, TX, areas. Rita's devastation ranges north, on through the Big Thicket up to Lufkin and Nacogdoches, TX. Old Jim Cowan was in Odessa during Katrina, but spent 23½ hours in the evacuation driving from Houston to Kilgore, TX, pre-Rita.	
2005	LAYNE buys Indiana contractor REYNOLDS, INC., making LAYNE one of the largest US supplier of water, and wastewater services.	

2005	Today, petroleum tankers comprise about 40% of all the merchant shipping fleet, world-wide. This year alone, 2.42 billion metric tons (2,200 lb. per metric ton) of petroleum is shipped by tanker.	
2005	**The recently introduced Lexion 590 R from CATERPILLAR is the world's largest grain combine.**	
2005	SARA LEE sells the HILLS BROS. COFFEE brand to MASSIMO ZANETTI BEVERAGE USA.	
2005	Wow! 6.4 million of the little CHEVROLET Cavalier cars have been sold since being introduced in 1982. However, only 6 million BUICK Le Sabres have been sold since their introduction way back in 1959.	
2005	USA; seatbelt usage saves about 16,700 lives this year, excluding passengers under the age of five. This is more than four times the number saved by front seat air bags.	
2005	The third busiest airport in the world is now DFW, between Dallas and Ft. Worth, TX.	(see 2007)
2005	MURPHY-HOFFMAN CO. is now a network of some thirty KENWORTH dealers in ten states across the central USA.	
2005	The previously publicly-traded YORK firm is purchased by JOHNSON CONTROLS.	
2005	FLINT acquires forty-nine percent of MACKENZIE VALLEY CONSTRUCTION. FLINT has revenues above one billion dollars this year.	(see 2006)
2005	In only 24 hours, 793 acres (320 hectares) is plowed with a 500 horsepower CASE-IH-STEIGER STX Quadtrac, pulling a disc plow, setting a new world record.	(see 2007)
2005	England; this is the 150th anniversary of FODEN, and to celebrate, PACCAR decides to cease production of FODEN vehicles. With this decision, PELICAN is able to move into the sale and distribution of HINO trucks, which presently have mostly replaced their FODEN business.	(see 2006)
2005	December 7; NASCAR signs A $4.5 billion television broadcast deal. *"Yeah Bubba, 'ats Billyun, wit a B."*	
2005	West Allis, WI; there will be no more UNIT cranes or shovels, but UNIT DROP FORGE continues making closed-die steel forgings for use in components in the off-highway equipment market, selling as Unit Forgings. This continues from the original plant on 62nd Street here in town.	
2005	The US Congress passes the "Energy Policy Act," promoting the use of coal through clean coal technologies.	
2006	January 1; R. C. CEMENT CO. INC. and LONE STAR INDUSTRIES merge into a new firm; BUZZI UNICEM USA INC.	
2006	January; another family-run business "bites the dust," as the 367 store BURLINGTON COAT FACTORY WAREHOUSE CORP. founder and CEO Monroe Milstein and other family members leave after selling to BAIN CAPITAL PARTNERS for $2.1 billion.	
2006	January; TEREX acquires HALCO HOLDINGS; including the subsidiaries HALCO DRILLING INT'L, HALCO AMERICA, HALCO DRILLING EQUIPMENT OF AUSTRALIA, and HALCO DRILLING OF IRELAND.	
2006	April; GM will sell its remaining 8% stake in ISUZU MOTORS of Japan, about $300,000,000 worth.	
2006	Texas; San Antonio is the new home for TOYOTA's new Tundra and Tacoma pickup manufacturing facility.	
2006	April; WHIRLPOOL completes its acquisition of MAYTAG for $2.7 billion; merging of the two firms begins immediately.	

2006	**WESTERN UNION ceases sending word telegrams; they will however, continue wiring money.**	
2006	Janjaap Ruijssenaars, a Dutch architect, invents a floating bed that "hovers" on magnets. $1,500,000 will buy it.	
2006	June; Oklahoma's KERR-McGEE is bought by ANANDARKO of Houston.	
2006	July 4; at Utah's Salt Flats, Bob Cleveland sets a new land speed record of 81 mph… on a riding lawn mower. However, Bob won't get in the *Guinness* book because his mower was modified and had no mower blade.	
2006	July; for the first time, TOYOTA outsells FORD, 241,826 units to 239, 989 units. *"Naw Bubba, I doubt that the $3 a gallon gasoline had any effect on that."*	
2006	Telephone companies Verizon and MCI merge; as do AT&T and SBC or Bell South.	
2006	The fifth generation of the Wright family are now at REED, manufacturing pipe wrenches and other pipe tools.	
2006	The planet Pluto is downgraded to "dwarf planet" status as leading astronomers meet in Prague.	
2006	August 26; President Idriss Déby of Chad orders CHEVRON and PETRONAS to leave his country, saying neither company has paid their taxes.	
2006	New York City; each year now 30,000,000 flags of all kinds are produced by ANNIN & COMPANY.	
2006	FEDEX is now a $32 billion company with more than 260,000 employees utilizing 70,000 vehicles and 670 airplanes to handle six million shipments each business day for customers in over 220 countries around the world.	
2006	Petroleum giant EXXON MOBIL makes a $ 39.5 billion profit this year!!! This is the largest profit ever made by any US business… I doubt that $3/gallon gasoline had any effect on this, either.	
2006	November; after nearly fifty years, the old STARDUST hotel and casino in Las Vegas closes its doors forever.	(see 2007)
2006	There are now only 932 million acres of farmland in the USA.	

BOYS & GIRLS CLUB

2006	This year, FORD MOTOR CO. loses $12.7 billion, this amounts to $4,700 lost for each new vehicle sold. *"Ya know Bubba, I really doubt that old Henry would understand that."*
2006	The Federated Boys Clubs of America, now the Boys and Girls Clubs, with 3,700 locations, are working with 4.5 million young people annually.
2006	Headquartered in Dusseldorf, Germany, having operations in over seventy nations with about 188,000 employees, THYSSEN-KRUPP has sales this year of $61 billion.
2006	Canada; R. P. M. TECH INC. liquidates EQUIPMENTS BLANCHET, LTD.

2006	In the twenty years since its inception, FORD has sold 7.4 million of its Taurus autos… and that's GOOD.	
2006	The ALAMO GROUP of Seguin, TX, buys GRADALL from JLG INDUSTRIES. However, the Gradall machines continue to be built in the original facility in New Philadelphia, OH, where more than 15,000 Gradalls have been built and shipped to customers all over the world, as of 2008.	
2006	FLINT acquires DENMAR ENERGY SERVICES in July, and TRANSCO ENERGY SVCS in December.	(see 2007)
2006	England; after SEDDON ATKINSON decides to cease production, PELICAN's Knottingley dealership moves to sell and distribute BMC Municipal Trucks. Richard Crump continues to manage PELICAN.	
2007	February; with 180 patents to his name, ninety-three-year-old Robert Adler, co-inventor of the television remote control, dies in Boise, ID.	(see 1956)

2007	March 19; two of the huge new AIRBUS A380 passenger planes land simultaneously in New York and Los Angeles; the first A380 landings in the USA.	
2007	According to the CIA, (I guess they keep track of this stuff, too), the USA now has 14,858 airports.	
2007	The Caterpillar 797B, at 400 ton capacity, is, today, the world's largest haul truck, costing about $5 million each.	
2007	The closed STARDUST is imploded by explosives. After the cleanup, BOYD GAMING CORP. will erect the $4 billion ECHELON PALACE RESORT, a 5,000 room hotel with 2 theatres, a shopping mall, and a million square feet of meeting space.	
2007	DUNKIN DONUTS, the world's largest coffee user, sells about a billion cups each year, or about 30 cups each second.	
2007	Staffed with more than 120 meteorologists, the Weather Channel now broadcasts into over than 93 million homes.	
2007	The largest crude oil refiner in North America, VALERO now operates sixteen refineries, including six in Texas, as well as one in Aruba.	
2007	RITE AID CORP. acquires about 1,850 Eckerd's and BROOKS stores, also six distribution centers, (most on the East Coast), from the Canadian firm, Jean Coutu Group, Inc.	
2007	The RCA-Victor puppy, Nipper will soon disappear from the labels on recordings; legal considerations prevent global use of the trademark. *"Ya know, Slim, that pup had a really good run."*	
2007	INGRAM COMPACTION is the oldest continuously operating asphalt compaction equipment manufacturer in the USA.	
2007	The "average" new US built automobile now contains three hundred and nineteen pounds of aluminum.	(see 1960)
2007	"Mrs. Stewart's Bluing" continues to be made today essentially the same way as in the 1880s. It continues to be a family-run outfit, and they continue to say, "If it ain't broke, don't fix it!"	
2007	UK; since 1931, RUSTON BUCYRUS has built more than 40,000 crawler cranes and excavators.	
2007	September; MARINE & MAINLAND CRANE SERVICES INC. is 100% acquired by ENERGY CRANES LLC.	
2007	A century after the accidental discovery of crude oil in Argentina, the need for continuing drilling and production is now considered more important than ever.	
2007	At age 56, Jean Daum, creator of *Coffee News,* dies of cancer. Jean's daughters will carry on the business.	
2007	Georgia, USA; eighty-nine MILLION passengers travelled through here last year, making Atlanta's Hartsfield Airport the busiest airport on the planet.	
2007	This year in the USA more than 5,200 megawatts of windpower equipment is installed… that is more than double the 2006 installations… and quadruples the capacity of the installations of 2001.	(see 2008)
2007	France, April 3; a new speed record of 356.4 mph (574.8 kph) for high-speed trains is set by SNCF, surpassing the existing record set by SCNF in 1990.	
2007	Today's "average" CEO in the USA is making about 275 times as much as his "average" worker. *"Yeah Bubba, this CEO is making in one day about what his employee makes all year."*	(see 2009)
2007	INGERSOLL-RAND says adios to the compressor industry, as they sell their entire line to DOOSAN INFRACORE. However, the compressors will continue to be branded I-R… at least for a while, anyhow.	
2007	November; CATERPILLAR acquires the assets of the forestry division of BLOUNT INTERNATIONAL INC. of Portland, OR, including facilities in the USA and Sweden.	(see 2003)

2007	November, Aransas Pass, TX; Having served excellent food with great service for 60 years, the Duck Inn restaurant closes its doors forever.	
2007	November 16; once professional baseball's youngest pitcher ever, "The Voice of the Reds," Joe Noxell dies at age 79.	
2007	November 30; daredevil stunt motorcyclist Evil Knievel dies at age 69.	
2007	Flint Transfield Services contracts with Suncor for plant maintenance at Fort McMurray and Sarnia Refinery. In North America, Flint now has 9,000 plus employees scattered from Mission, TX, to Norman Wells in the Northwest Territories of Canada.	(see 2008)
2007	An AGCO Challenger Model MT 875B tractor (430kw/576. 6 hp), pulling a group of Gregoire Besson XXL discs 46 feet (14 m) wide, discs 1,591 acres (644 hectares) while going 286 miles in 24 hours (11.91 mph) and setting a new world cultivation (discing) record. That's 66 acres each hour, using 1.16 gallons (4.42 l) of diesel per hectare. *"Yeah Slim, at's sixty–six acres an hour…at's about two months work fer you and old Dobbin!!"*	(see 2005)
2007	At 104 years old, the fourth Rolls Royce automobile ever built (1904) sells this year for US $7,300,000.	
2007	Texas; in Houston, Stewart & Stevenson acquires essentially all assets of Crown Energy Technologies Inc. Based in Calgary, Alberta, Canada, and with many US operations, Crown has 1,100 employees, and sales of $240 million the past twelve months.	
2007	Kansas; Caterpillar dealer, Foley Equipment Co. builds a new 125,000 square foot engine rebuild facility in Park City.	(see 2009)
2007	Chevron Corporation combines the Pittsburg & Midway Coal Mining Co. and Molycorp., both Chevron-owned subsidiaries, to form Chevron Mining Inc., with Mark A. Smith as president.	

2007	Texas; in Corpus Christi, Anderson Machinery Co. is still going strong after 50 years. They are now dealers for Grove cranes, Bomag rollers, and several other top brands of heavy equipment.	
2007	December (week 17); the NFL playoff game between the New England Patriots and the New York Jets, as the Pats are 15-0 and trying for a 16-0 season.	
2007	December 31; with more than 16,000 hours "on-camera," Regis Philbin has more "on-air" time than anyone else ever in the history of television. *"Yessir Bubba, thet's almost two years solid on telly vision."*	
2008	January 1; the Nascar Premier Series is renamed… the Sprint Cup.	
2008	January 2; in the commodities trading market, the price of crude oil hits $100 a barrel (42 US gallons) for the first time ever.	

2008	Texas, January 14; the directors of Lufkin Industries decides to "suspend its participation in the commercial trailer market." The trailer facilities will be closed as current contracts are honored, and existing parts inventories are run-out. *NOTE: Before long it will be rumored that Lufkin Industries soon tries to get some of Obama's "economic stimulus" money, but were unable to do so, because the company was too small.*	(see 2014)
2008	February 3; the Patriots and the Jets meet in Phoenix, Arizona, for Super Bowl XLII.	
2008	In the past fifteen years, the number of heavy trucks on US highways has increased by thirty percent.	
2008	March; the eighty-five-year-old investment bank, Bear Stearns, collapses; tolling the beginning of a finance industry induced recession… soon to be depression.	

2008	The US now has approximately six thousand truck stops.	
2008	Amherst, MA; the ninth generation of the Cowls family continues to operating the Cowls Lumber Yard.	
2008	The drivers of America are spending $700 billion, annually, on imported oil to traverse the three million miles of paved roads in the USA.	
2008	Texas; the OAKWOOD STATE BANK of Oakwood Texas, established January 1, 1900, in Leon County, some twenty miles southwest of Palestine, is the smallest operating bank in America. The president, eighty-four-year-old R. R. Wylie, says they have only 600 checking accounts, no savings accounts, no CDs, and no computers. Each of the 600 monthly statements are hand-typed on an old Waltham banking machine by seventy-five-years-young Lela Coates.	
2008	Privately held MARS, INC., collaborating with BERKSHIRE HATHAWAY, buys out the family-owned and operated WILLIAM WRIGLEY, JR., COMPANY.	
2008	The nation of Greece now produces seventy percent of the world's olive oil.	
2008	Sweetwater, TX; "Were it a country all by itself, Nolan County, TX, would rank sixth on the list of wind-energy producing nations," says Greg Wortham, the mayor. By end-of-year, Nolan county has 1,500 wind turbines, producing electricity equal to the production of two to three nuclear power plants.	
2008	August; CVS CAREMART CORP. buys LONG'S DRUG STORES of California in a $2.7 billion deal. LONG'S had 521 stores, giving CVS a total of 6,800 drugstores across 41 states and DC.	
2008	Sweden; August 20; in Lund, the ALFA LAVAL GROUP announces the acquisition of HUTCHINSON HAYES SEPARATION CO. of Houston, TX. Founded in 1927, H-H-S is a leader in manufacturing and marketing of separation equipment, parts, and service.	
2008	By trapping the natural hot water in underground reservoirs, and piping it through radiators, 99% of the homes in Reykjavík, Iceland, are heated using natural geothermal power.	
2008	October 3; thirteen years to the day after his acquittal for murder, O. J. Simpson is convicted of twelve criminal counts, including breaking and entering, kidnapping, and armed robbery.	
2008	October; the US Congress passes a $700 billion "bail-out" for financial/insurance institutions to (hopefully) avert a total market crash and depression!! ...and what a waste it is!!!!	(see 2009)
2008	October 30, Germany; late this evening, the last flight departs from Berlin's Templehof Airport. This flight marks the end of aviation here, spanning several decades, back to WWII. Just before midnight, two 1930 era planes, a DC-3 and a JU-52, takeoff, and the runway lights are now darkened forever.	
2008	Jack Daniel's Tennessee Whiskey is now sold in 135 countries around the world, however, a drink cannot be legally purchased in Lynchburg, TN, where Jack Daniels is brewed, as the town is dry.	
2008	Texas; having been refurbished in 1988, the Carnegie Library in Ballinger continues to function as a library, one of the few in the nation continuing to be utilized as originally intended.	
2008	The former ARDCO operates today as a division of PETTIBONE/TRAVERSE LIFT LLC, in Lafayette, LA.	
2008	USA; New York City is now the "World's Wine Auction Capital." Now take that, Paris!!!	
2008	This year, in seventy-eight nations around the world, more than a quarter of a BILLION guests checked in at the three-thousand, three-hundred hotel properties of the HILTON HOTELS CORPORATION. This is quite a step up from 1924 in Cisco, TX. *"Yeah Bubba, Ole Conrad would really be proud!"*	

2008	Johnston & Jennings continues to operate as a gray and ductile iron foundry in Chicago, IL.	
2008	Nine million Ford Mustangs have been sold since its 1964 debut. However, since Ford introduced their F-Series trucks in 1959, twenty-seven million of them have been bought. The little Ford Ranger pickup was introduced in 1982, and 5.5 million Rangers have been sold. Then, the Ford Explorer was introduced in 1990, and about 6.3 million Explorers have been sold up to now.	
2008	USA; Michigan, at 97%, now leads the country in seatbelt usage; Massachusetts brings up the rear with 67% usage, the national average is 83% usage.	
2008	From Tulsa Rig, Reel & Manufacturing's 1908 founding, Flint now celebrates 100 years. Now Flint has more than 10,000 employees working from over sixty locations in North America.	
2008	Qatar; the 40,318-foot (12,289 m) Al Shakeen offshore well drilled by Transocean for Maersk passes Russia's 40,230-foot (12,262 m) Kola Borehole in depth. NOTE: Remember that the Kola Borehole is a bored hole, and the rock samples were retrieved; it is NOT a drilled well, as such.	(see 2011)
2009	Franklin, MN; Alfred Woelbing's original formula Carmex lip balm can still be purchased in the tiny jars. "Seriously, we never test on animals. We don't need to because we've got so many Woelbing family members to use as test subjects." Carma Labs continue to be run by the Woelbing family.	
2009	March; Forbes Magazine estimates Mr. Frank Buck's worth at about $1.6 billion. That ain't too bad for a thousand buck investment in a sandwich shop made forty-four years ago.	
2009	USA; today in Le Mars, IA, more ice cream is produced here by a single company than in any other city on earth. The descendants of Fred H. Wells still live here and operate their business in "The Ice Cream Capital of The World."	
2009	**Boy, did this ever jump… there are some CEOs making 15,000 times what an "average" worker is making… it was easier after many workers took a good (12.5%) pay cut. The CEO then pulls $91 million total out for last year.**	

2009	The US average work week is 34.6 hours; in South Korea it is 43.6 hours and in Germany, folks work 26 hours per week.	
2009	It is said that Amazing Grace has been recorded by more artists than any other song in history, and that's good.	
2009	The Oak Ridge Boys of today have played and sang together for over 35 years. The two newest of the present group joined in 1973. Since their 1943 start, over forty "boys" have participated in this singing group.	
2009	There are now over 5,700 Dairy Queen shops in the U. S, and Texas has the most at over 600.	
2009	Salem, MA; Craig Burkinshaw, the fourth generation of his family, is now a candy-maker at Ye Olde Pepper Candy Company here in town. Two centuries later, he still makes the candy the old fashioned way… by hand!!	
2009	Cedar Rapids, IA, August 6; today, Terex Corp. announces that manufacturing operations at the local old Cedarapids plant, will cease by mid-year 2010. Engineering, sales, and service will remain here, but manufacturing will be transferred to their plants in Durand, MI, Oklahoma City, and various other North American locations.	
2009	Due to the popularity of the digital camera, Kodak retires its Kodachrome film after 75 years of success.	(see 2011)

2009	BUCYRUS INTERNATIONAL purchases the Mining Division of TEREX CORPORATION. This includes all brands formerly known as O&K, UNIT RIG, REEDRILL, SHM, as well as HALCO. The products are hydraulic excavators, haul trucks, rock drills, as well as high wall miners. The old O&K factory in Dortmund, Germany, also goes to BUCYRUS as part of the deal.	
2009	September 18; having been on the air for seventy-two years, *Guiding Light* airs its final episode today. The soap opera debuted on radio in 1937, and moved to television in 1952, but higher production costs, and lower ratings finally got it.	
2009	Arlington, TX; the DALLAS COWBOYS begin playing in their new home stadium here, next to the "Ballpark at Arlington." Just the super-scoreboard in this new stadium cost $75 million, more than twice the original cost of the entire old Texas Stadium.	
2009	October 3, New York; the Poughkeepsie Bridge reopens with ceremony today as "the Walkway Over the Hudson." The entire 6,767-foot long bridge has new concrete decking panels installed and is now open for pedestrian traffic across its entire length, making it the longest pedestrian bridge in the world.	
2009	Pennsylvania; after a century and three-quarter, horse-drawn for its first two decades or so, going steam-powered in 1853-1854, the STRASBURG RAIL ROAD is still running, the oldest short line railroad operating in the United States of America.	
2009	During the past three decades, the world's GDP has more than doubled, from +/- US $30 trillion in 1980 to US $72.5 trillion this year. The USA presently the world's largest economy, grew 119% during this time. Up-and-coming India's grew 455%, with the most fantastic increase of 1506% for China.	
2009	Ohio; one hundred and forty years after its founding, the A. I. Root Company, in the original brick building, continue forging onward, now producing some of the most exceptional candles, of the very highest quality.	
2009	**The movie *Avatar* earns $2.8 billion at the box office, making it the largest grossing "picture show" ever.** *"Ya know Slim, I git kinda blue sumtimes, but them folks is redikerlus."*	
2009	FOLEY acquires MARTIN TRACTOR CO., expanding their Cat territory from 55 counties to 99 counties.	(see 2012)
2010	California; celebrating their centennial this year, the family-owned EDWARD R. BACON COMPANY is still going strong.	
2010	England; after 304 years, TWININGS continues selling tea from Thomas' original shop on the Strand, as well as in more than 100 different countries all around the world.	
2010	Mississippi; in the town of Madison, the DeBeukelaer family continues baking Belgium Wafers. Their "Pirouline" is the only American made national brand of rolled wafers.	
2010	Houston now has more than twenty of the JAMES CONEY ISLAND restaurants.	
2010	During its first decade, T-3 ENERGY SERVICES acquires UNITED WELLHEAD of Robstown, TX, MANIFOLD VALVES of Jennings, LA, PIPELINE VALVE CO. and CUSTOM COATING APPLICATORS, both of Houston, OILCO of Nisku, Alberta, Canada, K. C. MACHINE of Rock Springs, WY, ENERGY EQUIPMENT CORP. of Houston, PINNACLE WELLHEAD of Oklahoma City, as well as AZUMA ENERGY WELLHEAD DIVISION with many locations.	
2010	Ohio; during this past decade, Cincinnati has lost 25% of the available jobs for its workforce.	

2010	This year General Motors sells more new cars in the Republic of China than in the United States of America. The sad note is that almost all of them are made in China. The UAW can be really proud of that.

2010	November; Caterpillar Inc. enters into an agreement under which Cat will acquire Bucyrus International for about $8.6 billion.
2010	The World Wide Web now has well over 200 million websites for communications and commerce.
2010	UAE; the "new" World's Tallest Building opens for business. At more than twice the height of the Empire State Building, the 2,717 foot tall "Burj Dubai, "called the "Burj Khalifa" after its inauguration, is more than one-half mile tall.
2010	As a part of the Columbus McKinnon family of companies, Chester Hoist continues making high quality hoisting products at the Hal Wright, Sr., original location in Lisbon, OH.
2010	USA; it is figured that about 13,000,000 household fires are extinguished this year with spray foam, carbon tetrachloride, or soda acid fire extinguishers; those are in addition to the many, many home fires simply put out with the old water hose.

2010	Washington; I-R Material Handling Division opens a new manufacturing facility in Kent. I-R's Powered Industrial Lifting Equipment is moved from Southern Pines, NC, to Kent. I-R's Winch & Hoist Solutions production is moved from Seattle to Kent.
2010	December; Pepsico announces it is buying a majority portion of Wimm-Bill-Dann Foods for $3.8 billion, making it the largest food and beverage company in Russia. This is the largest international acquisition ever for Pepsico; making Russia their second largest market area after the USA.
2011	January 4; although production officially ended with the 2010 fourth quarter, the very last Mercury automobile, a Grand Marquis, rolls off the assembly line as another good marque "bites the dust."
2011	On Valentine's Day, 91-year-old pianist George Shearing passes away. Though born blind, Shearing composed over 300 tunes.
2011	Over the last 50 years, the human population of earth has increased from three billion in 1960 to about seven billion now.
2011	Celebrating more than a century of manufacturing and marketing fire-fighting equipment, the W. S. Darley Company remains a family owned and operated business in Chicago.
2011	February; Seawell Ltd. Announces they plan on buying and merging Allis-Chalmers Energy, Inc., making it a wholly-owned subsidiary of Seawell Limited.
2011	June; converted to US gallons and US dollars, gasoline prices around the world average thusly: New York City, NY, $4 per gallon; Toronto, Ontario, Canada, $5.41; one gallon in London, UK is $8.39; and up to $10.02 in Istanbul, Turkey. With government subsidies it is $1.11 in Cairo, Egypt, and with Super Chavez subsidies it is less than 10 cents a gallon in Caracas, Venezuela. A barrel of crude oil varies little around the globe from the current price of $86 to $88 for the 42 gallons.
2011	The old Rolodex is passé now, as business (and personal) contact information is all stored on our computers, and in our hand held telephone iPod thingies. *Old Jim's NOTE: This applies mostly to the young'uns, as I still love the old Rolodex.*

2011	USA; a Nielsen survey shows that the number of homes with at least one television set has declined for the first time in over twenty years. This decline is probably due to the upsurge in "superphones," iPod thingies, etc.	
2011	USA; although native to the northeast US, more cranberries are now harvested from the 18,000 acres of bogs in Wisconsin than any other area.	
2011	The "Kodak Moment" has ended!!! Sadly, now, after almost a century and a quarter, Kodak is out of the camera business.	
2011	This year the 1,347,350,000 people of China purchase 18,000,000 new cars, and many of them can remember 1985.	
2011	USA; the American Space Shuttle completes its last voyage, having just made some repairs to the International Space Station.	
2011	United Airlines and Continental Airlines merge, and Continental's great service and schedules go south fast.	
2011	The best selling vehicle in the USA this year is the F-Series Ford pickups, and 584, 917 of these are sold.	
2011	In the USA 12 million new cars are sold this year.	
2011	Russia; the 40,327-foot (12,345 m) deep offshore Sakhalin-1/Odoptu OP-11 well is completed.	
2012	India; the largest employer on earth today is the Indian Railway System, with 1.6 million employees.	
2012	Texas; in Houston, retailer Star Furniture Company celebrates its centennial.	
2012	USA; WAKE UP AMERICANS!!! This year, only 2% of all new clothing sold here is made here… remember 1997?	
2012	UK; August 9; after selling off its last six vessels, Stevenson Clarke Shipping, Ltd., has now gone in to liquidation. Having survived dozens of economic downturns, the 282-year-old firm simply couldn't survive the current downturn. Stevie Clarke was the oldest shipping firm in Europe, and probably the oldest on the planet.	
2012	Canada; the private, family-owned Equipment Sales & Service Ltd. is the Link-Belt crane dealer in Edmonton, Alberta.	
2012	Tennessee; ninety-two-years-young Luther Massingil has now been in radio for 72 years. All that time on station KDEF in Chattanooga. Luther is a local hero of sorts for reuniting many hundreds of lost pets with their owners, as he advertises notices about the lost pets while performing his DJ duties. Luther is inducted into the Radio Hall of Fame this year.	
2012	Kansas; Caterpillar dealer Foley now acquires Dean Machinery, and they go from 19 locations in 14 cities to serving 104 of the 105 counties in this state, as well as 40 counties in western Missouri, including the Kansas City metro area.	
2012	The total revenue of National-Oilwell-Varco is $20. 4 billion this year, with a net income of $2.5 billion.	
2013	Scattered over six continents, in 1,160 Various facilities, about 60,250 persons are now employed by National-Oilwell-Varco.	
2013	After well over a century of successfully producing pumps and other items, Flygt has production facilities in the USA, India, China, Argentina, and of course in Emmaboda, Sweden.	

2014	January; at their apex, BLOCKBUSTER had 9,000 video rental stores. As technology bypasses them, the last one closes this month.	
2014	April; GE OIL & GAS acquires CAMERON, of BOP fame.	
2014	Growing from SCOTT TRUCK & TRACTOR, now SCOTT EQUIPMENT has 21 locations in five states, but maintaining their corporate office in their hometown of Monroe, LA. Scott continues to be a family-owned and managed business.	
2014	The WALT DISNEY COMPANY has been nominated for over 200 Oscars, and has won more than 50.	
2014	Ralph Lauren, born Ralph Lifshitz in 1939, is the 200th wealthiest person on earth, at $7.1 Billion. He did achieve his ambition.	
2015	The film soundtrack to the movie *Grease* has now sold more than 40 million copies around the world, making it the best selling film soundtrack of all time.	
2015	Texas; LUFKIN INDUSTRIES, a leading manufacturing of oil well pump jacks and other such equipment, closes it doors, shuts down, goes belly-up, after 113 years. A terrible blow to the small city of Lufkin.	

IMAGE SOURCES

4000 BC: "Ancient Egypt rope manufacture," Wikimedia Commons (commons.wikimedia.org); public domain.

1250 BC: "Ramses Reclining," by Jennifer Aitkens, Flickr (flickr.com); Creative Commons Attribution 2.0 Generic. Converted to grayscale, cropped.

625 BC: "Zagazig hoard of ancient Greek coins..." Wikimedia Commons (commons.wikimedia.org); public domain.

247 BC: "Qinshihuang," image ca. 1850, from *China's terracotta army and the First Emperor's mausoleum: the art and culture of Qin Shihuang's underground palace* by Zhongyi Yuan, via Wikimedia Commons (commons.wikimedia.org); public domain.

1023: "Jiao zi," Wikimedia Commons (commons.wikimedia.org); public domain.

1215: "Magna Carta (1297 version with seal, owned by David M Rubenstein)," Wikimedia Commons (commons.wikimedia.org); public domain.

1391: "MertonCollegeLibrary," Wikimedia Commons (commons.wikimedia.org); public domain.

1460s: "Leonardo da Vinci" by Raphael Morghen, Gift of Wallace L. De Wolf, Los Angeles County Museum of Art (www.lacma.org); public domain.

1500: "Taschenuhr Peter Henlein," Wikimedia Commons (commons.wikimedia.org); public domain.

1541: "Coronado sets out to the north," oil painting by Frederic Remington, Wikimedia Commons (commons.wikimedia.org); public domain.

1588: "The demise of the Spanish Armada..." Wikimedia Commons (commons.wikimedia.org); public domain.

1624: "Van Drebbel," Wikimedia Commons (commons.wikimedia.org); public domain.

1644: "Antonio Stradivarius," from *What We Hear in Music* by Anne Shaw Faulkner (1913), via Wikimedia Commons (commons.wikimedia.org); public domain.

1658: Figure from *Christiani Hugenii Zulichemii, const. f. Horologium oscillatorium, siue de motu pendulorum ad horologia aptato demonstrationes geometricæ*, by Christiaan Huygens (1643), Internet Archive (archive.org); public domain.

1679: "Portrait of Denis Papin..." from Wellcome Images, UK (id #L0017587), via Wikimedia Commons (commons.wikimedia.org); Creative Commons Attribution 4.0 International. Converted to grayscale, cropped.

1712: "Newcomen6325," from *Practical physics for secondary schools* by Newton Henry Black and Harvey Nathaniel Davis (1913), via Wikimedia Commons (commons.wikimedia.org); public domain.

1720: "Prairie schooner (PSF)," Wikimedia Commons (commons.wikimedia.org); public domain.

1723: *Poor Richard's Almanack*, "Title Page - no illus." from the Library of Congress (loc.gov/pictures/, item #2005692067); public domain.

1745: "The Process of Casting Crucible-melted Iron," from "The Development of American Industries Since Columbus" in *The Popular Science Monthly*, volume 38, page 158, via Wikimedia Commons (commons.wikimedia.org); public domain.

1752: "The philosopher & his kite," engraved by Henry S. Sadd, from the Library of Congress (loc.gov/pictures/, item #2006691772); public domain.

1762: "The Boy Mozart," oil painting possibly by Pietro Antonio Lorenzoni, 1763, from Cornell University's Division of Rare & Manuscript Collections; public domain.

1766: "Sketch of the Life of Dr. Priestley" from *The Popular Science Monthly*, Volume 5 August 1874, via Wikisource (wikisource.org); public domain.

1776: The Declaration of Independence, image from the National Archives of the United States (archives.gov); public domain.

1776: "TurtleSubmarine" from *The story of the submarine* by Farnham Bishop (1916), via Wikimedia Commons (commons.wikimedia.org); public domain.

1785: "Plan of Mr. Fitch's steam boat" from the Library of Congress (loc.gov/pictures/, item #2006691757); public domain.

1789: "Samuel Slater industrialist" from *The Biographical Cyclopedia of Representative Men of Rhode Island* (1881), via Wikimedia Commons (commons.wikimedia.org); public domain.

1794: "Whitney Cotton Gin," WPClipart (wpclipart.com); public domain.

1797: "USS Constitution, Outboard Profile with Sail Plan" from the National Archives of the United States (archives.gov. ID #5956232); public domain.

1802: "Humphry Davy Engraving 1830" from *The Life of Sir Humphry Davy* by John A. Paris (1831), via Wikimedia Commons (commons.wikimedia.org); public domain.

1804: "A la mémoire de J.M. Jacquard" engraving by Michel Marie Carquillat after Claude Bonnefond, via Wikimedia Commons (commons.wikimedia.org); public domain.

1807: "Tram on the Swansea and Mumbles Railway in Wales, 1807," Wikimedia Commons (commons.wikimedia.org); public domain.

1811: "FrameBreaking-1812," Wikimedia Commons (commons.wikimedia.org); public domain.

1814: "The Battle of New Orleans," designed by W. Momberger, engraved by H.B. Hall, from the Library of Congress (loc.gov/pictures/, item #2012645291); public domain.

1817: "Draisine1817," Wikimedia Commons (commons.wikimedia.org); public domain.

1821: "Coronation of George IV" painting by James Stephanoff, via Wikimedia Commons (commons.wikimedia.org); public domain.

1823: "Poinsettia" stock photo from Public Domain Pictures (publicdomainpictures.net); public domain.

1825: "Improved Electro Magnetic Apparatus," Trans. Royal Society of Arts,

Manufactures, and Commerce, Vol.43, Plate 3, fig.13 by W. Sturgeon (1824), via Wikimedia Commons (commons.wikimedia.org); public domain.

1829: "Stephenson's Rocket drawing" from *Mechanics* magazine (1829), via Wikimedia Commons (commons.wikimedia.org); public domain.

1830: "American bison" by Jack Dykinga, from the Agricultural Research Service, United States Department of Agriculture (ID #K5680-1); public domain.

1832: "Johan Theofron Munktell" from *Svenska industriens män* (1872), via Wikimedia Commons (commons.wikimedia.org); public domain.

1834: "Seed Planter" image from U.S. Patent #USI1X0008447 (granted to H. Blair, 1834), United States Patent and Trademark Office (uspto.gov); public domain.

1837: "Woman with original steel plow made by John Deere in Grand Detour, Illinois in 1838, at the Smithsonian Institution, Washington, D.C." photo by Harris & Ewing, from the Library of Congress (loc.gov/pictures/, item #hec2009013825); public domain.

1839: "Nasmyth's patent steam hammer, copied by permission of the inventor from the machine in the great exhibition" from the Library of Congress (loc.gov/pictures/, item #2006691796); public domain.

1840: "Penny Black Block of six," Wikimedia Commons (commons.wikimedia.org); public domain.

1842: "P.T. Barnum and General Tom Thumb" photograph by Samuel Root or Marcus Aurelius Root (ca 1850), from the National Portrait Gallery, Smithsonian Institution (item #NPG.93.154); public domain.

1843: "Scrooge's third visitor," from *A Christmas Carol. In Prose. Being a Ghost Story of Christmas* by Charles Dickens with Illustrations by John Leech (1843), via Wikimedia Commons (commons.wikimedia.org); public domain.

1846: "Improvement in Sugar Making" image from U.S. Patent #4879 (granted to Norbert Rilleux, 1846), via Google Patents (patents.google.com); public domain.

1848: "James Marshall, discoverer of gold, at Sutter's Mill" the from Library of Congress (loc.gov/pictures/, item #2007676072); public domain.

1849: "Pin" image from U.S. Patent #6281 (granted to Walter Hunt, 1849), via Google Patents (patents.google.com); public domain.

1850: "American Express shipping receipt 1853" from *The Cooper Collection of American Transportation History*, via Wikimedia Commons (commons.wikimedia.org); public domain.

1850: "Washing Table Furniture" image from U.S. Patent #7365 (granted to Joel Houghton, 1850), via Google Patents (patents.google.com); public domain.

1852: "Sir George Cayley's Governable Parachutes" illustration from *Mechanics'* magazine (1852), via Wikimedia Commons (commons.wikimedia.org); public domain.

1855: "The Niagara Falls suspension bridge. First opened: Aug. 1st. 1848" photograph from the Library of Congress (loc.gov/pictures/, item #2003664961); public domain.

1851: "Panama Railway in 1855" illustration from Panama, past and present by Farnham Bishop (1916), pg 101, Internet Archive (archive.org); public domain.

1857: "George M. Pullman" illustrations from *Contemporary American Biography: Biographical Sketches of Representative Men of the Day...*, Volume 1, Part 2, pg 258 (1895), via Google Books (books.google.com); public domain.

1858: "Instrument for Opening cans" image from U.S. Patent #19063 (granted to Ezra J. Warner, 1858), via Google Patents (patents.google.com); public domain.

1858: "New York Crystal Palace," frontispiece to *New York Crystal Palace: illustrated description of the building by Geo. Carstensen & Chs. Gildemeister, architects of the building...* by Karl Gildemeister (1854), via Wikimedia Commons (commons.wikimedia.org); public domain.

1859: "Charles Darwin," frontispiece of *The Life and Letters of Charles Darwin* by Francis Darwin (1887), via Wikimedia Commons (commons.wikimedia.org); public domain.

1860: "Abraham Lincoln by Alexander Hesler, 1860-crop" photograph by Alexander Hesler (1860), via Wikimedia Commons (commons.wikimedia.org); public domain.

1861: "Bombardment of Fort Sumter, 1861" by George Edward Perine, Wikimedia Commons (commons.wikimedia.org); public domain.

1862: "Old Faithful" by Albert Bierstadt, via Wikimedia Commons (commons.wikimedia.org) (commons.wikimedia.org); public domain.

Civil War: "Petersburg, Va. The 'Dictator,' a closer view" photograph by David Knox, from the Library of Congress (loc.gov/pictures/, item #cwpb.03851); public domain.

1865: "'Peace in Union" after a painting by Thomas Nast, via Wikimedia Commons (commons.wikimedia.org); public domain.

1866: "Improvement in irons for curling hair" image from U.S. Patent #57354A (granted to Hiram Maxim, 1866), via Google Patents (patents.google.com); public domain.

1866: "SS Great Eastern in New York Harbor, 1860" from a stereogram by George Stacy, via Wikimedia Commons (commons.wikimedia.org); public domain.

1868: "Windmill at Laramie," photograph by Andrew J. Russell (ca 1864-69), via Wikimedia Commons (commons.wikimedia.org); public domain.

1869: "East and West Shaking hands at the laying of last rail Union Pacific Railroad" photograph by Andrew J. Russell (1869), via Wikimedia Commons (commons.wikimedia.org); public domain.

1869: "Improvement in harrows" image from U.S. Patent #95458A (granted to David Garver, 1869), via Google Patents (patents.google.com); public domain.

1871: "The Great fire at Chicago. Scene in Wells Street - the terrified populace in front of the Briggs House, which has just caught fire" from *Harper's Weekly* (1871), from the Library of Congress (loc.gov/pictures/, item #94501371); public domain.

1871: "Improvement in cigar-lighters" image from U.S. Patent #121049A (granted to M. Gale, 1871), via Google Patents (patents.google.com); public domain.

1872: "Gottlieb Daimler 1890s2," Wikimedia Commons (commons.wikimedia.org); public domain.

1873: "Jesse James" from the Library of Congress (loc.gov/pictures/, item #2004672083); public domain.

1874: "The Sholes and Glidden typewriter" from *The Expert Typist* by Clarence Charles Smith (1922), via Wikimedia Commons (commons.wikimedia.org); public domain.

1875: "Cover" from Montgomery Ward *Catalogue no. 13, spring and summer, 1875*, Internet Archive (archive.org); public domain.

1876: "Opening day ceremonies at the Centennial Exhibition at Philadelphia, PA May 10, 1876" from *The Illustrated History of the Centennial Exposition Held In Commemoration of the One Hundredth Anniversary of American Independence* by James D. McCabe, via Wikimedia Commons (commons.wikimedia.org); public domain.

1877: "Thomas Edison" from the Brady-Handy Collection at the Library of Congress (loc.gov/pictures/, item #cwpbh.04044); public domain.

1878: "The Horse in motion. 'Abe Edgington,' owned by Leland Stanford; driven by C. Marvin, trotting at a 2:24 gait over the Palo Alto track, 15th June 1878" photographic series by Eadweard Muybridge (1878), from the Library of Congress (loc.gov/pictures/, item #91483062); public domain.

1878: "Joseph Wilson Swan 2," Wikimedia Commons (commons.wikimedia.org); public domain.

1880s: "View of Oldreive's new tricycle; the New Iron Horse, with a lady inside" photograph by Charles W. Oldrieve, from the Library of Congress (loc.gov/pictures/, item #2011660949); public domain.

1880: "Tunnel at Juneau Mine" photograph from the Library of Congress (loc.gov/pictures/, item #99614370); public domain.

1881: "The Wounded President--Ascertaining the Location of the Bullet" illustration from *Harper's Weekly* v.25 July-Dec.1881, via Hathi Trust's Digital Library (hathitrust.org); public domain.

1882: "Separable Pulley" image from U.S. Patent #260462A (granted to Wallace H. Dodge and George Peilion, 1882), via Google Patents (patents.google.com); public domain.

1883: "Kroger, B.H." photograph by Harris & Ewing (ca 1905), from the Library of Congress (loc.gov/pictures/, item #hec2009006806); public domain.

1883: "Pecos, Texas" stock image from Pixabay (pixabay.com); public domain.

1884: "Ringling Bros, world's greatest shows Raschetta brothers, marvelous somersaulting vaulters" poster by the Courier Company (c. 1900) from the Library of Congress (loc.gov/pictures/, item #2002695276); public domain.

1884: "Cleveland, Grover-President (BEP engraved portrait)" by the Bureau of Printing and Engraving, via Wikimedia Commons (commons.wikimedia.org); public domain.

1885: "Last Spike of the CPR - Craigellachie, British Columbia, Canada" photograph from the Library and Archives of Canada (1885), via Wikimedia Commons (commons. wikimedia.org); public domain.

1886: "Dish-washing machine" image from U.S. Patent #355139A (granted to Josephine Cochrane, 1886), via Google Patents (patents.google.com); public domain.

1887: "Heinrich Hertz" engraving by Robert Krewaldt (ca 1894), via Wikimedia Commons (commons.wikimedia.org); public domain.

1888: "N.Tesla," Wikimedia Commons (commons.wikimedia.org); public domain.

1889: "The Wall Street Journal first issue," by Dow Jones & Company (1889), via Wikimedia Commons (commons.wikimedia.org); public domain.

1890: "Oil wells just offshore at Summerland, California, c.1915" photograph by G.H. Eldridge, via Wikimedia Commons (commons.wikimedia.org); public domain.

1890: "Nellie Bly," photograph from the New York Public Library Digital Collection (digitalcollections.nypl.org, id #1121847); public domain.

1890: "John D Rockefeller" by Oscar White (ca 1900), via Wikimedia Commons (commons.wikimedia.org); public domain.

1891: "Endless Conveyor or Elevator" image from U.S. Patent #470918A (granted to J.W. Reno, 1892), via Google Patents (patents. google.com); public domain.

1892: "A Duryea Car of 1894: on the left Charles E. Duryea, pioneer motor manufacturer in the United States; with him his brother J.F. Duryea." photograph from The Outing Magazine (volume 51, pg 212, 1908), digitized by Google Books (books. google.com); public domain.

1892: "John Muir, full-length portrait, facing right, seated on rock with lake and trees in background" photograph ca 1902, from the Library of Congress (loc.gov/pictures/, item #95514008); public domain.

1893: "The fastest time on record" photograph by A.P. Yates (ca 1893), from the Library of Congress (loc.gov/pictures/, item #99401043); public domain.

1894: "Turbinia At Speed" photograph by Alfred John West (1897), via Wikimedia Commons (commons.wikimedia.org); public domain.

1895: "Bicycle-bearing" image from U.S. Patent #567851A (granted to Horace E. and John F. Dodge, 1896), via Google Patents (patents.google.com); public domain.

1895: "Drink Coca-Cola 5 cents" vintage ad from the Library of Congress (loc.gov/pictures/, item #2004671509); public domain.

1895: "Cinematographe Projection" illustration by Louis Poyot, via Wikimedia Commons (commons.wikimedia.org); public domain.

1895: "Mold" image from U.S. Patent #746971A (granted to Italo Marchiony, 1903), via Google Patents (patents.google. com); public domain.

1896: "Portrait of Alfred Nobel" by Gösta Florman (before 1896), via Wikimedia Commons (commons.wikimedia.org); public domain.

1897: "Pencil-sharpener" image from U.S. Patent #594114A (granted to John Lee Love, 1897), via Google Patents (patents.google. com); public domain.

1898: "Portrait of Caleb D. Bradham" ca 1910-15, from NC Collections (collections. ncdcr.gov); public domain.

1898: "Pierre and Marie Curie at work in their laboratory." historical image from Wellcome Images, UK (id #L0001761); Creative Commons Attribution 4.0 International. Converted to grayscale, cropped.

1899: "Charlie "Mile-a-Minute" Murphy" scanned image by Bob Hanson, Flickr (flickr.com, username Stronglight); Creative Commons Attribution 2.0 Generic. Converted to grayscale, cropped.

1899: "Photograph of the painting "Dog looking at and listening to a phonograph," by Francis Berraud in 1898" from the Library of Congress (loc.gov/pictures/, item #96521608); public domain.

1899: "Aspirin-Fläschchen" (1899), Wikimedia Commons (commons.wikimedia. org); public domain.

1900: "Gray's new trunk railway map of the United States, Dom. of Canada and portion of Mexico" from the Library of Congress (loc. gov, control #gm71000844); public domain.

1900: "New York Auto Show, 1900, New York Times," Wikimedia Commons (commons. wikimedia.org); public domain.

1900: "System of regulating steam-boilers" image from U.S. Patent #676790A (granted to Rollin H. White, 1900), via Google Patents (patents.google.com); public domain.

1901: "Singer Model27 Treadle Table," Wikimedia Commons (commons.wikimedia. org); public domain.

1901: "Logging-engine" image from U.S. Patent #674737A (granted to Alvin O. Lombard, 1900), via Google Patents (patents.google.com); public domain.

1901: "Automobile plow--in use in England," photograph by the American Stereoscopic Company (ca 1905), from the Library of Congress (loc.gov/pictures/, item #93508136); public domain.

1902: "The Prophet Ezekiel Airship," illustration from *Scientific American* (Vol. 85, No. 15, October 1901), via the Internet Archive (archive.org); public domain.

1902: "Ida M. Tarbell, No. 1," photograph by J. E. Purdy, from the Library of Congress (loc.gov/pictures/, item #97509168); public domain.

1901: "Glass-working machine" image from U.S. Patent #768034A (granted to Irving W. Colburn, 1903), via Google Patents (patents. google.com); public domain.

1903: "The Wright Brothers' Engine," photograph by the Smithsonian Institution, via Wikimedia Commons (commons. wikimedia.org); public domain.

1903: "Old97Wreck," Wikimedia Commons (commons.wikimedia.org); public domain.

1903: "Marcel Renault 1903," Wikimedia Commons (commons.wikimedia.org); public domain.

1904: "Glenn Curtiss on his V-8 motorcycle, Ormond Beach, Florida 1907," photograph from *The Motorcycle Illustrated* magazine, via Wikimedia Commons (commons. wikimedia.org); public domain.

1904: "1906 Adams-Farwell Runabout - National Automobile Museum" photograph by Douglas Wilkinson (remarkablecars. com); public domain.

1905: "White House caller" photograph by Harris & Ewing, from the Library of Congress (loc.gov/pictures/, item #hec2009010163); public domain.

1905: "Einstein patentoffice," photograph by Lucien Chavan (1904-5), via Wikimedia Commons (commons.wikimedia.org); public domain.

1905: "Potters wheel (PSF)," Wikimedia Commons (commons.wikimedia.org); public domain.

1906: "Apparatus for treating air" image from U.S. Patent #808897A (granted to Willis H. Carrier, 1906), via Google Patents (patents.google.com); public domain.

1906: "Alois Alzheimer," from Find A Grave (findagrave.com); public domain.

1906: "HMS Dreadnought 1906 H61017" photograph from the U. S. Naval Historical Center (1906) via Wikimedia Commons (commons.wikimedia.org); public domain.

1907: "Sven Wingquist," Wikimedia Commons (commons.wikimedia.org); public domain.

1907: "Florenz Ziegfield," photograph from the cover of *Time* magazine, Volume 11

Issue 20, 1928, via Wikimedia Commons (commons.wikimedia.org); public domain.

1907: "Paul-Cornu," Wikimedia Commons (commons.wikimedia.org); public domain.

1908: "E.F. [i.e., A.] Sperry," photograph by Bain News Service (ca 1910-15), from the Library of Congress (loc.gov/pictures/, item #ggb2005019687); public domain.

1908: "Photograph of Howard R. Hughes, Sr., with trench mining drill, Houston, Texas, September 29, 1917," from the University of Nevada-Las Vegas (digital. library.unlv.edu, ID #whh000052); public domain.

1908: "1910 Model T Ford, Salt Lake City, Utah," photograph by Harry Shipler (1910), via Wikimedia Commons (commons. wikimedia.org); public domain.

1909: "Electric heater" image from U.S. Patent #950058A (granted to Frank E. Shailor, 1910), via Google Patents (patents. google.com); public domain.

1909: "David Lloyd George," photograph from *The Rise of the Democracy* by Joseph Clayton (1911), via Wikimedia Commons (commons.wikimedia.org); public domain.

1910: "Girl Who Crossed US on Horseback" photograph from the *Kansas City Post* (1911), via The Long Riders' Guild (thelongridersguild.com); public domain.

1910: "The Barnum & Bailey greatest show on Earth, the world's largest, grandest, best amusement institution" poster by the Strobridge Litho. Co., from the Library of Congress (loc.gov/pictures/, item #92522393); public domain.

1910: "Three scenes of Harry Houdini as aviator; close-up in Voisin biplane cockpit (1910?); ascending in biplane; flying low," photograph from the Library of Congress (loc.gov/pictures/, item #2001705766); public domain.

1911: "Chevrolet in Sunbeam" photograph by Bain News Service, from the Library of Congress (loc.gov/pictures/, item #ggb2005022936); public domain.

1911: "Clyde Vernon Cessna (1917)," photograph by Textron, via Wikimedia Commons (commons.wikimedia.org); public domain.

1911: "Holt75pk," photograph from *The British Tanks 1915-19* by David Fletcher, via Wikimedia Commons (commons. wikimedia.org); public domain.

1912: "Wilson, Woodrow-President (BEP engraved portrait)" by the Bureau of Printing and Engraving, via Wikimedia Commons (commons.wikimedia.org); public domain.

1912: "Tarzan All Story," cover of *The All-Story* magazine (October 1912), via Public Domain Super Heroes (pdsh.wikia.com); public domain.

1912: "Selandia Bangkok 1912 600dpi," Wikimedia Commons (commons.wikimedia. org); public domain.

1912: "1911jeffers" newspaper advertisement from Saginaw, MI (1911), via Wikimedia Commons (commons.wikimedia.org); public domain.

1913: "A-line1913" photograph by the Ford Motor Company (1913), via Wikimedia Commons (commons.wikimedia.org); public domain.

1913: "Sikhorsky [i.e., Sikirsky] Aeroplane Russian Knight" photograph by Bain News Service, from the Library of Congress (loc. gov/pictures/, item #ggb2005017482); public domain.

1913: "John D. Rockefeller, full-length portrait, walking on street with John D. Rockefeller, Jr.," from the Library of Congress (loc.gov/pictures/, item #2005685460); public domain.

1914: "The Kroonland Passing through the Panama Canal," illustration from *The Book of History: Unites States* by James Bryce Bryce (1915), via Google Books (books.google. com); public domain.

1914: "Shackleton's expedition to the Antarctic a titanic upheaval," photograph by Underwood & Underwood, from the Library of Congress (loc.gov/pictures/, item #2013646125); public domain.

1914: "Hall Cyclecar" photograph by Fred Gildersleeve (prior to 1923), from Baylor University, The Texas Collection (blogs. baylor.edu/texascollection/); public domain.

1915: "Air cleaner" image from U.S. Patent #1405399A (granted to Frank A Donaldson,

1922), via Google Patents (patents.google. com); public domain.

1915: "Power lawn-mower" image from U.S. Patent #1131156A (granted to Ransom E. Olds, 1915), via Google Patents (patents. google.com); public domain.

WWI: "The Washington Times., July 26, 1914, Sunday Evening Edition, Image 1" from the Library of Congress and National Endowment for the Humanities, "Chronicling America" (chroniclingamerica. loc.gov); public domain.

WWI: "George S. Patton - France - 1918" photograph from the World War I Signal Corps Photograph Collection, via Wikimedia Commons (commons.wikimedia.org); public domain.

1916: "Hetty Howland Robinson Green, 1835-1916, half-length portrait, seated" from the Library of Congress (loc.gov/ pictures/, item #2005685231); public domain.

1916: "Boy with Baby Carriage," painting by Norman Rockwell (1916), via Wikimedia Commons (commons.wikimedia.org); public domain.

1917: "Separable fastener" image from U.S. Patent #1236783A (granted to Gideon Sundback, 1917), via Google Patents (patents. google.com); public domain.

1917: "C.M. Vought" photograph by Bain News Service, from the Library of Congress (loc.gov/pictures/, item #ggb2004010979); public domain.

1918: "1917 Albaugh-Dover Tractor" magazine advertisement, scanned by Don O'Brien, Flickr (flickr.com); Creative Commons Attribution 2.0 Generic. Converted to grayscale, cropped.

1918: "Electric Drill" image from U.S. Patent #D59678S (granted to Arno H. Petersen, 1921), via Google Patents (patents.google. com); public domain.

1918: "Crossing the timber line, Pike's Peak railway" photograph by the Detroit Photographic Co., from the Library of Congress (loc.gov/pictures/, item #2008676315); public domain.

1919: "Best 60 Tractor" photograph from the Caterpillar Company archives, via Wikimedia

Commons (commons.wikimedia.org); public domain.

1919: "Bread-toaster" image from U.S. Patent #1394450A (granted to Charles P. Strite, 1921), via Google Patents (patents. google.com); public domain.

1919: "New York City Deputy Police Commissioner John A. Leach, right, watching agents pour liquor into sewer following a raid during the height of prohibition," from the Library of Congress (loc.gov/pictures/, item #99405169); public domain.

1919: "Grand Canyon National Park canyon with ravine winding" photograph by Ansel Adams, National Archives (archives.gov, control #79-AAF-16); public domain.

1919: "Eisenhower transcontinental military convoy" photograph from the Eisenhower Presidential Museum archives, via Wikimedia Commons (commons.wikimedia.org); public domain.

1920: "Michigan & Griswold circa 1920" photograph from the Burton Historical Collection, Detroit Public Library, via Wikimedia Commons (commons.wikimedia. org); public domain.

1920: "Pitney-Bowes Model M postage meter c. 1920;" Wikimedia Commons (commons. wikimedia.org); public domain.

1920: "John A Macready" photograph by the U.S. Air Force, via Wikimedia Commons (commons.wikimedia.org); public domain.

1921: "Tera-ethyl-lead-chemical," by Wikimedia User EliseEtc, Wikimedia Commons (commons.wikimedia.org); Creative Commons Attribution-Share Alike 3.0. No changes made.

1921: "1921 Hudson Phaeton AACA Iowa 2012 fr," photograph by Christopher Ziemnowicz, via Wikimedia Commons (commons.wikimedia.org); public domain.

1921: "George Washington Carver," Pixabay (pixabay.com); public domain.

1922: "Where the North Begins 1923" poster, Warner Bros-Lithograph by Otis Lithograph, via Wikimedia Commons (commons. wikimedia.org); public domain.

1922: "Washing machine" image from U.S. Patent #1866779A (granted to Howard F

Image Sources

Snyder, 1932), via Google Patents (patents.google.com); public domain.

1923: "Hendee Mfg Co. Indian Motocycles" photograph by the Hendee Mfg. Co., via Wikimedia Commons (commons.wikimedia.org); public domain.

1923: "Amon G. Carter" by Bain News Service, from the Library of Congress (loc.gov, item #ggb2006014246); public domain.

1923: "USS Shenandoah" from the San Diego Air and Space Museum Archive, Flickr (flickr.com); public domain.

1924: "1920 Briggs & Stratton Flyer" photograph by Alfvan Beem, via Wikimedia Commons (commons.wikimedia.org); public domain.

1924: "Frozen confectionery" image from U.S. Patent #1505592A (granted to Frank W. Epperson, 1924), via Google Patents (patents.google.com); public domain.

1924: "1924WOlympicPoster," painted by Auguste Matisse, via Wikimedia Commons (commons.wikimedia.org); public domain.

1925: "Snow-removing machine" image from U.S. Patent #1703786A (granted to Arthur Sicard, 1929), via Google Patents (patents.google.com); public domain.

1925: "Mrs. Stewart's Bluing 02" photograph by Joe Mabel, via Wikimedia Commons (commons.wikimedia.org); Creative Commons Attribution-Share Alike 3.0. Converted to grayscale.

1926: "First Flight of a Liquid Propellant Rocket" from NASA, Flickr Commons (flickr.com); public domain.

1926: "Method and means for the atomizing or distribution of liquid or semiliquid materials" image from U.S. Patent #1800156A (granted to Erik Rotheim, 1931), via Google Patents (patents.google.com); public domain.

1927: "Portrait of Albert Einstein and Others (1879-1955), Physicist" from the Smithsonian Institution, Flickr Commons (flickr.com); public domain.

1927: "Charles A. Lindbergh, with Spirit of St. Louis in background, May 31, 1927," photograph from the Library of Congress

(loc.gov/pictures/, item #2002721494); public domain.

1927: "Aerial photograph of flood, unidentified stretch of lower Mississippi River," photograph from the National Archives of the United States (archives.gov, ID #285958); public domain.

1928: "Hoover, Herbert-President (BEP engraved portrait)" by the Bureau of Printing and Engraving, via Wikimedia Commons (commons.wikimedia.org); public domain.

1928: "225-357 Binder 1929 DeSoto Six 4 Door Sedan K Series" from VanDerBrink Auctions, LLC Yvette VanDerBrink-Auctioneer/owner, via Flickr (flickr.com, user Bill McChesney); Creative Commons Attribution 2.0 Generic. Converted to grayscale, cropped.

1928: "Bread slicing machine" image from U.S. Patent #1935996A (granted to Otto F Rohwedder, 1933), via Google Patents (patents.google.com); public domain.

1928: "1928 Okeechobee Aftermath 27," Wikimedia Commons (commons.wikimedia.org); public domain.

1929: "David Dunbar Buick," photograph from *Detroit in history and commerce* by James J. Mitchell (1891), via the Internet Archive (archive.org); public domain.

1929: "Carl Benz," Wikimedia Commons (commons.wikimedia.org); public domain.

1929: "Cord L-29 Cabriolet del 1929," Wikimedia Commons (commons.wikimedia.org); public domain.

1929: "Gulf Building, Houston, Texas," postcard published by Seawall Specialty Co, via Flickr (flickr.com, user MCAD Library); public domain.

1930s: "Combined thermoelectric safety shut-off and electroresponsive valve" image from U.S. Patent #2297854A (granted to Henry F Alfery, 1942), via Google Patents (patents.google.com); public domain.

1930: "Chrysler Building, New York, N.Y." photograph by Detroit Publishing Co., from the Library of Congress (loc.gov/pictures/, item #det1994022036); public domain.

1930: "Wiley Post, 1899-1935" photograph from the Library of Congress (loc.gov/pictures/, item #2002715783); public domain.

1930: "Clyde Tombaugh with 9-inch telescope," 1928 photograph from New Mexico State University Libraries (archphotos.nmsu.edu, ID #407000); public domain.

1931: "Piccard with his family and engineer in front of the capsule of a stratospheric balloon," photograph from the Spaarnestad Collection, via Flickr (flickr.com, Nationaal Archief of the Netherlands); public domain.

1931: "Lou Gehrig and Babe Ruth, New York Yankees, standing in front of a passenger train car in a railroad station," photograph by the Chicago Daily News, from the Library of Congress via Wikimedia Commons (commons.wikimedia.org); public domain.

1931: "Shirley sees her old friend the president," photograph by Harris & Ewing, from the Library of Congress (loc.gov/pictures/, item #hec2009011474); public domain.

1932: "Firestone, Harvey S. (1915), industrialist," photograph by Pirie MacDonald (1915), from the Library of Congress (loc.gov/pictures/, item #91795252); public domain.

1932: "Amelia Earhart at Derry," photograph from the National Library of Ireland, via Flickr (flickr.com); public domain.

1932: "Roosevelt, Franklin D-President (BEP engraved portrait)" by the Bureau of Printing and Engraving, via Wikimedia Commons (commons.wikimedia.org); public domain.

1933: "Douglas DC-1 "City of Los Angeles" of TWA" photograph from *L'Illustration*, volume 92, issue 4785 (1934), via Wikimedia Commons (commons.wikimedia.org); public domain.

1933: "Lunch time at CCC Camp, TVA #22, near Esco, Tennessee, November 1933," photograph by Lewis Hines, from the National Archives of the United States (archives.gov, ID #532777); public domain.

1933: "Looking upstream toward Boulder dam site showing outlet portals of all four diversion tunnels. Flow of Colorado River is approximately 70,000 cubic feet per second," photograph by the Department of the Interior, from the National Archives of the United States (archives.gov, ID #293890); public domain.

1934: "Radio signaling apparatus" image from U.S. Patent #2018569A (granted to Carleton D. Haigis and George W. Pettengill, 1935), via Google Patents (patents.google.com); public domain.

1934: "Lockheed 10A Electra" photograph from the Canadian Forces, via Wikimedia Commons (commons.wikimedia.org); public domain.

1935: "Hiawatha Milwaukee Road Postkarte 1935," postcard by Milwaukee Road, via Wikimedia Commons (commons.wikimedia.org); public domain.

1935: "Small Box Monopoly," Wikimedia Commons (commons.wikimedia.org); public domain.

1935: "Fallingwater (Kaufmann Residence) by Frank Lloyd Wright," Wikimedia Commons (commons.wikimedia.org); public domain.

1935: "Portrait photograph of Robert Watson-Watt" by Air Ministry of the United Kingdom, via Wikimedia Commons (commons.wikimedia.org); public domain.

1936: "Volkswagen Beetle Prototype 1936," photograph by Bruno Kussler Marques, via Flickr (flickr.com); Creative Commons Attribution 2.0 Generic. Converted to grayscale, cropped.

1936: "Gabor, Zsa Zsa," studio publicity photo via Wikimedia Commons (commons.wikimedia.org); public domain.

1937: "'Hindenburg' Disaster, May 6, 1937," photograph by Arthur Cofod, Jr., from the National Air and Space Museum Archives, Smithsonian Institution (airandspace.si.edu, ID #SI-98-15068); public domain.

1937: "Electrophotography" image from U.S. Patent #2297691A (granted to Chester F Carlson, 1942), via Google Patents (patents.google.com); public domain.

1938: "Münchener Abkommen, Chamberlain," from the German Federal Archive, via Wikimedia Commons (commons.wikimedia.org); Creative Commons Attribution-Share Alike 3.0 Germany. No changes made.

1938: "Douglas 'Wrong Way' Corrigan," 1938 photograph from the Illinois Digital Archives (idaillinois.org); public domain.

1938: "Portrait of Orson Welles," photograph by Carl Van Vechten (1937), from the Library of Congress (loc.gov/pictures/, item #2004663727); public domain.

1939: "An automobile on the sweeping curves of the Autobahn with view of the countryside," photograph by Wolf Strache, from the Library of Congress (loc.gov/pictures/, item #2001700458); public domain.

1939: "Igor Sikorsky in the last version of the VS-300, at the end of 1941," Wikimedia Commons (commons.wikimedia.org); public domain.

1939: "USS Texas Havana 1940," photograph by the U.S. Navy, via Wikimedia Commons (commons.wikimedia.org); public domain.

1940: "Winston Churchill as Prime Minister 1940-1945," photograph by Cecil Beaton, from the Imperial War Museums, UK (iwm.org.uk, catalog #MH 26392); public domain.

1940: "North American B-25 Mitchell," photograph from the U.S. Air Force, via Wikimedia Commons (commons.wikimedia.org); public domain.

1941: "Bethlehem Fairfield shipyards, near Baltimore, Maryland. Construction of a Liberty ship," photograph from the Office Of War Information (1943), from the Library of Congress (loc.gov/pictures/, item #owi2001046058); public domain.

1941: "K-ration supper unit" from the U.S. Army, Signal Corps (1943), via Wikimedia Commons (commons.wikimedia.org); public domain.

1942: "Poston, Ariz.--Evacuees of Japanese ancestry are being registered upon arrival at this War Relocation Authority center," photograph by Fred Clark (1942), from the Online Archive of California (oac.cdlib.org, ID WRA no. A-173); public domain.

1942: "Ernest Tubb," from Pixabay (pixabay.com); public domain.

1942: "Scrap Rubber Drive. Bing Crosby," photograph from the Franklin D. Roosevelt Library Public Domain Photographs, via the National Archives of the United States (archives.gov, ID #195573); public domain.

1943: "Sow the Seeds of Victory!" poster by the U.S. Food Administration (1917-19), from the National Archives of the United States (archives.gov, ID #512498); public domain.

WWII: "Baltimore, Maryland. Colonel H.J. Lawes..." photograph by the U.S. Army Signal Corps, from the Library of Congress (loc.gov/pictures/, item #owi2001045935); public domain.

WWII: "Operating a hand drill at Vultee-Nashville, woman is working on a 'Vengeance' dive bomber, Tennessee," photograph by Alfred T. Palmer (1943), from the Library of Congress (loc.gov/pictures/, item #fsa1992001211); public domain.

WWII: "Approaching Omaha," photograph from the Army Signal Corps Collection in the U.S. National Archives, via Wikimedia Commons (commons.wikimedia.org); public domain.

WWII: "US Army Detroit Tank Plant," Wikimedia Commons (commons.wikimedia.org); public domain.

WWII: "William Overstreet Jr," Wikimedia Commons (commons.wikimedia.org); public domain.

WWII: "Trinity device readied," photograph by the U.S. Department of Energy, via Wikimedia Commons (commons.wikimedia.org); public domain.

1944: "Wendell Wilkie and Charles McNary," photograph by Harris & Ewing, from the Library of Congress (loc.gov/pictures/, item #hec2009015589); public domain.

1945: "Harry S. Truman," photograph by the U.S. Department of Defense, from the National Archives of the United States (archives.gov, ID #530677); public domain.

1945: "Hirohito - in dress uniform," from the Library of Congress (loc.gov/pictures/, item #2002721830); public domain.

1945: "Glass phial of British Standard penicillin, London, England" from Wellcome Images, via Wikimedia Commons (commons.wikimedia.org); Creative Commons Attribution 4.0 International. Converted to grayscale, cropped.

1946: "1946 Dodge Power Wagon," advertisement by the Chrysler Corp. (1946), scan via Flickr (flickr.com, user Alden Jewell); public domain.

1946: "Chet Atkins," photograph by the Gretsch Guitar News, via Wikimedia Commons (commons.wikimedia.org); public domain.

1947: "Roswell Daily Record from July 9, 1947," Wikimedia Commons (commons. wikimedia.org); public domain.

1947: "First Mach flight propels Yeager, Air Force into history," photograph from the U.S. Air Force (af.mil, ID #071204-F-9999J-047); public domain.

1947: "Terracing machine" image from U.S. Patent #2527415A (granted to James E. Hancock, 1950), via Google Patents (patents.google.com); public domain.

1948: "Bernard Dickmann with President Harry S. Truman Holding Up the Newspaper 'Dewey Defeats Truman,'" from the Harry S. Truman Library & Museum (trumanlibrary. org, ID #44305); public domain.

1948: "Crazy Horse Memorial" by Jim Bowen, Flickr (flickr.com); Creative Commons Attribution 2.0 Generic. Converted to grayscale, cropped.

1948: "Berliners watching a C-54 land at Berlin Tempelhof Airport, 1948," photograph by the U.S. Air Force, via Wikimedia Commons (commons.wikimedia.org); public domain.

1949: "Living Large -- Argonne's First Computer (8056998342)," photograph by the U.S. Department of Energy, via Flickr (flickr. com, user energy.gov); public domain.

1949: "Chinese communists celebrated Stalin's seventy birthday," Wikimedia Commons (commons.wikimedia.org); public domain.

1949: "Valve mechanism for dispensing gases and liquids under pressure" image from U.S. Patent #2631814A (granted to Robert H. Abplanalp, 1953), via Google Patents (patents.google.com); public domain.

1950: "Greyhound Buses at Gorge Inn, 1952," photograph from the Seattle Municipal Archives, Flickr (flickr.com); Creative Commons Attribution 2.0 Generic. Converted to grayscale, cropped.

1950: "Museum of Science, Boston, MA - IMG 3163," Wikimedia Commons (commons. wikimedia.org); public domain.

1950: "Dwight and Mamie Eisenhower watching a television during the Republican National Convention, Chicago, Illinois," photograph by Thomas J. O'Halleran, from the Library of Congress (loc.gov/pictures/, item #2003673954); public domain.

1950: "Fulton: Airphibian," photograph from the San Diego Air and Space Museum, Flickr (flickr.com); public domain.

1951: "B-47," photograph from the U.S. Air Force (af.mil, ID #020903-O-9999R-001); public domain.

1951: "Diaper housing" image from U.S. Patent #2575164A (granted to Marion Donovan, 1951), via Google Patents (patents. google.com); public domain.

1952: "1952-allstate," Wikimedia Commons (commons.wikimedia.org); public domain.

1952: "Electric steam iron" image from U.S. Patent #2700236A (granted to Stanley Marvin and Roland Miller, 1955), via Google Patents (patents.google.com); public domain.

1953: "Dwight D. Eisenhower, three-quarter length portrait, standing, facing slightly left, hand on back of chair," from the Library of Congress (loc.gov/pictures/, item #96523007); public domain.

1953: "YB-52sideview," photograph by the U.S. Air Force, via Wikimedia Commons (commons.wikimedia.org); public domain.

1953: "Maclyn McCarty (June 9, 1911, to January 2, 2005) with Francis Crick and James D. Watson," photograph by Marjorie McCarty, from the Public Library of Science: Biology article "A Path to Discovery: The Career of Maclyn McCarty" by Joshua Lederberg and Emil C Gotschlich; Creative Commons Attribution. Converted to grayscale, cropped.

1954: "Boring head for continuous mining machine" image from U.S. Patent #2715524A (granted to James S. Robbins, 1955), via Google Patents (patents.google. com); public domain.

1954: "Ford Thunderbird 1955," Thunderbird Dealership Sales Photo by Milton Lewis, via Flickr (flickr.com, user Nick Morozov); Creative Commons Attribution 2.0 Generic. Converted to grayscale, cropped.

1954: "Filter unit" image from U.S. Patent #2937756A (granted to Humbert E. Kingsley, Jr., 1960), via Google Patents (patents.google.com); public domain.

1955: "Johnny Cash promotional picture" by Sun Records, via Wikimedia Commons (commons.wikimedia.org); public domain.

1955: "Postcard: Greyhound Scenicruiser," via Flickr (flickr.com, user blizzy63); public domain.

1955: "Control system" image from U.S. Patent #2903575A (granted to Eugene J. Polley, 1959), via Google Patents (patents. google.com); public domain.

1956: "Dyess Air Force Base," Wikimedia Commons (commons.wikimedia.org); public domain.

1956: "Elvis performing live at the Mississippi-Alabama Fairgrounds in Tupelo, Mississippi, September 26, 1956," photograph from the *TV Radio Mirror* (March 1957, Vol. 47, #4), via the Internet Archive (archive.org); public domain.

1956: "Rotary card" image from U.S. Patent #2731966A (granted to Hildaur L. Neilsen, 1961), via Google Patents (patents.google. com); public domain.

1957: "Sputnik 1," photograph from the NASA Space Science Data Coordinated Archive (nssdc.gsfc.nasa.gov); public domain.

1957: "Liquid vortex arc torch process" image from U.S. Patent #2906858A (granted to Harold S. Morton, Jr., 1959), via Google Patents (patents.google.com); public domain.

1958: "1958 Datsun 1000 210 rear," Wikimedia Commons (commons. wikimedia.org); public domain.

1958: "Modular electrical unit" image from U.S. Patent #3052822A (granted to Jack S. Kilby, 1962), via Google Patents (patents. google.com); public domain.

1959: "Buddy Holly publicity picture for Brunswick Records," Wikimedia Commons (commons.wikimedia.org); public domain.

1959: "Eisenhowers with Queen Elizabeth and Prince Phillip," photograph by Abbie Rowe of the National Park Service (1957), from the White House Historical Association (library.whitehousehistory.org), National

Archives and Records Administration; public domain.

1959: "1959 Studebaker Lark VIII," photograph by Jeremy, via Wikimedia Commons (commons.wikimedia.org); Creative Commons Attribution 2.0 Generic. Converted to grayscale, cropped.

1960: "Pilot Francis Gary Powers, half-length portrait, facing front, holding an airplane model, at hearings on the U-2 Incident in front of a Senate Armed Services Select Committee," photograph by Warren K. Leffler (1962), from the Library of Congress (loc.gov/pictures/, item #2015647010); public domain.

1960: "Moog Modular 55 img2," Wikimedia Commons (commons.wikimedia.org); Creative Commons Attribution 3.0 Unported (no author listed). Converted to grayscale, cropped.

1960: "Medical cardiac pacemaker" image from U.S. Patent #3057356A (granted to Wilson Greatbatch, 1962), via Google Patents (patents.google.com); public domain.

1961: "Man Enters Space," photograph from the Huntsville Times (1961), via NASA (nasa.gov); public domain.

1961: "Astronaut Alan Shepard - U.S.S. Champlain - Post-Recovery Mercury Capsule," photograph via NASA (nasa.gov); public domain.

1962: "Rafael Urdaneta Bridge, 1970s crop," from a photograph by Dilia Díaz Cisneros, via Wikimedia Commons (commons.wikimedia.org); Creative Commons Attribution 3.0 Unported. Converted to grayscale, cropped.

1962: "Space Needle under construction, 1961," photograph from the Seattle Municipal Archives (Item 165654), Flickr (flickr.com); Creative Commons Attribution 2.0 Generic. Converted to grayscale, cropped.

1963: "1963 Studebaker Avanti gold at Concord University," photograph by Christopher Ziemnowicz, via Wikimedia Commons (commons.wikimedia.org); public domain.

1963: "Aquatic vehicle" image from U.S. Patent #3369518A (granted to Clayton J. Jacobson, 1968), via Google Patents (patents.google.com); public domain.

1964: "Orville Redenbacher 1979," photograph by Hunt-Wesson, via Wikimedia Commons (commons.wikimedia.org); public domain.

1964: "Morrison Hotel Postcard," Wikimedia Commons (commons.wikimedia.org); public domain.

1965: "Astrodome 1965," photograph possibly by Ted Rozumalski from The Sporting News archives, via Wikimedia Commons (commons.wikimedia.org); public domain.

1965: "Superimposed model on an aerial photograph of the city - Miami, Florida," photoprint created by Florida State Road Department, from the State Library and Archives of Florida (floridamemory.com, image #Dot0448); public domain.

1966: "James Superswift Sports 250," photograph by Flickr user "Mick," via Wikimedia Commons (commons.wikimedia.org); Creative Commons Attribution 2.0 Generic. Converted to grayscale, cropped.

1967: "Muhammad Ali 1966," photograph from the Nationaal Archief of the Netherlands, via Wikimedia Commons (commons.wikimedia.org); Creative Commons Attribution-Share Alike 3.0 Netherlands. No changes made.

1967: "Ring-shaped tab for tear strips of containers" image from U.S. Patent #3349949A (granted to Omar L. Brown and Don B. Peters, 1967), via Google Patents (patents.google.com); public domain.

1968: "Prudhoe Bay, Alaska," photograph from the National Digital Library of the U.S. Fish and Wildlife Service (digitalmedia.fws.gov, data ID #04BAA320-CC21-4413-B37D8D0F90647A0C); public domain.

1968: "Wind-propelled apparatus" image from U.S. Patent #3487800A (granted to James Drake and Schweitzer Hoyle, 1970), via Google Patents (patents.google.com); public domain.

1969: "Saturn Apollo Program," photograph from NASA (nasa.gov, ID #6901250); public domain.

1969: "1970 Dodge Challenger photo-1," Wikimedia Commons (commons.wikimedia.org); public domain.

1970: "Lee A. Iacocca, President of Ford Motor Company, head-and-shoulders portrait, facing front, gesturing with one hand, during an interview," photograph by Thomas J. O'Halloran, from the Library of Congress (loc.gov/pictures/, item #2015645231); public domain.

1970: "Magnetic record disk cover" image from U.S. Patent #3668658A (granted to Ralph Flores and Herbert E. Thompson, 1972), via Google Patents (patents.google.com); public domain.

1971: "Walt Disney with company at press conference - Orlando, Florida," photograph from the State Library and Archives of Florida (floridamemory.com, image #C069089CV); public domain.

1971: "McDonnell Douglas DC-10 N1803U (C15-10)," photograph n. C15-10 released by McDonnell Douglas, via Wikimedia Commons (commons.wikimedia.org); public domain.

1972: "Ananda Mohan Chakrabarty - Kolkata 2009-11-08 3123," photograph by Biswarup Ganguly, via Wikimedia Commons (commons.wikimedia.org); Creative Commons Attribution 3.0 Unported. Converted to grayscale, cropped.

1973: "Xerox Alto mit Rechner," Wikimedia Commons (commons.wikimedia.org); public domain.

1973: "Egyptians Crossing Suez Canal," photograph from the Central Intelligence Agency, Flickr (flickr.com); public domain.

1974: "Ed Sullivan, three-quarter length portrait, seated, facing front," from the Library of Congress (loc.gov/pictures/, item #99471789); public domain.

1975: "Microburst crosssection (vectored)," image from the Federal Aviation Association, via Wikimedia Commons (commons.wikimedia.org); public domain.

1975: "SS Edmund Fitzgerald Upbound & In Ballast," photograph from the U.S. Coast Guard, via Wikimedia Commons (commons.wikimedia.org); public domain.

1976: "Electronic still camera" image from U.S. Patent #4131919A (granted to Gareth A. Lloyd and Steven J. Sasson, 1978), via Google Patents (patents.google.com); public domain.

1977: "Man Standing Next To Trans Alaska Pipeline," photograph by the U.S. Fish and

Wildlife Service, via Pixnio (pixnio.com); public domain.

1978: "William P. Lear with Turbine Engine," from the San Diego Air and Space Museum Archive, via Flickr (flickr.com); public domain.

1978: "Kraanwerkschip Thialf & diepwaterconstructieschip Balder - Calandkanaal - Port of Rotterdam," photograph by Frans Berkelaar, Flickr (flickr.com); Creative Commons Attribution 2.0 Generic. Converted to grayscale, cropped.

1979: "3MileIsland," photograph from the U.S. Department of Energy, via Wikimedia Commons (commons.wikimedia.org); public domain.

1980: "McNeil Street Pumping Station..." from the Library of Congress (loc.gov/pictures/, item #073665p); public domain.

1980: "Signing of the Staggers Rail Act of 1980," photograph from the White House, via Wikimedia Commons (commons.wikimedia.org); public domain.

1981: "First Appearance of the Space Shuttle," photograph from NASA (nasa.gov); public domain.

1982: "A Russian cargo plane, the Antonov 124..." photograph from NASA, JFK Space Center Media Gallery (mediaarchive.ksc.nasa.gov, photo #KSC-99PP-0287); public domain.

1983: "MASH TV cast 1974," publicity photo by CBS Television, via Wikimedia Commons (commons.wikimedia.org); public domain.

1983: "Sixteen Audio Cassettes," Public Domain Pictures (publicdomainpictures.net); public domain.

1984: "Renault alliance," Wikimedia Commons (commons.wikimedia.org); public domain.

1985: "C.F. Martin acoustic guitar," photograph by Yutaka Tsutano, Flickr (flickr.com); Creative Commons Attribution 2.0 Generic. Converted to grayscale, cropped.

1985: "Microsoft Windows 1.0 page4," brochure by Microsoft, scanned by Michael Holley, via Wikimedia Commons (commons.wikimedia.org); public domain.

1986: "Remembering the Challenger Crew," photograph from the NASA Goddard Space Flight Center, Flickr (flickr.com); public domain.

1986: "A V-22 Osprey prepares to land on the flight deck of amphibious assault ship USS Wasp," photograph from the U.S. Navy (navy.mil, image #070521-N-8923M-442); public domain.

1987: "BBKing07," photograph by Roland Godefroy, via Wikimedia Commons (commons.wikimedia.org); Creative Commons Attribution-Share Alike 3.0 Unported. No changes made.

1987: "Eagle Premier," Wikimedia Commons (commons.wikimedia.org); public domain.

1988: "Bullwinkle Offshore Platform," photograph by Jay Phagan, Flickr (flickr.com); Creative Commons Attribution 2.0 Generic. Converted to grayscale, cropped.

1989: "Boll Weevil" by Pearson Scott Foresman, via Wikimedia Commons (commons.wikimedia.org); public domain.

1989: "Berlin Wall - Brandenburg Gate," photograph by Sue Ream, via Wikimedia Commons (commons.wikimedia.org); Creative Commons Attribution 3.0 Unported. Converted to grayscale, cropped.

1990: "Hubble Floats Free," photograph by NASA, Astronomy Picture of the Day (apod.nasa.gov, 11/24/2002); public domain.

1991: "Sir Tim Berners-Lee at #WebWeWantFest," photograph by Belinda Lawley, via Flickr (flickr.com, user Southbank Centre London); Creative Commons Attribution 2.0 Generic. Converted to grayscale, cropped.

1991: "MacBook Pro Retina 13inch and PowerBook 100," photograph by Flickr user Raneko (flickr.com); Creative Commons Attribution 2.0 Generic. Converted to grayscale, cropped.

1992: "Anand-FSW-Figure1-B," by Anandwiki at English Wikipedia, via Wikimedia Commons (commons.wikimedia.org); Creative Commons Attribution 3.0 Unported. Converted to grayscale, cropped.

1993: "Reagan Goldwater pin star on Jimmy Doolittle 1985," photograph by Bill Fitz-Patrick, White House Photo Office, via Wikimedia Commons (commons.wikimedia.org); public domain.

1994: "Active pixel sensor with intra-pixel charge transfer" image from U.S. Patent #5471515A (granted to Eric R. Fossum, Sunetra Mendis, and Sabrina E. Kemeny, 1995), via Google Patents (patents.google.com); public domain.

1995: "Bezos' Iconic Laugh," photograph by Steve Jurvetson, Flickr (flickr.com); Creative Commons Attribution 2.0 Generic. Converted to grayscale, cropped.

1996: "Currency: $100, Issued: 1996-2013," U.S. Currency Education Program (uscurrency.gov); public domain.

1996: "Carl Sagan Astronomer Cosmologist," Pixabay (pixabay.com); public domain.

1997: "New Zealand Skyline Auckland," Pixabay (pixabay.com); public domain.

1997: "The team with ThrustSSC," photograph by Andrew Graves, via Wikimedia Commons (commons.wikimedia.org); public domain.

1998: "Caterpillar 797 Mining Truck," photograph by Wilson Hui, Flickr (flickr.com); Creative Commons Attribution 2.0 Generic. Converted to grayscale, cropped.

1998: "Eric Schmidt, Sergey Brin and Larry Page," photograph by Joi Ito, Flickr (flickr.com); Creative Commons Attribution 2.0 Generic. Converted to grayscale, cropped.

1999: "Dszpics1," photograph from the National Severe Storms Laboratory, via Wikimedia Commons (commons.wikimedia.org); public domain.

1999: "Chandra X-Ray Observatory (Chandra XRO)," image from NASA (nasa.gov); public domain.

1999: "1997-1999 Oldsmobile Cutlass," Wikimedia Commons (commons.wikimedia.org); public domain.

2000: "London Eye Ferris Wheel Buildings," Pixabay (pixabay.com); public domain.

2000: "Lockheed C130J Hercules 4," photograph by Ronnie Macdonald, Flickr (flickr.com); Creative Commons Attribution 2.0 Generic. Converted to grayscale, cropped.

2001: "OKC National Memorial & Museum," photograph by Josué Goge, Flickr (flickr.com); Creative Commons Attribution 2.0 Generic. Converted to grayscale, cropped.

2001: "London Stock Exchange," photograph by James Hume, Flickr (flickr.com); Creative Commons Attribution 2.0 Generic. Converted to grayscale, cropped.

2002: "Goodwill Store, 2015," photograph by Mike Mozart, Flickr (flickr.com); Creative Commons Attribution 2.0 Generic. Converted to grayscale, cropped.

2002: "Falkirk Wheel Scotland UK," Pixabay (pixabay.com); public domain.

2003: "Eurofighter Typhoon line drawing," Wikimedia Commons (commons.wikimedia.org); public domain.

2004: "Le Viaduc de Millau / Millau viaduct," photograph by Olivier Bacquet, Flickr (flickr.com); Creative Commons Attribution 2.0 Generic. Converted to grayscale, cropped.

2005: "Johnny Carson," autographed photograph from Alan Light, Flickr (flickr.com); Creative Commons Attribution 2.0 Generic. Converted to grayscale, cropped.

2005: "DFW airport," photo from NASA, via Wikimedia Commons (commons.wikimedia.org); public domain.

2006: "Boys and Girls Club of America Logo," Wikimedia Commons (commons.wikimedia.org); public domain.

2007: "A380 F-WWOW," photograph by Axel Péju, Flickr (flickr.com); Creative Commons Attribution 2.0 Generic. Converted to grayscale, cropped.

2007: "Regis Philbin at the 2009 Tribeca Film Festival," photograph by David Shankbone, via Wikimedia Commons (commons.wikimedia.org); Creative Commons Attribution 3.0 Unported. Converted to grayscale, cropped.

2008: "Wild horse wind turbines," photograph by Anna W. Jacobs, via Wikimedia Commons (commons.wikimedia.org); Creative Commons Attribution 3.0 Unported. Converted to grayscale, cropped.

2009: "The Oak Ridge Boys - Joe, Duane, William Lee & Richard," photograph by Flickr user cdnmusicdiva (flickr.com); Creative Commons Attribution 2.0 Generic. Converted to grayscale, cropped.

2009: "'Walkway Over The Hudson' State Historic Park -- Poughkeepsie (NY) September 2016," photograph by Ron Cogswell, Flickr (flickr.com); Creative Commons Attribution 2.0 Generic. Converted to grayscale, cropped.

2010: "Dubai Tower Arab Khalifa Burj," Pixabay (pixabay.com); public domain.

2011: "Concluding the STS-133 mission, Space Shuttle Discovery touches down at the Shuttle Landing Facility," photograph from NASA, via Wikimedia Commons (commons.wikimedia.org); public domain.

2014: "Preparing for the 84th Annual Academy Awards - giant Oscar statue," photograph by Doug Kline, Flickr (flickr.com); Creative Commons Attribution 2.0 Generic. Converted to grayscale, cropped.